Win32 Network Programming

Windows® 95 and Windows NT Network Programming Using MFC

Ralph Davis

Addison-Wesley Developers Press

Reading, Massachusetts • Menlo Park, California • New York
Don Mills, Ontario • Harlow, England • Amsterdam
Bonn • Sydney • Singapore • Tokyo • Madrid • San Juan
Paris • Seoul • Milan • Mexico City • Taipei

Library of Congress Cataloging-in-Publication Data

Davis, Ralph, 1947–

Win32 Network programming / Ralph Davis.

p. cm.

Includes index.

ISBN 0-201-48930-9

1. Microsoft Windows. 2. Microsoft Win32. 3. Operating systems (Computers) 4. Application software--Development. I. Title.

QA76.76.063D372 1996

005.2--dc20 96-9346

CIP

A-W Developers Press is a division of Addison-Wesley Publishing Company, Inc.

Sponsoring Editor: Ben Ryan
Project Manager: Sarah Weaver
Production Coordinator: Erin Sweeney
Cover design: Vicki Hochstedler
Set in 11 point Times Roman by Octal Publishing, Inc.

1 2 3 4 5 6 7 8 9 -MA- 0099989796
First printing, August 1996

Si tu no usas la cabeza, otro por ti la va a usar.

(If you don't use your brain, someone else will use it for you.)

—Ruben Blades, *Prohibido Olvidar*, on his album Caminando.

Contents

Acknowledgments

I have enjoyed the technical input of a number of highly skilled software engineers. The input I've gotten from several people has been of particular importance.

My technical editor, Jack Blundell of Fannie Mae, taught me a lot about programming Windows Sockets in a wide-area network environment. I am indebted to him for deepening my understanding of the issues involved.

My friend Steve Buck of Onpoint Technologies continues to be one of my most valued sources of information on a wide variety of subjects.

I also need to thank John Robbins, once of GE Fanuc, now at NuMega, for teaching me a lot about how NT works under the covers. I learned a lot from John during our many conversations over lunch in Charlottesville.

David Treadwell of Microsoft enlightened me considerably about the importance of overlapped I/O with Windows Sockets, and about how to do it right.

John Willard of Cabletron introduced me to I/O completion ports. I'm happy to say that, since then, I've never been the same.

As usual, the production staff at Addison-Wesley has been very pleasant to work with, and highly professional. I'd especially like to thank Claire Horne, Erin Sweeney, and Sarah Weaver.

Ralph Davis

Chapter 1

Introduction

This book picks up where my last book, *Windows NT Network Programming*, left off. Besides the fact that almost two years have passed, and I know more now than I did then, several external events have occurred:

- The release first of NT 3.51 (mostly an incremental upgrade) and now of NT 4.0.
- Windows 95.
- Microsoft's standardization on TCP/IP, Windows Sockets, and the emergence of Windows Sockets 2.0.
- The appearance of Visual C++ 2.0, the first version of Visual C++ with credible 32-bit functionality. Since then, we have moved to Visual C++ 4.1, which I used for this book.
- The growing acceptance of NT as a large-system, server-side operating system. In my role as a trainer, I see considerable interest in moving software systems that presently run under UNIX to NT—usually as a partner to the UNIX system, not a replacement. The attitude I see is very clear: NT has the horsepower to support UNIX-based software, and is likely to offer a significant market. (For an excellent discussion of NT vs. UNIX, see the May 1996 issue of *Byte* magazine.)

Each of these factors has had an influence on this book, and on how it has changed from *Windows NT Network Programming*.

Things I've Learned in the Last Two Years

The most important advance in my knowledge has centered on overlapped I/O, the Win32 vehicle for performing asynchronous operations. I have a much better understanding of how to do overlapped I/O right, and also of the importance that Microsoft is placing on it—particularly in the Windows Sockets context.

When I presented overlapped techniques in *Windows NT Network Programming*, my examples spun off a single operation, then waited for it to complete. What I now understand is that if you only do one operation, there's no point in doing overlapped I/O. It's more complex to code, and you don't get any real benefits from the complexity unless you have more than one operation in progress. My examples here issue at least two operations.

In *Windows NT Network Programming*, the only overlapped technique I really understood was the one that uses event handles. I did discuss I/O completion routines, but I had not really figured out how to use them. Since then, I have, and my discussion of them is based on a couple of years of working with them.

Most importantly, I knew nothing about I/O completion ports. They were introduced in NT 3.5, and *Windows NT Network Programming* came out in late 1994, about the same time as NT 3.5. I found out about them in early 1995. They occupy a key position here in the chapters that discuss and apply overlapped I/O (Chapters 6, 9, and 10), since Microsoft is touting them as the preferred vehicle for doing overlapped I/O.

Windows 95

The emergence of Windows 95 has had some effect on this book, but not that much. In fact, I was originally asked by Addison-Wesley to write this book as *Windows 95 Network Programming*. However, after some initial exploration of the subject, I became convinced that Windows 95 did not offer enough to warrant a complete book. For one thing, Windows 95 is a pale shadow of NT; it will never be seriously considered as an alternative to UNIX. As a developer, I have found it quite unsatisfying to go back five steps from NT, and look forward keenly to the day when Windows 95 is an anachronism. For another, this is primarily a book about writing server-side, back-end applications. Even Microsoft admits that Windows 95 is a client-side, front-end platform, which makes it mostly footnote material for me. (Another Addison-Wesley book, *Win32 Client/Server Developer's Guide* by Douglas J. Reilly, covers Windows 95 issues exclusively, and nicely complements the material in this book.)

Nevertheless, Windows 95 is the reason why this book is called *Win32 Network Programming*, and I have endeavored in my samples to provide code that will work in either environment. In most cases, the incompatibilities do not keep you from using a single binary image. At runtime, the GetVersionEx() function tells you which platform you're running on, and you don't ask Windows 95 to do anything it's not capable of doing.

In all cases where there is a difference between NT and Windows 95, the Windows 95 functionality is a subset of that offered by NT. There are no cases in the subject matter of this book where Windows 95 can do something NT can't.

There are surprisingly few major differences between the two operating systems. These are the ones we will encounter:

- Windows 95 can't do overlapped I/O against disk files. It can do it where it matters for our purposes, though—with Windows Sockets and Named Pipes. However, only NT supports I/O completion ports.
- Windows 95 is supposed to support I/O completion routines, but I cannot verify this. My own tests, using code that works fine under NT, don't work under Windows 95. I'm willing to take Microsoft's word that they work, though, and assume that eventually I'll figure out why I haven't been successful.
- NT services, which are the subject of Chapter 11, only work under NT. However, you can configure applications to start at boot time under Windows 95, just as you can under NT. And you can emulate the behavior of an NT service under Windows 95 without too much trouble. In Chapter 11, I use a couple of C++ classes to mask the differences between the two environments.
- You cannot implement a Named Pipes server on top of Windows 95. Named Pipes have always had this rather quaint notion of who's allowed to be a server and who isn't. This difference is mitigated by several things. First, Named Pipes are in their twilight years, and will probably continue to decline in significance. Second, the other APIs we will consider—Windows Sockets and RPC—will let you host a server application under Windows 95. Third, Windows 95 isn't supposed to be a server platform, anyhow.
- The most obtrusive difference between NT and Windows 95 appears in the LAN Manager API, discussed in Chapter 12. Windows 95 supports only a small, meaningless subset of the API. This would be harmless if the unsupported routines were just stubbed out in NETAPI32.DLL (the dynamic-link library that supports them under NT). However, this is not the case. If you link to NETAPI32.LIB, you won't even be able to

start your application under Windows 95. The few routines that are supported reside in an entirely different DLL, SVRAPI.DLL. But if you link to it, you get unresolved externals if you use any functions outside the Windows 95 subset. To have an application where a single binary image will work in either environment, you have to call GetVersionEx() to sense your operating system environment, call LoadLibrary() to load either NETAPI32.DLL or SVRAPI.DLL, then call GetProcAddress() to load pointers to the functions you want to call. But this is a cumbersome technique, requiring a lot of tedious, uninteresting code. In Chapter 12, therefore, I have adopted the policy of only supporting NT.

- Windows 95 does not support the Unicode 16-bit character set. Therefore, I have changed the code from "Windows NT Network Programming," which did use Unicode, so that it uses the 8-bit ANSI character set. From time to time, I use the WideCharToMultiByte() and MultiByteToWideChar() functions to switch character sets on the fly.
- Finally, there are some minor syntactic and behavioral differences between NT and Windows 95. I will discuss these in the chapters where they pop up.

Windows Sockets 2

Windows Sockets 2 is now part of NT 4.0, and will soon be included in Windows 95 as well. The Win32 SDK that Microsoft is distributing as part of the Developer Network subscription includes the Winsock 2 development tools. You can also download them from the World Wide Web, at http://www.stardust.com. The current version is beta 1.1, available in the file BETA1_1.ZIP (this may change by the time this book reaches the bookstores). The code in this book supports both versions, using different Visual C++ configurations that change the compiler switches.

Winsock 2 adds a number of features to Sockets 1.1, of which the most important for this book is standardization of overlapped I/O against Windows Sockets. Chapter 9 discusses the ramifications of Winsock 2 in some detail, and provides code examples that use both versions. Chapter 16 also presents a sample application that uses Winsock 2 if it's available.

C++ and the Microsoft Foundation Classes

One major difference in my approach for this book has been my move to a C++ and MFC environment. This move has been stimulated by these factors:

- The growth in acceptance for C++, MFC, and Visual C++, and the opportunities I've had to be involved in large-scale development efforts using them
- The ability of a C++ object-oriented approach to hide platform differences, while encouraging a modular programming style that focuses sharply on the Win32 techniques I want to illustrate

The code that forms the backbone of this book is a C++ class library that implements Win32 objects missing from the Microsoft Foundation Classes. This class library can be found on the book disk in the project \WIN32NET\CODE\WIN32OBJ\WIN32MFC.MDP. Table 1-1 shows what it adds to MFC.

Table 1-1. MFC Extension Classes Developed in This Book

Functionality	Class Name	Source Files	Where Introduced
Wrapping Win32 Exceptions in C++ Exceptions	CWin32Exception	WIN32EXC.H / .CPP	Chapter 2
Overlapped I/O on Files	COverlappedFile COverlapped	OVFILE.H / .CPP OVERLAP.H / .CPP	Chapter 6
I/O Completion Ports	CIoPort	IOPORT.H / .CPP	Chapter 6
Thread Local Storage	CTlsSlot	TLS.H / .CPP	Chapter 7
Memory-mapped Files	CMappedFile	MAPFILE.H	Chapter 7
Shared Memory	CSharedMemory	MAPFILE.H	Chapter 7
Overlapped Sockets	COverlappedSocket	OVSOCK.H / .CPP	Chapter 9
Windows Sockets 2	CXAsyncSocket	OVSOCK.H / .CPP	Chapter 9
Service Registration	CServiceInfo	NSPCLASS.H / .CPP	Chapter 9
Named Pipes	CNamedPipe	NAMEPIPE.H / .CPP	Chapter 10
Overlapped Pipes	COverlappedPipe	OVPIPE.H / .CPP	Chapter 10
Mailslots	CMailslot	MAILSLOT.H / .CPP	Chapter 10
RPC Clients	CRpcClient	RPCCLASS.H / .CPP	Chapter 11
RPC Servers	CRpcServer	RPCCLASS.H / .CPP	Chapter 11
Win32 Services	CWin32Service CWin32ComponentService	WIN32SRV.H / .CPP	Chapter 11
Security Objects	CSecurityAttributes CSecurityDescriptor	SECURITY.H / .CPP	Chapter 13

In addition, I have provided a separate class library to support the LAN Manager API. This project is in \WIN32NET\CODE\LANMAN\LMCLASS\LMCLASS.MDP. Table 1-2 shows the objects it implements and what they represent.

Table 1-2. C++ Objects Supporting the LAN Manager API

Object Represented	Class Name	Source Files
NT Servers	CNetServer	NETSRVR.H / .CPP
Users	CNetUser	NETUSER.H / .CPP
User Groups	CNetUserGroup	NETGROUP.H / .CPP

All the LAN Manager objects are developed in Chapter 12. I provide them in their own DLL because you can only use them under NT.

Installing the Disk

To install the course software, run A:SETUP in the directory under which you want the software installed. All of the binaries have been built.

SETUP will also set your environment appropriately. All the files will reside in the WIN32NET directory and its subdirectories. Refer to the README.TXT for more complete build instructions.

Using the Code

I have published the code in this book with the intention and expectation that you will use it to facilitate your own development efforts. My only request is this: if you want to use the code in a commercial product, I would appreciate a tip. You can contact me at my CompuServe address (71161.1060@compuserve.com) to discuss the details.

Problems, Assistance, and Upgrades

Let me know if you have any problems or questions. Also, I'll probably post upgrades to Addison-Wesley's FTP site from time to time. That address is ftp://ftp.aw.com/tcb/authors/davis.

I hope you find this book interesting and helpful. Writing it has been an exhilarating experience for me, since it gave me an opportunity to enhance my understanding of—and appreciation for—Windows NT.

Chapter 2

Exception Handling

Two kinds of exception handling are available to a Win32 program written in C++: C++ exception handling and Win32 Structured Exception Handling. Both provide a means by which applications can handle unexpected events. These include both software- and hardware-generated error conditions, called **exceptions**. Structured Termination Handling, which is an adjunct to Structured Exception Handling, protects a body of code from being abandoned while resources such as synchronization objects are in a locked or indeterminate state.

We will explore Win32 Structured Exception Handling and Structured Termination Handling first, then look at what C++ exception handling adds to them.

Win32 Exception Handling

Structured Exception Handling and Structured Termination Handling serve several purposes. By trapping your own exceptions, you can prevent the summary termination of your application and do something less drastic, such as rolling back the activity where the exception occurred. You can also use exceptions quite deliberately to implement algorithms such as lazy memory allocation. (See the virtual memory allocation discussion in Chapter 3.)

Structured Termination Handling can guarantee that a function will have a single exit point. Thus, all resource cleanup can be localized in a single block of code.

Win32 Syntax

As the names imply, Structured Exception Handling and Structured Termination Handling are implemented by the Microsoft C/C++ compiler using structured programming constructs. They add four keywords to the language: *__try, __except, __leave,* and *__finally.*

Here is the skeletal framework of an exception handler:

```
__try
   {
   // Guarded code
   }
__except ([exception-filter expression])
   {
   // [Exception-handling logic]
   }
```

The curly braces are mandatory, even if the *__try* and *__except* blocks consist of a single statement. The *__try* blocks cannot stand by themselves; they must be followed by either an *__except* or a *__finally.*

Win32 Semantics

First, the *__try* block is executed. If an exception occurs, Windows tries to notify a debugger. If the process is not being debugged, or if the debugger does not handle the exception, Windows begins climbing back up the stack ("unwinding") to find an exception handler. If it finds one, it evaluates the exception-filter expression. If the expression resolves to EXCEPTION_EXECUTE_HANDLER (1), Windows will enter the *__except* block. The exception filter can also return EXCEPTION_CONTINUE_EXECUTION (–1), telling Windows to retry the machine instruction that failed, or EXCEPTION_CONTINUE_SEARCH (0), indicating that the associated exception handler cannot deal with the exception that has occurred. If Windows does not find an application-defined exception handler, it tries to notify the debugger again. If there is no debugger, or the debugger still does not handle the exception, Windows executes its own exception-handling logic.

When Visual C++ or the Win32 SDK has been installed from a supported CD-ROM drive, you can start a post-mortem debugging session. When Windows reports the error, it presents a message box offering to debug or terminate the application. This is usually the best way to handle exceptions, because it takes you right to the line of code that caused the problem. The most common exceptions (access violations and division by zero) are generally the result of programming errors; post-mortem debugging is the best way to diagnose these problems.

Possible Exceptions

Undoubtedly, the most typical exception is a memory access violation (0xC0000005), defined as the constant EXCEPTION_ACCESS_VIOLATION. This indicates that somewhere in your application you have strayed into memory that you do not have permission to access. Table 2-1 lists all the exception codes that are currently defined. The codes are divided into bit fields as follows (the *typedef* is my own):

```
typedef struct _EXCEPTION_CODE
{
   unsigned dwSeverity  : 2;  // Bits 31 and 30
   unsigned dwOwner     : 1;  // Bit 29
   unsigned dwReserved  : 1;  // Bit 28
   unsigned dwFacility  : 12  // Bits 27-16
   unsigned dwException : 16  // Bits 15-0
} EXCEPTION_CODE;
```

The values for *dwSeverity* are:

- 0: Success
- 1: Informational
- 2: Warning
- 3: Error

The SDK header file WINNT.H provides macros for testing the error level:

- ERROR_SEVERITY_SUCCESS (0): Success
- ERROR_SEVERITY_INFORMATIONAL (0x40000000): Informational
- ERROR_SEVERITY_WARNING (0x80000000): Warning
- ERROR_SEVERITY_ERROR (0xC0000000): Error

All the codes listed in Table 2-1 are either warnings or errors.

Table 2-1. Win32 Exception Codes

Code	Defined As	Level
EXCEPTION_ACCESS_VIOLATION	STATUS_ACCESS_VIOLATION (0xC0000005)	Error
EXCEPTION_DATATYPE_MISALIGNMENT	STATUS_DATATYPE_MISALIGNMENT (0x80000002)	Warning
EXCEPTION_BREAKPOINT	STATUS_BREAKPOINT (0x80000003)	Warning (used by debuggers)
EXCEPTION_SINGLE_STEP	STATUS_SINGLE_STEP (0x80000004)	Warning (used by debuggers)
EXCEPTION_ARRAY_BOUNDS_EXCEEDED	STATUS_ARRAY_BOUNDS_EXCEEDED (0xC000008C)	Error
EXCEPTION_FLT_DENORMAL_OPERAND	STATUS_FLOAT_DENORMAL_OPERAND (0xC000008D)	Error
EXCEPTION_FLT_DIVIDE_BY_ZERO	STATUS_FLOAT_DIVIDE_BY_ZERO (0xC000008E)	Error
EXCEPTION_FLT_INEXACT_RESULT	STATUS_FLOAT_INEXACT_RESULT (0xC000008F)	Error
EXCEPTION_FLT_INVALID_OPERATION	STATUS_FLOAT_INVALID_OPERATION (0xC0000090)	Error
EXCEPTION_FLT_OVERFLOW	STATUS_FLOAT_OVERFLOW (0xC0000091)	Error
EXCEPTION_FLT_STACK_CHECK	STATUS_FLOAT_STACK_CHECK (0xC0000092)	Error
EXCEPTION_FLT_UNDERFLOW	STATUS_FLOAT_UNDERFLOW (0xC0000093)	Error

Table 2-1. Win32 Exception Codes *(continued)*

Code	Defined As	Level
EXCEPTION_INT_DIVIDE_BY_ZERO	STATUS_INTEGER_DIVIDE_BY_ZERO (0xC0000094)	Error
EXCEPTION_INT_OVERFLOW	STATUS_INTEGER_OVERFLOW (0xC0000095)	Error
EXCEPTION_PRIV_INSTRUCTION	STATUS_PRIVILEGED_INSTRUCTION (0xC0000096)	Error
EXCEPTION_IN_PAGE_ERROR	STATUS_IN_PAGE_ERROR (0xC0000006)	Error
EXCEPTION_ILLEGAL_INSTRUCTION	STATUS_ILLEGAL_INSTRUCTION (0xC000001D)	Error
EXCEPTION_NONCONTINUABLE_EXCEPTION	STATUS_NONCONTINUABLE_EXCEPTION (0xC0000025)	Error
EXCEPTION_STACK_OVERFLOW	STATUS_STACK_OVERFLOW (0xC00000FD)	Error
EXCEPTION_INVALID_DISPOSITION	STATUS_INVALID_DISPOSITION (0xC0000026)	Error
EXCEPTION_GUARD_PAGE	STATUS_GUARD_PAGE_VIOLATION (0X80000001)	Warning
CONTROL_C_EXIT	STATUS_CONTROL_C_EXIT (0xC000013A)	Error
STATUS_NO_MEMORY	0xC0000017	Error

The *dwOwner* bit indicates whether the code is generated by Microsoft (0) or defined by the developer (1). It can be tested using the APPLICATION_ERROR_MASK (0x20000000) macro.

dwReserved is always 0; Windows clears it automatically when processing an exception. Both *dwFacility* and *dwException* can be defined according to the needs of specific applications. All the codes in Table 2-1 have *dwFacility* set to 0.

The *#defines* for the EXCEPTION_ codes are in WINBASE.H; *#defines* for the STATUS_ constants are in WINNT.H. Both these headers are included by WINDOWS.H.

In addition to EXCEPTION_ACCESS_VIOLATION, programming errors may also trigger EXCEPTION_PRIV_INSTRUCTION or EXCEPTION_ILLEGAL_INSTRUCTION violations. EXCEPTION_PRIV_INSTRUCTION means that the CPU encountered an instruction in the code stream that is reserved for operating system software, such as an ARPL (Adjust Requestor Privilege Level) on an Intel chip. EXCEPTION_ILLEGAL_INSTRUCTION means that the CPU was given an instruction that it was unable to decode. These exceptions are most likely to result from attempting to execute data or from executing code that has been overwritten. EXCEPTION_BREAKPOINT and EXCEPTION_SINGLE_ STEP are used by debuggers. EXCEPTION_DATATYPE_ MISALIGNMENT indicates that a piece of data is not aligned on the proper byte boundary for the host processor. It will occur only under NT; Intel processors do not enforce datatype alignment, as do RISC chips like the MIPS or the Alpha.

The EXCEPTION_FLT_ and EXCEPTION_INT_ codes are triggered by errors that occur in floating-point and integer arithmetic operations. EXCEPTION_NONCONTINUABLE_EXCEPTION means that you attempted to retry an instruction after an exception that has been tagged as noncontinuable. EXCEPTION_GUARD_PAGE means that you entered a page of memory that you have designated as a guard page. Windows uses guard page exceptions internally for stack management. STATUS_ NO_MEMORY is used to report memory-allocation errors under certain conditions (see Chapter 3).

The Exception Filter

As we saw earlier, the exception-filter expression follows the *__except* keyword in parentheses. Windows evaluates exception-filter expressions as it looks for someone to handle a particular exception. The values it expects the filter expression to resolve to are:

- EXCEPTION_EXECUTE_HANDLER (1): Pass control to the block of code following the *__except* statement.
- EXCEPTION_CONTINUE_SEARCH (0): I can't handle the exception; look for someone else.
- EXCEPTION_CONTINUE_EXECUTION (−1): Retry the instruction.

Simple expression filters can be coded inline. Because EXCEPTION_EXECUTE_HANDLER and EXCEPTION_CONTINUE_SEARCH are defined as 1 and 0, you can use a simple Boolean test if you do not intend to reexecute an instruction. Here are two examples.

```
// Do the exception handler unconditionally
__except (EXCEPTION_EXECUTE_HANDLER)

// Handle access violations
// Pass all other exceptions up the stack
__except (GetExceptionCode() == EXCEPTION_ACCESS_VIOLATION)
```

More complex filter expressions require a filter function. In particular, you cannot request the reexecution of an instruction unless you call a filter function. This is the most powerful way to use Structured Exception Handling. It allows you, for instance, to delay allocating memory until you actually need it, and then to allocate only as much as you need.

Win32 provides two pseudofunctions (they are actually macros) that allow you to determine what caused the exception. GetExceptionCode() returns a DWORD containing the exception code.

```
DWORD GetExceptionCode(VOID);
```

GetExceptionCode() can be called in either the filter expression or the *__except* block; it cannot be called from a filter function.

GetExceptionInformation() returns complete information about the exception and the instruction that triggered it.

```
LPEXCEPTION_POINTERS GetExceptionInformation(VOID);
```

The return value is a pointer to an EXCEPTION_POINTERS structure, which contains pointers to two other structures.

```
typedef struct _EXCEPTION_POINTERS
   {
   PEXCEPTION_RECORD ExceptionRecord;
   PCONTEXT          ContextRecord;
   } EXCEPTION_POINTERS;
```

The EXCEPTION_RECORD structure that *ExceptionRecord* points to describes the exception in a machine-independent way. *ContextRecord* points to a CONTEXT structure, which is a snapshot of the register contents at the time the exception occurred. The EXCEPTION_RECORD is defined as follows:

```
typedef struct _EXCEPTION_RECORD
{
   DWORD ExceptionCode;
   DWORD ExceptionFlags;
   struct _EXCEPTION_RECORD *ExceptionRecord;
   PVOID ExceptionAddress;
   DWORD NumberParameters;
   DWORD ExceptionInformation[EXCEPTION_MAXIMUM_PARAMETERS];
} EXCEPTION_RECORD;
```

ExceptionCode reports the exception that occurred; it is the same value as that returned by GetExceptionCode(). *ExceptionFlags* indicates whether the instruction can be retried or not. Windows uses the *ExceptionRecord* field to build a linked list of EXCEPTION_RECORDs if nested exceptions (which are exceptions in exception handlers or filter functions) occur. *ExceptionAddress* points to the instruction that the application was executing when the exception was triggered. *NumberParameters* and *ExceptionInformation* contain any additional information required to more precisely describe the exception. At present, they are used only with access violations (*ExceptionCode* == EXCEPTION_ACCESS_VIOLATION) and C++ exceptions (*ExceptionCode* == 0xE06D7363). In the case of an access violation, the first element in the *ExceptionInformation* array is 0 if the application was attempting to read the address, and 1 if it was trying to write to it. The second element is the virtual address of the data that the application was accessing.

GetExceptionInformation() can be called only from the filter expression (that is, inside the parentheses following the *__except*). It cannot be called in a filter function or an exception handler.

The restrictions on where you can use GetExceptionCode() and GetExceptionInformation() may appear rather arbitrary. However, they make sense when you consider that GetExceptionCode() and GetExceptionInformation() are macros, not functions. They are expanded inline, and the stack environment is volatile during exception processing.

To summarize, there are three locations of interest during the processing of an exception. Each has different restrictions on the use of GetExceptionCode() and GetExceptionInformation(). One is the exception-filter expression, contained in the parentheses following the *__except* statement. Here, you can call either GetExceptionCode() or GetExceptionInformation(). Another is the filter function that is called from the filter expression. It may call neither GetExceptionCode() nor GetExceptionInformation(). The third is the exception handler, which is the code in curly braces after the *__except* statement. It can call GetExceptionCode(), but not GetExceptionInformation(). The easiest way to accommodate these restrictions is to pass the return value of GetExceptionCode() or GetExceptionInformation() as an argument to a filter function. The filter function can use this information as it needs to. Fortunately, you don't have to memorize these rules—the compiler displays a "bad context for intrinsic function" message—but it doesn't hurt to know what they are.

Here's a code fragment demonstrating the use of a filter function. It uses GetExceptionInformation() to obtain both the exception code and information on register contents.

```
char *p;
__try
   {
   strcpy(p, "Hi, folks");
   }
__except (CheckPointer(GetExceptionInformation(),
        &p))
   {
   // p could not be allocated
   MessageBox(NULL,
              "Memory allocation error",
              "My Application", MB_OK);
   ExitProcess(1);
   }
```

p is not initialized, so the strcpy() triggers an exception. CheckPointer(), the function called by the filter expression, examines the exception to determine how to proceed. If the exception was EXCEPTION_ACCESS_VIOLATION, CheckPointer() allocates memory for *p*. If the allocation is successful, CheckPointer() returns EXCEPTION_CONTINUE_EXECUTION. If it fails, CheckPointer() returns EXCEPTION_EXECUTE_HANDLER. The exception handler puts up a message box informing the user of the error. For any other exception, CheckPointer() returns EXCEPTION_CONTINUE_SEARCH.

Here is the listing for CheckPointer():

```
DWORD CheckPointer(LPEXCEPTION_POINTERS lpExc, char **pp)
{
   char *p;
   if (lpExc->ExceptionRecord->ExceptionCode !=
         EXCEPTION_ACCESS_VIOLATION)
      return (DWORD) EXCEPTION_CONTINUE_SEARCH;
   p = (char *) malloc(255);
   if (p == NULL)
      return (DWORD) EXCEPTION_EXECUTE_HANDLER;
   *pp = p;

   // We also have to change the register
   // contents by modifying a field
   // in the CONTEXT structure

#if _X86_
   // This is 80386-specific
   lpExc->ContextRecord->Edi = (DWORD) p;
#elif _MIPS_
   lpEx->ContextRecord->IntA0 =
      lpEx->ContextRecord->IntV0 = (DWORD) p;
   lpEx->ContextRecord->IntT5 = lpEx->ContextRecord->IntA0 + 3;
#endif
   return (DWORD) EXCEPTION_CONTINUE_EXECUTION;
}
```

Notice that CheckPointer(), in addition to allocating memory and storing its address in *p*, must also put the newly allocated pointer into the appropriate fields of the CONTEXT structure, pointed to by the *ContextRecord* field of the EXCEPTION_POINTERS structure. On an Intel platform, for example, this is the *Edi* field, representing the contents of the EDI register. When Windows reexecutes the instruction, it reloads the registers from the CONTEXT structure. The code shown here is both machine- and compiler-specific. Ordinarily, programming this way is a terrible practice, particularly under NT; to get the greatest advantage out of NT, you don't want to make any assumptions about the hardware you're running on. My intention here is only to show you how to do this if you ever need to—not to suggest that you do it regularly.

Raising Your Own Exceptions

You can use the exception-reporting mechanism for your own purposes by invoking the function RaiseException().

```
VOID RaiseException(DWORD   dwExceptionCode,
                    DWORD   dwExceptionFlags,
                    DWORD   dwArguments,
                    LPDWORD lpdwArguments);
```

dwExceptionCode is the exception that you want to raise. It will be reported in the *ExceptionCode* field of the EXCEPTION_RECORD or returned by GetExceptionCode(). It can be one of the predefined exceptions, or a code you define for your own purposes. As I discussed earlier in this chapter, exception codes are formatted as a bitfield, shown again here:

```
typedef struct _EXCEPTION_CODE
{
   unsigned dwSeverity  : 2;  // Bits 31 and 30
   unsigned dwOwner     : 1;  // Bit 29
   unsigned dwReserved  : 1;  // Bit 28
   unsigned dwFacility  : 12  // Bits 27-16
   unsigned dwException : 16  // Bits 15-0
} EXCEPTION_CODE;
```

dwFacility and *dwException* can be whatever you want them to be. By Win32 convention, *dwSeverity* uses a value of 1 to indicate an informational exception, 2 to indicate a warning, and 3 to specify an error. Set *dwOwner* to 1 to stamp this code as one of your own. *dwReserved* must be 0; in fact, Windows will automatically clear it. Here is an easy way to distinguish programmer-defined exceptions from those used by Microsoft: the high byte for programmer-defined codes will always be 0x60, 0xA0, or 0xE0, whereas for Microsoft's it will be 0x40, 0x80, or 0xC0.

dwExceptionFlags has one possible non-zero setting, EXCEPTION_NONCONTINUABLE. This indicates that the offending instruction cannot be retried, and any attempt to do so will itself trigger an exception (EXCEPTION_NONCONTINUABLE_EXCEPTION). Passing this argument as 0 says that the instruction can be reexecuted—provided, of course, that there is an exception-filter function that knows how to remedy the situation. For most exceptions, it is probably reasonable to reattempt the instruction, or at least give yourself the option to do so. Noncontinuable exceptions should be reserved for truly serious error conditions. *dwExceptionFlags* is reported in the *ExceptionFlags* field of the EXCEPTION_RECORD that GetExceptionInformation() returns.

dwArguments and *lpdwArguments* allow you to pass yourself additional information. They will be reported in the *NumberParameters* and *ExceptionInformation* fields of the EXCEPTION_RECORD.

I frequently use RaiseException() to report memory allocation errors. Raising an exception is quicker and easier than testing return values at many levels of a call tree. The exception I raise is STATUS_NO_MEMORY, which is the exception raised by the Heap Allocation routines under certain conditions (see Chapter 3). There is no reason to make this a noncontinuable exception; a smart exception-filter function might be able to adjust memory-usage conditions so that the request could be retried and succeed. I also pass the number of bytes I tried to allocate as the first element in the *lpdwArguments* array.

Structured Termination Handling

An important corollary to Win32 Structured Exception Handling is Structured Termination Handling. This sets up cleanup code that executes no matter how the normal flow of execution terminates, unless it kills the running thread or process.

```
__try
   {
   // [Normal flow of execution]
   }
__finally
   {
   // [Cleanup code here]
   }
```

Note that termination handlers and exception handlers must be separate. This code, for example, won't compile:

```
__try
   {
   // [Guarded statements]
   }
__except (EXCEPTION_EXECUTE_HANDLER)
   {
   // [Exception handler]
   }
__finally
   {
   // [Termination handler]
   }
```

However, this will:

```
__try
   {
   __try
      {
      // [Guarded statements]
      }
   __except (EXCEPTION_EXECUTE_HANDLER)
      {
      // [Exception handler]
      }
   }
__finally
   {
   // [Termination handler]
   }
```

The pseudofunction AbnormalTermination() can be used in the *__finally* block (and only in the *__finally* block) to determine whether the *__try* block terminated with some kind of specific transfer of control (*return, break, goto*, or an exception):

```
BOOL AbnormalTermination(VOID);
```

If the *__try* block executes to completion, it will fall through into the *__finally* block, and AbnormalTermination() will return FALSE. Any statement that causes an abnormal termination can be expensive because it causes Windows to search backward up the stack for termination and exception handlers. For instance, using *return* inside a *__try* block in response to an error, or as the last statement in a *__try* block, is considered an incorrect use of *__try/__finally.* Therefore, Microsoft C/C++ for Windows provides an additional keyword, *__leave*, which breaks out of a *__try* block without triggering either an abnormal termination or an unwind. It behaves the way a *break* statement behaves in a *for* loop, but its natural habitat is the *__try* block of a *__try/__finally.*

An important use of Structured Termination Handling is to guarantee that any resources your program claims, like memory or synchronization objects, are returned to the system when you are through with them. The recommended procedure is:

1. Initialize HANDLEs or pointers to the value that indicates an invalid object (NULL, INVALID_HANDLE_VALUE, INVALID_SOCKET, or whatever).

2. In the *__try* block, allocate your resources. Handles and pointers are set to correct values as the resources are successfully allocated. If any of the allocations fails, set a flag to indicate failure and issue a *__leave*.
3. In the *__finally* block, release each resource whose corresponding handle or pointer is valid.

C++ Exception Handling

Starting with Visual C++ 2.0, Microsoft C++ supports ANSI standard C++ exception handling. This is a higher-level model for exception handling than Win32 Structured Exception Handling, and the two are not 100-percent compatible.

Microsoft recommends using the C++ mechanism, as it is more portable. Many MFC classes use exceptions to report error conditions; in these cases, you must use C++ exceptions to handle the errors gracefully. Unlike Win32 exceptions, which are usually caused by bugs in an application, MFC exceptions do not necessarily signal a pathological condition.

Microsoft's implementation of C++ exception handling actually uses Win32 exceptions. A C++ exception is raised as exception number 0xE06D7363.

C++ Syntax

C++ exception handling uses three keywords: *try*, *catch*, and *throw*. *try* works exactly like *__try*; it introduces the normal path through your code. The *try* block is then followed by one or more *catch* statements. Each *catch* declares in parentheses a specific type of exception that you are prepared to deal with. The differentiation among exception types is done on the basis of C++ typing. You raise an exception with the *throw* keyword, followed by some sort of statement that creates an exception object. *throw* without an operand sends the current exception further up the stack; it can only be issued inside a *catch* block.

In looking for an exception handler, Windows evaluates *catch* statements in the order in which they appear in the source code. If an exception is thrown as a C++ object, a *catch* is considered a match if:

- Its operand type is the same type as the operand of the *throw*
- Its operand type is a reference to the same type of object as the one being thrown

- Its operand type meets one of the above criteria for a base class of the thrown object
- Its operand is (...), indicating that it will accept all exceptions not previously mentioned

Because of this, it is important to declare exception handlers in order of precision, from the most specific to the most generic.

Combining Win32 and C++ Exception Handling

The basic rule for combining Win32 and C++ exception handling is quite simple: you can't have a *try* and a *__try* in the same function, even if the *__try* introduces a *__try/__finally*. Because C++ exception handling can provide most of the functionality you need for Win32 exceptions, the place this limitation will cause you the greatest inconvenience is when you want to use a *__finally* block. There is no alternative: from your C++ *try* block, you must call functions that include *__try/__finally* logic (or vice versa). C++ exceptions, like Win32 exceptions, perform a stack unwind, and will execute any *__finally* blocks between the point of the exception and the *catch* block that handles it.

Handling Win32 Exceptions in C++ Code

A Win32 exception will only be dispatched to a generic *catch (...)* block. Your opportunities for evaluating the exception are limited; you cannot call either GetExceptionCode() or GetExceptionInformation(). It is normally more useful to install an exception-translator function with _set_se _translator(). The translator function will be called any time a Win32 exception occurs. Typically, you wrap the information in a C++ object, then *throw* an exception using that object.

Here are the prototypes for the translator function and _set_se_translator(), from the Win32 header file EH.H:

```
typedef void (_CRTAPI1 *_se_translator_function)(
   unsigned int, struct _EXCEPTION_POINTERS*);

_CRTIMP _se_translator_function _CRTAPI1
   _set_se_translator(_se_translator_function);
```

The translator function is passed the return codes from GetException-Code() and GetExceptionInformation(). You pass _set_se_translator() the address of your translator function, and it returns the address of the previously installed one. There is no default translator function, so typically the return value is NULL.

Here's a C++ class that wraps Win32 exception information. To conform to MFC's exception handling, I've made this class a subclass of CException, the base class for MFC exceptions.

```
#include <eh.h>

class AFX_EXT_CLASS CWin32Exception : public CException
{
private:
   // Force use of non-default constructor
   CWin32Exception();
protected:
   EXCEPTION_POINTERS m_ExceptionPointers;
public:
   CWin32Exception(LPEXCEPTION_POINTERS lpExc)
      {
      m_ExceptionPointers.ExceptionRecord =
         lpExc->ExceptionRecord;
      m_ExceptionPointers.ContextRecord   =
         lpExc->ContextRecord;
      }
   UINT GetExceptionCode(void)
      {
      return
         m_ExceptionPointers.ExceptionRecord->ExceptionCode;
      }
   static _se_translator_function SetTranslator(
      _se_translator_function pTranslator =
         CWin32Exception::TranslatorFunction);
   static void TranslatorFunction(
      UINT,
      LPEXCEPTION_POINTERS lpExc);

   DECLARE_DYNAMIC(CWin32Exception);
};
```

I define one nondefault constructor for the class. It captures the EXCEPTION_POINTERS describing the exception in the *m_ExceptionPointers* member variable.

I can then implement a translator function as a single statement. I also provide a SetTranslator() method so users of this object don't have to call _set_se_translator(). By default, it uses CWin32Exception::TranslatorFunction() to do the translation.

```
_se_translator_function CWin32Exception::SetTranslator(
      _se_translator_function pTranslator /* =
         CWin32Exception::TranslatorFunction*/)
{
   return
      _set_se_translator(pTranslator);
}

void CWin32Exception::TranslatorFunction(
      UINT,
      LPEXCEPTION_POINTERS lpExc)
{
   throw new CWin32Exception(lpExc);
}
```

Here again I mimic the way MFC behaves by throwing a pointer to a newly allocated object. The *catch* block is responsible for deleting it.

Here's a main() function that continues the example presented earlier in this chapter, now using C++ instead of Win32 exceptions. Because you cannot use C++ exception handling to retry an instruction, the *catch* block here just prints out the exception code, then re-throws the exception so I can take advantage of post-mortem debugging. When you trap Win32 exceptions in C++ code, this is usually what you want to do. Remember that a *catch (...)* will trap a Win32 exception in the absence of a more precisely defined *catch*.

```
void main(int argc, char *argv[])
{
   char *p = NULL;
   _set_se_translator(TranslatorFunction);

   try
      {
      printf("\nTrying strcpy\n");
      strcpy(p, "Hi, folks");
      }
   catch (CWin32Exception *e)
      {
      printf("\nCaught Win32 exception 0x%08X",
         e->GetExceptionCode());
      e->Delete();
      throw;
      }
   ExitProcess(0);
}
```

The CWin32Exception is the first object I have presented from my C++ class library, an MFC extension DLL which provides Win32 functionality that is lacking in MFC. In subsequent chapters, I'll add many more classes. The project is in the directory \WIN32NET\CODE\WIN32OBJ on the disk accompanying this book. The Visual C++ project file is WIN32MFC.MDP.

Termination Handling with C++ Destructors

Structured Termination Handling is a very valuable service available in Windows. Unfortunately, though, you cannot use it in functions where you have C++ objects. To get the equivalent of Structured Termination Handling in C++, you create stack-based C++ objects that contain the operating system resources you are consuming. The objects' destructors can then take responsibility for releasing the resources. The destructors for all stack-based objects are called when a function exits, no matter how it does so. In order for this to work, it is important that the constructors for the object initialize the variables representing the resources so that they can be recognized as valid or not. Here's an example of an object that contains a dynamically allocated pointer. Its constructor initializes the corresponding member variable to NULL, and the destructor frees the memory.

```
class CMyObject
{
public:
   CString *m_pszMyString;
   CMyObject() {m_pszMyString = NULL;}
   virtual ~CMyObject() {delete m_pszMyString;}
// [Other cool functionality]
};

BOOL MyFunction(void)
{
   CMyObject MyObject();
   MyObject.m_pszMyString = new CString("Hi George");

   // [...]

   return TRUE;
}
```

Handling C++ Exceptions Using __try / __except

When you throw a C++ exception, the C++ compiler actually raises the Win32 exception 0xE06D7363. Therefore, careless use of *__try / __except* logic can cause you to inadvertently trap a C++ exception in a Win32 exception handler. "Careless" means something very precise: providing an exception filter that unconditionally evaluates to EXCEPTION_EXECUTE_HANDLER. Here's an example:

```
void main(int argc, char *argv[])
{
   try
      {
      CPlusPlusFunction(NULL);
      }
   catch (char *pError)
      {
      printf("\n%s", pError);
      }
   ExitProcess(0);
}

void CPlusPlusFunction(char *pArg)
{
   __try
      {
      if (pArg == NULL)
         throw "Invalid argument to CPlusPlusFunction():"
               "  NULL pointer";
      printf("\nString %s passed to CPlusPlusFunction()",
         pArg);
      }
   __except (EXCEPTION_EXECUTE_HANDLER)
      {
      printf("\nCaught Win32 exception 0x%08X",
         GetExceptionCode());
      }
   return;
}
```

The output from this program is:

```
Caught Win32 exception 0xE06D7363
```

This tells us that the exception starts its life as a Win32 exception, and is delegated to the *__except (EXCEPTION_EXECUTE_HANDLER)* block in

CPlusPlusFunction(). Because this exception handler thinks it's the end of the line, the C++ *catch* block in main() never gets control.

A simple change solves the problem. The exception handler only needs to filter out the Microsoft C++ exception. Here's a corrected version of CPlusPlusFunction():

```
void CPlusPlusFunction(char *pArg)
{
   __try
      {
      if (pArg == NULL)
         throw (char *) "Invalid argument to CPlusPlusFunction():"
                        "  NULL pointer";
      printf("\nString %s passed to CPlusPlusFunction()",
         pArg);
      }
   __except (GetExceptionCode() != 0xE06D7363)
      {
      printf("\nCaught Win32 exception 0x%08X",
         GetExceptionCode());
      }
   return;
}
```

Now, the program's output is:

```
Invalid argument to CPlusPlusFunction():  NULL pointer
```

Surprisingly, it doesn't work to *throw* the exception again from the *__except* block, like this:

```
__except (EXCEPTION_EXECUTE_HANDLER)
      {
      if (GetExceptionCode() == 0xE06D7363)
         throw;
      else
         printf("\nCaught Win32 exception 0x%08X",
            GetExceptionCode());
      }
```

C++ treats this as an unhandled exception, and the only output from the program is the C++ default message:

```
Abnormal program termination
```

Conclusion

C++ exception handling is a useful mechanism, providing a different way of reporting software errors than function return values. Exceptions have certain advantages:

- Instead of checking all function return values, you can provide a single point to which all error handling is referred. A good example of how this works is the way MFC implements the *new* operator. You never have to check to see that a pointer allocated with *new* is non-NULL. If the allocation request fails, the next line of code will never execute, because MFC throws a CMemoryException. You can trap memory-allocation failures in certain circmstances if you want to, but you don't have to worry about reading or writing a NULL pointer.
- Exception objects can return more detailed information about an error than a simple function return code is able to carry.

C++ exceptions are, of course, available only in C++ applications. Except for the special use of C++ exception handling to trap Win32 exceptions discussed above, C++ exceptions are generated by the application, not by the operating system.

Win32 exceptions, on the other hand, report errors detected by the hardware or the operating system, and can occur in any development environment—C, C++, Visual Basic, or whatever. After an initial infatuation with Win32 exception handling, I have come to the conclusion that there are only three situations that warrant its use:

- In conjunction with the Virtual Memory API to implement lazy memory allocation or sparse arrays, as discussed in the next chapter
- As a back-door contrivance for making worker threads go away. As we will see in Chapter 4, there is no direct way to do this
- In RPC client applications to detect exceptions raised by the RPC client stub (see Chapter 11)

In all other circumstances, a Win32 exception probably indicates a bug in your program. And here, the post-mortem debugging capabilities that Windows provides are exactly what you want. They will report an error at the precise moment that it occurs, and take you right to the line of code that triggered it. So interestingly, the problem with Win32 exceptions in C++ exception handling gets turned inside out: what you want to do is make sure you *don't* handle the exception. The best way to do this is exactly as I did it earlier:

1. Install a translator function that wraps the exception in a C++ object and issues a *throw*.
2. Catch the exception in a *catch* block that states the type of the C++ object explicitly. Don't use *catch (...)* for Win32 exceptions.
3. In the *catch* block, process the exception information however you need to. It is quite possible that you will do nothing at all with it.
4. As the last statement in the exception handler, issue a *throw* with no operand.

Structured Termination Handling is a different matter. It is useful in a wide variety of situations, and coexists comfortably with C++ exceptions, with the limit I mentioned—you cannot have *try* and *__try* in the same function. C++ object destructor methods serve the same purpose. The destructors for all objects declared on the stack are also invoked in all circumstances.

Suggested Readings

Online References

Programming with MFC: Encyclopedia. "Exceptions."
"Exception Handling," in the *C++ Language Reference*.
"Structured Exception Handling," in the *C++ Language Reference*.
"C++ Exception Handling," in *Programming Techniques*.
"Mixing C and C++ Exceptions," in *Programming Techniques*.
"Structured Exception Handling," in *Programming Techniques*.
"Exception Handling Overview," in *Programming Techniques*.
"Using Structured Exception Handling with C++," in *Programming Techniques*.
"Exception Classes," in the *Class Library Overview*.
Structured Exception Handling Overview in the Win32 online help.
Microsoft Knowledge Base for Win32 SDK articles:
  "Application Exception Error Codes"
  "Choosing the Debugger That the System Will Spawn"
  "Correct Use of Try/Finally"
  "First and Second Chance Exception Handling"
  "Noncontinuable Exceptions"
  "Trapping Floating-Point Exceptions in a Win32-based App"
  "Using volatile to Prevent Optimization of try/except"

Print References

Richter, Jeff. *Advanced Windows*. Redmond, WA: Microsoft Press, 1995. Chapter 14.

Chapter 3

Win32 Memory Allocation

The Win32 API adds two function sets for memory allocation—the Virtual Memory API and the Heap Memory API. The first is the closest to how the operating system itself actually does things. The second provides a layer on top of the Virtual Memory API that is somewhat easier to work with. This is not to say that the Virtual Memory API set is difficult to use; it is not. As you will see, there are some stark tradeoffs that you have to make in choosing which API set to use. The Global and Local allocation routines (GlobalAlloc(), LocalAlloc(), and their related functions) are still supported, as are the C runtime functions such as malloc() and calloc(). In addition, C++ provides the *new* operator. However, it is not a memory allocation primitive; it is implemented using the other mechanisms. The Microsoft Foundation Classes, for instance, use malloc().

Windows uses a virtual memory scheme in which every process runs in its own separate address space. As befits a 32-bit environment, each process has 4GB of virtual memory available to it. The upper 2GB are used by the operating system; the lower 2GB are available to the application. The mapping of virtual addresses to physical addresses uses a page-based scheme. Because the page is the unit used by this scheme, it is the unit of granularity for Windows memory allocation. On Intel chips, a page is 4096 bytes. On the DEC Alpha, a page is 8192 bytes. On MIPS machines, the page size is configurable; NT uses a page size of 4096 bytes. You need never assume a particular page size; the GetSystemInfo() function reports this information.

Since the virtual address space of 4GB is unlikely to be supported by that much real memory (at least today), Windows swaps pages of physical memory to disk to satisfy memory allocation requests. Every process has a set of pages known as its **working set**; these are the pages of memory belonging to the process that are currently resident in RAM. Windows will dynamically adjust the working set of processes to respond to changing usage conditions. When a process requests a new page of memory and none is available, Windows swaps one of the other pages belonging to that process to disk on a first-allocated, first-discarded basis. In addition, Windows uses a demand-paging strategy; even after pages are allocated, they are not brought into physical memory until they are actually accessed.

States of Memory

Windows associates a couple of attributes with each page of virtual memory. One describes the extent to which the page has been allocated to a process. The three possibilities are:

1. The page is **free**; it has not been allocated.
2. The page is **reserved**. The process has been granted a given virtual address (or range of virtual addresses), but no physical memory or swap file space has been associated with it.
3. The page is **committed**. Here, a virtual address is fully supported by physical storage.

There are also three fundamental levels of memory access:

1. No access is allowed. Free and reserved memory, by definition, cannot be accessed. In addition, you can deny all access to a committed block for some algorithmic purpose, like having a guard page to detect the need for more heap space. (However, NT also allows you to set a page up as a guard page and generates an EXCEPTION_GUARD_PAGE exception to let you know you have entered it.)
2. The page may be accessed on a read-only basis. Committed memory can be set to allow read-only access. You might do this, for instance, to prevent sensitive data from being accidentally overwritten.
3. The page may be read from and written to. This allows full access to a page of committed memory, and is the most common usage.

The Virtual Memory API

The Virtual Memory API most closely reflects the underlying Windows memory management strategy. It consists of a small group of functions, of which the most important, as you would expect, are the ones that allocate and free memory—VirtualAlloc() and VirtualFree().

The innovation that Win32 provides is that memory allocation can be either a one-step or two-step process, depending on how you call VirtualAlloc(). This is because memory has three possible states (free, reserved, and committed), rather than just two (free and allocated). Thus, VirtualAlloc() lets you reserve memory for later commitment, commit memory that you have previously reserved, or reserve and commit memory in a single step.

```
LPVOID VirtualAlloc(
          LPVOID   lpAddress,
          DWORD    dwSize,
          DWORD    dwAllocationType,
          DWORD    dwProtect);
```

lpAddress is the virtual address of the region you are allocating. The first time you allocate a block, you will most likely pass *lpAddress* as NULL, although you can specify a base virtual address if you have some reason for doing so. In this case, the address must be aligned on a 64K boundary, and you can only reserve it. If the address is already in use, VirtualAlloc() will return NULL. If you reserve memory first and commit it later, you need to supply a non-NULL address when calling VirtualAlloc() later to commit the memory.

dwSize is the number of bytes you want to reserve or commit. Windows will scale *lpAddress* and *dwSize* so that they describe an even multiple of the system page size. Assuming a page size of 4096 bytes, if you call VirtualAlloc() with an *lpAddress* of NULL and *dwSize* of 16000, Windows will allocate a region of 16384 bytes. If you try to commit 100 bytes starting at address 5000, Windows will commit 4096 bytes at address 4096. You do not need to adjust the arguments; Windows will do this automatically. It will not fail the request.

dwAllocationType specifies whether you want to reserve memory, commit it, or do both at once. To reserve memory, pass the constant MEM_RESERVE; to commit it, pass MEM_COMMIT. For a one-step reserve/commit, MEM_COMMIT is sufficient.

The *dwProtect* argument indicates what level of access you need to the newly allocated memory. Even if you are reserving memory, this argument is relevant. You should request the access that you will need when you commit the memory. This makes the subsequent commitment work a little more efficiently. The most important values for *dwProtect*, and the only ones supported by Windows 95, are PAGE_NOACCESS, PAGE_READONLY, and PAGE_READWRITE. NT provides two page-protection modifiers, PAGE_GUARD and PAGE_NOCACHE, which can be ORed with one of the other protection constants. PAGE_GUARD causes NT to raise an EXCEPTION_GUARD_PAGE exception when the page is entered. This operates as a signal that a data structure (like a stack) needs to be expanded. PAGE_NOCACHE is more esoteric and of little use to application programs; its principal relevance is in device drivers.

Here is an example that reserves a block of memory, then commits it in response to an exception. This is a very common and important use of virtual memory allocation in conjunction with Structured Exception Handling. Notice also the use of a termination handler to release the memory when you are through with it, and the nesting of a *__try/__except* within a *__try/__finally*.

```
#include <windows.h>
#include <stdio.h>

DWORD CheckPointer(DWORD dwException, char **p)
{
   printf("\nCheckPointer() entered");
   if (dwException != EXCEPTION_ACCESS_VIOLATION)
      {
      printf("\nCheckPointer() returning EXCEPTION_CONTINUE_SEARCH");
      return EXCEPTION_CONTINUE_SEARCH;
      }

   *p = (char *) VirtualAlloc(*p, 4096, MEM_COMMIT, PAGE_READWRITE);

   if (*p == NULL)
      {
      printf("\nCheckPointer() returning EXCEPTION_EXECUTE_HANDLER");
      return EXCEPTION_EXECUTE_HANDLER;
      }
   printf("\nCheckPointer() returning EXCEPTION_CONTINUE_EXCEPTION");
   return EXCEPTION_CONTINUE_EXECUTION;
}

void main(int argc, char *argv[])
{
   char *p;

   p = (char *) VirtualAlloc(NULL, 4096, MEM_RESERVE,
                                     PAGE_READWRITE);
```

```
    __try
       {
       __try
          {
          strcpy(p, "Hi, folks");
          }
       __except (CheckPointer(GetExceptionCode(), &p))
          {
          printf("\nMemory allocation error");
          ExitProcess(1);
          }
       }
    __finally
       {
       if (p != NULL)
          {
          printf("\n%s\n", p);
          VirtualFree(p, 0, MEM_RELEASE);
          }
       }
    ExitProcess(0);
}
```

Other Virtual Memory Functions

The other virtual memory functions are of less significance, though they can be useful under certain circumstances. VirtualProtect() and VirtualProtect-Ex() change the access mode of a block of memory. This can be valuable in protecting sensitive data after you have allocated memory for it and written the data into the memory. Here are their prototypes:

```
BOOL VirtualProtect(
        LPVOID  lpAddress,
        DWORD   dwSize,
        DWORD   dwNewProtect,
        PDWORD  lpdwOldProtect);

BOOL VirtualProtectEx(
        HANDLE  hProcess,
        LPVOID  lpAddress,
        DWORD   dwSize,
        DWORD   dwNewProtect,
        PDWORD  lpdwOldProtect);
```

lpAddress points to the region you want to change. *dwSize* is the number of bytes. As with all the virtual memory functions, they will be scaled so that they describe complete pages of memory in the region. *dwNewProtect* is the new access mode, and *lpdwOldProtect* returns the previous protection assigned to the memory. All pages in the indicated region must be in the committed state, or the request will fail.

VirtualProtectEx() allows you to manipulate memory belonging to another process; it takes an additional argument, *hProcess*. This is the handle of the process that owns the memory. Usually, you will only have a handle to another process if you start it as a child by calling CreateProcess().

VirtualQuery() and VirtualQueryEx() return information about a given block of virtual memory. VirtualQueryEx(), like VirtualProtectEx(), works with the virtual memory of a child process.

```
BOOL VirtualQuery(
        LPCVOID lpBaseAddress,
        PMEMORY_BASIC_INFORMATION lpMBI,
        DWORD   dwLength);

BOOL VirtualQueryEx(
        HANDLE  hProcess,
        LPCVOID lpBaseAddress,
        PMEMORY_BASIC_INFORMATION lpMBI,
        DWORD   dwLength);
```

They populate a MEMORY_BASIC_INFORMATION structure, whose definition is as follows:

```
typedef struct _MEMORY_BASIC_INFORMATION
{
   PVOID   BaseAddress;
   PVOID   AllocationBase;
   DWORD   AllocationProtect;
   DWORD   RegionSize;
   DWORD   State;
   DWORD   Protect;
   DWORD   Type;
} MEMORY_BASIC_INFORMATION;
```

Each call to VirtualQuery() will report on the largest contiguous range of memory starting at *lpBaseAddress* for which all the pages have identical characteristics. *RegionSize* is the number of bytes in the region being reported. *State* is MEM_FREE, MEM_COMMIT, or MEM_RESERVE. *Protect* is the current access mode of the region; *AllocationProtect* is the access mode that was requested when the region was first allocated. *Type* can be MEM_IMAGE, indicating that the pages are an executable file image;

MEM_MAPPED, designating a memory-mapped view of a file; or MEM_PRIVATE, specifying that the memory is private to this process. *BaseAddress* is the beginning of the region being described; *AllocationBase* is the base of the block from which this region has been carved. In other words, *AllocationBase* is the address returned by the first call to VirtualAlloc(); *BaseAddress* was returned by a subsequent call that changed the state or access mode of this memory.

Why Reserve Memory?

I have found that the question inevitably arises: all right, so you *can* reserve and commit memory as separate operations, but why would you *want* to?

The primary reason is that reserving memory mimics the Windows policy of not consuming a resource until it is actually needed. The preceding example does not dramatically illustrate the value of this. Suppose, however, you have an array that under maximum (but highly unlikely) conditions will reach 10MB in size. Under most circumstances, it will probably never get bigger than 1MB. It is extremely wasteful and causes severe performance degradation to sit on 10MB of memory that you probably won't use. However, you must have contiguous virtual addresses since the data structure you are creating must be treated as an array. Windows itself uses this exact scheme to manage a process's stacks and heaps.

The two-step reserve/commit provides a very clean solution to this problem. When you first allocate the data structure, you reserve a 10MB region by calling VirtualAlloc().

```
LPBYTE lp;
lp = VirtualAlloc(NULL, 10 * 1024 * 1024, MEM_RESERVE,
                  PAGE_READWRITE);
```

You then surround reads and writes to the array with *__try/__except* logic. Your exception filter function will look very much like the one in the preceding example. This way, you have an object that looks like a simple large array to you but that uses only the physical memory that you really need.

By the way, note that the exception-filter function just presented does not assume that the call to committing the memory succeeds. Indeed, you cannot make this assumption; you must check to see if VirtualAlloc() returns NULL. Reserving the memory only assigns virtual address space; it does not in any way guarantee that the physical memory will be there when you need it.

VirtualFree() reverses the allocation process. Like VirtualAlloc(), it can be done in one-step or two-step fashion. Thus, you can decommit a committed block of memory. The virtual addresses continue to be reserved; they are available to be recommitted at a later time. The physical memory is returned to the operating system. You can also release a block of memory, thereby relinquishing both the virtual addresses and the underlying physical memory.

VirtualFree() takes one less argument than VirtualAlloc()—the access mode is irrelevant. Here too you specify the base address, the number of bytes being affected, and the operation you want to perform (decommit or release).

```
BOOL VirtualFree(
        LPVOID lpAddress,
        DWORD  dwBytes,
        DWORD  dwFreeType);
```

As with VirtualAlloc(), *lpAddress* will be rounded down to a page boundary, and *dwSize* will be rounded up to a multiple of the page size. *dwFreeType* can be either MEM_DECOMMIT or MEM_RELEASE. If you are releasing memory rather than decommitting it, these conditions must be met:

- *lpAddress* must be the base of the region you originally reserved when you called VirtualAlloc().
- *dwBytes* must be zero.
- All pages in the region must be in the same state (committed or reserved). You can satisfy this requirement by first decommitting the entire block. There is no requirement that all pages be committed for a decommit request to succeed.

```
LPBYTE pBase = (LPBYTE) VirtualAlloc(
                           NULL,
                           1024 * 1024,
                           MEM_RESERVE,
                           PAGE_READWRITE);
//
// [Use memory here, committing it as needed]
//
// Now decommit the memory, then release it
VirtualFree(pBase, 1024 * 1024, MEM_DECOMMIT);
VirtualFree(pBase, 0, MEM_RELEASE);
```

The only caveat is that if you reserve a very large block, decommitting the entire block (whether or not you have committed it) can be time-consuming. It is more efficient to decommit only the number of bytes that you have actually committed (assuming that you are committing from the base of the block and not fragmenting the block into reserved and committed sections). You can do this by either maintaining a running count of the number of committed bytes or by calling VirtualQuery() to find out the size of the committed region. This way, you will know exactly how many bytes you need to decommit, and the decommit request will execute much more quickly. You should also check to make sure the number of committed bytes is not zero. Decommitting an entire block where no bytes have been committed can also be expensive.

Here's a revision of the previous example that uses VirtualQuery() to determine how many bytes have been committed:

```
MEMORY_BASIC_INFORMATION mbi;
LPBYTE pBase = (LPBYTE) VirtualAlloc(
                            NULL,
                            1024 * 1024,
                            MEM_RESERVE,
                            PAGE_READWRITE);
//
// [Use memory here, committing it as needed]
//
ZeroMemory(&mbi, sizeof (MEMORY_BASIC_INFORMATION));
VirtualQuery(pBase, &mbi, sizeof (MEMORY_BASIC_INFORMATION));
if (mbi.State == MEM_COMMIT && mbi.RegionSize > 0)
   VirtualFree(pBase, mbi.RegionSize, MEM_DECOMMIT);
VirtualFree(pBase, 0, MEM_RELEASE);
```

Heap Memory Allocation

In Win32, heap memory allocation has two meanings. One specifically connotes the API set known as the Heap Memory API. The other is a more general usage, referring to all the memory allocation API sets that do subsegment memory allocation. These include the LocalAlloc() and GlobalAlloc() APIs inherited from Windows 3.x, the malloc() family of functions, the OLE 2 *IMalloc* interface, and the Heap Memory API itself. All of these are built on top of virtual memory allocation, but shield applications from the additional complexity of the Virtual Memory API. The subsegment allocation capabilities of these APIs are also important. The granularity of the Virtual Memory API is very coarse; the minimum amount of memory you can allocate is one page—which currently means either 4096 or 8192 bytes, depending on the hardware your program is running on. The other API sets give you much finer granularity. In exchange, they give you less control over how memory is managed and do not provide as much memory protection.

The Heap Memory API

The Heap Memory API, like the Virtual Memory API, is new to Win32. It exposes some of the underlying memory-management scheme, though not as much as the Virtual Memory API. There are only a few functions, the most important of which are HeapAlloc() and HeapFree(). The other functions in the group are:

- HeapCreate() and HeapDestroy(), which you can use to allocate and release a new region for subsegment allocation
- HeapReAlloc(), which lets you resize a memory object allocated by HeapAlloc()
- HeapSize(), which reports the size of an object
- HeapLock() and HeapUnlock(), which request exclusive access to a heap
- Diagnostic functions that compact, validate, and walk a heap (HeapCompact(), HeapValidate(), and HeapWalk())

In addition to creating private heaps, you can get a handle to the default heap of the process by calling GetProcessHeap(). When you call HeapAlloc() with this handle, you allocate memory from the same pages of virtual memory as GlobalAlloc(), LocalAlloc(), and IMalloc::Alloc().

```
HANDLE GetProcessHeap(VOID);
```

To create a new heap, you call HeapCreate().

```
HANDLE HeapCreate(DWORD dwOptions,
                  DWORD dwInitialCommitted,
                  DWORD dwTotalReserved);
```

If *dwOptions* is passed as zero, then (by default) memory allocations that fail will return NULL pointers, and Windows will automatically serialize access to the heap by multiple threads within your application. This is probably the behavior you will want most of the time; if you want to change it, you can specify two flags, HEAP_GENERATE_EXCEPTIONS and HEAP_NO_SERIALIZE. HeapAlloc() and HeapFree() also include a flags argument. If you pass the zero flag to HeapCreate(), you can override the default behavior by setting the corresponding flag for those functions. Any non-zero flags that you pass to HeapCreate() affect all subsequent activity against the heap, and cannot be overridden.

dwInitialCommitted is the number of bytes you want allocated in committed pages; typically, you will pass this as a small number, somewhere between 4096 and 16,384. *dwTotalReserved* is the number of bytes you want allocated as reserved memory. The heap allocation routines will automatically commit new pages from this region when it becomes necessary. The committed portion of the heap will always grow, but never shrink; once a page in the heap has been committed, Windows will not decommit it. You can pass *dwTotalReserved* as zero; this will permit the heap to grow to all of available memory.

The HANDLE returned by either HeapCreate() or GetProcessHeap(), which is just the base virtual address of the heap, is then passed to the rest of the heap functions: HeapAlloc(), HeapFree(), HeapDestroy(), HeapReAlloc(), HeapSize(), and the heap diagnostic functions.

HeapAlloc() allocates memory from a heap.

```
LPVOID HeapAlloc(HANDLE hHeap, DWORD dwFlags, DWORD dwBytes);
```

hHeap and *dwBytes* should be obvious. *dwFlags* can be the same nonzero values as specified above for HeapCreate(): HEAP_GENERATE_EXCEPTIONS, and HEAP_NO_SERIALIZE. No matter what you passed to HeapCreate(), these flags will take precedence if you set them when calling HeapAlloc(). If you do not set them, they will inherit whatever values you passed to HeapCreate(). HEAP_GENERATE_EXCEPTIONS means that if the allocation request cannot be satisfied, Windows will generate a STATUS_NO_MEMORY (0xC0000017) exception, rather than return a NULL pointer. HEAP_NO_SERIALIZE means that access to the heap will not be serialized among multiple threads during this call to HeapAlloc(). You can pass one additional flag, HEAP_ZERO_MEMORY. This tells Windows to clear the allocated block to zeroes.

HeapFree() releases memory obtained from HeapAlloc().

```
BOOL HeapFree(HANDLE hHeap, DWORD dwFlags, LPVOID lpMem);
```

lpMem is the pointer returned by HeapAlloc(); *hHeap*, again, is the handle generated by HeapCreate() or returned by GetProcessHeap(). HEAP_NO_SERIALIZE is the only setting currently defined for *dwFlags*, and means the same thing as it does with HeapAlloc()—don't serialize access to the heap while you are executing this function.

HeapDestroy() releases the memory originally allocated for the heap when you called HeapCreate(). Presumably, HeapDestroy() calls VirtualFree() twice, once with MEM_DECOMMIT and once with MEM_ RELEASE. You should not call HeapDestroy() with the heap handle returned by GetProcessHeap().

Less important functions are HeapSize(), which returns the size of an allocated block within a heap, and HeapReAlloc(), which resizes a previously allocated block.

```
DWORD HeapSize(HANDLE hHeap, DWORD dwFlags, LPCVOID lpMem);
```

lpMem is the pointer returned by HeapAlloc(). The only possible setting for *dwFlags* at this time is HEAP_NO_SERIALIZE. The return value of the function is the size of *lpMem*; it is zero if the function fails.

```
LPVOID HeapReAlloc(HANDLE hHeap,
                   DWORD dwFlags,
                   LPVOID lpMem,
                   DWORD dwBytes);
```

dwBytes is the new size that you want for *lpMem*. *dwFlags* can take on all the values described above for HeapAlloc() (HEAP_GENERATE_EXCEPTIONS, HEAP_NO_SERIALIZE, and HEAP_ZERO_MEMORY), as well as one additional setting, HEAP_REALLOC_IN_PLACE_ONLY, which prevents Windows from moving the block to satisfy the request. The return value is the new virtual address where the memory resides (unless the request cannot be satisfied, in which case you either get a NULL pointer or a STATUS_NO_MEMORY exception).

Global and Local Memory Allocation

The time-honored global and local memory allocation API sets are still supported in Windows NT and Windows 95. After all, there is a great deal of code that has been written using these functions; breaking them would cause major side effects and was no doubt judged to be politically impossible. However, they have none of their previous semantics; in fact, they are now just different names for the same operations. You can use the local and global functions interchangeably with the same piece of memory. For instance, this code is perfectly acceptable:

```
LPSTR lp;
lp = LocalAlloc(LPTR, 255);
...
GlobalFree(lp);
```

Of course, it makes no sense to do this. The point I am making here is not that it is now appropriate to engage in questionable coding practices; rather, because there is no longer a distinction between NEAR and FAR pointers, the LocalAlloc() and GlobalAlloc() family of functions behave exactly the same.

These functions reflect the memory management environment that Microsoft created for Windows 2.1, where memory had to be maintained in two states: as a handle most of the time and as a pointer when you needed to access it. This scheme became irrelevant when Windows 3.0 went to protected mode. From that time on, there has been no need to LocalAlloc() or GlobalAlloc() a HANDLE, then LocalLock() or GlobalLock() it to convert it to a pointer. In protected mode, pointers are just virtual addresses, so Windows can let you keep track of unchanging pointers and still be free to move memory around as it sees fit. In Windows 3.x, the distinction between NEAR and FAR pointers is still pertinent; it is rooted in the segmented architecture of the 80286, which is now also obsolete. Segmented memory has disappeared; for all intents and purposes, local and global memory allocation is obsolete.

A Little PWALK through Memory

In this section, I present a sample application, MEMTEST.EXE, whose Visual C++ project is in \WIN32NET\CODE\MEMORY\MEMTEST\MEMTEST.MDP on the disk. In concert with the Win32 SDK utility PWALK.EXE (Process Walker), it demonstrates how the various memory allocation APIs behave. From this, the relative advantages and disadvantages of each emerge in pretty clear relief. This data is gathered from Windows NT; PWALK doesn't work under Windows 95, though the considerations are the same.

Figures 3-1 and 3-2 show the PWALK screens that appear when MEMTEST.EXE first starts up.

In Figure 3-1, I have highlighted the lines showing the process's stack (beginning at virtual address 0x00030000) and its default heap (at address 0x00140000). Notice that the stack begins with a reserved region of 1,040,384 bytes. Next comes a single committed page with PAGE_READWRITE access; it has also been flagged as a guard page. Following this is the currently active stack region, consisting of 4096 bytes of committed, read-write memory. When the stack needs more than 4096 bytes, the guard page is entered, which triggers an EXCEPTION_GUARD_PAGE exception. At this point, NT removes the guard page protection on the guard page and commits a new guard page from the bottom of the reserved portion.

The default heap for the process is the 1MB region that begins at 0x00140000. The first two pages have been committed. If this proves insufficient, the committed portion will grow into the reserved area at virtual address 0x00142000. As you will see, calls to GlobalAlloc(), LocalAlloc(), IMalloc::Alloc(), and HeapAlloc(GetProcessHeap(), ...) are satisfied from this location. The last highlighted line in Figure 3-1 shows a 1.8MB free region at 0x00240000, from which calls to malloc() will be carved.

Process Walker - memtest.exe

Process Sort View Options

Address	State	Prot	Size	BaseAddr	Object	Section	Na
00000000	Free	NA	65536	00000000			
00010000	Commit	RW	4096	00010000			
00011000	Free	NA	61440	00000000			
00020000	Commit	RW	4096	00020000			
00021000	Free	NA	61440	00000000			
00030000	Reserve	NA	1040384	00030000	stack		
0012E000	Commit	RW	4096	00030000	stack	guard	
0012F000	Commit	RW	4096	00030000	stack		
00130000	Commit	RW	4096	00130000			
00131000	Free	NA	61440	00000000			
00140000	Commit	RW	8192	00140000			
00142000	Reserve	NA	1040384	00140000			
00240000	Free	NA	1835008	00000000			
00400000	Commit	RO	4096	00400000	exe		

Ready Rewalk

Figure 3-1. PWALK Display at Startup—Screen 1

Process Walker - memtest.exe

Process Sort View Options

Address	State	Prot	Size	BaseAddr	Object	Section
00401000	Commit	NA	16384	00400000	exe	.text
00405000	Commit	NA	4096	00400000	exe	.bss
00406000	Commit	RO	4096	00400000	exe	.rdata
00407000	Commit	NA	4096	00400000	exe	.data
00408000	Commit	RW	4096	00400000	exe	.idata
00409000	Commit	NA	4096	00400000	exe	.rsrc
0040A000	Commit	RO	4096	00400000	exe	.reloc
0040B000	Free	NA	2005618688	00000000		
77CC0000	Commit	RO	4096	77CC0000	dll	
77CC1000	Commit	NA	454656	77CC0000	dll	.text
77D30000	Commit	RO	40960	77CC0000	dll	.rdata
77D3A000	Commit	NA	20480	77CC0000	dll	.data

Ready Rewalk

Figure 3-2. PWALK Display at Startup—Screen 2

In Figure 3-2, I have highlighted a free region at 0x0040B000. This is where my calls to VirtualAlloc() and HeapCreate() will be fulfilled. Notice the size of the region; it's over 2GB.

MEMTEST does three experiments: the first one allocates memory, the second tests memory access violations, and the third tests writes to released memory. Figure 3-3 shows the results of the first experiment.

The program first calls VirtualAlloc() with a base address of NULL and asks for 32 bytes. This is represented by the pointer *lpVirtual1*. As Figure 3-3 shows,

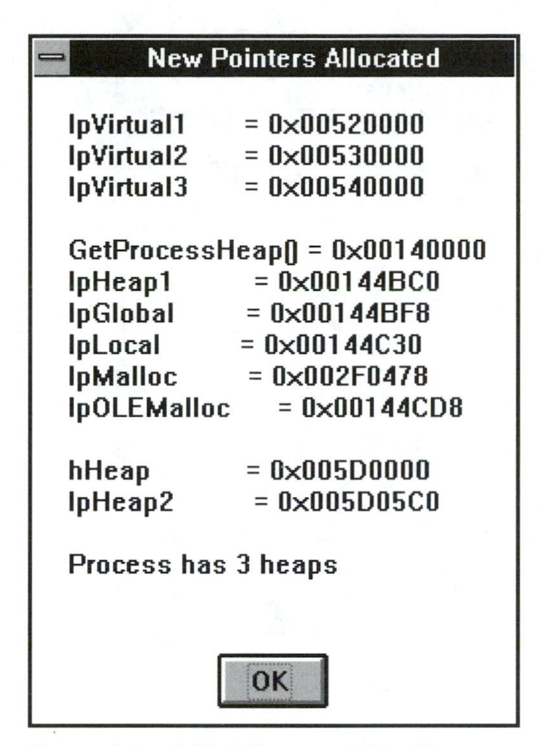

Figure 3-3. Initial Memory Allocations

the address assigned is 0x00520000. Next it adds 4096 bytes to *lpVirtual1* and calls VirtualAlloc() to reserve 32 bytes at this specific address. It keeps adding 4096 bytes until it gets a non-NULL address. This is the pointer *lpVirtual2*—allocated on the next 64K boundary. The next thing the program does is VirtualAlloc() another buffer using a NULL base address; this is *lpVirtual3*. As Figure 3-3 shows, this too is allocated on the next 64K boundary.

To test heap-based allocation routines [HeapAlloc(), GlobalAlloc(), LocalAlloc(), malloc(), and IMalloc::Alloc()], MEMTEST next allocates five pointers, four of which are from the default process heap. The function GetProcessHeap() returns the HANDLE of the process's heap; as you can see, it is just the base address of the heap (0x00140000). *lpHeap1* is returned by a call to HeapAlloc(GetProcessHeap(), ...). *lpGlobal* results from a call to GlobalAlloc(), *lpLocal* from one to LocalAlloc(). *lpMalloc* is generated by malloc(). Notice that it is not allocated from the default heap. *lpOLEMalloc* is returned by CoTaskMemAlloc() (which wraps the OLE 2 memory allocator, IMalloc::Alloc()). Finally, MEMTEST creates a new heap by calling HeapCreate() and asking for 8192 bytes of committed memory from a total of 65,536 bytes reserved. This is the variable *hHeap*; it is the base virtual

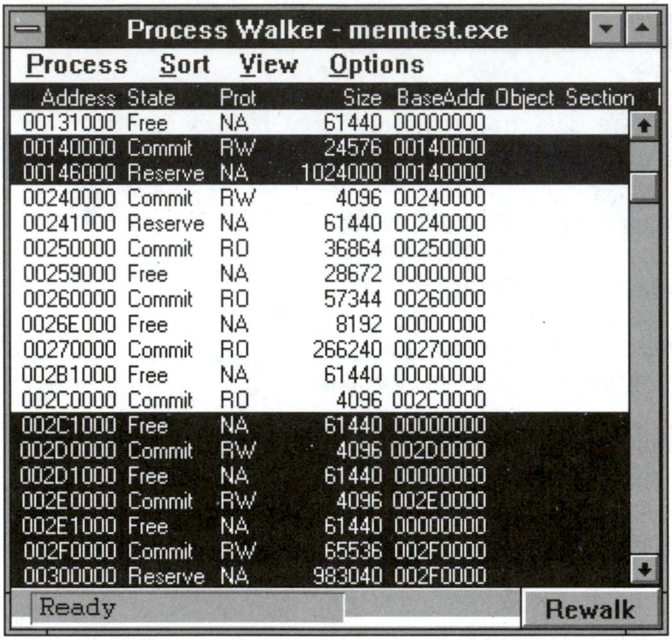

Process Walker - memtest.exe

Process Sort View Options

Address	State	Prot	Size	BaseAddr	Object	Section
00131000	Free	NA	61440	00000000		
00140000	Commit	RW	24576	00140000		
00146000	Reserve	NA	1024000	00140000		
00240000	Commit	RW	4096	00240000		
00241000	Reserve	NA	61440	00240000		
00250000	Commit	RO	36864	00250000		
00259000	Free	NA	28672	00000000		
00260000	Commit	RO	57344	00260000		
0026E000	Free	NA	8192	00000000		
00270000	Commit	RO	266240	00270000		
002B1000	Free	NA	61440	00000000		
002C0000	Commit	RO	4096	002C0000		
002C1000	Free	NA	61440	00000000		
002D0000	Commit	RW	4096	002D0000		
002D1000	Free	NA	61440	00000000		
002E0000	Commit	RW	4096	002E0000		
002E1000	Free	NA	61440	00000000		
002F0000	Commit	RW	65536	002F0000		
00300000	Reserve	NA	983040	002F0000		

Ready Rewalk

Figure 3-4. Heap-Based Memory Allocations

address of a newly committed region of memory. *lpHeap2* is HeapAlloc()'d from this new heap.

In Figure 3-4, PWALK has highlighted the memory regions that have changed. The default process heap is the first highlighted line, at address 0x00140000. The pointers from HeapAlloc(GetProcessHeap(), ...), GlobalAlloc(), LocalAlloc(), and CoTaskMemAlloc() are all from this region (0x00144BC0, 0x00144BF8, 0x00144C30, and 0x00144CD8). Notice that the committed size of the heap has tripled from what it was in Figure 3-1.

The next-to-last highlighted line in Figure 3-4 is the newly committed region where *lpMalloc* was allocated. As you can see, one megabyte has been reserved for these allocations, and the first 64K of it has been committed.

Figure 3-5 shows the memory allocated for *lpVirtual1*, *lpVirtual2*, and *lpVirtual3*. Although I only asked for 32 bytes for each of them, I got 4096—and this is not the only overhead. Notice that the 4096 bytes of committed memory at 0x00520000, 0x00530000, and 0x00540000 are followed by 61,440 bytes of free memory. Part of the experiment I did in TestMemoryAllocations() was to see if I could get to this free memory (starting at 0x00521000, 0x00531000, and 0x00541000). I couldn't. No matter what you do, the rest of the 64K block is unavailable. In other words, an allocation of 32 bytes consumes 4K (actually, one pageful) of physical memory and 64K of virtual memory!

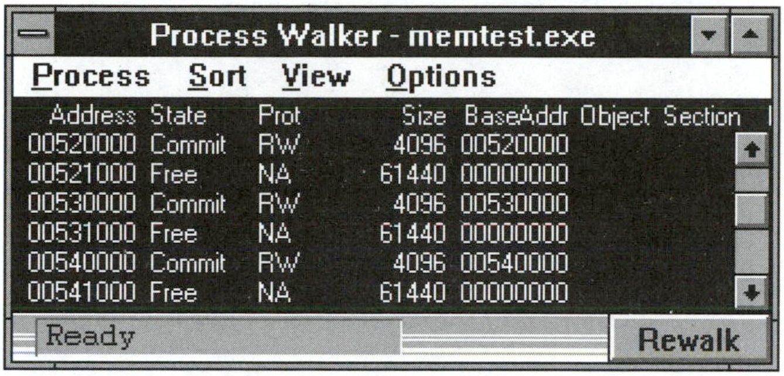

Process Walker - memtest.exe

Process Sort View Options

Address	State	Prot	Size	BaseAddr	Object	Section
00520000	Commit	RW	4096	00520000		
00521000	Free	NA	61440	00000000		
00530000	Commit	RW	4096	00530000		
00531000	Free	NA	61440	00000000		
00540000	Commit	RW	4096	00540000		
00541000	Free	NA	61440	00000000		

Ready Rewalk

Figure 3-5. Virtual Memory Allocations

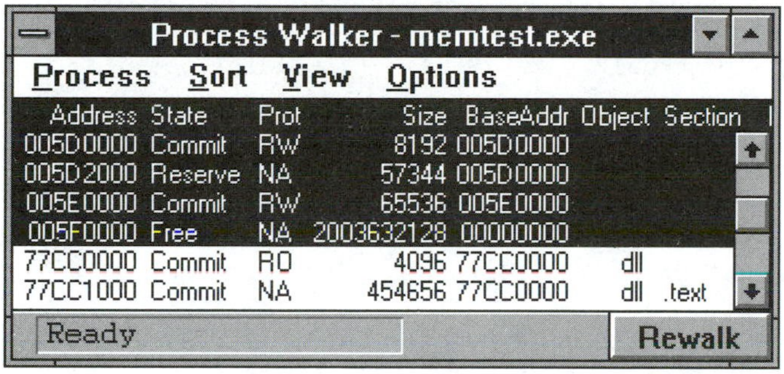

Process Walker - memtest.exe

Process Sort View Options

Address	State	Prot	Size	BaseAddr	Object	Section
005D0000	Commit	RW	8192	005D0000		
005D2000	Reserve	NA	57344	005D0000		
005E0000	Commit	RW	65536	005E0000		
005F0000	Free	NA	2003632128	00000000		
77CC0000	Commit	RO	4096	77CC0000	dll	
77CC1000	Commit	NA	454656	77CC0000	dll	.text

Ready Rewalk

Figure 3-6. PWALK Display Showing Newly Created Heap

The top two lines in Figure 3-6 show the newly created heap, represented by *hHeap* (0x005D0000). It has exactly the characteristics we requested: 8192 bytes in committed pages, and 64K reserved.

Clearly, the prime disadvantage of using VirtualAlloc() is its exceedingly coarse granularity.

Here is the function TestMemoryAllocations():

```
DWORD WINAPI TestMemoryAllocations(HWND hWnd)
{
   CHAR  szMessage[16384];

   lpVirtual1 = (LPBYTE) VirtualAlloc(NULL, 32,
      MEM_COMMIT, PAGE_READWRITE);
   lstrcpy((LPSTR) lpVirtual1, "lpVirtual1 (VirtualAlloc())");
   lpVirtual3 = lpVirtual1 + 4096;

   while (TRUE)
      {
      // An interesting phenomenon occurs here
      // If we try to reserve the next page up from lpVirtual1,
```

```
        // it fails, but as soon as we get to the next
        // 64K boundary, we're in business.

        // However, if we try to commit lpVirtual2 in this
        // call to VirtualAlloc, it does not succeed until
        // we get into virtual addresses over 0x7F000000

        lpVirtual2 = (LPBYTE) VirtualAlloc(
           lpVirtual3, 32, MEM_RESERVE, PAGE_READWRITE);
        if (lpVirtual2 != NULL)
           break;
        lpVirtual3 += 4096;
        }
    // This commit call succeeds
    VirtualAlloc(lpVirtual2, 32, MEM_COMMIT, PAGE_READWRITE);

    lstrcpy((LPSTR) lpVirtual2, "lpVirtual2 (VirtualAlloc())");

    // But this one fails
    VirtualAlloc(lpVirtual1, 8192, MEM_COMMIT, PAGE_READWRITE);

    lpVirtual3 = (LPBYTE) VirtualAlloc(NULL, 32, MEM_COMMIT, PAGE_READWRITE);
    lstrcpy((LPSTR) lpVirtual3, "lpVirtual3 (VirtualAlloc())");

    lpHeap1 = (LPBYTE) HeapAlloc(GetProcessHeap(), 0, 32);
    lstrcpy((LPSTR) lpHeap1, "lpHeap1 (HeapAlloc())");

    hGlobal = GlobalAlloc(GMEM_MOVEABLE, 32);
    lpGlobal = (LPBYTE) GlobalLock(hGlobal);
    lstrcpy((LPSTR) lpGlobal, "lpGlobal (GlobalAlloc())");

    hLocal = LocalAlloc(LMEM_MOVEABLE, 32);
    lpLocal = (LPBYTE) LocalLock(hLocal);
    lstrcpy((LPSTR) lpLocal, "lpLocal (LocalAlloc())");

    lpMalloc = (LPBYTE) malloc(32);
    lstrcpy((LPSTR) lpMalloc, "lpMalloc (malloc())");

    lpOLEMalloc = (LPBYTE) CoTaskMemAlloc(32);
    lstrcpy((LPSTR) lpOLEMalloc, "lpOLEMalloc (CoTaskMemAlloc())");

    hHeap = HeapCreate(0, 8192, 65536);
    lpHeap2 = (LPBYTE) HeapAlloc(hHeap, 0, 32);
    lstrcpy((LPSTR) lpHeap2, "lpHeap2 (HeapAlloc())");

    DWORD dwHeaps;
    HANDLE hHeapHandles[256];
```

```
    if (!bWindows95)
       dwHeaps = GetProcessHeaps(256, hHeapHandles);

    wsprintf(szMessage, "lpVirtual1       = 0x%08X\n"
                        "lpVirtual2       = 0x%08X\n"
                        "lpVirtual3       = 0x%08X\n\n"
                        "GetProcessHeap() = 0x%08X\n"
                        "lpHeap1          = 0x%08X\n"
                        "lpGlobal         = 0x%08X\n"
                        "lpLocal          = 0x%08X\n"
                        "lpMalloc         = 0x%08X\n"
                        "lpOLEMalloc      = 0x%08X\n\n"
                        "hHeap            = 0x%08X\n"
                        "lpHeap2          = 0x%08X\n\n",
        lpVirtual1, lpVirtual2, lpVirtual3,
        GetProcessHeap(), lpHeap1, lpGlobal, lpLocal, lpMalloc,
        lpOLEMalloc, hHeap, lpHeap2);

        if (!bWindows95)
           wsprintf(&szMessage[lstrlen(szMessage)],
                        "Process has %d heaps\n", dwHeaps);

    // We use an event to govern our response
    // to WM_INITMENUPOPUP
    GlobalUnlock(hGlobal);
    LocalUnlock(hLocal);
    SetEvent(hEvent);
    MessageBox(hWnd, szMessage, "New Pointers Allocated", MB_OK);

    return 0;
}
```

The second thing MEMTEST tests is what you have to do to trigger an exception. My hypothesis was that only memory accesses outside of committed, read-write pages would trigger exceptions. Thus, if you are doing heap allocations, you can read or write anywhere within the heap without causing an exception. In other words, if you use the heap allocation APIs, your memory objects are protected from other processes, but they are not protected from you. Let's see what the results show us.

Figure 3-7 shows the message box displayed by the function TestAccessViolations(), which tries to find the point where an exception will happen.

With *lpVirtual1*, I call VirtualQuery() to get the size of the allocated region, then read the next byte. For heap objects (*lpHeap1, lpGlobal, lpLocal, lpMalloc*, *lpOLEMalloc*, and *lpHeap2*), I call the corresponding function that reports the size of the object [HeapSize(), GlobalSize(), LocalSize(), IMalloc::GetSize(), and _msize()]. I then read the byte that should be one

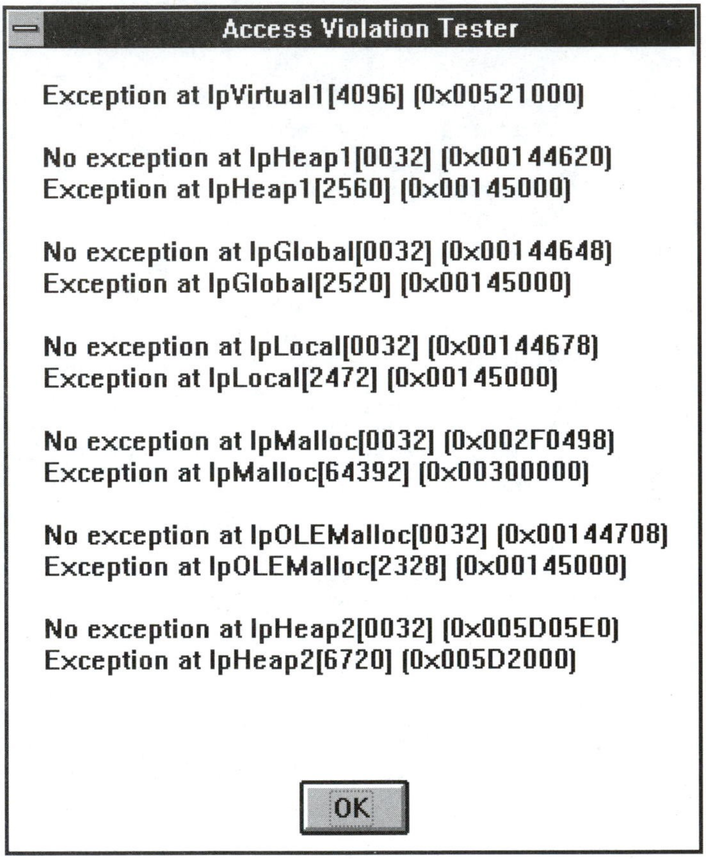

Access Violation Tester

Exception at lpVirtual1[4096] (0x00521000)

No exception at lpHeap1[0032] (0x00144620)
Exception at lpHeap1[2560] (0x00145000)

No exception at lpGlobal[0032] (0x00144648)
Exception at lpGlobal[2520] (0x00145000)

No exception at lpLocal[0032] (0x00144678)
Exception at lpLocal[2472] (0x00145000)

No exception at lpMalloc[0032] (0x002F0498)
Exception at lpMalloc[64392] (0x00300000)

No exception at lpOLEMalloc[0032] (0x00144708)
Exception at lpOLEMalloc[2328] (0x00145000)

No exception at lpHeap2[0032] (0x005D05E0)
Exception at lpHeap2[6720] (0x005D2000)

OK

Figure 3-7. Exceptions Caused by Invalid Memory Accesses

byte past the end of the object. For instance, with a size of 32, I first try to read *lpHeap1[32]*. If this succeeds (which it does), I keep bumping the array index and reading the next byte until I get an exception. Figure 3-7 shows that the read from *lpVirtual1[4096]* triggers an exception, but that with all the heap objects, no exception is triggered while you are reading a byte within the pages of committed memory that belong to the heap. The first time you read from the uncommitted page that follows it, you get an exception.

The conclusion here is inescapable: heap objects cannot be protected from each other. On the other hand, memory objects gotten from VirtualAlloc() are secure, with one loophole: if you commit a region of 65,536 bytes (or some multiple of it), then commit the following page; a read or write past the end of the first region will not cause an exception. Here's a code fragment that demonstrates this:

```
LPBYTE lpVirtual1, lpVirtual2;
lpVirtual1 = (LPBYTE) VirtualAlloc(NULL, 65536, MEM_COMMIT,
                                   PAGE_READWRITE);
lpVirtual2 = (LPBYTE) VirtualAlloc(NULL, 4096, MEM_COMMIT,
                                   PAGE_READWRITE);
// lpVirtual2 will equal lpVirtual1 + 65536
// This line of code will NOT cause an exception
lpVirtual1[65536] = '\0';
// No exception occurs until you write to lpVirtual1[65536 + 4096],
// which is past the region committed for lpVirtual2
```

Here is the listing for TestAccessViolations() and the function it calls, TryMemoryAccess():

```
VOID TestAccessViolations(HWND hWnd)
{
   char szMsg[16384];
   MEMORY_BASIC_INFORMATION mbi;
   DWORD   dwGlobalSize, dwLocalSize, dwMallocSize, dwOLEMallocSize;

   // Remember the sizes of our heap-based memory objects
   dwGlobalSize = GlobalSize(hGlobal);
   dwLocalSize = LocalSize(hLocal);
   dwMallocSize = _msize(lpMalloc);
   dwOLEMallocSize = lpIMalloc->GetSize(lpOLEMalloc);

   lstrcpy(szMsg, "");

   // Try to read from lpVirtual1[size of lpVirtual1]
   // This will trigger an exception
   VirtualQuery(lpVirtual1, &mbi, sizeof (mbi));

   TryMemoryAccess(szMsg, lpVirtual1, mbi.RegionSize, "lpVirtual1",
                   TRUE);

   // Try reading from lpHeap1 + HeapSize(lpHeap1)
   // This should not trigger an exception

   TryMemoryAccess(szMsg, lpHeap1,
      HeapSize(GetProcessHeap(), 0, lpHeap1), "lpHeap1", TRUE);

   // Try reading from lpGlobal + GlobalSize(lpGlobal)
   // This should not trigger an exception
   lpGlobal = (LPBYTE) GlobalLock(hGlobal);
   TryMemoryAccess(szMsg, lpGlobal, dwGlobalSize,
      "lpGlobal", TRUE);
   GlobalUnlock(hGlobal);
```

```
   // Try reading from lpLocal + LocalSize(lpLocal)
   // This should not trigger an exception
   lpLocal = (LPBYTE) LocalLock(hLocal);
   TryMemoryAccess(szMsg, lpLocal, dwLocalSize, "lpLocal", TRUE);
   LocalUnlock(hLocal);

   // Try reading from lpMalloc + _msize(lpMalloc)
   // This should not trigger an exception

   TryMemoryAccess(szMsg, lpMalloc, dwMallocSize, "lpMalloc", TRUE);

   // Try reading from lpOLEMalloc + lpIMalloc->GetSize(lpMalloc)
   // This should not trigger an exception

   TryMemoryAccess(szMsg, lpOLEMalloc, dwOLEMallocSize, "lpOLEMalloc", TRUE);

   // Try reading from lpHeap2 + HeapSize(lpHeap2)
   // This should not trigger an exception

   TryMemoryAccess(szMsg, lpHeap2,
      HeapSize(hHeap, 0, lpHeap2), "lpHeap2", TRUE);

   MessageBox(hWnd, szMsg, "Access Violation Tester", MB_OK);
}

VOID TryMemoryAccess(LPSTR lpszMsg, LPBYTE lpMem, DWORD dwOffset,
                     LPSTR lpVariable, BOOL bContinueUntilException)
{
   BOOL bExceptionRaised = FALSE;
   BYTE byMem;

   // Try reading from lpMem + dwOffset

   __try
      {
      byMem = lpMem[dwOffset];
      }
   __except (EXCEPTION_EXECUTE_HANDLER)
      {
      bExceptionRaised = TRUE;
      }

   if (bExceptionRaised)
      wsprintf(&lpszMsg[lstrlen(lpszMsg)],
         "Exception at %s[%04d] (0x%08X)\n",
         lpVariable, dwOffset, lpMem + dwOffset);
```

```
    else
       {
       wsprintf(&lpszMsg[lstrlen(lpszMsg)],
          "No exception at %s[%04d] (0x%08X)\n",
          lpVariable, dwOffset, lpMem + dwOffset);

       if (bContinueUntilException)
          {
          // See how far we have to go till we get an exception
          while (!bExceptionRaised)
             {
             __try
                {
                byMem = lpMem[++dwOffset];
                }
             __except (EXCEPTION_EXECUTE_HANDLER)
                {
                bExceptionRaised = TRUE;
                }
             }
          wsprintf(&lpszMsg[lstrlen(lpszMsg)],
             "Exception at %s[%04d] (0x%08X)\n",
             lpVariable, dwOffset, lpMem + dwOffset);
          }
       }

    lstrcat(lpszMsg, "\n");
}
```

And, as you can see in Figure 3-8, it gets worse; even after you free a heap object, you can *still* read and write it.

Figure 3-8 is generated by the routine TestMemoryReleases(), which frees the memory allocated by TestMemoryAllocations(), then tries to read it. It VirtualFree()s *lpVirtual1*, HeapFree()s *lpHeap1,* GlobalFree()s *lpGlobal,* LocalFree()s *lpLocal*, free()s *lpMalloc*, and CoTaskMemFree()s *lpOLEMalloc*. As you have probably surmised, only one of the subsequent reads triggers an exception: the read from *lpVirtual1*.

Here is the listing for TestMemoryReleases():

```
VOID TestMemoryReleases(HWND hWnd)
{
   char szMsg[8192];

   szMsg[0] = '\0';
   // Free lpVirtual1, then try to read from it
   // This will cause an exception
```

```
VirtualFree(lpVirtual1, 0, MEM_RELEASE);

TryMemoryAccess(szMsg, lpVirtual1, 0, "lpVirtual1", FALSE);

// Free lpHeap1, then read from it
// This should not cause an exception
HeapFree(GetProcessHeap(), 0, lpHeap1);
TryMemoryAccess(&szMsg[lstrlen(szMsg)], lpHeap1, 0, "lpHeap1",
   FALSE);

// Free lpGlobal, then read from it
// This should not cause an exception
lpGlobal = (LPBYTE) GlobalLock(hGlobal);
GlobalUnlock(hGlobal);
GlobalFree(hGlobal);
TryMemoryAccess(&szMsg[lstrlen(szMsg)], lpGlobal, 0, "lpGlobal",
   FALSE);

// Free lpLocal, then read from it
// This should not cause an exception
lpLocal = (LPBYTE) LocalLock(hLocal);
LocalUnlock(hLocal);
LocalFree(hLocal);
```

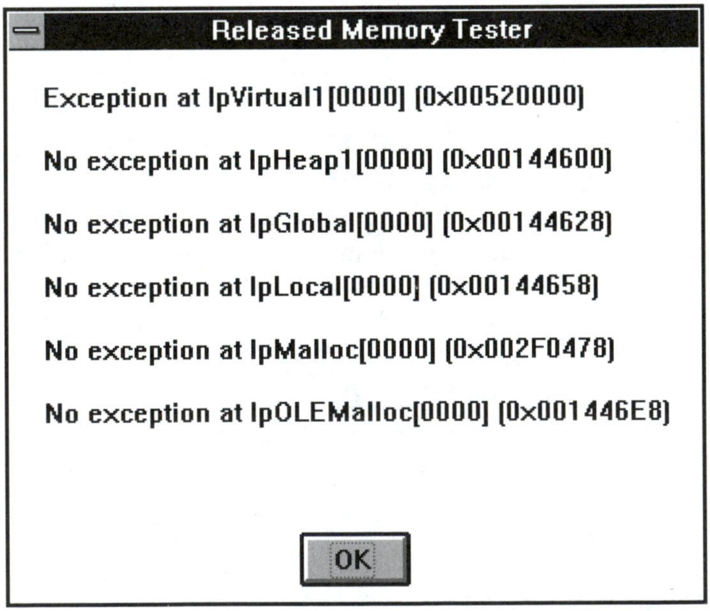

Released Memory Tester

Exception at lpVirtual1[0000] (0x00520000)

No exception at lpHeap1[0000] (0x00144600)

No exception at lpGlobal[0000] (0x00144628)

No exception at lpLocal[0000] (0x00144658)

No exception at lpMalloc[0000] (0x002F0478)

No exception at lpOLEMalloc[0000] (0x001446E8)

OK

Figure 3-8. Exceptions Caused by Accessing Freed Memory

```
    TryMemoryAccess(&szMsg[lstrlen(szMsg)], lpLocal, 0, "lpLocal", FALSE);

    // Free lpMalloc, then read from it
    // This won't cause an exception, either
    free(lpMalloc);
    TryMemoryAccess(&szMsg[lstrlen(szMsg)], lpMalloc, 0, "lpMalloc",
       FALSE);

    // Free lpOLEMalloc, then read from it
    // This won't cause an exception, either
    CoTaskMemFree(lpOLEMalloc);
    TryMemoryAccess(&szMsg[lstrlen(szMsg)], lpOLEMalloc, 0, "lpOLEMalloc",
       FALSE);

    // Free other pointers just to be polite
    VirtualFree(lpVirtual2, 0, MEM_RELEASE);
    VirtualFree(lpVirtual3, 0, MEM_RELEASE);
    HeapFree(hHeap, 0, lpHeap2);
    HeapDestroy(hHeap);

    // Reset event so menu can be initialized properly
    ResetEvent(hEvent);
    MessageBox(hWnd, szMsg, "Released Memory Tester", MB_OK);
}
```

The tradeoff between virtual memory and heap-based memory can thus be depicted in stark detail and bold hues: you can have fine granularity or tight protection, but not both. Win32 does not offer any way to balance the two—but C++ does.

C++ and MFC Considerations

Memory is allocated and released in C++ with the *new* and *delete* operators. These are not memory-allocation primitives; rather, they are virtual operations that are implemented on top of the other memory-allocation mechanisms. For any C++ objects you create, you can override them. Therefore, I cannot say that *new* behaves this way or that way; how it behaves depends on how it is implemented. In Visual C++ 4.x, *::operator new* uses malloc(). This is inherited in turn by all the MFC classes.

In a C++ program, you may use *new* and *delete* with non-C++ objects, though there is no particular advantage to doing so. For example:

```
char *p = new char[512];
// [Use the array]
// [...]
// Now free it
delete [] p;
```

You must use *new* and *delete* with true C++ objects; otherwise, the object's constructor and destructor are not invoked.

MFC Use of C++ Exceptions

The normal behavior of the *new* operator is to return a NULL pointer if it fails. However, MFC overrides this behavior to *throw* a CMemoryException instead. So when you use *new* in an MFC program, you know that the next line of code won't execute if the allocation fails.

Here's an example that shows how to trap a CMemoryException and use the conventional method of returning a NULL pointer. Here, I attempt to allocate a CString object. (The CString class is one of the most useful general-purpose MFC classes).

```
CString *pString;

try
   {
   pString  = new CString("My String");
   }
catch (CMemoryException *e)
   {
   pString = NULL;
   e->Delete();
   }
```

Throwing Your Own Memory Exceptions

You can use the MFC exception mechanism to report memory-allocation errors that occur in other places as well. The easiest way to do this is to call the MFC function AfxThrowMemoryException(). Suppose you override the *new* operator for a class of your own to use HeapAlloc() in a privately created heap. Here's a declaration of a class that does that. The constructor creates the heap; the destructor gets rid of it.

```
class CMyObject : public CObject
{
private:
   static HANDLE m_hHeap;
   static int    nRefCount;
public:
   CMyObject()
```

```
      {
      if (nRefCount == 0)
         m_hHeap = ::HeapCreate(0, 4096, 0);
      ++nRefCount;
      }
   virtual ~CMyObject()
      {
      if (--nRefCount == 0)
         ::HeapDestroy(m_hHeap);
      }
   LPVOID operator new(size_t nSize);
};
```

And here is the implementation of CMyObject::operator *new*:

```
static HANDLE CMyObject::m_hHeap = NULL;
static int    CMyObject::nRefCount = 0;

LPVOID CMyObject::operator new(size_t nSize)
{
   LPVOID lp;

   ASSERT(m_hHeap != NULL);
   lp = ::HeapAlloc(m_hHeap, 0, (DWORD) nSize);
   if (lp == NULL)
      AfxThrowMemoryException();
   return lp;
}
```

Protecting Heap-Based Arrays

C++ gives us a way to avoid the coarse granularity of virtual memory allocation, and still get some measure of memory protection. This involves overriding the array subscripting operator (*[ ]*), then trapping array indices that are invalid. The MFC array classes, for example, assert that the array index is between zero and the upper bound of the array. They also include the intelligence to dynamically grow the array as new elements are added to it. Table 3-1 lists these classes.

The use of an assertion means that the array index is only checked in debug builds (when the constant _DEBUG is defined). The assumption is that an invalid array index is a programming error, and should be cleaned up by release time.

A second version of MEMTEST, MFCARRAY, uses a CByteArray instead of the OLE 2 task memory allocator. Its project is in \WIN32NET\CODE\MEMORY\MFCARRAY\MFCARRAY.MDP on the disk. Here is the code that allocates the array and sets its size:

Table 3-1. MFC Array Classes and Templates

Class	Type of Object
CString	Character strings
CByteArray	8-bit numbers or characters
CWordArray	16-bit numbers
CDWordArray	32-bit numbers
CUIntArray	Unsigned integers
CPtrArray	Pointers
CObArray	MFC objects derived from CObject
CStringArray	CStrings
CArray	Template for user-defined array
CTypedPtrArray	Template for array of user-defined types

```
CByteArray *lpArray;
// ...
// ...
lpArray = new CByteArray;
lpArray->SetSize(32);
```

To read beyond the last element in the array, I try to access (*lpArray)[lpArray->GetSize()]. Figure 3-9 shows the message box that MFC puts up.

If I click the Ignore button, I do not get an exception, but at least I have some indication that I've made a mistake.

Another possible mechanism is to raise an exception. Win32 defines the exception code EXCEPTION_ARRAY_BOUNDS_EXCEEDED. However, the underlying hardware must support array bounds-checking, and in fact this exception is not supported on any platforms that Windows runs on. But it is certainly reasonable to raise this exception in an override of the *[]* operator.

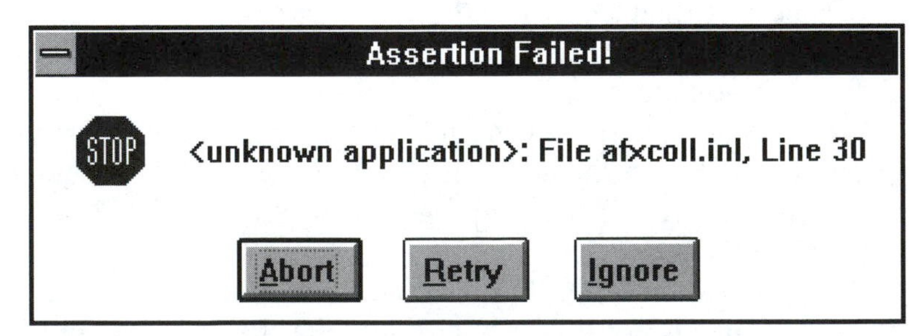

Figure 3-9. MFC Message Box Warning of Invalid Array Index

Here's an array template class, CMyArray. It provides two *[]* overrides, mimicking MFC's way of doing things. One returns an object in the array, the other returns a reference to an object.

```
template <class ARRAYTYPE, int ARRAYSIZE>
class CMyArray
{
public:
   ARRAYTYPE m_Elements[ARRAYSIZE];
   int GetSize(void) {return ARRAYSIZE;}
   ARRAYTYPE operator[](int nIndex) const;
   ARRAYTYPE& operator[](int nIndex);
}
```

The implementation of the operator[] method checks *nIndex* to make sure it is within bounds. If not, it raises an EXCEPTION_ARRAY_BOUNDS_EXCEEDED exception.

```
template <class ARRAYTYPE, int ARRAYSIZE>
ARRAYTYPE operator[](int nIndex) const
{
   if (nIndex < 0 || nIndex >= ARRAYSIZE)
      RaiseException(EXCEPTION_ARRAY_BOUNDS_EXCEEDED,
                     0,
                     0,
                     NULL);
   return m_Elements[nIndex];
}
```

A third sample application, CPPARRAY, on the disk in \WIN32NET\CODE\MEMORY\CPPARRAY\CPPARRAY.MDP, uses an object of this class. Here is how I declare and allocate it:

```
CMyArray<BYTE, 32>  *lpMyArray;
// ...
// ...
lpMyArray = new CMyArray<BYTE, 32>;
```

To test the behavior of this object, I try to read (*lpMyArray)[lpMyArray->GetSize()]. Figure 3-10 shows the message box that CPPARRAY presents. I have indeed succeeded in triggering an exception.

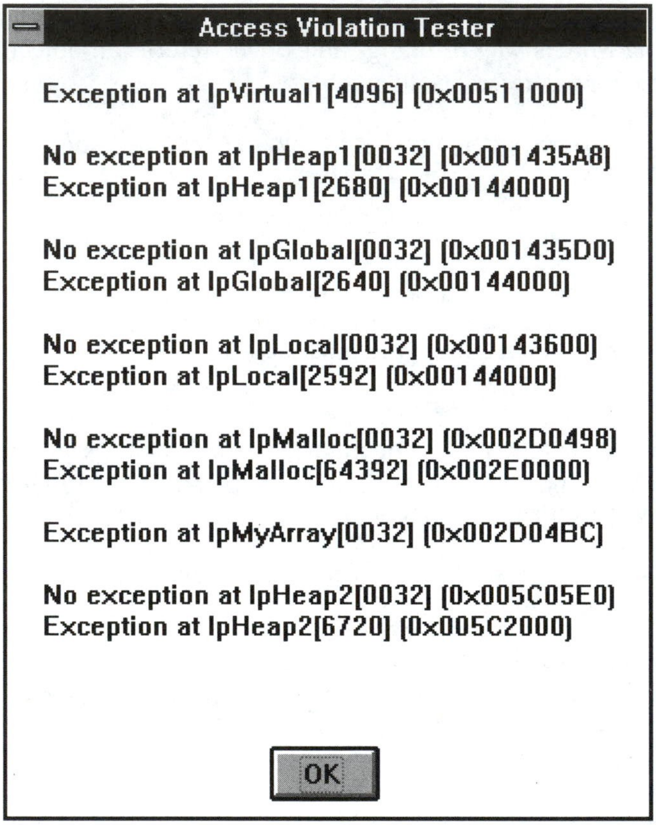

Access Violation Tester

Exception at lpVirtual1[4096] (0x00511000)

No exception at lpHeap1[0032] (0x001435A8)
Exception at lpHeap1[2680] (0x00144000)

No exception at lpGlobal[0032] (0x001435D0)
Exception at lpGlobal[2640] (0x00144000)

No exception at lpLocal[0032] (0x00143600)
Exception at lpLocal[2592] (0x00144000)

No exception at lpMalloc[0032] (0x002D0498)
Exception at lpMalloc[64392] (0x002E0000)

Exception at lpMyArray[0032] (0x002D04BC)

No exception at lpHeap2[0032] (0x005C05E0)
Exception at lpHeap2[6720] (0x005C2000)

OK

Figure 3-10. Exceptions Reported by MEMTST3.EXE Using Guarded C++ Array

Conclusion

Windows offers a very powerful, flexible memory-management scheme. To give developers more direct access to the underlying mechanism, the Win32 API adds two memory-management APIs: the Virtual Memory API and the Heap Memory API. Virtual Memory is the most powerful and allows you the most control over your own memory management. Its principal innovation is the ability to reserve large contiguous blocks of virtual memory without consuming any physical resources. You can then commit portions of this block, thereby obtaining physical storage, as you actually need them. You can decommit memory when you are done using it; the virtual addresses remain valid until you finally release the entire region. In conjunction with Structured Exception Handling, you can defer committing memory until the very moment when you actually access it. You can also change the access allowed to a block of memory, which keeps you from accidentally overwriting read-only memory objects.

The Heap Memory API lets you take advantage of the reserve/commit scheme without having to be aware of what goes on behind the scenes. Windows reserves and commits pages on your behalf as they are needed. The Heap Memory API allows finer granularity than the Virtual Memory API; it gives you a subsegment allocation API that operates within the parameters of the virtual memory management scheme.

The other heap-based memory-management schemes behave the same as the Heap Memory API. These include the global and local allocation APIs from earlier versions of Windows, malloc(), the OLE 2 memory allocator, and the C++ *new* operator (depending, of course, on how it is implemented).

The principal disadvantage of virtual memory allocation is that its unit of granularity is quite coarse. Any memory allocated with VirtualAlloc(), no matter how little, results in using at least one page of physical memory, and 64K of virtual memory. On the other hand, the memory is completely protected; you cannot inadvertently go outside the memory thus obtained without causing an exception. In contrast, heap-based memory allocations carve out much more precise units. The memory objects allocated using these functions are the size that you ask for (with a small amount of memory management header). Unfortunately, the Windows Virtual Memory Manager considers all objects residing in the same heap to be part of the same set of committed pages. Thus, wayward writes to variables in a heap can easily corrupt other objects in the heap, as well as the control information that precedes each object. These kinds of bugs can be very insidious and difficult to trace; their effects may not be felt until long after the offending code has been executed.

C++ provides a very reasonable compromise between the two. In most cases, the amount of waste you incur from using the Virtual Memory API is too high. C++ affords you the fine granularity of heap-based objects, but also gives you a way to implement your own memory protection by overriding the *[]* operator. The MFC array classes already do this, and raise an assertion (not an exception) if you trespass outside the bounds of an array.

Suggested Readings

Online References

Memory Management Overview in the Win32 online help.
"Templates," in *Programming Topics*.
"Collections," *Programming with MFC: Encyclopedia.*

Microsoft Knowledge Base for Win32 SDK articles:

"Copy on Write Page Protection for Windows NT"
"How Windows 95 Manages Virtual Memory"
"Improve System Performance by Using Proper Working Set Size"
"Memory Handle Allocation"
"Non-Addressable Range in Address Space"
"Overview of the Windows 95 Virtual Address Space Layout"
"PAGE_READONLY May Be Used as Discardable Memory"
"The Use of PAGE_WRITECOPY"
"VirtualLock() Only Locks Pages into Working Set"
"Windows NT Virtual Memory Manager Uses FIFO"
"Working Set Size, Nonpaged Pool, and VirtualLock()"

Print References

Custer, Helen. *Inside Windows NT.* Redmond, WA: Microsoft Press, 1992. Chapter 6.

King, Adrian. *Inside Windows 95*. Redmond, WA: Microsoft Press, 1995.

Pietrek, Matt. "An Exclusive Tour of the New TOOLHELP32 Functions for Windows 95," in *Microsoft Systems Journal*, Vol. 10, No. 9, September 1995.

Richter, Jeff. *Advanced Windows*. Redmond, WA: Microsoft Press, 1995. Chapters 4, 5, 6, and 8.

Chapter 4

Multithreading

In exploring how to multithread a Windows application, very little discussion needs to revolve around the actual mechanics. The API sets are simple; they center on the functions that start a new thread, none of which are difficult or complex. Instead, most of the discussion concerns integrating a multithreaded design into applications, particularly server-side applications. The question, then, is not how to implement a multithreaded application—simply put, you invoke functions through the thread-creation functions instead of calling them directly. The question is deciding what kinds of applications lend themselves to multithreading, and, within that context, what is the best division of labor among the threads you create.

What Are Threads?

Threads are the basic objects that Windows schedules for execution; they compete for and share the CPU (or CPUs). Threads allow a single application to multitask its own execution. On a single-processor machine, threads give the appearance of simultaneous, concurrent execution. On a multiple-processor machine, multiple threads do indeed execute simultaneously.

Threads provide four essential services. First, they allow portions of an application to execute asynchronously and in parallel. Second, they let you run multiple copies of a code section so that you can do things like provide identical services to multiple clients. Third, they make it possible to call functions that are likely to block without keeping your program's user from doing other things with it. Fourth, only multithreaded applications can take advantage of a multiprocessor machine.

Parallel, Asynchronous Execution

The first benefit provided by threads is allowing asynchronous and parallel execution. Frequently, the component tasks that make up an application do not need to execute consecutively. As long as task B does not need the output of task A, it does not have to wait for task A to complete. A single-threaded operating system forces sequential execution; a multithreaded one allows a design that more accurately reflects the interrelationships among parts of an application.

For instance, here are two functions that perform separate, unrelated tasks:

```
int a = 2, b = 3, c;
int d = 4, e = 5, f;

VOID FuncA()
{
    c = a + b;
}

VOID FuncB()
{
    f = d + e;
}
```

A single-threaded environment forces you to call FuncA(), wait for it to complete, and then call FuncB().

```
FuncA();
FuncB();
```

However, FuncB() deals with data that is entirely different from that manipulated by FuncA(). There is no need to make FuncB() stand in line behind FuncA(); why not do something like this (assuming a programming language statement "spin off")?

```
spin off FuncA();
spin off FuncB();
```

Now, the calling module can go about its business. Only when it needs the output of FuncA() and FuncB() does it need to make sure they're finished. Suppose, for instance, that you have a function FuncC() that returns the sum of *c* and *f*.

```
int FuncC()
{
   return c + f;
}
```

You cannot call FuncC() until you know that FuncA() and FuncB() have calculated the correct values of *c* and *f*. Thus, the top-level module needs to do something like this:

```
spin off FuncA();
spin off FuncB();
do other stuff
make sure FuncA() and FuncB() are done
printf("\nc + f = %d", FuncC());
```

Execution of Multiple Copies of Code Simultaneously

The second benefit provided by threads is the ability to run multiple copies of a given code stream. This is important, for instance, in Windows Sockets and Named Pipes server applications, where a one-thread-per-client division of labor is often an intelligent design. A single thread in the server application can listen for connection requests. As connections get established, the server spins off a new thread (represented by a single function) that handles the data exchange. This allows the server to provide a higher level of availability than it can achieve with a single thread of execution. We will see this kind of architecture in Chapters 9 and 10.

Harmless Execution of Blocking Calls

The third benefit provided by threads is the harmless execution of functions that block. When a thread running under Windows issues a blocking function call, it goes to sleep until the function completes. If the function call is issued by the main thread of an application (the one that manages the user interface), it shuts the application down; the user can do nothing with it. Some blocking functions—particularly those involving network communications—may block for a long time. This situation becomes innocuous if you make the blocking call in a secondary thread, perhaps one created for that sole purpose. When the function completes, the threads can use some kind of asynchronous notification, like posting a message, to let the responsible authorities know what has happened.

Symmetric Multiprocessing

A final benefit provided by threads is that only multithreaded applications can take advantage of a multiprocessor machine. Multiprocessing is one of the major advances that NT provides. A single-threaded application cannot possibly reap the performance benefits that multiple CPUs can yield. My own informal tests with a dual-processor machine indicate that these benefits are substantial.

The fact that Windows 95 can only use a single processor is one of the most important reasons why it is a pale shadow of NT as a platform for back-end, server-based applications.

Multithreaded Application Architectures

There are several application architectures that lend themselves to a multithreaded approach. The *OSF/DCE Application Development Guide* (see "Suggested Readings" at the end of this chapter) identifies three of them:

1. The boss/worker model
2. The work crew model
3. The pipelining model

The Boss/Worker Model

In this approach, a master thread assigns tasks to worker threads. Typically, the worker threads perform independent, parallel tasks. For example, a Windows Sockets server application listens for client connection requests on a single socket by calling the accept() function. This function creates a new socket that the server uses for data exchange with the client. It therefore makes sense to have a master thread that waits for connections and spins off worker threads to handle the data exchange. In this situation, the worker threads do not need to interact with each other at all.

The Work Crew Model

Here again, the threads work in parallel, but now they cooperate as equals to complete a single task. Each worker thread is responsible for one part of the task. A real-life example of the work crew model given in the *OSF/DCE Guide* is a group of people cleaning a house.

The Pipelining Model

In this architecture, there are several tasks that must be performed sequentially. Task 1 passes its output to Task 2, which in turn passes its output to Task 3. This becomes a candidate for multithreading when the tasks that must be performed sequentially can also be performed concurrently to produce more than one copy of the final output. The *OSF/DCE Guide* offers a factory assembly line as an example of the pipelining model.

CreateThread()

CreateThread() is the Win32 function that starts up a new thread. Here is its prototype:

```
HANDLE CreateThread(
   LPSECURITY_ATTRIBUTES  lpSecurityAttributes,
   DWORD                  dwStackSize,
   LPTHREAD_START_ROUTINE lpThreadFunction,
   LPVOID                 lpArgument,
   DWORD                  dwFlags,
   LPDWORD                lpdwThreadID);
```

lpSecurityAttributes points to a SECURITY_ATTRIBUTES structure that determines whether the thread handle can be inherited by child processes, and who can do what with the handle.

```
typedef struct _SECURITY_ATTRIBUTES
{
   DWORD   nLength;
   LPVOID  lpSecurityDescriptor;
   BOOL    bInheritHandle;
} SECURITY_ATTRIBUTES;
```

nLength is used for version control; you always set it to *sizeof* (SECURITY_ATTRIBUTES). *bInheritHandle* indicates whether the handle can be inherited by child processes. *lpSecurityDescriptor* points to a SECURITY_DESCRIPTOR structure, which is used to specify what rights other processes will have to the thread handle. The SECURITY_ DESCRIPTOR is an opaque type; that is, its format is not published, and applications may only access it indirectly, through the functions in the Security API (see Chapter 13). With thread handles, though, the use of a non-NULL SECURITY_DESCRIPTOR is highly esoteric; I have never encountered a situation where it was appropriate. Ordinarily, if you use security attributes at all, it is only to make the thread handle inheritable—and even this is pretty rare.

The second argument to CreateThread(), *dwStackSize*, specifies the number of bytes to commit at the bottom of the thread's stack. Every thread gets its own stack space; some of the figures in Chapter 3 show the stack space set aside for the MEMTEST application. If you pass *dwStackSize* to CreateThread() as zero, the new thread will be given a stack with the same characteristics as the calling thread. Passing it as non-zero asks to have more or fewer bytes committed at the bottom of the stack; the reserved area is still the same size as that reserved for the startup thread. If you are reasonably certain that your stack will not grow beyond a certain size, you can economize on your use of physical memory by making *dwStackSize* small—keeping in mind that at least one page of memory will be committed.

The third argument to CreateThread(), *lpThreadFunction*, is a pointer to the function where Windows will enter the thread. LPTHREAD_START_ROUTINE defines a function with the following prototype:

```
DWORD WINAPI ThreadFunction(LPVOID lpv);
```

The fourth argument to CreateThread(), *lpArgument*, is any data you want to pass to the thread. If it will not fit in 32 bits, or if there is more than one piece of information, you typically allocate memory for some type of structure or C++ object and pass its address. It is important that any pointer be valid for the life of the thread. If the function that creates the new thread passes a pointer to a stack variable, then exits, the pointer stands a superb chance of being invalid in the thread, thereby triggering an EXCEPTION_ACCESS_VIOLATION.

The *dwFlags* parameter controls the initial scheduling of the thread. If you set it to zero, Windows will immediately schedule the thread for execution. The only non-zero flag, CREATE_SUSPENDED, indicates that you do not want the thread to run until you specifically release it by passing its handle to ResumeThread().

The last argument, *lpdwThreadID*, points to a DWORD variable that returns the thread ID. Although the thread ID is generally of little interest, you cannot pass *lpdwThreadID* as NULL. The thread ID, incidentally, is not the same as the HANDLE returned by CreateThread(). The handle is used for synchronization, and it embodies the security protection requested in the security attributes. As a synchronization object, the thread handle stays non-signalled as long as the thread is running.

Most thread management functions need the thread handle. Only a few take the thread ID, the most useful of which is PostThreadMessage(). As with all Win32 handles, you need to close the thread handle (by passing it to CloseHandle()) when you are through with it. This has no effect on the thread itself; closing the thread handle is not equivalent to killing the thread. Failing to do so leaves system resources allocated, but not used, until your program finally exits.

The Thread Entry-Point Function

Windows calls the thread entry-point function to start executing your new thread. Here is its prototype again:

```
DWORD WINAPI ThreadFunction(LPVOID lpv);
```

lpv is the fourth argument you passed to CreateThread().

If the thread you are spinning off is a worker thread that performs a background task, it will often run as an infinite loop. To get this kind of thread to go away requires some imagination, as Win32 provides no direct way to kill a thread. We'll see some ways of doing this later in this chapter.

A thread can terminate itself by simply returning, or by calling the ExitThread() function:

```
VOID ExitThread(DWORD dwExitCode);
```

ExitThread() has a VOID return value for a very good reason: it doesn't return. *dwExitCode* is remembered as the final status of the thread; it can be retrieved by calling GetExitCodeThread().

```
BOOL GetExitCodeThread(
   HANDLE  hThread,
   LPDWORD lpdwExitCode);
```

As long as the thread is running, GetExitCodeThread() reports the exit code as STILL_ACTIVE.

If the thread just issues a *return* statement, Windows calls ExitThread() on its behalf, passing whatever value was included in the *return*. This is why the entry-point function is typed with a DWORD return value. Because there is more than one way to start a thread, and each way requires a different exit function, it is probably better to just *return* from the thread.

Other less important functions in the API set allow you to stop and restart a thread (SuspendThread() and ResumeThread()); to get and set the thread's priority (GetThreadPriority() and SetThreadPriority()); to obtain handles and IDs for the current thread (GetCurrentThread() and GetCurrentThreadID()); and to abort a running thread (TerminateThread()). When a thread first starts, it takes on the priority class of its owning process and runs at normal priority within that class. You should adjust the priority of a thread very carefully, and only if necessary. A thread whose priority gets reduced may get starved for CPU time; a thread whose priority gets boosted may hog the CPU. Windows' policy for scheduling threads is to schedule them in the order of their priorities. All threads at the same priority run in first-in, first-out order. A good guideline is: the higher a thread's priority, the more of its time it should spend asleep.

_beginthread() / _beginthreadex()

CreateThread() is fine if your thread uses nothing but Win32 functions. However, if it makes C runtime library calls, you must use _beginthread() or _beginthreadex(). The first is quite simple:

```
#include <process.h>

unsigned long _beginthread(
   void   (*lpThreadEntryPoint)(void *lpArgList),
   unsigned uStackSize,
   void    *lpArgList);
```

lpThreadEntryPoint is the address of the function through which the thread will be entered. As with CreateThread(), it is passed a single 32-bit argument; this is just the *lpArgList* that you pass to _beginthread(). Note that it is typed as a *void* function; this is a slight variation from CreateThread(). The function is expected to run to completion and not bother returning a value. *uStackSize* has the same meaning as the corresponding argument to CreateThread(): it is the number of bytes that will be committed at the base of the thread's stack. Passing it as zero tells Windows to commit the same number of bytes that it committed for the parent thread.

_beginthreadex() exactly parallels CreateThread(). It includes a SECURITY_ATTRIBUTES pointer, a startup flag (zero or CREATE_SUSPENDED), and a pointer to a DWORD that receives the thread ID. Use _beginthreadex() if you want to start the thread in the suspended state, or if you plan to use the thread ID with PostThreadMessage(). Another consideration is that only threads started with _beginthreadex() can set an exit code. If you do not need any of these features, the syntactic simplicity of _beginthread() argues for its use.

```
unsigned long _beginthreadex(
   void                *lpSecurityAttributes,
   unsigned             uStackSize,
```

```
unsigned (WINAPI *lpThreadEntryPoint) (void *lpArgList),
void              *lpArgList,
unsigned           uInitFlag,
unsigned          *lpThreadID)
```

The arguments are exactly the same as those for CreateThread(), and have the same meaning. The Microsoft documentation is a little unclear whether the first argument points to a SECURITY_ATTRIBUTES or a SECURITY_DESCRIPTOR. The source code for the MFC CWinThread class (THRDCORE.CPP in the MFC source directory) shows that it is a SECURITY_ATTRIBUTES pointer.

With _beginthreadex(), *lpThreadEntryPoint* is typed as returning an *unsigned* value. This is exactly the same as the CreateThread() LPTHREAD_START_ROUTINE, and is best accomplished by the thread issuing a *return* statement when it completes.

Return Information

Like CreateThread(), both _beginthread() and _beginthreadex() return the thread handle. It can be used with the thread-manipulation functions (SuspendThread(), ResumeThread(), SetThreadPriority()). If you use _beginthread(), you do not need to close the handle; the C runtime library does this automatically.

_beginthreadex(), on the other hand, does require you to close the thread handle yourself. In addition, _beginthreadex() returns the thread ID, which can be passed to PostThreadMessage() if you need to post messages to the new thread.

_endthread() / _endthreadex()

_endthread() and _endthreadex() are provided for a thread to terminate itself.

```
void _endthread(void);
void _endthreadex(unsigned uExitCode);
```

They should be paired with _beginthread() and _beginthreadex(), respectively. Actually, it is never necessary to call these functions explicitly; when the thread function returns, Windows itself shuts the thread down. A thread started by _beginthreadex() is expected to return a value. It can be retrieved by calling GetExitCodeThread(), as we discussed earlier in this chapter.

AfxBeginThread() and the CWinThread Class

MFC supports multithreading with the CWinThread class and the AfxBeginThread() function. MFC provides supports for two kinds of threads: worker threads and user-interface threads. MFC treats worker threads as invisible background threads. In this role, CWinThread serves mostly as a wrapper for the thread-management API. User-interface threads, on the other hand, create windows, and therefore need MFC's message-pumping support.

Worker Threads

Here is the version of AfxBeginThread() that spins off a worker thread:

```
CWinThread *AfxBeginThread(
   AFX_THREADPROC          lpfnThreadProc,
   LPVOID                  lpParam,
   int                     nPriority = THREAD_PRIORITY_NORMAL,
   UINT                    uStackSize = 0,
   DWORD                   dwCreateFlags = 0,
   LPSECURITY_ATTRIBUTES lpSecurityAttributes = NULL );
```

The arguments are the same as for CreateThread(), with two exceptions. The type AFX_THREADPROC is defined as a function that returns a UINT (unsigned integer), and does *not* have the WINAPI attribute. WINAPI sets up the prologue and epilogue code so a function can be invoked from outside a process's address space. *lpfnThreadProc* doesn't need this code; it is not the actual thread-entry function. That function is the internal MFC routine _AfxThreadEntry(), in THRDCORE.CPP. _AfxThreadEntry() in turn calls the thread-entry function that you provide here.

Secondly, the *nPriority* argument allows you to change the priority of the new thread from the default value, normal priority. If you call CreateThread() or _beginthreadex(), you have to make an additional call to SetThreadPriority().

The CWinThread Class and the Win32 Thread-Management API

The return value from AfxBeginThread() points to a CWinThread object representing your thread. This object contains the thread handle and the thread ID, in the member variables *m_hThread* and *m_nThreadID*. CWinThread also offers several methods that encapsulate the Win32 thread-management API. They are:

```
int CWinThread::GetThreadPriority();
```

This is implemented inline as ::GetThreadPriority(m_hThread).

```
BOOL CWinThread::SetThreadPriority(int nNewPriority);
```

This is implemented inline as ::SetThreadPriority(m_hThread, nNewPriority).

```
DWORD CWinThread::SuspendThread();
```

This method is implemented inline as ::SuspendThread(m_hThread). And finally,

```
DWORD CWinThread::ResumeThread();
```

is implemented inline as ::ResumeThread(m_hThread).

CWinThread also has a CreateThread() method, but it is not a wrapper for CreateThread(). In fact, it doesn't call CreateThread(), it calls _beginthreadex(). By default, too, CWinThread::CreateThread() creates a user-interface thread, not a worker thread. You rarely need to call this method, as AfxBeginThread() calls it for you.

User-Interface Threads

User-interface threads are nothing more than threads that create windows. Every thread is responsible for the windows that it creates. Specifically, this means that it must fetch messages for them. MFC user-interface threads provide this functionality. Any thread created in this fashion inherits the MFC message-dispatching mechanism. In fact, CWinThread provides the CWinApp behavior that you are probably very familiar with by now: the InitInstance(), Run(), and ExitInstance() methods. Since the release of MFC 3.0, CWinApp has been a subclass of CWinThread.

User-interface threads behave differently from worker threads. Here, you do not provide a thread-entry function. Instead, you:

1. Derive a class from CWinThread.
2. Override InitInstance() and any other methods you are interested in.
3. Call the second flavoring of AfxBeginThread().

Again, Windows will enter the new thread through the MFC function _AfxThreadEntry(). Now, however, it invokes InitInstance() in your derived class. InitInstance() is responsible for creating the windows that the thread will be using. From that point on, the new thread behaves exactly the same as the primary thread set up by CWinApp::InitInstance(). That is, any activity in windows owned by the thread triggers event notifications from MFC.

Here is the prototype for AfxBeginThread() used this way:

```
CWinThread *AfxBeginThread(
   CRuntimeClass *pThreadClass,
   int nPriority = THREAD_PRIORITY_NORMAL,
   UINT nStackSize = 0,
   DWORD dwCreateFlags = 0,
   LPSECURITY_ATTRIBUTES lpSecurityAttrs = NULL );
```

The last four arguments are the same as in the other version. Instead of an entry point and an argument to pass to it, the first argument here is the CRuntimeClass of your CWinThread-derived class. For instance, if you derive a class called CMyThread, you would call AfxBeginThread() as follows (assuming that you accept the default parameters):

```
CMyThread *pThread = (CMyThread *)
   AfxBeginThread(RUNTIME_CLASS(CMyThread));
```

The class declaration must include the DECLARE_DYNCREATE() macro, and the implementation requires its IMPLEMENT_DYNCREATE() complement. AfxBeginThread() creates a new object of your CWinThread class, calls its InitInstance() method, then invokes the Run() method, which drives the message loop for the thread.

You terminate a user-interface thread by posting a WM_QUIT message to one of its windows, or to the thread itself. After all, the Run() method is basically doing a *while (GetMessage(...))* loop. WM_QUIT causes GetMessage() to return FALSE, and exits the loop.

AfxEndThread()

AfxEndThread() has the same effect as ExitThread(), _endthread(), and _endthreadex()—it shuts down the thread that calls it.

```
void AfxEndThread(UINT uExitCode);
```

As we have seen with those other functions, it is not necessary to call AfxEndThread(); the thread in question need only issue a *return uExitCode*.

When a thread terminates, MFC closes the thread handle and deletes the CWinThread object.

Which API Should You Use?

The function call you use depends on what your thread plans to do. If it will only use Win32 calls, you can use CreateThread(). If it needs to call C runtime library functions, you must use _beginthread() or _beginthreadex(). Lastly, if the thread will use MFC, you have to call AfxBeginThread(). Because AfxBeginThread() calls _beginthreadex(), a thread started by AfxBeginThread() can use all three levels of APIs: MFC, the C runtime library, and Win32 system calls.

Table 4-1 summarizes the thread execution mechanisms, and the levels of functionality that they support.

Table 4-1. Thread Execution APIs

Function Call	Level of Support
CreateThread()	Win32 only
_beginthread() / _beginthreadex()	C runtime library Win32
AfxBeginThread()	MFC C runtime library Win32

Killing Threads

A thread can terminate itself, as we have seen, by returning or by explicitly calling ExitThread(), _endthreadex(), or AfxEndThread(). The memory allocated for the thread's stack is released, and any DLLs that the process is using are notified of the thread's disappearance. But there is no graceful way to kill one thread from another one. TerminateThread() will kill a specific thread (other than the one that calls it), but it is an abortive termination—the stack is not released and DLLs are not informed. It should be used only if no other strategy works.

```
BOOL TerminateThread(
   HANDLE hThread,
   DWORD  dwExitCode);
```

To kill a worker thread that is running as an infinite loop, you have to use some kind of back-door contrivance. I have found three methods that are effective. The first is as follows:

1. Pass the thread a pointer that you VirtualAlloc(). Within the loop, the thread refers to the pointer.
2. When you want to kill the thread, VirtualFree() the pointer. The thread includes an exception handler that detects the exception and handles it by breaking out of the loop.

Note that this will only work with a pointer created by VirtualAlloc(). As discussed in Chapter 3, pointers allocated by any other means do not cause exceptions when you write to the memory after freeing the pointer. There is an example of this technique later in this chapter.

The second method uses PostThreadMessage():

```
BOOL PostThreadMessage(
   DWORD  dwThreadID,
   UINT   uMsg,
   WPARAM wParam,
   LPARAM lParam);
```

PostThreadMessage() is one of the few functions that takes the thread ID rather than the thread handle. PostThreadMessage() has the appearance of a standard message-passing function, like PostMessage() or SendMessage(), but it targets a thread, not a window. You can post either a user-defined message or a predefined message that the thread knows how to interpret, like WM_COMMAND, WM_DESTROY, or WM_QUIT. The thread can check its messages by calling GetMessage(), which will block until a message comes in, or PeekMessage(), which returns immediately. A better alternative, which lets you avoid blocking forever or polling relentlessly, is MsgWaitForMultipleObjects(). This function indicates if you have any messages, but also lets you specify a determinate timeout period. I present an example that uses it later in this chapter, and discuss it fully in the next chapter.

If the thread that is the target of a PostThreadMessage() has created windows, it will also have to retrieve messages for them. Only the thread that creates a window gets messages for it. However, a thread message has no target window; the *hwnd* member of the MSG structure is reported as NULL. So it will not be enough for the thread to do a traditional message loop like this one:

```
MSG msg;
while (GetMessage(&msg, NULL, 0, 0))
   {
   TranslateMessage(&msg);
   DispatchMessage(&msg);
   }
```

DispatchMessage() will not be able to determine which window procedure to call; it retrieves this information by calling GetWindowLong(lpMsg ->hwnd, GWL_WNDPROC). As a result, the message loop must be prepared for NULL window handles and deal with them appropriately. Here is a revised message loop that can manage messages posted by PostThreadMessage():

```
MSG msg;
while (GetMessage(&msg, NULL, 0, 0))
   {
   if (msg.hwnd == NULL)
      {
      // Deal with thread-specific message
      }
   else
      {
      TranslateMessage(&msg);
      DispatchMessage(&msg);
      }
   }
```

You can use PostThreadMessage() with threads created by CreateThread(), _beginthreadex(), and AfxBeginThread(). Both CreateThread() and _beginthreadex() return the thread ID through one of their arguments. AfxBeginThread() returns a pointer to the new CWinThread object that it creates. The CWinThread member variable *m_nThreadID* remembers the thread ID. There is one exception: you cannot post a message to an MFC user-interface thread. This is because the CWinThread::PumpMessage() method does essentially what I have just shown you—issues a GetMessage() followed by a DispatchMessage(). To post a message to one of these threads, you must post it to one of its windows.

The third method for killing a thread—and the cleanest one—uses Win32 event objects to tell the thread that it's time to go away. Events are presented in the next chapter, along with an example of killing a thread using them.

Thread Synchronization

Unlike separate processes, each of which runs in its own virtual address space, all threads of a process share the same address space. Therefore, they can all access the static data of the process. They also share all objects owned by the process—window handles, GDI objects, file handles, and synchronization objects, to name some of them. Thus, threads are very tightly coupled, and you must synchronize their access to any process-wide data items or objects. Win32 provides a wide array of tools for doing this (see Chapter 5).

Code Listings

There is a Visual C++ project on your source code disk (\WIN32NET\CODE\THRDEXC\THRDEXC.MDP) that demonstrates exception handling, virtual memory allocation, and multithreading. Figure 4-1 shows what it looks like on one of my NT workstations.

The information in the Processor Information group box is constant; it is retrieved by a call to GetSystemInfo(), and the fields are populated in the OnInitDialog() method of my dialog class (CThreadsDlg). On the other hand, the Memory Usage statistics on the bottom of the screen are dynamic. In order to update them periodically, the dialog procedure spins off a thread that runs in an infinite loop. The loop works as follows:

1. It captures the memory statistics by calling GlobalMemoryStatus().
2. It displays them in the fields of the dialog box.
3. It gathers its strength for the next cycle by sleeping for five seconds.

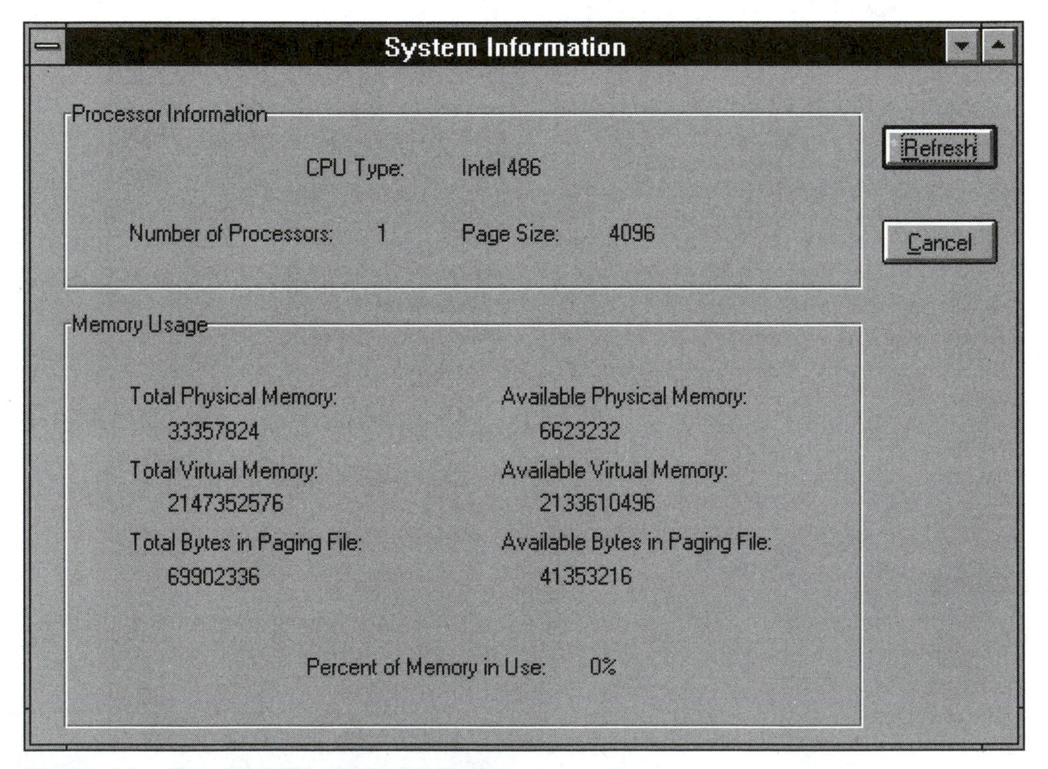

Figure 4-1. System Information Dialog Box

In order to support the Cancel button that you see in the dialog box, you need some way to kill the thread. For the reasons I discussed earlier, TerminateThread() is not an acceptable solution. Therefore, when the dialog procedure starts the thread, it passes it a pointer that it obtains from VirtualAlloc(). This points to a structure typed as follows in THRDEDLG.H:

```
struct SYSTEM_INFO_PARMS
{
   HWND  hDlg;
   TCHAR szBuffer[150];
};
```

Here is the fragment of code that allocates the memory and spins off the thread. I have added three member variables to CThreadsDlg. *m_lpSystemInfo* remembers the pointer I pass to the thread; *m_hThread* captures the thread handle; and *m_dwThreadID* receives the thread ID passed back from CreateThread(). I use CreateThread() here because the thread makes no C runtime library calls, and knows nothing about MFC.

```
// [Excerpt from class declaration in THRDEDLG.H]
class CThreadsDlg : public CDialog
{
   // ...
protected:
   HANDLE m_hThread;
   DWORD  m_dwThreadID;
   SYSTEM_INFO_PARMS *m_lpSystemInfo;
   // ...
};

// [Code excerpt]
m_lpSystemInfo = (SYSTEM_INFO_PARMS *)
      ::VirtualAlloc(NULL, sizeof (SYSTEM_INFO_PARMS),
         MEM_COMMIT, PAGE_READWRITE);

m_lpSystemInfo->hDlg = GetSafeHwnd();

m_hThread = ::CreateThread(NULL, 0, SystemInfoThread,
   m_lpSystemInfo, 0, &m_dwThreadID);
```

The thread updates the dialog box through the window handle passed in the SYSTEM_INFO_PARMS structure (*m_lpSystemInfo->hDlg*). When the user presses the Cancel button, CThreadsDlg::OnCancel() calls VirtualFree() to release the memory, then wakes the thread up and waits for it to finish.

The last thing it does before delegating to CDialog::OnCancel() is to close the thread handle.

```
void CThreadsDlg::OnCancel()
{
   ::VirtualFree(m_lpSystemInfo, 0, MEM_RELEASE);

   // Now wake the guy up so he can go away
   ::PostThreadMessage(m_dwThreadID, WM_COMMAND, 0, 0L);

   // WaitForSingleObject() is discussed in Chapter 5
   ::WaitForSingleObject(m_hThread, INFINITE);
   ::CloseHandle(m_hThread);
   CDialog::OnCancel();
}
```

When the thread wakes up, it tries to write to the dialog box using the window handle in the structure and gets an EXCEPTION_ACCESS_VIOLATION. It uses a *catch (...)* to trap this and break out of the infinite loop.

To implement the Refresh button, you need a way to wake the thread up if it is in its five-second nap. And this is where it will spend 99.99999999 percent of its time. If the thread just calls Sleep(5000), there is nothing you can do to roust it out. Therefore, the thread calls MsgWaitForMultipleObjects() instead:

```
if (::MsgWaitForMultipleObjects(0, NULL, FALSE,
            5000, QS_ALLEVENTS) == 0)
   {
   // Got a message--we'll look for WM_DESTROY
   // as a terminate message, although nobody's
   // sending it to us right now
   // WM_COMMAND means refresh the memory display

   if (::PeekMessage(&msg, NULL, 0, 0, PM_REMOVE) &&
       msg.message == WM_DESTROY)
      bContinue = FALSE;
   }
```

MsgWaitForMultipleObjects() normally deals with an array of object handles, but in this case there are none; the first argument indicates a zero-element array and the second is a NULL pointer to it. The fourth argument is the timeout value, with the special value INFINITE (–1), saying to wait forever. Finally, the last argument is a flag specifying what kinds of messages should wake the thread up. QS_ALLEVENTS means that you want to know about everything that happens. (QS is an abbreviation for Queue Status; the full suite of flags is documented with the GetQueueStatus() function.) MsgWaitForMultipleObjects() returns either the zero-based index into the array of handles of the object that satisfied the wait or the count of handles if a message arrives. We have an empty array, so a return value of zero indicates a message. The only other possible response using MsgWaitForMultipleObjects() this way is WAIT_TIMEOUT, which means that the timeout period expired.

To implement the Refresh button, I post the thread a message with PostThreadMessage(). It doesn't matter what message I post, but I use WM_COMMAND because it makes sense in this context. Here's the CThreadsDlg::OnRefresh() method, which handles a click on the Refresh button:

```
void CThreadsDlg::OnRefresh()
{
   ::PostThreadMessage(m_dwThreadID, WM_COMMAND, 0, 0L);
}
```

Here are the listings of the thread function, SystemInfoThread(), and CThreadsDlg::OnInitDialog(). The source file on the disk is \WIN32NET\CODE\THRDEXC\THRDEDLG.CPP.

```
DWORD WINAPI SystemInfoThread(LPVOID lp)
{
   SYSTEM_INFO_PARMS *lpSysInfo = (SYSTEM_INFO_PARMS *) lp;
   MEMORYSTATUS MemoryStatus;
   MSG    msg;
   BOOL   bContinue = TRUE;

   try
      {
      while (bContinue)
         {
         MemoryStatus.dwLength = sizeof (MEMORYSTATUS);
         ::GlobalMemoryStatus(&MemoryStatus);

         ::SetDlgItemInt(lpSysInfo->hDlg, IDB_TOTAL_PHYSICAL,
                      MemoryStatus.dwTotalPhys, FALSE);
         ::SetDlgItemInt(lpSysInfo->hDlg, IDB_AVAIL_PHYSICAL,
                      MemoryStatus.dwAvailPhys, FALSE);
         ::SetDlgItemInt(lpSysInfo->hDlg, IDB_TOTAL_VIRTUAL,
                      MemoryStatus.dwTotalVirtual, FALSE);
         ::SetDlgItemInt(lpSysInfo->hDlg, IDB_AVAIL_VIRTUAL,
                      MemoryStatus.dwAvailVirtual, FALSE);
         ::SetDlgItemInt(lpSysInfo->hDlg, IDB_TOTAL_PAGING,
                      MemoryStatus.dwTotalPageFile,
                      FALSE);
```

```
            ::SetDlgItemInt(lpSysInfo->hDlg, IDB_AVAIL_PAGING,
                            MemoryStatus.dwAvailPageFile,
                            FALSE);

            wsprintf(lpSysInfo->szBuffer, TEXT("%d%%"),
                         MemoryStatus.dwMemoryLoad);
            ::SetDlgItemText(lpSysInfo->hDlg, IDB_MEMORY_PERCENT,
                             lpSysInfo->szBuffer);

            // Sleep for five seconds, but check for
            // messages

            if (::MsgWaitForMultipleObjects(0, NULL, FALSE,
               5000, QS_ALLEVENTS) == 0)
               {
               // Got a message--we'll look for WM_DESTROY
               // as a terminate message, although nobody's
               // sending it to us right now
               // WM_COMMAND means refresh the memory display

               if (::PeekMessage(&msg, NULL, 0, 0, PM_REMOVE) &&
                   msg.message == WM_DESTROY)
                  bContinue = FALSE;
               }
            }
        }
   catch (...)
      {
      TRACE("\nC++ exception caught");
      }
   TRACE(TEXT("\nSystemInfoThread terminating\n"));
   return 0;
}

BOOL CThreadsDlg::OnInitDialog()
{
   CenterWindow();

   SYSTEM_INFO SystemInfo;

   GetSystemInfo(&SystemInfo);

   switch (SystemInfo.dwProcessorType)
      {
      case PROCESSOR_INTEL_386:
         m_ProcessorType = TEXT("Intel 386");
         break;
```

```
        case PROCESSOR_INTEL_486:
            m_ProcessorType = TEXT("Intel 486");
            break;
        case PROCESSOR_INTEL_PENTIUM:
            m_ProcessorType = TEXT("Intel Pentium");
            break;
        case PROCESSOR_MIPS_R4000:
            m_ProcessorType = TEXT("MIPS R4000");
            break;
        case PROCESSOR_ALPHA_21064:
            m_ProcessorType = TEXT("DEC Alpha");
            break;
        default:
            m_ProcessorType = TEXT("Unknown processor");
            break;
        }
    SetDlgItemInt(IDB_PROCESSOR_COUNT, SystemInfo.dwNumberOfProcessors);
    SetDlgItemInt(IDB_PAGE_SIZE, SystemInfo.dwPageSize);

    m_lpSystemInfo = (SYSTEM_INFO_PARMS *)
        ::VirtualAlloc(NULL, sizeof (SYSTEM_INFO_PARMS),
            MEM_COMMIT, PAGE_READWRITE);

    m_lpSystemInfo->hDlg = GetSafeHwnd();

    m_hThread = ::CreateThread(NULL, 0, SystemInfoThread,
        m_lpSystemInfo, 0, &m_dwThreadID);

    CDialog::OnInitDialog();
    return TRUE;  // return TRUE  unless you set the focus to a control
}
```

Conclusion

Multithreading allows you to create software that more closely reflects the way logical components of an application interact with each other. Instead of imposing a sequential, serial mode of execution, applications can be written to run concurrently and asynchronously. This is the only way a Win32 application can take advantage of a multiprocessor hardware platform; multiple threads of an application can run on any available CPU. Multithreading plays a crucial role in network server applications, because it permits the server to pay attention to everyone who wants to talk to it. It is not so essential on the client side, but it does allow an application to remain responsive to the end user even while waiting for a lengthy operation to complete.

The thread management API is not complex. The thread-creation functions (CreateThread(), _beginthread(), _beginthreadex(), and AfxBeginThread()) are the most important functions, and may be the only ones you'll use in many applications. SuspendThread() and ResumeThread() allow you to suspend and resume threads, and SetThreadPriority() lets you control their priority. A thread can call ExitThread(), _endthread(), _endthreadex(), or AfxEndThread() to stop its own execution, or simply *return*.

Challenges arise in three areas when using threads:

1. Because there is no direct way for one thread to stop another thread, you have to use indirect means, such as purposely causing exceptions, posting thread-specific messages, or signalling an event object.
2. Threads are tightly coupled; they share the same virtual address space, the same static data, and the same object handles. Therefore, without proper synchronization they can get in each other's way. The use of synchronization objects is essential in managing the interaction among threads.
3. Much design work and thinking needs to happen before writing a multithreaded application. You must decide if multithreading is a good idea for your application, what the best division of labor is among the threads, and what the tradeoffs are between having one thread bear too much responsibility and having too many threads competing for CPU time.

One important thing to keep in mind is that it is easier to build thread safety into an application right from the start than it is to retrofit it later on. Even if you don't multithread your application initially, coding as if you were making it multithreaded makes it much simpler to change your mind subsequently. A couple of guidelines suffice:

- Use stack-based variables and dynamically allocated memory as much as possible.
- If you use static or global variables, protect your access to them by using the techniques discussed in Chapter 5.

Suggested Readings

Online References

"Multithreading," in *Programming MFC: Encyclopedia.*
Processes and Threads Overview in the Win32 online help.
"Creating Multithread Applications for Win32," in *Programming Techniques*.

Microsoft Knowledge Base for Win32 SDK articles:
"CPU Quota Limits Not Enforced"
"Creating Windows in a Multithreaded Application"
"Getting Real Handle to Thread/Process Requires Two Calls"
"How to Design Multithread Applications to Avoid Deadlock"
"How to Set Foreground/Background Responsiveness in Code"
"Physical Memory Limits Number of Processes/Threads"
"Priority Inversion and Windows NT Scheduler"
"Thread Handles and Thread IDs"

Print References

Custer, Helen. *Inside Windows NT.* Redmond, WA: Microsoft Press, 1992. Chapters 4 and 7.

King, Adrian. *Inside Windows 95.* Redmond, WA: Microsoft Press, 1995.

Open Software Foundation. *OSF/DCE Application Development Guide.* Englewood Cliffs, NJ: Prentice-Hall, Inc., 1993.

Richter, Jeff. *Advanced Windows.* Redmond, WA: Microsoft Press, 1995. Chapters 2 and 3.

Chapter 5

Synchronization Objects

Synchronization objects are the traffic-control mechanisms of a multitasking, multithreaded operating system. They allow threads and processes to coordinate their activities by determining things like when a certain task or operation has completed, or when a shared global resource is available.

Windows provides three object types for interprocess as well as interthread synchronization, and one object type solely for interthread synchronization. The interprocess mechanisms are **semaphores**, **events**, and **mutexes**. They are represented by HANDLEs generated by the operating system. **Critical sections** serve only for coordinating the threads of a single process; they are represented by a CRITICAL_SECTION structure, not as HANDLEs.

Win32 objects have two significant states for synchronization purposes: signalled and nonsignalled. These are the green-light and red-light states, respectively. When an object is signalled, any thread waiting on its handle is allowed to proceed. If the object is nonsignalled, threads waiting on it go to sleep. This behavior is common to all Win32 objects—even those not normally considered synchronization mechanisms, such as file, thread, and process handles. Chapter 4 showed briefly how it applies to threads, where a handle stays nonsignalled until the thread it represents terminates.

The meaning of the signalled and nonsignalled states depends on the type of object. A semaphore is nonsignalled if its current count is 0—that is, all the resources that it is protecting are in use. Its state reverts to signalled when a thread using one of the resources surrenders ownership of the semaphore. A mutex is nonsignalled if a thread has claimed it; it is signalled otherwise. An event is nonsignalled while an operation with which it is linked is pending; it is signalled when the operation completes.

For the programming techniques presented in this book, mutexes and events are the synchronization objects that need to be considered. Semaphores and mutexes are closely related; a mutex can be thought of as a semaphore whose count is always 1. Mutexes are necessary in this book to control access to shared global data structures in dynamic-link libraries. Mutexes and critical sections do exactly the same thing; they provide mutually exclusive (one-at-a-time) access to shared resources. However, since critical sections do not provide interprocess synchronization, they are of little use here.

Events are important because they are used by the API sets we will be considering—File I/O, Windows Sockets, and Named Pipes. Events are being standardized in Windows Sockets version 2. Therefore, a thorough understanding of events is crucial. However, before examining mutexes and events any further, I want to consider the wait functions. They are essential tools for using Win32 synchronization objects effectively.

The Wait Functions

The three wait functions provide the same service. They put the calling thread to sleep until needed resources become available or until an operation completes. For instance, a thread might suspend itself until it can safely write a message to a window. The main thread of an application might spin off several worker threads, then wait until all of them finish their work.

The wait functions provide these variations on the same theme:

- Wait for one object.
- Wait for any one of a set of objects.
- Wait for all of a set of objects.
- Wait for a set of objects (which may be empty), and also let me know if a message comes in.

Because all of these functions take a timeout value, you have control over the duration of a wait.

WaitForSingleObject()

WaitForSingleObject() waits for one object at a time.

```
DWORD WaitForSingleObject(HANDLE hObject, DWORD dwTimeout);
```

The timeout value is in milliseconds. If specified as the constant INFINITE (−1), WaitForSingleObject() will block indefinitely. You can also pass it as 0, which allows you to test the state of the object without waiting for it to signal. There are four possible return values from WaitForSingleObject():

- WAIT_OBJECT_0: The object has entered the signalled state. With mutexes and semaphores, this also confers ownership.
- WAIT_TIMEOUT: The timeout expired before the object became available.
- WAIT_ABANDONED_0: The object is a mutex in the signalled state, and the thread that owned it terminated without releasing it. It is safe to use it.
- WAIT_FAILED: Uh oh! Call GetLastError(). (*hObject* is probably a bogus object handle.)

WaitForMultipleObjects()

WaitForMultipleObjects() allows you to wait for a set of objects.

```
DWORD WaitForMultipleObjects(
        DWORD           dwCount,
        CONST HANDLE   *lpHandles,
        BOOL            bWaitAll,
        DWORD           dwTimeout);
```

dwCount is the number of handles in the array that *lpHandles* points to. The objects do not have to be of the same type; you can pass a set consisting of any combination of handles that makes sense to your application. *bWaitAll* indicates whether you want to wait until *all* of the objects go signalled (TRUE), or whether it will be sufficient for just *one* of them to signal (FALSE). *dwTimeout* is the timeout in milliseconds. The return value from WaitForMultipleObjects(), in addition to WAIT_TIMEOUT or WAIT_FAILED, can be the index of the signalling object into *lpHandles* added to either WAIT_OBJECT_0 (defined as 0) or WAIT_ABANDONED_0 (which is only appropriate for mutexes).

Suppose you pass a five-element array and indicate with *bWaitAll* that you need only one of the objects to signal. The third object in the array *(lpHandles[2])* signals first, so the return value is WAIT_OBJECT_0 + 2 (which at present happens to be just 2, since WAIT_OBJECT_0 is defined as 0). Or perhaps you have five mutexes you are interested in, again being content if only one of them signals. The fourth object *(lpHandles[3])* belongs to a thread that crashes without having a termination handler to make sure the mutex gets released. The return value will be WAIT_ABANDONED_0 + 3.

If you need for all of the objects to go signalled, then you pass *bWaitAll* as TRUE. In this case, when the wait is satisified, the return value will be between WAIT_OBJECT_0 and (WAIT_OBJECT_0 + (*dwCount* – 1)). If the return value falls between WAIT_ABANDONED_0 and (WAIT_ABANDONED_0 + (dwCount – 1)), then all of the objects in the array are signalled, and at least one of them is an abandoned mutex.

MsgWaitForMultipleObjects()

MsgWaitForMultipleObjects() behaves like WaitForMultipleObjects(); the first four arguments are the same.

```
DWORD MsgWaitForMultipleObjects(
          DWORD    dwCount,
          LPHANDLE lpHandles,      // sic!
                                   // prototype for
                                   // WaitForMultipleObjects()
                                   // says CONST HANDLE *
          BOOL     bWaitAll,
          DWORD    dwTimeout,
          DWORD    dwEventFlags)
```

In addition, MsgWaitForMultipleObjects() has a PeekMessage() flavoring; it will return if a message is posted to the thread's message queue. The fifth argument is a filter specifying what messages you are interested in. I normally pass this as QS_ALLEVENTS, which will report any message that comes in. Other possibilities allow you to narrow the scope of messages you want. They are described in the documentation for the GetQueueStatus() function.

You saw in the last chapter that MsgWaitForMultipleObjects() allows you to pass an empty array, where the first argument is 0 and the second is NULL. In this case, the function gives you the equivalent of an interruptible Sleep(). Sleep() expects only one argument—the amount of time to sleep. But if you call Sleep() and in the meantime a message comes in, you can do nothing about it—you're asleep and that's all there is to it. MsgWaitForMultipleObjects() lets you say, "Put me to sleep for this much time, but wake me up if anybody calls." MsgWaitForMultipleObjects() is often preferable to PeekMessage() as well because it puts the calling thread to sleep, whereas PeekMessage() necessitates polling. Polling is always undesirable because it wastes CPU time.

The Mechanics of the API

For semaphores, mutexes, and events—and for other types of Win32 objects—the synchronization procedure is pretty much the same:

1. The object is created by calling the appropriate Create<object>() function, such as CreateMutex(), CreateSemaphore(), or Create-Event().
2. If another process wants to synchronize on the object using its name, it can get a handle by calling the Open<object>() function, or by just calling the Create<object>() function again. For most object types, an attempt to create an object that already exists does not fail—it just works like an Open. The only difference is that the Create<object>() call implicitly requests all access to the object, whereas Open<object>() allows you to specify the exact access you want. It is more efficient to ask only for the level of access you actually need. However, I must be candid and admit that I often just ask for all access anyway; this way I know that if I get a handle to the object, I can use it however I want to. Being more precise invites unanticipated ERROR_ACCESS_DENIED failures.
3. The threads or processes using an object gain and release control of it by calling the appropriate functions.
4. When a process is finished using an object, it closes the handle by calling CloseHandle().

The next discussion focuses on mutexes and events, the object types I will be using for the code presented in the rest of the book.

Mutexes

CreateMutex() is the function that creates a new mutex object, or opens a handle to an existing one.

```
HANDLE CreateMutex(
          LPSECURITY_ATTRIBUTES lpSecurityAttributes,
          BOOL                  bClaimedAtCreation,
          LPCTSTR               lpName);
```

Most of the Create<object>() functions mimic this syntax: the first argument contains the SECURITY_ATTRIBUTES you want to tie to the object, and the last is the name you want to assign to it. The intermediate arguments are dependent on the type of object; they are different for semaphores, mutexes, and events. The security attributes determine whether the handle can be inherited by child processes and what kinds of access other processes are allowed to have. The Win32 Security API is complicated. Until it is discussed in Chapter 13, I will pass the security attributes as NULL, except when it's necessary to do otherwise (like when a server application creates a Named Pipe). The question "Should I use security attributes?" is like "Should I program in assembler?" The answer is, not unless you have to. If you need to ask, you probably don't have to. With synchronization objects, NULL security attributes allow open access.

Objects are assigned names so that other processes can use them for synchronization. If you don't need to do interprocess synchronization with an object, or you're synchronizing with a child process that knows the object's handle, you don't need to name it. There are no conventions for naming Win32 objects, unlike Named Pipes, which have a required prefix (\PIPE\). However, to minimize the likelihood of name-space collisions, I think it's a good idea to adopt some discipline in how you name objects. I imitate the convention for Named Pipes. In addition to the required prefix, I usually follow \PIPE\ with a component that stamps the pipe as belonging to my application, say \PIPE\WNET\. This decreases the chances that someone else will give a pipe the same name. Table 5-1 shows the prefixes I use for different object types. I also follow them with a signature component. I use forward slashes because the backslash is an illegal character in a Win32 object name.

Table 5-1. Prefixes for Naming Win32 Objects

Object Type	Prefix
Semaphore	/SEMAPHORE/
Mutex	/MUTEX/
Event	/EVENT/
Shared Memory	/SHARED_MEM/
Memory-mapped File	/FILE_MAP/

The type of the name is LPCTSTR, a pointer to a string that is either 16-bit Unicode or 8-bit ANSI. LPCTSTR is actually typed as a pointer to a TCHAR array. If the constant UNICODE is defined, the *typedef* for TCHAR is a *wchar_t*, or *unsigned short*. If UNICODE is not defined, TCHAR is a *char*.

Getting back to CreateMutex(), its second argument, *bClaimedAtCreation*, allows you to create a mutex and claim ownership of it in a single atomic operation. If you pass *bClaimedAtCreation* as FALSE, the mutex is created in the unowned (signalled) state. Under most circumstances, you don't need to claim a mutex when you create it, so you will usually pass *bClaimedAtCreation* as FALSE.

Once a mutex has been created, OpenMutex() returns a handle to it.

```
HANDLE OpenMutex(DWORD   dwDesiredAccess,
                 BOOL    bInheritable,
                 LPCTSTR lpName);
```

All the Open<object>() functions take the same set of arguments, except for those derived from previous versions of Windows. The first is the access mode you want. This will vary with the type of object. SYNCHRONIZE access allows you to claim and release a mutex and close its handle, which is all you need to do with it. The constant MUTEX_ALL_ACCESS requests "all possible access." Specifically, this grants every access right that makes sense for a mutex. Microsoft literature recommends that you request the lowest level of access that you actually need; higher levels require additional security checks and therefore degrade performance.

The second argument to the Open<object>() functions, *bInheritable*, indicates whether the handle can be inherited by child processes. A child process can inherit a handle and use it for synchronization without knowing its name. However, named objects are much more common for synchronization among processes—and are easier to code.

The third argument, the name of the object, must correspond to the name of an object that already exists. You can also call the Create<object>() function with the name of an existing object; for most object types, this is just interpreted as a call to Open<object>() requesting all possible access. The Create<object>() function will behave normally, returning a valid handle. You can detect that someone else created the object by calling GetLastError(); it will report ERROR_ALREADY_EXISTS.

Once you have a handle to a mutex, you claim ownership of it by calling one of the wait functions and surrender it with ReleaseMutex():

```
BOOL ReleaseMutex(HANDLE hMutex);
```

To prevent synchronization objects from getting stuck or abandoned, it's a good idea to put the release function in the *__finally* block of a Structured Termination handler, or to wrap it in the destructor of a C++ object. This is exactly what the MFC CSingleLock and CMultiLock classes do.

Let's take a look at a function printfConsole(). It uses a mutex to synchronize writes to a console window, created by a call to AllocConsole() when a GUI application starts up. printfConsole() is in a DLL; this code fragment from the DLL's initialization code creates the mutex:

```
extern HANDLE hPrintfMutex;
hPrintfMutex = CreateMutex(NULL, FALSE,
                    TEXT("/MUTEX/WNET/WNET_PRINTF_MUTEX"));
```

Here is the listing of printfConsole():

```
int _CRTAPI2 printfConsole(LPCTSTR format, ...)
{
   va_list argp;
   TCHAR   szBuffer[1024];
   HANDLE  hStdout;
   DWORD   dwBytes = ((DWORD) -1);

   va_start(argp, format);
   wvsprintf(szBuffer, format, argp);

   hStdout = GetStdHandle(STD_OUTPUT_HANDLE);

   // Protect write to the console with a mutex
   WaitForSingleObject(hPrintfMutex, INFINITE);

   __try
      {
      if (!WriteFile(hStdout, szBuffer, lstrlen(szBuffer),
                  &dwBytes, NULL))
         dwBytes = (DWORD) -1;
      }
   __finally
      {
      // Make sure we release the mutex, no matter how we got here
      ReleaseMutex(hPrintfMutex);
      va_end(argp);
      }

   return (int) dwBytes;
}
```

Events

Events are open-ended objects that report the completion of I/O operations. They are built into the File I/O, Windows Sockets, and Named Pipes APIs. When used in this context, they are set to the nonsignalled state when you make the call that starts the operation and set to the signalled state when the operation completes.

Events come in two types—auto-reset and manual-reset. An auto-reset event allows one thread to proceed when it signals, then immediately reverts to nonsignalled. A manual-reset event allows any thread to run once it has entered the signalled state. It does not become nonsignalled again until it is tied to a new I/O operation or explicitly reset by a call to ResetEvent(). For the APIs we will be dealing with, manual-reset events are required, so that is all I consider here.

As with mutexes, CreateEvent() creates a new event or returns a handle to an existing one; OpenEvent() returns a handle to an event created somewhere else.

```
HANDLE CreateEvent(
          LPSECURITY_ATTRIBUTES lpSecurityAttributes,
          BOOL    bManualReset,
          BOOL    bInitialState,
          LPCTSTR lpName);
```

lpSecurityAttributes and *lpName* are the same as they are for CreateMutex(). *bManualReset* determines the type of event—manual-reset (TRUE) or auto-reset (FALSE). *bInitialState* indicates whether the event should be created in the signalled (TRUE) or nonsignalled (FALSE) state.

OpenEvent() has the same arguments as OpenMutex; here is its prototype:

```
HANDLE OpenEvent(
          DWORD   dwDesiredAccess,
          BOOL    bInheritable,
          LPCTSTR lpName);
```

The only difference between OpenEvent() and OpenMutex() is the types of access that are appropriate. SYNCHRONIZE access allows you to wait on the event handle, either implicitly by tying it to an I/O operation, or explicitly by passing it to one of the wait functions. EVENT_MODIFY_STATE lets you change the state of the event by calling SetEvent(), ResetEvent(), or PulseEvent(). EVENT_ALL_ACCESS requests that you be given all possible access (that is, all accesses that are supported). If you pass CreateEvent() the name of an existing event, it behaves like a call to OpenEvent() with a desired access of EVENT_ALL_ACCESS.

When an event is used with an I/O operation, there is no need to directly change its state (except that there's a bug in Windows 95, which I'll discuss in due course). You associate an event with an operation by putting its handle in a field of a structure. Next, you invoke the function that begins the operation, for example, ReadFile(), and tell it to execute asynchronously. The function returns before the operation completes. You then test the status of the operation by passing the event handle to one of the wait functions, or to GetOverlappedResult() (see Chapter 6).

Three functions directly change the state of an event:

- ResetEvent(), which puts the event into the nonsignalled state.
- SetEvent(), which puts it into the signalled state.
- PulseEvent(), which signals the event, then immediately forces it back to the nonsignalled state. For manual-reset events, all waiting threads are released before the event goes nonsignalled. For auto-reset events, only one thread is released.

All of these functions take one argument, the event handle, and return TRUE or FALSE to indicate success or failure.

Code Listing

In the last chapter, I showed how to terminate a thread by deliberately triggering an exception. As I mentioned there, another way to make a thread go away is to use an event handle. A different version of the application presented there, included on your disk as the Visual C++ project \WIN32NET\CODE\THREADS\THREADS.MDP, demonstrates the latter technique. I use two events here: one to tell the thread to wake up and refresh the memory statistics, the other to tell it to go away. The CThreadsDlg class changes accordingly; here are the appropriate excerpts:

```
class CThreadsDlg : public CDialog
{
// [...]
public:
   enum {WAKEUP_EVENT = 0, GOAWAY_EVENT = 1};
   DWORD GetEventCount() CONST
      {
      return GOAWAY_EVENT - WAKEUP_EVENT + 1;
      }
   CONST HANDLE *GetEventArray() CONST
      {
      return m_hEvents;
      }

   CWinThread *GetSystemInfoThread() CONST
      {
      return m_pSystemInfoThread;
      }
protected:
   // [...]
   CWinThread *m_pSystemInfoThread;
   HANDLE m_hEvents[2];
   // [...]

};
```

In this version, I start the thread by calling AfxBeginThread(), and pass it a pointer to the current CThreadsDlg object.

```
// Create two non-signalled, manual-reset events
m_hEvents[GOAWAY_EVENT] =
   ::CreateEvent(NULL, TRUE, FALSE, NULL);
m_hEvents[WAKEUP_EVENT] =
   ::CreateEvent(NULL, TRUE, FALSE, NULL);
m_pSystemInfoThread =
   AfxBeginThread(SystemInfoThread, (LPVOID) this);
```

The thread uses this object to update the dialog box, and passes its array of event handles to WaitForMultipleObjects(). Here is the revised implementation of SystemInfoThread():

```
UINT SystemInfoThread(LPVOID lp)
{
   CThreadsDlg *pDlg = (CThreadsDlg *) lp;
   MEMORYSTATUS MemoryStatus;
   BOOL         bContinue = TRUE;
   CString      szBuffer;
   DWORD        dwEventIndex;

   while (bContinue)
      {
      MemoryStatus.dwLength = sizeof (MEMORYSTATUS);
      ::GlobalMemoryStatus(&MemoryStatus);

      pDlg->SetDlgItemInt(IDB_TOTAL_PHYSICAL,
                    MemoryStatus.dwTotalPhys);
      pDlg->SetDlgItemInt(IDB_AVAIL_PHYSICAL,
                    MemoryStatus.dwAvailPhys);
      pDlg->SetDlgItemInt(IDB_TOTAL_VIRTUAL,
                    MemoryStatus.dwTotalVirtual);
      pDlg->SetDlgItemInt(IDB_AVAIL_VIRTUAL,
                    MemoryStatus.dwAvailVirtual);
      pDlg->SetDlgItemInt(IDB_TOTAL_PAGING,
                    MemoryStatus.dwTotalPageFile);
      pDlg->SetDlgItemInt(IDB_AVAIL_PAGING,
                    MemoryStatus.dwAvailPageFile);
      szBuffer.Format(TEXT("%d%%"),
               MemoryStatus.dwMemoryLoad);
      pDlg->SetDlgItemText(IDB_MEMORY_PERCENT,
                     szBuffer);

      dwEventIndex = ::WaitForMultipleObjects(
         pDlg->GetEventCount(),
```

```
            pDlg->GetEventArray(),
            FALSE,
            5000);
        if (dwEventIndex != WAIT_TIMEOUT)
            {
            // One of our boys signalled--see if it's
            // refresh or go away
            if (dwEventIndex == pDlg->GOAWAY_EVENT)
                bContinue = FALSE;
            }
        }

    TRACE(TEXT("\nSystemInfoThread terminating\n"));
    return 0;
}
```

To terminate the thread, all I have to do is set the handle of the appropriate event, as shown in the new CThreadsDlg::OnCancel():

```
void CThreadsDlg::OnCancel()
{
   ::SetEvent(m_hEvents[GOAWAY_EVENT]);
   ::WaitForSingleObject(m_pSystemInfoThread->m_hThread, INFINITE);
   CDialog::OnCancel();
}
```

CThreadsDlg::OnRefresh() needs to signal the wakeup event handle, but wants it to immediately revert to the nonsignalled state so it does not cause WaitForMultipleObjects() to wake up again. PulseEvent() is exactly the function it needs. (Or we could use an auto-reset event.)

```
void CThreadsDlg::OnRefresh()
{
   ::PulseEvent(m_hEvents[WAKEUP_EVENT]);
}
```

I don't think it will be controversial if I say that this is a better implementation than the one I presented in Chapter 4.

C++ and MFC Considerations

MFC 4 adds classes to represent Win32 synchronization objects. They are declared in the header file AFXMT.H, and implemented in MTCORE.CPP and MTEX.CPP. Functionality common to all of the objects is collected in the CSyncObject abstract base class. Each specific object type then derives from it: CMutex, CSemaphore, CEvent, and CCriticalSection. There are two additional classes that can be used to claim ownership of an object: CSingleLock and CMultiLock. CSingleLock locks one object at a time; its use is optional, since you can accomplish the same purpose with the native object. CMultiLock locks an array of CSyncObject pointers; it uses WaitForMultipleObjects() or MsgWaitForMultipleObjects(). Both CSingleLock and CMultiLock add a level of automatic cleanup—their destructors release ownership of the object (or objects) if they have been claimed.

The CSyncObject Class

Here is the essential class declaration for CSyncObject, from AFXMT.H. (I have removed the debug-only elements.) The class implementation is in MTCORE.CPP. One method—the HANDLE() operator—can be found in AFXMT.INL.

```
class CSyncObject : public CObject
{
   DECLARE_DYNAMIC(CSyncObject)

// Constructor
public:
   CSyncObject(LPCTSTR pstrName);

// Attributes
public:
   operator HANDLE() const;
   HANDLE  m_hObject;

// Operations
   virtual BOOL Lock(DWORD dwTimeout = INFINITE);
   virtual BOOL Unlock() = 0;
   virtual BOOL Unlock(LONG /* lCount */, LPLONG /* lpPrevCount=NULL */)
                  { return TRUE; }

// Implementation
public:
   virtual ~CSyncObject();
   friend class CSingleLock;
   friend class CMultiLock;
};
```

The constructor does nothing—in debug mode, it just remembers the object name. The destructor closes the object handle. The heart of this class is the Lock() and Unlock() methods. Lock() is inherited by all the subclasses except CCriticalSection. Here's what it does:

```
BOOL CSyncObject::Lock(DWORD dwTimeout)
{
   if (::WaitForSingleObject(m_hObject, dwTimeout)
         == WAIT_OBJECT_0)
      return TRUE;
   else
      return FALSE;
}
```

The CSyncObject::Unlock() methods must be overridden—the first version because it is a pure virtual function, the second because it does nothing. This method cannot possibly be implemented in the base class, because it means something different for each type of object. For a mutex, you call ReleaseMutex(). For a semaphore, you call ReleaseSemaphore(). For an event, you do nothing. Finally, a critical section calls LeaveCriticalSection(). Therefore, the Unlock() method is the main place where the specific object classes impose their own views of the world. Their constructors will also invoke the appropriate Create<object>() function.

The CMutex Class

CMutex is also declared in AFXMT.H, and implemented in MTEX.CPP.

```
class CMutex : public CSyncObject
{
   DECLARE_DYNAMIC(CMutex)

// Constructor
public:
   CMutex(BOOL bInitiallyOwn = FALSE, LPCTSTR lpszName = NULL,
         LPSECURITY_ATTRIBUTES lpsaAttribute = NULL);

// Implementation
public:
   virtual ~CMutex();
   BOOL Unlock();
};
```

This is a very lean class. The constructor calls CreateMutex(); Unlock() calls ReleaseMutex(). That's it; the destructor doesn't do anything (but it must be included in order for CSyncObject::~CSyncObject() to close the handle).

The CSemaphore Class

The CSemaphore class is only slightly bigger than CMutex. Here's its declaration, from AFXMT.H:

```
class CSemaphore : public CSyncObject
{
   DECLARE_DYNAMIC(CSemaphore)

// Constructor
public:
   CSemaphore(LONG lInitialCount = 1, LONG lMaxCount = 1,
              LPCTSTR pstrName=NULL,
              LPSECURITY_ATTRIBUTES lpsaAttributes = NULL);

// Implementation
public:
   virtual ~CSemaphore();
   virtual BOOL Unlock();
   virtual BOOL Unlock(LONG lCount, LPLONG lprevCount = NULL);
};
```

The constructor calls CreateSemaphore(); the destructor does nothing (but it does give the CSyncObject destructor a chance). There are two versions of Unlock(). The ReleaseSemaphore() function, which they both call, allows you to bump the semaphore count by more than one, if you have a reason for doing so. Usually, you don't, so the simplest version of Unlock() (defined in AFXMT.INL) just increments the count. The second version, implemented in MTEX.CPP (like the other CSemaphore methods) bumps the count by the amount indicated in its *lCount* argument.

The CEvent Class

The CEvent class is also declared in AFXMT.H. Here is its declaration:

```
class CEvent : public CSyncObject
{
   DECLARE_DYNAMIC(CEvent)
```

```
// Constructor
public:
   CEvent(BOOL bInitiallyOwn = FALSE, BOOL bManualReset = FALSE,
          LPCTSTR lpszName = NULL,
          LPSECURITY_ATTRIBUTES lpsaAttribute = NULL);

// Operations
public:
   BOOL SetEvent();
   BOOL PulseEvent();
   BOOL ResetEvent();
   BOOL Unlock();

// Implementation
public:
   virtual ~CEvent();
};
```

The constructor, destructor, and the Unlock() method are implemented in MTEX.CPP. The constructor calls CreateEvent(); the destructor does nothing except allow CSyncObject::~CSyncObject() to be called. By the way, I would suggest that the default value for the constructor's *bManualReset* argument should be TRUE, not FALSE. In my Win32 programming, I need manual-reset events much more often than auto-reset ones.

It is meaningless to unlock an event, so the Unlock() method just returns FALSE. SetEvent(), PulseEvent(), and ResetEvent() are implemented in AFXMT.INL. They just pass the object handle (*m_hObject*) through to the Win32 function of the same name, after ASSERTing that the handle is valid.

The CCriticalSection Class

CCriticalSection is declared in AFXMT.H, and its entire implementation is in AFXMT.INL.

```
class CCriticalSection : public CSyncObject
{
   DECLARE_DYNAMIC(CCriticalSection)

// Constructor
public:
   CCriticalSection();

// Attributes
public:
   operator CRITICAL_SECTION*();
   CRITICAL_SECTION m_sect;
```

```
// Operations
public:
   BOOL Unlock();
   BOOL Lock();
   BOOL Lock(DWORD dwTimeout);

// Implementation
public:
   virtual ~CCriticalSection();
};
```

Notice that there's no reason to derive CCriticalSection from CSyncObject. Strictly speaking, a critical section is not a Win32 synchronization object. Furthermore, CCriticalSection inherits no functionality whatsoever from CSyncObject. All of its methods replace the methods in the base class.

There are four Win32 functions that manipulate critical sections—InitializeCriticalSection(), EnterCriticalSection(), LeaveCriticalSection(), and DeleteCriticalSection(). The constructor calls the first, Lock() calls the second, Unlock() calls the third, and the destructor invokes the fourth. The version of Unlock() with a timeout argument is provided to keep you from accidentally calling the corresponding CSyncObject::Unlock(). Critical sections don't let you time out; this version just calls the version that has no arguments.

The CSingleLock Class

This class has really only one role to play. It remembers whether you have locked an object or not, and its destructor unlocks it if you have. Here is the class declaration excerpted from AFXMT.H:

```
class CSingleLock
{
// Constructors
public:
   CSingleLock(CSyncObject* pObject, BOOL bInitialLock = FALSE);

// Operations
public:
   BOOL Lock(DWORD dwTimeOut = INFINITE);
   BOOL Unlock();
   BOOL Unlock(LONG lCount, LPLONG lPrevCount = NULL);
   BOOL IsLocked();
```

```
// Implementation
public:
   ~CSingleLock();

protected:
   CSyncObject* m_pObject;
   HANDLE  m_hObject;
   BOOL    m_bAcquired;
};
```

With CSingleLock, you first construct the specific object you want to lock (either a CMutex, a CSemaphore, or a CEvent). You then pass its address to the CSingleLock constructor.

The Lock() method invokes the Lock() method in the underlying object, and remembers its return value in *m_bAcquired*. The CSingleLock destructor (the only CSingleLock method defined in AFXMT.INL instead of MTEX.CPP) calls Unlock(), which in turn calls the object's own Unlock() method if *m_bAcquired* is TRUE.

The CMultiLock Class

Whereas CSingleLock is a convenience, CMultiLock is a necessity. It uses WaitForMultipleObjects() or MsgWaitForMultipleObjects() to lock an array of CSyncObjects. It takes care of setting up a contiguous array of object HANDLEs, as these functions require. Here is the class declaration from AFXMT.H:

```
class CMultiLock
{
// Constructor
public:
   CMultiLock(CSyncObject* ppObjects[],
              DWORD dwCount,
              BOOL bInitialLock = FALSE);

// Operations
public:
   DWORD Lock(DWORD dwTimeOut = INFINITE,
              BOOL bWaitForAll = TRUE,
              DWORD dwWakeMask = 0);
   BOOL Unlock();
   BOOL Unlock(LONG lCount, LPLONG lPrevCount = NULL);
   BOOL IsLocked(DWORD dwItem);
```

```
// Implementation
public:
   ~CMultiLock();

protected:
   HANDLE  m_hPreallocated[8];
   BOOL    m_bPreallocated[8];

   CSyncObject* const * m_ppObjectArray;
   HANDLE* m_pHandleArray;
   BOOL*   m_bLockedArray;
   DWORD   m_dwCount;
};
```

You first instantiate an array of CSyncObject pointers. You then construct a CMultiLock object, passing it a pointer to this array. The constructor builds an array of the object HANDLEs in *m_pHandleArray.*

The Lock() method calls WaitForMultipleObjects() if its *dwWakeMask* argument comes in as zero; otherwise, it calls MsgWaitForMultipleObjects(), passing *dwWakeMask* along as its last argument. It remembers which HANDLEs in the array are locked in the *m_bLockedArray.* Then, the Unlock() method scans this array and calls the object-specific Unlock() method for all locked objects.

The CMultiLock destructor calls its Unlock() method to make sure you release ownership of all your locked objects.

Using the MFC Synchronization Object Classes

To demonstrate the use of the MFC classes, I provide an additional implementation of the THREADS sample application, which you will find in the \WIN32NET\CODE\THRDSYNC directory on the disk. The version of THREADS presented earlier used native Win32 events. This one uses an array of CEvent objects stored in a CMultiLock array.

The CThreadsDlg class changes from the version presented above. Here are the relevant portions of the class declaration:

```
class CThreadsDlg : public CDialog
{
// Construction
public:
   CMultiLock& GetEventArray() CONST
      {
      return (CMultiLock&) *m_pEventArray;
      }
```

```
// [...]
// Implementation
protected:
   CMultiLock *m_pEventArray;
   CEvent *m_pEvents[2];

// [...]
};
```

When I start up the background thread, I set up both the CEvent array (*m_pEvents*) and the CMultiLock object (*m_pEventArray*).

```
// Create two non-signalled, manual-reset events
m_pEvents[0] = new CEvent(FALSE, TRUE);
m_pEvents[1] = new CEvent(FALSE, TRUE);

m_pEventArray = new CMultiLock(
     (CSyncObject **) m_pEvents, 2);
m_pSystemInfoThread =
   AfxBeginThread(SystemInfoThread, (LPVOID) this);
```

The thread itself calls CMultiLock::Lock() instead of calling WaitForMultipleObjects() directly.

```
dwEventIndex = pDlg->GetEventArray().Lock(
                     5000, FALSE);
```

The OnRefresh() and OnCancel() methods change to use CEvent methods instead of direct Win32 function calls.

```
void CThreadsDlg::OnCancel()
{
   m_pEvents[GOAWAY_EVENT]->SetEvent();

   ::WaitForSingleObject(
      m_pSystemInfoThread->m_hThread, 5000);

   delete m_pEventArray;
   delete m_pEvents[GOAWAY_EVENT];
   delete m_pEvents[WAKEUP_EVENT];
   CDialog::OnCancel();
}

void CThreadsDlg::OnRefresh()
{
   m_pEvents[WAKEUP_EVENT]->PulseEvent();
}
```

Conclusion

Synchronization objects are an important tool for safe programming in a multithreaded environment. Windows provides several kinds of them. The choice of which one to use depends on what you need to accomplish.

- Semaphores regulate access to a shared resource where more than one instance of the resource may be used concurrently. Examples of this are modem pools or software licenses.
- Mutexes can be thought of as semaphores where there is never more than one instance of a resource. The term mutex is shorthand for mutual exclusion. Mutexes allow one thread at a time to use a shared object.
- Critical sections are less expensive mutual-exclusion objects that work only between threads of a single process.
- Events are open-ended objects that signal the completion of an I/O operation. They are required by some of the other Win32 API sets.

Structured Termination Handling (or intelligent C++ destructors) help assure the proper use of synchronization objects, because they guarantee that a thread that owns an object will relinquish it.

In Chapters 6 and 7, we will see how events and mutexes are used with file I/O and dynamic-link libraries.

Suggested Readings

Online References

"Multithreading: How to Use the Synchronization Classes," in *Programming MFC: Encyclopedia.*

Handles and Objects Overview in the Win32 online help.

Synchronization Overview in the Win32 online help.

Microsoft Knowledge Base for Win32 SDK articles:

"Critical Sections Versus Mutexes"

"Interrupting Threads in Critical Sections"

"Mutex Wait Is FIFO But Can Be Interrupted"

Print References

Custer, Helen. *Inside Windows NT.* Redmond, WA: Microsoft Press, 1992. Chapter 3.

Richter, Jeff. *Advanced Windows.* Redmond, WA: Microsoft Press, 1995. Chapter 9.

Chapter 6

Win32 File I/O

This chapter introduces the powerful file I/O capabilities of the Win32 programming interface. The Win32 file I/O API is rich and interesting in and of itself. For my purposes, it is especially pertinent, because overlapped, or asynchronous, I/O is the backbone of the network communication APIs we'll study later in this book. It is also the optimal way to use Windows Sockets, which is maturing into the peer-to-peer programming interface of choice.

This chapter is also the first place where we encounter a significant divergence between Windows NT and Windows 95. Specifically, Windows 95 cannot do overlapped I/O on disk files. However, this is less important than you might think, because Windows 95 can do overlapped I/O where we need it to—with Windows Sockets and Named Pipes.

The Win32 API offers a complete set of file I/O functions. You can still use standard C runtime library functions, but these are provided primarily for console applications and for backward compatibility. The Win32 file I/O calls offer the most hooks into the operating system kernel, and are the only way to use the advanced capabilities of the NT file system, which include:

- Attaching security restrictions to files and directories on NTFS partitions
- Support for 64-bit (that is, unlimited) file sizes
- Asynchronous I/O
- I/O completion ports
- Callback functions with read and write calls (I/O completion routines)

Only NT supports all of these. Windows 95 does not support the last three (when applied to disk files), and MFC supports none of them. It seems fair to say that the MFC CFile class aims to achieve lowest-common-denominator Win32 functionality.

Basic File I/O Operations

The Win32 functions that perform the basic set of file operations (open, read, write, and close) are CreateFile(), ReadFile(), WriteFile(), and CloseHandle().

CreateFile()

The name CreateFile() would seem to suggest that this function is responsible for creating new files, and that OpenFile() should be used with existing files. However, the name CreateFile() is used because it is consistent with the other object functions in Win32; that is, it creates a Win32 file object representing some kind of a disk object. The associated disk operation is included as one of the arguments to CreateFile():

```
HANDLE CreateFile(
          LPCTSTR lpFileName,
          DWORD   dwDesiredAccess,
          DWORD   dwShareMode,
          LPSECURITY_ATTRIBUTES lpSecurityAttributes,
          DWORD   dwCreationDisposition,
          DWORD   dwFlagsAndAttributes,
          HANDLE  hTemplateFile);
```

The first three arguments should be more or less self-explanatory, as they are common to most file I/O APIs. The operating system needs to know the name of the file *(lpFileName)*, it needs to know how you intend to access the file *(dwDesiredAccess)*, and it needs to know what access to allow other processes while you have the file open *(dwShareMode)*. *lpFileName* is an LPCTSTR, a pointer to a Unicode or ANSI string. You can access files on remote machines using a redirected drive, or with the full Universal Naming Convention (UNC) filename. UNC filenames have this format:

```
\\<Machine name>\<Share name>\<Rest of path to file>\<Filename>
```

For instance, if the machine NUMBER1 is sharing the directory C:\ under the share name ROOT, you use the UNC name \\NUMBER1\ROOT\AUTOEXEC.BAT to open the AUTOEXEC.BAT file in that directory. As you will see in Chapter 10, this is how a Named Pipes client connects to a Named Pipes server.

The next argument to CreateFile(), *dwDesiredAccess*, indicates whether you want to open the file for read access, write access, or both. The constants defined by Win32 for this purpose are GENERIC_READ and GENERIC_WRITE. These constants are so-named because there is a plethora of Win32 object types, and many different kinds of rights that apply to them. The Win32 API allows you to request access by specifying a more abstract, generic set of rights, which are then mapped to the specific set of rights that make sense for a given object type. For files, GENERIC_READ and GENERIC_WRITE map to FILE_GENERIC_READ and FILE_GENERIC_WRITE, which are defined as follows in WINNT.H:

```
#define FILE_GENERIC_READ          (STANDARD_RIGHTS_READ      |\
                                    FILE_READ_DATA            |\
                                    FILE_READ_ATTRIBUTES      |\
                                    FILE_READ_EA              |\
                                    SYNCHRONIZE)

#define FILE_GENERIC_WRITE         (STANDARD_RIGHTS_WRITE     |\
                                    FILE_WRITE_DATA           |\
                                    FILE_WRITE_ATTRIBUTES     |\
                                    FILE_WRITE_EA             |\
                                    FILE_APPEND_DATA          |\
                                    SYNCHRONIZE)
```

STANDARD_RIGHTS_READ and STANDARD_RIGHTS_WRITE are the same. They grant permission to alter the security characteristics of a file. FILE_READ_EA and FILE_WRITE_EA let you read and write the extended attributes of a file. SYNCHRONIZE lets you use a file handle as a synchronization object—that is, it lets you pass it to functions like WaitForSingleObject(). The other constants should be self-explanatory.

dwShareMode specifies the ways in which other threads and processes may access the file while you are working with it. A value of zero requests exclusive access. The constants FILE_SHARE_READ and FILE_SHARE_WRITE grant read and write access and may be ORed together.

lpSecurityAttributes is significant if you are creating a new file on an NTFS partition or if you need the file handle to be inheritable. You can pass it as NULL if child processes do not need to use the handle, and if you are not setting explicit security limitations. Be aware that creating a file with NULL security attributes or passing a SECURITY_ATTRIBUTES structure with a NULL security descriptor does not make it available to everyone. Rather, it causes the file to inherit the security restrictions of the directory where it resides. Usually, these allow administrative users (those belonging to the group Administrators) full access and give other users (members of the group Everyone) read access. You will see how to grant universal access to a file in Chapter 10 when I apply security attributes to Named Pipes. I defer the bulk of the discussion of Win32 security until Chapter 13.

Most of the syntactic complexity of CreateFile() is contained in *dwCreationDisposition* and *dwFlagsAndAttributes*. CreateFile() can do a number of things; *dwCreationDisposition* tells CreateFile() what I/O operation you want. Possible values for *dwCreationDisposition* are:

- CREATE_NEW: Create a new file, but fail the function if the file already exists.
- CREATE_ALWAYS: Create a new file unconditionally; if the file already exists, truncate its contents.
- OPEN_EXISTING: Open an existing file, but fail the function if the file does not already exist.
- OPEN_ALWAYS: Open an existing file, and create a new one if the file does not already exist.
- TRUNCATE_EXISTING: Open an existing file, and truncate it to zero bytes. If the file does not exist, fail the function.

dwFlagsAndAttributes specifies the attributes of a newly created file. It is ignored when you open an existing file. These are the standard normal, read-only, hidden, system, and archive attributes. The corresponding Win32 constants are FILE_ATTRIBUTE_NORMAL, FILE_ATTRIBUTE_READONLY, FILE_ATTRIBUTE_HIDDEN, FILE_ATTRIBUTE_SYSTEM, and FILE_ATTRIBUTE_ARCHIVE. Another interesting attribute is FILE_ATTRIBUTE_TEMPORARY, which tells Windows that you are creating the file as a temporary file. Windows tries to keep all file accesses in cache. In combination with the flag bit FILE_FLAG_DELETE_ON_CLOSE, it lets you set up a temporary file that you do not have to worry about deleting when you are through with it. Windows will delete it when the last handle to the file is closed. Another new attribute is FILE_ATTRIBUTE_COMPRESSED, which tells Windows that you want to store the file in compressed format.

The flag bits of *dwFlagsAndAttributes* govern the way in which the file will be accessed. The most interesting for our purposes is FILE_FLAG_OVERLAPPED. This enables overlapped (asynchronous) file I/O for both normal disk files and named pipes. FILE_FLAG_WRITE_THROUGH may be desirable for certain kinds of named pipes; it prevents local buffering of data, forcing all writes to the named pipe to be immediately transmitted to the partner station. FILE_FLAG_RANDOM_ACCESS and FILE_FLAG_SEQUENTIAL_SCAN inform Windows how you intend to access the file, and influence its caching policy.

The final argument to CreateFile(), *hTemplateFile*, is a handle to an open file whose extended attributes will be inherited by a newly created file. It is ignored when you are opening an existing file.

CreateFile() returns a HANDLE that you use for subsequent operations on the file. If the function fails, it returns INVALID_HANDLE_VALUE (−1), not NULL. When I first starting writing code for NT, this was one of my most common mistakes. This is an annoying inconsistency in the Win32 API: most functions that return HANDLEs return NULL to signal failure, but some return INVALID_HANDLE_VALUE. There does appear to be some rhyme or reason for this: the functions that return INVALID_HANDLE_VALUE—that is, CreateConsoleScreenBuffer(), CreateFile(), CreateMailslot(), CreateNamedPipe(), FindFirstChangeNotification(), FindFirstFile(), and GetStdHandle()—are primarily file-related. However, so is CreateFileMapping(), but it returns NULL if it fails.

ReadFile() / WriteFile()

Reads and writes are done using ReadFile() and WriteFile(), which have identical syntax:

```
BOOL ReadFile(
        HANDLE       hFile,
        LPVOID       lpBuffer,
        DWORD        dwBytes,
        LPDWORD      lpBytes,
        LPOVERLAPPED lpOverlapped);

BOOL WriteFile(
        HANDLE       hFile,
        LPVOID       lpBuffer,
        DWORD        dwBytes,
        LPDWORD      lpBytes,
        LPOVERLAPPED lpOverlapped);
```

The first four arguments (*hFile, lpBuffer, dwBytes,* and *lpBytes*) are standard. The operating system needs to know which file you are targeting (*hFile*), where to read the data to or write it from (*lpBuffer*), and how many bytes to read or write. It also needs to inform you how many bytes were read or written. Some file I/O APIs, like the C runtime functions _read() and _write(), use the function return value to report this. Win32 uses the *lpBytes* argument.

Overlapped I/O

The last argument to ReadFile() and WriteFile() is the most interesting. It is a pointer to an OVERLAPPED structure. For files created with the FILE_FLAG_OVERLAPPED flag, the structure allows you to do file I/O in the background while your program goes about its other tasks. With files created for non-overlapped I/O, you can use the OVERLAPPED structure to specify the file offset where you want the read or write operation to begin. Ordinarily, you do this by calling SetFilePointer() before you invoke ReadFile() or WriteFile().

A reminder: though Windows 95 cannot do overlapped I/O against disk files, it can with communications objects. So the ensuing discussion is relevant for both platforms.

The OVERLAPPED Structure

There are three ways of doing overlapped I/O: standard overlapped I/O using event handles, I/O completion ports, and I/O completion routines. All of them require you to pass a pointer to an OVERLAPPED structure, defined as follows:

```
typedef struct _OVERLAPPED
{
   DWORD   Internal;
   DWORD   InternalHigh;
   DWORD   Offset;
   DWORD   OffsetHigh;
   HANDLE  hEvent;
} OVERLAPPED;
```

Not surprisingly, *Internal* and *InternalHigh* are used for internal purposes. Their meaning is documented, however: when an operation has completed, *Internal* is any error that occurred or NO_ERROR (zero) if none did, and *InternalHigh* is the number of bytes transferred. *Offset* and *OffsetHigh* specify the file position at which the read or write should begin. NT will seek to the indicated location in the file before performing the operation. For overlapped I/O, you must specify the offset; NT does not automatically adjust the file pointer. The offset is expressed as two DWORD variables to accommodate 64-bit file sizes. With virtual files like named pipes and Windows Sockets, the offset is irrelevant, but must be set to zero.

A common error is to forget to initialize the *OffsetHigh* field when reading a disk file. This causes NT to attempt a read at a fabulously high address. The function call does not fail, but when you block waiting for the operation to complete, you never wake up. A good practice is to zero out the OVERLAPPED structure before you start populating the fields:

```
OVERLAPPED ov;

ZeroMemory(&ov, sizeof (OVERLAPPED));
```

An even better approach is to derive a C++ class from the OVERLAPPED structure, then initialize the fields in the class constructor. That way, you can't possibly forget. I'll be using such a class a lot in this book. Here's what its declaration might look like:

```
class COverlapped : public OVERLAPPED
{
public:
   COverlapped()
   {
   Internal     = 0;
   InternalHigh = 0;
   Offset       = 0;
   OffsetHigh   = 0;
   hEvent       = NULL;
   }
// [Rest of class declaration]
};
```

As we will see, there are other reasons for extending the OVERLAPPED structure.

Standard Overlapped I/O Using Event Handles

I should confess at once that I made up the term "Standard Overlapped I/O" for the technique I'm about to discuss. Microsoft does not refer to it as "standard." In this approach, you create a manual-reset event for each operation you want to execute. You then put the handle of the event in the *hEvent* field of the OVERLAPPED structure. When the operation commences, Windows automatically puts the event into the nonsignalled state. At this point, a FALSE return value from ReadFile() or WriteFile() may not indicate a true failure; if GetLastError() returns ERROR_IO_PENDING, the operation is being done in the background. When it completes, Windows will signal the event. As I type this manuscript, there is a bug in Windows 95 4.0 (build 950). By the time the book reaches the bookstores, the bug may have been fixed. At present, Windows 95 forgets to put the event into the nonsignalled state, so you must do this yourself for code you want to run in both environments.

Windows does reserve the right to overrule your request. For example, if you spin off an overlapped read or write against a file that is already cached in memory, the function will return TRUE. You cannot assume that the I/O will always be overlapped.

An overlapped operation does not update **lpBytes*, the variable reporting the number of bytes read or written. After all, the operation is still pending at this point; its final result is not known until you call GetOverlappedResult().

GetOverlappedResult(). After you have spun off overlapped operations, you can test for their completion by calling GetOverlappedResult():

```
BOOL GetOverlappedResult(
        HANDLE       hFile,
        LPOVERLAPPED lpOverlapped,
        LPDWORD      lpBytesTransferred,
        BOOL         bWait);
```

hFile and *lpOverlapped* are the file handle and OVERLAPPED structure that you previously passed to ReadFile() or WriteFile(). *lpBytesTransferred* returns the number of bytes moved. *bWait* specifies whether you want GetOverlappedResult() to block until the operation completes (TRUE), or return immediately with a code indicating the current status of the operation (FALSE). If you pass *bWait* as FALSE and the operation is still not complete, GetOverlappedResult() returns FALSE, and GetLastError() reports the error as ERROR_IO_INCOMPLETE (*not* ERROR_IO_PENDING, for some reason). Because *bWait* is a BOOL, you cannot request a timeout; you either wait forever or you return immediately.

WaitForMultipleObjects(). GetOverlappedResult() has two important limitations: it only reports on a single operation, and it does not let you specify a timeout. The power of overlapped I/O comes in spinning off multiple operations against a file, pipe, or socket. It is more common to set up an array of event handles, then pass it to WaitForMultipleObjects() or MsgWaitForMultipleObjects(). When an operation completes, you call GetOverlappedResult() to find out its final disposition.

I/O Completion Ports

Another way to do overlapped I/O is to use I/O completion ports. You do this by associating file handles with an I/O completion port. Once you have done so, I/O events against those files (or pipes, or sockets) are queued to the port asynchronously. Because I/O completion ports are specifically designed for a multiprocessor environment, they are only supported under NT.

CreateIoCompletionPort(). To associate a file with an I/O completion port, you pass its handle to CreateIoCompletionPort():

```
BOOL CreateIoCompletionPort(
        HANDLE hFile,
        HANDLE hExistingPort,
        DWORD  dwCompletionKey,
        DWORD  dwConcurrentThreads);
```

hFile identifies an open file. To create a new I/O completion port, pass *hExistingPort* as NULL. To associate an additional file with an already existing port, pass it as the value returned by a previous call to CreateIoCompletionPort(). You can also pass *hFile* as INVALID_HANDLE_VALUE to create an I/O completion port that is not connected to a file. Then, typically, you will use PostQueuedCompletionStatus() to post events to the queue by hand, so to speak. *dwCompletionKey* serves as the unique identifier for the files you link to a port; it will be the piece of information passed back by NT when the operation completes. *dwConcurrentThreads* requests the number of active threads you want to have supporting the I/O port. Passing it as zero asks NT to allocate one thread for each CPU on your system.

Now, you issue ReadFile() and WriteFile() calls against the file. The only fields of the OVERLAPPED structure carrying pertinent information are the *Offset* and *OffsetHigh* fields. With pipes and sockets, even these fields have no meaning. In other words, none of the fields apply to your I/O call, but you are still required to pass this argument.

Microsoft is currently recommending I/O completion ports as the most efficient way to do overlapped file I/O, because it allows the system to tailor the number of threads to the ability of your hardware to support them. Threads are not free; spinning off more threads to get better throughput can actually be counterproductive. Passing *dwConcurrentThreads* as zero uses I/O completion ports in the most optimized way.

This is particularly relevant for Windows Sockets programming. Windows Sockets have full overlapped capabilities, and overlapped I/O is the fastest way to use them, as we will see in Chapter 9. I/O completion ports are said to be the fastest way to do overlapped I/O (I have not been able to verify this).

GetQueuedCompletionStatus(). The return value from CreateIoCompletionPort() is a HANDLE to the port. You then find out the status of your I/O operations by passing this handle to GetQueuedCompletionStatus(). This function combines the action of WaitForMultipleObjects() and GetOverlappedResult(), with the difference that you do not specify the I/O operations of interest explicitly. With WaitForMultipleObjects(), you pass the array of event handles you have set up to represent your operations. With GetQueuedCompletionStatus(), the completion port knows which files you have associated with it. This gets around one of the limitations of WaitForMultipleObjects()—it can only accept an array of 64 handles. In a large server application, you could conceivably have many more handles than this to manage. Here is the prototype:

```
BOOL GetQueuedCompletionStatus(
        HANDLE         hPort,
        LPDWORD        lpdwBytesTransferred,
        LPDWORD        lpdwCompletionKey,
        LPOVERLAPPED *lplpOverlapped,
        DWORD          dwTimeout);
```

hPort is the port handle created by CreateIoCompletionPort(). *lpdwBytesTransferred* points to a DWORD variable that will return the number of bytes read or written. *lpdwCompletionKey* returns the *dwCompletionKey* that you passed to CreateIoCompletionPort() to uniquely stamp each file you connect to the port. **lplpOverlapped* will be set to point to the OVERLAPPED structure that was submitted to the original I/O call. *dwTimeout* is the usual timeout argument, with INFINITE indicating an indefinite block.

If GetQueuedCompletionStatus() returns TRUE, an I/O operation has completed, and the output variables contain the information describing it. If it returns FALSE, and **lplpOverlapped* is set to NULL, there is no event on the queue; GetQueuedCompletionStatus() just timed out. If the return value is FALSE, and **lplpOverlapped* is non-NULL, an operation completed with an error. Call GetLastError() to find out what the specific problem was.

PostQueuedCompletionStatus(). You can use an I/O completion port to report operations against files that you have not associated with the port by calling PostQueuedCompletionStatus(). Usually, you will do this when you call CreateIoCompletionPort() with an invalid file handle (*hFile* == INVALID_HANDLE_VALUE).

```
BOOL PostQueuedCompletionStatus(
        HANDLE       hPort,
        DWORD        dwBytesTransferred,
        DWORD        dwCompletionKey,
        LPOVERLAPPED lpOverlapped);
```

hPort is the port you want to post the event to; the other arguments are the ones that you want GetQueuedCompletionStatus() to return.

Using Event Handles. You can override the posting of operations to the completion port by putting an event handle in the *hEvent* field, and setting its low bit. In this case, NT signals the event when the operation completes, so you use standard overlapped techniques.

Setting the low bit is a bit messy syntactically, since the HANDLE type is a void *. You have to do something ugly like this:

```
OVERLAPPED ov;

ZeroMemory(&ov, sizeof (OVERLAPPED));
ov.hEvent = CreateEvent(NULL, TRUE, FALSE, NULL);
(*((int *) &ov.hEvent)) |= 1;
```

Callback Functions with Overlapped File I/O

The third overlapped technique uses ReadFileEx() and WriteFileEx() instead of ReadFile() and WriteFile(). These functions allow you to specify a call-back function that is then invoked when operations complete. Here is the prototype for ReadFileEx(); WriteFileEx() is exactly the same:

```
BOOL ReadFileEx(
        HANDLE       hFile,
        LPVOID       lpBuffer,
        DWORD        dwBytesToRead,
        LPOVERLAPPED lpOverlapped,
        LPOVERLAPPED_COMPLETION_ROUTINE lpRoutine);
```

The first three arguments are the same as for ReadFile() and WriteFile(), as is the pointer to the OVERLAPPED structure. The function pointed to by lpRoutine has the following prototype:

```
VOID WINAPI FileIOCompletionRoutine(
               DWORD        dwError,
               DWORD        dwBytesTransferred,
               LPOVERLAPPED lpOverlapped);
```

dwError will either be 0 to indicate successful completion of the operation, or ERROR_HANDLE_EOF if ReadFileEx() tried to read past the end of the file. All other error conditions cause ReadFileEx() to fail when you call it—but so can ERROR_HANDLE_EOF. Be prepared for both conditions, because if ReadFileEx() returns FALSE, the I/O completion routine won't be called.

dwBytesTransferred reports the number of bytes read or written. *lpOverlapped* points to the OVERLAPPED structure that was originally passed to ReadFileEx() or WriteFileEx(). The event handle, reported in the *hEvent* field of *lpOverlapped*, is not used, so you can pass other information to the completion routine using this field if you need to.

The completion routine is executed when the thread that called ReadFileEx() or WriteFileEx() enters what is known as an alertable wait state. It does this by calling extended versions of Sleep(), WaitForSingleObject(), or WaitForMultipleObjects()—SleepEx(), WaitForSingleObjectEx(), and WaitForMultipleObjectsEx(). They have the same syntax as the non-extended versions, but add one argument that specifies whether you want to enter an alertable wait state or not. Here is the prototype for WaitForSingleObjectEx():

```
DWORD WaitForSingleObjectEx(
        HANDLE hObject,
        DWORD  dwTimeout,
        BOOL   bAlertable);
```

If *bAlertable* is passed as TRUE, the thread calling WaitForSingleObjectEx() enters an alertable wait state, in which the I/O completion routine can be called. The I/O routine runs in the context of the thread that calls WaitForSingleObjectEx(), which must be the same thread that calls ReadFileEx() or WriteFileEx(). If, on the other hand, you pass *bAlertable* as FALSE, WaitForSingleObjectEx() becomes exactly equivalent to WaitForSingleObject().

Because the event handle is not used to signal the completion of the operation, it is often sufficient to call SleepEx(). If you pass the timeout value as INFINITE, SleepEx() wakes up only when all I/O completion events have been delivered to the completion routine. If the callback function is invoked in response to WaitForSingleObjectEx() or WaitForMultipleObjectsEx(), the function returns the value WAIT_IO_COMPLETION. It can also return the standard values for the other wait functions that I discussed in Chapter 5.

Because the callback function cannot be called until you enter an alertable wait state, using callbacks does not relieve you of having to block at some point.

I/O completion routines are usually the easiest way to code overlapped I/O. For one thing, the return codes from ReadFileEx() and WriteFileEx() are less ambiguous. A TRUE return value *always* means that the operation was spun off successfully; FALSE means the operation failed. The failure may be a benign condition like end-of-file; but if either function returns FALSE, the operation is not pending—it's done, plain and simple. Second, there is no way for Windows to report the status of the operation except by calling the completion routine. You can see that ReadFileEx() and WriteFileEx() don't even provide an argument that reports the number of bytes transferred, as do ReadFile()

and WriteFile(). Finally, it appears that Windows does more bookkeeping for you with I/O completion routines. You'll see in the code listings that you don't have to keep track of as much information as with the other two methods.

Extending the OVERLAPPED Structure

With standard overlapped techniques, you know which operation completes from the return value of WaitForMultipleObjects()—it returns the index into the array of event handles. Typically, you will have parallel arrays of the OVERLAPPED structures you are using, and of the buffers where your data is located.

With I/O completion ports and completion routines, Windows tells you which operation completes by passing back the OVERLAPPED structure that you originally turned over to it. GetQueuedCompletionStatus() sets an output pointer variable; the completion routine receives the OVERLAPPED structure as one of its arguments. However, the OVERLAPPED structure by itself usually does not include enough information for you to know what to do next. When you're working with a disk file, only the offset fields tell you anything. With pipes and sockets, none of the fields are significant. With an asynchronous read operation, you probably need to be able to find the buffer that you read the data into. Often, too, you want to reissue the original call. For this, you need to know what that call was, and what file handle you're issuing it against.

Because of this, you usually need to extend the basic OVERLAPPED structure so that you can easily retrieve this information in an I/O completion routine, or following a call to GetQueuedCompletionStatus(). One way to do this is to simply build a longer C structure whose first element is an OVERLAPPED structure. Here's an XOVERLAPPED structure that also remembers the file handle and buffer:

```
typedef struct tagXOVERLAPPED
{
   OVERLAPPED ov;
   HANDLE     hFile;
   LPVOID     lpBuffer;
} XOVERLAPPED;
```

This structure does the job, but there are some problems with it. For one thing, it makes your syntax a bit more complicated. Now you have to access the elements of the OVERLAPPED structure through the XOVERLAPPED structure in which they reside. Plus, you'll usually be working with an array of them, since you'll be spinning off multiple overlapped operations. For example:

```
XOVERLAPPED xov[2];

::ZeroMemory(xov, sizeof (xov));
xov[0].ov.Offset = 0;
xov[1].ov.Offset = 4096;
xov[0].ov.hEvent = CreateEvent(NULL, TRUE, FALSE, NULL);
xov[1].ov.hEvent = CreateEvent(NULL, TRUE, FALSE, NULL);
```

Whenever you pass a pointer to an XOVERLAPPED to a function, you'll either have to type-cast it, or point to the OVERLAPPED member of the structure. The compiler won't recognize that XOVERLAPPED is in any way related to the OVERLAPPED structure that it wants. You have to placate it as follows:

```
ReadFile(..., (LPOVERLAPPED) &xov[0]);
```

or:

```
ReadFile(..., &xov[0].ov);
```

Perhaps a more fundamental problem is that a C structure can only carry data around—it possesses no built-in intelligence, no knowledge of what to do with the data.

For this reason, I use a C++ class that I call COverlapped to extend the OVERLAPPED structure. I mentioned this class earlier in this chapter; the actual implementation deviates a little from what I showed there.

C++ allows you to refer to the base structure elements directly, and so simplifies the syntax. Most important, I can set up my COverlapped objects so they know how to recycle themselves. I do this by including a member variable, *m_PreviousOperation*, that remembers the operation with which I associated the COverlapped object. I then implement a Recycle() method that reissues the original function call:

```
BOOL  Recycle(DWORD dwBytesToTransfer,
              LPDWORD lpdwBytesTransferred,
              LPOVERLAPPED_COMPLETION_ROUTINE lpCompletion = NULL);

enum Operation {Invalid = -1,
                ConnectNamedPipe = 0,
                ReadFile = 1,
                WriteFile = 2,
                ReadFileEx = 3,
                WriteFileEx = 4};
```

```
BOOL COverlapped::Recycle(DWORD dwBytesToTransfer,
                    LPDWORD lpdwBytesTransferred,
                    LPOVERLAPPED_COMPLETION_ROUTINE lpCompletion)
{
   BOOL bRetcode;

   switch (m_PreviousOperation)
      {
      case ConnectNamedPipe:
         bRetcode = ::ConnectNamedPipe(m_hFile, this);
         break;
      case ReadFile:
         bRetcode = ::ReadFile(m_hFile, m_lpBuffer, dwBytesToTransfer,
                           lpdwBytesTransferred, this);
         break;
      case WriteFile:
         bRetcode = ::WriteFile(m_hFile, m_lpBuffer, dwBytesToTransfer,
                           lpdwBytesTransferred, this);
         break;
      case ReadFileEx:
         bRetcode = ::ReadFileEx(m_hFile, m_lpBuffer, dwBytesToTransfer,
                           this, lpCompletion);
         break;
      case WriteFileEx:
         bRetcode = ::WriteFileEx(m_hFile, m_lpBuffer, dwBytesToTransfer,
                           this, lpCompletion);
         break;
      default:
         bRetcode = FALSE;
         break;
      }
   return bRetcode;
}
```

The other member variables are *m_hFile*, the file handle, and *m_lpBuffer*, the buffer. I also provide a GetResult() method that wraps a call to GetOverlappedResult(). As is often the case with C++, it simplifes the syntax; a blocking call to GetResult() requires only one argument, while GetOverlappedResult() wants four. It needs the file handle, which I've remembered in *m_hFile*. It needs a pointer to the OVERLAPPED structure, which in this case is just the C++ *this* pointer. It needs a pointer to a DWORD where it will report the number of bytes transferred—the only required argument to GetResult(). Finally, it needs a flag that tells it whether to block or not; GetResult() provides a default argument of TRUE.

```
BOOL GetResult(LPDWORD lpdwBytes, BOOL bBlock = TRUE);

BOOL COverlapped::GetResult(LPDWORD lpdwBytes, BOOL bBlock)
{
   return ::GetOverlappedResult(m_hFile, this, lpdwBytes, bBlock);
}
```

I've also provided a constructor that expects one nondefault argument, a boolean flag that tells it whether to create an event or not. Using this constructor, the variable declaration is sufficient to set up an OVERLAPPED structure to use with any of the three techniques.

```
COverlapped ovWithEvent(TRUE), ovWithoutEvent(FALSE);
```

Here's the header file from my MFC extension DLL that declares the COverlapped class, \WIN32NET\CODE\WIN32OBJ\OVERLAP.H on the disk:

```
/********
*
* OVERLAP.H
*
* Copyright (c) 1995-1996 Ralph P. Davis
*
* All Rights Reserved
*
*****/

#ifndef _OVERLAP_INCLUDED
#define _OVERLAP_INCLUDED

extern CWinApp *g_pMyApp;

class AFX_EXT_CLASS COverlapped : public OVERLAPPED
{
public:
    enum Operation {Invalid = -1,
                    ConnectNamedPipe = 0,
                    ReadFile = 1,
                    WriteFile = 2,
                    ReadFileEx = 3,
                    WriteFileEx = 4,
                    TransactNamedPipe = 5
                   };
```

```
protected:
    HANDLE m_hFile;
    LPVOID m_lpBuffer;
    Operation m_PreviousOperation;  // For recycling
public:
    COverlapped(BOOL bCreateEvent,
                HANDLE hNewFile = INVALID_HANDLE_VALUE,
                LPVOID lpNewBuffer = NULL);
    COverlapped(HANDLE hNewEvent = NULL,
                HANDLE hNewFile = INVALID_HANDLE_VALUE,
                LPVOID lpNewBuffer = NULL);
    COverlapped(LPOVERLAPPED lpOverlapped,
                HANDLE hFile = INVALID_HANDLE_VALUE,
                LPVOID lpBuffer = NULL);
    COverlapped(COverlapped& Overlapped);

    BOOL   GetResult(LPDWORD lpdwBytes, BOOL bBlock = TRUE);
    BOOL   Recycle(DWORD dwBytesToTransfer,
                   LPDWORD lpdwBytesTransferred,
                   LPOVERLAPPED_COMPLETION_ROUTINE lpCompletion = NULL);

    // Get/set methods
    VOID      SetFile(HANDLE hFile);
    LPVOID    GetBuffer(void);
    VOID      SetBuffer(LPVOID lpBuffer);
    Operation GetPreviousOperation(void);
    VOID      SetPreviousOperation(Operation op);
    HANDLE    GetEventHandle(void);
    VOID      SetEventHandle(HANDLE hEvent);
    DWORD     GetOffset(void);
    VOID      SetOffset(DWORD dwOffset);
    DWORD&    FileOffset(void);   // Allows direct += assignment
    DWORD&    FileOffsetHigh(void);
};

#endif
```

The implementation file, \WIN32NET\CODE\WIN32OBJ\OVERLAP.CPP, follows:

```
/********
*
* OVERLAP.CPP
*
* Copyright (c) 1995-1996 Ralph P. Davis
*
* All Rights Reserved
*
*****/
```

```
/*===== Includes =====*/

#include "stdafx.h"
#include "overlap.h"

COverlapped::COverlapped(BOOL bCreateEvent,
                         HANDLE hNewFile,
                         LPVOID lpNewBuffer)
{
   if (AfxGetApp() == NULL)
      {
      g_pMyApp = new CWinApp;
      }
   Internal     = 0;
   InternalHigh = 0;
   Offset       = 0;
   OffsetHigh   = 0;

   if (bCreateEvent)
      {
      hEvent    = ::CreateEvent(NULL, TRUE, FALSE, NULL);

      if (hEvent == NULL)
         {
         AfxThrowResourceException();
         }
      }
   else
      hEvent    = NULL;
   m_hFile      = hNewFile;
   m_lpBuffer   = lpNewBuffer;
}

COverlapped::COverlapped(HANDLE hNewEvent,
                         HANDLE hNewFile,
                         LPVOID lpNewBuffer)
{
   if (AfxGetApp() == NULL)
      {
      g_pMyApp = new CWinApp;
      }
   Internal     = 0;
   InternalHigh = 0;
   Offset       = 0;
   OffsetHigh   = 0;
   hEvent       = hNewEvent;
   m_hFile      = hNewFile;
   m_lpBuffer   = lpNewBuffer;
}
```

```
COverlapped::COverlapped(COverlapped& Overlapped)
{
   if (AfxGetApp() == NULL)
      {
      g_pMyApp = new CWinApp;
      }
   Internal     = Overlapped.Internal;
   InternalHigh = Overlapped.InternalHigh;
   Offset       = Overlapped.Offset;
   OffsetHigh   = Overlapped.OffsetHigh;
   hEvent       = Overlapped.hEvent;
   m_hFile      = Overlapped.m_hFile;
   m_lpBuffer   = Overlapped.m_lpBuffer;
}

COverlapped::COverlapped(LPOVERLAPPED lpOverlapped,
                         HANDLE hFile, LPVOID lpBuffer)
{
   if (AfxGetApp() == NULL)
      {
      g_pMyApp = new CWinApp;
      }
   Internal     = lpOverlapped->Internal;
   InternalHigh = lpOverlapped->InternalHigh;
   Offset       = lpOverlapped->Offset;
   OffsetHigh   = lpOverlapped->OffsetHigh;
   hEvent       = lpOverlapped->hEvent;
   m_hFile      = hFile;
   m_lpBuffer   = lpBuffer;
}

BOOL COverlapped::GetResult(LPDWORD lpdwBytes, BOOL bBlock)
{
   return ::GetOverlappedResult(m_hFile, this, lpdwBytes, bBlock);
}

BOOL COverlapped::Recycle(DWORD dwBytesToTransfer,
                          LPDWORD lpdwBytesTransferred,
                          LPOVERLAPPED_COMPLETION_ROUTINE lpCompletion)
{
   BOOL bRetcode;

   switch (m_PreviousOperation)
      {
      case ConnectNamedPipe:
         bRetcode = ::ConnectNamedPipe(m_hFile, this);
         break;
```

```
      case ReadFile:
         bRetcode = ::ReadFile(m_hFile, m_lpBuffer, dwBytesToTransfer,
                              lpdwBytesTransferred, this);
         break;
      case WriteFile:
         bRetcode = ::WriteFile(m_hFile, m_lpBuffer, dwBytesToTransfer,
                              lpdwBytesTransferred, this);
         break;
      case ReadFileEx:
         bRetcode = ::ReadFileEx(m_hFile, m_lpBuffer, dwBytesToTransfer,
                              this, lpCompletion);
         break;
      case WriteFileEx:
         bRetcode = ::WriteFileEx(m_hFile, m_lpBuffer, dwBytesToTransfer,
                              this, lpCompletion);
         break;
      default:
         bRetcode = FALSE;
         break;
      }
   return bRetcode;
}

//********* GET/SET METHODS **********

VOID COverlapped::SetFile(HANDLE hFile)
{
   m_hFile = hFile;
}

LPVOID COverlapped::GetBuffer()
{
   return m_lpBuffer;
}

VOID COverlapped::SetBuffer(LPVOID lpBuffer)
{
   m_lpBuffer = lpBuffer;
}

COverlapped::Operation COverlapped::GetPreviousOperation(void)
{
   return m_PreviousOperation;
}

VOID COverlapped::SetPreviousOperation(Operation op)
```

```
{
   m_PreviousOperation = op;
}

HANDLE COverlapped::GetEventHandle(void)
{
   return hEvent;
}

VOID COverlapped::SetEventHandle(HANDLE hEvent)
{
   this->hEvent = hEvent;
}

DWORD COverlapped::GetOffset(void)
{
   return Offset;
}

VOID COverlapped::SetOffset(DWORD dwOffset)
{
   Offset = dwOffset;
}

DWORD& COverlapped::FileOffset(void)
{
   return (DWORD&) Offset;
}

DWORD& COverlapped::FileOffsetHigh(void)
{
   return (DWORD&) OffsetHigh;
}
```

Using Overlapped I/O—The *cat* Utility

To demonstrate the use of overlapped I/O, I provide three implementations of the UNIX *cat* utility. Its role is very simple: it copies its standard input to its standard output. You can also enter file specifications on the command line to write disk files.

This program admits of a very brief implementation. Assuming that *hStdInput* represents the file you are reading from—standard input or a named disk file—the core of the program can be just this modest loop:

```
while (ReadFile(hStdInput, ...))
   WriteFile(GetStdHandle(STD_OUTPUT_HANDLE), ...);
```

In my implementations, if the user enters files on the command line, I read them using overlapped I/O, then write them out using a synchronous WriteFile() call. There is no good reason for using overlapped I/O here, beyond my specifically pedagogical mission. As often happens in code for a book like this, I have done things in a way that demonstrates as many techniques as possible. If I were doing a real-life version of *cat*, I'd probably do this:

```
while (ReadFile(hStdInput, ...))
   WriteFile(GetStdHandle(STD_OUTPUT_HANDLE), ...);
```

Considerations Common to All Implementations

All of these implementations do several things in the same way. They all issue two simultaneous reads of 4096 bytes. The number of reads and the buffer size are represented by the C++ manifest constants *nNumReads* and *nBufferSize*. I declare them as follows in the file \WIN32NET\CODE\FILEUTIL\CATHLPR.H:

```
const int nBufferSize = 4096;
const int nNumReads   = 2;
```

My first read is at offset zero, and my second at offset 4096. When a read completes, and there is data remaining to be read from the file, I reissue the original read after setting the file offset (the *Offset* field of the OVERLAPPED structure) to the next unread location in the file. To accommodate 64-bit file sizes, I compare the new offset to its old value. If the new one is less than the old one, I know that a 64-bit wraparound has occurred, and I bump the *OffsetHigh* field of the OVERLAPPED structure.

There are a few considerations that apply to all my implementations of *cat.* One of the most important is making sure the program's output is properly sequenced. Although I have observed my read requests to complete in the order in which I submit them, I cannot assume that this will occur. Therefore, I collect the output for each file in a buffer that I VirtualAlloc() according to the file size reported by GetFileSize(). (Ironically, even though my arithmetic can handle 64-bit file sizes, my memory allocation cannot.)

I have also observed that you have to write to standard output in relatively small chunks. You can't buffer a large file, then write it out in a single WriteFile(). WriteFile() returns FALSE, and GetLastError() tells you ERROR_NOT_ENOUGH_MEMORY. The largest size I've ever succeeded in writing is 65,536 bytes, but this is not consistent. Therefore, I limit writes to 16,384 bytes, and handle them in the helper function WriteStdOutputBuffer(), here excerpted from \WIN32NET\CODE\FILEUTIL\CATHLPR.CPP:

```
BOOL WriteStdOutputBuffer(LPBYTE lpBuffer, DWORD dwFileSize)
{
   DWORD dwBytesToWrite;
   DWORD dwBytesWritten;
   BOOL  bRetcode = TRUE;

   for (DWORD j = 0; j < dwFileSize;
        j += (4 * nBufferSize))
      {
      dwBytesToWrite = min(dwFileSize - j,
                           (4 * nBufferSize));

      if (!::WriteFile(
               ::GetStdHandle(STD_OUTPUT_HANDLE),
               &lpBuffer[j],
               dwBytesToWrite,
               &dwBytesWritten,
               NULL))
         {
         bRetcode = FALSE;
         break;
         }
      }
   return bRetcode;
}
```

Standard Overlapped I/O and I/O Completion Ports

I group these implementations together because they are very similar. Indeed, they both use the same helper functions—SpinOffRead(), which issues a ReadFile(), and IsReadComplete(), which buffers the data for later dumping to standard output, then calls SpinOffRead() to read the next buffer. (We'll look at these functions shortly.)

Setup Sequence. The setup sequence for both methods is also pretty much the same. In one case, I create events for each read I spin off. In the other, I call CreateIoCompletionPort() to tie the file I'm reading to a completion port.

Here's the setup for the standard overlapped implementation, excerpted from \WIN32NET\CODE\FILEUTIL\TWOREADS\CAT.CPP:

```
HANDLE     hStdInput, hStdOutput;
TCHAR      szBuffer[nNumReads][nBufferSize];
OVERLAPPED ov[nNumReads];
HANDLE     hEvents[nNumReads];
DWORD      dwBytesRead, dwBytesWritten;
```

```
int         i, j;
int         nOVIndex;
BOOL        bIOComplete = FALSE;
DWORD       dwFileSize;
LPBYTE      lpBuffer;
DWORD       dwOutstandingReads = 0;
DWORD       dwReadOffset = 0;

// [...]

dwFileSize = ::GetFileSize(hStdInput, NULL);
lpBuffer = (LPBYTE) ::VirtualAlloc(NULL,
   dwFileSize, MEM_COMMIT, PAGE_READWRITE);
::ZeroMemory(ov, sizeof (ov));

bIOComplete = FALSE;
for (j = 0; j < nNumReads; ++j)
   {
   hEvents[j] = ov[j].hEvent =
      ::CreateEvent(NULL, TRUE, FALSE, NULL);
   bIOComplete |=
      SpinOffRead(hStdInput,
                  &ov[j],
                  szBuffer[j],
                  &dwOutstandingReads,
                  &dwReadOffset,
                  NULL);
   }
```

Here's the same sequence for I/O completion ports, taken from WIN32NET\CODE\FILEUTIL\IOPORTS\CAT.CPP:

```
HANDLE hStdInput, hStdOutput;
int    i, j;
TCHAR  szBuffer[nNumReads][nBufferSize];
DWORD  dwBytesRead, dwBytesWritten;
HANDLE hPort;
DWORD  dwKey = 1;
BOOL   bIOComplete = FALSE;
DWORD  dwFileSize;
DWORD  dwOutstandingReads = 0;
DWORD  dwReadOffset = 0;
LPBYTE lpBuffer;

// [...]
```

```
hPort = ::CreateIoCompletionPort(hStdInput,
             NULL,
             1,
             0);
if (hPort != NULL)
   {
   COverlapped  ov[nNumReads];
   LPOVERLAPPED lpOverlapped;

   dwFileSize = GetFileSize(hStdInput, NULL);
   lpBuffer = (LPBYTE) VirtualAlloc(NULL,
      dwFileSize, MEM_COMMIT, PAGE_READWRITE);

   bIOComplete = FALSE;
   for (j = 0; j < nNumReads; ++j)
      {
      ov[j].SetFile(hStdInput);
      ov[j].SetBuffer(szBuffer[j]);

      bIOComplete |=
         SpinOffRead(
            hStdInput,
            &ov[j],
            szBuffer[j],
            &dwOutstandingReads,
            &dwReadOffset,
            NULL);
      }
```

There are only two real differences between these setup sequences:

- With standard overlapped I/O, I create events; with I/O completion ports, I create a single port that reports all the I/O against *hStdInput*.
- With I/O completion ports, I use my extension of the OVERLAPPED structure, the COverlapped class. This class remembers the file handle and the buffer used with each of my read operations. With standard overlapped I/O, I can just use the OVERLAPPED structure; the return value from WaitForMultipleObjects() tells me everything I need to know.

Action Loops. The action loops do not differ much, either. With standard overlapped I/O, I call WaitForMultipleObjects() in an infinite loop. When it completes, I use its return value to find the OVERLAPPED structure I need to pass to GetOverlappedResult(). With I/O completion ports, GetQueued-CompletionStatus() combines the action of WaitForMultipleObjects() and

GetOverlappedResult(); I stay in my loop as long as it returns TRUE (and I have more data to read). In both cases, if I have a successful operation, I call my helper function IsReadComplete() to write the data to standard output and issue another read.

Here's the implementation using WaitForMultipleObjects() and GetOverlappedResult():

```
while (!bIOComplete)
   {
   nOVIndex =
      ::WaitForMultipleObjects(nNumReads, hEvents,
         FALSE, INFINITE);

   if (nOVIndex < nNumReads)
      {
      if (::GetOverlappedResult(hStdInput,
            &ov[nOVIndex],
            &dwBytesRead,
            TRUE))
         bIOComplete = IsReadComplete(
            hStdInput,
            &ov[nOVIndex],
            szBuffer[nOVIndex],
            dwBytesRead,
            &dwOutstandingReads,
            &dwReadOffset,
            NULL,
            lpBuffer);
      }
   }
```

Using GetQueuedCompletionStatus(), it reads like this:

```
while (!bIOComplete &&
         ::GetQueuedCompletionStatus(hPort,
            &dwBytesRead,
            &dwKey,
            &lpOverlapped,
            INFINITE))
   {
   if (lpOverlapped != NULL)
      {
      bIOComplete =
         IsReadComplete(hStdInput,
            lpOverlapped,
            ((COverlapped *)
               lpOverlapped)->GetBuffer(),
```

```
                dwBytesRead,
                &dwOutstandingReads,
                &dwReadOffset,
                NULL,
                lpBuffer);
        }
    }
```

The main difference here, besides the function calls, is that I can find the buffer directly using the index returned by WaitForMultipleObjects(). GetQueuedCompletionStatus(), on the other hand, does not provide enough information, so I retrieve the buffer pointer from the COverlapped object I used to extend the OVERLAPPED structure.

The Helper Functions. Both implementations use the helper functions SpinOffRead() and IsReadComplete(). SpinOffRead() is the workhorse; it is responsible for issuing a ReadFile(), then determining whether we've finished reading the file. There are two conditions that indicate that we're finished:

- ReadFile() returns TRUE, and the number of bytes read is zero.
- ReadFile() returns FALSE, and GetLastError() returns anything other than ERROR_IO_PENDING. Strictly speaking, the error code for end-of-file is ERROR_HANDLE_EOF, but I interpret all errors as terminating the read operation.

In addition to this, I have to keep track of the number of reads I have issued. I don't want to terminate the action loop until all my outstanding reads are complete. So the condition for ending the read of one file, and moving on to the next one, is that either of the conditions just mentioned occurs, and all my reads have completed.

In the case of standard overlapped I/O—where the *hEvent* field of the OVERLAPPED structure is not NULL—to remove an OVERLAPPED structure from circulation, I call ResetEvent() to force the event into the non-signalled state. This makes sure this operation will never cause WaitForMultipleObjects() to wake up.

The return value from SpinOffRead() is used as my loop control variable, *bIOComplete*, in the cat() function.

Here's the function listing, from the file \WIN32NET\CODE\FILEUTIL\CATHLPR.CPP:

```
#include <windows.h>
#include "cathlpr.h"

BOOL SpinOffRead(HANDLE        hFile,
```

```
                LPOVERLAPPED lpOverlapped,
                LPVOID       lpBuffer,
                LPDWORD      lpdwOutstandingReads,
                LPDWORD      lpdwReadOffset,
                LPDWORD      lpdwReadOffsetHigh)
{
   DWORD dwBytesRead = 0;
   DWORD dwOldReadOffset = *lpdwReadOffset;

   dwBytesRead = 0;

   // For each read we spin off, bump the count of
   // outstanding operations
   ++(*lpdwOutstandingReads);

   lpOverlapped->Offset     = *lpdwReadOffset;

   if (lpdwReadOffsetHigh != NULL)
      lpOverlapped->OffsetHigh = *lpdwReadOffsetHigh;
   else
      lpOverlapped->OffsetHigh = 0;


   BOOL bStatus = ::ReadFile (
      hFile,
      lpBuffer,
      nBufferSize,
      &dwBytesRead,
      lpOverlapped);

   BOOL bTerminateRead;
   BOOL bIOPending;

   // Termination condition is:
   //    ReadFile() returns TRUE and bytes read is 0
   //    ReadFile() returns FALSE and GetLastError() is
   //    not ERROR_IO_PENDING
   if (bStatus)
      {
      bTerminateRead = (dwBytesRead == 0);
      }
   else
      {
      bTerminateRead = (::GetLastError() != ERROR_IO_PENDING);
      }

   if (bTerminateRead)
```

```
        {
        if (lpOverlapped->hEvent != NULL)
            {
            // Reset event if using events with standard overlapped I/O
            // This makes sure this operation will never cause
            // WaitForMultipleObjects() to wake up
            ::ResetEvent(lpOverlapped->hEvent);
            }

        // Decrement count of outstanding reads
        --(*lpdwOutstandingReads);
        return ((*lpdwOutstandingReads) == 0);
        }

    bIOPending = !bStatus;  // False return from ReadFile()
                            // means I/O is pending if we've
                            // gotten this far
    if (bIOPending)
        {
        (*lpdwReadOffset) += nBufferSize;

        if (lpdwReadOffsetHigh != NULL)
            {
            // Check for 64-bit wraparound

            if ((*lpdwReadOffset) < dwOldReadOffset)
                {
                ++(*lpdwReadOffsetHigh);
                }
            }
        return FALSE;
        }

    // Synchronous operation completed successfully
    (*lpdwReadOffset) += dwBytesRead;

    if (lpdwReadOffsetHigh != NULL)
        {
        if ((*lpdwReadOffset) < dwOldReadOffset)
            {
            ++(*lpdwReadOffsetHigh);
            }
        }
    return FALSE;
}
```

The other helper function, IsReadComplete(), buffers the data read for eventual writing to standard output, then calls SpinOffRead().

```
BOOL IsReadComplete(HANDLE       hFile,
                    LPOVERLAPPED lpOverlapped,
                    LPVOID       lpBuffer,
                    DWORD        dwBytesRead,
                    LPDWORD      lpdwOutstandingReads,
                    LPDWORD      lpdwReadOffset,
                    LPDWORD      lpdwReadOffsetHigh,
                    LPBYTE       lpWriteBuffer)
{
   --(*lpdwOutstandingReads);
   ::CopyMemory(&lpWriteBuffer[lpOverlapped->Offset],
                lpBuffer,
                dwBytesRead);
   return SpinOffRead(
             hFile, lpOverlapped, lpBuffer,
             lpdwOutstandingReads, lpdwReadOffset,
             lpdwReadOffsetHigh);
}
```

I/O Completion Routines

It takes much less code to implement *cat* using I/O completion routines. I mentioned some of the reasons for this earlier:

- NT does more of the bookkeeping for you.
- There is no ambiguity in the return value from ReadFileEx() or WriteFileEx().

Setup Sequence. The setup sequence is quite simple. It only needs to remember the file handle and the buffer pointer in the COverlapped object, and set the *Offset* field. I also use a single manual-reset event as a loop-control object. This will tell me that I am done reading a file. Here is the code, from \WIN32NET\CODE\FILEUTIL\IOCOMP\CAT.CPP:

```
HANDLE hStdInput, hStdOutput;
int    i, j;
TCHAR  szBuffer[nNumReads][nBufferSize];
DWORD  dwBytesRead, dwBytesWritten;
DWORD  dwFileSize;
BOOL   bSuccess;
HANDLE hMyEvent;
```

```
// [...]

COverlapped ov[nNumReads];

dwFileSize = GetFileSize(hStdInput, NULL);
g_lpBuffer = (LPBYTE) VirtualAlloc(NULL,
   dwFileSize, MEM_COMMIT, PAGE_READWRITE);

hMyEvent = ::CreateEvent(NULL, TRUE, FALSE, NULL);
bSuccess = FALSE;
for (j = 0; j < nNumReads; ++j)
   {
   ov[j].SetEventHandle(hMyEvent);
   ov[j].SetBuffer(szBuffer[j]);
   ov[j].SetFile(hStdInput);
   ov[j].FileOffset() = (j * nBufferSize);

   bSuccess |=
      ::ReadFileEx(hStdInput, szBuffer[j], nBufferSize,
         &ov[j], FileIOCompletionRoutine);
   }
```

Action Loop. The action loop is very simple. It blocks on a call to WaitForSingleObjectEx(). I use this function, rather than SleepEx(), because I am using an event handle *(hMyEvent)* to tell me that I'm done reading a particular file. While the I/O is still in progress, WaitForSingleObjectEx() returns WAIT_IO_COMPLETION. When the event is signalled (in the I/O completion routine), WaitForSingleObjectEx() returns WAIT_OBJECT_0 (defined as zero). In actuality, because the I/O completion routine recycles the read request, WaitForSingleObjectEx() stays asleep until the whole file is read:

```
while (::WaitForSingleObjectEx(
          hMyEvent, INFINITE, TRUE)
            != WAIT_OBJECT_0)
   ;
```

The I/O Completion Routine. All the real work is done in the I/O completion routine. Its job is to buffer the data for eventual output, recycle the request, and set the event handle when the I/O is complete. Remember that the I/O completion routine is passed three arguments:

- A DWORD representing the status of the operation, which will either be NO_ERROR (zero) or ERROR_HANDLE_EOF

- A DWORD reporting the number of bytes read in the operation being reported
- A pointer to the original OVERLAPPED structure

The read operation is complete when the status argument comes in as ERROR_HANDLE_EOF, or when the recycled ReadFileEx() returns FALSE. At this point, the I/O completion routine calls SetEvent(). There is no need to keep track of outstanding reads. Because of the way I/O completion routines work, the action loop will not wake up from WaitForSingleObjectEx() until *all* the outstanding reads have been posted to the completion routine.

Here's the code listing:

```
VOID WINAPI FileIOCompletionRoutine(
   DWORD        dwError,
   DWORD        dwBytesTransferred,
   LPOVERLAPPED lpOverlapped)
{
   COverlapped  *lpCOverlapped = (COverlapped *) lpOverlapped;

   if (dwError != NO_ERROR)
      ::SetEvent(lpCOverlapped->GetEventHandle());
   else
      {
      ::CopyMemory(&g_lpBuffer[lpCOverlapped->GetOffset()],
         lpCOverlapped->GetBuffer(),
         dwBytesTransferred);
      // Reissue ReadFileEx()
      lpCOverlapped->FileOffset() += (nNumReads * nBufferSize);

      lpCOverlapped->SetPreviousOperation(COverlapped::ReadFileEx);
      if (!(lpCOverlapped->Recycle(nBufferSize, NULL,
            FileIOCompletionRoutine)))
         ::SetEvent(lpCOverlapped->GetEventHandle());
      }
}
```

Note that recycling the request in the I/O completion routine does not cause it to be entered recursively. The completion routine cannot be called again until it returns. When the recycle request completes, it is placed at the end of the queue for delivery to the completion routine.

Additional Win32 File I/O Functions

Win32 provides a full set of functions for all the standard file I/O operations. Like CreateFile(), they support remote file operations using UNC filenames or redirected drives. Much of this API set is based on the OS/2 file I/O services. Some of the most useful functions are shown in Table 6-1.

Table 6-1. Additional Win32 File I/O Functions

Function	Action Performed
CopyFile	Copies one file to another
CreateDirectory	Makes a new directory
DeleteFile	Erases a file
FindFirstFile	Enumerates files and directories
FindNextFile	Continues file enumeration
FindClose	Closes file enumeration
FlushFileBuffers	Forces writing of dirty buffers to disk
GetCurrentDirectory	Returns the current working directory
GetDiskFreeSpace	Gets statistics on disk usage
GetDriveType	Characterizes a drive as removable, fixed, network, CD-ROM, or RAM
GetFileAttributes	Retrieves a file's attributes
GetFileSize	Gets file size with full support for 64-bit file sizes
GetFullPathName	Returns the full path specification for a file
GetVolumeInformation	Reports file-system information for a given drive
LockFile	Locks a byte range in a file for exclusive access
LockFileEx	Locks a byte range in a file; permits shared or exclusive access
MoveFile	Moves or renames a file
MoveFileEx	Moves or renames a file; supports inter-volume moves
RemoveDirectory	Deletes a directory
SearchPath	Searches a set of directories for a given file
SetCurrentDirectory	Changes the current working directory
SetEndOfFile	Sets the size of a file
SetFileAttributes	Changes a file's attributes
SetFilePointer	Moves the file pointer
SetFileTime	Touches a file
UnlockFile	Unlocks a byte range locked by LockFile()
UnlockFileEx	Unlocks a byte range locked by LockFileEx()

C++ and MFC Considerations

The Microsoft Foundation Classes offer file I/O services through the CFile class. The methods of this class wrap the Win32 file I/O functions. However, they provide lowest-common-denominator (that is, Windows 95) functionality—specifically, they do not support overlapped I/O. But the class is worth studying, because it makes no sense to build a class that does support overlapped I/O on any other foundation.

The MFC CFile Class

Table 6-2 lists the CFile methods and the Win32 functions that they use. I built the table by examining the CFile source file, FILECORE.CPP (in your MFC source directory).

Table 6-2. CFile Methods and Corresponding Win32 Functions

CFile Method	Purpose	Win32 Functions Used
Abort	Closes a file, ignores errors	CloseHandle
Close	Closes a file	CloseHandle
Duplicate	Copies a CFile object with a new file handle	DuplicateHandle
Flush	Forces write of dirty buffers	FlushFileBuffers
GetLength	Gets size of a file	<None—calls other CFile methods>
GetPosition	Returns current file position	SetFilePointer
LockRange	Locks byte range in a file	LockFile
Open	Creates or opens a file	CreateFile
Read	Reads data from a file	ReadFile
Remove	Deletes a file	DeleteFile
Rename	Moves or renames a file	MoveFile
Seek	Moves to a specific file offset	SetFilePointer
SetLength	Sets size of a file	SetEndOfFile
UnlockRange	Unlocks byte range in a file	UnlockFile
Write	Writes data to a file	WriteFile

The only methods we need to override to support overlapped I/O are Open(), Read(), and Write().

Extending CFile to Support Overlapped I/O: COverlappedFile

Before we take a close look at how this class is implemented, and why I implemented it the way I did, let's look at the class declaration on the disk in \WIN32NET\CODE\WIN32OBJ\OVFILE.H.

```
/********
*
* OVFILE.H
*
* Copyright (c) 1995-1996 Ralph P. Davis
*
* All Rights Reserved
*
********/

#ifndef _OVFILE_INCLUDED
#define _OVFILE_INCLUDED

class CFile;
class COverlapped;
class CIoPort;

typedef BOOL (CALLBACK *RECEIVECALLBACK)(LPBYTE lpData, DWORD dwData,
                                         HANDLE hConnection);

extern CWinApp *g_pMyApp;

class AFX_EXT_CLASS COverlappedFile : public CFile
{
   DECLARE_DYNAMIC(COverlappedFile)

protected:
   CIoPort *m_lpIoPort;  // If we tie the file to an I/O completion port
   RECEIVECALLBACK m_lpReceiveCallback;

public:
   COverlappedFile();
   COverlappedFile(HANDLE hFile);
   COverlappedFile(LPCTSTR lpszFileName, BOOL bAlways = FALSE);

   virtual ~COverlappedFile();

   virtual RECEIVECALLBACK GetReceiveCallback(void)
      {
      return m_lpReceiveCallback;
      }
```

```
virtual VOID SetReceiveCallback(RECEIVECALLBACK lpReceiveCallback)
   {
   m_lpReceiveCallback = lpReceiveCallback;
   }

virtual BOOL CallReceiveCallback(LPBYTE lpData,
   DWORD dwDataLength, HANDLE hConnection)
   {
   ASSERT(m_lpReceiveCallback != NULL);
   return m_lpReceiveCallback(lpData, dwDataLength, hConnection);
   }
virtual BOOL Create(
   LPCTSTR lpszFileName,
   BOOL    bAlways = FALSE);

// Default implementation, inherited from MFC
virtual BOOL Open(LPCTSTR        lpszFileName,
                  UINT           nOpenFlags,
                  CFileException *pError = NULL);

virtual BOOL Open(
   LPCTSTR lpszFileName,
   BOOL    bAlways = FALSE);

// Override that knows more about overlapped I/O
virtual BOOL Open(
   LPCTSTR lpszFileName,
   DWORD   dwOperation,
   DWORD   dwAccess = GENERIC_WRITE | GENERIC_READ,
   DWORD   dwShareMode = 0,
   DWORD   dwFlags = FILE_FLAG_OVERLAPPED,
   DWORD   dwAttributes = FILE_ATTRIBUTE_NORMAL,
   BOOL    bInherit = FALSE);

virtual BOOL Read(LPVOID lpBuffer, DWORD dwCount, DWORD *lpBytesRead,
      COverlapped *lpOverlapped);
virtual BOOL Read(LPVOID lpBuffer, DWORD dwCount,
      COverlapped *lpOverlapped,
      LPOVERLAPPED_COMPLETION_ROUTINE lpCompletionRoutine);
virtual BOOL Write(const void *lpBuffer, DWORD dwCount,
   COverlapped *pOverlapped);
virtual BOOL Write(LPVOID lpBuffer, DWORD dwCount,
      COverlapped *lpOverlapped,
      LPOVERLAPPED_COMPLETION_ROUTINE lpCompletionRoutine);

virtual HANDLE GetFileHandle(void)
   {
   return (HANDLE) m_hFile;
   }
```

```
    virtual VOID SetFileHandle(HANDLE hFile)
       {
       m_hFile = (UINT) hFile;
       }
    virtual VOID InvalidateFileHandle(void)
       {
       m_hFile = (UINT) INVALID_HANDLE_VALUE;
       }

    CIoPort *GetIoPort(void);
    VOID    SetIoPort(CIoPort *lpPort);
    BOOL    Post(COverlapped  *lpOverlapped,
                 DWORD         dwBytes);    // For posting to
                                            // an I/O completion port
    BOOL    Post(CIoPort     *lpPort,
                 COverlapped *lpOverlapped,
                 DWORD        dwBytes);
};

#endif
```

The Open() and Create() Methods. I provide three versions of the Open() method. One is the core routine that actually does the CreateFile() call. Although it takes seven arguments, you can see from its prototype that it provides default values for the last five. The defaults open the file for exclusive, read-write, uninherited access. Here is the prototype of this method:

```
virtual BOOL Open(
      LPCTSTR lpszFileName,
      DWORD   dwOperation,
      DWORD   dwAccess = GENERIC_WRITE | GENERIC_READ,
      DWORD   dwShareMode = 0,
      DWORD   dwFlags = FILE_FLAG_OVERLAPPED,
      DWORD   dwAttributes = FILE_ATTRIBUTE_NORMAL,
      BOOL    bInherit = FALSE);
```

As you can see from the implementation, this method thinly wraps CreateFile(). Its arguments are presented to CreateFile() in the format that that function expects. Here is the excerpt from \WIN32NET\CODE\WIN32OBJ\OVFILE.CPP:

```
BOOL COverlappedFile::Open(
      LPCTSTR lpszFileName,
      DWORD dwOperation,
      DWORD dwAccess,
      DWORD dwShareMode,
```

```
        DWORD dwFlags,
        DWORD dwAttributes,
        BOOL  bInherit)
{
    SECURITY_ATTRIBUTES sa;
    LPSECURITY_ATTRIBUTES lpsa = NULL;

    m_hFile = hFileNull;

    if (bInherit)
        {
        sa.nLength = sizeof(sa);
        sa.lpSecurityDescriptor = NULL;
        sa.bInheritHandle = bInherit;
        lpsa = &sa;
        }

    dwFlags |= FILE_FLAG_OVERLAPPED;  // Make sure overlapped I/O is set

    dwFlags |= dwAttributes;  // Two arguments get galomphed together
    HANDLE hFile = ::CreateFile(lpszFileName,
                                dwAccess,
                                dwShareMode,
                                lpsa,
                                dwOperation,
                                dwFlags,
                                NULL);

    SetFileHandle(hFile);  // Remember file handle even if it's bogus
    return (hFile != INVALID_HANDLE_VALUE);
}
```

The other versions of Open() call this one, as does the Create() method. Here are the prototypes for Open() and Create(); the only argument they need, besides the filename, is a flag indicating whether the open or create is unconditional. This determines whether the operation is OPEN_EXISTING or OPEN_ALWAYS, in the case of Open(), or CREATE_NEW instead of CREATE_ALWAYS for Create(). Here, too, the second argument defaults to FALSE (the safe assumption), so that Open() will fail if the file doesn't exist and Create() will fail if it does.

```
virtual BOOL Open(
        LPCTSTR lpszFileName,
        BOOL    bAlways = FALSE);
```

```
virtual BOOL Create(
      LPCTSTR lpszFileName,
      BOOL    bAlways = FALSE);
```

Both implementations delegate to the first version of Open().

```
BOOL COverlappedFile::Open(
      LPCTSTR lpszFileName,
      BOOL    bAlways)
{
   return Open(lpszFileName, bAlways ? OPEN_ALWAYS : OPEN_EXISTING,
               GENERIC_READ | GENERIC_WRITE);
}

BOOL COverlappedFile::Create(
      LPCTSTR lpszFileName,
      BOOL    bAlways)
{
   return Open(lpszFileName, bAlways ? CREATE_ALWAYS : CREATE_NEW,
               GENERIC_READ | GENERIC_WRITE);
}
```

In both cases, I call Open() with three arguments—even though the third one passes the default values—so the compiler can tell which version of Open() I want. Otherwise, I might have an infinite recursion.

The third implementation of Open() is a strict override of CFile::Open(). CFile::Open() hard-codes the flags argument that it passes to CreateFile(), so I have to replace it outright—I cannot inherit any of its functionality. Here is the prototype:

```
virtual BOOL Open(LPCTSTR         lpszFileName,
                  UINT            nOpenFlags,
                  CFileException *pError = NULL);
```

nOpenFlags encodes the operation parameters in an abstract way. Here is how the flags are defined in the CFile class. This excerpt is from the MFC header file AFX.H:

```
enum OpenFlags {
       modeRead =         0x0000,
       modeWrite =        0x0001,
       modeReadWrite =    0x0002,
       shareCompat =      0x0000,
       shareExclusive =   0x0010,
       shareDenyWrite =   0x0020,
       shareDenyRead =    0x0030,
```

```
shareDenyNone =       0x0040,
modeNoInherit =       0x0080,
modeCreate =          0x1000,
modeNoTruncate =      0x2000,
typeText =            0x4000,
typeBinary =     (int)0x8000
};
```

The job of the implementation is to test the flag bits and convert them into the corresponding arguments expected by CreateFile(). My implementation invokes the core version of COverlappedFile::Open() that I presented earlier.

The final task performed by this method is to return error information through the third argument, an optional pointer to a CFileException object. This has two members of interest: *m_lOsError* captures the operating-system specific error, in this case by calling GetLastError(). The other, *m_cause*, describes the error in an abstract way. The CFileException::OsErrorToException() method does this conversion. (Some of the conversions are a little bit forced, by the way—take a look at the the MFC source file FILEX.CPP.) Here is my replacement, from \WIN32NET\CODE\WIN32OBJ\OVFILE.CPP:

```
BOOL COverlappedFile::Open(LPCTSTR lpszFileName,
      UINT nOpenFlags,
      CFileException* pError)
{
   // This is the Microsoft MFC version of CFile::Open(),
   // modified to do overlapped I/O.
   // CFile hardcodes the flags and attributes argument
   // so we can't inherit the behavior, we have to
   // replace it.
   m_bCloseOnDelete = FALSE;

   DWORD dwDesiredAccess = 0;

   // Test access bits of nOpenFlags
   if (nOpenFlags & modeReadWrite)
      dwDesiredAccess = GENERIC_READ | GENERIC_WRITE;
   else if (nOpenFlags & modeWrite)
      dwDesiredAccess = GENERIC_WRITE;
   else
      dwDesiredAccess = GENERIC_READ;

   DWORD dwShareMode = 0;

   if (nOpenFlags & shareDenyNone)
      dwShareMode = FILE_SHARE_READ | FILE_SHARE_WRITE;
```

```
    else if ((nOpenFlags & shareDenyRead) == shareDenyRead)
       // shareDenyRead is two bits
       dwShareMode = FILE_SHARE_WRITE;
    else if (nOpenFlags & shareDenyWrite)
       dwShareMode = FILE_SHARE_READ;
    else
       dwShareMode = 0;   // Exclusive access

    // modeNoInherit is the non-zero flag
    BOOL bInheritHandle = (nOpenFlags & modeNoInherit) == 0;

    DWORD dwCreationDisposition;

    if (nOpenFlags & modeCreate)  // modeCreate is the non-zero bit
       dwCreationDisposition = CREATE_ALWAYS;
    else
      dwCreationDisposition = OPEN_EXISTING;

    // Use our own override of Open()

    BOOL bStatus;
    bStatus = Open(
             lpszFileName,
             dwCreationDisposition,
             dwDesiredAccess,
             dwShareMode,
             FILE_FLAG_OVERLAPPED,
             FILE_ATTRIBUTE_NORMAL,
             bInheritHandle);

    if (!bStatus && (pError != NULL))
       {
       pError->m_lOsError = ::GetLastError();
       pError->m_cause =
          CFileException::OsErrorToException(pError->m_lOsError);
       }
    m_bCloseOnDelete = TRUE;
    return TRUE;
}
```

The COverlappedFile Constructors. I like to provide constructors that generate fully usable objects. Some philosophies of C++ programming say don't do anything in constructors that can fail, because you can't return a value. True enough; but you can raise exceptions. And the beauty of C++ is in being able to do so much with so little. So I include one version of the constructor that opens the file. By the way, this mimics CFile itself; one of its constructors does the same thing. Here are the prototype and implementation of the constructor.

```
COverlappedFile(LPCTSTR lpszFileName, BOOL bAlways = FALSE);

COverlappedFile::COverlappedFile(LPCTSTR lpszFileName, BOOL bAlways)
{
   m_lpIoPort = NULL;

   if (!Open(lpszFileName, bAlways))
      {
      CFileException::ThrowOsError((LONG)::GetLastError());
      }
}
```

The Read() and Write() Methods. CFile has Read() and Write() methods, as you would expect. They do nonoverlapped operations, so COverlappedFile must provide overloaded versions of these methods. I provide two versions of each. One uses ReadFile() (or WriteFile()), either with events or an I/O completion port. The other uses ReadFileEx() (or WriteFileEx()) with an I/O completion routine. Both versions allow the caller to pass his own OVERLAPPED structure, wrapped in a COverlapped object.

Here are the prototypes and implementations of the Read() methods. Notice that I use the COverlapped object to remember everything I need to know to recycle the request. The Write() implementations differ in only one respect (other than the functions they call, of course): a failed write request throws an MFC CFileException. My thought here is that a write failure is more likely to be some pathological condition like insufficient disk space.

```
// Prototypes
// Standard or I/O completion ports
virtual BOOL Read(LPVOID lpBuffer, DWORD dwCount,
                  DWORD *lpBytesRead,
                  COverlapped *lpOverlapped);

// I/O completion routines
virtual BOOL Read(LPVOID lpBuffer, DWORD dwCount,
      COverlapped *lpOverlapped,
      LPOVERLAPPED_COMPLETION_ROUTINE lpCompletionRoutine);

// Implementations
// Version 1. Calls ReadFile(), supports either
// standard overlapped I/O or I/O completion ports
BOOL COverlappedFile::Read(LPVOID lpBuffer, DWORD dwCount,
         DWORD *lpBytesRead,
         COverlapped *lpOverlapped)
```

```
{
   ASSERT(dwCount != 0);
   ASSERT(lpBuffer != NULL);
   ASSERT (lpBytesRead != NULL);

   if (lpOverlapped != NULL)
      {
      lpOverlapped->SetBuffer(lpBuffer);
      lpOverlapped->SetFile(GetFileHandle());
      lpOverlapped->SetPreviousOperation(COverlapped::ReadFile);
      if (lpOverlapped->GetEventHandle() != NULL)
         ::ResetEvent(lpOverlapped->GetEventHandle());
      }

   return ::ReadFile(GetFileHandle(), lpBuffer, dwCount,
           lpBytesRead,
           lpOverlapped);
}

// Version 2. Calls ReadFileEx(), supports
// I/O completion routines only
BOOL COverlappedFile::Read(LPVOID lpBuffer, DWORD dwCount,
          COverlapped *lpOverlapped,
          LPOVERLAPPED_COMPLETION_ROUTINE lpCompletionRoutine)
{
   ASSERT(dwCount != 0);
   ASSERT(lpBuffer != NULL);
   ASSERT (lpCompletionRoutine != NULL);

   if (lpOverlapped != NULL)
      {
      lpOverlapped->SetBuffer(lpBuffer);
      lpOverlapped->SetFile(GetFileHandle());
      lpOverlapped->SetPreviousOperation(
         COverlapped::ReadFileEx);
      }

   return ::ReadFileEx(
           GetFileHandle(),
           lpBuffer,
           dwCount,
           lpOverlapped,
           lpCompletionRoutine);
}
```

The Receive Callback Routine. The member variable *m_lpReceiveCallback* is a placeholder for a function that will be called to report the completion of asynchronous reads. I intend it for use in later chapters, when I derive classes from COverlappedFile to represent overlapped Windows Sockets and Named Pipes. There is no reason why it cannot be used with disk files as well, but this is not my main purpose in including it.

When subclasses need to invoke the callback routine, they will do so by calling the CallReceiveCallback() method. The arguments passed to the callback function are a pointer to the incoming data, the number of bytes of data, and a HANDLE representing the connection over which it has arrived. Here is the definition of CallReceiveCallback(), implemented in \WIN32NET\CODE\WIN32OBJ\OVFILE.H:

```
virtual BOOL CallReceiveCallback(LPBYTE lpData,
   DWORD dwDataLength, HANDLE hConnection)
   {
   ASSERT(m_lpReceiveCallback != NULL);
   return m_lpReceiveCallback(lpData,
                              dwDataLength,
                              hConnection);
   }
```

So that you can see everything in its complete context, here is the complete listing of the COverlappedFile implementation file, \WIN32NET\CODE\WIN32OBJ\OVFILE.CPP.

```
/********
*
* OVFILE.CPP
*
* Copyright (c) 1995-1996 Ralph P. Davis
*
* All Rights Reserved
*
********/

/*===== Include Files =====*/

#define IMPLEMENT_OVFILE
#include "stdafx.h"
#include "ovfile.h"
#include "overlap.h"
#include "ioport.h"

IMPLEMENT_DYNAMIC(COverlappedFile, CFile)

COverlappedFile::COverlappedFile()
```

```
{
   if (AfxGetApp() == NULL)
      {
      g_pMyApp = new CWinApp;
      }
   m_lpIoPort = NULL;
   m_lpReceiveCallback = NULL;
}

COverlappedFile::COverlappedFile(LPCTSTR lpszFileName, BOOL bAlways)
{
   if (AfxGetApp() == NULL)
      {
      g_pMyApp = new CWinApp;
      }
   m_lpIoPort = NULL;
   m_lpReceiveCallback = NULL;

   if (!Open(lpszFileName, bAlways))
      {
      CFileException::ThrowOsError((LONG)::GetLastError());
      }
}

COverlappedFile::COverlappedFile(HANDLE hFile) : CFile((int) hFile)
{
   if (AfxGetApp() == NULL)
      {
      g_pMyApp = new CWinApp;
      }

   m_lpIoPort = NULL;
   m_lpReceiveCallback = NULL;
}

COverlappedFile::~COverlappedFile()
{
   if (m_lpIoPort != NULL)
      {
      m_lpIoPort->Remove(this);
      m_lpIoPort = NULL;
      }
}

BOOL COverlappedFile::Create(
      LPCTSTR lpszFileName,
      BOOL    bAlways)
```

```
{
   BOOL bRetcode =
      Open(lpszFileName, bAlways ? CREATE_ALWAYS : CREATE_NEW,
               GENERIC_READ | GENERIC_WRITE);
   return bRetcode;
}

BOOL COverlappedFile::Open(LPCTSTR lpszFileName,
      UINT nOpenFlags,
      CFileException* pError)
{
   // This is the Microsoft MFC version of CFile::Open(),
   // modified to do overlapped I/O.
   // CFile hardcodes the flags and attributes argument
   // so we can't inherit the behavior, we have to
   // replace it.
   m_bCloseOnDelete = FALSE;

   DWORD dwDesiredAccess = 0;

   // Test access bits of nOpenFlags
   if (nOpenFlags & modeReadWrite)
      dwDesiredAccess = GENERIC_READ | GENERIC_WRITE;
   else if (nOpenFlags & modeWrite)
      dwDesiredAccess = GENERIC_WRITE;
   else
      dwDesiredAccess = GENERIC_READ;

   DWORD dwShareMode = 0;

   if (nOpenFlags & shareDenyNone)
      dwShareMode = FILE_SHARE_READ | FILE_SHARE_WRITE;
   else if ((nOpenFlags & shareDenyRead) == shareDenyRead)
      // shareDenyRead is two bits
      dwShareMode = FILE_SHARE_WRITE;
   else if (nOpenFlags & shareDenyWrite)
      dwShareMode = FILE_SHARE_READ;
   else
      dwShareMode = 0;   // Exclusive access

   // modeNoInherit is the non-zero flag
   BOOL bInheritHandle = (nOpenFlags & modeNoInherit) == 0;

   DWORD dwCreationDisposition;

   if (nOpenFlags & modeCreate)  // modeCreate is the non-zero bit
      dwCreationDisposition = CREATE_ALWAYS;
```

```
    else
      dwCreationDisposition = OPEN_EXISTING;

    // Use our own override of Open()

    BOOL bStatus;
    bStatus = Open(
                lpszFileName,
                dwCreationDisposition,
                dwDesiredAccess,
                dwShareMode,
                FILE_FLAG_OVERLAPPED,
                FILE_ATTRIBUTE_NORMAL,
                bInheritHandle);

    if (!bStatus && (pError != NULL))
        {
        pError->m_lOsError = ::GetLastError();
        pError->m_cause =
            CFileException::OsErrorToException(pError->m_lOsError);
        }
    m_bCloseOnDelete = TRUE;
    return TRUE;
}

BOOL COverlappedFile::Open(
        LPCTSTR lpszFileName,
        BOOL    bAlways)
{
    return Open(lpszFileName,
                bAlways ? OPEN_ALWAYS : OPEN_EXISTING,
                GENERIC_READ | GENERIC_WRITE);
}

BOOL COverlappedFile::Open(
        LPCTSTR lpszFileName,
        DWORD dwOperation,
        DWORD dwAccess,
        DWORD dwShareMode,
        DWORD dwFlags,
        DWORD dwAttributes,
        BOOL  bInherit)
{
    SECURITY_ATTRIBUTES sa;
    LPSECURITY_ATTRIBUTES lpsa = NULL;

    m_hFile = hFileNull;
```

```
    if (bInherit)
        {
        sa.nLength = sizeof(sa);
        sa.lpSecurityDescriptor = NULL;
        sa.bInheritHandle = bInherit;
        lpsa = &sa;
        }

    dwFlags |= FILE_FLAG_OVERLAPPED;  // Make sure overlapped I/O is set

    dwFlags |= dwAttributes;  // Two arguments get galomphed together
    HANDLE hFile = ::CreateFile(lpszFileName,
                                dwAccess,
                                dwShareMode,
                                lpsa,
                                dwOperation,
                                dwFlags,
                                NULL);

    SetFileHandle(hFile);  // Remember file handle even if it's bogus
    return (hFile != INVALID_HANDLE_VALUE);
}

BOOL COverlappedFile::Read(LPVOID lpBuffer, DWORD dwCount,
          DWORD *lpBytesRead,
          COverlapped *lpOverlapped)
{
    ASSERT(dwCount != 0);
    ASSERT(lpBuffer != NULL);
    ASSERT (lpBytesRead != NULL);

    if (lpOverlapped != NULL)
        {
        lpOverlapped->SetBuffer(lpBuffer);
        lpOverlapped->SetFile(GetFileHandle());
        lpOverlapped->SetPreviousOperation(COverlapped::ReadFile);
        if (lpOverlapped->GetEventHandle() != NULL)
            ::ResetEvent(lpOverlapped->GetEventHandle());
        }

    return ::ReadFile(GetFileHandle(), lpBuffer, dwCount,
            lpBytesRead,
            lpOverlapped);
}

BOOL COverlappedFile::Read(LPVOID lpBuffer, DWORD dwCount,
          COverlapped *lpOverlapped,
          LPOVERLAPPED_COMPLETION_ROUTINE lpCompletionRoutine)
```

```
{
   ASSERT(dwCount != 0);
   ASSERT(lpBuffer != NULL);
   ASSERT (lpCompletionRoutine != NULL);

   if (lpOverlapped != NULL)
      {
      lpOverlapped->SetBuffer(lpBuffer);
      lpOverlapped->SetFile(GetFileHandle());
      lpOverlapped->SetPreviousOperation(COverlapped::ReadFileEx);
      }

   return ::ReadFileEx(GetFileHandle(), lpBuffer, dwCount,
           lpOverlapped,
           lpCompletionRoutine);
}

BOOL COverlappedFile::Write(const void *lpBuffer, DWORD dwCount,
      COverlapped *lpOverlapped)
{
   ASSERT(dwCount != 0);
   ASSERT(lpBuffer != NULL);

   DWORD dwWritten;

   if (lpOverlapped != NULL)
      {
      lpOverlapped->SetBuffer((LPVOID) lpBuffer);
      lpOverlapped->SetFile(GetFileHandle());
      lpOverlapped->SetPreviousOperation(COverlapped::WriteFile);
      if (lpOverlapped->GetEventHandle() != NULL)
         ::ResetEvent(lpOverlapped->GetEventHandle());
      }

   return ::WriteFile(GetFileHandle(),
                      lpBuffer,
                      dwCount,
                      &dwWritten,
                      lpOverlapped);
}

BOOL COverlappedFile::Write(LPVOID lpBuffer, DWORD dwCount,
         COverlapped *lpOverlapped,
         LPOVERLAPPED_COMPLETION_ROUTINE lpCompletionRoutine)
{
   ASSERT(dwCount != 0);
   ASSERT(lpBuffer != NULL);
   ASSERT (lpCompletionRoutine != NULL);
```

```
   if (lpOverlapped != NULL)
      {
      lpOverlapped->SetBuffer(lpBuffer);
      lpOverlapped->SetFile(GetFileHandle());
      lpOverlapped->SetPreviousOperation(COverlapped::WriteFileEx);
      }

   BOOL bStatus = ::WriteFileEx(GetFileHandle(), lpBuffer, dwCount,
           lpOverlapped,
           lpCompletionRoutine);
   if (!bStatus)
      CFileException::ThrowOsError((LONG)::GetLastError());
   return bStatus;
}

CIoPort *COverlappedFile::GetIoPort()
{
   return m_lpIoPort;
}

VOID COverlappedFile::SetIoPort(CIoPort *lpIoPort)
{
   m_lpIoPort = lpIoPort;
}

BOOL COverlappedFile::Post(COverlapped  *lpOverlapped,
                           DWORD         dwBytes)
{
   BOOL bRetcode;

   ASSERT(m_lpIoPort != NULL);
   return Post(m_lpIoPort, lpOverlapped, dwBytes);
}

BOOL COverlappedFile::Post(CIoPort     *lpPort,
                           COverlapped *lpOverlapped,
                           DWORD        dwBytes)
{
   BOOL bRetcode;
   ASSERT(lpPort != NULL);
   return lpPort->Post(this, lpOverlapped, dwBytes);
}
```

The cat Program Using COverlappedFile

I'd like to present one more version of *cat*, this one using the MFC objects I've developed. The listing that follows uses I/O completion routines. I show only the setup sequence and the action loop; the rest of the code is the same as shown earlier. I pass a pointer to the output buffer to the I/O completion routine using Thread Local Storage, a technique we'll look at in the next chapter.

```
HANDLE hStdInput, hStdOutput;
COverlappedFile   InputFile;
int               i, j;
TCHAR             szBuffer[nNumReads][nBufferSize];
DWORD             dwBytesRead, dwBytesWritten;
DWORD             dwFileSize;
BOOL              bSuccess;
LPBYTE            lpBuffer;

if (InputFile.Open(lpszFileName[i], FALSE))
   {
   COverlapped ov[nNumReads];

   dwFileSize = InputFile.GetLength();
   lpBuffer = (LPBYTE) ::VirtualAlloc(NULL,
      dwFileSize, MEM_COMMIT, PAGE_READWRITE);

   TlsWriteBuffer = (LPVOID) lpBuffer;

   CEvent MyEvent;
   bSuccess = FALSE;
   for (j = 0; j < nNumReads; ++j)
      {
      ov[j].SetEventHandle((HANDLE) MyEvent);
      ov[j].SetBuffer(szBuffer[j]);
      ov[j].SetFile(&InputFile);
      ov[j].SetOffset(j * nBufferSize);

      bSuccess |= InputFile.Read(
         szBuffer[j],
         nBufferSize,
         &ov[j],
         FileIOCompletionRoutine);
      }
   if (!bSuccess)  // No successful reads were issued
      MyEvent.SetEvent();

   while (::WaitForSingleObjectEx(
            (HANDLE) MyEvent, INFINITE, TRUE))
      ;
```

```
WriteStdOutputBuffer(lpBuffer, dwFileSize);
::VirtualFree(lpBuffer, 0, MEM_RELEASE);
InputFile.Close();
}
```

I/O Completion Ports—The CIoPort Class

To wrap I/O completion ports, I use a class I call CIoPort. This class is derived from the root class in my Win32 object library, CWin32Object. CWin32Object encapsulates Win32 objects that the operating system represents as HANDLEs, but that have no synchronization properties.

As you saw above, COverlappedFile has a member variable, *m_lpIoPort*, that points to a CIoPort object for any files using I/O completion ports. The CIoPort class, for its part, maintains an array of COverlappedFile objects that have been associated with it, in its member variable *m_FileArray*. The array is represented using the MFC CArray template class. CIoPort provides two methods that pertain to this array: Add() and Remove():

```
BOOL Add(COverlappedFile *lpNewElement);
BOOL Remove(COverlappedFile *lpFile);
```

Add() invokes the CArray::Add() method, then uses the index into the array as the *dwCompletionKey* argument for CreateIoCompletionPort(). The port handle is remembered as the object handle (*m_hObject*) of the CWin32Object base class. Also, the *m_lpIoPort* member of the COverlappedFile remembers the CIoPort object. It is set in CIoPort::Add() by calling the SetIoPort() method.

Notice that the first time this method is invoked, it will create a new I/O completion port, since the object handle is initialized to NULL. Then each subsequent call (for a new file) will associate the new file objects with the existing port handle.

```
BOOL CIoPort::Add(COverlappedFile *lpNewElement)
{
   HANDLE hPort;
   DWORD dwKey = (DWORD) m_FileArray.Add(lpNewElement);

   if (dwKey == ((DWORD) -1))
      {
      return FALSE;
      }
   hPort = ::CreateIoCompletionPort(
                 lpNewElement->GetFileHandle(),
                 GetHandle(),
                 dwKey,
```

```
                0);
    if (hPort != NULL)
        {
        if (GetHandle() == NULL)
            {
            Attach(hPort);
            lpNewElement->SetIoPort(this);  // Set back-pointer
                                            // to I/O completion port
            }
        }
    else
        {
        m_FileArray.RemoveAt((int) dwKey);
        }
    return (hPort != NULL);
}
```

Figure 6-1 shows the relationships among these three classes:

- *CWin32Object::m_hObject* remembers the NT HANDLE identifying the I/O completion port.
- *CIoPort::m_FileArray* stores pointers to the COverlappedFile objects that have been tied to the port. The relationship between the port and the files is one-to-many; hence the use of an array.
- *COverlappedFile::m_lpIoPort* keeps a pointer to the CIoPort object with which the file is associated.

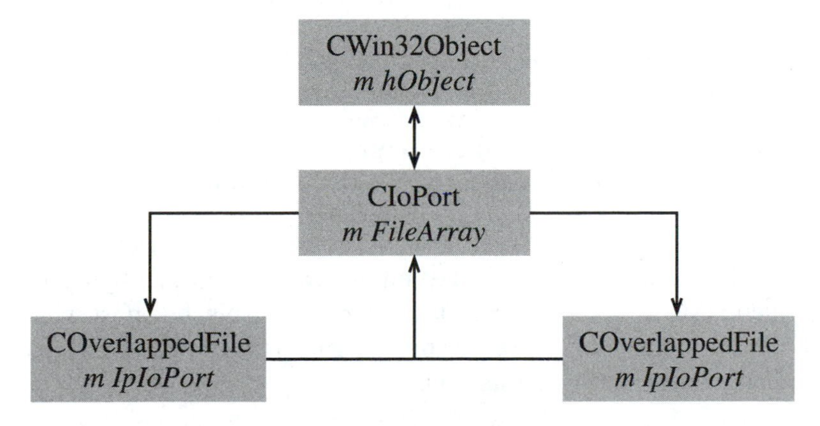

Figure 6-1. Relationships Among CWin32Object, CIoPort, and COverlapped-File Objects

The Remove() method just removes a COverlappedFile object from *m_FileArray.* There is no way to disassociate an open file from an I/O completion port, short of closing the file or port handle. Remove() also sets the embedded CIoPort pointer in the COverlappedFile object by invoking its SetIoPort() method.

```
BOOL CIoPort::Remove(COverlappedFile *lpFile)
{
   BOOL bRetcode = FALSE;
   for (int i = 0; !bRetcode && (i < m_FileArray.GetSize()); ++i)
      {
      if (m_FileArray[i] == lpFile)
         {
         m_FileArray.RemoveAt(i);
         // Set back pointer appropriately
         // This breaks the link between the
         // COverlappedFile and the CIoPort
         // as far as we're concerned
         // (but not as far as NT is concerned)
         lpFile->SetIoPort(NULL);
         bRetcode = TRUE;
         }
      }
   return bRetcode;
}
```

The two other methods on this class, Wait() and Post(), wrap the GetQueuedCompletionStatus() and PostQueuedCompletionStatus() functions:

```
COverlappedFile *Wait(LPOVERLAPPED *lplpOverlapped,
                      LPDWORD       lpdwBytes,
                      DWORD         dwTimeout = INFINITE);
BOOL Post(COverlappedFile *lpFile,
          COverlapped     *lpOverlapped,
          DWORD            dwBytes);
```

The Wait() method uses the completion key returned by GetQueuedCompletionStatus() to fetch the COverlappedFile object against which an operation is completing. The other three arguments are passed along unaltered to GetQueuedCompletionStatus().

```
COverlappedFile *CIoPort::Wait(LPOVERLAPPED *lplpOverlapped,
                               LPDWORD lpdwBytes,
                               DWORD dwTimeout)
```

```
{
   COverlappedFile *lpFile = NULL;
   DWORD dwKey;

   if (::GetQueuedCompletionStatus(
                  GetHandle(),
                  lpdwBytes,
                  &dwKey,
                  lplpOverlapped,
                  dwTimeout))
      {
      // Make sure item still exists
      if (dwKey < (DWORD) m_FileArray.GetSize())
         lpFile = m_FileArray[dwKey];
      }

   return lpFile;
}
```

The Post() method expects a COverlappedFile pointer as its first argument. It looks this object up in *m_FileArray*, then uses its index as the *dwCompletionKey* argument for PostQueuedCompletionStatus. The other two arguments—the count of bytes transferred, and the OVERLAPPED structure (wrapped in a COverlapped object)—are passed along as is.

```
BOOL CIoPort::Post(COverlappedFile *lpFile,
                   COverlapped     *lpOverlapped,
                   DWORD            dwBytes)
{
   // Find file in array
   BOOL bFound = FALSE;
   for (int i = 0; !bFound && (i < m_FileArray.GetSize()); ++i)
      {
      bFound = (m_FileArray[i] == lpFile);
      }

   if (bFound)
      {
      // We know about this guy (as indeed we should)
      return ::PostQueuedCompletionStatus(
                  GetHandle(),
                  dwBytes,
                  (DWORD) i,  // Completion key is index in array
                  lpOverlapped);
      }
   return FALSE;
}
```

The CIoPort class is declared in \WIN32NET\CODE\WIN32OBJ\IOPORT.H:

```
/********
*
* IOPORT.H
*
* Copyright (c) 1995-1996 Ralph P. Davis
*
* All Rights Reserved
*
********/

#ifndef _IOPORT_INCLUDED
#define _IOPORT_INCLUDED
#include "win32obj.h"
#include "ovfile.h"

class AFX_EXT_CLASS CIoPort : public CWin32Object
{
protected:
   CArray<COverlappedFile *, COverlappedFile *> m_FileArray;
public:
   CIoPort();
   virtual ~CIoPort();
   BOOL Add(COverlappedFile *lpNewElement);
   BOOL Remove(COverlappedFile *lpFile);
   COverlappedFile *Wait(LPOVERLAPPED *lplpOverlapped,
                         LPDWORD       lpdwBytes,
                         DWORD         dwTimeout = INFINITE);
   BOOL Post(COverlappedFile *lpFile,
             COverlapped *lpOverlapped,
             DWORD        dwBytes);
   DECLARE_DYNAMIC(CIoPort)
};
#endif
```

The implementation of the class is in \WIN32NET\CODE\WIN32OBJ\IOPORT.CPP:

```
/********
*
* IOPORT.CPP
*
* Copyright (c) 1995-1996 Ralph P. Davis
*
* All Rights Reserved
*
********/
```

```
/*===== Includes =====*/

#include "stdafx.h"
#include "ioport.h"
#include "overlap.h"


/*===== Function Definitions =====*/

IMPLEMENT_DYNAMIC(CIoPort, CWin32Object)

CIoPort::CIoPort()
{
   // Create an unattached port (not associated with a file)
   // This will allow posting to the port using
   // CIoPort::Post(), which calls ::PostQueuedCompletionStatus()
   HANDLE hPort =
      ::CreateIoCompletionPort(INVALID_HANDLE_VALUE,
                               NULL,
                               (DWORD) -1,
                               0);
   if (hPort != NULL)
      {
      Attach(hPort);
      }
   else
      {
      AfxThrowResourceException();
      }
}

CIoPort::~CIoPort()
{
   for (int i = 0; i < m_FileArray.GetSize(); ++i)
      {
      // Remove back pointers from associated
      // files
      m_FileArray[i]->SetIoPort(NULL);
      }
   m_FileArray.RemoveAll();
}

BOOL CIoPort::Add(COverlappedFile *lpNewElement)
{
   HANDLE hPort;
   DWORD dwKey = (DWORD) m_FileArray.Add(lpNewElement);
```

```
    if (dwKey == ((DWORD) -1))
        {
        return FALSE;
        }
    hPort = ::CreateIoCompletionPort(
                    lpNewElement->GetFileHandle(),
                    GetHandle(),
                    dwKey,
                    0);
    if (hPort != NULL)
        {
        if (GetHandle() == NULL)
            {
            Attach(hPort);
            }
        lpNewElement->SetIoPort(this);  // Set back-pointer
                                        // to I/O completion port
        }
    else
        {
        m_FileArray.RemoveAt((int) dwKey);
        }
    return (hPort != NULL);
}

BOOL CIoPort::Remove(COverlappedFile *lpFile)
{
    BOOL bRetcode = FALSE;
    for (int i = 0; !bRetcode && (i < m_FileArray.GetSize()); ++i)
        {
        if (m_FileArray[i] == lpFile)
            {
            m_FileArray.RemoveAt(i);
            // Set back pointer appropriately
            // This breaks the link between the
            // COverlappedFile and the CIoPort
            // as far as we're concerned
            // (but not as far as NT is concerned)
            lpFile->SetIoPort(NULL);
            bRetcode = TRUE;
            }
        }
    return bRetcode;
}

COverlappedFile *CIoPort::Wait(LPOVERLAPPED *lplpOverlapped,
                               LPDWORD lpdwBytes,
                               DWORD dwTimeout)
```

```
{
   COverlappedFile *lpFile = NULL;
   DWORD dwKey;

   if (::GetQueuedCompletionStatus(
                  GetHandle(),
                  lpdwBytes,
                  &dwKey,
                  lplpOverlapped,
                  dwTimeout))
      {
      // Make sure item still exists
      if (dwKey < (DWORD) m_FileArray.GetSize())
         lpFile = m_FileArray[dwKey];
      }
   return lpFile;
}

BOOL CIoPort::Post(COverlappedFile *lpFile,
                   COverlapped *lpOverlapped,
                   DWORD        dwBytes)
{
   // Find file in array
   BOOL bFound = FALSE;
   for (int i = 0; !bFound && (i < m_FileArray.GetSize()); ++i)
      {
      bFound = (m_FileArray[i] == lpFile);
      }

   if (bFound)
      {
      // We know about this guy (as indeed we should)
      return ::PostQueuedCompletionStatus(
                  GetHandle(),
                  dwBytes,
                  (DWORD) i,  // Completion key is index in array
                  lpOverlapped);
      }
   return FALSE;
}
```

Additional Source Code Listings

In this section, I present Win32 versions of two additional file utilities that run as console applications. *ls*, like *cat*, comes from UNIX. *which* finds a requested file by searching either the PATH or a given set of directories.

which

which uses the SearchPath() function to tell you which copy of a file it will select from a given set of directories. Suppose you have more than one copy of a utility like *ls.exe* on your path, and you want to make sure the one that gets executed is the most up-to-date version. *which* gives you that information.

Here is the prototype for SearchPath():

```
DWORD SearchPath(
        LPCTSTR   lpszPath,
        LPCTSTR   lpszFile,
        LPCTSTR   lpszExtension,
        DWORD     dwOutputBufferSize,
        LPTSTR    lpszReturnBuffer,
        LPTSTR   *lplpFileNameComponent);
```

lpszPath is the list of directories you want SearchPath() to scan. Directories in this string are delimited by semicolons. If you want SearchPath() to look in the directories that Windows normally searches to run a program, you can pass *lpszPath* as NULL. In this case, the search order is:

1. The directory from which the application started
2. The current directory
3. The Windows system directory, identified by GetSystemDirectory() This will probably be %SystemRoot%\SYSTEM32
4. The Windows directory, reported by GetWindowsDirectory() (most likely %SystemRoot%)
5. The directories listed in the PATH environment variable

lpszFile is the name of the file you want SearchPath() to locate. *lpszExtension* is the default extension that Windows will append to the filename if *lpszFile* does not include one. *dwOutputBufferSize* and *lpszReturnBuffer* describe the location where you want the answer deposited. *lplpFileNameComponent* can be handy. It will return a pointer to the last component of the filename (that is, the filename without the path preceding it). For example, if SearchPath() finds a file named C:\WIN32NET\BIN\LS.EXE, **lplpFileNameComponent* will point to LS.EXE. This can save you some trouble parsing the filename.

which takes one required and one optional argument. The first argument is the file you want it to locate. You also have the option of specifying the set of directories you want *which* to search. If you do not pass this, *which* passes the *lpszPath* argument to SearchPath() as NULL.

which also shows my first use of the FormatMessage() function. This is the Win32 version of perror(). Its syntax is quite a bit more complicated than perror(), but its error messages are much more informative. You can also use FormatMessage() to display application-specific messages that you have compiled with the Message Compiler and linked into your application (or a DLL). This gives you easy internationalization. My use of FormatMessage() in *which* is taken almost verbatim from the Win32 SDK Knowledge Base, article number Q94999, entitled "FormatMessage() Converts GetLastError() Codes." In *ls*, following *which*, I also use it to display my own messages, which are included on the source code disk in broken French and Spanish, as well as English.

Here's what FormatMessage() looks like:

```
DWORD FormatMessage(
        DWORD   dwFlags,
        LPCVOID lpSource,
        DWORD   dwMessageID,
        DWORD   dwLanguageID,
        LPTSTR  lpBuffer,
        DWORD   dwSize,
        va_list *pArgs);
```

dwFlags specifies how the output message is to be constructed. Some of the most important flags are:

- FORMAT_MESSAGE_ALLOCATE_BUFFER says that you want Windows to allocate the memory for the message. When this flag is set, *lpBuffer* is a pointer to a pointer for which memory will be LocalAlloc()'d. When you are through with the message, you need to LocalFree() it.
- FORMAT_MESSAGE_FROM_SYSTEM identifies the message as a system message; *dwMessageID* is a GetLastError() code.
- FORMAT_MESSAGE_FROM_STRING indicates that *lpSource* points to a format string. It may contain "insert sequences," which are similar to *printf()* format specifiers. However, FormatMessage() uses *%n* sequences, where *n* designates a one-based index into the array pointed to by *pArgs*. The *%n* may be followed by printf()-type format codes, enclosed in exclamation points. Thus, the insert sequence *%1!08x!* says to substitute the value of the first element in *lpArgs* (that is, *lpArgs[0]*) and format it as an eight-digit hexadecimal number, padded on the left with zeroes.

- FORMAT_MESSAGE_FROM_HMODULE tells Windows that the message is contained in an executable image or a DLL. *lpSource* will be either the module handle (obtained by a call to LoadLibrary() or GetModuleHandle()) or NULL to identify the current process.
- FORMAT_MESSAGE_ARGUMENT_ARRAY says that *lpArgs* is not a *va_list* *, but rather an array of 32-bit data items.

lpSource is ignored unless either the FORMAT_MESSAGE_FROM_HMODULE or the FORMAT_MESSAGE_FROM_STRING flags are set.

dwMessageID identifies the message that you want to render. If FORMAT_MESSAGE_FROM_SYSTEM is set, *dwMessageID* is a GetLastError() code. The Win32 header file WINERROR.H is generated by the Message Compiler; it has the definitions of all the GetLastError() codes and includes the strings that will be returned by FormatMessage() as comments.

dwLanguageID specifies the language in which you want the message to be rendered. A version of the message in the requested language must have been defined when the Message Compiler processed the messages. For system-defined messages, you will normally pass this as either LANG_USER_DEFAULT or as GetUserDefaultLangID(), so that the message is generated in the language for which the user's machine is configured. For application-defined messages, it will be whatever numeric code you have associated with the languages you are supporting. For *ls*, I use the low 8 bits returned by GetUserDefaultLangID(). These identify the language; the high 8 bits describe dialectical flavorings, like British, American, or Australian English.

lpBuffer points to the buffer where you want the message to be placed. If you set the FORMAT_MESSAGE_ALLOCATE_BUFFER flag, Windows will LocalAlloc() the memory for you. In this case, *lpBuffer* points to the pointer that you want Windows to allocate. *dwSize* specifies the maximum length of a message, unless you set FORMAT_MESSAGE_ALLOCATE_BUFFER, in which case it designates the smallest size you want Windows to allocate.

Finally, *lpArgs* points to the values that will be substituted into the message string for insert sequences. If the FORMAT_MESSAGE_ARGUMENT_ARRAY flag is set, this is an array of DWORDs.

Here is the complete listing of \WIN32NET\CODE\FILEUTIL\WHICH.CPP:

```
/********
*
* WHICH.CPP
*
* Copyright (c) 1993-1996 Ralph P. Davis, All Rights Reserved
*
* Finds a given file on a given path
*
* USAGE:
*
*     which <filename> [<path>]
*
*     If <path> is not specified, uses Windows' default searching algorithm
*
********/

/*===== Includes=====*/

#include <windows.h>
#include <stdio.h>


/*===== Function Definitions =====*/

VOID main(int argc, char *argv[])
{
   LPCTSTR lpFileName;
   LPCTSTR lpPath = NULL;
   char    szPathName[MAX_PATH + 1];
   LPTSTR  lpFilePart;
   LPSTR   lpMsg;

   if (argc == 1)
      {
      fprintf(stderr, "\nUsage:  which <filename> [<path>]\n");
      ExitProcess(1);
      }

   lpFileName = (LPCTSTR) argv[1];

   if (argc < 3)
      lpPath = NULL;
   else
      lpPath = (LPCTSTR) argv[2];

   // SearchPath() returns the length of the full filename
   if (SearchPath(lpPath, lpFileName, NULL, MAX_PATH, szPathName,
                  &lpFilePart) > 0)
```

```
        printf("\n%s\n", szPathName);
    else
        {
        FormatMessage(
          FORMAT_MESSAGE_ALLOCATE_BUFFER | FORMAT_MESSAGE_FROM_SYSTEM,
          NULL, GetLastError(), LANG_USER_DEFAULT,
          (LPSTR) &lpMsg, 0, NULL );

        fprintf(stderr, "\nSearchPath() failed\n%s\n",
                lpMsg);
        LocalFree(lpMsg);
        }
}
```

ls

The last application I present here is *ls*, a Win32 implementation of the UNIX utility that lists files. The Win32 file-enumeration functions are FindFirstFile(), FindNextFile(), and FindClose():

```
HANDLE FindFirstFile(
          LPCTSTR lpszFileSpec,
          LPWIN32_FIND_DATA lpWin32FindData);
BOOL FindNextFile(
          HANDLE hSearch,
          LPWIN32_FIND_DATA lpWin32FindData);
BOOL FindClose(HANDLE hSearch);
```

The WIN32_FIND_DATA structure captures information about each enumerated file. For *ls*, the field of interest is the *cFileName* field, which reports the native name of the file in its own file system. The *cAlternateFileName* field provides an 8.3 FAT-compatible filename for NTFS names that do not conform to FAT conventions. For instance, for the filename "george washington.c," which is legal in NTFS, NT generates the 8.3 name "GEORGE~1.C". If I have another file in the same directory called "george jones.c," *cAlternateFileName* gives it as "GEORGE~2.C".

A very simple *ls* can be written with only a few lines of code. Here's what it might look like:

```
/********
*
* LS1.CPP
*
* Very simple implementation of LS using Win32 functions
*
********/
```

```
/*===== Includes =====*/

#include <windows.h>
#include <stdio.h>


/*===== Function Definitions =====*/

VOID ls(LPCTSTR lpszFileSpec)
{
   HANDLE hSearch;
   WIN32_FIND_DATA Win32FindData;

   hSearch = FindFirstFile(lpszFileSpec, &Win32FindData);

   if (hSearch == INVALID_HANDLE_VALUE)
      {
      fprintf(stderr,
         "\nFindFirstFile() for %s failed, GetLastError() = %d\n",
         lpszFileSpec, GetLastError());
      return;
      }

   do
      {
      printf("\n%s", Win32FindData.cFileName);
      }
   while (FindNextFile(hSearch, &Win32FindData));

   FindClose(hSearch);
}

VOID main(int argc, char *argv[])
{
   int i;

   if (argc == 1)
      ls("./*.*");
   else
      {
      for (i = 1; i < argc; ++i)
         ls(argv[i]);
      }
   ExitProcess(0);
}
```

However, I have chosen to provide a more ambitious version that demonstrates all of the techniques we've studied so far in this book. My *ls* is multithreaded; for each *argv*, I execute the ls() function in a new thread. Each thread captures its output in a local buffer, which it concatenates to a single global buffer when it finishes. The main thread, after starting the secondary threads, waits until they all complete, then prints the contents of the global buffer.

Because multiple threads append their output to a single common buffer, their activities must be synchronized. I use a mutex for traffic control. Since I have no idea how much memory to allocate for the buffers, it makes sense to reserve an amount that is probably more than I'll need. You can then commit it as necessary when an exception occurs. I reserve 16MB for each thread, and 16MB times the number of threads for the global buffer. I also need an array of thread handles; I allocate this by calling HeapAlloc(GetProcessHeap(), ...).

ls uses FormatMessage() to report all errors. Even if it is unable to load the DLL that contains the messages (WNETMSGS.DLL), it does not use a hard-coded message. In this case, it asks the system why it couldn't load it by passing GetLastError() to FormatMessage(). It displays its messages by calling WriteFile(GetStdHandle(STD_OUTPUT_HANDLE), ...) or WriteFile(GetStdHandle(STD_ERROR_HANDLE), ...), rather than printf().

Here is the listing:

```
/********
*
* LS.CPP
*
* Copyright (c) 1993-1996 Ralph P. Davis, All Rights Reserved
*
* Win32 Multithreaded Implementation of LS
*
********/


/*===== Includes =====*/

#include <windows.h>
#include <stdio.h>
#include "wnetmsgs.h"     // Generated by the Message Compiler


/*===== Constants =====*/

#define LOCAL_BUFFSIZE (16384 * 1024)
```

```
/*===== Global Variables =====*/

LPSTR     lpBuffer    = NULL;
HANDLE    hMutex      = NULL;
HINSTANCE hMessageDLL = NULL;

/*===== Function Definitions =====*/

DWORD CommitBuffer(LPSTR lpBuffer)
{
   // Find out how much is committed, and commit one more
   // page
   SYSTEM_INFO SystemInfo;
   MEMORY_BASIC_INFORMATION mbi;

   if (VirtualQuery(lpBuffer, &mbi, sizeof (MEMORY_BASIC_INFORMATION))
      != sizeof (MEMORY_BASIC_INFORMATION))
      // Uh oh! lpBuffer is probably a bogus pointer
      return EXCEPTION_EXECUTE_HANDLER;

   if (mbi.State != MEM_COMMIT)
      // No memory has been committed yet,
      // start at offset zero.
      mbi.RegionSize = 0;

   // Get the system page size
   GetSystemInfo(&SystemInfo);

   if (VirtualAlloc(&lpBuffer[mbi.RegionSize], SystemInfo.dwPageSize,
         MEM_COMMIT, PAGE_READWRITE) == NULL)
      return EXCEPTION_EXECUTE_HANDLER;
   else
      return (DWORD) EXCEPTION_CONTINUE_EXECUTION;
}

DWORD WINAPI ls(LPSTR lpszFileSpec)
{
   HANDLE hSearch;
   WIN32_FIND_DATA Win32FindData;
   char  szMessage[1024];
   LPSTR lpLocalBuffer;
   DWORD dwBytes;
   DWORD dwError = NO_ERROR;
   LPSTR lpMsg;
   MEMORY_BASIC_INFORMATION mbi;
   LPSTR lpArgs[2];

   // Reserve a local buffer for this thread's output
```

```
lpLocalBuffer = (LPSTR) VirtualAlloc(NULL, LOCAL_BUFFSIZE,
                             MEM_RESERVE, PAGE_READWRITE);

if (lpLocalBuffer != NULL)
   {
   hSearch = FindFirstFile(lpszFileSpec, &Win32FindData);

   if (hSearch != INVALID_HANDLE_VALUE)
      {
      do
         {
         __try
            {
            lstrcat(lpLocalBuffer, Win32FindData.cFileName);

            // If file name has an 8.3 rendition,
            // display that too
            if (lstrlen(Win32FindData.cAlternateFileName) > 0)
               {
               lstrcat(lpLocalBuffer, " (");
               lstrcat(lpLocalBuffer,
                  Win32FindData.cAlternateFileName);
               lstrcat(lpLocalBuffer, ")");
               }
            lstrcat(lpLocalBuffer, "\n");
            }
         __except (CommitBuffer(lpLocalBuffer))
            {
            // Couldn't commit the memory
            // Whine to the user

            // The English message text is
            // "Unable to commit memory"

            // We use the low sixteen bits of
            // GetUserDefaultLangID().  These identify
            // the main language (English, French, German, etc.)
            // The high sixteen bits distinguish dialects

            FormatMessage(FORMAT_MESSAGE_FROM_HMODULE,
                          (LPCVOID) hMessageDLL,
                          MSG_CANTCOMMITMEMORY,
                          GetUserDefaultLangID() & 0x00FF,
                          szMessage,
                          sizeof (szMessage),
                          NULL);
            WriteFile(GetStdHandle(STD_ERROR_HANDLE), szMessage,
               lstrlen(szMessage), &dwBytes, NULL);
```

```
            ExitProcess(dwError = GetLastError());
            return dwError;
            }
         }
      while (FindNextFile(hSearch, &Win32FindData));
      FindClose(hSearch);
      }
   else
      {
      // We're going to include the system-generated
      // message in one of our private message
      FormatMessage(
        FORMAT_MESSAGE_ALLOCATE_BUFFER | FORMAT_MESSAGE_FROM_SYSTEM,
        NULL, dwError = GetLastError(),
        LANG_USER_DEFAULT,
        (LPSTR) &lpMsg, 0, NULL );

      // Our message string has two insert sequences
      // Its text is:
      //    Error on file spec %1!s!: %2!s!
      //
      // %1 points to the first element in lpArgs (lpArgs[0]),
      // which is the file specification that caused the failure.
      // !s! indicates that it points to a NULL-terminated string

      // %2 (lpArgs[1]) is the text of the system error message
      // for the GetLastError() code triggered by FindFirstFile()
      lpArgs[0] = lpszFileSpec;
      lpArgs[1] = lpMsg;
      FormatMessage(
         FORMAT_MESSAGE_FROM_HMODULE |
         FORMAT_MESSAGE_ARGUMENT_ARRAY,
         (LPCVOID) hMessageDLL,
         MSG_FILESPECERROR,
         GetUserDefaultLangID() & 0x00FF,
         szMessage,
         sizeof (szMessage),
         lpArgs);
      LocalFree(lpMsg);
      WriteFile(GetStdHandle(STD_ERROR_HANDLE), szMessage,
         lstrlen(szMessage), &dwBytes, NULL);
      }
   }
else
   {
   // Our message string is "Unable to allocate memory"
   FormatMessage(FORMAT_MESSAGE_FROM_HMODULE,
```

```
        (LPCVOID) hMessageDLL,
        MSG_CANTALLOCATE_MEMORY,
        GetUserDefaultLangID() & 0x00FF,
        szMessage,
        sizeof (szMessage),
        NULL);
    WriteFile(GetStdHandle(STD_ERROR_HANDLE), szMessage,
        lstrlen(szMessage), &dwBytes, NULL);
    }

if (lpLocalBuffer != NULL)
    {
    // See if we've committed memory
    // If no memory is committed, we've got
    // nothing to report
    VirtualQuery(lpLocalBuffer, &mbi,
        sizeof (MEMORY_BASIC_INFORMATION));

    if (mbi.State == MEM_COMMIT && mbi.RegionSize > 0)
        {
        // Grab the mutex
        WaitForSingleObject(hMutex, INFINITE);

        __try
            {
            __try
                {
                lstrcat(lpBuffer, lpLocalBuffer);
                }
            __except (CommitBuffer(lpBuffer))
                {
                FormatMessage(FORMAT_MESSAGE_FROM_HMODULE,
                              (LPCVOID) hMessageDLL,
                              MSG_CANTCOMMITMEMORY,
                              GetUserDefaultLangID() & 0x00FF,
                              szMessage,
                              sizeof (szMessage),
                              NULL);
                WriteFile(GetStdHandle(STD_ERROR_HANDLE), szMessage,
                    lstrlen(szMessage), &dwBytes, NULL);
                leave;
                }
            }
        __finally
            {
            ReleaseMutex(hMutex);
```

```
            // Decommit what we've committed
            VirtualFree(lpLocalBuffer, mbi.RegionSize, MEM_DECOMMIT);
            }
         }
      VirtualFree(lpLocalBuffer, 0, MEM_RELEASE);
      }

   ExitThread(dwError);

   // Humor the compiler
   return dwError;
}


VOID main(int argc, char *argv[])
{
   int      nThreads;
   LPHANDLE lpThreadHandles;
   DWORD    dwThreadID;
   int      i;
   MEMORY_BASIC_INFORMATION mbi;
   DWORD    dwBytes;
   char     szMessage[1024];

   if (argc > 1)
      nThreads = argc - 1;
   else
      nThreads = 1;

   // Load our messages (they're in WNETMSGS.DLL)
   hMessageDLL = LoadLibrary("WNETMSGS.DLL");
   if (hMessageDLL == NULL)
      {
      lstrcpy(szMessage, "\nWNETMSGS.DLL: ");
      FormatMessage(
        FORMAT_MESSAGE_FROM_SYSTEM,
        NULL, GetLastError(),
        LANG_USER_DEFAULT,
        &szMessage[lstrlen(szMessage)],
        sizeof (szMessage) - lstrlen(szMessage),
        NULL );
      WriteFile(GetStdHandle(STD_ERROR_HANDLE), szMessage,
         lstrlen(szMessage), &dwBytes, NULL);
      ExitProcess(GetLastError());
      }

   // Get a little bit of heap memory for the
   // array of thread handles
```

```
lpThreadHandles = (LPHANDLE)
   HeapAlloc(GetProcessHeap(),
      HEAP_ZERO_MEMORY,
      nThreads * sizeof (HANDLE));

if (lpThreadHandles == NULL)
   {
   // Our message is "Unable to allocate memory"
   FormatMessage(FORMAT_MESSAGE_FROM_HMODULE,
      (LPCVOID) hMessageDLL,
      MSG_CANTALLOCATE_MEMORY,
      GetUserDefaultLangID() & 0x00FF,
      szMessage,
      sizeof (szMessage),
      NULL);
   WriteFile(GetStdHandle(STD_ERROR_HANDLE), szMessage,
      lstrlen(szMessage), &dwBytes, NULL);
   ExitProcess(GetLastError());
   }

// Reserve enough memory for all our threads to use
// the global buffer
lpBuffer = (LPSTR) VirtualAlloc(NULL,
                     nThreads * LOCAL_BUFFSIZE,
                     MEM_RESERVE, PAGE_READWRITE);


__try
   {
   // Create an unnamed mutex
   hMutex = CreateMutex(NULL, FALSE, NULL);
   for (i = 0; i < nThreads; ++i)
      {
      // Note that we can use the forward slash for a file
      // name component.  Do you know anyone who likes
      // backslashes better?
      if (argc == 1)
         lpThreadHandles[0] = CreateThread(NULL, 0,
            (LPTHREAD_START_ROUTINE) ls, "./*.*", 0, &dwThreadID);
      else
         lpThreadHandles[i] = CreateThread(NULL, 0,
            (LPTHREAD_START_ROUTINE) ls, argv[i + 1], 0,
            &dwThreadID);
      }

   // Wait for all the threads to terminate
   // Third argument (bWaitAll) is TRUE
   WaitForMultipleObjects(nThreads, lpThreadHandles, TRUE, INFINITE);
```

```
        // See if any memory has been committed
        // If not, we don't have anything to report
        VirtualQuery(lpBuffer, &mbi, sizeof (MEMORY_BASIC_INFORMATION));

        if (mbi.State == MEM_COMMIT && mbi.RegionSize > 0)
           {
           WriteFile(GetStdHandle(STD_OUTPUT_HANDLE), lpBuffer,
              lstrlen(lpBuffer), &dwBytes, NULL);
           VirtualFree(lpBuffer, mbi.RegionSize, MEM_DECOMMIT);
           }
        }
   __finally
        {
        HeapFree(GetProcessHeap(), 0, lpThreadHandles);

        if (lpBuffer != NULL)
           VirtualFree(lpBuffer, 0, MEM_RELEASE);

        if (hMutex != NULL)
           CloseHandle(hMutex);
        FreeLibrary(hMessageDLL);
        }
   ExitProcess(GetLastError());
}
```

The next two listings are the header file WNETMSGS.H that was generated by the Message Compiler, and the message file from which it was produced (\WIN32NET\CODE\WNETMSGS.MC).

```
/********
*
* WNETMSGS.H
*
* Messages for WNet Modules that use the Message Compiler
*
*********/
//
//  Values are 32 bit values layed out as follows:
//
//   3 3 2 2 2 2 2 2 2 2 2 2 1 1 1 1 1 1 1 1 1 1
//   1 0 9 8 7 6 5 4 3 2 1 0 9 8 7 6 5 4 3 2 1 0 9 8 7 6 5 4 3 2 1 0
//  +---+-+-+-----------------------+-----------------------+
//  |Sev|C|R|     Facility          |          Code         |
//  +---+-+-+-----------------------+-----------------------+
//
//  where
//
```

```
//      Sev - is the severity code
//
//          00 - Success
//          01 - Informational
//          10 - Warning
//          11 - Error
//
//      C - is the Customer code flag
//
//      R - is a reserved bit
//
//      Facility - is the facility code
//
//      Code - is the facility's status code
//
//
// Define the facility codes
//


//
// Define the severity codes
//
#define STATUS_SEVERITY_WARNING          0x2
#define STATUS_SEVERITY_SUCCESS          0x0
#define STATUS_SEVERITY_INFORMATIONAL    0x1
#define STATUS_SEVERITY_ERROR            0x3


//
// MessageId: MSG_FILESPECERROR
//
// MessageText:
//
//  Error on file specification %1!s!: %2!s!
//
#define MSG_FILESPECERROR                0xA0000001L

//
// MessageId: MSG_CANTCOMMITMEMORY
//
// MessageText:
//
//  Unable to commit memory
//
#define MSG_CANTCOMMITMEMORY             0xE0000002L

//
```

```
// MessageId: MSG_CANTALLOCATE_MEMORY
//
// MessageText:
//
//  Unable to allocate memory
//
#define MSG_CANTALLOCATE_MEMORY          0xE0000003L

//
// MessageId: MSG_RPC_SERVER_FAILED
//
// MessageText:
//
//  %1!s! failed. %2!s!
//
#define MSG_RPC_SERVER_FAILED            0xE0000004L

;/********
;*
;* WNETMSGS.MC
;*
;* Messages for WNet Modules that use the Message Compiler
;*
;*********/

SeverityNames=(Success=0x0:STATUS_SEVERITY_SUCCESS
               Informational=0x1:STATUS_SEVERITY_INFORMATIONAL
               Warning=0x2:STATUS_SEVERITY_WARNING
               Error=0x3:STATUS_SEVERITY_ERROR
              )

LanguageNames=(English=0x0009:MSG00001
              French=0x000c:MSG00002
              Spanish=0x000a:MSG00003
              )

MessageId=
Severity=Warning
SymbolicName=MSG_FILESPECERROR
Language=English
Error on file specification %1!s!: %2!s!
.
Language=French
Erreur sur spécification de fichier %1!s!: %2!s!
.
Language=Spanish
Error sobre la especificación de archivo %1!s!: %2!s!
.
```

```
MessageID=
Severity=Error
SymbolicName=MSG_CANTCOMMITMEMORY
Language=English
Unable to commit memory
.
Language=French
Incapable engager à la mémoire
.
Language=Spanish
Incapaz de comprometer memoria
.

MessageID=
Severity=Error
SymbolicName=MSG_CANTALLOCATE_MEMORY
Language=English
Unable to allocate memory
.
Language=French
Incapable allouer la mémoire
.
Language=Spanish
Incapaz de destinar memoria
.

MessageID=
Severity=Error
SymbolicName=MSG_RPC_SERVER_FAILED
Language=English
%1!s! failed. %2!s!
.
Language=French
%1!s! a manqué. %2!s!
.
Language=Spanish
%1!s! fracasó. %2!s!
.
```

Conclusion

Win32 provides a complete set of file I/O APIs to support the capabilities of Windows NT and Windows 95, and of the NT file system in particular. This API set is implicitly a network API because the functions can be used to access files on other machines. Later, you will see that the Named Pipes and Mailslots API is built on top of the file I/O API, since Named Pipes and

Mailslots are NT file systems. You will also see how Windows Sockets uses features of Win32 files, most importantly overlapped I/O. Win32 provides a number of advanced capabilities, including:

- Support for 64-bit file sizes
- Asynchronous, or overlapped, I/O
- Security restrictions on NTFS files

Overlapped I/O is an important and pervasive technique that generally yields the best I/O throughput. There are three ways of doing overlapped I/O:

- Standard overlapped I/O using events
- I/O completion routines with ReadFileEx() and WriteFileEx()
- I/O completion ports with ReadFile() and WriteFile()

The Microsoft Foundation Classes support the basic Win32 file I/O set with the CFile class. This class, however, has no support for overlapped I/O in any of its flavors. It is necessary to extend the MFC class hierarchy in order to provide an object-oriented interface for these advanced and important capabilities.

Suggested Readings

Online References

File Systems Overview in the Win32 SDK online help.
Files Overview in the Win32 SDK online help.
"Files," in *Programming with MFC: Encyclopedia.*
Microsoft Knowledge Base for Win32 SDK articles:
"Cancelling Overlapped I/O"
"FormatMessage() Converts GetLastError() Codes"
"How to Open Volumes under Windows 95"
"Increased Performance Using FILE_FLAG_SEQUENTIAL_SCAN"
"Limit on the Number of Bytes Written Asynchronously"
"Limitations of Overlapped I/O in Windows 95"
"Long Filenames on Windows NT FAT Partitions"
"ReadFile() at EOF Changed in Windows NT 3.5"
"Types of File I/O Under Win32"
"Using NTFS Alternate Data Streams"
"Using Temporary File Can Improve Application Performance"

Print References

Custer, Helen. *Inside Windows NT.* Redmond, WA: Microsoft Press, 1992. Chapter 8.

Richter, Jeff. *Advanced Windows*. Redmond, WA: Microsoft Press, 1995. Chapter 13.

Chapter 7

Dynamic-Link Libraries in Windows NT and Windows 95

Much of the code I present in this book comprises a small set of dynamic-link libraries (DLLs). I have already mentioned one of them in Chapters 2 and 6—a C++ class library that extends the Microsoft Foundation Classes by adding Win32 capabilities neglected by MFC. In later chapters, I present another DLL that uses my class library, but exposes a C function-call interface. It offers an API for peer-to-peer communications under Windows, and hides some of the messiness of the Windows Sockets Service Registration API.

In this chapter, we'll look at the mechanics of building DLLs with Visual C++, and consider some issues involved in implementing a Win32 DLL. Also, because of the way Windows manages data in a DLL, this is a good place to look at Thread Local Storage and shared memory.

The Two Kinds of Dynamic-Link Libraries

The choice of which kind of dynamic-link library to create depends on how you want to expose the code in the DLL. An MFC extension DLL exports C++ classes; client applications can either use the objects directly or derive new classes from them. Though a C++ class library usually offers a cleaner programming interface than a conventional C function-call interface, it is not as universal. It can only be used by an application that is compiled with the same C++ compiler. The client application does not have to be an MFC application. From what I have seen, it may not have to do anything more than include AFX.H. Some of the sample programs presented in Chapter 6 use my Win32 object library, but are not themselves MFC applications.

The principal advantage of a C-language function-call interface is that it can be used by a much wider range of development tools, including high-level tools like Visual Basic that do not use C at all. A common technique, and the one that I use, is to offer a C interface through one DLL, and implement the calls by translating them into operations on C++ objects.

Building the Two Kinds of DLLs

Visual C++ makes it simple to build either kind of DLL, without having to know anything about the build procedure. Figure 7-1 shows the Visual C++ 4.X New Project Workspace screen, with the MFC AppWizard(dll) project type selected. This generates an MFC extension DLL. Figure 7-2 shows the same screen, with a conventional DLL selected.

When you create an MFC extension DLL, Visual C++ generates several source files for you. For a standard DLL, it only generates the project files. You can add source files to the project as you create them by clicking on the right mouse button.

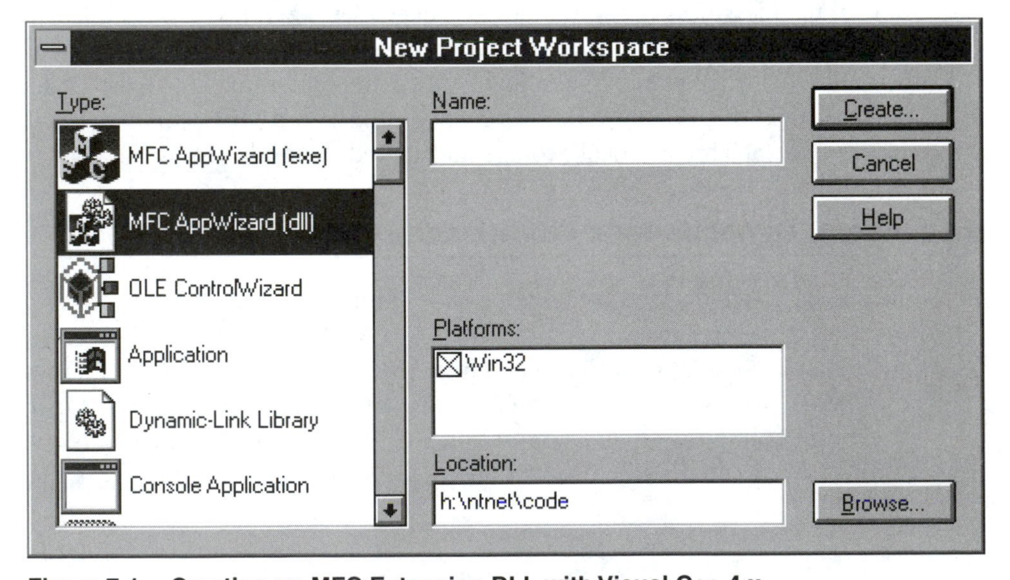

Figure 7-1. Creating an MFC Extension DLL with Visual C++ 4.x

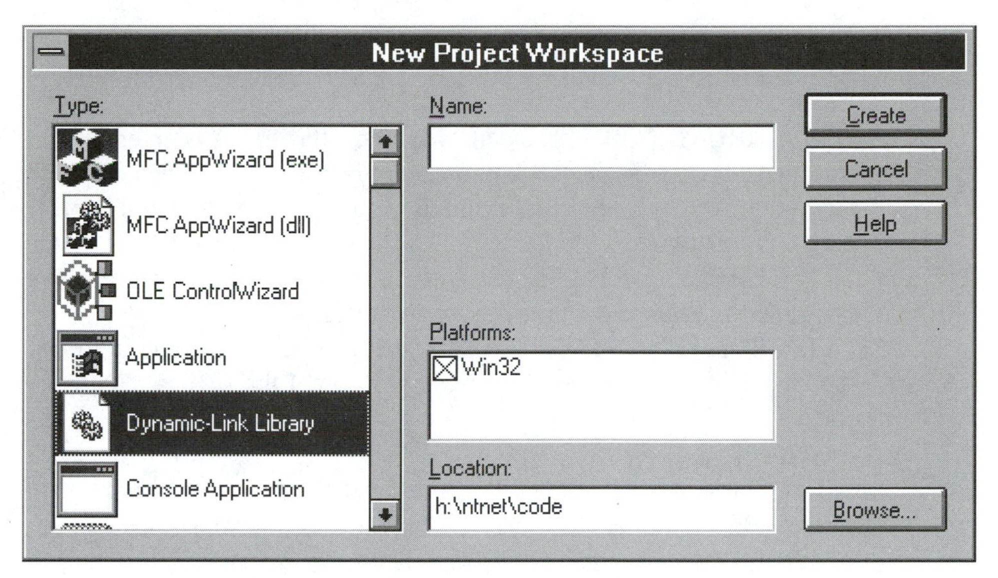

Figure 7-2. Creating a Standard DLL with Visual C++ 4.x

The DLL Entry Point

The **DLL entry point** is the function that Windows calls to initialize and shut down the DLL. If your DLL has no special initialization or termination sequence, you do not have to provide an entry-point function. You can call the function anything you want, but the preferred name is DllMain(). Using this name buys you automatic initialization of the C runtime library on behalf of your DLL. It is also required for MFC extension DLLs—in fact, Visual C++ generates a DLLMain() function when it creates a new project.

In the Win32 environment, the entry-point function is called on several occasions. For this reason, one of the arguments that Windows passes to the function is a code indicating why it is being called. Here is the complete prototype:

```
BOOL DllEntryPoint(
        HINSTANCE hDll,
        DWORD     dwReason,
        LPVOID    lpReserved);
```

hDll is the module or instance handle for the DLL. Like the instance handle of a standard executable, it is the base virtual address where Windows maps the DLL. You will need it if you have resources to pull from the DLL (like dialog boxes or message strings). *dwReason* is the most important argument and may well be the only one you ever look at. It can take on one of the following values, to let the DLL know why it is being called:

- DLL_PROCESS_ATTACH says that a new client application is loading the DLL, either automatically at load time or by an explicit call to LoadLibrary() or LoadLibraryEx().
- DLL_THREAD_ATTACH means that a new thread has been created in an attached process. The DLL entry point is not called on behalf of the startup thread of an application; the DLL_PROCESS_ATTACH notification is considered sufficient.
- DLL_THREAD_DETACH means that a thread in an attached process has called ExitThread(), either explicitly or implicitly.
- DLL_PROCESS_DETACH indicates that a process is detaching from the DLL, by calling either ExitProcess() or FreeLibrary().

Exporting Symbols from a DLL

To export symbols from a Win32 DLL, you can use the Microsoft storage-class modifiers. These use the *__declspec* keyword, followed by *dllexport*. You can export any globally visible symbol—functions, C++ classes, even data items. Here are several examples:

```
// C++ class
class __declspec(dllexport) CMyClass : public CYourClass
{
};

// C function
extern "C" __declspec(dllexport) MyCFunction()
{
}

// Data item
__declspec(dllexport) int nWindows = 0;
```

There are several things to notice here. First, adding *__declspec(dllexport)* to the class declaration, as I have done here, exports every public symbol in the class. You can also export individual members of the class by tagging them with *__declspec(dllimport)*. Second, to make sure that C functions get exported as is (that is, without name-mangling in the C++ fashion), you have to add *extern "C"* to the function declaration. You can also force all functions declared in a header file to have C names by placing these lines at the top of the header file:

```
#ifdef __cplusplus
extern "C"
{
#endif
```

At the bottom of the file, add:

```
#ifdef __cplusplus
}
#endif
```

You'll see these lines in many of the Windows header files themselves.

In the header file that publishes your interface, the exported items should be declared with the *dllimport* storage-class modifier. This optimizes the loading of the symbols from the DLL. It also causes a slight problem, because typically you will also include this header file in the source file where you implement the object. The compiler will issue this warning:

```
warning C4273: 'MyCFunction' : inconsistent dll linkage.  dllexport assumed.
```

This is a harmless condition, but it can be irritating. There are two ways to deal with this problem. One is to define a constant that takes on the value *__declspec(dllexport)* in your implementation file, and *__declspec(dllimport)* everywhere else. In an MFC extension DLL, for instance, you can use AFX_EXT_CLASS—it's predefined by MFC for exactly that purpose. Another way is just to tell the compiler to shut up by adding this *#pragma()* to a central header file:

```
#pragma warning(disable:4273)
```

Data in a DLL

By default, every process that uses a DLL gets its own private copy of the DLL's data. This means, for instance, that global variables declared in the DLL will contain different values for each client application. You can override this behavior by using a module definition (.DEF) file and adding a SECTIONS statement. To add the .DEF file to a Visual C++ project, select the *File...* item on the *Insert* menu, then select the .DEF file. Visual C++ will add all the necessary commands to the build procedure.

To declare that all initialized and uninitialized data is to be shared, add the following lines to the .DEF file:

```
SECTIONS
   .DATA   READ WRITE SHARED       ; Share initialized data
   .BSS    READ WRITE SHARED       ; Share uninitialized data
```

You can also share specific data items by putting them into named data segments. You name a segment using the *data_seg #pragma*. Section names must begin with a period and contain no more than eight characters. Here, the variable *nWindows* is assigned to the .MYDATA segment:

```
#pragma data_seg(".MYDATA")
int nWindows = 0;
#pragma data_seg()
```

The declaration of *nWindows* must initialize it. Otherwise, the compiler puts it in the .BSS segment. You also need to add this SECTIONS statement to the .DEF file:

```
SECTIONS
   .MYDATA READ WRITE SHARED    ; Share .MYDATA segment
```

Normally, it is highly desirable for every process to have its own private copy of global data. Otherwise, each process using a DLL is subject to having the DLL's supporting data corrupted by a wayward sister. Also, there are some types of data that are process-specific, even if you make them visible across many processes. Window handles and handles to GDI objects fall into this category.

There is a serious limitation with *#pragma data_seg()*. Windows will try to load the named data section at the same address in every process using the DLL. If it cannot, it will load it at the next available address, and the data item will not be shared. What's worse, this will be done quietly and behind the scenes. You get no warning, no error code, no exceptions—data items you thought would be shared aren't shared, and that's it. So when you need to share DLL data among client processes, the most powerful, reliable, and flexible way to do so is with shared memory, which I address a bit later in this chapter.

Thread-Specific Data

Because Windows gives every process that uses a DLL its own copy of the DLL's static data, no effort is required to get process-specific data. There are two places where some programming effort is required, both having to do with changing this default behavior:

- When you want global data to be shared among processes
- When you want data to be private to each thread in a client process, not just to each process

Shared memory gives you the first. For the second, Windows provides the Thread Local Storage API, a small group of functions that lets you pigeonhole data on a thread-specific basis. Thread Local Storage (TLS) is similar to extra bytes in a window structure because it gives you a convenient place to tuck data for later retrieval.

Syntax of the Thread Local Storage API

Syntactically, the TLS API is simple. TlsAlloc() generates a new TLS index, which can be thought of as a set of lockers, one for every thread that the process creates.

```
DWORD TlsAlloc(VOID);
```

Each process can allocate at least 64 (TLS_MINIMUM_AVAILABLE) TLS indexes, and every thread can use them all, so many levels of thread-specific storage are available. Once you have a TLS index, you use TlsSetValue() to save thread-specific data for the calling thread.

```
BOOL TlsSetValue(DWORD dwTlsIndex, LPVOID lpTlsValue);
```

No argument indicating which thread owns the data is needed; Windows keeps track of each thread's pigeonholes for you.

TlsGetValue() retrieves the data you have stored for the current thread.

```
LPVOID TlsGetValue(DWORD dwTlsIndex);
```

Finally, when you are finished with a TLS index, you free it by passing it to TlsFree().

```
BOOL TlsFree(DWORD dwTlsIndex);
```

Using Thread Local Storage in DLLs

You can use the TLS functions anywhere you need to store information on a per-thread basis. They are not restricted to DLLs, though that is a very important usage of them. In DLLs, the TLS functions are typically used as follows:

1. When the DLL entry point gets a DLL_PROCESS_ATTACH notification, it calls TlsAlloc() to obtain as many Thread Local Storage indexes as it needs for the new process. It can store them in global variables, since every attaching process gets its own copy of the global variables in a DLL. It also calls TlsSetValue() to store any thread-specific data for the initial thread of the process.
2. When the DLL entry point gets a DLL_THREAD_ATTACH message, it calls TlsSetValue() to store data on behalf of the new thread. This data will not destroy the data the DLL has stored for any other threads.
3. When a function in the DLL is called, it can call TlsGetValue() to retrieve any information belonging to the current thread.
4. When the DLL entry point gets a DLL_THREAD_DETACH notification, it can call TlsGetValue() to retrieve the thread-specific data it has previously stored. If it allocated memory and stored a pointer, this is the time to free the memory.
5. When the DLL receives a DLL_PROCESS_DETACH notification, it calls TlsFree() to free the TLS indexes it originally allocated.

Using Storage-Class Modifiers to Obtain Thread-Specific Data

You can also declare variables to be per-thread variables using the thread storage-class modifier. Here's how you would declare a thread-specific variable *nWindows:*

```
__declspec (thread) int nWindows;
```

The declaration must be exactly as it appears above and can be applied only to global and static variables. Automatic (stack-based) variables are always thread-specific.

There is a major problem with *__declspec(thread)* variables in dynamic-link libraries. If a client application loads your DLL by calling LoadLibrary() or LoadLibraryEx(), the application will suffer an access violation the first time you access any such data item. That's too bad, because:

- Loading DLLs with LoadLibrary() is a perfectly reasonable thing to do.
- You cannot detect how your DLL has been loaded.
- You cannot prevent your DLL from being loaded by LoadLibrary().

The conclusion is inescapable: don't use *__declspec(thread)* in dynamic-link libraries.

Memory-Mapped File I/O

The Win32 API provides a set of functions for mapping files to memory addresses. This API provides three services:

- It allows a program to view file I/O as simple memory accesses and relieves it from doing seeks, reads, and writes on the file.
- It allows two processes to share disk files.
- It allows two processes to share memory.

Because data in a DLL is private to each attached process, DLLs are one place where shared memory becomes very important.

Using the Memory-Mapping API

Mapping a view of a file is a three-step process:

1. Open the file by calling CreateFile(). It is strongly recommended that you open it for exclusive access. Otherwise, other processes can manipulate the file using standard I/O calls. The result will be that your view of the file will not reflect any changes those processes make, nor will their image of the file reflect your changes. If you are creating a shared memory region, you do not need to call CreateFile(); you will use file handle INVALID_HANDLE_VALUE (–1) in Step 2 instead.
2. Obtain a handle for a file mapping by calling CreateFileMapping(), passing the file handle you obtained in Step 1.
3. Obtain a memory address to access the file by calling MapViewOfFile().

When you are creating a shared-memory region to use in a DLL, a good place to do this is during your DLL_PROCESS_ATTACH handling.

Syntax of Memory-Mapping Functions

Here's what CreateFileMapping() looks like:

```
HANDLE CreateFileMapping(
         HANDLE  hFile,
         LPSECURITY_ATTRIBUTES lpSecurityAttributes,
         DWORD   dwProtection,
         DWORD   dwMaximumSizeHigh,
         DWORD   dwMaximumSizeLow,
         LPCTSTR lpName);
```

hFile is the handle returned by CreateFile(), or INVALID_HANDLE_VALUE if you are allocating shared memory. *dwProtection* specifies the access to the memory and uses the same constants as VirtualAlloc(), discussed in Chapter 3. Normally you will pass either PAGE_READWRITE or PAGE_READONLY. PAGE_READONLY makes little sense with shared memory, but can be used to set up a read-only view of a file. Another interesting usage with disk files is to pass *dwProtection* as PAGE_WRITECOPY, then request FILE_MAP_COPY access in the call to MapViewOfFile(). This initializes the memory from the contents of the file; however, if you write to the memory, it creates a new copy of the memory region that is not linked to the file. In this manner, you can prevent the underlying file from being altered. This is useful, for instance, with debugger applications, which may need to write breakpoints into the code. When Windows loads an executable file, it maps a view of it into your virtual address space. If it were not loaded for PAGE_WRITECOPY access, then all instances of the processes, and the file itself, would be affected by the activity of the debugger. As it is, when the debugger alters the original contents of the executable, Windows makes a new copy of it that is divorced from the underlying .EXE file.

dwProtection must be consistent with the file access specified in the call to CreateFile(). You cannot open a file for GENERIC_READ access and then map a PAGE_READWRITE view. When you are allocating a shared-memory region, you can take advantage of the reserve-commit behavior discussed in Chapters 2 and 3. You do this by ORing the SEC_RESERVE flag into *dwProtection*. This tells Windows to reserve the virtual memory for the shared region, rather than commit it as it will otherwise. You then commit the memory using VirtualAlloc() in response to an EXCEPTION_ACCESS_VIOLATION. The only restriction here is that once you have committed pages, you cannot decommit them. You also don't want to release the memory by calling VirtualFree(); use the standard mechanisms for destroying a memory-mapped file, discussed a little later in this chapter.

lpSecurityAttributes specifies whether the handle can be inherited by child processes; it can also be used to restrict how other processes can access the shared memory. If either *lpSecurityAttributes* or its member field *lpSecurityDescriptor* is NULL, access to the memory is unrestricted.

dwMaximumSizeHigh and *dwMaximumSizeLow* together specify the size of the region you want to allocate. If passed as zero, they say to map a region that is the same size as the file. There are two arguments to support 64-bit file sizes. For shared memory *(hFile == INVALID_HANDLE_VALUE), dwMaximumSizeHigh* must be zero, and *dwMaximumSizeLow* must not be; a shared-memory region can be described only by a 32-bit quantity.

By the way, if you are working with a disk file and specify a non-zero value that is larger than the file's size, the file will grow to that size if you don't do anything else to change it. Suppose you have a 16,384-byte file and you want to append some data to it. You can't do this with a memory-mapped view of the file if you pass *dwMaximumSizeHigh* and *dwMaximumSizeLow* as zero; Windows will save the file with its original size. Well, you say, no problem; I'll map a 2MB view of the file. You then append 4096 bytes, close the mapped view, and close the file. At this point, how big is the file? 20,480 bytes? No, it's 2MB. What you have to do is close the mapped view of the file, call SetFilePointer() to move to what you intend to be the new end of the file, then call SetEndOfFile(). It may be easier in this case to do your file I/O using ReadFile() and WriteFile(); Windows will increase the file size as it needs to.

lpName is the name you want to assign to the mapping object. The name is needed only to share the view among processes; other processes can pass it to OpenFileMapping() to obtain their own handles. As you saw with synchronization objects in Chapter 5, Windows does not enforce any naming constraints, but it is best to adopt some discipline to prevent accidental name-space collisions. I use the names /SHARED_MEM/<app signature>/<rest of name> for shared memory and /FILE_MAP/<app signature>/<rest of name> for memory-mapped files.

Unlike CreateFile() (but like the other object-creation functions discussed in Chapter 5), CreateFileMapping() returns NULL if it fails. If the object has already been created, CreateFileMapping() still succeeds. You can detect this by calling GetLastError() and checking to see if it returns ERROR_ALREADY_EXISTS. This is how you will normally use CreateFileMapping() when you set up shared memory in a DLL. As each new process loads your DLL, you call CreateFileMapping() in response to DLL_PROCESS_ATTACH notification. The first call creates the shared memory; all subsequent calls open a new HANDLE to it. Windows does not destroy the shared memory until the last HANDLE is closed.

OpenFileMapping() has the same syntax as the other Open<object>() functions you have seen—OpenMutex() and OpenEvent().

```
HANDLE OpenFileMapping(
          DWORD   dwDesiredAccess,
          BOOL    bInheritHandle,
          LPCTSTR lpName);
```

OpenFileMapping() is useful if you need a handle to a memory-mapped view of a file created by someone else. It succeeds even if *lpName* designates a view of a disk file that was opened for exclusive access, provided you have been granted the access you request. This is also the only way you can share the file because you do not need to call CreateFile(). If someone has opened the file for exclusive access, CreateFile() will fail.

dwDesiredAccess can be FILE_MAP_READ, FILE_MAP_WRITE, FILE_MAP_COPY, or FILE_MAP_ALL_ACCESS (which is equivalent to FILE_MAP_WRITE). The access requested must be consistent with that given the file-mapping object by the creating thread. If CreateFileMapping() specified PAGE_READWRITE, then FILE_MAP_READ and FILE_MAP_WRITE are fine, but FILE_MAP_COPY is not. (Incidentally, FILE_MAP_WRITE is understood to imply FILE_MAP_READ; you do not have to specify FILE_MAP_READ | FILE_MAP_WRITE.) If you called CreateFileMapping() and asked for PAGE_WRITECOPY protection, then FILE_MAP_COPY is the only argument you can pass to OpenFileMapping().

Once you have obtained a handle from CreateFileMapping() or OpenFileMapping(), you call MapViewOfFile() to convert it to a pointer. Here's the prototype:

```
LPVOID MapViewOfFile(
          HANDLE hFileMapping,
          DWORD  dwDesiredAccess,
          DWORD  dwFileOffsetHigh,
          DWORD  dwFileOffsetLow,
          DWORD  dwBytesToMap);
```

hFileMapping is the handle returned by CreateFileMapping() or OpenFileMapping(). As with OpenFileMapping(), *dwDesiredAccess* can be FILE_MAP_READ, FILE_MAP_WRITE, FILE_MAP_COPY, or FILE_MAP_ALL_ACCESS. Again, it must be consistent with the access previously requested.

dwOffsetLow and *dwOffsetHigh* specify the offset into the file where mapping is to begin, and *dwBytesToMap* states how many bytes to include in the mapping. A value of zero says to include the entire file. Although file sizes can be 64 bits, memory pointers cannot; for this reason, you cannot map more than a DWORD's worth of bytes at once. For shared memory, *dwOffsetLow, dwOffsetHigh,* and *dwBytesToMap* are irrelevant and should be passed as zero.

There is another version of MapViewOfFile(), MapViewOfFileEx(), which adds an argument requesting a specific base address for the region. However, unless you have a good reason for wanting a certain address, you should content yourself with MapViewOfFile(). If the address is not available, MapViewOfFileEx() does not search for one that is; it just returns NULL.

You can access the mapped region through the pointers you obtain from MapViewOfFile() or MapViewOfFileEx(). No automatic synchronization is provided, however. To coordinate reads and writes to the area, you must use one of the synchronization objects discussed in Chapter 5.

Cleaning up is also a three-step process. Typically, a DLL does this during DLL_PROCESS_DETACH handling. To clean up a memory-mapped file:

1. Call UnmapViewOfFile() to disconnect from the shared memory. This also writes dirty buffers to a memory-mapped disk file.
2. Call CloseHandle() with the handle of the file mapping object. If you are closing the last instance, Windows destroys the mapped view.
3. If you are viewing a disk file, call CloseHandle() with the file handle.

UnmapViewOfFile() requires only one argument—the pointer returned by MapViewOfFile().

```
BOOL UnmapViewOfFile(LPVOID lpBaseAddress);
```

You can also call FlushViewOfFile() from time to time to force dirty buffers to be written:

```
BOOL FlushViewOfFile(
        LPVOID lpBaseAddress,
        DWORD  dwBytesToFlush);
```

FlushViewOfFile() writes *dwBytesToFlush* bytes to the associated file, starting at the address *lpBaseAddress*.

C++ and MFC Considerations

We have seen that Visual C++ generates dynamic-link library projects. Beyond this, there are no classes for any of the Win32 object types I have discussed here—Thread Local Storage and memory-mapped files. These are powerful tools, and C++ can simplify your use of them. For this reason, I have added three more classes to my Win32 object library:

- CTlsSlot, which represents a single TLS index
- CMappedFile, which wraps both memory-mapped files and shared memory
- CSharedMemory, derived from CMappedFile to simplify the use of CMappedFile in creating shared memory

The source code for these classes is in the \WIN32NET\CODE\WIN32OBJ directory, in the files TLS.H, TLS.CPP, and MAPFILE.H. There is no MAPFILE.CPP, because I implement the last two classes as C++ template classes. Their implementation must be defined in the class header file.

CTlsSlot

The Thread Local Storage API is already very simple. In designing a C++ class to represent it, I had to be careful not to make the interface more complicated. Accordingly, the CTlsSlot has only one member variable—*m_dwTLSIndex*, which stores the Thread Local Storage index—and a few methods:

- The constructor CTlsSlot(), which calls :TlsAlloc() to initialize *m_dwTLSIndex*.
- An operator=() method, which calls ::TlsSetValue(). This allows you to tuck data behind the TLS index by saying:

```
CTlsSlot MyTlsSlot;
char *p = new char[256];

MyTlsSlot = (LPVOID) p;
```

- An LPVOID operator, which calls ::TlsGetValue() to retrieve the data stored. Here's how you would use it:

```
char *p = (char *) (LPVOID) MyTlsSlot;
```

- The destructor ~CTlsSlot(), which calls :TlsFree() to release *m_dwTLSIndex*.

Because the constructor and destructor create and destroy the TLS slot, you can get a global TLS index in a DLL by declaring a CTlsSlot object (instead of a DWORD TLS index) as a global variable.

The source code for this class is in \WIN32NET\CODE\WIN32OBJ\TLS.H and TLS.CPP, which I list here.

```
/********
*
* TLS.H
*
* Copyright (c) 1995-1996 Ralph P. Davis
*
* All Rights Reserved
*
*****/

#ifndef TLS_INCLUDED
#define TLS_INCLUDED
```

```
extern CWinApp *g_pMyApp;

class AFX_EXT_CLASS CTlsSlot
{
protected:
   DWORD m_dwTLSIndex;
public:
   CTlsSlot();
   virtual ~CTlsSlot();
   CTlsSlot& operator=(LPVOID lp);
   operator LPVOID() const;
};
#endif

/********
*
* TLS.CPP
*
* Copyright (c) 1995-1996 Ralph P. Davis
*
* All Rights Reserved
*
*****/

#include "stdafx.h"
#include "tls.h"

CTlsSlot::CTlsSlot()
{
   m_dwTLSIndex = ::TlsAlloc();

   if (m_dwTLSIndex == (DWORD) (-1))
      AfxThrowResourceException();
}

CTlsSlot::~CTlsSlot()
{
   ::TlsFree(m_dwTLSIndex);
}

CTlsSlot& CTlsSlot::operator=(LPVOID lp)
{
   ::TlsSetValue(m_dwTLSIndex, lp);
   return (*this);
}

CTlsSlot::operator LPVOID() const
{
   return ::TlsGetValue(m_dwTLSIndex);
}
```

CMappedFile

Because a memory-mapped file behaves like an array, I have made the CMappedFile class a template. I have no idea what kinds of objects the caller will want to store in the memory; by making CMappedFile a template, I allow callers to store anything they want to.

With a template class, all the code is implemented in the class's header file, and it is not exported. Client applications use the class by including the header file. It is not possible to build the code into a DLL, since the compiler cannot know how big the constituent objects are until someone using the template instantiates an object.

In designing methods for CMappedFile, I have tried to do two things:

- Provide methods that wrap the underlying SDK calls very thinly, so calling applications have the option of providing most of the intelligence themselves
- Provide methods and constructors that simplify the calling sequence as much as possible

As is always the case with C++ classes, some of the most important choices are which function arguments should be defaulted, what the default values should be, and what order the argument lists should declare them in. The arguments you are most likely to override should be first in the list. My assumption is that a caller is most likely to map a file for read-write access, using the size of the file as the size of its memory-mapped view. I also accept the limitation of not being able to support files with 64-bit file sizes. This is not unprecedented—the MFC CFile class also has this limitation.

The arguments also allow callers to use CMappedFile to set up shared memory, but because the assumptions (and defaults) are a little different in that case, I also implement a CSharedMemory class.

The thinnest level of wrapping should wrap ::CreateFileMapping(), ::OpenFileMapping(), ::MapViewOfFile(), ::UnmapViewOfFile(), and ::FlushViewOfFile(). I take care of closing the mapping handle by deriving CMappedFile from CWin32Object, which I mentioned in Chapter 6. Its Close() method will dispose of the mapping handle, and I don't need to call it explicitly; the CWin32Object destructor does so automatically.

To begin with, here is the CMappedFile class declaration:

```
template<class TYPE>
class CMappedFile : public CWin32Object
{
protected:
   HANDLE m_hFile;
```

```
    BOOL   m_bCloseOnDelete;
    TYPE  *m_lpAddress;
    DWORD  m_dwObjectsMapped;
public:
    CMappedFile();

    // Does everything
    CMappedFile(LPTSTR lpszFileName,
                LPTSTR lpszMapName = NULL,
                DWORD  dwObjects = 0,
                BOOL   bReadOnly = FALSE);
    virtual ~CMappedFile();

    // Assumes caller opens the file
    BOOL Create(DWORD  dwObjects = 0,
                HANDLE hFile = INVALID_HANDLE_VALUE,
                DWORD  dwProtection = PAGE_READWRITE,
                LPTSTR lpName = NULL,
                LPSECURITY_ATTRIBUTES lpsa = NULL);

    // Opens the file for the caller
    BOOL Create(LPTSTR lpszFileName,
                DWORD  dwObjects    = 0,
                DWORD  dwProtection = PAGE_READWRITE,
                LPTSTR lpName = NULL,
                LPSECURITY_ATTRIBUTES lpsa = NULL);

    // Assumes file-mapping object has been created
    // by a prior call to one of the Create() methods
    BOOL Map(DWORD dwAccess = FILE_MAP_WRITE,
             DWORD dwOffset = 0,
             DWORD dwObjectsToMap = 0);

    // Does everything
    BOOL Map(LPTSTR lpszFileName,
             DWORD  dwObjects = 0,
             BOOL   bReadOnly = FALSE,
             LPTSTR lpszMapName = NULL);

    // Assumes the caller has opened the file,
    // does everything else
    BOOL Map(HANDLE hFile,
             DWORD  dwObjects = 0,
             BOOL   bReadOnly = FALSE,
             LPTSTR lpszMapName = NULL);
    BOOL Open(LPTSTR lpszName,
              DWORD  dwAccess = FILE_MAP_WRITE,
              DWORD  bInherit = FALSE);
```

```
    BOOL Unmap(void);
    BOOL Flush(int nObjectIndex = 0,
               DWORD dwObjects  = 0); // Meaning all objects

    TYPE  operator[](int nIndex) const;
    TYPE& operator[](int nIndex);     // Allows assignment to
                                      // array element
    operator TYPE *() const;
};
```

Member Variables. CMappedFile has four protected data members:

- *HANDLE m_hFile*. This remembers the handle of the file associated with the memory-mapped view. If CMappedFile opens it for the caller, it also closes it.
- *BOOL m_bCloseOnDelete*. This keeps track of whether CMappedFile is responsible for closing the file handle. The assumption is that if CMappedFile opens the file, it must also close it.
- *TYPE *m_lpAddress*. This is the virtual address of the memory-mapped region. CMappedFile does not return this to the caller except in response to the *operator TYPE *()* method.
- *DWORD m_dwObjectsMapped*. This is the logical size of the memory-mapped view, in terms of the objects the caller is storing in it. It is converted to the byte size of the region by multiplying it by *sizeof(TYPE)*.

CreateFileMapping(). To wrap CreateFileMapping(), CMappedFile implements a very basic Create() method, which assumes that the caller has already opened the file (or is using shared memory). Here's its prototype again:

```
BOOL Create(DWORD  dwObjects = 0,
            HANDLE hFile = INVALID_HANDLE_VALUE,
            DWORD  dwProtection = PAGE_READWRITE,
            LPTSTR lpName = NULL,
            LPSECURITY_ATTRIBUTES lpsa = NULL);
```

Because the caller is setting up an array of typed objects, the first argument, *dwObjects*, is not the byte size of the region, as expected by CreateFileMapping(), but its object count. Create() maps this to the byte size (which CreateFileMapping() requires) by multiplying it by the size of the objects contained in the array. Next, Create() calls CreateFileMapping(), and if it succeeds, remembers the HANDLE returned by calling CWin32Object::SetHandle(). Finally, it remembers the number of objects in the array in *m_dwObjectsMapped*.

```
template<class TYPE>
BOOL CMappedFile<TYPE>::Create(
                        DWORD  dwObjects /* = 0*/,
                        HANDLE hFile /* = INVALID_HANDLE_VALUE*/,
                        DWORD  dwProtection /* = PAGE_READWRITE*/,
                        LPTSTR lpName /* = NULL*/,
                        LPSECURITY_ATTRIBUTES lpsa /* = NULL*/)

{
   DWORD dwSize = dwObjects * sizeof (TYPE);

   if (hFile == INVALID_HANDLE_VALUE)
      {
      // For shared memory, size must be greater than zero.
      ASSERT(dwSize > 0);
      }

   HANDLE hMap =
            ::CreateFileMapping(hFile,
                                lpsa,
                                dwProtection,
                                0,      // Not worrying about 64-bit
                                        // file sizes
                                dwSize,
                                lpName);

   SetHandle(hMap);

   if (dwSize > 0)
      {
      m_dwObjectsMapped = dwObjects;
      }
   else
      {
      m_dwObjectsMapped =
         ::GetFileSize(hFile, NULL) / sizeof (TYPE);
      }

   return (hMap != NULL);
}
```

The next level of abstraction is to open the file for the caller. Therefore, I provide another Create() method that takes the filename instead of its HANDLE. It calls CreateFile() to open the file, then invokes the first form of the Create() method. A NULL filename is interpreted as asking for shared memory. Here's the prototype for this method:

```
BOOL Create(LPTSTR lpszFileName,
            DWORD  dwObjects    = 0,
            DWORD  dwProtection = PAGE_READWRITE,
            LPTSTR lpName = NULL,
            LPSECURITY_ATTRIBUTES lpsa = NULL);
```

I assume here that the caller wants to open the file for exclusive, non-overlapped access, and that if the file does not exist, it is okay to create it. The access mode for opening the file can be inferred from *dwProtection*: if it is PAGE_READONLY, the file should be opened for GENERIC_READ access. Otherwise, I open it for GENERIC_READ | GENERIC_WRITE access.

I also need to set the *m_bCloseOnDelete* flag to indicate that it is CMappedFile's responsibility to close the file. I do not return the HANDLE to the caller, so only CMappedFile can close the file.

```
template<class TYPE>
BOOL CMappedFile<TYPE>::Create(
                         LPTSTR lpszFileName,
                         DWORD  dwObjects /* = 0*/,
                         DWORD  dwProtection /* = PAGE_READWRITE*/,
                         LPTSTR lpName /* = NULL*/,
                         LPSECURITY_ATTRIBUTES lpsa /* = NULL*/)
{
   HANDLE hFile;

   if (lpszFileName != NULL)
      {
      DWORD  dwFileAccess;

      if (dwProtection == PAGE_READONLY)
         {
         dwFileAccess = GENERIC_READ;
         }
      else
         {
         dwFileAccess = GENERIC_READ | GENERIC_WRITE;
         }

      hFile = ::CreateFile(lpszFileName,
                           dwFileAccess,
                           0,
                           NULL,
                           OPEN_ALWAYS,
                           0,
                           NULL);
```

```
        if (hFile == INVALID_HANDLE_VALUE)
            {
            return FALSE;
            }
        m_hFile          = hFile;
        m_bCloseOnDelete = TRUE;
        }
    else
        {
        hFile = INVALID_HANDLE_VALUE;
        ASSERT(dwObjects > 0);
        }

    BOOL bRetcode;

    bRetcode = Create(dwObjects, hFile, dwProtection, lpName, lpsa);

    if (!bRetcode)
        {
        ::CloseHandle(hFile);
        }

    return bRetcode;
}
```

MapViewOfFile(). After obtaining a HANDLE to the file-mapping object, the next step is to call MapViewOfFile() to convert it to a pointer. Here I provide two levels of abstraction: the lowest level, which assumes that the caller has already invoked one of the Create() methods, and the highest level, which does everything.

The default arguments for the lowest-level Map() method request read-write access from the beginning to the end of the file. Here is its prototype:

```
BOOL Map(DWORD dwAccess = FILE_MAP_WRITE,
         DWORD dwOffset = 0,
         DWORD dwObjectsToMap = 0);
```

This method does very little: it converts the object count to a byte count, calls MapViewOfFile(), and remembers the pointer it returns in *m_lpAddress*. Here's the code:

```
template<class TYPE>
BOOL CMappedFile<TYPE>::Map(DWORD dwAccess /* = FILE_MAP_WRITE*/,
                            DWORD dwOffset /* = 0*/,
                            DWORD dwObjectsToMap /* = 0*/)
```

```
{
   ASSERT(GetHandle() != NULL);

   if (dwObjectsToMap == 0)
      {
      // Map entire region
      dwObjectsToMap = m_dwObjectsMapped;
      }

   DWORD dwBytesToMap =
      dwObjectsToMap * sizeof (TYPE);

   TYPE *lp = (TYPE *) ::MapViewOfFile(
                                 GetHandle(),
                                 dwAccess,
                                 0,    // Offset high
                                 dwOffset,
                                 dwBytesToMap);


   m_lpAddress = lp;
   return (lp != NULL);
}
```

The highest level, in contrast, does everything. This means that the caller only needs to make a single call to one of these Map() methods; it is not necessary to call Create(), then the lowest level Map() method. Here again, CMappedFile gives the caller the flexibility to pass either a file handle or a filename.

```
BOOL Map(LPTSTR lpszFileName,
         DWORD  dwObjects = 0,
         BOOL   bReadOnly = FALSE,
         LPTSTR lpszMapName = NULL);

BOOL Map(HANDLE hFile,
         DWORD  dwObjects = 0,
         BOOL   bReadOnly = FALSE,
         LPTSTR lpszMapName = NULL);
```

Both versions of Map() call the corresponding Create() method, then the low-level Map() shown earlier.

```
template<class TYPE>
BOOL CMappedFile<TYPE>::Map(LPTSTR lpszFileName,
                            DWORD  dwObjects /* = 0*/,
                            BOOL   bReadOnly /* = FALSE*/,
                            LPTSTR lpszMapName /* = NULL*/)
```

```
{
  BOOL bRetcode =
       Create(lpszFileName,
              dwObjects,
              (bReadOnly ? PAGE_READONLY : PAGE_READWRITE),
              lpszMapName);
   if (bRetcode)
      {
      bRetcode = Map((bReadOnly ? FILE_MAP_READ : FILE_MAP_WRITE));
      if (!bRetcode)
         {
         Close();
         }
      }

   return (bRetcode);
}

template<class TYPE>
BOOL CMappedFile<TYPE>::Map(
            HANDLE hFile,
            DWORD  dwObjects /* = 0*/,
            BOOL   bReadOnly /* = FALSE*/,
            LPTSTR lpszMapName /* = NULL*/)
{
   BOOL bRetcode =
       Create(dwObjects,
              hFile,
              (bReadOnly ? PAGE_READONLY : PAGE_READWRITE),
              lpszMapName);
   if (bRetcode)
      {
      bRetcode = Map((bReadOnly ? FILE_MAP_READ : FILE_MAP_WRITE));
      if (!bRetcode)
         {
         Close();
         }
      }

   return (bRetcode);
}
```

OpenFileMapping(). The OpenFileMapping() function is not as general-purpose as the other components of this API. However, if a thread or process wants a HANDLE to a memory-mapped file created by someone else, and the file was opened for exclusive access (as is recommended), OpenFileMapping() is the only way to do this.

Therefore, CMappedFile offers an Open() method whose three arguments are the same ones expected by OpenFileMapping(). Open() lets you default all but the name of the region, which is the only link to the memory-mapped view and cannot be inferred.

```
BOOL Open(LPTSTR lpszName,
          DWORD  dwAccess = FILE_MAP_WRITE,
          DWORD  bInherit = FALSE);
```

Open() also takes responsibility for converting the HANDLE into a pointer by invoking the low-level Map() method. The implementation is quite brief:

```
template<class TYPE>
BOOL CMappedFile<TYPE>::Open(LPTSTR lpszName,
                             DWORD  dwAccess /* = FILE_MAP_WRITE*/,
                             DWORD  bInherit /* = FALSE*/)
{
   ASSERT(lpszName != NULL);  // Have to supply a name

   BOOL   bRetcode = TRUE;
   HANDLE hMap     = ::OpenFileMapping(dwAccess,
                                       bInherit,
                                       lpszName);

   bRetcode = (hMap != NULL);
   if (bRetcode)
      {
      bRetcode = Map(dwAccess);
      if (!bRetcode)
         {
         ::CloseHandle(hMap);
         }
      else
         {
         SetHandle(hMap);
         }
      }
   return bRetcode;
}
```

Wrapping Everything in the Constructor. The highest level of abstraction is achieved by providing a constructor that creates a complete object:

```
CMappedFile(LPTSTR lpszFileName,
            LPTSTR lpszMapName = NULL,
            DWORD  dwObjects = 0,
            BOOL   bReadOnly = FALSE);
```

It just passes its arguments along to one of the high-level Map() methods, and throws a CResourceException if it fails.

```
template<class TYPE>
CMappedFile<TYPE>::CMappedFile(
                         LPTSTR lpszFileName,
                         LPTSTR lpszMapName /* = NULL*/,
                         DWORD  dwObjects /* = 0*/,
                         BOOL   bReadOnly /* = FALSE*/)
{
   m_hFile             = INVALID_HANDLE_VALUE;
   m_bCloseOnDelete    = FALSE;
   m_dwObjectsMapped   = 0;

   if (!Map(lpszFileName,
            dwObjects,
            bReadOnly
            lpszMapName))
      {
      AfxThrowResourceException();
      }
}
```

Now, the caller can map a read-write, unnamed view of MAPFILE.H simply by saying:

```
CMappedFile<BYTE> *pMappedFile = new CMappedFile<BYTE>("MAPFILE.H");
```

UnmapViewOfFile(). The caller does not have to explicitly unmap the view of the file; the CMappedFile destructor will do so automatically if it has not already been done. However, it is nice to offer this flexibility, since a caller may want to map successive views of a disk file starting at different offsets—if the file is too big to be mapped to a single view, for instance. Therefore, CMappedFile has an Unmap() method. It does not need any arguments, since the only information it requires—the pointer to unmap—is stored in the *m_lpAddress* member variable.

```
template<class TYPE>
BOOL CMappedFile<TYPE>::Unmap()
{
   BOOL bRetcode = FALSE;
```

```
    if (m_lpAddress != NULL)
        {
        bRetcode = ::UnmapViewOfFile(m_lpAddress);
        m_lpAddress = NULL;
        }

    return bRetcode;
}
```

FlushViewOfFile(). The CMappedFile::Flush() method wraps Flush-ViewOfFile() very thinly. It expects its arguments in units of the objects stored in the array, rather than bytes. Its default parameters flush the entire region starting at byte offset zero.

```
template<class TYPE>
BOOL CMappedFile<TYPE>::Flush(int nObjectIndex /* = 0*/,
                              DWORD dwObjects  /* = 0*/)
{
   ASSERT(nObjectIndex >= 0 &&
          nObjectIndex < (int) m_dwObjectsMapped);
   ASSERT(((DWORD) nObjectIndex + dwObjects) < m_dwObjectsMapped);

   if (dwObjects == 0)
      {
      // Flush the rest of the mapped view starting
      // with nObjectIndex
      dwObjects = (m_dwObjectsMapped - ((DWORD) nObjectIndex));
      }

   DWORD dwSize = dwObjects * sizeof (TYPE);

   return ::FlushViewOfFile(&m_lpAddress[nObjectIndex],
                            dwSize);
}
```

Accessing the Data Stored in the Memory-Mapped File. CMappedFile does not return the address of the memory-mapped region to its caller. Rather, it stores it in a protected data member, *m_lpAddress*. Therefore, it must provide some way for a using application to get at the data. It does so by overriding the array subscripting operator and by implementing a operator TYPE *() method that returns the base address of the region:

```
TYPE  operator[](int nIndex) const;
TYPE& operator[](int nIndex);     // Allows assignment to
                                  // array element
operator TYPE *() const;
```

The array-subscript overrides give CMappedFile control over how callers store and retrieve data—specifically, they let CMappedFile check the array index. The reason for providing two overrides is that a TYPE& can be used on the left side of an assignment statement. (This technique, by the way, pervades the implementation of the MFC array classes.) The TYPE * operator lets the caller manipulate a pointer to the region directly—after all, the memory does belong to the calling process. Here are the implementations:

```
template<class TYPE>
TYPE CMappedFile<TYPE>::operator[](int nIndex) const
{
  ASSERT(nIndex >= 0 && nIndex < (int) m_dwObjectsMapped);

   return m_lpAddress[nIndex];
}

template<class TYPE>
TYPE& CMappedFile<TYPE>::operator[](int nIndex)
{
   ASSERT(nIndex >= 0 && nIndex < (int) m_dwObjectsMapped);

   return (TYPE&) m_lpAddress[nIndex];
}

template<class TYPE>
CMappedFile<TYPE>::operator TYPE *() const
{
   return m_lpAddress;
}
```

CSharedMemory

The CMappedFile class is sufficient to offer shared-memory support, by passing NULL filenames or file handles of INVALID_HANDLE_VALUE. However, to simplify the interface, I have derived the CSharedMemory class from CMappedFile. It doesn't offer much additional functionality—it just overrides the nondefault constructor and one of the Map() methods. (The default constructor just prints debug trace messages to announce that it has been called.)

```
template<class TYPE>
class CSharedMemory: public CMappedFile<TYPE>
{
   // Class to simplify calling syntax for CMappedFile
   // objects used for shared memory
```

```
public:
   CSharedMemory();
   CSharedMemory(DWORD  dwObjects,
                 LPTSTR lpszMapName = NULL,
                 BOOL   bReadOnly = FALSE);

   BOOL Map(DWORD  dwObjects,
            BOOL   bReadOnly = FALSE,
            LPTSTR lpszMapName = NULL);
};
```

The nondefault constructor delegates to its CMappedFile counterpart passing a NULL filename:

```
template<class TYPE>
CSharedMemory<TYPE>::CSharedMemory(
                 DWORD  dwObjects,
                 BOOL   bReadOnly   /* = FALSE*/,
                 LPTSTR lpszMapName /* = NULL*/) :
   CMappedFile<TYPE>(NULL, lpszMapName, dwObjects, bReadOnly)
{
}
```

There is no point in doing any argument-checking in the body of the function. If one of the arguments is invalid, say *dwObjects* is zero, the CMappedFile constructor will throw a CResourceException, and the body of this function will never be entered.

The CSharedMemory::Map() method is quite similar, but it does get a chance to look at the arguments.

```
BOOL CSharedMemory<TYPE>::Map(
            DWORD  dwObjects,
            BOOL   bReadOnly   /* = FALSE*/,
            LPTSTR lpszMapName /* = NULL*/)
{
   ASSERT(dwObjects > 0);

   return CMappedFile<TYPE>::Map(INVALID_HANDLE_VALUE,
                                 dwObjects,
                                 bReadOnly,
                                 lpszMapName);
}
```

The complete listing of \WIN32NET\CODE\WIN32OBJ\MAPFILE.H follows:

```
/********
*
* MAPFILE.H
*
* Copyright (c) 1995-1996 Ralph P. Davis
*
* All Rights Reserved
*
*****/

#ifndef MAPFILE_INCLUDED
#define MAPFILE_INCLUDED

#include "win32obj.h"

extern CWinApp *g_pMyApp;

template<class TYPE>
class CMappedFile : public CWin32Object
{
protected:
   HANDLE m_hFile;
   BOOL   m_bCloseOnDelete;
   TYPE  *m_lpAddress;
   DWORD  m_dwObjectsMapped;
public:
   CMappedFile();

   // Does everything
   CMappedFile(LPTSTR lpszFileName,
               LPTSTR lpszMapName = NULL,
               DWORD  dwObjects = 0,
               BOOL   bReadOnly = FALSE);
   virtual ~CMappedFile();

   // Assumes caller opens the file
   BOOL Create(DWORD  dwObjects = 0,
               HANDLE hFile = INVALID_HANDLE_VALUE,
               DWORD  dwProtection = PAGE_READWRITE,
               LPTSTR lpName = NULL,
               LPSECURITY_ATTRIBUTES lpsa = NULL);

   // Opens the file for the caller
   BOOL Create(LPTSTR lpszFileName,
               DWORD  dwObjects    = 0,
               DWORD  dwProtection = PAGE_READWRITE,
               LPTSTR lpName = NULL,
               LPSECURITY_ATTRIBUTES lpsa = NULL);
```

```
   // Assumes file-mapping object has been created
   // by a prior call to one of the Create() methods
   BOOL Map(DWORD dwAccess = FILE_MAP_WRITE,
            DWORD dwOffset = 0,
            DWORD dwObjectsToMap = 0);

   // Does everything
   BOOL Map(LPTSTR lpszFileName,
            DWORD  dwObjects = 0,
            BOOL   bReadOnly = FALSE,
            LPTSTR lpszMapName = NULL);

   // Assumes the caller has opened the file,
   // does everything else
   BOOL Map(HANDLE hFile,
            DWORD  dwObjects = 0,
            BOOL   bReadOnly = FALSE,
            LPTSTR lpszMapName = NULL);
   BOOL Open(LPTSTR lpszName,
             DWORD  dwAccess = FILE_MAP_WRITE,
             DWORD  bInherit = FALSE);

   BOOL Unmap(void);
   BOOL Flush(int nObjectIndex = 0,
              DWORD dwObjects  = 0); // Meaning all objects

   TYPE  operator[](int nIndex) const;
   TYPE& operator[](int nIndex);    // Allows assignment to
                                    // array element
   operator TYPE *() const;
};

template<class TYPE>
class CSharedMemory: public CMappedFile<TYPE>
{
   // Class to simplify calling syntax for CMappedFile
   // objects used for shared memory
public:
   CSharedMemory();
   CSharedMemory(DWORD  dwObjects,
                 BOOL   bReadOnly = FALSE,
                 LPTSTR lpszMapName = NULL);
   BOOL Map(DWORD  dwObjects,
            BOOL   bReadOnly = FALSE,
            LPTSTR lpszMapName = NULL);
};
```

```
template<class TYPE>
CMappedFile<TYPE>::CMappedFile()
{
   if (AfxGetApp() == NULL)
      {
      g_pMyApp = new CWinApp;
      }

   m_hFile          = INVALID_HANDLE_VALUE;
   m_bCloseOnDelete = FALSE;
   m_dwObjectsMapped  = 0;
}

template<class TYPE>
CMappedFile<TYPE>::CMappedFile(
                        LPTSTR lpszFileName,
                        LPTSTR lpszMapName /* = NULL*/,
                        DWORD  dwObjects /* = 0*/,
                        BOOL   bReadOnly /* = FALSE*/)
{
   m_hFile            = INVALID_HANDLE_VALUE;
   m_bCloseOnDelete   = FALSE;
   m_dwObjectsMapped  = 0;

   if (!Map(lpszFileName,
            dwObjects,
            bReadOnly,
            lpszMapName))
      {
      AfxThrowResourceException();
      }
}

template<class TYPE>
CMappedFile<TYPE>::~CMappedFile()
{
   // If m_lpAddress is not NULL, caller has not
   // unmapped the view of the file
   if (m_lpAddress != NULL)
      {
      Unmap();
      }

   // m_bCloseOnDelete is set to TRUE if
   // we open the file
   if ((m_hFile != INVALID_HANDLE_VALUE) && (m_bCloseOnDelete))
```

```
        {
        ::CloseHandle(m_hFile);
        }
}

template<class TYPE>
BOOL CMappedFile<TYPE>::Create(
                          DWORD  dwObjects /* = 0*/,
                          HANDLE hFile /* = INVALID_HANDLE_VALUE*/,
                          DWORD  dwProtection /* = PAGE_READWRITE*/,
                          LPTSTR lpName /* = NULL*/,
                          LPSECURITY_ATTRIBUTES lpsa /* = NULL*/)

{
   DWORD dwSize = dwObjects * sizeof (TYPE);

   if (hFile == INVALID_HANDLE_VALUE)
      {
      // For shared memory, size must be greater than zero.
      ASSERT(dwSize > 0);
      }

   HANDLE hMap =
            ::CreateFileMapping(hFile,
                                lpsa,
                                dwProtection,
                                0,      // Not worrying about 64-bit
                                        // file sizes
                                dwSize,
                                lpName);

   SetHandle(hMap);

   if (dwSize > 0)
      {
      m_dwObjectsMapped = dwObjects;
      }
   else
      {
      m_dwObjectsMapped =
         ::GetFileSize(hFile, NULL) / sizeof (TYPE);
      }
   return (hMap != NULL);
}

template<class TYPE>
BOOL CMappedFile<TYPE>::Create(
                          LPTSTR lpszFileName,
                          DWORD  dwObjects /* = 0*/,
```

```
                              DWORD  dwProtection /* = PAGE_READWRITE*/,
                              LPTSTR lpName /* = NULL*/,
                              LPSECURITY_ATTRIBUTES lpsa /* = NULL*/)
{
   HANDLE hFile;

   if (lpszFileName != NULL)
      {
      DWORD  dwFileAccess;

      if (dwProtection == PAGE_READONLY)
         {
         dwFileAccess = GENERIC_READ;
         }
      else
         {
         dwFileAccess = GENERIC_READ | GENERIC_WRITE;
         }

      hFile = ::CreateFile(lpszFileName,
                           dwFileAccess,
                           0,
                           NULL,
                           OPEN_ALWAYS,
                           0,
                           NULL);
      if (hFile == INVALID_HANDLE_VALUE)
         {
         return FALSE;
         }
      m_hFile          = hFile;
      m_bCloseOnDelete = TRUE;
      }
   else
      {
      hFile = INVALID_HANDLE_VALUE;
      ASSERT(dwObjects > 0);
      }

   BOOL bRetcode;

   bRetcode = Create(dwObjects, hFile, dwProtection, lpName, lpsa);

   if (!bRetcode)
      {
      ::CloseHandle(hFile);
      }
   return bRetcode;
}
```

```
template<class TYPE>
BOOL CMappedFile<TYPE>::Map(DWORD dwAccess /* = FILE_MAP_WRITE*/,
                            DWORD dwOffset /* = 0*/,
                            DWORD dwObjectsToMap /* = 0*/)
{
   ASSERT(GetHandle() != NULL);

   if (dwObjectsToMap == 0)
      {
      // Map entire region
      dwObjectsToMap = m_dwObjectsMapped;
      }

   DWORD dwBytesToMap =
      dwObjectsToMap * sizeof (TYPE);

   TYPE *lp = (TYPE *) ::MapViewOfFile(
                               GetHandle(),
                               dwAccess,
                               0,   // Offset high
                               dwOffset,
                               dwBytesToMap);
   m_lpAddress = lp;
   return (lp != NULL);
}

template<class TYPE>
BOOL CMappedFile<TYPE>::Map(LPTSTR lpszFileName,
                            DWORD  dwObjects /* = 0*/,
                            BOOL   bReadOnly /* = FALSE*/,
                            LPTSTR lpszMapName /* = NULL*/)
{
   BOOL bRetcode =
       Create(lpszFileName,
              dwObjects,
              (bReadOnly ? PAGE_READONLY : PAGE_READWRITE),
              lpszMapName);
   if (bRetcode)
      {
      bRetcode = Map((bReadOnly ? FILE_MAP_READ : FILE_MAP_WRITE));
      if (!bRetcode)
         {
         Close();
         }
      }
   return (bRetcode);
}
```

```
template<class TYPE>
BOOL CMappedFile<TYPE>::Map(
            HANDLE hFile,
            DWORD  dwObjects /* = 0*/,
            BOOL   bReadOnly /* = FALSE*/,
            LPTSTR lpszMapName /* = NULL*/)
{
   BOOL bRetcode =
       Create(dwObjects,
              hFile,
              (bReadOnly ? PAGE_READONLY : PAGE_READWRITE),
              lpszMapName);
   if (bRetcode)
      {
      bRetcode = Map((bReadOnly ? FILE_MAP_READ : FILE_MAP_WRITE));
      if (!bRetcode)
         {
         Close();
         }
      }
   return (bRetcode);
}

template<class TYPE>
BOOL CMappedFile<TYPE>::Open(LPTSTR lpszName,
                             DWORD  dwAccess /* = FILE_MAP_WRITE*/,
                             DWORD  bInherit /* = FALSE*/)
{
   ASSERT(lpszName != NULL);  // Have to supply a name

   BOOL   bRetcode = TRUE;
   HANDLE hMap     = ::OpenFileMapping(dwAccess,
                                       bInherit,
                                       lpszName);

   bRetcode = (hMap != NULL);
   if (bRetcode)
      {
      bRetcode = Map(dwAccess);
      if (!bRetcode)
         {
         ::CloseHandle(hMap);
         }
      else
         {
         SetHandle(hMap);
         }
      }
```

```
   return bRetcode;
}

template<class TYPE>
BOOL CMappedFile<TYPE>::Unmap()
{
   BOOL bRetcode = FALSE;
   if (m_lpAddress != NULL)
      {
      bRetcode = ::UnmapViewOfFile(m_lpAddress);
      m_lpAddress = NULL;
      }
   return bRetcode;
}

template<class TYPE>
BOOL CMappedFile<TYPE>::Flush(int nObjectIndex /* = 0*/,
                              DWORD dwObjects  /* = 0*/)
{
   BOOL bRetcode;

   ASSERT(nObjectIndex >= 0 &&
          nObjectIndex < (int) m_dwObjectsMapped);
   ASSERT(((DWORD) nObjectIndex + dwObjects) < m_dwObjectsMapped);

   if (dwObjects == 0)
      {
      // Flush the rest of the mapped view starting
      // with nObjectIndex
      dwObjects = (m_dwObjectsMapped - ((DWORD) nObjectIndex));
      }

   DWORD dwSize = dwObjects * sizeof (TYPE);

   bRetcode = ::FlushViewOfFile(&m_lpAddress[nObjectIndex],
                                 dwSize);
   return bRetcode;
}

template<class TYPE>
TYPE CMappedFile<TYPE>::operator[](int nIndex) const
{
   ASSERT(nIndex >= 0 && nIndex < (int) m_dwObjectsMapped);
   return m_lpAddress[nIndex];
}

template<class TYPE>
TYPE& CMappedFile<TYPE>::operator[](int nIndex)
```

```
{
   ASSERT(nIndex >= 0 && nIndex < (int) m_dwObjectsMapped);
   return (TYPE&) m_lpAddress[nIndex];
}

template<class TYPE>
CMappedFile<TYPE>::operator TYPE *() const
{
   return m_lpAddress;
}


/*========= CSharedMemory implementation =========*/

template<class TYPE>
CSharedMemory<TYPE>::CSharedMemory()
{
}

template<class TYPE>
CSharedMemory<TYPE>::CSharedMemory(
                  DWORD  dwObjects,
                  BOOL   bReadOnly /* = FALSE*/,
                  LPTSTR lpszMapName /* = NULL*/) :
   CMappedFile<TYPE>(NULL, lpszMapName, dwObjects, bReadOnly)
{
}

template<class TYPE>
BOOL CSharedMemory<TYPE>::Map(
            DWORD  dwObjects,
            BOOL   bReadOnly   /* = FALSE*/,
            LPTSTR lpszMapName /* = NULL*/)
{
   ASSERT(dwObjects > 0);

   return CMappedFile<TYPE>::Map(INVALID_HANDLE_VALUE,
                                 dwObjects,
                                 bReadOnly,
                                 lpszMapName);
}

#endif
```

Conclusion

DLLs are convenient repositories for code that you want to make generally available. With MFC, you can create DLLs that export C++ classes, or more general DLLs that offer a C function-call interface.

All data in a DLL is private to each attaching process, unless you force it to be shared. You can alter this default behavior in two ways. The Thread Local Storage API makes data even more private, by giving each thread its own slot for storing data. Memory-mapped files let you create data structures that are global to all processes that the DLL supports. Because Windows does not synchronize access to shared memory, synchronization objects become very important. Typically, a DLL creates and destroys Thread Local Storage, shared memory objects, and synchronization objects in its DllMain() function, which is called many times during the life of a DLL:

- When a new process loads the DLL (DLL_PROCESS_ATTACH)
- When an attached process creates a new thread (DLL_THREAD_ATTACH)
- When a thread in an attached process terminates (DLL_THREAD_DETACH)
- When an attached process terminates (DLL_PROCESS_DETACH)

The DLL can also declare these resources as global C++ objects. In this case, the object's constructor is called when the DLL is loaded, and the destructor when it is unloaded.

Suggested Readings

Online References

DLL Overview in the Win32 API online help.
File Mapping Overview in the Win32 API online help.
Processes and Threads Overview in the Win32 API online help (for discussion of Thread Local Storage).
"Dynamic-Link Libraries," in *Programming with MFC: Encyclopedia.*
"Thread Local Storage," in the *C/C++ Language Reference.*
"Thread Local Storage (TLS)," in *Programming Techniques.*
"Creating DLLs for Win32," in *Programming Techniques.*
Microsoft Knowledge Base for Win32 SDK articles:
"Alternatives to Using GetProcAddress() with LoadLibrary()"
"Common File Mapping Problems and Platform Differences"
"Copying Compressed Files"
"CreateFileMapping() SEC_* Flags"

"Debugging a Dynamic-Link Library (DLL) in Windows"
"Debugging DLLs Using WinDbg"
"Dynamic Loading of Win32 DLLs"
"Dynamically Loading Dynamic-Link Libraries in Windows NT"
"Exporting Data from a DLL or an Application"
"FlushViewOfFile() on Remote Files"
"How to Share Data Between Different Mappings of a DLL"
"How to Specify Shared and Nonshared Data in a DLL"
"How to Use __declspec(dllexport) in an MFC Extension DLL"
"Sharing All Data in a DLL"
"The Use of PAGE_WRITECOPY"
"Thread Local Storage Overview"
"TNO11: Using MFC as Part of a DLL"
"Why LoadLibraryEx() Returns an HINSTANCE"
"Why to Use _declspec(dllimport) & _declspec(dllexport) in Code"

Print References

Richter, Jeff. *Advanced Windows*. Redmond, WA: Microsoft Press, 1995. Chapters 7, 11, and 12.

Chapter 8

Peer-to-Peer Concepts and API Design

Horizontal applications are those that take advantage of peer-to-peer networking services. Windows offers a rich set of these services. In this chapter, I discuss the terminology and concepts of peer-to-peer communications and develop specifications for a network-independent peer-to-peer API set. The next chapter implements this API on top of Windows Sockets and the Service Registration API.

Peer-to-Peer Communications

Peer-to-peer communications are communications on an equal basis among network stations. The defining characteristic of peer-to-peer networking is that any station can play the role of either client or server. This is the situation on a Windows network, whether or not you are running NT Server. Any station can share resources with any other station. I am sitting at a Windows 95 workstation, and I logged on through an NT Server. I'm editing a file stored on a NetWare server, and my MFC 4.x DLLs reside on an NT workstation.

Peer-to-peer communications use established communications protocols so that machines know what to expect in the data stream. The protocols represent the common language that the computers understand. Each protocol has rules dictating both the format of the data units, or packets, that the stations will exchange, as well as the sequence in which packets of varying types should be expected. It is not my purpose here to present an in-depth analysis of peer-to-peer protocols. That is a highly detailed, technical subject, on which many books have already been written. Besides, well-designed peer-to-peer programming interfaces shield developers from having to know anything about the protocols that underlie them.

NT and Windows 95 provide built-in support for several major protocols, including:

- NetBEUI (short for NetBIOS Extended User Interface)
- TCP/IP (the Transmission Control Protocol/Internet Protocol)
- Microsoft's implementation of Novell's IPX/SPX (Internet Packet Exchange/Sequenced Packet Exchange)

They also support these programming interfaces:

- Named Pipes
- Windows Sockets
- NetBIOS
- Remote Procedure Calls (RPC)

To varying degrees, all of these APIs are independent of the underlying protocol.

Types of Peer-to-Peer Service

Two types of peer-to-peer service are generally recognized as being required:

- Connectionless service, also referred to as datagram service
- Connection-oriented service

Connectionless (Datagram) Service

Connectionless service is intended for single-packet exchanges of information. It is the lowest level of service, offering speed of communication while sacrificing some reliability. On local-area networks, datagram service is normally highly reliable. It is primarily when you enter a wide-area network that it becomes more chancy. Most of the connectionless protocols specify that datagram packets can be discarded at any time by any router that detects an abnormal condition. These conditions can include:

- A corrupted packet (one whose checksum does not tally correctly)
- A packet that appears to be lost (as identified by an excessively high "hop count," which keeps track of how many bridges and routers a packet has gone through)

Datagrams can be sent to more than one station at a time. A transmission to all network stations is called a **broadcast**; a transmission to a group of related stations is referred to as a **multicast**.

Two levels of connectionless service, **acknowledged** and **unacknowledged**, have been specified in the standards. Acknowledged connectionless service implements a simple request-response protocol. Packets are sent one at a time, and the receiving station is expected to acknowledge receipt of each packet; thus, delivery is guaranteed. Unfortunately, not many commercially available protocol suites (and none that ship with Windows) implement this level of service. In contrast, unacknowledged connectionless service does not guarantee delivery. A packet is placed onto the network for transmission, but the sending station has no way of knowing if it ever arrives at its destination. As I stated earlier, if a host or router along the way detects a corrupted packet or decides that the packet is lost, it quietly discards it. Also, routers can be configured to give datagrams low priority. If a router is busy, it just doesn't bother forwarding datagrams.

It is also possible that a packet A sent at time X will arrive at its destination after a packet B that goes out at some later time Y. This can happen, for instance, on a network with intelligent routers and multiple paths between stations. When packet A is first transmitted, the geographically shortest route to the destination may be overloaded, and the routers will send it over a longer circuit. Then when packet B is placed onto the network, if the congestion in the shortest circuit has cleared up, B is likely to travel that route and get to its destination before packet A. This is why connection-oriented protocols also enforce sequenced delivery of packets; if packet B is sent after packet A but before packet C, it will arrive after packet A and before packet C.

Because of its simplicity, connectionless service supports only two operations: sending a datagram and receiving a datagram.

Connection-Oriented Service

Connection-oriented service is intended for the reliable exchange of streams of data between two stations. Streams consist of multiple sequenced packets. It is guaranteed that they will be delivered, and in the same sequence in which they were transmitted. Specifically, the guarantee is that if a packet cannot be delivered, the sender will be informed. Packets are not just dropped without notification.

Connection-oriented service is always point-to-point (or, more precisely, end-to-end; on a wide-area network, what appears to be a point-to-point connection between one host machine and another may actually consist of several intermediate point-to-point connections). There are no connection-oriented broadcasts or multicasts. However, you can have multipoint connections, or conference calls. Windows Sockets 2 adds explicit API support for multipoint connections.

Like connectionless service, connection-oriented service must support send and receive operations, as the exchange of data, after all, is the whole purpose of peer-to-peer communications. In addition, there are three operations required for setting up and destroying the communications channel. **Listen** makes a server application available for clients to connect to. **Call** attempts to establish a connection from a client to a server. **Hangup** destroys a connection when it is no longer needed.

Developing a Standardized API

Since all protocols implement these same basic operations, it should be possible to code to a single peer-to-peer API, without regard for the protocols that the network supports. No such API exists under Windows, though Windows Sockets, RPC, and Named Pipes are natural candidates.

Windows Sockets

Microsoft's clear intention is to standardize on Windows Sockets as their preferred programming interface, just as they are standardizing on TCP/IP. Berkeley and Windows Sockets, though, provide what I will refer to as protocol independence—but not protocol transparency. The Sockets API is indeed the same for all underlying protocols, but you must select a protocol when you write your code. If you want to develop a Sockets application that supports more than one protocol, you must build a separate binary file for each protocol you want to support.

True protocol transparency, on the other hand, allows a single binary file to support all your target protocols by selecting a protocol based on runtime conditions. To achieve full protocol transparency with Windows Sockets, Microsoft introduced the Service Registration API with Windows NT 3.5. This allows client and server applications on a network to locate each other, and tells both types of application what arguments to pass to Windows Sockets functions. Windows Sockets 2 expands this support, and provides a much better foundation for protocol transparency.

Remote Procedure Calls (RPC)

RPC appears to be an important component of Microsoft's distributed application environment, and does offer full protocol transparency. For client-server applications that lend themselves to the remote procedure call paradigm, RPC is a very good platform. Its main deficiency is the fact that there is more than one RPC standard—but Microsoft only supports one.

Named Pipes

Named Pipes offer a very good programming interface. However, they are not widely supported outside the Windows and OS/2 environments, so they cannot provide rich internetworking capabilities. NetBIOS suffers from the same limitation, and is not a pretty API—it began its life as an assembly language interrupt call back in the early 1980s, and its roots still show through, even though Windows has moved the interface up to the C level.

Distributed OLE Objects

In the future, OLE will most likely offer protocol-transparent distributed capabilities as well. In the Win32 environment, it is implemented on top of RPC, so it should not be difficult to extend it to a fully networked environment. In order to do so, the RPC layer must be well-optimized; even locally, OLE is not especially quick.

The WNet() API

In my two previous books on distributed Windows programming, *Windows Network Programming* and *Windows NT Network Programming* (Addison-Wesley, 1993 and 1994), I centered the code around a small API set that provides a single entry point for network services. This API was offered in a level-one DLL (WNETLVL1.DLL), which then loaded level-zero DLLs for all the protocols I wanted to support (WNETTCP.DLL, WNETNW.DLL, WNETPIPE.DLL, and WNETNB.DLL).

Windows Sockets, in conjunction with the Service Registration API, now provides this capability. In the next chapter, you'll see how it does so, and I'll present some new C++ classes that wrap both APIs. To make these services available to non-C++ users, I will implement a new version of my level-one DLL, offering the same API (slightly modified). It will continue to be a C-interface DLL, but instead of loading a succession of level-zero DLLs, it will link to WIN32MFC.DLL and use the classes I present in the next chapter. In this chapter, we'll look at the design of this API set; the code appears in Chapter 9.

By the way, Windows Sockets itself uses level-one/level-zero layering. The core Sockets 1.1 DLL, WSOCK32.DLL, loads helper DLLs that support the underlying protocols when you create sockets that use them. In Windows Sockets 2, the operating system provides the level-one DLL, WS2_32.DLL. Underlying layers are provided by any protocol implementor wishing to support Windows Sockets.

Because peer-to-peer communications require only a handful of operations, an API that offers them can be quite small and uncomplicated. I have mentioned seven operations so far in this chapter: **Call, Listen, Hangup, Send, Receive, Send Datagram,** and **Receive Datagram**; these will be excellent candidates for inclusion. Because it is normally a good idea to have initialization and cleanup functions, **Init** and **Shutdown** operations should also be provided.

To translate the abstract notion of these operations into callable functions, I have borrowed Microsoft's naming convention. Windows provides a small group of functions with a WNet() prefix. They are not general-purpose by any means; even in NT, they continue to be a miscellaneous API set, useful only for mapping local drives and print devices to remote resources. However, the naming convention is catchy: I'll use the WNet() prefix followed by the name of the operation. Thus, I have a nine-function API set. These functions are shown in Table 8-1 and described in greater detail following the table.

Table 8-1. WNet() Functions

Type of Function	Function Name
Initialization/cleanup	WNetInit()
	WNetShutdown()
Connection-oriented service	WNetCall()
	WNetListen()
	WNetHangup()
	WNetSend()
	WNetReceive()
Connectionless service	WNetSendDatagram()
	WNetReceiveDatagram()

These functions constitute the core API and are contained on the disk in the Visual C++ project \WIN32NET\CODE\NEWDLLS\WNETLVL1.MDP. The C++ classes are in \WIN32NET\CODE\WIN32OBJ\WIN32MFC.MDP.

WNetInit(). An application wishing to use my API calls WNetInit() to register, then uses the remaining functions as appropriate. WNetInit() creates server-side sockets to listen for client connection requests and to receive datagrams, though it can be instructed to do client-only initialization and to omit datagrams. In my earlier books, WNetInit() expected to be passed a window handle, because all event notifications were handled by percolating window messages from the bottom layers to the top. Now, it just expects a pointer to a callback function, typed as a RECEIVECALLBACK. This simplifies the event-notification mechanism, making it leaner and more general-purpose. Here is the type definition:

```
typedef BOOL (CALLBACK *RECEIVECALLBACK)(
                              LPBYTE lpData,
                              DWORD  dwData,
                              HANDLE hConnection);
```

This function receives a pointer to the incoming data (*lpData*), the size in bytes of the data (*dwData*), and the socket over which it has arrived (*hConnection*), passed as the more abstract HANDLE type.

Here's the prototype for WNetInit():

```
BOOL WINAPI WNetInit(RECEIVECALLBACK lpReceiveCallback,
                     LPVOID          lpEndpoint,
                     LPHANDLE        lphUser,
                     BOOL            bClientOnly = FALSE,
                     BOOL            bUseDatagrams = TRUE);
```

lpEndpoint is the service name that the caller wants to register. *bClientOnly* tells WNetInit() not to do any server-side initializations. *bUseDatagrams* says whether the caller wants to receive incoming datagrams. *lphUser* returns a pointer to a C++ object representing this user of my DLL, typed as a HANDLE. This HANDLE is then passed as an argument to other functions in the API. Among other things, the object contains the sockets that have been set up on behalf of the calling application.

WNetListen(). WNetListen() puts the server into the listening state, ready to receive client connection requests. It actually has nothing to do; WNetInit() has already done everything this operation requires.

```
BOOL WINAPI WNetListen(HANDLE hUser);
```

hUser is the user handle generated by a previous call to WNetInit().

WNetCall(). WNetCall() is the client-side counterpart to WNetListen(); it tries to connect to a listening server application.

```
HANDLE WINAPI WNetCall(HANDLE hUser,
                       LPVOID lpTargetStation,
                       LPVOID lpEndpoint);
```

lpTargetStation is the machine where the server application lives, and *lpEndpoint* is the service name under which it is offering its services. The HANDLE that WNetCall() returns is the socket representing the connection to the server application; it will be passed in subsequent calls to WNetSend(), WNetReceive(), and WNetHangup().

WNetSend(). WNetSend() sends data over a connection.

```
BOOL WINAPI WNetSend(HANDLE hConnection,
                     LPVOID lpData,
                     DWORD  dwDataLength,
                     DWORD  dwTimeout = 5000);
```

hConnection represents the connection to the partner station. It is either the HANDLE returned by WNetCall(), or the one passed to the RECEIVE-CALLBACK function when data is received asynchronously. *lpData* points to the data; *dwDataLength* is its byte length. *dwTimeout* allows the caller to get bored waiting for a jammed socket to open up.

WNetReceive(). WNetReceive() receives data from a connected partner.

```
BOOL WINAPI WNetReceive(HANDLE  hConnection,
                        LPVOID  lpData,
                        DWORD   dwDataLength,
                        LPDWORD lpdwBytesRead,
                        DWORD   dwTimeout = 5000);
```

The first three arguments are the same as for WNetSend(). *lpdwBytesRead* returns the number of bytes read. *dwTimeout* is a timeout value in milliseconds, with INFINITE meaning to block forever. In addition, a timeout value of zero is interpreted as requesting a nonblocking receive.

WNetHangup(). WNetHangup() completes the suite of functions necessary to support connection-oriented communications. It closes a connection with a partner station.

```
void WINAPI WNetHangup(HANDLE hConnection);
```

WNetSendDatagram(). WNetSendDatagram() transmits a datagram to a target station or group of stations.

```
BOOL WINAPI WNetSendDatagram(HANDLE hUser,
                             LPVOID lpTargetStation,
                             LPVOID lpEndpoint,
                             LPVOID lpData,
                             DWORD  dwDataLength);
```

lpTargetStation is the name of the machine you want to send a datagram to, with a NULL pointer indicating a broadcast. *lpEndpoint* is the name of the service that the receiving application is using to accept datagrams. *lpData* and *dwDataLength* describe the data, and *hUser* is the HANDLE returned by WNetInit().

WNetReceiveDatagram(). WNetReceiveDatagram() expresses your willingness to receive datagrams. Logically, its sole purpose is to make an endpoint available for asynchronous reception of datagrams; it does not have a synchronous mode of operation. In fact, it is implemented as a no-operation; WNetInit() does this automatically if you tell it you want datagram support.

```
BOOL WINAPI WNetReceiveDatagram(HANDLE hUser,
                                LPVOID lpBuffer,
                                DWORD  dwBufferSize);
```

WNetShutdown(). The last function in this API suite is WNetShutdown(), which closes down the application's network operations. Its only argument is the user handle returned by WNetInit().

```
void WINAPI WNetShutdown(HANDLE hUser);
```

The source code for this DLL appears in the next chapter. Some sample applications that use it are presented in Chapter 16.

Conclusion

The theory and practice of peer-to-peer communications has evolved over the last 25 years into a stable and mature body of thought. A standard set of operations is widely agreed to be required; these operations lend themselves to standardization in a generic API. Such an API has been very slow in coming to Windows; with Windows Sockets, the Service Registration API, and RPC, it is probably safe to say that it has. Networking is built into the operating system, even if you do not have NT Server. Windows supports several important protocols, among them NetBEUI, TCP/IP, and Novell's IPX/SPX. On top of these protocols, Windows provides several programming interfaces: Named Pipes, Windows Sockets, NetBIOS, and RPC.

The next chapter implements the generic API specified in this chapter over Windows Sockets and the Service Registration API. With these tools, you do not need to decide at design time which protocol to use. You can use whatever protocol the stations you want to talk to have indicated they support.

Suggested Readings

Davis, Ralph. *Windows Network Programming*, Reading, MA: Addison-Wesley Publishing Company, 1993. Chapter 2.

———. *Windows NT Network Programming*, Reading, MA: Addison-Wesley Publishing Company, 1994. Chapter 9.

Stallings, William. *Handbook of Computer-Communications Standards. Volume 1: The Open Systems (OSI) Model and OSI-Related Standards*. Carmel, IN: SAMS, 1990.

———. *Handbook of Computer-Communications Standards. Volume 2: Local Area Network Standards*. Carmel, IN: SAMS, 1990.

———. *Handbook of Computer-Communications Standards. Volume 3: The TCP/IP Protocol Suite*. Carmel, IN: SAMS, 1989.

Chapter 9

Windows Sockets

The Windows Sockets API is a specification originally developed by a consortium of companies to standardize the TCP/IP programming interface under Windows. TCP (the Transmission Control Protocol) and IP (the Internet Protocol) have an established history dating back a quarter of a century. They were originally developed to support the U.S. Department of Defense's DARPA Internet. The Department of Defense has continued to play an important role in the extension of TCP and IP as the Internet has expanded to include civilian networks.

Programming Interfaces for TCP/IP

Several programming interfaces have evolved to allow applications to communicate over TCP/IP networks. The most widely used is the **Berkeley Sockets** interface, developed at the University of California (Berkeley) as one of Berkeley's extensions to the UNIX operating system. Berkeley's version of UNIX is referred to as the **Berkeley Software Distribution (BSD)**. The Windows Sockets API is based on Berkeley Sockets, BSD version 4.3.

Another more recent API is AT&T's **Transport Layer Interface (TLI)**, developed at Bell Labs as a protocol-independent interface for requesting network transport services. Though superior to Berkeley Sockets in many ways, TLI does not yet have the acceptance enjoyed by Berkeley Sockets.

However, Novell's stake in UNIX and its present emphasis on TLI could give it a significant boost.

Through Windows NT version 3.51, Microsoft has supported Windows Sockets version 1.1. Windows Sockets 2 is now a reality, and NT 4.0 implements both a Sockets 1.1 and a Sockets 2.0 layer.

Sockets and Protocol Independence

Berkeley Sockets, Windows Sockets, and TLI are protocol-independent. Nothing in these APIs necessitates the use of TCP/IP as the supporting protocol. In fact, under both NT and Windows 95, Windows Sockets serves as the programming interface to several underlying protocols, including:

- Novell's IPX/SPX protocols. Sockets are a much better API than Novell's Event Control Block (ECB) interface, which mires you in the details of the protocol.
- The NetBEUI protocol suite, where it replaces the NetBIOS programming interface, to which it is also superior.
- The AppleTalk protocol family, for communication with Macintosh machines.
- The ISO TP/4 protocol suite, which is not widely used in the U.S., but has a following in Europe.

The TCP/IP, IPX/SPX, and NetBEUI protocol layers ship with both Windows NT and Windows 95. However, as we will see in this chapter, sockets give you protocol independence, but not full protocol transparency. When you create a socket, you have to specify in your code the protocol that you want to use. From this point on, the data exchange knows nothing about the protocol. But you cannot use a single binary image with all the protocols you might want to take advantage of; you have to have a separate binary for each of them.

Portability between Berkeley and Windows Sockets

One of the original goals of Windows Sockets was to facilitate the porting of code already written for Berkeley Sockets so that Windows stations could be easily integrated into TCP/IP networks. With some exceptions, Windows Sockets supports the complete Berkeley Sockets API. Windows Sockets also provides extended (and nonportable) functions that are tailored to the Win32 environment. They all have *WSA* prefixes in their names (WSA stands for Windows Sockets Asynchronous). One of these functions, WSAAsyncSelect(), is the foundation for the MFC sockets classes (CAsyncSocket and CSocket).

Overlapped I/O

Windows Sockets also have full overlapped I/O capabilities, and provide their best data-transfer rate using them. This is an extension to Windows Sockets, originally introduced in NT 3.5. Windows 95 supports overlapped operations on Windows Sockets, except with I/O completion ports. To standardize the use of overlapped I/O with Windows Sockets, the Winsock 2 specification includes functions that abstract the underlying Win32 API. Under Windows NT and Windows 95, these functions are implemented using the calls I discussed in Chapter 6. The abstraction of overlapped I/O in Winsock 2 is intended to allow 16-bit Windows applications to use it. For the purposes of this book, 16-bit Windows is just a fading memory, so there is no strong argument for using the Winsock 2 abstractions.

Protocol Transparency with the Service Registration API

To make Windows Sockets a truly protocol-transparent API—where a single binary image does work with all protocol suites—Microsoft added the Service Registration API with NT 3.5. This API allows Sockets servers to register their presence on a network, and to ask the underlying support layers what arguments they need to pass to the Sockets functions. With this mechanism, both client and server applications can be written so that they make no assumptions about the network environment. Windows Sockets 2 extends the Service Registration API in several ways, and irons out some of the ugliness of the original API.

Because of the importance that Microsoft is attaching to overlapped I/O with Sockets, and the protocol transparency you get from the Service Registration API, I will present a considerable amount of code in this chapter using both techniques. The first I will encapsulate in the COverlappedSocket class. The second I will provide through several classes, each of which wraps a different aspect of the Service Registration API. Finally, I will implement the WNet API I presented in the last chapter on top of these classes. As you will see, the classes make the implementation of the API much simpler than it was in my last two books.

Berkeley Sockets to Windows Sockets

Because one of the purposes of Windows Sockets is to ease porting of code between Berkeley and Windows environments, I will first discuss the most generic (that is, Berkeley-compatible) way to use Windows Sockets. This yields a very simple programming model. Its simplicity in no way argues against it; this approach is perfectly adequate in many situations—particularly in code targeted for Windows 95. As is always the case, the asynchronous model is more complicated to program. Even though it yields faster throughput, the difference may not always be worth it.

Basic Windows Sockets

WSAStartup()

Before making any other Windows Sockets calls, you must initialize the Windows Sockets DLL by calling WSAStartup(), which, of course, is not portable.

```
int WSAStartup(
        WORD      wVersionRequired,
        LPWSADATA lpWSAData);
```

wVersionRequired indicates the highest version of the Windows Sockets DLL you need. You use it to negotiate version compatibility with the DLL. The low byte specifies the major version you want, and the high byte indicates the minor version. MAKEWORD(1, 1), or 0x0101, requests version 1.1, the version supported by Windows NT 3.51 and Windows 95 4.0. MAKEWORD(2, 0) (0x0002) requests version 2.0 under NT 4.0. If the DLL cannot support the version you request, WSAStartup() returns −1, and WSAGetLastError(), which is a Sockets macro for GetLastError(), reports WSAVERNOTSUPPORTED. A return value of zero indicates a successful initialization.

It is not at all uncommon to call WSAStartup() twice, once to initialize Sockets 1.1 and once for Sockets 2. In code later in this chapter, I do exactly this.

lpWSAData points to a WSADATA structure that returns information on the configuration of the DLL. Here is its *typedef* from WINSOCK2.H:

```
typedef struct WSAData
{
   WORD                 wVersion;
   WORD                 wHighVersion;
   char                 szDescription[WSADESCRIPTION_LEN+1];
   char                 szSystemStatus[WSASYS_STATUS_LEN+1];
   unsigned short       iMaxSockets;
   unsigned short       iMaxUdpDg;
   char FAR *           lpVendorInfo;
} WSADATA;
```

wVersion is the version of Windows Sockets that the DLL thinks the application will use; *wHighVersion* is the highest version it can support. Normally, these two fields are the same. *szDescription* is a signature string, and *szSystemStatus* can be used to report status or configuration information.

iMaxSockets is the maximum number of sockets available to the application; *iMaxUdpDg* is the largest datagram the application can send. *lpVendorInfo* is not defined in the documentation; its use is vendor-specific.

A DLL should call WSAStartup() once for each process it is supporting, and should balance each call to WSAStartup() with a call to WSACleanup(). The logical place to do this is in the DLL_PROCESS_ATTACH and DLL_PROCESS_DETACH handlers in the DllMain() function.

In an MFC application, you do not need to call WSAStartup() or WSACleanup(). AfxSocketInit() calls WSAStartup(), and WSACleanup() is invoked when MFC cleans up after each process. However, MFC 4.1 is bound to Windows Sockets 1.1. If you also want to use Sockets 2, you need to call WSAStartup() to initialize it as well. I usually do this by loading pointers to WSAStartup() and WSACleanup() from WS2_32.DLL to avoid any possibility of ambiguity. Here's some code that does this. (I assume success to simplify the code.)

```
#define INCL_WINSOCK_API_TYPEDEFS 1
#include <winsock2.h>

HINSTANCE hSocketLib =
    ::LoadLibrary(_T("WS2_32.DLL"));

LPFN_WSASTARTUP lpfnWSAStartup =
    (LPFN_WSASTARTUP) ::GetProcAddress(
                        hSocketsLib,
                        "WSAStartup");

WSADATA WSAData;
lpfnWSAStartup(0x0002, &WSAData);
```

Once you have initialized the DLL by calling WSAStartup(), you are ready to begin using Windows Sockets. The next thing a server application must do is obtain a socket to use in listening for client connection requests. It does this by calling the socket() function, then calling bind() to associate the socket with its machine address and service endpoint.

Opening a Socket

socket() opens a socket. Sockets are analogous to HANDLEs; they are just communications channels. In fact, in Windows a socket *is* a HANDLE, or at least behaves very much like one.

```
typedef unsigned int SOCKET;
SOCKET PASCAL FAR socket(int af, int type, int protocol);
```

af denotes the address family. For Internet addresses, the address family is AF_INET or PF_INET (both defined as 2). For NetWare addressing, the address family is AF_NS, where NS comes from XNS (Xerox Network Systems) or AF_IPX (both of which are 6). Table 9-1 shows the address family constants currently defined in WINSOCK2.H, the comments describing them in that file, and the associated Win32 header file, where relevant. The fact that a constant is defined for a particular protocol does not mean that it is now, or will ever be, supported; it just leaves room for it.

Table 9-1. Address Family Constants Defined in WINSOCK2.H

Constant	Protocol	Win32 Header File
AF_UNIX (1)	Local to host (pipes, portals)	None
AF_INET (2)	Internetwork: UDP, TCP, etc.	WINSOCK.H (1.1), WINSOCK2.H (2.0)
AF_IMPLINK (3)	Arpanet imp addresses	None
AF_PUP (4)	Pup protocols: e.g., BSP	None
AF_CHAOS (5)	MIT CHAOS protocols	None
AF_IPX (6)	IPX and SPX	WSIPX.H, WSNWLINK.H
AF_NS (6)	XEROX NS protocols	WSIPX.H, WSNWLINK.H
AF_ISO (7)	ISO protocols	WSHISOTP.H
AF_OSI (7)	OSI is ISO	WSHISOTP.H
AF_ECMA (8)	European computer manufacturers	None
AF_DATAKIT (9)	Datakit protocols	None
AF_CCITT (10)	CCITT protocols, X.25 etc.	None
AF_SNA (11)	IBM SNA	None
AF_DECnet (12)	DECnet	None
AF_DLI (13)	Direct data link interface	None
AF_LAT (14)	LAT	None

Table 9-1. Address Family Constants Defined in WINSOCK2.H *(continued)*

Constant	Protocol	Win32 Header File
AF_HYLINK (15)	NSC Hyperchannel	None
AF_APPLETALK (16)	AppleTalk	ATALKWSH.H
AF_NETBIOS (17)	NetBios-style addresses	WSNETBS.H
AF_VOICEVIEW (18)	VoiceView	WSVV.H
AF_FIREFOX (19)	Protocols from Firefox	None
AF_BAN (21)	Banyan	WSVNS.H
AF_ATM (22)	Native ATM Services	None

type specifies whether you want connection-oriented or datagram communications. SOCK_DGRAM requests datagram service. Over TCP/IP, SOCK_STREAM specifies connection-oriented service. TCP/IP is stream-oriented; that is, all transmissions are viewed just as a raw byte stream. Many other protocols (including IPX/SPX and NetBEUI) are message-oriented. They add an extra level of structuring to data transmission, converting a sequence of packets into a discrete message. With these protocols, it is usually better to request a socket type of SOCK_SEQPACKET (sequenced-packet socket) for connection-oriented service. I have generally observed, for instance, that IPX/SPX gives you better performance with a sequenced-packet socket than with a stream socket (though you can use either).

For Internet addresses, the address family and socket type determine the protocol, so you just pass *protocol* as zero. Stream sockets use TCP (IPPROTO_TCP); datagram sockets use UDP (the User Datagram Protocol, identified by IPPROTO_UDP). This is not the case for NetWare addresses, or addresses in other protocols; you must pass *protocol* as NSPROTO_IPX for a datagram socket, and as NSPROTO_SPXII for a connection-oriented socket.

The arguments to socket() are what give you protocol independence, but they are also what deny you protocol transparency. You must choose an address family, and for each address family, the *type* and *protocol* arguments will vary. Using the Sockets API alone, there is no way to avoid hard-wiring your choices into your code. You have protocol independence because your use of the API does not differ from one protocol to another. You do not have protocol transparency, because you cannot determine at run time what arguments to pass—you have to know them when you develop your application. The Service Registration API, as we will see, tells you exactly what information to pass to socket(), and thereby gives you protocol transparency.

Binding to a Machine Address and Service Endpoint

The next thing the server must do is bind the socket to its machine address and service endpoint. The bind() function accomplishes this.

```
int PASCAL bind(SOCKET s, const struct sockaddr *addr, int namelen);
```

s is the socket returned by socket(). Because machine addresses and endpoints vary from one address family to another, *addr* points to a structure (actually, it is a discriminated union) that represents the information in a neutral way.

```
struct sockaddr
{
   u_short sa_family;
   char    sa_data[14];
};
typedef struct sockaddr SOCKADDR, *PSOCKADDR, FAR *LPSOCKADDR;
```

sa_family is the address family and describes the format of the address. The *sa_data* field maps to a protocol-specific address representation.

For TCP/IP, the *sockaddr_in* type holds this specific data:

```
struct sockaddr_in
{
   short   sin_family;
   u_short sin_port;
   struct  in_addr sin_addr;
   char    sin_zero[8];
};
typedef struct sockaddr_in SOCKADDR_IN, *PSOCKADDR_IN,
                           FAR *LPSOCKADDR_IN;
```

The *sa_data* field of *sockaddr* corresponds to *sin_port, sin_addr,* and *sin_zero* in *sockaddr_in. sin_addr* is a 4-byte Internet address; the *struct in_addr* is actually a union that lets you view the address as four bytes, two shorts, or one long. *sin_zero* is padding; I always set it to zero.

For an IPX address, the address is represented by a *struct sockaddr_ipx*, defined in WSIPX.H:

```
typedef struct sockaddr_ipx
{
   short          sa_family;
   char           sa_netnum[4];
   char           sa_nodenum[6];
```

```
    unsigned short sa_socket;
} SOCKADDR_IPX, *PSOCKADDR_IPX, FAR *LPSOCKADDR_IPX;
```

An IPX machine address consists of a 4-byte network number (*sa_netnum*) followed by a 6-byte node number (*sa_nodenum*). The service endpoint is an IPX socket (*sa_socket*).

Before you can bind to your address, you need to find out what it is. The way you do this differs radically among the various protocols; the Sockets API only standardizes name-to-address resolution for TCP/IP. In fact, at this point, Sockets ceases to be protocol independent; you have to invent your own mechanism with any other protocols. The Service Registration API provides protocol-independent name-to-address resolution.

The TCP/IP binding process takes a human-readable host name, service name, and protocol, and maps it to a binary address. How the mapping is done depends on the underlying TCP/IP implementation. Some versions use database files; by convention, these are called **hosts** and **services** and stored in the /etc directory on UNIX systems. Other implementations use a **Domain Name Server (DNS)**, where the address translation requires a network exchange. Windows supports either scheme; I have my network configured to use local hosts and services files, which are stored in %SystemRoot%\SYSTEM32\DRIVERS\ETC under NT, and in the Windows directory under Windows 95. My HOSTS file provides for machines named NUMBER1 through NUMBER12; each of these maps to a fictitious Internet address from 126.0.0.1 to 126.0.0.12. Here's what it looks like:

```
# Copyright (c) 1993 Microsoft Corp.
#
# This is a sample HOSTS file used by Microsoft TCP/IP for Windows NT
# 3.1
#
# This file contains the mappings of IP addresses to host names. Each
# entry should be kept on an individual line. The IP address should
# be placed in the first column followed by the corresponding host name.
# The IP address and the host name should be separated by at least one
# space.
#
# Additionally, comments (such as these) may be inserted on individual
# lines or following the machine name denoted by a '#' symbol.
#
# For example:
#
#      102.54.94.97     rhino.acme.com          # source server
#       38.25.63.10     x.acme.com              # x client host
```

```
127.0.0.1       localhost

126.0.0.1       NUMBER1
126.0.0.2       NUMBER2
126.0.0.3       NUMBER3
126.0.0.4       NUMBER4
126.0.0.5       NUMBER5
126.0.0.6       NUMBER6
126.0.0.7       NUMBER7
126.0.0.8       NUMBER8
126.0.0.9       NUMBER9
126.0.0.10      NUMBER10
126.0.0.11      NUMBER11
126.0.0.12      NUMBER12
```

The binary Internet address (in dot notation) is the first field on the line. The translation scheme finds the requested machine name and returns the corresponding Internet address as a long integer in big-endian format. For instance, a request to look up the address of my NT server (NUMBER1) returns the bytes 0x7E 0 0 1, in that order.

In Berkeley Sockets, gethostbyname() maps a name to an Internet address. Here is the prototype from WINSOCK2.H:

```
struct hostent FAR * PASCAL FAR gethostbyname(const char FAR *name);
```

WINSOCK2.H also defines a Microsoft-style type LPHOSTENT for the return value. The FAR specifiers vanish in Win32; here's a simplified prototype, using Microsoft types:

```
LPHOSTENT PASCAL gethostbyname(LPCSTR name);
```

name is the human-readable machine name. The *hostent* structure is defined as follows (omitting the unnecessary and irritating FARs):

```
struct hostent
{
   char   *h_name;
   char  **h_aliases;
   short   h_addrtype;
   short   h_length;
   char  **h_addr_list;
#define h_addr h_addr_list[0]
};
```

h_name returns the host's primary network name. A machine can also be known by aliases; these follow the primary name on the line of the HOSTS file. *h_aliases* is an array of pointers to them. *h_addrtype* is the address family. *h_length* tells you how long the address is, and *h_addr_list* is an array of addresses. The definition of *h_addr* as *h_addr_list[0]* is for backward compatibility. Normally, *h_addr* is the machine address you need to bind to.

There is one important concern here. If you bind to a specific IP address, you cannot receive communications at any other IP address your machine may have. You could have multiple IP addresses, for instance, if you are connected to a local-area network, but also connect to a wide-area network with a dialup connection. You may also have multiple IP addresses if your machine has more than one network card. To solve this problem, you can specify INADDR_ANY as your IP address, instead of a specific address. Because INADDR_ANY is just defined as zero, you can do this by zeroing the SOCKADDR_IN, then setting the address family and the port. If you do this, clients can connect to you using any of your IP addresses.

The Berkeley Sockets function getservbyname() takes a service name and protocol and returns the corresponding port number. Here is its Microsoft-style prototype:

```
LPSERVENT PASCAL getservbyname(LPCSTR name,
                               LPCSTR proto);
```

In a file-based TCP/IP implementation like mine, this information is fetched from the SERVICES file. This file is quite long; it has entries for all the standard TCP/IP services. I show here only the portion that describes ports and protocols that I use.

```
# Copyright (c) 1993 Microsoft Corp.
#
# This file contains port numbers for well-known services as defined by
# RFC 1060 (Assigned Numbers).
#
# Format:
#
# <service name>  <port number>/<protocol>  [aliases...]   [#<comment>]
#
wnetsrvr        20000/tcp
wnetsrvr_dgram  20001/udp
wnetsrvr        17990/spx
wnetsrvr_dgram  17733/ipx
wnetsrvr        3500/nbc    # NetBIOS connection-oriented port
wnetsrvr_dgram  3600/nbd    # NetBIOS datagram port
```

```
wnetbnch          30000/tcp
wnetbnch          18247/spx
wnetbnch          4500/nbc
```

The service name is the first field on the line. The next field has the port number and protocol name.

getservbyname() returns a pointer to a *struct servent*.

```
struct servent
{
   char      *s_name;
   char     **s_aliases;
   short      s_port;
   char      *s_proto;
};
```

s_name returns the service's primary name; *s_proto* parrots the *proto* argument passed to getservbyname(). Like hosts, services can also have aliases, and these are reported in *s_aliases*. Most importantly, *s_port* is the endpoint needed for binding.

Here is a function WNetGetHostAddress() that takes a machine name, a service name, and a protocol name, and returns a SOCKADDR structure formatted so that it can be immediately passed to bind(). If the host name is passed as NULL, it sets the IP address to INADDR_ANY.

```
// WNetGetHostAddress() populates a SOCKADDR structure with the
// Internet address of the local machine, and the port number of
// the requested process

BOOL WINAPI WNetGetHostAddress(LPCSTR lpszHost, LPCSTR lpszService,
                               LPCSTR lpszProto,
                               LPSOCKADDR lpAddr)
{
   LPHOSTENT   lpHost;
   LPSERVENT   lpServ;
   SOCKADDR_IN sin;
   BOOL        bRetcode = FALSE;

   ZeroMemory(&sin, sizeof (SOCKADDR_IN));
   sin.sin_family = AF_INET;

   if (lpszHost != NULL)
      {
      lpHost = gethostbyname(lpszHost);
      if (lpHost != NULL)
```

```
            {
            CopyMemory(&sin.sin_addr, lpHost->h_addr_list[0],
                       lpHost->h_length);
            }
        else
            {
            return FALSE;
            }
        }
    lpServ = getservbyname(lpszService, lpszProto);
    if (lpServ != NULL)
        {
        // The port number is required, so we don't
        // return TRUE if we can't determine what it is
        bRetcode = TRUE;
        sin.sin_port = lpServ->s_port;
        }
    CopyMemory(lpAddr, &sin, sizeof (SOCKADDR));
    return bRetcode;
}
```

For example, to get the binding address of the WNETSRVR service using TCP on the local machine, I would call WNetGetHostAddress() as follows:

```
SOCKADDR sa;

WNetGetHostAddress(NULL, "wnetsrvr", "tcp", &sa);
```

Once the server has bound a socket to its address and endpoint, it is ready to call listen(). This makes it fully available for client applications to connect to.

Putting a Server into the Listening State

listen() takes the server application from the bound to the listening state.

```
int PASCAL listen(SOCKET s, int backlog);
```

backlog indicates the number of connection requests you are willing to have queued at the socket; it must be from 1 to 5. If you pass an argument outside this range, Windows Sockets will quietly scale it so that it is within the limits; it won't fail the function. The *backlog* number is in addition to any client already being serviced. With a *backlog* of 1, for example, one client application can connect to the server and exchange data. While this is going on, another client application that tries to connect on a blocking socket will go into orbit. To be precise, it will think that it has actually connected to the server, but its first attempt to transmit data will block until the server calls accept().

Accepting Client Connections

As soon as the server has called listen(), it must turn around and invoke accept(). The call to listen() puts the socket into the listening state; it does not block. accept(), on the other hand, does not return until a client request comes in.

```
SOCKET PASCAL accept(SOCKET s, LPSOCKADDR lpAddr, LPINT lpLength);
```

s is the socket on which the server is listening. *lpAddr* will return the address of a connecting client, and *lpLength* will report the length of the address. The return value from accept() is a new socket descriptor; this socket is the one that the server uses to exchange data with the client. The socket that you pass to listen() is never used for any other purpose.

Client-Side Calls

To establish a connection to a server, a client must also open a socket. It is not necessary for the client to bind the socket; Windows Sockets will assign an unbound socket a unique port number when it connects to a server. The function that requests a connection is connect().

```
int PASCAL connect(SOCKET s, const struct sockaddr *name, int namelen);
```

s is the socket that the client has obtained by calling socket(). *name* is a SOCKADDR containing the machine address and service endpoint of the server. This must be populated in the same way that the server found out its own address, using the calls shown earlier (gethostbyname(), getserv-byname()).

Exchange of Data

Once a connection is established, the partner stations have several ways to exchange data: recv()/send(), _read()/_write(), and overlapped I/O.

recv()/send(). One option uses the recv() and send() functions, which are standard Berkeley Sockets calls. They have identical arguments.

```
int PASCAL send(SOCKET s, LPCSTR buf, int len, int flags);

int PASCAL recv(SOCKET s, LPSTR buf, int len, int flags);
```

flags is the only argument needing explanation. For send(), the flag MSG_OOB indicates that the data should be sent on an urgent basis (OOB stands for out-of-band). There is also a Win32 extension to Windows Sockets, the MSG_PARTIAL flag. This indicates to the underlying transport driver that the packet you are sending constitutes a fragment of a larger message, and that more transmissions will follow. For recv(), the MSG_OOB flag says that you want to receive out-of-band data. MSG_PEEK can be used to look at the data without removing it from the incoming queue.

The send() and recv() functions return the number of bytes written or read, or SOCKET_ERROR (−1) if they fail. As with all Windows Sockets functions, you can get the specific error code by calling WSAGetLastError().

I have observed one very important quirk. Microsoft TCP/IP WILL fragment your packets. If you expect to receive 4096 bytes of data, it is not enough to call recv() and ask for 4096 bytes. You have to accumulate the number of bytes you receive until it totals 4096. For example:

```
int nReceived, nTotalReceived;

for (nTotalReceived = 0; nTotalReceived < 4096; )
   {
   nReceived = recv( ...);
   if (nReceived > 0)
      {
      nTotalReceived += nReceived;
      }
   }
```

According to the documentation, send() may also manifest this behavior. I have never seen it do so, but it may be best to use send() this way also.

Using send() and recv() is the most Berkeley-compatible way to exchange data.

_read()/_write(). On the few UNIX projects I have worked on, it was more common to use _read() and _write(), because UNIX treats sockets as files. The syntax is very much like send() and recv(), omitting only the *flags* argument.

```
int _read(int handle, void *buffer, unsigned int count);
int _write(int handle, const void *buffer, unsigned int count);
```

You can use these functions with Windows Sockets under Win32, but you have to take a couple of additional steps. In Sockets 1.1, before you open a socket, you must tell Windows that you want it created as a non-overlapped handle. You do this by calling setsockopt() with the SO_OPENTYPE socket option, as follows:

```
int nOption = SO_SYNCHRONOUS_NONALERT;
setsockopt(INVALID_SOCKET, SOL_SOCKET, SO_OPENTYPE,
   (char *) &nOption, sizeof (int));

SOCKET s = socket(AF_INET, SOCK_STREAM, 0);
```

The call to setsockopt() only affects sockets created after you call it, and only those sockets belonging to the current thread. Notice that you pass the first argument—normally, the socket you are configuring—as INVALID_SOCKET.

In Windows Sockets 2, this is not necessary (in fact, it's not even supported). The socket() function only creates non-overlapped sockets. The WSASocket() function (new in Sockets 2) includes the FILE_FLAG_OVERLAPPED bit in one of its arguments, so you can request a non-overlapped socket.

Next, you have to convert the socket to a file handle by calling _open_osfhandle(), which is a Win32 extension to the C runtime library.

```
int _open_osfhandle (long osfhandle, int flags);
```

Pass the socket as the *osfhandle* argument; *flags* takes on the same values as when you open a file: _O_RDWR (read-write access), _O_RDONLY (read-only access), _O_BINARY or _O_TEXT (to request raw or translated I/O). The return value is a handle you can then use with _read() or _write(). For example:

```
#include <winsock.h>
#include <io.h>
#include <fcntl.h>

// In Sockets 2, this isn't necessary--the constants
// SO_SYNCHRONOUS_NONALERT and SO_OPENTYPE aren't
// even defined in WINSOCK2.H
int nOption = SO_SYNCHRONOUS_NONALERT;
setsockopt(INVALID_SOCKET, SOL_SOCKET, SO_OPENTYPE,
   (char *) &nOption, sizeof (int));

SOCKET s = socket(AF_INET, SOCK_STREAM, 0);
```

```
int     nFileHandle;
nFileHandle = _open_osfhandle(s, _O_RDWR | _O_BINARY);
```

Now, you can use *nFileHandle* as input to _read() and _write().

Overlapped I/O. By default, Windows Sockets 1.1 opens sockets as overlapped Win32 file handles. Therefore, you can pass a socket to ReadFile(), ReadFileEx(), WriteFile(), or WriteFileEx() without modification. The socket behaves exactly like the file handles discussed in Chapter 6. Because it is opened for overlapped I/O, you have to follow the procedures I outlined there, using event handles, I/O completion routines, or I/O completion ports. Overlapped I/O is the most powerful and efficient way to use Windows Sockets, especially on the server side.

In Sockets 2.0, the socket() function no longer creates overlapped sockets. You get an overlapped socket by calling WSASocket() and setting the WSA_FLAG_OVERLAPPED bit. Then there is a whole suite of functions that abstract the underlying Win32 calls. In either NT or Windows 95, you can just call the Win32 functions directly; it is not necessary to use the Sockets 2 calls. They are provided so you can use Sockets 2 in the Win16 environment. Table 9-2 shows the correspondence between Win32 and Sockets 2 functions.

Table 9-2. Windows Sockets 2.0 and Win32 Functions Associated with Overlapped I/O

Windows Sockets 2.0	Win32
WSARecv()	ReadFile()/ReadFileEx()
WSARecvFrom()	ReadFile()/ReadFileEx()
WSASend()	WriteFile()/WriteFileEx()
WSASendTo()	WriteFile()/WriteFileEx()
WSAWaitForMultipleEvents()	WaitForMultipleObjectsEx()
WSACreateEvent()	CreateEvent()
WSACloseEvent()	CloseHandle()
WSASetEvent()	SetEvent()
WSAResetEvent()	ResetEvent()
WSAGetOverlappedResult()	GetOverlappedResult()

I would like to spend a little time here looking at WSARecv(), WSASend(), and WSAGetOverlappedResult(). Because I am only developing for the 32-bit Windows environment, I don't use them in the code I present in this chapter, being content to use the native Win32 calls that they map to (ReadFile(), ReadFileEx(), WriteFile(), and WriteFileEx()). The Win32 Benchmark application in Chapter 16 includes an example of using them.

Here are the prototypes for WSASend() and WSARecv():

```
int WSASend(
    SOCKET                             s,
    LPWSABUF                           lpSendBuffers,
    DWORD                              dwBuffers,
    LPDWORD                            lpdwBytesSent,
    DWORD                              dwFlags,
    LPWSAOVERLAPPED                    lpOverlapped,
    LPWSAOVERLAPPED_COMPLETION_ROUTINE lpCompletionRoutine);

int WSARecv(
    SOCKET                             s,
    LPWSABUF                           lpRecvBuffers,
    DWORD                              dwBuffers,
    LPDWORD                            lpdwBytesReceived,
    LPDWORD                            lpdwFlags,
    LPWSAOVERLAPPED                    lpOverlapped,
    LPWSAOVERLAPPED_COMPLETION_ROUTINE lpCompletionRoutine);
```

The arguments are the same, except that the flags are solely an input argument for WSASend(), whereas they are an input/output argument for WSARecv(). You can see that they are also very similar to, and combine, the arguments for WriteFile() / WriteFileEx() and ReadFile() / ReadFileEx(). The socket *s* replaces the file handle; both functions include an argument that returns the number of bytes sent or received. *lpOverlapped* points to a WSAOVERLAPPED structure, which is just another name for the OVERLAPPED structure.

Here are the differences:

- WSASend() and WSARecv() pass their send and receive buffers as arrays of WSABUF structures. The WSABUF has two fields: *len* is the byte length of the data, and *buf* points to it:

  ```
  typedef struct _WSABUF
  {
     u_long len;
     char  *buf;
  } WSABUF, *LPWSABUF;
  ```

Because the input and output buffers are passed as arrays of WSABUFs, WSASend() and WSARecv() support what is referred to as **scatter/gather I/O**. They will concatenate the separate buffers passed to WSASend() into a single packet, and they will distribute arriving packets to the buffers passed to WSARecv(). This can save you some trouble in situations where what you are sending needs to be collected from dispersed locations in memory (from a noncontiguous data structure like a linked list, for example). To tell Windows Sockets how many WSABUFs are in the array, WSASend() and WSARecv() include the *dwBuffers* argument.

- These functions combine the arguments of WriteFile() and WriteFileEx() (for WSASend()) and ReadFile() and ReadFileEx() (for WSARecv()). If you pass *lpCompletionRoutine* as a non-NULL address, you will receive completion notifications through it. Otherwise, if *lpOverlapped->hEvent* is not NULL, the event handle will be signalled when the operation completes. If you want to use an I/O completion port, you can pass *lpCompletionRoutine* as NULL, *lpOverlapped* as non-NULL, and *lpOverlapped->hEvent* as NULL.

  Winsock 2 has one additional difference from native Win32 overlapped I/O. Even if you open the socket for overlapped I/O, you can pass both *lpOverlapped* and *lpCompletionRoutine* as NULL. In this case, you will get non-overlapped I/O for that particular operation.
- The flags argument passes information that only applies to Windows Sockets. The flags for WSASend() are the same as for send(). For WSARecv(), *lpdwFlags* is an output argument to tell the caller if a partial message has arrived. If this is the case, the data you asked for is delivered, and the MSG_PARTIAL bit is set. You can call WSARecv() again to receive the rest of the message. You can also set the MSG_PARTIAL bit on input to tell WSARecv() that you are willing to receive partial messages, so it does not need to flag them.
- Because the flags are part of the output data returned by WSARecv(), they will not be returned immediately when WSARecv() is executed in overlapped fashion. Therefore, the flags must be reported through the asynchronous reporting mechanisms used by Win32 overlapped I/O. WSAGetOverlappedResult() adds the flags as one of its output arguments; this is the only difference between it and GetOverlappedResult().

```
BOOL WSAAPI WSAGetOverlappedResult(
    SOCKET          s,
    LPWSAOVERLAPPED lpOverlapped,
    LPDWORD         lpdwTransfer,
    BOOL            nWait,
    LPDWORD         lpdwFlags);
```

The Winsock 2 I/O completion routine adds the output flags to the arguments passed to a Win32 I/O completion routine.

```
typedef void (CALLBACK * LPWSAOVERLAPPED_COMPLETION_ROUTINE)(
    DWORD           dwError,
    DWORD           dwBytesTransferred,
    LPWSAOVERLAPPED lpOverlapped,
    DWORD           dwFlags);
```

The completion routine is called when you call WSAWaitForMultipleEvents() (an exact analog to WaitForMultipleObjectsEx()) to put your thread into an alertable wait state.

- WSASend() and WSARecv() use Sockets conventions for their return codes. If an overlapped operation completes synchronously, the functions return zero. Otherwise, they return SOCKET_ERROR, and WSAGetLastError() tells you the specific reason for failure. WSA_IO_PENDING says that the operation is being performed in overlapped mode; it is defined as the standard Win32 code ERROR_IO_PENDING.

send() and recv() are the simplest and most Berkeley-compatible functions, as they do not require any special handling. _read() and _write() oblige you to convert a socket into a C runtime file handle. I have not observed a difference in performance between these two approaches. Overlapped I/O, though it is more complex to code, yields a significant performance improvement—consistently 100K per second faster than any other technique, from what I have seen. (Chapter 16 presents specific benchmark data.)

Datagram Service

For datagram service, there is no need for the server to call listen(), nor for the client to call connect(). To receive datagrams, however, a station must bind to a local endpoint using a datagram protocol (UDP in the TCP/IP suite).

Once the datagram sockets are opened, the stations send and receive data using sendto() and recvfrom(). sendto() and recvfrom() take the same arguments as send() and recv(), but add two for the partner station.

```
int PASCAL sendto(SOCKET s, LPCSTR buf, int len, int flags,
                  const struct sockaddr *to, int tolen);

int PASCAL recvfrom(SOCKET s, LPSTR buf, int len, int flags,
                    LPSOCKADDR from, LPINT fromlen);
```

With sendto(), *to* and *tolen* indicate where to send the data. With recvfrom(), *from* and *fromlen* capture the address of the sending station.

WSASendTo() and WSARecvFrom() are the Winsock 2 extensions to sendto() and recvfrom(). Like these functions, they add two arguments to WSASend() and WSARecv(), designating the socket address of the target server (in the case of WSASendTo()) or providing an output variable to capture the address of a sending station (WSARecvFrom()).

```
int WSASendTo(
    SOCKET                             s,
    LPWSABUF                           lpSendBuffers,
    DWORD                              dwBuffers,
    LPDWORD                            lpdwBytesSent,
    DWORD                              dwFlags,
    const struct sockaddr             *lpTargetSockAddr,
    int                                nAddressLength,
    LPWSAOVERLAPPED                    lpOverlapped,
    LPWSAOVERLAPPED_COMPLETION_ROUTINE lpCompletionRoutine);

int WSARecvFrom(
    SOCKET                             s,
    LPWSABUF                           lpRecvBuffers,
    DWORD                              dwBuffers,
    LPDWORD                            lpdwBytesReceived,
    LPDWORD                            lpdwFlags,
    struct sockaddr                   *lpSendingSockAddr,
    LPINT                              lpnAddressLength,
    LPWSAOVERLAPPED                    lpOverlapped,
    LPWSAOVERLAPPED_COMPLETION_ROUTINE lpCompletionRoutine);
```

Though they are intended primarily to support datagram communications, sendto() / WSASendTo() and recvfrom() / WSARecvFrom() can also be used with connection-oriented sockets—the address-related arguments are ignored.

sendto() and recvfrom() provide the simplest and most Berkeley-compatible means of data exchange on a datagram socket.

Closing a Socket

When you are done exchanging data, you close the socket. In standard Berkeley Sockets, you can just call close(), because the socket is a file. This is not true in Windows, so Windows Sockets provides a closesocket() function.

```
int PASCAL closesocket(SOCKET s);
```

For connection-oriented communications, the server application closes the socket created by accept(), not the one originally returned by socket(). Only when the server goes out of service altogether should it close its listening socket.

Shutting Down

The last thing you have to do is call WSACleanup() to let the Windows Sockets DLL know you are finished using it. Of course, this function is also nonportable.

```
int PASCAL WSACleanup(void);
```

Each call to WSAStartup() must be balanced by a WSACleanup(). It appears that Sockets keeps a reference count, and removes itself from memory when the count falls to zero.

Other Portability Considerations

So far, I have discussed only how Sockets calls behave in blocking mode. Frequently, it is desirable to put a socket into nonblocking mode. In Berkeley Sockets, this is done using the ioctl() function, which is a UNIX system call for configuring an I/O device. There is no ioctl() in the C runtime library for either Windows 95 or Windows NT, so Windows Sockets provides ioctlsocket().

```
int PASCAL ioctlsocket(SOCKET s, long cmd, u_long *argp);
```

Winsock 2 adds the WSAIoctl() function.

```
int WSAIoctl(
    SOCKET                              s,
    DWORD                               dwCommand,
    LPVOID                              lpInBuffer,
    DWORD                               dwInBufferSize,
    LPVOID                              lpOutBuffer,
    DWORD                               dwOutBufferSize,
    LPDWORD                             lpdwBytesReturned,
    LPWSAOVERLAPPED                     lpOverlapped,
    LPWSAOVERLAPPED_COMPLETION_ROUTINE lpCompletionRoutine);
```

WSAIoctl() supports new command codes that are specific to Winsock 2, and allows protocol- and vendor-specific commands to be added. For requests that may require some time to complete, it supports overlapped execution.

These functions play several roles with respect to sockets. To put a socket into nonblocking mode, pass *cmd* as the constant FIONBIO, and point *argp* or *lpInBuffer* to a non-zero variable. On a blocking socket in standard Berkeley usage, the functions accept(), connect(), send(), recv(), sendto(), and recvfrom() do not return until they have completed the requested action. On a nonblocking socket, on the other hand, they return immediately. You can call the select() function to detect the occurrence of an event—a client connection request, the arrival of a packet, and so on—before you call the relevant function. The select() function blocks until an event of interest occurs. It also lets you specify a timeout. In many respects, select() is similar to WaitForMultipleObjects().

However, select() is cumbersome to use (and inefficient, according to Microsoft, because it triggers context switches). Windows Sockets offers several useful alternatives. For one thing, you can use blocking, overlapped sockets and specify timeouts. Win32 also offers extensions that allow you to set send() and recv() timeouts using setsockopt(). They use the SO_SNDTIMEO and SO_RCVTIMEO socket options, and pass the timeout value in milliseconds. Zero requests an infinite timeout. For example:

```
SOCKET s;
int nTimeout = 5000;  // 5-second timeout

// socket() works OK in Sockets 1.1
// s = socket(AF_INET, SOCK_STREAM, 0);

// In Winsock 2, you have to call WSASocket()
// with the WSA_FLAG_OVERLAPPED flag
s = WSASocket(AF_INET, SOCK_STREAM, 0, NULL, 0,
              WSA_FLAG_OVERLAPPED);
setsockopt(s, SOL_SOCKET, SO_RCVTIMEO, (char *) &nTimeout,
   sizeof (int));
```

Once you have done this, the send() and recv() functions will only block for the amount of time you have specified; they will not block indefinitely. This only works on sockets opened for overlapped I/O.

Windows Sockets also offers the WSAAsyncSelect() function, which puts a socket into nonblocking mode and requests notification of events that occur on it. WSAAsyncSelect() constitutes the bulk of the next section of this chapter, so I defer my discussion until then. Sockets 2 adds WSAEventSelect(). This function also requests asynchronous notification and makes the socket nonblocking, but rather than posting a message to a window, as WSAAsyncSelect() does, it causes a Win32 event object to signal. It too is discussed later in this chapter.

Berkeley to Windows Sockets—A Brief Summary

To summarize, standard Berkeley Sockets calls will port to Windows Sockets, with these exceptions:

- You must call WSAStartup() to initialize the Windows Sockets DLL.
- You must use ioctlsocket() or WSAIoctl() (which are not portable) to configure the socket.
- You can use _read() and _write() to receive and send data, but only after converting the socket descriptor to a file handle by calling _open_ofshandle. However, you can use send() and recv() in the standard Berkeley fashion.
- You must use closesocket() (which is not portable), rather than close() (which is), to close a socket.
- You must call WSACleanup() to shut down the DLL.

The following core functions work the same in both environments, with subtle variations, because a socket is an *unsigned int* in Windows Sockets and an *int* in Berkeley. Therefore, with functions like socket() or accept(), you must test for return values of INVALID_SOCKET (defined as ~0) instead of –1.

- socket()
- bind()
- listen()
- accept()
- connect()
- send()
- recv()
- sendto()
- recvfrom()

The Windows Sockets implementation of select() is syntactically the same as the Berkeley version, but uses arrays of SOCKETs, rather than bit strings. The Berkeley macros (FD_CLR(), FD_ISSET(), FD_SET(), and FD_ZERO()) shield you from the differences.

Windows Sockets Extensions

There are two levels of extensions. The first are the Windows Sockets 1 extensions to Berkeley Sockets. These are a handful of functions with WSA prefixes that offer asynchronous execution and message-posting. By far the most important of them is WSAAsyncSelect(). The second level consists of the Windows Sockets 2.0 extensions, the most important of which address overlapped I/O.

WSAAsyncSelect()

WSAAsyncSelect() has two effects: it puts a socket into nonblocking mode, and it asks to have a message posted to a window when certain events occur. Here is its prototype:

```
int PASCAL WSAAsyncSelect(SOCKET s, HWND hWnd, u_int wMsg, long lEvent);
```

What WSAAsyncSelect() says in effect is this: when any of the events described in *lEvent* occur on the socket *s*, post message *wMsg* to window *hWnd*. The possible bit settings for *lEvent*, and the events they represent, are as follows:

- FD_READ: Data is available for reading.
- FD_WRITE: The socket can be written to.
- FD_OOB: Urgent data needs to be read.
- FD_ACCEPT: A client request for a connection has arrived.
- FD_CONNECT: A client's attempt to connect to a server has completed.
- FD_CLOSE: The socket has been closed by the partner station.
- FD_QOS: The socket's quality of service has been changed (Windows Sockets 2.0 only).
- FD_GROUP_QOS: The quality of service of the socket's group has changed (Windows Sockets 2.0 only).
- FD_ALL_EVENTS: All of the above.

Each call to WSAAsyncSelect() overrides the previous call. Thus, if you want notification of multiple events, as you often do, you must OR the appropriate flags together. Passing *lEvent* as zero cancels notification for the socket.

When the window procedure for the notification window is called, *wParam* contains the socket number. *lParam* contains the event code and any error that may have occurred. The event status can be retrieved using the WSAGETSELECTERROR() macro, as follows:

```
WORD wError;
wError = WSAGETSELECTERROR(lParam);
```

If the error code is zero, the operation was successful. For a list of the possible errors, see Error Codes in the Windows Sockets online help. The reference page for each function describes the possible errors more thoroughly. I have found it a helpful practice to print the return value of WSAGetLastError() whenever a problem occurs. Table 9-3 shows some of the error codes I have encountered and the situations that provoked them.

Table 9-3. Some Common Windows Sockets Error Codes

Defined Constant	Numeric Value	Possible Causes of Error
WSAENOTSOCK	10038	A socket created in one process is used by another process.
WSAEADDRINUSE	10048	Triggered by bind() because a process went down without closing a socket. When you attempt to start the process again, the socket is still bound to the previous socket, and the new bind() fails.
WSAENOBUFS	10055	One of the asynchronous database routines such as WSAGetHostByName() was called with an output buffer that was too small.
WSAETIMEDOUT	10060	A client application got bored waiting for connect() to complete. (The server application is probably not running.) A read or write operation timed out.
WSAECONNREFUSED	10061	A client application could not connect to a server because the server backlog was full.
WSAVERNOTSUPPORTED	10092	Calling WSAStartup() and asking for version 1.0.
WSANOTINITIALISED	10093	You didn't call WSAStartup().

The WSAGETSELECTEVENT() macro reports the event.

```
WORD wEvent;
wEvent = WSAGETSELECTEVENT(lParam);
```

It is not necessary to reissue WSAAsyncSelect(); it is automatically reactivated when you call the enabling function. For FD_READ or FD_OOB events, these are ReadFile(), ReadFileEx(), read(), recv(), recvfrom(), WSARecv(), and WSARecvFrom(). For FD_ACCEPT, it is accept() or WSAAccept(). For FD_WRITE, they are WriteFile(), WriteFileEx(), write(), send(), sendto(), WSASend(), and WSASendTo(). You only need to call WSAAsyncSelect() again when you want notification of different events, or when you want to cancel notification altogether.

Use of WSAAsyncSelect() on the Server Side. This is a typical sequence of events in a server application:

1. Create a socket and bind your address to it.
2. Call WSAAsyncSelect(), and request FD_ACCEPT notification.
3. Call listen(), and go on to other tasks (or put your server application to sleep).
4. When a connection request comes in, the notification window receives the message and the FD_ACCEPT notification. Respond by calling accept() or WSAAccept() to complete the connection.
5. Call WSAAsyncSelect() to request FD_READ | FD_OOB | FD_CLOSE notification for the socket created by accept(). This causes notifications to be sent to you when the client sends data, or closes the socket it is using.
6. When you receive FD_READ or FD_OOB notification, call ReadFile(), read(), recv(), recvfrom(), WSARecv(), or WSARecvFrom() to retrieve the data.
7. Respond to FD_CLOSE notification by calling closesocket() with the socket returned by accept().

Use of WSAAsyncSelect() on the Client Side. For the client, a typical scenario might be:

1. Create a socket.
2. Call WSAAsyncSelect() and request FD_CONNECT notification.
3. Call connect() or WSAConnect(). They return immediately, and you are free to do something else.
4. When the FD_CONNECT notification comes in telling you that the connection you requested has been established, request FD_WRITE | FD_READ | FD_OOB | FD_CLOSE notification on the socket (reported in *wParam*).
5. When an FD_WRITE event is reported, the socket is available for the client to send requests to the server.

6. When data from the server arrives, the notification window receives FD_READ or FD_OOB events. You respond by calling ReadFile(), read(), recv(), recvfrom(), WSARecv(), or WSARecvFrom().

Normally, the client initiates the closing of the connection because the client knows when it no longer needs the services that the server is offering. However, the client should be prepared for an FD_CLOSE notification and close its own socket in response to it.

WSAAsyncSelect() is a very powerful function. The MFC CAsyncSocket class is built on top of it. If you use WSAAsyncSelect(), you don't need to multithread a Windows Sockets server; WSAAsyncSelect() provides implicit multithreading. It also removes the need to allocate buffer space before you post an asynchronous receive request. Windows Sockets buffers the data for you, then tells you to come and get it. You can allocate space at the precise moment when you need it. To find out exactly how much memory to allocate, you call ioctlsocket() with the command code FIONREAD. Notice that you need to call recv() in a loop, and accumulate the number of bytes it returns.

```
SOCKET s;
u_long ulBytesAvailable;
int    nBytesReceived,
u_long ulTotalReceived;
LPBYTE lpBuffer;

if ((ioctlsocket(s, FIONREAD, &ulBytesAvailable) == 0) &&
     (ulBytesAvailable > 0))
    {
    lpBuffer = (LPBYTE) VirtualAlloc(NULL, ulBytesAvailable,
                              MEM_COMMIT, PAGE_READWRITE);
    for (ulTotalReceived == 0;
          ulTotalReceived < ulBytesAvailable;
         )
        {
        nBytesReceived =
           recv(s,
                &lpBuffer[ulTotalReceived],
                ulBytesAvailable - ulTotalReceived,
                0);
        if (nBytesReceived > 0)
           {
           ulTotalReceived += (u_long) nBytesReceived;
           }
```

```
    else
       {
       // Error or partner has closed its socket
       }
    }
```

WSAEventSelect()

WSAEventSelect() is a Sockets 2.0 addition that works a lot like WSAAsyncSelect(), but uses event signalling instead of message posting.

```
int WSAAPI WSAEventSelect(
    SOCKET   s,
    WSAEVENT hEvent,
    long     lEvents);
```

The first and last arguments are the same as for WSAAsyncSelect(). But where the middle arguments to WSAAsyncSelect() specify a window handle and a message, the *hEvent* argument to WSAEventSelect() specifies an event handle. The event must be a manual-reset event created by calling WSACreateEvent() or CreateEvent(). WSACreateEvent() requires no arguments, and creates an unnamed manual-reset event.

```
#define WSAEVENT HANDLE

WSAEVENT WSAAPI WSACreateEvent(void);
```

Like WSAAsyncSelect(), WSAEventSelect() returns zero if it succeeds, SOCKET_ERROR if it fails.

To detect the completion of the operation, you wait on the event handle by calling one of the wait functions discussed in Chapters 5 and 6 (WaitForSingleObject(), WaitForMultipleObjects(), MsgWaitForMultipleObjects(), WaitForSingleObjectEx(), or WaitForMultipleObjectsEx()). Sockets 2 provides its own function, WSAWaitForMultipleEvents(), whose prototype reveals it to be WaitForMultipleObjectsEx() in disguise:

```
DWORD WSAAPI WSAWaitForMultipleEvents(
    DWORD          dwEvents,
    const WSAEVENT *lphEvents,
    BOOL           bWaitAll,
    DWORD          dwTimeout,
    BOOL           bAlertable);
```

dwEvents is the number of WSAEVENT objects in the array pointed to by *lphEvents*. *bWaitAll* says to wait for all the events to signal (TRUE), or to wake up when any one of them signals (FALSE). *dwTimeout* is the timeout in milliseconds; WSA_INFINITE (which is just defined as INFINITE) says to block forever. Pass *bAlertable* as TRUE if you are using I/O completion routines, FALSE otherwise.

The return value from WSAWaitForMultipleEvents() is the index into *lphEvents* of the event that has signalled. To find out what network occurrence has caused this to happen, you call WSAEnumNetworkEvents().

```
int WSAAPI WSAEnumNetworkEvents(
    SOCKET             s,
    WSAEVENT           hEvent,
    LPWSANETWORKEVENTS lpNetworkEvents);
```

WSAEnumNetworkEvents() fills a WSANETWORKEVENTS structure with the status of all operations that have completed.

```
typedef struct _WSANETWORKEVENTS {
       long lNetworkEvents;
       int  iErrorCode[FD_MAX_EVENTS];
} WSANETWORKEVENTS, FAR * LPWSANETWORKEVENTS;
```

lNetworkEvents will contain the FD_* codes of any complete operations. *iErrorCode* contains the status of the operation, with zero indicating that it was successful. At this point, the interface starts to look a lot like the Berkeley select() function. For each bit that is set in *lNetworkEvents*, you fetch its status from *iErrorCode*. All the notification codes have a corresponding index into *iErrorCode*. Its constant is the notification constant (FD_READ, FD_WRITE, etc.) with a suffix of _BIT. This is how you process the WSANETWORKEVENTS structure:

```
SOCKET s = WSASocket(AF_INET, SOCK_STREAM, 0, NULL, 0,
                     WSA_FLAG_OVERLAPPED);

// [Bind the socket, and do whatever else is appropriate]

WSAEVENT hEvent = WSACreateEvent();

WSAEventSelect(s, hEvent, FD_ALL_EVENTS);

if (WSAWaitForMultipleEvents(1, &hEvent, TRUE, INFINITE, FALSE)
      == WSA_WAIT_EVENT_0)
   {
   WSANETWORKEVENTS NetworkEvents;

   WSAEnumNetworkEvents(s, hEvent, &NetworkEvents);
```

```
// Is the partner station sending us data?
if (NetworkEvents.lNetworkEvents & FD_READ)
   {
   if (NetworkEvents.iErrorCode[FD_READ_BIT] == 0)
      {
      // Successful read, data is available
      }
   }

// We don't say else if--event notifications are not
// mutually exclusive
// Can we write to the socket?
if (NetworkEvents.lNetworkEvents & FD_WRITE)
   {
   if (NetworkEvents.iErrorCode[FD_WRITE_BIT] == 0)
      {
      // We can write to the socket
      }
   }

// Is the partner station sending us urgent data?
if (NetworkEvents.lNetworkEvents & FD_OOB)
   {
   if (NetworkEvents.iErrorCode[FD_OOB_BIT] == 0)
      {
      // OOB data has arrived--go get it
      }
   }

// Is a client trying to connect to us?
if (NetworkEvents.lNetworkEvents & FD_ACCEPT)
   {
   if (NetworkEvents.iErrorCode[FD_ACCEPT_BIT] == 0)
      {
      // Client is trying to connect to us
      // Call accept() or WSAAccept()
      }
   }

// Are we connected to a server?
if (NetworkEvents.lNetworkEvents & FD_CONNECT)
   {
   if (NetworkEvents.iErrorCode[FD_CONNECT_BIT] == 0)
      {
      // Connection established--send server request
      // for service or information
      }
   }
```

```
// Did the partner station say goodbye?
if (NetworkEvents.lNetworkEvents & FD_CLOSE)
   {
   // Don't need to check status--just close our own socket
   closesocket(s);
   }

// Has quality of service changed for this socket?
if (NetworkEvents.lNetworkEvents & FD_QOS)
   {
   if (NetworkEvents.iErrorCode[FD_QOS_BIT] == 0)
      {
      // [Respond in an appropriate manner]
      }
   }

// Has group's quality of service changed?
if (NetworkEvents.lNetworkEvents & FD_GROUP_QOS)
   {
   if (NetworkEvents.iErrorCode[FD_GROUP_QOS_BIT] == 0)
      {
      // [Respond accordingly]
      }
   }
```

In one important respect, WSAAsyncSelect() and WSAEventSelect() behave the same way. Each call to one of these functions for a given socket overrides the previous call *to either function*. So if you want notification of multiple events, you OR the FD_* flags together. An event mask of zero cancels notifications on the socket. To emphasize: WSAAsyncSelect() and WSAEventSelect() cancel each other out. A call to WSAAsyncSelect() replaces any previous call to either WSAAsyncSelect() *or* WSAEventSelect(), and vice versa.

TransmitFile()

TransmitFile() is another handy Windows Sockets extension to Berkeley Sockets. It sends an open file over a Sockets connection.

```
BOOL TransmitFile(
    SOCKET   hSocket,
    HANDLE   hFile,
    DWORD    nNumberOfBytesToWrite,
    DWORD    nNumberOfBytesPerSend,
    LPOVERLAPPED  lpOverlapped,
    LPTRANSMIT_FILE_BUFFERS  lpTransmitBuffers,
    DWORD    dwReserved);
```

hSocket must be a connected socket; the file (identified by *hFile*) will be sent to the partner station. The transmission will be faster if you set the FILE_FLAG_SEQUENTIAL_SCAN bit when you open the file. *nNumberOfBytesToWrite* is the total number of bytes you want to send from the file; zero says to send the entire file. *nNumberOfBytesPerSend* lets you specify how big each chunk transmitted over the network should be; zero lets the Sockets layer make its own decision. The OVERLAPPED structure (*lpOverlapped*) pertains to the socket, not the file. If the socket has been opened for overlapped I/O, you must pass a non-NULL pointer. You can use either an event handle or an I/O completion port; you cannot use I/O completion routines.

lpTransmitBuffers points to a TRANSMIT_FILE_BUFFERS structure.

```
typedef struct _TRANSMIT_FILE_BUFFERS {
    PVOID Head;
    DWORD HeadLength;
    PVOID Tail;
    DWORD TailLength;
} TRANSMIT_FILE_BUFFERS;
```

This allows you to attach headers and trailers to the file transmission. The header information might include the name of the file on the sending station. The trailer might include some indication that the file transmission is complete.

dwReserved must be passed as zero.

Miscellaneous WSA Functions

There are several other miscellaneous WSA functions. Most of them are asynchronous versions of functions like gethostbyname() and getservbyname() and are referred to as the WSAAsyncGetXByY() functions. They are provided because some TCP/IP implementations call a Domain Name Server (DNS) to do the mappings, so the getXbyY() calls trigger network activity, and can block. The complete set of WSAAsyncGetXByY() functions are listed in Table 9-4.

WSAAsyncGetHostByName(), the asynchronous counterpart to gethostbyname(), is typical.

```
HANDLE PASCAL WSAAsyncGetHostByName(
                 HWND   hWnd,
                 u_int  wMsg,
                 LPCSTR name,
                 LPSTR  lpBuffer,
                 int    buflen);
```

Table 9-4. WSAAsyncGetXByY() Functions

Function Name	Purpose
WSAAsyncGetServByName	Retrieve service information based on the service name ("telnet", "ftp", "wnetsrvr", and so on).
WSAAsyncGetServByPort	Retrieve service information based on the service's port number.
WSAAsyncGetProtoByName	Get protocol information based on the protocol name ("tcp", "udp", and so on).
WSAAsyncGetProtoByNumber	Get protocol information based on the protocol number (IPPROTO_TCP, NSPROTO_SPX, and so on).
WSAAsyncGetHostByName	Get machine's Internet address based on its name.
WSAAsyncGetHostByAddr	Get machine information based on its Internet address.

When invoked, WSAAsyncGetHostByName() returns immediately; its return value is a task handle. When the asynchronous activity completes, the Windows Sockets DLL copies the *hostent* structure to the buffer pointed to by *lpBuffer*, then posts the *wMsg* message to *hWnd*. The *wParam* for the message will be the task handle originally returned by WSAAsyncGetHost-ByName(). The high word of *lParam* will contain the status of the operation, with zero indicating success. The error code can be extracted with the WSAGETASYNCERROR() macro.

```
WORD wError;
wError = WSAGETASYNCERROR(lParam);
```

If the error code is WSAENOBUFS, *lpBuffer* was not large enough to accommodate all the output information. In this case, the low word of *lParam* tells you how much space you need to allocate. The WSAGETA-SYNCBUFLEN() macro returns this value:

```
WORD wError;
WORD wBuflen;
wError = WSAGETASYNCERROR(lParam);
if (wError == WSAENOBUFS)
   wBuflen = WSAGETASYNCBUFLEN(lParam);
```

You can cancel the request by calling WSACancelAsyncRequest() with the handle returned by WSAAsyncGetHostByName().

```
int PASCAL WSACancelAsyncRequest(HANDLE hTask);
```

The WSAGetXByY() functions are cumbersome, and were intended for the Windows 3.x environment, where blocking is death. They can be considered obsolete in Win32.

MFC Support for Windows Sockets

The Microsoft Foundation Classes version 4.1 support Windows Sockets 1.1 through two primary classes: CAsyncSocket and CSocket. They are declared in the header file AFXSOCK.H, and implemented in SOCKCORE.CPP. Many of the methods are implemented as inline calls in the file AFXSOCK.INL. At present (June 1996), MFC does not support Windows Sockets 2.

AfxSocketInit()

When you use the MFC Sockets classes, you need to call AfxSocketInit() instead of WSAStartup(), which AfxSocketInit() calls for you. When you create a project with Visual C++ and ask for Sockets support, it will generate the call to AfxSocketInit().

CAsyncSocket

CAsyncSocket is a thin wrapper around the Sockets API. In fact, many of its methods are just inline invocations of the corresponding function. For example, here is the Bind() method as it appears in AFXSOCK.INL:

```
_AFXSOCK_INLINE BOOL CAsyncSocket::Bind(
               const SOCKADDR* lpSockAddr,
               int nSockAddrLen)
{
   return (SOCKET_ERROR != bind(
                                m_hSocket,
                                lpSockAddr,
                                nSockAddrLen));
}
```

As its name implies, CAsyncSocket is intended to provide asynchronous processing, and relies heavily on the capabilities of WSAAsyncSelect(). Socket event notifications are handled internally by the CSocketWnd class, which you never need to deal with directly. To use the services of CAsyncSocket, you call the AsyncSelect() method to declare the events you are interested in. AsyncSelect() only needs one argument: the notification flags.

```
BOOL AsyncSelect(long lEvent =
      FD_READ | FD_WRITE | FD_OOB | FD_ACCEPT |
                FD_CONNECT | FD_CLOSE);
```

The other pieces of information needed by WSAAsyncSelect() are inferred as follows:

- The socket handle is the *m_hSocket* member of CAsyncSocket.
- The window handle is kept in Thread Local Storage as part of MFC's state information for the socket. It is the HWND of a CSocketWnd object created the first time you call Socket() (either directly or via the Create() method).
- The notification message is WM_SOCKET_NOTIFY, a private message used only by MFC (defined as 0x0373 in AFXPRIV.H).

You then override the notification handlers that are called when an event is posted to CSocketWnd. Table 9-5 shows the handler methods and the corresponding event code.

Table 9-5. CAsyncSocket Notification Handlers

CAsyncSocket Method	WSAAsyncSelect() Event Code
OnReceive	FD_READ
OnSend	FD_WRITE
OnOutOfBandData	FD_OOB
OnAccept	FD_ACCEPT
OnConnect	FD_CONNECT
OnClose	FD_CLOSE

Each of these methods has an empty implementation in CAsyncSocket, so you must override them to use the class in this manner. All of them take one argument—the error code extracted from the *lParam* by calling WSAGETSELECTERROR().

Setup. The calls that set up the client and server sides of a connection are similar to the ones we studied earlier. To obtain a socket, you call the Socket() method:

```
BOOL Socket(int nSocketType=SOCK_STREAM, long lEvent =
      FD_READ | FD_WRITE | FD_OOB | FD_ACCEPT |
                FD_CONNECT | FD_CLOSE,
      int nProtocolType = 0, int nAddressFormat = PF_INET);
```

The default arguments create a connection-oriented socket using TCP, and register the socket to receive all possible asynchronous notifications.

The next step is to bind the socket. As we have seen, this is obligatory for the server, optional (but harmless) for the client. The Bind() method has two versions, one of which we have already seen. The other one allows you to pass your machine address as a string, either an IP address in dot notation ("126.0.0.1") or your machine name ("NUMBER1").

```
BOOL Bind(UINT nSocketPort, LPCTSTR lpszSocketAddress = NULL);

BOOL Bind (const SOCKADDR* lpSockAddr, int nSockAddrLen);
```

The first version limits you to using TCP/IP, since the address resolution mechanism it uses only exists in that protocol suite. Passing *lpszSocketAddress* as NULL (or not passing it at all, which is the same thing) causes the socket to be bound to IP address INADDR_ANY, the most flexible binding available. The second version of Bind() is more general, and supports any underlying protocol. It requires you to figure out your socket address between the time you create the socket and the time you bind it.

The Create() method simplifies socket creation and binding for sockets that use TCP/IP. It combines calls to the Socket() and Bind() methods, using TCP/IP name-to-address resolution.

```
BOOL Create(UINT nSocketPort = 0, int nSocketType=SOCK_STREAM,
      long lEvent = FD_READ | FD_WRITE | FD_OOB | FD_ACCEPT |
                    FD_CONNECT | FD_CLOSE,
      LPCTSTR lpszSocketAddress = NULL);
```

The next thing the server has to do is put itself into the listening state. The Listen() method accomplishes this. It is very simple, and is implemented as an inline call to the listen() function.

```
BOOL Listen(int nConnectionBacklog=5);
```

The client establishes a connection with a server by calling Connect(). Here also there are two versions: one requires the fully populated socket address of the server, the other takes a string representing the server (and only supports TCP/IP).

```
BOOL Connect(LPCTSTR lpszHostAddress, UINT nHostPort);

BOOL Connect(const SOCKADDR* lpSockAddr, int nSockAddrLen);
```

To complete the connection, the server must call Accept(). The logical place for it to do this is in the OnAccept() notification handler. Accept() expects a reference to an empty CAsyncSocket object as its first argument. Accept() will finish initializing this object, which will then represent the connection to the client, and will be used for all data exchange. The Accept() method uses the accept() function to accomplish its task.

```
virtual BOOL Accept(CAsyncSocket& rConnectedSocket,
       SOCKADDR* lpSockAddr = NULL, int* lpSockAddrLen = NULL);
```

The last two arguments are the same as the corresponding arguments to accept(). If passed as non-NULL pointers, they return the socket address of the connecting client.

Tables 9-6 and 9-7 summarize the method calls required to put a server and client into the connected state. The first column shows the calls when you're using TCP/IP, the second those required for other protocol suites.

Table 9-6. CAsyncSocket Server-Side Methods for Establishing a Connection

Using TCP/IP	Using Other Protocols
getservbyname() to find out server's port ID	Socket()
Create()	Population of SOCKADDR structure by protocol-specific address-resolution techniques)
	Bind() (with fully populated SOCKADDR structure)
Listen()	Listen()
Accept()	Accept()

Table 9-7. CAsyncSocket Client-Side Methods for Establishing a Connection

Using TCP/IP	Using Other Protocols
Create()	Socket()
	Population of SOCKADDR structure by protocol-specific address-resolution techniques)
	Bind() (with fully populated SOCKADDR structure)
getservbyname() to find out server's port ID	Population of SOCKADDR structure with server's address by protocol-specific address-resolution techniques)
Connect() (with name of target machine)	Connect() (with fully populated SOCKADDR structure)

Data Exchange. Once the client and server are connected, they exchange data by calling the Send() and Receive() methods. (You can also use SendTo() and ReceiveFrom()). If you have requested FD_WRITE notifications in your call to AsyncSelect(), you do your Send() calls in the OnSend() notification handler. Similarly, if you've asked for FD_READ notifications, you do your Receive() calls in the OnReceive() handler.

Here's an important thing to remember: WSAAsyncSelect() puts the socket into nonblocking mode. This means that Send() and Receive() will not block. They may fail, however, and set the last-error code to WSAE-WOULDBLOCK. If you call these functions anywhere other than the notification handler, you must be prepared for this to happen.

Terminating a Connection. The Close() method breaks a connection by calling closesocket(). Usually, a client will call Close() when it no longer needs anything from the server, and the server will call Close() in its OnClose() notification handler. By the way, the CAsyncSocket destructor calls Close(), so as long as you destroy a CAsyncSocket object, you don't need to explicitly call Close().

Class Declaration. The following listing shows the declaration of the CAsyncSocket class, excerpted from AFXSOCK.H. I include only the methods and data members that you will normally need to access.

```
class CAsyncSocket : public CObject
{
public:
   BOOL Create(UINT nSocketPort = 0,
               int nSocketType=SOCK_STREAM,
               long lEvent = FD_READ | FD_WRITE | FD_OOB |
                             FD_ACCEPT | FD_CONNECT | FD_CLOSE,
               LPCTSTR lpszSocketAddress = NULL);

// Attributes
public:
   SOCKET m_hSocket;

   operator SOCKET() const;

   BOOL GetPeerName(CString& rPeerAddress, UINT& rPeerPort);
   BOOL GetPeerName(SOCKADDR* lpSockAddr, int* lpSockAddrLen);

   BOOL GetSockName(CString& rSocketAddress, UINT& rSocketPort);
   BOOL GetSockName(SOCKADDR* lpSockAddr, int* lpSockAddrLen);
```

```
   BOOL SetSockOpt(int nOptionName, const void* lpOptionValue,
                   int nOptionLen, int nLevel = SOL_SOCKET);
   BOOL GetSockOpt(int nOptionName, void* lpOptionValue,
                   int* lpOptionLen, int nLevel = SOL_SOCKET);

   static int PASCAL GetLastError();

// Operations
public:

   virtual BOOL Accept(CAsyncSocket& rConnectedSocket,
      SOCKADDR* lpSockAddr = NULL, int* lpSockAddrLen = NULL);

   BOOL Bind(UINT nSocketPort, LPCTSTR lpszSocketAddress = NULL);
   BOOL Bind (const SOCKADDR* lpSockAddr, int nSockAddrLen);

   virtual void Close();

   BOOL Connect(LPCTSTR lpszHostAddress, UINT nHostPort);
   BOOL Connect(const SOCKADDR* lpSockAddr, int nSockAddrLen);

   BOOL IOCtl(long lCommand, DWORD* lpArgument);

   BOOL Listen(int nConnectionBacklog=5);

   virtual int Receive(void* lpBuf, int nBufLen, int nFlags = 0);

   int ReceiveFrom(void* lpBuf, int nBufLen,
      CString& rSocketAddress, UINT& rSocketPort, int nFlags = 0);
   int ReceiveFrom(void* lpBuf, int nBufLen,
      SOCKADDR* lpSockAddr, int* lpSockAddrLen, int nFlags = 0);

   virtual int Send(const void* lpBuf, int nBufLen, int nFlags = 0);

   int SendTo(const void* lpBuf, int nBufLen,
      UINT nHostPort, LPCTSTR lpszHostAddress = NULL,
      int nFlags = 0);
   int SendTo(const void* lpBuf, int nBufLen,
      const SOCKADDR* lpSockAddr, int nSockAddrLen, int nFlags = 0);

   BOOL AsyncSelect(long lEvent =
      FD_READ | FD_WRITE | FD_OOB | FD_ACCEPT |
      FD_CONNECT | FD_CLOSE);

// Overridable callbacks
protected:
   virtual void OnReceive(int nErrorCode);
   virtual void OnSend(int nErrorCode);
```

```
    virtual void OnOutOfBandData(int nErrorCode);
    virtual void OnAccept(int nErrorCode);
    virtual void OnConnect(int nErrorCode);
    virtual void OnClose(int nErrorCode);

// Implementation
public:
    BOOL Socket(int nSocketType=SOCK_STREAM, long lEvent =
        FD_READ | FD_WRITE | FD_OOB | FD_ACCEPT |
        FD_CONNECT | FD_CLOSE,
        int nProtocolType = 0, int nAddressFormat = PF_INET);

};
```

CSocket

It can be somewhat cumbersome to use CAsyncSocket without overriding some of its asynchronous behavior. On the client side, you often want an operation to execute synchronously, or at least appear to. When a client tries to connect to a server, for instance, you'd like to know whether it did or not, within a reasonable amount of time. Frequently, too, the client needs to perform a transaction with the server—it wants to send a request and get an answer. This kind of behavior can be difficult to model using asynchronous notifications.

For this reason, MFC provides another Sockets-related class, CSocket, which pretends to offer a synchronous interface. That is, it uses the asynchronous capabilities of CAsyncSocket (from which it is derived), but the interface it offers hides this fact. When you call its Send() or Receive() methods, they do not return until the operation is complete. They call the corresponding CAsyncSocket method, and if CAsyncSocket::GetLastError() returns WSAEWOULDBLOCK, they retrieve messages until they get the one they want (WM_SOCKET_NOTIFY with the appropriate WSAGETSELECTEVENT() code). Here's the listing of CSocket::Receive(). Send() uses the exact same logic.

```
int CSocket::Receive(void* lpBuf, int nBufLen, int nFlags)
{
    if (m_pbBlocking != NULL)
        {
        WSASetLastError(WSAEINPROGRESS);
        return  FALSE;
        }
    int nResult;
    while ((nResult = CAsyncSocket::Receive(
                lpBuf, nBufLen, nFlags)) == SOCKET_ERROR)
```

```
        {
        if (GetLastError() == WSAEWOULDBLOCK)
            {
            if (!PumpMessages(FD_READ))
                return SOCKET_ERROR;
            }
        else
            return SOCKET_ERROR;
        }
    return nResult;
}
```

Class Declaration. Here is the declaration of CSocket, again excerpted from AFXSOCK.H. The methods that override the corresponding CAsyncSocket methods impose the pseudosynchronous model exemplified by CSocket::Receive(). The Create() override just makes sure that all WSAAsyncSelect() events get reported asynchronously.

```
class CSocket : public CAsyncSocket
{
public:
    BOOL Create(UINT nSocketPort = 0, int nSocketType=SOCK_STREAM,
        LPCTSTR lpszSocketAddress = NULL);

// Implementation
public:
    virtual BOOL Accept(CAsyncSocket& rConnectedSocket,
        SOCKADDR* lpSockAddr = NULL, int* lpSockAddrLen = NULL);
    virtual void Close();
    virtual int Receive(void* lpBuf, int nBufLen, int nFlags = 0);
    virtual int Send(const void* lpBuf, int nBufLen, int nFlags = 0);
};
```

It seems pretty clear that this class is built around the limitations of Windows 3.1—limitations that no longer obtain in the Win32 environment. There's nothing wrong now with just issuing a call and letting it block. Later in this chapter, I will develop a class that I call COverlappedSocket, which uses CAsyncSocket as a blocking socket on the client side, and borrows some of its asynchronous functionality on the server. To make sure the socket gets created as a blocking socket, I override the Create() and Socket() methods to force the AsyncSelect() event code to be passed as zero, which turns off asynchronous notifications. And just to make sure my point is clear, I force the socket into blocking mode by calling CAsyncSocket::IOCtl(). Here's my COverlappedSocket::Socket() method. (It calls the CAsyncSocket methods through an embedded CAsyncSocket-derived member, *m_AsyncSocket*).

```
BOOL COverlappedSocket::Socket(int  nSocketType,
                               long lEvent,
                               int  nProtocolType,
                               int  nAddressFormat)
{
   BOOL bRetcode;

   bRetcode = m_AsyncSocket.Socket(nSocketType, 0, nProtocolType,
                                   nAddressFormat);
   if (bRetcode)
      {
      DWORD dwIOMode = FALSE;  // Not nonblocking I/O
      m_AsyncSocket.IOCtl(FIONBIO, &dwIOMode);
      SetFileHandle((HANDLE) m_AsyncSocket.m_hSocket);
      }
   return bRetcode;
}
```

One capability that CSocket does offer is serialization with an MFC CArchive object. This enables you to associate a CSocket with a CArchive, then do I/O to the socket using the << and >> operators. CSocket can't do this by itself, though; it requires the services of a CFile-derived class, because CArchive can only work with CFile objects. Therefore, MFC adds a third class, CSocketFile. It is a simple class, implementing only the Read(), Write(), and Close() methods (as required by CArchive). It also overrides the other CFile methods, but only to disable them (since they are irrelevant for sockets). Here is an excerpt from its declaration:

```
class CSocketFile : public CFile
{
public:
//Constructors
   CSocketFile(CSocket* pSocket, BOOL bArchiveCompatible = TRUE);

// Implementation
public:
   CSocket* m_pSocket;
   BOOL m_bArchiveCompatible;

   virtual ~CSocketFile();

   virtual UINT Read(void* lpBuf, UINT nCount);
   virtual void Write(const void* lpBuf, UINT nCount);
   virtual void Close();
```

```
// Unsupported APIs
   virtual BOOL Open(LPCTSTR lpszFileName, UINT nOpenFlags,
                     CFileException* pError = NULL);
   virtual CFile* Duplicate() const;
   virtual DWORD GetPosition() const;
   virtual LONG Seek(LONG lOff, UINT nFrom);
   virtual void SetLength(DWORD dwNewLen);
   virtual DWORD GetLength() const;
   virtual void LockRange(DWORD dwPos, DWORD dwCount);
   virtual void UnlockRange(DWORD dwPos, DWORD dwCount);
   virtual void Flush();
   virtual void Abort();
};
```

Now you can do I/O to the socket via the archive. The socket must be in the connected state to tie it to an archive. Once it is, you instantiate a CSocketFile object, passing it a pointer to the CSocket. You then create two CArchive objects, one to send (or store) the data, the other to receive (or load) it.

```
CSocket MySocket;

MySocket.Create();
// Connect to TCP echo service on local machine (port number 7)
MySocket.Connect("localhost", 7);

CSocketFile MySocketFile(&MySocket);
CArchive    arTransmit(&MySocketFile, CArchive::store);
CArchive    arReceive(&MySocketFile, CArchive::load);

CString OutString, InString;

LPTSTR lpString = OutString.GetBufferSetLength(8192);

::FillMemory(lpString, 8191, 'A');
lpString[8191] = '\0';

OutString.ReleaseBuffer();

// Send 100 packets

for (int i = 0; i < 100; ++i)
   {
   arTransmit << OutString;
   arTransmit.Flush();
   arReceive  >> InString;
   }
```

```
arTransmit.Close();
arReceive.Close();

MySocket.Close();
```

Extensions to the MFC Sockets Classes

The MFC Sockets classes have some shortcomings. CAsyncSocket is fairly lean and efficient; it does not impose a significant performance penalty, from what I have observed. However, using it in its full asynchronous implementation requires some messy coding. The CSocket class adds a pseudosynchronous layer on top of CAsyncSocket, and offers a very simple coding model, with some cost in performance. These classes do not attempt to take advantage of Win32's overlapped capabilities. They are thus unable to use advanced features like I/O completion routines or I/O completion ports. Furthermore, they are currently rooted in Windows Sockets 1.1. To get Sockets 2 support now (while we wait for MFC to incorporate it), we have to take matters into our own hands by deriving new classes.

COverlappedSocket / CXAsyncSocket

Therefore, I have implemented an overlapped Sockets class as part of my Win32 object library (WIN32MFC.DLL). This class is called COverlapped-Socket. It uses the COverlappedFile class developed in Chapter 6 to inherit its overlapped I/O capabilities. To this, it adds Sockets-specific functionality to handle all of the communications requirements (setting up connections, listening for clients, and so on).

I first thought to borrow the functionality of COverlappedFile and CAsyncSocket by multiple inheritance. However, I found this difficult to work with, for a variety of reasons. A simpler implementation derives from COverlappedFile alone, and includes an embedded data member, *m_AsyncSocket*, that belongs to a new class I create called CXAsyncSocket. This class, a subclass of CAsyncSocket, does not have a great deal of functionality; its main purpose is to act as a conduit between COverlappedSocket and CAsyncSocket. When COverlappedSocket requires Sockets-related services, it calls CAsyncSocket methods through *m_AsyncSocket*. In the other direction, *m_AsyncSocket* receives the asynchronous notifications the COverlappedSocket is interested in, then delegates them to COverlappedSocket, through its own member variable *m_pOwningSocket*. Therefore, both CXAsyncSocket and COverlappedSocket override OnAccept(), OnReceive(), OnOutOfBandData(), and OnClose(). CXAsyncSocket uses Windows

Sockets 2, if it can. Thus, it overrides CAsyncSocket::Create() and CAsyncSocket::Socket() and calls WSASocket(); it replaces CAsyncSocket::Connect(), and calls WSAConnect(); and it implements its own version of Accept(), which calls WSAAccept().

CXAsyncSocket. Here is the class declaration of CXAsyncSocket, from \WIN32NET\CODE\WIN32OBJ\OVSOCK.H:

```
class AFX_EXT_CLASS CXAsyncSocket : public CAsyncSocket
{
protected:
   COverlappedSocket *m_pOwningSocket; // Where I live
public:
   CXAsyncSocket(COverlappedSocket *pOwningSocket)
      {
      m_pOwningSocket = pOwningSocket;
      }
   virtual void OnAccept( int nErrorCode );
   virtual void OnReceive( int nErrorCode );
   virtual void OnOutOfBandData( int nErrorCode );
   virtual void OnClose(int nErrorCode );

   // Override Create(), Socket(), and Accept()
   // to use Winsock 2 if it's available
   BOOL Create(UINT nSocketPort = 0, int nSocketType=SOCK_STREAM,
               long lEvent = 0,
               LPCTSTR lpszSocketAddress = NULL);
   BOOL Socket(int nSocketType = SOCK_STREAM, long lEvent = 0,
               int nProtocolType = 0, int nAddressFormat = PF_INET);
   BOOL Connect(const SOCKADDR* lpSockAddr, int nSockAddrLen);

   virtual BOOL Accept(CAsyncSocket& rConnectedSocket,
                       SOCKADDR* lpSockAddr = NULL,
                       int* lpSockAddrLen = NULL);

   DECLARE_DYNAMIC(CXAsyncSocket);
};
```

Both Create() and Socket() create new sockets; the only difference is that Create() assumes the Internet address family, while Socket() lets the caller choose one. In the Winsock 2 version, they call WSASocket() to open the socket.

```
SOCKET WSAAPI WSASocket(
    int                  iAddressFamily,
    int                  iSocketType,
    int                  iProtocol,
```

```
LPWSAPROTOCOL_INFO lpProtocolInfo,
GROUP              g,
DWORD              dwFlags);
```

The first three arguments are the same as the arguments for the socket() function. However, if *lpProtocolInfo* is passed as a non-NULL pointer, they are ignored. *lpProtocolInfo* points to a WSAPROTOCOL_INFO structure that offers a more complete description of the target protocol. Its *iAddressFamily*, *iSocketType*, and *iProtocol* fields pass the same information as the corresponding arguments. The WSAPROTOCOL_INFO structure is also populated by the WSAEnumProtocols() function. You can enumerate your protocols and create sockets for each of them by passing the WSAPROTOCOL_INFO structure directly to WSASocket(). This same capability exists in Sockets 1.1, but you have to call EnumProtocols() to enumerate your protocols, then pull the fields out of the PROTOCOL_INFO structure (an earlier version of WSAPROTOCOL_INFO) and pass them to socket() as its arguments.

The group identifier *g* specifies the identifier of a socket group that you want the new socket to join. To create a new group, pass *g* as SG_UNCONSTRAINED_GROUP or SG_CONSTRAINED_GROUP. An unconstrained group can contain any type of socket (stream-oriented, message-oriented, or datagram) as long as they are all part of the same protocol family. Constrained groups can only contain connection-oriented sockets, and they must all be connected to the same server process. Socket groups serve two main purposes:

- They allow you to set quality of service for a group of sockets as a whole, rather than for each individual socket.
- They allow you to set relative priorities for the sockets in a group. You do this by calling setsockopt() with the SO_GROUP_PRIORITY option (new to Winsock 2).

Because *g* is only an input parameter, you have to call getsockopt() with the SO_GROUP_ID option to find out the ID of a newly created group. For sockets that you subsequently create that you want to join the group, you pass this ID as *g*.

Passing *g* as zero creates a socket that is not associated with a group.

The last argument, *dwFlags*, includes several options. Some of them provide explicit support for multipoint connections (Sockets conference calls). The one of highest interest for us is the WSA_FLAG_OVERLAPPED flag, which is just defined as FILE_FLAG_OVERLAPPED. In Winsock 2, this is the only way to create an overlapped socket. You can also create a non-overlapped socket by omitting this flag.

Because CXAsyncSocket::Create() and CXAsyncSocket::Socket() are very similar, I show only the Socket() method. After creating the socket, it calls the CAsyncSocket::AttachHandle() method. This allows MFC to complete its initialization of the socket object.

```
BOOL CXAsyncSocket::Socket(
               int nSocketType /*= SOCK_STREAM*/,
               long lEvent /* = 0*/,
               int nProtocolType /*= 0*/,
               int nAddressFormat /*= PF_INET*/)
{
#ifndef _USE_WINSOCK2_
   return CAsyncSocket::Socket(nSocketType, lEvent,
                               nProtocolType,
                               nAddressFormat);
#else
   m_hSocket =
      ::WSASocket(nAddressFormat, nSocketType, nProtocolType,
          NULL,  // WSAPROTOCOL_INFO
          0,     // Socket group
          WSA_FLAG_OVERLAPPED);

   if (m_hSocket != INVALID_SOCKET)
      {
      AttachHandle(m_hSocket, this, FALSE);
      return AsyncSelect(lEvent);
      }
   return FALSE;
#endif
}
```

The Connect() method calls WSAConnect(), a Winsock 2 extension to the Berkeley connect() function. It allows the client to send data to the server along with the connect request, if the underlying protocol supports this capability. It also lets the client request a specific quality of service.

```
int WSAAPI WSAConnect(
    SOCKET                 s,
    const struct sockaddr *lpServerAddress,
    int                    nServerAddressLength,
    LPWSABUF               lpCallerData,
    LPWSABUF               lpCalleeData,
    LPQOS                  lpSQOS,
    LPQOS                  lpGQOS);
```

The first three arguments are the same as for connect()—the client's socket, the server's socket address, and the size of the address information. The fourth argument points to a WSABUF structure pointing to data the client wants to send along with the connection request. The fifth argument is provided for the server to return data to the client. On input, the client sets *len* to the size of the buffer. On output, the server sets *len* to the amount of data it is returning, with zero indicating there is no data.

Both *lpCallerData* and *lpCalleeData* can be passed as NULL if no exchange of data needs to take place. Over protocols that do not support this feature, WSAConnect() will fail if you do not pass NULL pointers.

The sixth and seventh arguments request quality of service for the client's socket and the socket's group, respectively. Quality of service is represented by the QOS structure type. It in turn contains one member indicating the quality of service for client-to-server transmissions, and another requesting the server-to-client quality of service:

```
typedef struct _QualityOfService
{
    FLOWSPEC SendingFlowspec;
    FLOWSPEC ReceivingFlowspec;
    WSABUF   ProviderSpecific;
} QOS, *LPQOS;
```

Here are the *typedef*s for the FLOWSPEC structure and the GUARANTEE enumeration it uses from WINSOCK2.H, including the comments for each field. Quality of service in Windows Sockets 2 is a highly technical and specialized topic, and one I don't fully understand. For a detailed discussion, I refer you to the Windows Sockets 2 specification. You can download it from the World Wide Web at the address http://www.stardust.com. The name of the file is WSAPI21.DOC.

```
typedef enum
{
    BestEffortService,
    PredictiveService,
    GuaranteedService
} GUARANTEE;

typedef long int32;

typedef struct _flowspec
{
    int32       TokenRate;              /* In Bytes/sec */
    int32       TokenBucketSize;        /* In Bytes */
    int32       PeakBandwidth;          /* In Bytes/sec */
```

```
    int32        Latency;               /* In microseconds */
    int32        DelayVariation;        /* In microseconds */
    GUARANTEE    LevelOfGuarantee;      /* Guaranteed, Predictive */
                                        /*   or Best Effort      */
    int32        CostOfCall;            /* Reserved for future use, */
                                        /*   must be set to 0 now    */
    int32        NetworkAvailability;   /* read-only:         */
                                        /*   1 if accessible, */
                                        /*   0 if not         */
} FLOWSPEC, *LPFLOWSPEC;
```

CXAsyncSocket::Connect() uses only the first three arguments, the standard ones for connect(). Here is the listing:

```
BOOL CXAsyncSocket::Connect(const SOCKADDR* lpSockAddr,
                            int nSockAddrLen)
{
#ifndef _USE_WINSOCK2_
   return CAsyncSocket::Connect(lpSockAddr, nSockAddrLen);
#else
   return (::WSAConnect(m_hSocket, lpSockAddr, nSockAddrLen,
           NULL, NULL, NULL, NULL) == 0);
#endif
}
```

Lastly, the CXAsyncSocket::Accept() method calls WSAAccept().

```
SOCKET WSAAPI WSAAccept(
    SOCKET            s,
    struct sockaddr *lpClientAddress,
    LPINT             lpnClientAddressLength,
    LPCONDITIONPROC   lpfnCondition,
    DWORD             dwCallbackData
    );
```

The first three arguments are the same as for the accept() function. The fourth argument specifies a callback function, called a **condition procedure**, where the server can do these things:

- Receive any data the client has sent in its WSAConnect() call.
- Return data to the client.
- Decide whether the client should be allowed to connect to the server.
- Determine whether the server can provide the quality of service that the client wants.

Here's the prototype for the condition procedure:

```
typedef
int
(CALLBACK * LPCONDITIONPROC)(
    LPWSABUF lpCallerId,
    LPWSABUF lpCallerData,
    LPQOS    lpSQOS,
    LPQOS    lpGQOS,
    LPWSABUF lpCalleeId,
    LPWSABUF lpCalleeData,
    GROUP    *g,
    DWORD    dwCallbackData
    );
```

lpCallerId is the protocol-specific address of the calling application, and *lpCallerData* is the data it transmitted with its connection request. *lpSQOS* and *lpGQOS* are the qualities of service the client has requested for the socket on which it is connecting to the server, and for the group to which the socket belongs. *lpCalleeId* is the protocol-specific address of the server application. To return data to the client, the server copies the data to the address specified by *lpCalleeData->buf*. The amount of data copied must not exceed *lpCalleeData->len*. The server must set *lpCalleeData->len* to indicate how much data it is returning, with zero meaning that no data is available. The GROUP pointer *g* lets the server assign the socket to a new or existing socket group if it has a reason to do so. *dwCallbackData* is application-specific information; it is the last argument the server passed to WSAAccept(). The return code from the condition procedure is CF_ACCEPT if the server accepts the connection, CF_REJECT if not.

The only other wrinkle in CXAsyncSocket::Accept() is the call to CAsyncSocket::AttachHandle(). This is how you attach a socket you have created outside of MFC to an MFC CAsyncSocket object.

```
BOOL CXAsyncSocket::Accept(
      CAsyncSocket& rConnectedSocket,
      SOCKADDR      *lpSockAddr    /*= NULL*/,
      int           *lpSockAddrLen /*= NULL*/)
{
#ifndef _USE_WINSOCK2_
   return CAsyncSocket::Accept(rConnectedSocket,
            lpSockAddr, lpSockAddrLen);
#else
   SOCKET hSocket =
      ::WSAAccept(m_hSocket, lpSockAddr, lpSockAddrLen,
         NULL, 0);

   if (hSocket != INVALID_SOCKET)
```

```
            {
            rConnectedSocket.m_hSocket = hSocket;
            CAsyncSocket::AttachHandle(hSocket, &rConnectedSocket);
            }
        return (hSocket != INVALID_SOCKET);
    #endif
    }
```

COverlappedSocket. COverlappedSocket provides overlapped I/O by inheriting from COverlappedFile, presented in Chapter 6. Most of its intelligence resides in a couple of key methods. I mentioned earlier that I override the CAsyncSocket Create() and Socket() methods so they create blocking sockets, with asynchronous notifications turned off. When I use a COverlappedSocket object as a server endpoint, I ask for FD_ACCEPT notifications initially. The OnAccept() handler then accepts the connection and spins off a background thread to receive data. I also call AsyncSelect() and ask for FD_CLOSE notification. If I am running under Windows 95, I content myself with using the standard AsyncSelect() mechanism, asking for FD_READ | FD_OOB | FD_CLOSE events; I don't feel that comfortable yet with Windows 95's ability to handle overlapped I/O.

I also have to call the COverlappedFile::SetFileHandle() method; the socket handle (CAsyncSocket::m_hSocket) must also be remembered as the file handle (CFile::m_hFile).

Here is my OnAccept() handler, from \WIN32NET\CODE\WIN32OBJ\OVSOCK.CPP:

```
void COverlappedSocket::OnAccept( int nErrorCode )
{
   if (nErrorCode == 0)
      {
      COverlappedSocket *pConnectedSocket =
         new COverlappedSocket;

      if (m_AsyncSocket.Accept(pConnectedSocket->m_AsyncSocket))
         {
         // Set callback function for incoming data
         pConnectedSocket->SetReceiveCallback(
            GetReceiveCallback());
         pConnectedSocket->SetFileHandle(
            (HANDLE) pConnectedSocket->m_AsyncSocket.m_hSocket);

         // Spin off thread to handle reads
         // using overlapped I/O
         if (CWin32Object::IsWindowsNT())
```

```
            {
            AfxBeginThread(NTSocketsThread,
               (LPVOID) pConnectedSocket);
            pConnectedSocket->AsyncSelect(FD_CLOSE);
            }
         else
            {
            pConnectedSocket->AsyncSelect(FD_READ | FD_OOB | FD_CLOSE);
            }
         }
      else
         {
         delete pConnectedSocket;
         }
      }
}
```

NTSocketsThread() is a COverlappedSocket static member function (it must be static to be used as a thread entry point). It ties the socket to an I/O completion port (represented as a CIoPort object). It then spins off overlapped reads, using COverlappedFile::Read(), to listen for incoming data. When data arrives, it is posted upstairs by invoking COverlappedFile::CallReceiveCallback(). This activates the callback function that was provided by the host application. Because it implements a higher-level protocol, my classes cannot provide a reasonable default implementation of the callback. The sample applications in Chapter 16 show a couple of examples.

The operation is then recycled using the Recycle() method of my COverlapped class.

Here is the listing:

```
UINT COverlappedSocket::NTSocketsThread(LPVOID lp)
{
   COverlappedSocket *pSocket =
      (COverlappedSocket *) lp;
   CIoPort      IOPort;
   COverlapped  Overlapped[OVERLAPPED_READS];
   LPBYTE       lpData[OVERLAPPED_READS];
   LPOVERLAPPED lpOverlapped;
   int          i;
   BOOL         bOK = TRUE;

   pSocket->m_hThread = ::GetCurrentThread();
   IOPort.Add(pSocket);

   int nReadBufSize = 64000;
   int nSizeSize = sizeof (int); // sizeof nReadBufSize
```

```
    // Set size of receive buffer
    pSocket->m_AsyncSocket.SetSockOpt(
       SO_RCVBUF, &nReadBufSize, nSizeSize);
    DWORD dwBytesRead;

    for (i = 0; i < OVERLAPPED_READS; ++i)
       {
       lpData[i] = new BYTE[nReadBufSize];
       Overlapped[i].SetFile((HANDLE) pSocket->GetFileHandle());
       Overlapped[i].SetBuffer(lpData[i]);
       if (!pSocket->Read(lpData[i], nReadBufSize, &dwBytesRead,
          &Overlapped[i]) && (::GetLastError() != ERROR_IO_PENDING))
          bOK = FALSE;
       }

    COverlapped *pThisOverlapped;
    while (bOK &&
          (IOPort.Wait(&lpOverlapped, &dwBytesRead) != NULL) &&
          (dwBytesRead > 0))
       {
       pThisOverlapped = (COverlapped *) lpOverlapped;
       pSocket->CallReceiveCallback(
             (LPBYTE) pThisOverlapped->GetBuffer(),
             dwBytesRead,
             (HANDLE) pSocket);
       if (!pThisOverlapped->Recycle(nReadBufSize, &dwBytesRead)
          && (::GetLastError() != ERROR_IO_PENDING))
          bOK = FALSE;
       }
    for (i = 0; i < OVERLAPPED_READS; ++i)
       {
       delete [] lpData[i];
       }
    DWORD dwError = pSocket->m_AsyncSocket.GetLastError();
    return dwError;
}
```

The last method of interest is the OnClose() handler, called when a client application hangs up. It closes the socket, waits for the background thread to go away, then deletes the *this* pointer. Closing the socket causes the thread to exit because GetQueuedCompletionStatus() reports an error on the I/O completion port. In response, CIoPort::Wait() returns NULL, which is one of the conditions of the loop.

```
void COverlappedSocket::OnClose(int nErrorCode )
{
   Close();
   SetFileHandle(INVALID_HANDLE_VALUE);
```

```
   if (m_hThread != NULL)
      ::WaitForSingleObject(m_hThread, 2000);
   delete this;
}
```

The OnReceive() method is a fairly conventional implementation. It calls CAsyncSocket::IOCtl(), passing it the FIONREAD verb to ask it how much data is available. It allocates the memory, reads the data, and posts it upstairs. This method, as I mentioned, is provided so COverlappedSocket objects can be used for Windows 95 server applications—although I don't recommend using Windows 95 as a host for server applications (and neither does Microsoft).

```
void COverlappedSocket::OnReceive( int nErrorCode )
{
   BOOL bRetcode;

   if (nErrorCode == 0)
      {
      // Hi, you got any data for me?
      DWORD dwBytesToRead;

      bRetcode = m_AsyncSocket.IOCtl(FIONREAD, &dwBytesToRead);

      int nBytesReceived, nTotalReceived;

      while (bRetcode &&
             (dwBytesToRead > 0))
         {
         LPBYTE lpData = new BYTE[dwBytesToRead];

         for (nTotalReceived = 0;
              nTotalReceived < (int) dwBytesToRead;
             )
            {
            nBytesReceived =
               m_AsyncSocket.Receive(
                  &lpData[nTotalReceived],
                  dwBytesToRead - (DWORD) nTotalReceived);

            if (nBytesReceived > 0)
               {
               nTotalReceived += nBytesReceived;
               }
```

```
                else
                   {
                   // Error
                   bRetcode = (nBytesReceived == SOCKET_ERROR);
                   break;
                   }
                }
             if (bRetcode)
                {
                CallReceiveCallback(lpData, dwBytesToRead,
                                    (HANDLE) this);
                bRetcode =
                   m_AsyncSocket.IOCtl(FIONREAD, &dwBytesToRead);
                }
             delete lpData;
             }
          }
}
```

Code Listings

Here are the complete source files for CXAsyncSocket and COverlapped-Socket, \WIN32NET\CODE\WIN32OBJ\OVSOCK.H and \WIN32NET\CODE\WIN32OBJ\OVSOCK.CPP.

```
/********
*
* OVSOCK.H
*
* Copyright (c) 1995-1996 Ralph P. Davis
*
* All Rights Reserved
*
********/

#ifndef _OVSOCK_INCLUDED
#define _OVSOCK_INCLUDED

#include "ovfile.h"
#include "tls.h"

class COverlappedSocket;
class CXAsyncSocket;

class AFX_EXT_CLASS CXAsyncSocket : public CAsyncSocket
{
protected:
   COverlappedSocket *m_pOwningSocket; // Where I live
```

```
public:
   CXAsyncSocket(COverlappedSocket *pOwningSocket)
      {
      m_pOwningSocket = pOwningSocket;
      }
   virtual void OnAccept( int nErrorCode );
   virtual void OnReceive( int nErrorCode );
   virtual void OnOutOfBandData( int nErrorCode );
   virtual void OnClose(int nErrorCode );

   // Override Create(), Socket(), and Accept()
   // to use Winsock 2 if it's available
   BOOL Create(UINT nSocketPort = 0, int nSocketType=SOCK_STREAM,
               long lEvent = 0,
               LPCTSTR lpszSocketAddress = NULL);
   BOOL Socket(int nSocketType = SOCK_STREAM, long lEvent = 0,
               int nProtocolType = 0, int nAddressFormat = PF_INET);
   BOOL Connect(const SOCKADDR* lpSockAddr, int nSockAddrLen);

   virtual BOOL Accept(CAsyncSocket& rConnectedSocket,
                       SOCKADDR* lpSockAddr = NULL,
                       int* lpSockAddrLen = NULL);

   DECLARE_DYNAMIC(CXAsyncSocket);
};

class AFX_EXT_CLASS COverlappedSocket : public COverlappedFile
{
protected:
   long          m_lEventMask;
   static UINT NTSocketsThread(LPVOID lp);
   HANDLE m_hThread;
   enum {OVERLAPPED_READS = 2};
   CXAsyncSocket m_AsyncSocket;

public:
   COverlappedSocket();
   virtual ~COverlappedSocket();

   virtual void OnAccept( int nErrorCode );
   virtual void OnReceive( int nErrorCode );
   virtual void OnOutOfBandData( int nErrorCode );
   virtual void OnClose(int nErrorCode );

   BOOL AsyncSelect(long lEvent =
        FD_READ | FD_WRITE | FD_OOB | FD_ACCEPT | FD_CONNECT | FD_CLOSE);
```

```
    CXAsyncSocket& GetSocket(void)
        {
        return m_AsyncSocket;
        }
    const CXAsyncSocket *GetSocket(void) const
        {
        return &m_AsyncSocket;
        }

    long GetEventMask(void)
        {
        return m_lEventMask;
        }

    // Override CAsyncSocket methods so we create a
    // blocking socket with no asynchronous notifications
    // These pass through to the embedded m_AsyncSocket member
    BOOL Create(UINT nSocketPort = 0, int nSocketType=SOCK_STREAM,
                long lEvent = 0,
                LPCTSTR lpszSocketAddress = NULL);
    BOOL Socket(int nSocketType = SOCK_STREAM, long lEvent = 0,
                int nProtocolType = 0, int nAddressFormat = PF_INET);

    virtual void Close();

    DECLARE_DYNAMIC(COverlappedSocket)
};

#endif


/********
*
* OVSOCK.CPP
*
* Copyright (c) 1995-1996 Ralph P. Davis
*
* All Rights Reserved
*
********/

/*===== Include Files =====*/

#include "stdafx.h"

#include "win32obj.h"
#include "ovsock.h"
#include "overlap.h"
#include "ovfile.h"
#include "ioport.h"
```

```
IMPLEMENT_DYNAMIC(COverlappedSocket, COverlappedFile)
IMPLEMENT_DYNAMIC(CXAsyncSocket, CAsyncSocket)

COverlappedSocket::COverlappedSocket() : m_AsyncSocket(this)
{
   m_bCloseOnDelete = FALSE;  // Tell CFile not to close me
   m_lEventMask = 0;
}

COverlappedSocket::~COverlappedSocket()
{
   Close();
}

BOOL COverlappedSocket::Create(UINT nSocketPort, int nSocketType,
      long lEvent, LPCTSTR lpszSocketAddress)
{
   BOOL bRetcode;

   bRetcode = m_AsyncSocket.Create(nSocketPort, nSocketType,
       0, lpszSocketAddress);

   if (bRetcode)
      {
      DWORD dwIOMode = FALSE;  // Not nonblocking I/O
      m_AsyncSocket.IOCtl(FIONBIO, &dwIOMode);
      SetFileHandle((HANDLE) m_AsyncSocket.m_hSocket);
      }
   return bRetcode;
}

BOOL COverlappedSocket::Socket(int  nSocketType,
                               long lEvent,
                               int  nProtocolType,
                               int  nAddressFormat)
{
   BOOL bRetcode;

   bRetcode = m_AsyncSocket.Socket(nSocketType, 0, nProtocolType,
                                   nAddressFormat);
   if (bRetcode)
      {
      DWORD dwIOMode = FALSE;  // Not nonblocking I/O
      m_AsyncSocket.IOCtl(FIONBIO, &dwIOMode);
      SetFileHandle((HANDLE) m_AsyncSocket.m_hSocket);
      }
   return bRetcode;
}
```

```
void COverlappedSocket::Close(void)
{
   m_AsyncSocket.Close();
   m_AsyncSocket.m_hSocket = INVALID_SOCKET;
   SetFileHandle(INVALID_HANDLE_VALUE);
}

UINT COverlappedSocket::NTSocketsThread(LPVOID lp)
{
   COverlappedSocket *pSocket =
      (COverlappedSocket *) lp;
   CIoPort      IOPort;
   COverlapped  Overlapped[OVERLAPPED_READS];
   LPBYTE       lpData[OVERLAPPED_READS];
   LPOVERLAPPED lpOverlapped;
   int          i;
   BOOL         bOK = TRUE;

   pSocket->m_hThread = ::GetCurrentThread();
   IOPort.Add(pSocket);

   int nReadBufSize = 64000;
   int nSizeSize = sizeof (int); // sizeof nReadBufSize

   // Set size of receive buffer
   pSocket->m_AsyncSocket.SetSockOpt(
      SO_RCVBUF, &nReadBufSize, nSizeSize);
   DWORD dwBytesRead;

   for (i = 0; i < OVERLAPPED_READS; ++i)
      {
      lpData[i] = new BYTE[nReadBufSize];
      Overlapped[i].SetFile((HANDLE) pSocket->GetFileHandle());
      Overlapped[i].SetBuffer(lpData[i]);
      if (!pSocket->Read(lpData[i], nReadBufSize, &dwBytesRead,
         &Overlapped[i]) && (::GetLastError() != ERROR_IO_PENDING))
         bOK = FALSE;
      }

   COverlapped *pThisOverlapped;
   while (bOK &&
         (IOPort.Wait(&lpOverlapped, &dwBytesRead) != NULL) &&
         (dwBytesRead > 0))
      {
      pThisOverlapped = (COverlapped *) lpOverlapped;
      pSocket->CallReceiveCallback(
            (LPBYTE) pThisOverlapped->GetBuffer(),
            dwBytesRead,
            (HANDLE) pSocket);
```

```
      if (!pThisOverlapped->Recycle(nReadBufSize, &dwBytesRead)
         && (::GetLastError() != ERROR_IO_PENDING))
         bOK = FALSE;
      }
   for (i = 0; i < OVERLAPPED_READS; ++i)
      {
      delete [] lpData[i];
      }
   DWORD dwError = pSocket->m_AsyncSocket.GetLastError();
   return dwError;
}

void COverlappedSocket::OnAccept( int nErrorCode )
{
   if (nErrorCode == 0)
      {
      COverlappedSocket *pConnectedSocket =
         new COverlappedSocket;

      if (m_AsyncSocket.Accept(pConnectedSocket->m_AsyncSocket))
         {
         // Set callback function for incoming data
         pConnectedSocket->SetReceiveCallback(
            GetReceiveCallback());
         pConnectedSocket->SetFileHandle(
            (HANDLE) pConnectedSocket->m_AsyncSocket.m_hSocket);

         // Spin off thread to handle reads
         // using overlapped I/O
         if (CWin32Object::IsWindowsNT())
            {
            AfxBeginThread(NTSocketsThread,
               (LPVOID) pConnectedSocket);
            pConnectedSocket->AsyncSelect(FD_CLOSE);
            }
         else
            {
            pConnectedSocket->AsyncSelect(FD_READ | FD_OOB | FD_CLOSE);
            }
         }
      else
         {
         delete pConnectedSocket;
         }
      }
}
```

```
void COverlappedSocket::OnReceive( int nErrorCode )
{
   BOOL bRetcode;

   if (nErrorCode == 0)
      {
      // Hi, you got any data for me?
      DWORD dwBytesToRead;

      bRetcode = m_AsyncSocket.IOCtl(FIONREAD, &dwBytesToRead);

      int nBytesReceived, nTotalReceived;

      while (bRetcode &&
             (dwBytesToRead > 0))
         {
         LPBYTE lpData = new BYTE[dwBytesToRead];

         for (nTotalReceived = 0;
              nTotalReceived < (int) dwBytesToRead;
             )
            {
            nBytesReceived =
               m_AsyncSocket.Receive(
                  &lpData[nTotalReceived],
                  dwBytesToRead - (DWORD) nTotalReceived);

            if (nBytesReceived > 0)
               {
               nTotalReceived += nBytesReceived;
               }
            else
               {
               // Error
               bRetcode = (nBytesReceived == SOCKET_ERROR);
               break;
               }
            }
         if (bRetcode)
            {
            CallReceiveCallback(lpData, dwBytesToRead,
                                (HANDLE) this);
            bRetcode =
               m_AsyncSocket.IOCtl(FIONREAD, &dwBytesToRead);
            }
         delete lpData;
         }
      }
}
```

```
void COverlappedSocket::OnOutOfBandData( int nErrorCode )
{
   OnReceive(nErrorCode);
}

void COverlappedSocket::OnClose(int nErrorCode )
{
   Close();
   SetFileHandle(INVALID_HANDLE_VALUE);

   if (m_hThread != NULL)
      ::WaitForSingleObject(m_hThread, 2000);

   delete this;
}

BOOL COverlappedSocket::AsyncSelect(long lEvent)
{
   m_lEventMask = lEvent;
   return m_AsyncSocket.AsyncSelect(lEvent);
}

//=========== CXAsyncSocket class ==========

BOOL CXAsyncSocket::Create(
               UINT nSocketPort /*= 0*/,
               int nSocketType /*=SOCK_STREAM*/,
               long lEvent /* = 0*/,
               LPCTSTR lpszSocketAddress /*= NULL*/)
{
#ifndef _USE_WINSOCK2_
   return CAsyncSocket::Create(nSocketPort, nSocketType, lEvent,
                               lpszSocketAddress);
#else
   m_hSocket =
      ::WSASocket(AF_INET, nSocketType, 0,
          NULL,  // WSAPROTOCOL_INFO
          0,
          WSA_FLAG_OVERLAPPED);

   if (m_hSocket != INVALID_SOCKET)
      {
      AttachHandle(m_hSocket, this, FALSE);
      return AsyncSelect(lEvent);
      }
   return FALSE;
#endif
}
```

```
BOOL CXAsyncSocket::Socket(
                int nSocketType /*= SOCK_STREAM*/,
                long lEvent /* = 0*/,
                int nProtocolType /*= 0*/,
                int nAddressFormat /*= PF_INET*/)
{
#ifndef _USE_WINSOCK2_
   return CAsyncSocket::Socket(nSocketType, lEvent,
                                nProtocolType,
                                nAddressFormat);
#else
   m_hSocket =
      ::WSASocket(nAddressFormat, nSocketType, nProtocolType,
          NULL,  // WSAPROTOCOL_INFO
          0,     // Socket group
          WSA_FLAG_OVERLAPPED);

   if (m_hSocket != INVALID_SOCKET)
      {
      AttachHandle(m_hSocket, this, FALSE);
      return AsyncSelect(lEvent);
      }
   return FALSE;
#endif
}

BOOL CXAsyncSocket::Accept(
      CAsyncSocket& rConnectedSocket,
      SOCKADDR     *lpSockAddr    /*= NULL*/,
      int          *lpSockAddrLen /*= NULL*/)
{
#ifndef _USE_WINSOCK2_
   return CAsyncSocket::Accept(rConnectedSocket,
            lpSockAddr, lpSockAddrLen);
#else
   SOCKET hSocket =
      ::WSAAccept(m_hSocket, lpSockAddr, lpSockAddrLen,
          NULL, 0);

   if (hSocket != INVALID_SOCKET)
      {
      rConnectedSocket.m_hSocket = hSocket;
      CAsyncSocket::AttachHandle(hSocket, &rConnectedSocket);
      }

   return (hSocket != INVALID_SOCKET);
#endif
}
```

```
BOOL CXAsyncSocket::Connect(const SOCKADDR* lpSockAddr,
                            int nSockAddrLen)
{
#ifndef _USE_WINSOCK2_
   return CAsyncSocket::Connect(lpSockAddr, nSockAddrLen);
#else
   return (::WSAConnect(m_hSocket, lpSockAddr, nSockAddrLen,
           NULL, NULL, NULL, NULL) == 0);
#endif
}

void CXAsyncSocket::OnAccept( int nErrorCode )
{
   m_pOwningSocket->OnAccept(nErrorCode);
}

void CXAsyncSocket::OnReceive( int nErrorCode )
{
   m_pOwningSocket->OnReceive(nErrorCode);
}

void CXAsyncSocket::OnOutOfBandData( int nErrorCode )
{
   m_pOwningSocket->OnOutOfBandData(nErrorCode);
}

void CXAsyncSocket::OnClose(int nErrorCode )
{
   m_pOwningSocket->OnClose(nErrorCode);
}
```

The Service Registration API

The Service Registration API is an important adjunct to the Windows Sockets API, because it is the missing link that makes Windows Sockets truly protocol-transparent, not just protocol-independent. Using this API, you register server class information, associating a server name with a class identifier. When a server starts up, it uses this information to determine what sockets to open, and how to bind them to ports and machine addresses. It can also advertise its presence on the network, so client applications can find it and connect to it. The client, for its part, uses the API to determine where a desired server resides, and what sockets it needs to talk to it.

Unfortunately, the Service Registration API is messy. Although it consists of only a few functions, the most important of them require you to populate variable-length structures. It usually takes a lot of code to do so. It might be fair to say, "Don't worry about the fact that the structures have 91 fields—you never have to populate more than 57 of them at a time." (Those numbers are fictitious, and mild exaggerations.) The situation is helped by the fact that a handful of sample applications ship with the Win32 SDK (in the directory \MSTOOLS\SAMPLES\RNR). Not only do they give you a clear idea of how to use the API, but, as a comment in the code says, they give you a good body of code you can "leverage." And apparently, I'm not the only person who thinks this API is awful in Sockets 1.1. Sockets 2 simplifies it quite a bit, and adds some missing functionality.

To reduce the complexity of the API, my strategy has been to hide the ugly details in a C++ class, CServiceInfo. This class in turn offers a very simple interface to its users, and thereby allows me to tap into the power of Service Registration while avoiding its horrors. Indeed, the usefulness of the API is such that I have rewritten my WNet API (originally presented in my last two books, and discussed in Chapter 8) using it, with CServiceInfo and COverlappedSocket acting as intermediaries. The new implementation is presented later in this chapter.

It also helps if we think first of what the API does, then look at how it does it. There are only a few operations, and not all of them are required:

- It allows you to register a service class. When you register, you associate a service class name with a **Globally Unique Identifier (GUID)**. GUIDs are 16-byte unique numbers that are also used to identify OLE server applications and RPC interfaces. You also declare the protocols you want to use and the endpoints (TCP ports and so on) through which you can be contacted. If you are only using TCP/IP, this step is unnecessary; somebody monitors changes to your SERVICES file, and automatically creates GUIDs for all the TCP and UDP services named there.
- When a server application comes online, it reads the registration information. This tells it what arguments to pass to socket() / WSASocket() and bind(), based on the information recorded in the step above. After creating its sockets and putting them into the listening state, the server then tells the registration database that it is online.
- When a client application starts up, it too reads the registration information to find a target server. This tells it what to pass to socket() / WSASocket(), bind(), and connect() / WSAConnect().

Registering a New ServiceType

The first step in registering a new service class is to associate the service class name with a GUID. The GUID type is a standard type that Microsoft has borrowed from the Open Software Foundation's Distributed Computing Environment. It is defined as follows in RPCDCE.H:

```
typedef struct _GUID
{
    unsigned long  Data1;
    unsigned short Data2;
    unsigned short Data3;
    unsigned char  Data4[8];
} GUID;
```

Creating a New GUID. You can create a new GUID for your service. At build time, there are two tools that generate them: GUIDGEN is part of the OLE development suite, and UUIDGEN comes with the RPC development tools. GUIDGEN puts a new GUID declaration onto the clipboard for pasting into your code as a global variable. Here's an example of what it creates:

```
// {17B34121-6D18-11cf-8515-02608C3E9938}
static const GUID <<name>> =
{ 0x17b34121, 0x6d18, 0x11cf,
  { 0x85, 0x15, 0x2, 0x60, 0x8c, 0x3e, 0x99, 0x38 } };
```

UUIDGEN outputs the GUID in a format that is more appropriate to the RPC setting; we'll see what it does in Chapter 11.

You can also generate new GUIDs in software by calling the RPC function UuidCreate(), passing it a pointer to the GUID variable where you want to capture the GUID.

Using a Predefined GUID Group. The header file SVCGUID.H defines GUIDs for many of the standard TCP/IP and NetWare services. In addition, it defines template GUIDs for these two environments. The TCP template GUID is 0x00090000, 0, 0, 0xC0, 0, 0, 0, 0, 0, 0, 0x46. You can give yourself a GUID just by plugging your own server endpoint information into the low 16 bits of the first field (*Data1*). For TCP and UDP, this is your port ID. SVCGUID.H has macros you can use to define TCP and UDP GUIDs, SVCID_TCP(PortID) and SVCID_UDP(PortID).

Using Automatically Generated GUIDs. If your server will be accessed over TCP/IP (as it should be), the easiest way to get a GUID is to let the TCP drivers generate one automatically. My environment is set up to use local HOSTS and SERVICES files for network configuration. It appears that someone is monitoring changes to SERVICES, and generating GUIDs for all the TCP and UDP services declared there. In fact, all the service registration is done automatically, and this first step becomes unnecessary; all you have to do is have specific servers announce their presence when they come online.

Registering the Service. To register the service, you call the SetService() function. You pass it the information it needs as an array of records. Each record describes one of the protocols you want to use. For TCP and UDP, the only required data is the port your service is using. For NetWare, two records are required. One states whether you are doing connection-oriented service or not, the other declares the SAP ID you want to associate with your service. (SAP is an acronym for Novell's Service Advertising Protocol.) The records are passed in two structures: a SERVICE_TYPE_INFO_ABS and a SERVICE_TYPE_VALUE_ABS, defined in the header file NSPAPI.H. ("ABS" indicates that the structures are in absolute format—that is, they contain pointers to the data.)

```
typedef struct _SERVICE_TYPE_INFO_ABS {
    LPTSTR                 lpTypeName ;
    DWORD                  dwValueCount ;
    SERVICE_TYPE_VALUE_ABS Values[1] ;
} SERVICE_TYPE_INFO_ABS;
```

lpTypeName is the logical name you are associating with the service. *dwValueCount* says how many records are in the value array that starts in the *Values* field. I mentioned that variable-length structures complicate this API; here is the first one we've encountered.

The SERVICE_TYPE_VALUE_ABS structure is defined as follows:

```
typedef struct _SERVICE_TYPE_VALUE_ABS  {
    DWORD   dwNameSpace ;
    DWORD   dwValueType ;
    DWORD   dwValueSize ;
    LPTSTR  lpValueName ;
    PVOID   lpValue ;
} SERVICE_TYPE_VALUE_ABS;
```

dwNameSpace indicates the target protocol. NS_DNS means the TCP/IP suite, NS_SAP specifies NetWare. There are other name-space constants defined, but these are the only ones supported in Sockets 1.1.

dwValueType is the type of data being passed in this record, using constants defined for the Registry. All the values currently supported are REG_DWORD, indicating a DWORD. *dwValueSize* is its size, and is *sizeof(DWORD).*

lpValueName uses strings defined in NSPAPI.H (Sockets 1.1) and WINSOCK2.H (Winsock 2) to indicate which attribute we're setting. *lpValue* points to a program variable containing the desired value. For TCP and UDP, the value name is either SERVICE_TYPE_VALUE_TCPPORT ("TCPPort") or SERVICE_TYPE_VALUE_UDPPORT ("UDPPort"); the value is the port at which your service can be accessed. NetWare requires two records if you are offering connection-oriented service. The first says that you are doing connection-oriented service; the value name is SERVICE_TYPE_VALUE_CONN ("ConnectionOriented"), and the value is TRUE. The next record has the value name SERVICE_TYPE_VALUE_SAPID ("SapID"), and the value is the SAP ID you want to use. WINSOCK2.H defines two additional constants, SERVICE_TYPE_VALUE_IPXPORT ("IpxSocket") and SERVICE_TYPE_VALUE_OBJECTID ("ObjectID"). As of the Winsock 2 Beta 1.1, there is no explanation of how to use them.

My CServiceInfo class has an AddClass() method that encapsulates this functionality.

```
BOOL AddClass(LPTSTR lpszServiceClass,
              DWORD dwTCPPort,
              DWORD dwUDPPort,
              DWORD dwSAPObjectType = INVALID_SOCKET,
              DWORD dwIPXSocket = INVALID_SOCKET,
              GUID *lpGUID = NULL);
```

It in turn calls a helper function, SetupServiceInfo(). Here are the lines from that function that populate the SERVICE_TYPE_INFO_ABS and SERVICE_TYPE_VALUE_ABS structures (plus the declarations of the member variables it uses).

```
DWORD CServiceInfo::m_dwTRUE  = TRUE;
DWORD CServiceInfo::m_dwFALSE = FALSE;

LPSERVICE_TYPE_INFO_ABS  m_lpServiceClassInfo;
LPSERVICE_TYPE_VALUE_ABS m_lpServiceClassValues;
CString                  m_szServiceClassName;
DWORD                    m_dwTCPPort;
DWORD                    m_dwUDPPort;
DWORD                    m_dwSAPObjectType;

// The class name is required. In addition to specifying the
// protocols and endpoints we're using, we also have to
// provide a name-to-GUID mapping
m_lpServiceClassInfo->lpTypeName    =
   (LPTSTR) (const char *) m_szServiceClassName;
```

```
// The dwValueCount field of the SERVICE_TYPE_INFO_ABS
// structure says how many records are being passed.
// We initialize it to zero, then bump it as we add records
m_lpServiceClassInfo->dwValueCount = 0;

int i = 0;

// Registering for TCP connection-oriented communications?
if (m_dwTCPPort != INVALID_SOCKET)
   {
   ++m_lpServiceClassInfo->dwValueCount;
   m_lpServiceClassValues[i].dwNameSpace = NS_DNS ;
   m_lpServiceClassValues[i].dwValueType = REG_DWORD ;
   m_lpServiceClassValues[i].dwValueSize = sizeof (DWORD) ;
   m_lpServiceClassValues[i].lpValueName = SERVICE_TYPE_VALUE_TCPPORT;
   m_lpServiceClassValues[i].lpValue     = &m_dwTCPPort;
   ++i;
   }
// No--how about UDP
else if (m_dwUDPPort != INVALID_SOCKET)
   {
   ++m_lpServiceClassInfo->dwValueCount;
   m_lpServiceClassValues[i].dwNameSpace = NS_DNS ;
   m_lpServiceClassValues[i].dwValueType = REG_DWORD ;
   m_lpServiceClassValues[i].dwValueSize = sizeof (DWORD) ;
   m_lpServiceClassValues[i].lpValueName = SERVICE_TYPE_VALUE_UDPPORT;
   m_lpServiceClassValues[i].lpValue     = &m_dwUDPPort;
   ++i;
   }

// Registering for NetWare?
if (m_dwSAPObjectType != INVALID_SOCKET)
   {
   if (m_dwTCPPort != INVALID_SOCKET)
      {
      // If caller registered a TCP port, then
      // we know we want connection-oriented communication
      ++m_lpServiceClassInfo->dwValueCount;
      m_lpServiceClassValues[i].dwNameSpace = NS_SAP ;
      m_lpServiceClassValues[i].dwValueType = REG_DWORD ;
      m_lpServiceClassValues[i].dwValueSize = sizeof (DWORD) ;
      m_lpServiceClassValues[i].lpValueName = SERVICE_TYPE_VALUE_CONN ;

      m_lpServiceClassValues[i].lpValue     = &m_dwTRUE;
      ++i;
      }
```

```
    ++m_lpServiceClassInfo->dwValueCount;
    m_lpServiceClassValues[i].dwNameSpace = NS_SAP ;
    m_lpServiceClassValues[i].dwValueType = REG_DWORD ;
    m_lpServiceClassValues[i].dwValueSize = sizeof (DWORD) ;
    m_lpServiceClassValues[i].lpValueName = SERVICE_TYPE_VALUE_SAPID;
    m_lpServiceClassValues[i].lpValue     = &m_dwSAPObjectType;
    }
```

Populating these structures is the worst part of service registration.

The next step is to put the records into a SERVICE_INFO structure. This will then serve as one of the arguments to SetService(). Because CServiceInfo is declared as a subclass of SERVICE_INFO, I can refer to the fields directly.

```
typedef struct _SERVICE_INFO {
    LPGUID    lpServiceType ;
    LPTSTR    lpServiceName ;
    LPTSTR    lpComment ;
    LPTSTR    lpLocale ;
    DWORD     dwDisplayHint ;
    DWORD     dwVersion ;
    DWORD     dwTime ;
    LPSTR     lpMachineName ;
    LPSERVICE_ADDRESSES lpServiceAddress ;
    BLOB      ServiceSpecificInfo ;
} SERVICE_INFO;
```

The last field, *ServiceSpecificInfo,* points to the array of records we have just built. The only other field of interest for service registration is *lpServiceType*, which points to our GUID. The BLOB type contains two fields: *pBlobData*, which points to the data, and *cbSize*, the size of the data in bytes.

Here are the additional lines from CServiceInfo::SetupServiceInfo() that populate *lpServiceType* and *ServiceSpecificInfo*.

```
GUID                                  m_ServiceGUID;
LPBYTE                                m_lpServiceInfoBuffer;
DWORD                                 m_dwBlobSize;

lpServiceType                      = &m_ServiceGUID;

enum {EXTRA_VALUE_RECORDS = 3};

m_dwBlobSize = sizeof (SERVICE_TYPE_INFO) +
      (EXTRA_VALUE_RECORDS * sizeof (SERVICE_TYPE_VALUE));
m_lpServiceInfoBuffer = new BYTE[m_dwBlobSize];
ServiceSpecificInfo.pBlobData =  m_lpServiceInfoBuffer;
ServiceSpecificInfo.cbSize    =  m_dwBlobSize;
```

Now we're ready to call SetService(). Here is the listing of the AddClass() method, which ends with the call to this function:

```
BOOL CServiceInfo::AddClass(LPTSTR lpszServiceClass,
                            DWORD dwTCPPort,
                            DWORD dwUDPPort,
                            DWORD dwSAPObjectType,
                            DWORD dwIPXSocketType,
                            GUID *lpGUID)
{
   GUID NewGUID;
   INT   nRetcode;
   DWORD dwStatusFlags;

   // Get a new GUID for this service class
   if (lpGUID == NULL)
      {
      ::UuidCreate(&NewGUID);
      lpGUID = &NewGUID;
      }

   m_ServiceClassId      = *lpGUID;
   m_szServiceClassName =  lpszServiceClass;
   m_dwTCPPort           =  dwTCPPort;
   m_dwUDPPort           =  dwUDPPort;
   m_dwSAPObjectType     =  dwSAPObjectType;
   m_dwIPXSocket         =  dwIPXSocketType;
   SetUpServiceInfo();
   nRetcode = SetService(
                  NS_DEFAULT,
                  SERVICE_ADD_TYPE,
                  0,
                  this,
                  NULL,
                  &dwStatusFlags
                  );

   if (nRetcode == SOCKET_ERROR)
      {
      TRACE(_T("\nSetService() failed, GetLastError() = %d"),
         GetLastError());
      }
   return (nRetcode != SOCKET_ERROR);
}
```

The first argument to SetService() is the target name space; NS_DEFAULT means that we have (or may have) multiple records targeting more than one protocol, and is normally the argument you will pass. The second argument is the verb; SERVICE_ADD_TYPE is the relevant one here (we'll see others). The third argument is a set of flags; none apply here, so we pass it as zero. The fourth argument is a pointer to our SERVICE_INFO structure; passing the *this* pointer works because CServiceInfo is derived from SERVICE_INFO. The fifth argument is reserved and must be passed as NULL. The last argument is an output variable, returning specific status information if SetService() fails. Like most Sockets functions, SetService() returns SOCKET_ERROR if something goes wrong.

Registering for Both Connection-Oriented and Connectionless Service. If your service wants to be accessible using both types of protocols, you have to create two classes: one for the connection-oriented protocols, and one for the datagram ones. I don't know why this is the case; there's nothing in the documentation stating this (but then again, there's very little in the documentation on this API anyway). However, trial and error has shown me that it is indeed the case.

The Good News. This setup sequence is the worst part of this API. There are three pieces of good news:

- The worst is behind us.
- If you're satisfied to use TCP and UDP, you don't need to do this step.
- Windows Sockets 2 cleans up the interface, providing a new function, WSAInstallServiceClass().

Windows Sockets 2: The WSAInstallServiceClass() Function. The complexity of the registration process comes from having so many levels of embedded pointers. First, there is a SERVICE_INFO structure. It contains a *ServiceSpecificInfo* field, which is a BLOB structure. The BLOB structure contains a field *pBlobData*, which is set to point to a SERVICE_ TYPE_ INFO_ABS structure. This structure is the header for an array of SERVICE_TYPE_VALUE_ABS structures. WSAInstallServiceClass() eliminates the first two levels. Its only argument, as you can see from the prototype, is a pointer to a WSASERVICECLASSINFO structure, the Winsock 2 equivalent of the SERVICE_TYPE_INFO_ABS.

```
INT WINAPI WSAInstallServiceClass(
   LPWSASERVICECLASSINFO lpWSAServiceClassInfo);
```

The WSASERVICECLASSINFO structure contains the name-to-GUID mapping for the service type, and a pointer to an array of WSANSCLASSINFO structures.

```
typedef struct _WSAServiceClassInfoA
{
    LPGUID            lpServiceClassId;
    LPSTR             lpszServiceClassName;
    DWORD             dwCount;
    LPWSANSCLASSINFO lpClassInfos;
} WSASERVICECLASSINFO, *PWSASERVICECLASSINFO,
  *LPWSASERVICECLASSINFO;
```

The WSANSCLASSINFO structure is just a rearrangement of the SERVICE_TYPE_VALUE_ABS structure from Windows Sockets 1.1.

```
typedef struct _WSANSCLASSINFO
{
   LPTSTR lpszName;
   DWORD  dwname space;
   DWORD  dwValueType;
   DWORD  dwValueSize;
   LPVOID lpValue;
} WSANSCLASSINFO;
```

Here is the Winsock 2 version of CServiceInfo::AddClass():

```
BOOL CServiceInfo::AddClass(LPTSTR lpszServiceClass,
                            DWORD dwTCPPort,
                            DWORD dwUDPPort,
                            DWORD dwSAPObjectType,
                            DWORD dwIPXSocket,
                            GUID *lpGUID)
{
   GUID NewGUID;
   INT   nRetcode;

   // Get a new GUID for this service class
   if (lpGUID == NULL)
      {
      ::UuidCreate(&NewGUID);
      lpGUID = &NewGUID;
      }

   m_ServiceClassId      = *lpGUID;
   m_szServiceClassName =  lpszServiceClass;
   m_dwTCPPort           =  dwTCPPort;
   m_dwUDPPort           =  dwUDPPort;
```

```
    m_dwSAPObjectType       =  dwSAPObjectType;
    m_dwIPXSocket           =  dwIPXSocket;

    SetUpServiceInfo();
    nRetcode = ::WSAInstallServiceClass(
                 &m_ServiceClassInfo);

    if (nRetcode == SOCKET_ERROR)
       {
       TRACE(_T("\nWSAInstallServiceClass() failed, GetLastError() = %d"),
          GetLastError());
       }
    return (nRetcode != SOCKET_ERROR);
}
```

Starting a Server Application

When a server application starts up, it has two tasks to perform:

1. It must call GetAddressByName() to get the protocol-specific information that was previously registered for its service type. This function tells it the arguments to pass to socket() / WSASocket() and bind(). If the server is offering connection-oriented service, it will also call listen() for all sockets it creates.
2. It must then pass an array of SOCKADDR structures, representing the addresses to which it has bound its sockets, to SetService(). This is the final step in server initialization.

GetAddressByName() returns an array of CSADDR_INFO structures. Within these structures are all the information you need to pass to socket() / WSASocket() and bind().

```
typedef struct _SOCKET_ADDRESS {
    LPSOCKADDR lpSockaddr ;
    INT iSockaddrLength ;
} SOCKET_ADDRESS;

//
// CSAddr Information
//
typedef struct _CSADDR_INFO {
    SOCKET_ADDRESS LocalAddr ;
    SOCKET_ADDRESS RemoteAddr ;
    INT iSocketType ;
    INT iProtocol ;
} CSADDR_INFO;
```

The socket() arguments are in *LocalAddr.lpSockaddr->sa_family*, *iSocketType*, and *iProtocol*. The bind() arguments are *LocalAddr.lpSockaddr* and *LocalAddr.iSockaddrLength*.

CServiceInfo has a Register() method that calls GetAddressByName(). It is using COverlappedSocket objects, so it invokes the CAsyncSocket methods that wrap the Sockets API. For each socket it creates, it adds its SOCKADDR to a SERVICE_ADDRESSES structure. This is required for its next call to SetService(), which advertises its presence. SERVICE_ADDRESSES, in turn, contains an array of SERVICE_ADDRESS structures. CServiceInfo keeps track of the sockets it creates in a CArray member variable, *m_SocketsInUse*.

```
typedef struct _SERVICE_ADDRESSES {
    DWORD           dwAddressCount ;
    SERVICE_ADDRESS Addresses[1] ;
} SERVICE_ADDRESSES;

typedef struct _SERVICE_ADDRESS {
    DWORD   dwAddressType ;
    DWORD   dwAddressFlags ;
    DWORD   dwAddressLength ;
    DWORD   dwPrincipalLength ;
    BYTE   *lpAddress ;
    BYTE   *lpPrincipal ;
} SERVICE_ADDRESS;
```

In the SERVICE_ADDRESS structure, only *dwAddressType*, *dwAddressLength*, and *lpAddress* are relevant. *dwAddressType* is the address family (AF_INET, AF_IPX, etc.). *dwAddressLength* is the size of the address, and *lpAddress* points to the SOCKADDR.

The logic for the CServiceInfo::Register() is:

```
Convert the service name to its GUID (as required by GetAddressByName())
    GetTypeByName() is the Service Registration function that does this
Call GetAddressByName() with a zero-length buffer to find out how much
    memory we actually need
Call GetAddressByName() to get the CSADDR_INFO structures
For each element in the array
    Instantiate a new COverlappedSocket
    Call COverlappedSocket::Socket()
    Call CAsyncSocket::Bind()
    If a connection-oriented socket, call CAsyncSocket::Listen()
    Add SOCKADDR to SERVICE_ADDRESSES array
    Remember socket in m_SocketsInUse array
```

Here is the actual listing. Notice that the calling sequence for this method has only two arguments: the service class name, and the name of this particular instance of the service.

```
BOOL CServiceInfo::Register(LPTSTR lpszServiceClass,
                            LPTSTR lpszServerName)
{
   int          nRetcode;
   LPBYTE       lpBuffer;
   DWORD        dwBytesRequired = 0;
   PCSADDR_INFO lpAddressInfo;
   GUID         ServiceGUID;

   // Convert the service name to its GUID
   // (as required by GetAddressByName())
   if (::GetTypeByName(lpszServiceClass, &ServiceGUID) == SOCKET_ERROR)
      {
      return FALSE;
      }

   m_szServiceClassName = lpszServiceClass;
   m_szServerName       = lpszServerName;

   m_ServiceClassId     = ServiceGUID;

   // Call GetAddressByName() with a zero-length buffer
   // to find out how much memory we actually need
   nRetcode = GetAddressByName(
                 NS_DEFAULT,
                 &m_ServiceClassId,
                 lpszServerName,
                 NULL,
                 RES_SERVICE | RES_FIND_MULTIPLE,
                 NULL,
                 NULL,
                 &dwBytesRequired,
                 NULL,
                 NULL);
   if (::GetLastError() != ERROR_INSUFFICIENT_BUFFER)
      dwBytesRequired = 32768;

   lpBuffer = new BYTE[dwBytesRequired];

   // Call GetAddressByName() to get the CSADDR_INFO structures
   nRetcode = GetAddressByName(
                 NS_DEFAULT,
                 &ServiceGUID,
                 lpszServerName,
```

```
                NULL,
                RES_SERVICE | RES_FIND_MULTIPLE,
                NULL,
                lpBuffer,
                &dwBytesRequired,
                NULL,
                NULL);

if (nRetcode != SOCKET_ERROR)
   {
   // Parse the array, consisting of CSADDR_INFO structures
   lpAddressInfo = (PCSADDR_INFO) lpBuffer;
   COverlappedSocket *lpSocket;
   BOOL              bSuccess;

   // SERVICE_ADDRESSES structure is header for list of
   // SERVICE_ADDRESS structures.  Contains one,
   // allocate enough for all of them.
   lpServiceAddress =
      (SERVICE_ADDRESSES *)
         new BYTE[sizeof (SERVICE_ADDRESSES) +
            ((nRetcode - 1) * sizeof (SERVICE_ADDRESS))];
   lpServiceAddress->dwAddressCount = (DWORD) nRetcode;

   // For each element in the array
   for (INT i = 0; i < nRetcode; i++)
      {
      // Instantiate a new COverlappedSocket
      lpSocket = new COverlappedSocket;

      // Call COverlappedSocket::Socket()
      bSuccess = lpSocket->Socket(lpAddressInfo[i].iSocketType, 0,
                      lpAddressInfo[i].iProtocol,
                      lpAddressInfo[i].LocalAddr.lpSockaddr->sa_family);
      if (bSuccess)
         {
         // Call CAsyncSocket::Bind()
         bSuccess = lpSocket->GetSocket().Bind(
                 lpAddressInfo[i].LocalAddr.lpSockaddr,
                 lpAddressInfo[i].LocalAddr.iSockaddrLength);

         if (bSuccess)
            {
            // If a connection-oriented socket,
            // call CAsyncSocket::Listen()
            if (lpAddressInfo[i].iSocketType != SOCK_DGRAM )
               {
```

```
                bSuccess = lpSocket->GetSocket().Listen();
                }
            }
        }
    if (bSuccess)
        {
        // Add SOCKADDR to SERVICE_ADDRESSES array
        lpServiceAddress->Addresses[i].dwAddressType =
            lpAddressInfo[i].LocalAddr.lpSockaddr->sa_family;
        lpServiceAddress->Addresses[i].dwAddressFlags = 0;
        lpServiceAddress->Addresses[i].dwAddressLength =
            lpAddressInfo[i].LocalAddr.iSockaddrLength;
        lpServiceAddress->Addresses[i].dwPrincipalLength = 0 ;
        lpServiceAddress->Addresses[i].lpAddress =
           new BYTE[lpAddressInfo[i].LocalAddr.iSockaddrLength];

        // Copy the address--pointer won't be valid for long
        ::CopyMemory(lpServiceAddress->Addresses[i].lpAddress,
           &lpAddressInfo[i].LocalAddr,
           lpAddressInfo[i].LocalAddr.iSockaddrLength);
        lpServiceAddress->Addresses[i].lpPrincipal = NULL ;

        // Remember socket in m_SocketsInUse array
        m_SocketsInUse.Add(lpSocket);
        }
    else
        {
        delete lpSocket;
        }
    }
  }
  delete [] lpBuffer;
  return (m_SocketsInUse.GetSize() > 0);
}
```

Before we move on, let's take a closer look at the call to GetAddressByName(). Here is the invocation once again:

```
nRetcode = GetAddressByName(
                NS_DEFAULT,
                &ServiceGUID,
                lpszServerName,
                NULL,
                RES_SERVICE | RES_FIND_MULTIPLE,
                NULL,
                lpBuffer,
```

```
        &dwBytesRequired,
        NULL,
        NULL);
```

As with SetService(), the first argument is the name space; NS_ DEFAULT says to give us all registered addresses. The second argument points to our service GUID. The third argument is ignored here, because we set the RES_SERVICE flag in the fifth one. Later, we'll see that on the client side, it targets the specific machine that the client wants to talk to.

The fourth argument can be a pointer to an array of protocol numbers (IPPROTO_TCP, NSPROTO_SPXII, and so on), if you want to restrict the protocols that GetAddressByName() enumerates. I pass it as NULL here because I want all address information. The RES_SERVICE flag in the fifth argument says to use the GUID to retrieve the service information. The RES_FIND_MULTIPLE flag says to report all address information registered for the service.

Finally, the seventh argument designates the output buffer, and the eighth points to a variable containing the length of the buffer. If it is too small, the call to GetAddressByName() will fail, GetLastError() will say ERROR_INSUFFICIENT_BUFFER, and the variable pointed to will tell you how much memory you need.

At least, that's what it's supposed to do. Under Windows 95, it doesn't work quite right, and I had to add this kludge:

```
if (::GetLastError() != ERROR_INSUFFICIENT_BUFFER)
      dwBytesRequired = 32768;
```

In Windows Sockets 2, GetAddressByName() becomes WSAGetAddress-ByName().

```
INT WSAAPI WSAGetAddressByName(
   LPSTR         lpszServiceInstanceName,
   LPGUID        lpServiceClassId,
   DWORD         dwNameSpace,
   LPDWORD       lpdwBufferLength,
   LPWSAQUERYSET lpResults,
   DWORD         dwResolution,
   LPSTR         lpszAliasBuffer,
   LPDWORD       lpdwAliasBufferLength);
```

Here, *lpszServiceInstanceName* is the name of the specific server instance; it is ignored if *dwResolution* includes the RES_SERVICE flag. *lp-ServiceClassId* points to the GUID that has been assigned to the type.

dwNameSpace is the name space, and can be passed as either NS_ALL or NS_DEFAULT (both defined as zero) to return information on all name spaces. The output information is returned in a WSAQUERYSET structure, pointed to by *lpResults*. On input, **lpdwBufferLength* has the size of the buffer at *lpResults*; on output, it reports the amount of data actually written there. The buffer must include padding, as the WSAQUERYSET structure points to data outside of itself.

```
typedef struct _WSAQuerySet
{
    DWORD           dwSize;
    LPSTR           lpszServiceInstanceName;
    LPGUID          lpServiceClassId;
    LPWSAVERSION    lpVersion;
    LPSTR           lpszComment;
    DWORD           dwNameSpace;
    LPGUID          lpNSProviderId;
    LPSTR           lpszContext;
    DWORD           dwNumberOfProtocols;
    LPAFPROTOCOLS   lpafpProtocols;
    LPSTR           lpszQueryString;
    DWORD           dwNumberOfCsAddrs;
    LPCSADDR_INFO   lpcsaBuffer;
    LPBLOB          lpBlob;
} WSAQUERYSET, *PWSAQUERYSET, *LPWSAQUERYSET;
```

The fields of interest are *dwNumberOfCsAddrs* and *lpcsaBuffer*. For the client, these contain the information it needs to pass to socket() / WSASocket(), bind(), and connect() / WSAConnect(). The server only needs to pass the WSAQUERYSET along to WSASetService() to complete its initialization.

Here is the Winsock 2 version of the CServiceInfo::Register() method.

```
BOOL CServiceInfo::Register(LPTSTR lpszServiceClass,
                            LPTSTR lpszServerName)
{
   int          nRetcode;
   GUID         ServiceGUID;

   // Convert the service name to its GUID
   // (as required by WSAGetAddressByName())
   if (::WSAGetServiceClassIdByClassName(
        lpszServiceClass,
        &ServiceGUID) == SOCKET_ERROR)
      {
      return FALSE;
      }
```

```
m_szServiceClassName = lpszServiceClass;
m_szServerName       = lpszServerName;
m_ServiceClassId     = ServiceGUID;

DWORD dwQuerySetSize = m_dwQuerySetSize;

nRetcode = ::WSAGetAddressByName(
              lpszServerName,
              &m_ServiceClassId,
              NS_ALL,
              &dwQuerySetSize,
              m_lpWSAQuerySet,
              RES_SERVICE | RES_FIND_MULTIPLE,
              NULL,
              NULL);

if (nRetcode != SOCKET_ERROR)
   {
   // Parse the array, consisting of CSADDR_INFO structures
   PCSADDR_INFO lpAddressInfo =
      (PCSADDR_INFO) m_lpWSAQuerySet->lpcsaBuffer;
   COverlappedSocket *lpSocket;
   BOOL                bSuccess;

   for (DWORD i = 0;
        i < m_lpWSAQuerySet->dwNumberOfCsAddrs;
        i++)
      {
      // Instantiate a new COverlappedSocket
      lpSocket = new COverlappedSocket;

      // Call COverlappedSocket::Socket()
      bSuccess = lpSocket->Socket(lpAddressInfo[i].iSocketType, 0,
                   lpAddressInfo[i].iProtocol,
                   lpAddressInfo[i].LocalAddr.lpSockaddr->sa_family);
      if (bSuccess)
         {
         // Call CAsyncSocket::Bind()
         bSuccess = lpSocket->GetSocket().Bind(
                 lpAddressInfo[i].LocalAddr.lpSockaddr,
                 lpAddressInfo[i].LocalAddr.iSockaddrLength);

         if (bSuccess)
            {
            // If a connection-oriented socket,
            // call CAsyncSocket::Listen()
            if (lpAddressInfo[i].iSocketType != SOCK_DGRAM )
```

```
                {
                bSuccess = lpSocket->GetSocket().Listen();
                }
             }
          }
       if (bSuccess)
          {
          // Remember socket in m_SocketsInUse array
          m_SocketsInUse.Add(lpSocket);
          }
       else
          {
          delete lpSocket;
          }
       }
    }
  return (m_SocketsInUse.GetSize() > 0);
}
```

Advertising the Server's Presence on the Network. Because Register() has already set up the SERVICE_ADDRESSES array (represented by the *lpServiceAddress* field in SERVICE_INFO), very little work needs to be done to advertise. CServiceInfo has an Advertise() method that sets the few remaining fields that are required—*lpServiceType* (pointing to the GUID), *lpServiceName* (the name of this server instance), and *dwVersion*.

```
BOOL CServiceInfo::Advertise()
{
   int   nRetcode;
   DWORD dwStatusFlags;

   lpServiceType                  = &m_ServiceClassId;
   lpServiceName                  =
      (LPTSTR) (const char *) m_szServerName;
   lpComment                      =  NULL;
   lpLocale                       =  NULL;
   lpMachineName                  =  NULL ;
   dwVersion                      =  1;
   dwDisplayHint                  =  0;
   dwTime                         =  0;
   ServiceSpecificInfo.cbSize     =  0 ;
   ServiceSpecificInfo.pBlobData  =  NULL ;

   nRetcode =  SetService(
                  NS_DEFAULT,
                  SERVICE_REGISTER,
                  0,
```

```
                this,
                NULL,
                &dwStatusFlags) ;

    ClearServiceAddress();
    return (nRetcode != SOCKET_ERROR) ;
}
```

This call to SetService() differs from the one we made in CService-Info::AddType() only in the second argument, the verb—here SERVICE_REGISTER instead of SERVICE_ADD_TYPE.

In Winsock 2, SetService() becomes WSASetService(). It too eliminates a level of indirection, because it accepts the address information as a WSAQUERYSET, exactly the way in which WSAGetAddressByName() returns it. There is no need to convert CSADDR_INFOs to SERVICE_ADDRESSes.

```
typedef enum _WSAESETSERVICEOP
{
    REGISTER=0,
    DEREGISTER,
    FLUSH
} WSAESETSERVICEOP;

INT WSAAPI WSASetService(
   LPWSAQUERYSET      lpServiceInfo,
   WSAESETSERVICEOP essOperation,
   DWORD              dwFlags);
```

essOperation is REGISTER if the server is coming online, DEREGISTER if it is shutting down, or FLUSH to write a series of deferred registrations. The *dwFlags* can be one of these values, or zero:

- SERVICE_DEFER: Cache the registration information until a FLUSH command is issued.
- SERVICE_HARD: Issue the command immediately.
- SERVICE_MULTIPLE: Multiple instances of the server can be registered.

lpServiceInfo is a pointer to a WSAQUERYSET structure that contains all the server's registration data.

lpServiceInfo->lpszServiceInstanceName is the name of this specific server instance. *lpServiceInfo->lpServiceClassId* points to the GUID for the class of service. *lpServiceInfo->lpVersion* points to a WSAVERSION structure indicating the version that this server instance supports.

```
typedef struct _WSAVersion
{
   DWORD       dwVersion;
   ECOMPARATOR ecHow;
} WSAVERSION, *PWSAVERSION, *LPWSAVERSION;
```

lpServiceInfo->lpszComment is a comment string that is not interpreted by the Sockets layer. *lpServiceInfo->lpszContext* is provided to support hierarchical name spaces, like Novell's NetWare Directory Services (NDS). If *lpServiceInfo->dwNameSpace* is passed as NS_ALL, it should be set to "" or "\\". If *lpServiceInfo->dwNameSpace* designates something like NS_NDS (Novell's NDS), *lpServiceInfo->lpszContext* can be a specific context with the Directory Services tree. A zero-length string "" or NULL pointer registers the server at the default context; "\\" registers it at the root of the tree. *lpServiceInfo->dwNumberOfCsAddrs* is the number of CSADDR_INFO structures in the *lpServiceInfo->lpcsaBuffer* array.

Here is the Winsock 2 version of CServiceInfo::Advertise():

```
BOOL CServiceInfo::Advertise()
{
   INT nRetcode = ::WSASetService(
                     m_lpWSAQuerySet,
                     REGISTER,
                     0);
   return (nRetcode != SOCKET_ERROR) ;
}
```

At this point, the server is all taken care of. Now, let's go back and see what the client has to do to get connected.

Connecting a Client to a Server

The client's activity is analogous to the server's startup sequence. It too calls GetAddressByName(), asking it for the socket information it needs to connect to the server. The client calls socket() / WSASocket() and bind() exactly as the server did. But instead of calling listen(), the client is going to call connect() / WSAConnect(). To do this, it uses the remote address information returned by GetAddressByName().

Here is the CSADDR_INFO structure again:

```
typedef struct _CSADDR_INFO {
    SOCKET_ADDRESS LocalAddr ;
    SOCKET_ADDRESS RemoteAddr ;
    INT iSocketType ;
    INT iProtocol ;
} CSADDR_INFO;
```

In this case, it's the *RemoteAddr* we're interested in. We'll pass *RemoteAddr.lpSockaddr* and *RemoteAddr.iSockaddrLength* to connect() / WSA-Connect().

One other difference is that the client does not need to connect to all the possible server endpoints; one is enough. Once it has a connection to the server, it breaks out of its loop.

CServiceInfo has a Connect() method that implements this logic. It takes only two arguments: the service GUID and the target machine. To simplify the interface, there's another version of Connect() that takes the service name instead of the GUID. It calls GetTypeByName() to retrieve its GUID, then calls the other version. Here are both of them:

```
COverlappedSocket *CServiceInfo::Connect(LPTSTR lpszServiceClass,
                                         LPTSTR lpszServerName)
{
   COverlappedSocket *lpSocket = NULL;
   GUID ServiceGUID;

   if (::GetTypeByName(lpszServiceClass, &ServiceGUID) != SOCKET_ERROR)
      {
      lpSocket = Connect(&ServiceGUID, lpszServerName);
      }
   return lpSocket;
}

COverlappedSocket *CServiceInfo::Connect(LPGUID lpGUID,
                                         LPTSTR lpszServerName)
{
   INT           nRetcode;
   LPBYTE        lpBuffer;
   DWORD         dwBytesRequired = 0;
   PCSADDR_INFO lpAddressInfo;
   COverlappedSocket *lpSocket = NULL;
   INT           i;

   // Find out how big a buffer we need
   nRetcode = GetAddressByName(
                NS_DEFAULT,
                lpGUID,
                lpszServerName,
                NULL,
                RES_FIND_MULTIPLE,
                NULL,
                NULL,
```

```
                 &dwBytesRequired,
                 NULL,
                 NULL);
    if (::GetLastError() != ERROR_INSUFFICIENT_BUFFER)
       dwBytesRequired = 32768;

    lpBuffer = new BYTE[dwBytesRequired];

    // Now we can call GetAddressByName() for real
    nRetcode = GetAddressByName(
                 NS_DEFAULT,
                 lpGUID,
                 lpszServerName,
                 NULL,
                 RES_FIND_MULTIPLE,
                 NULL,
                 lpBuffer,
                 &dwBytesRequired,
                 NULL,
                 NULL);

    if (nRetcode != SOCKET_ERROR)
       {
       // Parse the array, consisting of CSADDR_INFO structures
       lpAddressInfo = (PCSADDR_INFO) lpBuffer;
       BOOL               bSuccess;

       for (i = 0, bSuccess = FALSE; i < nRetcode && !bSuccess; i++)
          {
          lpSocket = new COverlappedSocket;
          bSuccess = lpSocket->Socket(lpAddressInfo[i].iSocketType, 0,
                         lpAddressInfo[i].iProtocol,
                         lpAddressInfo[i].LocalAddr.lpSockaddr->sa_family);
          if (bSuccess)
             {
             bSuccess = lpSocket->GetSocket().Bind(
                      lpAddressInfo[i].LocalAddr.lpSockaddr,
                      lpAddressInfo[i].LocalAddr.iSockaddrLength);

             if (bSuccess)  // OK for both stream and datagram sockets
                {
                bSuccess = lpSocket->GetSocket().Connect(
                   lpAddressInfo[i].RemoteAddr.lpSockaddr,
                   lpAddressInfo[i].RemoteAddr.iSockaddrLength);
                }
             }
          if (!bSuccess)
```

```
                {
                delete lpSocket;
                lpSocket = NULL;
                }
            }
        }
    delete [] lpBuffer;
    return lpSocket;
}
```

This listing is very similar to CServiceInfo::Register(). There is one important difference in the way I call GetAddressByName(). Here is the client-side call again:

```
nRetcode = GetAddressByName(
                    NS_DEFAULT,
                    lpGUID,
                    lpszServerName,
                    NULL,
                    RES_FIND_MULTIPLE,
                    NULL,
                    lpBuffer,
                    &dwBytesRequired,
                    NULL,
                    NULL);
```

Notice that the flags argument (the fifth one) specifies only the RES_FIND_MULTIPLE flag—not RES_SERVICE. This causes the third argument—designating the target machine—to become relevant. We have to tell GetAddressByName() where the server application lives, since it is going to feed us remote addressing information.

The Winsock 2 version differs in that it uses WSAGetAddressByName() instead of GetAddressByName(). The addressing information is returned in the *lpcsaBuffer* field of the WSAQUERYSET that we pass.

```
COverlappedSocket *CServiceInfo::Connect(LPTSTR lpszServiceClass,
                                         LPTSTR lpszServerName)
{
    COverlappedSocket *lpSocket = NULL;
    GUID ServiceGUID;

    if (::WSAGetServiceClassIdByClassName(
            lpszServiceClass, &ServiceGUID) != SOCKET_ERROR)
        {
        lpSocket = Connect(&ServiceGUID, lpszServerName);
        }
```

```
   return lpSocket;
}

COverlappedSocket *CServiceInfo::Connect(LPGUID lpGUID,
                                         LPTSTR lpszServerName)
{
   INT          nRetcode;
   PCSADDR_INFO lpAddressInfo;
   COverlappedSocket *lpSocket = NULL;
   DWORD        i;

   DWORD dwQuerySetSize = m_dwQuerySetSize;

   nRetcode = ::WSAGetAddressByName(
                 lpszServerName,
                 &m_ServiceClassId,
                 NS_ALL,
                 &dwQuerySetSize,
                 m_lpWSAQuerySet,
                 RES_FIND_MULTIPLE,
                 NULL,
                 NULL);

   if (nRetcode != SOCKET_ERROR)
      {
      // Parse the array, consisting of CSADDR_INFO structures
      lpAddressInfo = (PCSADDR_INFO) m_lpWSAQuerySet->lpcsaBuffer;
      BOOL              bSuccess;

      for (i = 0, bSuccess = FALSE;
           i < m_lpWSAQuerySet->dwNumberOfCsAddrs && !bSuccess;
           i++)
         {
         lpSocket = new COverlappedSocket;
         bSuccess = lpSocket->Socket(lpAddressInfo[i].iSocketType, 0,
                          lpAddressInfo[i].iProtocol,
                          lpAddressInfo[i].LocalAddr.lpSockaddr->sa_family);
         if (bSuccess)
            {
            bSuccess = lpSocket->GetSocket().Bind(
                          lpAddressInfo[i].LocalAddr.lpSockaddr,
                          lpAddressInfo[i].LocalAddr.iSockaddrLength);

            if (bSuccess)  // OK for both stream and datagram sockets
               {
               bSuccess = lpSocket->GetSocket().Connect(
                  lpAddressInfo[i].RemoteAddr.lpSockaddr,
```

```
                lpAddressInfo[i].RemoteAddr.iSockaddrLength);
            }
        }
      if (!bSuccess)
        {
        delete lpSocket;
        lpSocket = NULL;
        }
      }
    }
  return lpSocket;
}
```

Additional Functions

The above examples used these functions: SetService(), GetAddressByName(), and GetTypeByName() in Sockets 1.1, and WSAInstallServiceClass(), WSASetService(), WSAGetAddressByName(), and WSAGetServiceClassId-ByClassName() in Sockets 2. WSAInstallServiceClass(), (WSA)SetService(), and (WSA)GetAddressByName() are the core of the Service Registration API.

GetTypeByName() has a converse, GetNameByType(). Surprisingly, these functions are not entirely reversible. The TCP echo service can be accessed using either TCP or UDP. Both protocols use port number 7. SVCGUID.H defines two GUIDs for echo, SVCID_ECHO_TCP and SVCID_ECHO_UDP.

```
static GUID EchoGuid = SVCID_ECHO_UDP;
TCHAR  szEchoService[256];

GetNameByType(&EchoGuid, szEchoService);
// szEchoService now says "echo"

GetTypeByName(szEchoService, &EchoGuid);

// EchoGuid now equals SVCID_ECHO_TCP
```

The problem here is that both service types have the same name. When you ask for the GUID of "echo," GetTypeByName() looks up the TCP one first, and returns its GUID, without worrying about whether it has another one.

In Winsock 2, these functions become WSAGetServiceClassIdByClass-Name() and WSAGetServiceClassNameByClassId(), which are just different names for GetTypeByName() and GetNameByType().

The EnumProtocols() function reports on the protocols that are installed on a machine. It populates an array of PROTOCOL_INFO structures. These describe many aspects of the protocols, including:

- The address family, the preferred socket type, and the preferred protocol (all the arguments you need to pass to socket(), in other words)
- Whether the protocol is connection-oriented or connectionless
- Whether the protocol is stream- or message-oriented
- Whether the protocol supports urgent data

In Winsock 2, EnumProtocols() becomes WSAEnumProtocols(), and the PROTOCOL_INFO structure becomes a WSAPROTOCOL_INFO. The function behaves the same, but the structure returns additional information describing which Winsock 2 features the protocol supports, such as multipoint connections, connect and disconnect data, and quality of service.

Finally, the GetService() function retrieves information about a specific service, packed in an array of NS_SERVICE_INFO structures. This structure contains a SERVICE_INFO structure, and a field telling you what name space it belongs to. Winsock 2 has no GetService() equivalent, but replaces it with functions that enumerate services known to the name space: WSALookupServiceBegin(), WSALookupServiceNext(), and WSALookupServiceDone().

WSALookupServiceBegin(). This function initiates a name-space enumeration. To allow for the widest range of underlying name spaces, it lets you walk a name-space hierarchy. Although the Microsoft TCP/IP name space is not hierarchical, some other important ones are, most notably Novell's NetWare Directory Services.

```
INT WSAAPI WSALookupServiceBegin(
   LPWSAQUERYSET lpRestrictions,
   DWORD         dwFlags,
   LPHANDLE      lphLookup);
```

dwFlags specifies the scope of the service enumeration. LUP_DEEP says to report all levels of a hierarchical name space. LUP_CONTAINERS asks for the enumeration of container objects. In Novell's NDS, for instance, organizations (O=) and organizational units (OU=) are containers. LUP_NOCONTAINERS requests the enumeration of leaf (noncontainer) objects only. In the Novell context, common name objects (CN=) would be reported. LUP_NEAREST asks the name-space provider to return the service entries ordered by their proximity to the current machine. "Proximity" has no universal significance; its meaning is provider-specific (and it may not have any meaning). LUP_DEEP and LUP_NEAREST can be ORed with the other two flags; LUP_CONTAINERS and LUP_NOCONTAINERS are mutually exclusive. The LUP_RETURN_* flags restrict the amount of information reported. LUP_RETURN_ALL requests all data; the other ones are LUP_RETURN_NAME, LUP_RETURN_TYPE, LUP_RETURN_VERSION, LUP_RETURN_ COMMENT, LUP_RETURN_ ADDR, and LUP_RETURN_BLOB.

The handle returned in *lphLookup* is passed to WSALookupServiceNext() to iterate the matching name-space entries.

lpRestrictions points to a WSAQUERYSET structure that specifies the parameters for your search.

lpRestrictions->lpszServiceInstanceName specifies the name of the specific server instance you are interested in. Passing it as NULL requests all active servers using the GUID specified in *lpRestrictions->lpServiceClassId*. *lpRestrictions->lpszServiceInstanceName* can also contain wildcards, but the specific wildcard characters are provider-dependent.

lpRestrictions->lpServiceClassId specifies the service type you want to find out about; a NULL pointer asks to enumerate all service types.

lpRestrictions->dwNameSpace is the name space you want to browse. If you pass it as NS_ALL, all name spaces will be reported. In this case, you should pass *lpRestrictions->lpszContext* as either “” or “\\”, since these are the only contexts that are required to be recognized by all name-space providers.

lpRestrictions->lpszContext is the location in the name space where you want the lookup to begin. Its meaning is specific to the underlying name-space provider; in many name spaces, it will have no meaning. *lpRestrictions->lpszContext* is primarily intended for hierarchical name spaces like Novell’s NDS. Passing *lpRestrictions->lpszContext* as “” says to start at the current context; passing “\\” says to start at the top of the name space (the meaning of “top” is provider-specific).

lpRestrictions->lpafpProtocols points to an array of AF_PROTOCOL structures.

```
typedef struct _AFPROTOCOLS {
   INT iAddressFamily;
   INT iProtocol;
} AFPROTOCOLS, *PAFPROTOCOLS, *LPAFPROTOCOLS;
```

These specify the address family and protocol identifiers expected as the first and third arguments to socket() and WSASocket() (AF_INET, IPPROTO_TCP, NSPROTO_SPXII, and so on). Passing it as a non-NULL pointer restricts the report to servers accessible over the protocols you specify; a NULL pointer requests a report for all protocols.

lpRestrictions->lpBlob means nothing to WSALookupServiceBegin(); it is passed through to the name-space provider, and can be used for any provider-specific purpose.

lpRestrictions->lpVersion points to a WSAVERSION structure that specifies the version you want, and how to determine whether a given version should be considered a match or not.

```
typedef enum _WSAEcomparator
{
   COMP_EQUAL=0,
   COMP_NOTLESS
} WSAECOMPARATOR, *PWSAECOMPARATOR, *LPWSAECOMPARATOR;

typedef struct _WSAVersion
{
   DWORD       dwVersion;
   ECOMPARATOR ecHow;
} WSAVERSION, *PWSAVERSION, *LPWSAVERSION;
```

dwVersion is the version number you want. *ecHow* says whether you require an exact version match (COMP_EQUAL), or if it will be adequate for the server to support at least your preferred version (COMP_NOTLESS). If you want version 2.0, for instance, and the server is offering version 2.1, COMP_EQUAL will suppress enumeration of the server, while COMP_NOTLESS will report it.

WSALookupServiceNext(). This function takes the lookup handle generated by WSALookupServiceBegin() and returns the name-space entries matching the selection criteria.

```
INT WSAAPI WSALookupServiceNext(
   HANDLE          hLookup,
   DWORD           dwControlFlags,
   LPDWORD         lpdwBufferLength,
   LPWSAQUERYSET   lpResults);
```

On input, **lpdwBufferLength* passes the byte size of the buffer at *lpResults*. On return, it contains the number of WSAQUERYSET structures that have been populated.

lpResults points to an array of WSAQUERYSET structures, and their accompanying data. Be sure to leave a lot of space in *lpResults*, since the output data will contain not only the structures, but also all the information they point to. The fields that are of most interest are *lpcsaBuffer* and *dwNumberOfCsAddrs*. These provide the information that the caller will need to open sockets and connect to the server.

WSALookupServiceNext() will return zero as long as it has information to report. When it is done, it returns SOCKET_ERROR, and WSAGetLastError() says WSA_E_NO_MORE. Note that *lpResults* may still contain valid data when WSALookupServiceNext() says it's done.

WSALookupServiceEnd(). To terminate a name-space query, pass the lookup handle to WSALookupServiceEnd().

```
INT WINAPI WSALookupServiceEnd(HANDLE hLookup);
```

Code Listings

The complete source code for CServiceInfo (and a couple of other ancillary classes) follows. The header file is \WIN32NET\CODE\WIN32OBJ\NSPCLASS.H, and the implementation is in \WIN32NET\CODE\WIN32OBJ\NSPCLASS.CPP.

```
/********
*
* NSPCLASS.H
*
* Copyright (c) 1995-1996 Ralph P. Davis
*
* All Rights Reserved
*
********/

#ifndef _NSPCLASS_INCLUDED
#define _NSPCLASS_INCLUDED

#include <nspapi.h>

#include "ovsock.h"

extern CWinApp *g_pMyApp;

// Several wrapper classes derived directly from the
// Win32 structures

#ifdef _USE_WINSOCK2_
#define PROTOCOL_INFO_BASE_CLASS WSAPROTOCOL_INFO
#define ENUM_PROTOCOLS(a, b, c) WSAEnumProtocols(a, b, c)

#else
#define PROTOCOL_INFO_BASE_CLASS PROTOCOL_INFO
#define ENUM_PROTOCOLS(a, b, c) EnumProtocols(a, b, c)
```

```
#endif

class AFX_EXT_CLASS CProtocolInfo :
   public PROTOCOL_INFO_BASE_CLASS
{
public:
   CProtocolInfo(INT nProtocolID);
   CProtocolInfo(PROTOCOL_INFO_BASE_CLASS& ProtocolInfo);
   GetProtocolInfo(INT nProtocolID);
};

class AFX_EXT_CLASS CProtocols : public CObject
{
protected:
   CArray<CProtocolInfo *, CProtocolInfo *&> Protocols;
public:
   CProtocols();          // Enumerate protocols

   virtual ~CProtocols();

   DECLARE_DYNAMIC(CProtocols)
};

#ifndef _USE_WINSOCK2_
class AFX_EXT_CLASS CServiceInfo : public SERVICE_INFO
{
protected:
   enum {EXTRA_VALUE_RECORDS = 3};

   CArray<COverlappedSocket *,
          COverlappedSocket *&> m_SocketsInUse;

   GUID                        m_ServiceClassId;

   DWORD                       m_dwBlobSize;
   LPBYTE                      m_lpServiceInfoBuffer;
   LPSERVICE_TYPE_INFO_ABS     m_lpServiceClassInfo;
   LPSERVICE_TYPE_VALUE_ABS    m_lpServiceClassValues;
   SERVICE_ADDRESS            *m_lpServiceAddresses;
   CString                     m_szServiceClassName;
   CString                     m_szServerName;
   DWORD                       m_dwTCPPort;
   DWORD                       m_dwUDPPort;
   DWORD                       m_dwIPXSocket;
   DWORD                       m_dwSAPObjectType;
private:
```

```
    VOID SetUpServiceInfo();
    VOID ClearServiceAddress();
    static DWORD m_dwTRUE;
    static DWORD m_dwFALSE;
public:
    CString GetServiceClassName(void);
    DWORD GetTCPPort(void);

    BOOL  IsReceivingDatagrams(void);

    CServiceInfo();
    virtual ~CServiceInfo();
    CArray<COverlappedSocket *, COverlappedSocket *&>& GetSockets();
    RECEIVECALLBACK GetReceiveCallback(void);


    // Server-side operations
    BOOL Register(LPTSTR lpszServiceClass,
                  LPTSTR lpszServerName);
    BOOL Deregister(LPTSTR lpszServiceClass,
                    LPTSTR lpszServerName);
    BOOL Advertise();
    BOOL AddClass(LPTSTR lpszServiceClass,
                  DWORD dwTCPPort,
                  DWORD dwUDPPort,
                  DWORD dwSAPObjectType = INVALID_SOCKET,
                  DWORD dwIPXSocketType = INVALID_SOCKET,
                  GUID *lpGUID = NULL);
    BOOL DeleteClass(LPTSTR lpszServiceClass,
                     DWORD  dwTCPPort,
                     DWORD  dwUDPPort,
                     DWORD  dwSAPObjectType,
                     DWORD  dwIPXSocket,
                     GUID  *lpGUID = NULL);

    // Client operations
    COverlappedSocket *Connect(LPTSTR lpszServiceClass,
                               LPTSTR lpszServerName);
    COverlappedSocket *Connect(LPGUID lpGUID,
                               LPTSTR lpszServerName);
};
#else
class AFX_EXT_CLASS CServiceInfo
{
protected:
    enum {EXTRA_VALUE_RECORDS = 4};
```

```
    CArray<COverlappedSocket *,
           COverlappedSocket *&> m_SocketsInUse;

    GUID                        m_ServiceClassId;

    WSASERVICECLASSINFO         m_ServiceClassInfo;
    LPWSANSCLASSINFO            m_lpServiceClassValues;
    LPWSAQUERYSET               m_lpWSAQuerySet;
    DWORD                       m_dwQuerySetSize;
    CString                     m_szServiceClassName;
    CString                     m_szServerName;
    DWORD                       m_dwTCPPort;
    DWORD                       m_dwUDPPort;
    DWORD                       m_dwIPXSocket;
    DWORD                       m_dwSAPObjectType;
private:

    VOID SetUpServiceInfo();
    static DWORD m_dwTRUE;
    static DWORD m_dwFALSE;
public:
    CString GetServiceClassName(void);
    DWORD GetTCPPort(void);

    BOOL  IsReceivingDatagrams(void);

    CServiceInfo();
    virtual ~CServiceInfo();
    CArray<COverlappedSocket *, COverlappedSocket *&>& GetSockets();
    RECEIVECALLBACK GetReceiveCallback(void);


    // Server-side operations
    BOOL Register(LPTSTR lpszServiceClass,
                  LPTSTR lpszServerName);
    BOOL Deregister(LPTSTR lpszServiceClass,
                    LPTSTR lpszServerName);
    BOOL Advertise();
    BOOL AddClass(LPTSTR lpszServiceClass,
                 DWORD dwTCPPort,
                 DWORD dwUDPPort,
                 DWORD dwSAPObjectType = INVALID_SOCKET,
                 DWORD dwIPXSocket = INVALID_SOCKET,
                 GUID *lpGUID = NULL);
    BOOL DeleteClass(LPTSTR lpszServiceClass,
                    DWORD  dwTCPPort,
                    DWORD  dwUDPPort,
                    DWORD  dwSAPObjectType,
```

```
                    DWORD  dwIPXSocket,
                    GUID  *lpGUID = NULL);

   // Client operations
   COverlappedSocket *Connect(LPTSTR lpszServiceClass,
                              LPTSTR lpszServerName);
   COverlappedSocket *Connect(LPGUID lpGUID,
                              LPTSTR lpszServerName);
};
#endif

#endif




/********
*
* NSPCLASS.CPP
*
* Copyright (c) 1995-1996 Ralph P. Davis
*
* All Rights Reserved
*
********/

/*===== Includes =====*/

#include "stdafx.h"

#include "ovsock.h"
#include "nspclass.h"


/*===== Function Definitions =====*/

IMPLEMENT_DYNAMIC(CProtocols, CObject)

CProtocolInfo::CProtocolInfo(
   PROTOCOL_INFO_BASE_CLASS& ProtocolInfo)
{
   if (AfxGetApp() == NULL)
      {
      g_pMyApp = new CWinApp;
      }
#ifdef _USE_WINSOCK2_
   dwServiceFlags1    = ProtocolInfo.dwServiceFlags1;
   dwServiceFlags2    = ProtocolInfo.dwServiceFlags2;
   dwServiceFlags3    = ProtocolInfo.dwServiceFlags3;
```

```
   dwServiceFlags4     = ProtocolInfo.dwServiceFlags4;
   dwProviderFlags     = ProtocolInfo.dwProviderFlags;
   dwProviderId        = ProtocolInfo.dwProviderId;
   dwCatalogEntryId    = ProtocolInfo.dwCatalogEntryId;
   ProtocolChain       = ProtocolInfo.ProtocolChain;
   iVersion            = ProtocolInfo.iVersion;
   iProtocolMaxOffset = ProtocolInfo.iProtocolMaxOffset;
   iNetworkByteOrder   = ProtocolInfo.iNetworkByteOrder;
   iSecurityScheme     = ProtocolInfo.iSecurityScheme;
   dwMessageSize       = ProtocolInfo.dwMessageSize;
   dwProviderReserved = ProtocolInfo.dwProviderReserved;
   lstrcpy(szProtocol, ProtocolInfo.szProtocol);
#else
   dwServiceFlags = ProtocolInfo.dwServiceFlags;
   lpProtocol     = ProtocolInfo.lpProtocol;
#endif
   iAddressFamily = ProtocolInfo.iAddressFamily;
   iMaxSockAddr   = ProtocolInfo.iMaxSockAddr;
   iMinSockAddr   = ProtocolInfo.iMinSockAddr;
   iSocketType    = ProtocolInfo.iSocketType;
   iProtocol      = ProtocolInfo.iProtocol;
   dwMessageSize  = ProtocolInfo.dwMessageSize;
}

CProtocolInfo::CProtocolInfo(INT nProtocolID)
{
   if (AfxGetApp() == NULL)
      {
      g_pMyApp = new CWinApp;
      }
   if (GetProtocolInfo(nProtocolID) == SOCKET_ERROR)
      AfxThrowResourceException();
}

INT CProtocolInfo::GetProtocolInfo(INT nProtocolID)
{
   INT   nProtocols[2];
   DWORD dwBufferSize = sizeof (PROTOCOL_INFO_BASE_CLASS);

   nProtocols[0] = nProtocolID;
   nProtocols[1] = 0;
   return ENUM_PROTOCOLS(nProtocols, this, &dwBufferSize);
}

CProtocols::CProtocols()
{
   // Enumerate the protocols
   LPBYTE         lpBuffer;
   PROTOCOL_INFO_BASE_CLASS *lpInfo;
```

```
    CProtocolInfo *lpProtocolInfo;
    DWORD          dwBufferSize;
    INT            i, nProtocols;

    if (AfxGetApp() == NULL)
       {
       g_pMyApp = new CWinApp;
       }
    // First, find out how big a buffer we need
    dwBufferSize = 0;
    ENUM_PROTOCOLS(NULL, NULL, &dwBufferSize);

    if (::GetLastError() != ERROR_INSUFFICIENT_BUFFER)
       {
       dwBufferSize = 32768;  // Windows 95 bug?
       }
    lpBuffer = new BYTE[dwBufferSize];

    nProtocols = ENUM_PROTOCOLS(
       NULL,
       (PROTOCOL_INFO_BASE_CLASS *) lpBuffer,
       &dwBufferSize);

    if (nProtocols == SOCKET_ERROR)
       {
       AfxThrowResourceException();
       }

    lpInfo = (PROTOCOL_INFO_BASE_CLASS *) lpBuffer;
    for (i = 0; i < nProtocols; ++i)
       {
       lpProtocolInfo = new CProtocolInfo(lpInfo[i]);
       if (Protocols.Add(lpProtocolInfo) == (-1))
          AfxThrowResourceException();
       }
    delete lpBuffer;
}

CProtocols::~CProtocols()
{
    int i;

    for (i = 0; i < Protocols.GetSize(); ++i)
       delete Protocols[i];
    Protocols.RemoveAll();
}

DWORD CServiceInfo::m_dwTRUE  = TRUE;
DWORD CServiceInfo::m_dwFALSE = FALSE;
```

```
#ifndef _USE_WINSOCK2_

CServiceInfo::CServiceInfo()
{
   if (AfxGetApp() == NULL)
      {
      g_pMyApp = new CWinApp;
      }
   lpServiceType     = NULL;
   lpServiceName     = NULL;
   lpComment         = NULL;
   lpLocale          = NULL;
   dwDisplayHint     = 0;
   dwVersion         = 0;
   dwTime            = 0;
   lpMachineName     = NULL;
   lpServiceAddress = NULL;
   ::ZeroMemory(&ServiceSpecificInfo, sizeof (ServiceSpecificInfo));

   m_dwBlobSize = sizeof (SERVICE_TYPE_INFO) +
      (EXTRA_VALUE_RECORDS * sizeof (SERVICE_TYPE_VALUE));
   m_lpServiceInfoBuffer = new BYTE[m_dwBlobSize];
   m_lpServiceClassInfo    =
      (LPSERVICE_TYPE_INFO_ABS) m_lpServiceInfoBuffer;;
   m_lpServiceClassValues = m_lpServiceClassInfo->Values;
}

CServiceInfo::~CServiceInfo()
{
   for (int i = 0; i < m_SocketsInUse.GetSize(); ++i)
      {
      delete m_SocketsInUse[i];
      }

   if (m_SocketsInUse.GetSize() > 0)
      {
      m_SocketsInUse.RemoveAll();
      }

   delete [] m_lpServiceInfoBuffer;
}

BOOL CServiceInfo::AddClass(LPTSTR lpszServiceClass,
                            DWORD dwTCPPort,
                            DWORD dwUDPPort,
                            DWORD dwSAPObjectType,
                            DWORD dwIPXSocketType,
                            GUID *lpGUID)
```

```
{
   GUID NewGUID;
   INT   nRetcode;
   DWORD dwStatusFlags;

   // Get a new GUID for this service class
   if (lpGUID == NULL)
      {
      ::UuidCreate(&NewGUID);
      lpGUID = &NewGUID;
      }

   m_ServiceClassId      = *lpGUID;
   m_szServiceClassName =  lpszServiceClass;
   m_dwTCPPort           =  dwTCPPort;
   m_dwUDPPort           =  dwUDPPort;
   m_dwSAPObjectType     =  dwSAPObjectType;
   m_dwIPXSocket         =  dwIPXSocketType;
   SetUpServiceInfo();
   nRetcode = SetService(
                  NS_DEFAULT,
                  SERVICE_ADD_TYPE,
                  0,
                  this,
                  NULL,
                  &dwStatusFlags
                  );

   if (nRetcode == SOCKET_ERROR)
      {
      TRACE(_T("\nSetService() failed, GetLastError() = %d"),
         GetLastError());
      }
   return (nRetcode != SOCKET_ERROR);
}

BOOL CServiceInfo::DeleteClass(LPTSTR lpszServiceClass,
                              DWORD  dwTCPPort,
                              DWORD  dwUDPPort,
                              DWORD  dwSAPObjectType,
                              DWORD  dwIPXSocket,
                              GUID  *lpGUID)
{
   INT   nRetcode;
   DWORD dwStatusFlags;
   GUID  ServiceGUID;

   m_szServiceClassName = lpszServiceClass;
   m_dwTCPPort          = dwTCPPort;
```

```
    m_dwUDPPort          = dwUDPPort;
    m_dwSAPObjectType    = dwSAPObjectType;
    m_dwIPXSocket        = dwIPXSocket;

    if (lpGUID == NULL)
        {
        if (::GetTypeByName(lpszServiceClass, &ServiceGUID) == SOCKET_ERROR)
            return FALSE;
        lpGUID = &ServiceGUID;
        }
    m_ServiceClassId = *lpGUID;

    SetUpServiceInfo();
    nRetcode = SetService(
                    NS_DEFAULT,
                    SERVICE_DELETE_TYPE,
                    0,
                    this,
                    NULL,
                    &dwStatusFlags
                    );

    if (nRetcode == SOCKET_ERROR)
        {
        TRACE(_T("\nSetService() failed, GetLastError() = %d"),
            GetLastError());
        }
    return (nRetcode != SOCKET_ERROR);
}

BOOL CServiceInfo::Register(LPTSTR lpszServiceClass,
                            LPTSTR lpszServerName)
{
    int          nRetcode;
    LPBYTE       lpBuffer;
    DWORD        dwBytesRequired = 0;
    PCSADDR_INFO lpAddressInfo;
    GUID         ServiceGUID;

    // Convert the service name to its GUID
    // (as required by GetAddressByName())
    if (::GetTypeByName(lpszServiceClass, &ServiceGUID) == SOCKET_ERROR)
        {
        return FALSE;
        }

    m_szServiceClassName = lpszServiceClass;
    m_szServerName       = lpszServerName;
```

```
m_ServiceClassId     = ServiceGUID;

// Call GetAddressByName() with a zero-length buffer
// to find out how much memory we actually need
nRetcode = GetAddressByName(
               NS_DEFAULT,
               &m_ServiceClassId,
               lpszServerName,
               NULL,
               RES_SERVICE | RES_FIND_MULTIPLE,
               NULL,
               NULL,
               &dwBytesRequired,
               NULL,
               NULL);
if (::GetLastError() != ERROR_INSUFFICIENT_BUFFER)
   dwBytesRequired = 32768;

lpBuffer = new BYTE[dwBytesRequired];

// Call GetAddressByName() to get the CSADDR_INFO structures
nRetcode = GetAddressByName(
               NS_DEFAULT,
               &ServiceGUID,
               lpszServerName,
               NULL,
               RES_SERVICE | RES_FIND_MULTIPLE,
               NULL,
               lpBuffer,
               &dwBytesRequired,
               NULL,
               NULL);

if (nRetcode != SOCKET_ERROR)
   {
   // Parse the array, consisting of CSADDR_INFO structures
   lpAddressInfo = (PCSADDR_INFO) lpBuffer;
   COverlappedSocket *lpSocket;
   BOOL              bSuccess;

   // SERVICE_ADDRESSES structure is header for list of
   // SERVICE_ADDRESS structures.  Contains one,
   // allocate enough for all of them.
   lpServiceAddress =
      (SERVICE_ADDRESSES *)
         new BYTE[sizeof (SERVICE_ADDRESSES) +
            ((nRetcode - 1) * sizeof (SERVICE_ADDRESS))];
   lpServiceAddress->dwAddressCount = (DWORD) nRetcode;
```

```
// For each element in the array
for (INT i = 0; i < nRetcode; i++)
   {
   // Instantiate a new COverlappedSocket
   lpSocket = new COverlappedSocket;

   // Call COverlappedSocket::Socket()
   bSuccess = lpSocket->Socket(lpAddressInfo[i].iSocketType, 0,
                     lpAddressInfo[i].iProtocol,
                     lpAddressInfo[i].LocalAddr.lpSockaddr->sa_family);
   if (bSuccess)
      {
      // Call CAsyncSocket::Bind()
      bSuccess = lpSocket->GetSocket().Bind(
              lpAddressInfo[i].LocalAddr.lpSockaddr,
              lpAddressInfo[i].LocalAddr.iSockaddrLength);

      if (bSuccess)
         {
         // If a connection-oriented socket,
         // call CAsyncSocket::Listen()
         if (lpAddressInfo[i].iSocketType != SOCK_DGRAM )
            {
            bSuccess = lpSocket->GetSocket().Listen();
            }
         }
      }
   if (bSuccess)
      {
      // Add SOCKADDR to SERVICE_ADDRESSES array
      lpServiceAddress->Addresses[i].dwAddressType =
          lpAddressInfo[i].LocalAddr.lpSockaddr->sa_family;
      lpServiceAddress->Addresses[i].dwAddressFlags = 0;
      lpServiceAddress->Addresses[i].dwAddressLength =
          lpAddressInfo[i].LocalAddr.iSockaddrLength;
      lpServiceAddress->Addresses[i].dwPrincipalLength = 0 ;
      lpServiceAddress->Addresses[i].lpAddress =
         new BYTE[lpAddressInfo[i].LocalAddr.iSockaddrLength];

      // Copy the address--pointer won't be valid for long
      ::CopyMemory(lpServiceAddress->Addresses[i].lpAddress,
         &lpAddressInfo[i].LocalAddr,
         lpAddressInfo[i].LocalAddr.iSockaddrLength);
      lpServiceAddress->Addresses[i].lpPrincipal = NULL ;

      // Remember socket in m_SocketsInUse array
      m_SocketsInUse.Add(lpSocket);
      }
```

```
            else
               {
               delete lpSocket;
               }
            }
         }
   delete [] lpBuffer;
   return (m_SocketsInUse.GetSize() > 0);
}

BOOL CServiceInfo::Deregister(LPTSTR lpszServiceClass,
                              LPTSTR lpszServerName)
{
   return TRUE;
}

BOOL CServiceInfo::Advertise()
{
   int   nRetcode;
   DWORD dwStatusFlags;

   lpServiceType                  = &m_ServiceClassId;
   lpServiceName                  =
      (LPTSTR) (const char *) m_szServerName;
   lpComment                      =  NULL;
   lpLocale                       =  NULL;
   lpMachineName                  =  NULL ;
   dwVersion                      =  1;
   dwDisplayHint                  =  0;
   dwTime                         =  0;
   ServiceSpecificInfo.cbSize     =  0 ;
   ServiceSpecificInfo.pBlobData =  NULL ;

   nRetcode =  SetService(
                  NS_DEFAULT,
                  SERVICE_REGISTER,
                  0,
                  this,
                  NULL,
                  &dwStatusFlags) ;

   ClearServiceAddress();
   return (nRetcode != SOCKET_ERROR) ;
}

VOID CServiceInfo::ClearServiceAddress()
{
   for (DWORD i = 0; i < lpServiceAddress->dwAddressCount; ++i)
```

```
        {
        delete [] lpServiceAddress->Addresses[i].lpAddress;
        }
    delete lpServiceAddress;
    lpServiceAddress = NULL;
}

VOID CServiceInfo::SetUpServiceInfo()
{
    lpServiceType                  = &m_ServiceClassId;
    ServiceSpecificInfo.pBlobData =  m_lpServiceInfoBuffer;
    ServiceSpecificInfo.cbSize    =  m_dwBlobSize;

    // The class name is required. In addition to specifying the
    // protocols and endpoints we're using, we also have to
    // provide a name-to-GUID mapping
    m_lpServiceClassInfo->lpTypeName   =
        (LPTSTR) (const char *) m_szServiceClassName;

    // The dwValueCount field of the SERVICE_TYPE_INFO_ABS
    // structure says how many records are being passed.
    // We initialize it to zero, then bump it as we add records
    m_lpServiceClassInfo->dwValueCount = 0;

    int i = 0;

    // Registering for TCP connection-oriented communications?
    if (m_dwTCPPort != INVALID_SOCKET)
        {
        ++m_lpServiceClassInfo->dwValueCount;
        m_lpServiceClassValues[i].dwNameSpace = NS_DNS ;
        m_lpServiceClassValues[i].dwValueType = REG_DWORD ;
        m_lpServiceClassValues[i].dwValueSize = sizeof (DWORD) ;
        m_lpServiceClassValues[i].lpValueName = SERVICE_TYPE_VALUE_TCPPORT;
        m_lpServiceClassValues[i].lpValue     = &m_dwTCPPort;
        ++i;
        }
    // No--how about UDP
    else if (m_dwUDPPort != INVALID_SOCKET)
        {
        ++m_lpServiceClassInfo->dwValueCount;
        m_lpServiceClassValues[i].dwNameSpace = NS_DNS ;
        m_lpServiceClassValues[i].dwValueType = REG_DWORD ;
        m_lpServiceClassValues[i].dwValueSize = sizeof (DWORD) ;
        m_lpServiceClassValues[i].lpValueName = SERVICE_TYPE_VALUE_UDPPORT;
        m_lpServiceClassValues[i].lpValue     = &m_dwUDPPort;
        ++i;
        }

    // Registering for NetWare?
    if (m_dwSAPObjectType != INVALID_SOCKET)
```

```
      {
      if (m_dwTCPPort != INVALID_SOCKET)
         {
         // If caller registered a TCP port, then
         // we know we want connection-oriented communication
         ++m_lpServiceClassInfo->dwValueCount;
         m_lpServiceClassValues[i].dwNameSpace = NS_SAP ;
         m_lpServiceClassValues[i].dwValueType = REG_DWORD ;
         m_lpServiceClassValues[i].dwValueSize = sizeof (DWORD) ;
         m_lpServiceClassValues[i].lpValueName = SERVICE_TYPE_VALUE_CONN ;

         m_lpServiceClassValues[i].lpValue     = &m_dwTRUE;
         ++i;
         }
      ++m_lpServiceClassInfo->dwValueCount;
      m_lpServiceClassValues[i].dwNameSpace = NS_SAP ;
      m_lpServiceClassValues[i].dwValueType = REG_DWORD ;
      m_lpServiceClassValues[i].dwValueSize = sizeof (DWORD) ;
      m_lpServiceClassValues[i].lpValueName = SERVICE_TYPE_VALUE_SAPID;
      m_lpServiceClassValues[i].lpValue     = &m_dwSAPObjectType;
      }
}

COverlappedSocket *CServiceInfo::Connect(LPTSTR lpszServiceClass,
                                         LPTSTR lpszServerName)
{
   COverlappedSocket *lpSocket = NULL;
   GUID ServiceGUID;

   if (::GetTypeByName(lpszServiceClass, &ServiceGUID) != SOCKET_ERROR)
      {
      lpSocket = Connect(&ServiceGUID, lpszServerName);
      }
   return lpSocket;
}

COverlappedSocket *CServiceInfo::Connect(LPGUID lpGUID,
                                         LPTSTR lpszServerName)
{
   INT          nRetcode;
   LPBYTE       lpBuffer;
   DWORD        dwBytesRequired = 0;
   PCSADDR_INFO lpAddressInfo;
   COverlappedSocket *lpSocket = NULL;
   INT          i;

   // Find out how big a buffer we need
   nRetcode = GetAddressByName(
                 NS_DEFAULT,
```

```
                lpGUID,
                lpszServerName,
                NULL,
                RES_FIND_MULTIPLE,
                NULL,
                NULL,
                &dwBytesRequired,
                NULL,
                NULL);
if (::GetLastError() != ERROR_INSUFFICIENT_BUFFER)
   dwBytesRequired = 32768;

lpBuffer = new BYTE[dwBytesRequired];

// Now we can call GetAddressByName() for real
nRetcode = GetAddressByName(
                NS_DEFAULT,
                lpGUID,
                lpszServerName,
                NULL,
                RES_FIND_MULTIPLE,
                NULL,
                lpBuffer,
                &dwBytesRequired,
                NULL,
                NULL);

if (nRetcode != SOCKET_ERROR)
   {
   // Parse the array, consisting of CSADDR_INFO structures
   lpAddressInfo = (PCSADDR_INFO) lpBuffer;
   BOOL              bSuccess;

   for (i = 0, bSuccess = FALSE; i < nRetcode && !bSuccess; i++)
      {
      lpSocket = new COverlappedSocket;
      bSuccess = lpSocket->Socket(lpAddressInfo[i].iSocketType, 0,
                     lpAddressInfo[i].iProtocol,
                     lpAddressInfo[i].LocalAddr.lpSockaddr->sa_family);
      if (bSuccess)
         {
         bSuccess = lpSocket->GetSocket().Bind(
                 lpAddressInfo[i].LocalAddr.lpSockaddr,
                 lpAddressInfo[i].LocalAddr.iSockaddrLength);

         if (bSuccess)  // OK for both stream and datagram sockets
            {
            bSuccess = lpSocket->GetSocket().Connect(
               lpAddressInfo[i].RemoteAddr.lpSockaddr,
```

```
                    lpAddressInfo[i].RemoteAddr.iSockaddrLength);
                }
            }
        if (!bSuccess)
            {
            delete lpSocket;
            lpSocket = NULL;
            }
        }
    }
    delete [] lpBuffer;
    return lpSocket;
}

#else
CServiceInfo::CServiceInfo()
{
    if (AfxGetApp() == NULL)
        {
        g_pMyApp = new CWinApp;
        }

    m_ServiceClassInfo.dwCount = 0;
    m_ServiceClassInfo.lpServiceClassId    = &m_ServiceClassId;
    m_ServiceClassInfo.lpszServiceClassName = NULL;
    m_ServiceClassInfo.lpClassInfos =
        new WSANSCLASSINFO[EXTRA_VALUE_RECORDS];

    m_lpServiceClassValues = m_ServiceClassInfo.lpClassInfos;
    m_dwQuerySetSize = 16384;
    m_lpWSAQuerySet =
        (LPWSAQUERYSET) new BYTE[m_dwQuerySetSize];

    ::ZeroMemory(m_lpWSAQuerySet, sizeof (WSAQUERYSET));
    m_lpWSAQuerySet->dwSize = sizeof (WSAQUERYSET);
}

CServiceInfo::~CServiceInfo()
{
    for (int i = 0; i < m_SocketsInUse.GetSize(); ++i)
        {
        delete m_SocketsInUse[i];
        }

    if (m_SocketsInUse.GetSize() > 0)
        {
        m_SocketsInUse.RemoveAll();
        }
```

```
   delete [] m_ServiceClassInfo.lpClassInfos;
   delete [] m_lpWSAQuerySet;
}

BOOL CServiceInfo::AddClass(LPTSTR lpszServiceClass,
                            DWORD dwTCPPort,
                            DWORD dwUDPPort,
                            DWORD dwSAPObjectType,
                            DWORD dwIPXSocket,
                            GUID *lpGUID)
{
   GUID NewGUID;
   INT   nRetcode;

   // Get a new GUID for this service class
   if (lpGUID == NULL)
      {
      ::UuidCreate(&NewGUID);
      lpGUID = &NewGUID;
      }

   m_ServiceClassId      = *lpGUID;
   m_szServiceClassName =  lpszServiceClass;
   m_dwTCPPort           =  dwTCPPort;
   m_dwUDPPort           =  dwUDPPort;
   m_dwSAPObjectType     =  dwSAPObjectType;
   m_dwIPXSocket         =  dwIPXSocket;

   SetUpServiceInfo();
   nRetcode = ::WSAInstallServiceClass(
                 &m_ServiceClassInfo);

   if (nRetcode == SOCKET_ERROR)
      {
      TRACE(_T("\nWSAInstallServiceClassInfo() failed, GetLastError() = %d"),
         GetLastError());
      }
   return (nRetcode != SOCKET_ERROR);
}

BOOL CServiceInfo::DeleteClass(LPTSTR,
                               DWORD,
                               DWORD,
                               DWORD,
                               DWORD,
                               GUID *)
{
```

```
    INT   nRetcode;
    nRetcode = ::WSARemoveServiceClass(&m_ServiceClassId);

    if (nRetcode == SOCKET_ERROR)
       {
       TRACE(_T("\nSetService() failed, GetLastError() = %d"),
          GetLastError());
       }
    return (nRetcode != SOCKET_ERROR);
}

BOOL CServiceInfo::Register(LPTSTR lpszServiceClass,
                            LPTSTR lpszServerName)
{
    int          nRetcode;
    GUID         ServiceGUID;

    // Convert the service name to its GUID
    // (as required by WSAGetAddressByName())
    // Winsock 2 Beta 1.1 has
    // WSAGetServiceClassIdByClassName() in WINSOCK2.H,
    // but forgets to export it from WS2_32.DLL
    if (::GetTypeByName( //::WSAGetServiceClassIdByClassName(
          lpszServiceClass,
          &ServiceGUID) == SOCKET_ERROR)
       {
       return FALSE;
       }

    m_szServiceClassName = lpszServiceClass;
    m_szServerName       = lpszServerName;
    m_ServiceClassId     = ServiceGUID;

    DWORD dwQuerySetSize = m_dwQuerySetSize;

    nRetcode = ::WSAGetAddressByName(
                  lpszServerName,
                  &m_ServiceClassId,
                  NS_ALL,
                  &dwQuerySetSize,
                  m_lpWSAQuerySet,
                  RES_SERVICE | RES_FIND_MULTIPLE,
                  NULL,
                  NULL);

    if (nRetcode != SOCKET_ERROR)
       {
       // Parse the array, consisting of CSADDR_INFO structures
```

```
    PCSADDR_INFO lpAddressInfo =
       (PCSADDR_INFO) m_lpWSAQuerySet->lpcsaBuffer;
    COverlappedSocket *lpSocket;
    BOOL               bSuccess;

    for (DWORD i = 0;
         i < m_lpWSAQuerySet->dwNumberOfCsAddrs;
         i++)
       {
       // Instantiate a new COverlappedSocket
       lpSocket = new COverlappedSocket;

       // Call COverlappedSocket::Socket()
       bSuccess = lpSocket->Socket(lpAddressInfo[i].iSocketType, 0,
                    lpAddressInfo[i].iProtocol,
                    lpAddressInfo[i].LocalAddr.lpSockaddr->sa_family);
       if (bSuccess)
          {
          // Call CAsyncSocket::Bind()
          bSuccess = lpSocket->GetSocket().Bind(
                  lpAddressInfo[i].LocalAddr.lpSockaddr,
                  lpAddressInfo[i].LocalAddr.iSockaddrLength);

          if (bSuccess)
             {
             // If a connection-oriented socket,
             // call CAsyncSocket::Listen()
             if (lpAddressInfo[i].iSocketType != SOCK_DGRAM )
                {
                bSuccess = lpSocket->GetSocket().Listen();
                }
             }
          }
       if (bSuccess)
          {
          // Remember socket in m_SocketsInUse array
          m_SocketsInUse.Add(lpSocket);
          }
       else
          {
          delete lpSocket;
          }
       }
    }
  return (m_SocketsInUse.GetSize() > 0);
}

BOOL CServiceInfo::Deregister(LPTSTR lpszServiceClass,
                              LPTSTR lpszServerName)
```

```
{
   INT nRetcode = ::WSASetService(
                     m_lpWSAQuerySet,
                     DEREGISTER,
                     0);
   return (nRetcode == 0);
}

BOOL CServiceInfo::Advertise()
{
   INT nRetcode = ::WSASetService(
                     m_lpWSAQuerySet,
                     REGISTER,
                     0);
   return (nRetcode != SOCKET_ERROR) ;
}

VOID CServiceInfo::SetUpServiceInfo()
{
   // The class name is required. In addition to specifying the
   // protocols and endpoints we're using, we also have to
   // provide a name-to-GUID mapping
   m_ServiceClassInfo.lpszServiceClassName =
      (LPSTR) (LPCTSTR) m_szServiceClassName;

   // The dwCount field of the WSASERVICECLASSINFO
   // structure says how many records are being passed.
   // We initialize it to zero, then bump it as we add records
   m_ServiceClassInfo.dwCount = 0;

   int i = 0;

   // Registering for TCP connection-oriented communications?
   if (m_dwTCPPort != INVALID_SOCKET)
      {
      ++m_ServiceClassInfo.dwCount;
      m_lpServiceClassValues[i].dwNameSpace = NS_DNS ;
      m_lpServiceClassValues[i].dwValueType = REG_DWORD ;
      m_lpServiceClassValues[i].dwValueSize = sizeof (DWORD) ;
      m_lpServiceClassValues[i].lpszName = SERVICE_TYPE_VALUE_TCPPORT;
      m_lpServiceClassValues[i].lpValue     = &m_dwTCPPort;
      ++i;
      }
   // No--how about UDP
   else if (m_dwUDPPort != INVALID_SOCKET)
      {
      ++m_ServiceClassInfo.dwCount;
      m_lpServiceClassValues[i].dwNameSpace = NS_DNS ;
```

```
      m_lpServiceClassValues[i].dwValueType = REG_DWORD ;
      m_lpServiceClassValues[i].dwValueSize = sizeof (DWORD) ;
      m_lpServiceClassValues[i].lpszName = SERVICE_TYPE_VALUE_UDPPORT;
      m_lpServiceClassValues[i].lpValue     = &m_dwUDPPort;
      ++i;
      }

   // Registering for NetWare?
   if (m_dwSAPObjectType != INVALID_SOCKET)
      {
      if (m_dwTCPPort != INVALID_SOCKET)
         {
         // If caller registered a TCP port, then
         // we know we want connection-oriented communication
         ++m_ServiceClassInfo.dwCount;
         m_lpServiceClassValues[i].dwNameSpace = NS_SAP ;
         m_lpServiceClassValues[i].dwValueType = REG_DWORD ;
         m_lpServiceClassValues[i].dwValueSize = sizeof (DWORD) ;
         m_lpServiceClassValues[i].lpszName = SERVICE_TYPE_VALUE_CONN ;

         m_lpServiceClassValues[i].lpValue     = &m_dwTRUE;
         ++i;
         }
      ++m_ServiceClassInfo.dwCount;
      m_lpServiceClassValues[i].dwNameSpace = NS_SAP ;
      m_lpServiceClassValues[i].dwValueType = REG_DWORD ;
      m_lpServiceClassValues[i].dwValueSize = sizeof (DWORD) ;
      m_lpServiceClassValues[i].lpszName = SERVICE_TYPE_VALUE_SAPID;
      m_lpServiceClassValues[i].lpValue     = &m_dwSAPObjectType;
      ++i;

      if (m_dwIPXSocket != INVALID_SOCKET)
         {
         ++m_ServiceClassInfo.dwCount;
         m_lpServiceClassValues[i].dwNameSpace = NS_SAP ;
         m_lpServiceClassValues[i].dwValueType = REG_DWORD ;
         m_lpServiceClassValues[i].dwValueSize = sizeof (DWORD) ;
         m_lpServiceClassValues[i].lpszName =
            SERVICE_TYPE_VALUE_IPXPORT;
         m_lpServiceClassValues[i].lpValue     = &m_dwIPXSocket;
         }
      }
}

COverlappedSocket *CServiceInfo::Connect(LPTSTR lpszServiceClass,
                                          LPTSTR lpszServerName)
{
   COverlappedSocket *lpSocket = NULL;
   GUID ServiceGUID;
```

```
    // Winsock 2 Beta 1.1 has
    // WSAGetServiceClassIdByClassName() in WINSOCK2.H,
    // but forgets to export it from WS2_32.DLL
    if (::GetTypeByName(//::WSAGetServiceClassIdByClassName(
            lpszServiceClass, &ServiceGUID) != SOCKET_ERROR)
        {
        lpSocket = Connect(&ServiceGUID, lpszServerName);
        }
    return lpSocket;
}

COverlappedSocket *CServiceInfo::Connect(LPGUID lpGUID,
                                         LPTSTR lpszServerName)
{
    INT          nRetcode;
    PCSADDR_INFO lpAddressInfo;
    COverlappedSocket *lpSocket = NULL;
    DWORD        i;

    DWORD dwQuerySetSize = m_dwQuerySetSize;

    nRetcode = ::WSAGetAddressByName(
                    lpszServerName,
                    &m_ServiceClassId,
                    NS_ALL,
                    &dwQuerySetSize,
                    m_lpWSAQuerySet,
                    RES_FIND_MULTIPLE,
                    NULL,
                    NULL);

    if (nRetcode != SOCKET_ERROR)
        {
        // Parse the array, consisting of CSADDR_INFO structures
        lpAddressInfo = (PCSADDR_INFO) m_lpWSAQuerySet->lpcsaBuffer;
        BOOL              bSuccess;

        for (i = 0, bSuccess = FALSE;
             i < m_lpWSAQuerySet->dwNumberOfCsAddrs && !bSuccess;
             i++)
            {
            lpSocket = new COverlappedSocket;
            bSuccess = lpSocket->Socket(lpAddressInfo[i].iSocketType, 0,
                            lpAddressInfo[i].iProtocol,
                            lpAddressInfo[i].LocalAddr.lpSockaddr->sa_family);
            if (bSuccess)
                {
                bSuccess = lpSocket->GetSocket().Bind(
```

```
                    lpAddressInfo[i].LocalAddr.lpSockaddr,
                    lpAddressInfo[i].LocalAddr.iSockaddrLength);

            if (bSuccess)  // OK for both stream and datagram sockets
               {
               bSuccess = lpSocket->GetSocket().Connect(
                  lpAddressInfo[i].RemoteAddr.lpSockaddr,
                  lpAddressInfo[i].RemoteAddr.iSockaddrLength);
               }
            }
         if (!bSuccess)
            {
            delete lpSocket;
            lpSocket = NULL;
            }
         }
      }
   return lpSocket;
}

#endif

CArray<COverlappedSocket *, COverlappedSocket *&>&
CServiceInfo::GetSockets()
{
   return m_SocketsInUse;
}

RECEIVECALLBACK CServiceInfo::GetReceiveCallback()
{
  return m_SocketsInUse[0]->GetReceiveCallback();

}

CString CServiceInfo::GetServiceClassName(void)
{
   return m_szServiceClassName;
}

DWORD CServiceInfo::GetTCPPort(void)
{
   return m_dwTCPPort;
}

BOOL CServiceInfo::IsReceivingDatagrams(void)
{
   return (m_dwUDPPort != INVALID_SOCKET ||
           m_dwSAPObjectType != INVALID_SOCKET);
}
```

The WNet DLLs Using the Service Registration API

With CServiceInfo and COverlappedSocket in place, I can now reimplement my WNet DLLs using them. I no longer have layered DLLs, with multiple DLLs to build and load; I just have to write one. Windows Sockets takes care of dispatching my requests to the correct protocol support layer.

To remind you, these are the functions that I specified for this API in the last chapter:

- WNetInit(): Initialize the DLL for a new user.
- WNetListen(): Listen for client connection requests.
- WNetCall(): Try to connect to a server.
- WNetHangup(): Break a connection.
- WNetSend(): Transmit data over a connection.
- WNetReceive(): Receive data over a connection.
- WNetSendDatagram(): Send a datagram packet.
- WNetReceiveDatagram(): Receive a datagram packet.
- WNetShutdown(): Disconnect a user from the DLL.

WNetInit()

WNetInit() is the most involved function in this series. It uses CServiceInfo to set up a listening server. If a GUID does not already exist for the service type, it calls CServiceInfo::AddClass(). It follows this with calls to CServiceInfo::Register() and CServiceInfo::Advertise(). Once this is complete, WNetInit() scans the array of sockets that have been opened. For each one that it finds, it calls CAsyncSocket::AsyncSelect(FD_ACCEPT) to put it into the accepting state.

WNetInit() creates an additional GUID for datagram communications if requested to do so. This uses substantially the same sequence of steps as the first procedure, with some nuances.

WNetInit() is in the file \WIN32NET\CODE\NEWDLLS\WNETINIT.CPP. Here is its listing:

```
BOOL WINAPI WNetInit(RECEIVECALLBACK lpReceiveCallback,
                     LPVOID          lpEndpoint,
                     LPHANDLE        lphUser,
                     BOOL            bClientOnly,
                     BOOL            bUseDatagrams)
{
   CHAR    szHostName[256];
   DWORD   dwTCPPort;
   DWORD   dwUDPPort;
```

```
DWORD    dwSPXPort;
DWORD    dwIPXPort;
GUID     ConnectionOrientedGUID;
GUID     DGramGUID;
CServiceInfo *pServiceInfo;
BOOL     bAddType = FALSE;

if (AfxGetModuleState()->m_hCurrentInstanceHandle == NULL)
   AfxGetModuleState()->m_hCurrentInstanceHandle =
               g_hDLLInstance;

TlsReceiveCallback = lpReceiveCallback;

if (bClientOnly)
   {
   *lphUser = (HANDLE) new CServiceInfo;
   return TRUE;
   }

if (lpEndpoint == NULL)
   lpEndpoint = _T("wnetsrvr");

// Find out our TCP host name
gethostname(szHostName, sizeof (szHostName));

// Initialize the CServiceInfo object for client-only
// initialization, and add the type, but don't
// register the server

// Get TCP port to use
LPSERVENT lpServ = getservbyname(
                     (LPCTSTR) lpEndpoint,
                     _T("tcp"));
if (lpServ == NULL)
   {
   return FALSE;
   }

// Have to convert port number order--getservbyname()
// returns it in network byte order
dwTCPPort = (DWORD) ntohs(lpServ->s_port);

if (::GetTypeByName((LPTSTR) lpEndpoint,
      &ConnectionOrientedGUID) == SOCKET_ERROR)
   {
   // Set TCP GUID using appropriate endpoint
   SET_TCP_SVCID(&ConnectionOrientedGUID, dwTCPPort);
   bAddType = TRUE;
   }
```

```
// See if we have an SPX port registered
lpServ = getservbyname((LPCTSTR) lpEndpoint, "spx");
if (lpServ != NULL)
   {
   dwSPXPort = (DWORD) ntohs(lpServ->s_port);
   }
else
   {
   dwSPXPort = INVALID_SOCKET;
   }

// Instantiate a CServiceInfo object to register
// with Service Registration API
pServiceInfo = new CServiceInfo;

if (bAddType && (!pServiceInfo->AddClass((LPTSTR) lpEndpoint,
                          dwTCPPort,
                          INVALID_SOCKET,
                          dwSPXPort,
                          (LPGUID) &ConnectionOrientedGUID)))
   {
   return FALSE;
   }

if (!pServiceInfo->Register((LPTSTR) lpEndpoint,
                         szHostName))
   {
   return FALSE;
   }

if (!pServiceInfo->Advertise())
   {
   return FALSE;
   }

CArray<COverlappedSocket *, COverlappedSocket *&>&
   SocketArray =
      pServiceInfo->GetSockets();

// Put sockets into accepting mode
COverlappedSocket *pThisSocket;

ASSERT(lpReceiveCallback != NULL);

for (int i = 0; i < SocketArray.GetSize(); ++i)
   {
   pThisSocket = SocketArray[i];
   pThisSocket->SetReceiveCallback(lpReceiveCallback);
```

```
    pThisSocket->AsyncSelect(FD_ACCEPT);
    }

// CServiceInfo object will identify this user of our
// services
*lphUser = (HANDLE) pServiceInfo;

if (bUseDatagrams)
    {
    bAddType = FALSE;
    // Now, let's register for datagram services
    // Look for a UDP port

    CString szDgramEndpoint;
    szDgramEndpoint = (LPTSTR) lpEndpoint;

    // Type name will have _dgram suffix
    szDgramEndpoint += _T("_dgram");

    lpServ = getservbyname(
                        (LPCTSTR) szDgramEndpoint,
                        _T("udp"));
    if (lpServ == NULL)
        {
        dwUDPPort = INVALID_SOCKET;
        }
    else
        {
        dwUDPPort = (DWORD) ntohs(lpServ->s_port);
        }

    // Look for an IPX port
    lpServ = getservbyname(
                        (LPCTSTR) szDgramEndpoint,
                        _T("ipx"));
    if (lpServ == NULL)
        {
        dwIPXPort = INVALID_SOCKET;
        }
    else
        {
        dwIPXPort = (DWORD) ntohs(lpServ->s_port);
        }

    if (dwUDPPort != INVALID_SOCKET ||
         dwIPXPort != INVALID_SOCKET)
        {
        pServiceInfo = new CServiceInfo;
```

```
if (::GetTypeByName((LPTSTR) (LPCTSTR) szDgramEndpoint,
     &DGramGUID) == SOCKET_ERROR)
   {
   // Set UDP GUID using UDP port
   SET_UDP_SVCID(&DGramGUID, dwUDPPort);
   bAddType = TRUE;
   }

if (bAddType && (!pServiceInfo->AddClass((LPTSTR)
                              (const char *) szDgramEndpoint,
                              INVALID_SOCKET,
                              dwUDPPort,
                              dwIPXPort,
                              (LPGUID) &DGramGUID)))
   {
   TRACE(_T("\nCServiceInfo::AddClass() failed, GetLastError()
      = %d"),
      ::GetLastError());
   }

else if (!pServiceInfo->Register((LPTSTR)
                              (const char *) szDgramEndpoint,
                              szHostName))
   {
   TRACE(_T("\nCServiceInfo::Register() failed, GetLastError()
      = %d"),
      ::GetLastError());
   }
else if (!pServiceInfo->Advertise())
   {
   TRACE(_T("\nCServiceInfo::Advertise() failed,
      GetLastError() = %d"),
      ::GetLastError());
   }
else
   {
   CArray<COverlappedSocket *, COverlappedSocket *&>&
      DgramSocketArray =
         pServiceInfo->GetSockets();

   // Put sockets into receiving mode
   for (int i = 0; i < DgramSocketArray.GetSize(); ++i)
      {
      pThisSocket = DgramSocketArray[i];
      pThisSocket->SetReceiveCallback(lpReceiveCallback);
      pThisSocket->AsyncSelect(FD_READ);
      }
   }
delete pServiceInfo;
```

```
        }
    }
    return TRUE;
}
```

WNetListen()

Because WNetInit() puts the server into the listening state (actually, CServiceInfo::Register() does this), WNetListen() is redundant. My implementation just checks to see if the CServiceInfo object contains a valid TCP port. If it doesn't, one of two things has occurred:

- The user never called WNetInit(), which is wrong.
- The user called WNetInit() and requested client-only initialization. This is okay, but it's not okay for the user to then turn around and put itself into the listening state.

If neither of these things has happened, the user is already listening.

The code for WNetListen(), and for the rest of the WNet API, is in \WIN32NET\CODE\NEWDLLS\WNETFUNC.CPP.

```
BOOL WINAPI WNetListen(HANDLE hUser)
{
    BOOL bRetcode = TRUE;

    // See if we're already listening
    CServiceInfo *pServiceInfo = (CServiceInfo *)
        hUser;

    if (pServiceInfo->GetTCPPort() == INVALID_SOCKET)
        {
        // We did WNetInit() without setting up the
        // server, which is totally bogus
        bRetcode = FALSE;
        }
    return bRetcode;
}
```

WNetCall()

WNetCall() uses CServiceInfo::Connect() to connect to the server application. Internally, my classes are using the ANSI character set, as required by Windows Sockets. However, I want to allow callers to use UNICODE if they so desire, so I call my local helper function UnicodeToANSI() to convert the target station and service names (if necessary). The only other setup required is to set the socket's receive callback function, in case the caller wants to receive data asynchronously. I do this by borrowing the receive callback function from one of the sockets I've already created. If WNetInit() was asked to do client-only initialization, it drops the callback function into Thread Local Storage using the CTlsSlot object TlsReceiveCallback. WNetCall() gets it from there if it is not available anywhere else.

WNetCall() returns a pointer to the COverlappedSocket object that CServiceInfo::Connect() creates, cast to a HANDLE. In subsequent calls, this represents the connection between the client and the server.

```
HANDLE WINAPI WNetCall(HANDLE hUser,
                       LPVOID lpTargetStation,
                       LPVOID lpEndpoint)
{
   CServiceInfo *pServiceInfo =
      (CServiceInfo *) hUser;

   char szEndpointANSI[256];
   char szTargetStationANSI[256];

   if (lpEndpoint == NULL)
      {
      lpEndpoint = _T("wnetsrvr");
      }

   UnicodeToANSI((LPSTR) lpEndpoint,
      szEndpointANSI, sizeof (szEndpointANSI));
   UnicodeToANSI((LPSTR) lpTargetStation,
      szTargetStationANSI, sizeof (szTargetStationANSI));

   COverlappedSocket *pSocket =
      pServiceInfo->Connect((LPTSTR) szEndpointANSI,
                            (LPTSTR) szTargetStationANSI);

   if (pSocket != NULL)
      {
      if (pServiceInfo->GetSockets().GetSize() > 0)
         {
         pSocket->SetReceiveCallback(
            pServiceInfo->GetReceiveCallback());
         }
      else
         {
         pSocket->SetReceiveCallback((RECEIVECALLBACK)
            (LPVOID) TlsReceiveCallback);
         }
      }
   return ((HANDLE) pSocket);
}
```

WNetHangup()

WNetHangup() terminates a connection by closing its socket. The way it does this is very simple; it deletes the COverlappedSocket object, whose destructor is smart enough to close the socket.

```
void WINAPI WNetHangup(HANDLE hConnection)
{
   COverlappedSocket *pSocket =
      (COverlappedSocket *) hConnection;

   ASSERT(pSocket != NULL);
   delete pSocket;
}
```

WNetSend()

WNetSend() uses CAsyncSocket::Send() to transmit data over a connection. One convenience I have added to this function is the ability to specify a timeout. This is very easy to implement. I call CAsyncSocket::SetSockOpt() and set the SO_SNDTIMEO option to the value specified. I have to check a couple of things first. If *dwTimeout* is passed as INFINITE, I have to convert it to zero, which SO_SNDTIMEO interprets as an infinite wait. On the other hand, if *dwTimeout* is passed as zero—meaning the caller doesn't want to wait at all—I have to change it to a very small non-zero value, or it will have exactly the opposite effect.

```
BOOL WINAPI WNetSend(HANDLE hConnection,
                     LPVOID lpData,
                     DWORD  dwDataLength,
                     DWORD  dwTimeout)
{
   COverlappedSocket *pSocket =
      (COverlappedSocket *) hConnection;

   int nSent;

   if (dwTimeout == INFINITE)
      {
      dwTimeout = 0;    // Zero means INFINITE
                        // for SO_SNDTIMEO
      }
   else if (dwTimeout == 0)
      {
      // No-wait
      // Set timeout to a very small non-zero value
```

```
      // (Zero means infinite)
      dwTimeout = 1;
      }

   pSocket->GetSocket().SetSockOpt(
      SO_SNDTIMEO, &dwTimeout, sizeof (DWORD));

   nSent = pSocket->GetSocket().Send(lpData, (int) dwDataLength);

   if (nSent != SOCKET_ERROR)
      {
      ASSERT(nSent == (int) dwDataLength);
      }
   return (nSent != SOCKET_ERROR);
}
```

WNetReceive()

WNetReceive() comes in two varieties—blocking and nonblocking. A nonblocking receive is indicated by a timeout value of zero. In this case, the caller does not expect data in hand; he or she is just providing buffer space to receive data asynchronously. This is typically server-side behavior, so I assume that if you're initialized, you're already receiving data in the background, and just return TRUE.

A blocking receive, where the caller wants the data right now, is more likely to be a client-side operation. My procedure here is:

1. Disable asynchronous FD_READ notifications by calling CAsyncSocket::AsyncSelect(0).
2. Use CAsyncSocket::SetSockOpt() to set SO_RCVTIMEO, the receive timeout. The logic here is the same as for WNetSend(), except that I've already dealt with a zero timeout.
3. Make sure the socket's receive buffer is large enough to accommodate the request. I do this by calling CAsyncSocket::GetSockOpt() and asking for SO_RCVBUF, then calling CAsyncSocket::SetSockOpt() to reset it if it's not currently big enough.
4. Call CAsyncSocket::Receive() to get the data, making sure I call it in a loop until I get the number of bytes I want or I time out.

```
BOOL WINAPI WNetReceive(HANDLE   hConnection,
                        LPVOID   lpData,
                        DWORD    dwDataLength,
                        LPDWORD lpdwBytesRead,
                        DWORD    dwTimeout
                        )
```

```
{
   DWORD dwOriginalDataLength = dwDataLength;

   if (dwTimeout == 0)
      {
      // Already waiting for data in the background
      return TRUE;
      }
   else
      {
      DWORD dwStartTime;
      BOOL   bRetval;

      COverlappedSocket *pSocket =
          (COverlappedSocket *) hConnection;

      LPBYTE lpbData = (LPBYTE) lpData;

      long lOldEventMask = pSocket->GetEventMask();

      if (lOldEventMask != 0)
         {
         // Disable async notifications
         pSocket->AsyncSelect(0);
         }

      // Make sure receive buffer is big enough
      int nReceiveBufSize = 0;
      int nSizeSize        = sizeof (nReceiveBufSize);

      if (pSocket->GetSocket().GetSockOpt(
            SO_RCVBUF, (void *) &nReceiveBufSize,
            &nSizeSize))
         {
         if (nReceiveBufSize < (int) dwDataLength)
            {
            if (!pSocket->GetSocket().SetSockOpt(
               SO_RCVBUF, (const void *) &dwDataLength,
               sizeof (dwDataLength)))
               {
               TRACE(TEXT(
                  "\n\tUnable to set receive buffer size in
                     WNetReceive()"));
               }
            }
         }
```

```
        else
            {
            TRACE(TEXT(
                "\n\tUnable to get receive buffer size in WNetReceive()"));
            }

        int nTotalReceived, nReceived;
        if (dwTimeout == INFINITE)
            {
            dwTimeout = 0;    // Zero means INFINITE
                              // for SO_RCVTIMEO
            }

        pSocket->GetSocket().SetSockOpt(
            SO_RCVTIMEO, &dwTimeout, sizeof (DWORD));

        bRetval = TRUE;
        for (nTotalReceived = 0, dwStartTime = GetCurrentTime();
               (nTotalReceived < (int) dwDataLength) &&
                  ((GetCurrentTime() - dwStartTime) < dwTimeout);
               )
           {
           nReceived = pSocket->GetSocket().Receive(
               &lpbData[nTotalReceived],
               ((int) dwDataLength) - nTotalReceived);

           if (nReceived == 0 || nReceived == SOCKET_ERROR)
               {
               bRetval = FALSE;
               break;
               }
           nTotalReceived += nReceived;
           }

        if (bRetval && lpdwBytesRead != NULL)
            {
            *lpdwBytesRead = (DWORD) nTotalReceived;
            }
        if (lOldEventMask != 0)
            {
            pSocket->AsyncSelect(lOldEventMask);
            }
        return bRetval;
        }
}
```

WNetSendDatagram()

WNetSendDatagram() is the only function that uses neither a CServiceInfo object nor a COverlappedSocket. It just creates a new CAsyncSocket, then lets CAsyncSocket::SendTo() do most of its work for it. Whereas WNet-SendDatagram() expects the target process to be passed as a string (actually an LPVOID), CAsyncSocket::SendTo() wants its port number. For this reason, WNetSendDatagram() is limited to sending UDP datagrams; it converts the endpoint name to a port number by calling getservbyname(). CAsync-Socket::SendTo() interprets a NULL target station name as a request for a broadcast datagram.

```
BOOL WINAPI WNetSendDatagram(HANDLE,
                             LPVOID lpTargetStation,
                             LPVOID lpEndpoint,
                             LPVOID lpData,
                             DWORD  dwDataLength)
{
   int nSent = SOCKET_ERROR;

   if (lpEndpoint == NULL)
      {
      lpEndpoint = _T("wnetsrvr");
      }

   LPSERVENT lpServ = getservbyname(
      (LPCTSTR) lpEndpoint,
      "udp");

   if (lpServ != NULL)
      {
      // Have to convert port number to host order
      // SendTo() converts it back to network order
      short sPort = ntohs(lpServ->s_port);

      CAsyncSocket *pSocket = new CAsyncSocket;

      if (pSocket->Socket(SOCK_DGRAM, 0))
         {
         // Now all we have to do is SendTo()
         nSent = pSocket->SendTo(
            lpData, dwDataLength,
            sPort, (LPCTSTR) lpTargetStation);
         }
      delete pSocket;
      }
   return ((nSent != SOCKET_ERROR) && (nSent == (int) dwDataLength));
}
```

WNetReceiveDatagram()

Receiving datagrams is always an asynchronous operation. Here, too, WNet-Init() will have spun off datagram reception if it was instructed to do so. Thus, WNetReceiveDatagram() just checks to see if this has happened. The return value (TRUE or FALSE) indicates whether the socket is already waiting for datagrams.

```
BOOL WINAPI WNetReceiveDatagram(HANDLE hUser,
                                LPVOID /*lpBuffer*/,
                                DWORD  /*wBufferSize*/
                                )
{
   BOOL bRetcode;

   CServiceInfo *pServiceInfo =
      (CServiceInfo *) hUser;

   // Already receiving asynchronously?
   // Make sure CServiceInfo object is set up for datagram
   // service
   bRetcode = pServiceInfo->IsReceivingDatagrams();
   return bRetcode;
}
```

WNetShutdown()

The last function in my WNet API just deletes the CServiceInfo object allocated by WNetInit(). The CServiceInfo destructor closes all of its open sockets.

```
void WINAPI WNetShutdown(HANDLE hUser)
{
   CServiceInfo *pServiceInfo =
      (CServiceInfo *) hUser;
   delete pServiceInfo;
}
```

Code Listings

There are four source files for the WNet DLL: WNETLVL1.H, WNET-INIT.CPP, WNETFUNC.CPP, and WNETMISC.CPP. Here are the complete listings for WNETINIT.CPP and WNETFUNC.CPP, which contain all the functions just discussed. WNETMISC.CPP contains helper functions (UnicodeToANSI(), ANSIToUnicode()). All the source files are in \WIN32NET\CODE\NEWDLLS.

```
/********
*
* WNETINIT.CPP
*
* Copyright (c) 1993-1996 Ralph P. Davis
*
* All Rights Reserved
*
********/

/*===== Includes =====*/

#include "stdafx.h"
#include <rpc.h>
#include <svcguid.h>

#define WNET_DLLFUNCTION __declspec(dllexport)

#include "wnetlvl1.h"
#include "ovsock.h"
#include "nspclass.h"
#include "tls.h"


/*===== Global Variables =====*/

CTlsSlot  TlsReceiveCallback;
HINSTANCE g_hDLLInstance;


/*===== Function Definitions =====*/

extern "C" WNET_DLLFUNCTION
INT APIENTRY DllMain(HINSTANCE hInstance,
                     DWORD     dwReason,
                     LPVOID    lpReserved)
{
   switch (dwReason)
      {
      case DLL_PROCESS_ATTACH:
         g_hDLLInstance = hInstance;

         if (!AfxSocketInit())
            {
            return 0;
            }
         break;
      }
```

```
   return TRUE;
}

extern "C" WNET_DLLFUNCTION
BOOL WINAPI WNetInit(RECEIVECALLBACK lpReceiveCallback,
                     LPVOID          lpEndpoint,
                     LPHANDLE        lphUser,
                     BOOL            bClientOnly,
                     BOOL            bUseDatagrams)
{
   CHAR    szHostName[256];
   DWORD   dwTCPPort;
   DWORD   dwUDPPort;
   DWORD   dwSPXPort;
   DWORD   dwIPXPort;
   GUID    ConnectionOrientedGUID;
   GUID    DGramGUID;
   CServiceInfo *pServiceInfo;
   BOOL    bAddType = FALSE;

   if (AfxGetModuleState()->m_hCurrentInstanceHandle == NULL)
      AfxGetModuleState()->m_hCurrentInstanceHandle =
                  g_hDLLInstance;

   TlsReceiveCallback = lpReceiveCallback;

   if (bClientOnly)
      {
      *lphUser = (HANDLE) new CServiceInfo;
      return TRUE;
      }

   if (lpEndpoint == NULL)
      lpEndpoint = _T("wnetsrvr");

   // Find out our TCP host name
   gethostname(szHostName, sizeof (szHostName));

   // Initialize the CServiceInfo object for client-only
   // initialization, and add the type, but don't
   // register the server

   // Get TCP port to use
   LPSERVENT lpServ = getservbyname(
                         (LPCTSTR) lpEndpoint,
                         _T("tcp"));
   if (lpServ == NULL)
```

```
    {
    return FALSE;
    }

// Have to convert port number order--getservbyname()
// returns it in network byte order
dwTCPPort = (DWORD) ntohs(lpServ->s_port);

if (::GetTypeByName((LPTSTR) lpEndpoint,
        &ConnectionOrientedGUID) == SOCKET_ERROR)
    {
    // Set TCP GUID using appropriate endpoint
    SET_TCP_SVCID(&ConnectionOrientedGUID, dwTCPPort);
    bAddType = TRUE;
    }

// See if we have an SPX port registered
lpServ = getservbyname((LPCTSTR) lpEndpoint, "spx");
if (lpServ != NULL)
    {
    dwSPXPort = (DWORD) ntohs(lpServ->s_port);
    }
else
    {
    dwSPXPort = INVALID_SOCKET;
    }

// Instantiate a CServiceInfo object to register
// with Service Registration API
pServiceInfo = new CServiceInfo;

if (bAddType && (!pServiceInfo->AddClass((LPTSTR) lpEndpoint,
                            dwTCPPort,
                            INVALID_SOCKET,
                            dwSPXPort,
                            (LPGUID) &ConnectionOrientedGUID)))
    {
    return FALSE;
    }

if (!pServiceInfo->Register((LPTSTR) lpEndpoint,
                            szHostName))
    {
    return FALSE;
    }

if (!pServiceInfo->Advertise())
```

```
    {
    return FALSE;
    }

CArray<COverlappedSocket *, COverlappedSocket *&>&
    SocketArray =
        pServiceInfo->GetSockets();

// Put sockets into accepting mode
COverlappedSocket *pThisSocket;

ASSERT(lpReceiveCallback != NULL);

for (int i = 0; i < SocketArray.GetSize(); ++i)
    {
    pThisSocket = SocketArray[i];
    pThisSocket->SetReceiveCallback(lpReceiveCallback);
    pThisSocket->AsyncSelect(FD_ACCEPT);
    }

// CServiceInfo object will identify this user of our
// services
*lphUser = (HANDLE) pServiceInfo;

if (bUseDatagrams)
    {
    bAddType = FALSE;
    // Now, let's register for datagram services
    // Look for a UDP port

    CString szDgramEndpoint;
    szDgramEndpoint = (LPTSTR) lpEndpoint;

    // Type name will have _dgram suffix
    szDgramEndpoint += _T("_dgram");

    lpServ = getservbyname(
                        (LPCTSTR) szDgramEndpoint,
                        _T("udp"));
    if (lpServ == NULL)
        {
        dwUDPPort = INVALID_SOCKET;
        }
    else
        {
        dwUDPPort = (DWORD) ntohs(lpServ->s_port);
        }
```

```
// Look for an IPX port
lpServ = getservbyname(
                        (LPCTSTR) szDgramEndpoint,
                        _T("ipx"));
if (lpServ == NULL)
   {
   dwIPXPort = INVALID_SOCKET;
   }
else
   {
   dwIPXPort = (DWORD) ntohs(lpServ->s_port);
   }

if (dwUDPPort != INVALID_SOCKET ||
    dwIPXPort != INVALID_SOCKET)
   {
   pServiceInfo = new CServiceInfo;

   if (::GetTypeByName((LPTSTR) (LPCTSTR) szDgramEndpoint,
         &DGramGUID) == SOCKET_ERROR)
      {
      // Set UDP GUID using UDP port
      SET_UDP_SVCID(&DGramGUID, dwUDPPort);
      bAddType = TRUE;
      }

   if (bAddType && (!pServiceInfo->AddClass((LPTSTR)
                                (const char *) szDgramEndpoint,
                                INVALID_SOCKET,
                                dwUDPPort,
                                dwIPXPort,
                                (LPGUID) &DGramGUID)))
      {
      TRACE(_T("\nCServiceInfo::AddClass() failed, GetLastError()
         = %d"),
         ::GetLastError());
      }

   else if (!pServiceInfo->Register((LPTSTR)
                                (const char *) szDgramEndpoint,
                                szHostName))
      {
      TRACE(_T("\nCServiceInfo::Register() failed, GetLastError()
         = %d"),
         ::GetLastError());
      }
   else if (!pServiceInfo->Advertise())
```

```
            {
            TRACE(_T("\nCServiceInfo::Advertise() failed,
               GetLastError() = %d"),
               ::GetLastError());
            }
         else
            {
            CArray<COverlappedSocket *, COverlappedSocket *&>&
               DgramSocketArray =
                  pServiceInfo->GetSockets();

            // Put sockets into receiving mode
            for (int i = 0; i < DgramSocketArray.GetSize(); ++i)
               {
               pThisSocket = DgramSocketArray[i];
               pThisSocket->SetReceiveCallback(lpReceiveCallback);

               pThisSocket->AsyncSelect(FD_READ);
               }
            }
         delete pServiceInfo;
         }
      }
   return TRUE;
}


/********
*
* WNETFUNC.CPP
*
* Copyright (c) 1992-1996 Ralph P. Davis
*
* All Rights Reserved
*
********/

/*===== Includes =====*/

#include "stdafx.h"

#define WNET_DLLFUNCTION __declspec(dllexport)

#include "wnetlvl1.h"
#include "win32obj.h"
#include "ovsock.h"
#include "overlap.h"
#include "nspclass.h"
#include "tls.h"
```

```
/*===== External Variables =====*/

extern CTlsSlot TlsReceiveCallback;


/*===== External Functions =====*/

extern "C" VOID WINAPI ANSIToUnicode(LPSTR  lpInputString,
                          LPTSTR lpszOutputString,
                          int nOutStringLen);
extern "C" BOOL WINAPI UnicodeToANSI(LPTSTR lpInputString,
                          LPSTR lpszOutputString,
                          int nOutStringLen);


/*===== Function Definitions =====*/

extern "C" __declspec(dllexport)
BOOL WINAPI WNetIsWindowsNT(void)
{
   return CWin32Object::IsWindowsNT();
}

extern "C" __declspec(dllexport)
BOOL WINAPI WNetIsWindows95(void)
{
   return !WNetIsWindowsNT();
}

extern "C" __declspec(dllexport)
BOOL WINAPI WNetListen(HANDLE hUser)
{
   BOOL bRetcode = TRUE;

   // See if we're already listening
   CServiceInfo *pServiceInfo = (CServiceInfo *)
      hUser;

   if (pServiceInfo->GetTCPPort() == INVALID_SOCKET)
      {
      // We did WNetInit() without setting up the
      // server, which is bogus
      bRetcode = FALSE;
      }
   return bRetcode;
}

extern "C" __declspec(dllexport)
```

```
BOOL WINAPI WNetReceive(HANDLE  hConnection,
                        LPVOID  lpData,
                        DWORD   dwDataLength,
                        LPDWORD lpdwBytesRead,
                        DWORD   dwTimeout
                        )
{
   DWORD dwOriginalDataLength = dwDataLength;

   if (dwTimeout == 0)
      {
      // Already waiting for data in the background
      return TRUE;
      }
   else
      {
      DWORD dwStartTime;
      BOOL  bRetval;

      COverlappedSocket *pSocket =
          (COverlappedSocket *) hConnection;

      LPBYTE lpbData = (LPBYTE) lpData;

      long lOldEventMask = pSocket->GetEventMask();

      if (lOldEventMask != 0)
         {
         // Disable async notifications
         pSocket->AsyncSelect(0);
         }

      // Make sure receive buffer is big enough
      int nReceiveBufSize = 0;
      int nSizeSize       = sizeof (nReceiveBufSize);

      if (pSocket->GetSocket().GetSockOpt(
            SO_RCVBUF, (void *) &nReceiveBufSize,
            &nSizeSize))
         {
         if (nReceiveBufSize < (int) dwDataLength)
            {
            if (!pSocket->GetSocket().SetSockOpt(
               SO_RCVBUF, (const void *) &dwDataLength,
               sizeof (dwDataLength)))
               {
               TRACE(TEXT(
                  "\n\tUnable to set receive buffer size in
                     WNetReceive()"));
```

```
                }
            }
        }
    else
        {
        TRACE(TEXT(
            "\n\tUnable to get receive buffer size in WNetReceive()"));
        }

    int nTotalReceived, nReceived;
    if (dwTimeout == INFINITE)
        {
        dwTimeout = 0;      // Zero means INFINITE
                            // for SO_RCVTIMEO
        }

    pSocket->GetSocket().SetSockOpt(
        SO_RCVTIMEO, &dwTimeout, sizeof (DWORD));

    bRetval = TRUE;
    for (nTotalReceived = 0, dwStartTime = GetCurrentTime();
           (nTotalReceived < (int) dwDataLength) &&
              ((GetCurrentTime() - dwStartTime) < dwTimeout);
           )
      {
      nReceived = pSocket->GetSocket().Receive(
          &lpbData[nTotalReceived],
          ((int) dwDataLength) - nTotalReceived);

      if (nReceived == 0 || nReceived == SOCKET_ERROR)
          {
          bRetval = FALSE;
          break;
          }
      nTotalReceived += nReceived;
      }

    if (bRetval && lpdwBytesRead != NULL)
        {
        *lpdwBytesRead = (DWORD) nTotalReceived;
        }
    if (lOldEventMask != 0)
        {
        pSocket->AsyncSelect(lOldEventMask);
        }
    return bRetval;
    }
}
```

```
extern "C" __declspec(dllexport)
BOOL WINAPI WNetSend(HANDLE hConnection,
                     LPVOID lpData,
                     DWORD  dwDataLength,
                     DWORD  dwTimeout)
{
   COverlappedSocket *pSocket =
      (COverlappedSocket *) hConnection;

   int nSent;

   if (dwTimeout == INFINITE)
      {
      dwTimeout = 0;    // Zero means INFINITE
                        // for SO_SNDTIMEO
      }
   else if (dwTimeout == 0)
      {
      // No-wait
      // Set timeout to a very small non-zero value
      // (Zero means infinite)
      dwTimeout = 1;
      }

   pSocket->GetSocket().SetSockOpt(
      SO_SNDTIMEO, &dwTimeout, sizeof (DWORD));

   nSent = pSocket->GetSocket().Send(lpData, (int) dwDataLength);

   if (nSent != SOCKET_ERROR)
      {
      ASSERT(nSent == (int) dwDataLength);
      }
   return (nSent != SOCKET_ERROR);
}

extern "C" __declspec(dllexport)
HANDLE WINAPI WNetCall(HANDLE hUser,
                       LPVOID lpTargetStation,
                       LPVOID lpEndpoint)
{
   CServiceInfo *pServiceInfo =
      (CServiceInfo *) hUser;

   char szEndpointANSI[256];
   char szTargetStationANSI[256];

   if (lpEndpoint == NULL)
```

```
        {
        lpEndpoint = _T("wnetsrvr");
        }

    UnicodeToANSI((LPSTR) lpEndpoint,
        szEndpointANSI, sizeof (szEndpointANSI));
    UnicodeToANSI((LPSTR) lpTargetStation,
        szTargetStationANSI, sizeof (szTargetStationANSI));

    COverlappedSocket *pSocket =
        pServiceInfo->Connect((LPTSTR) szEndpointANSI,
                              (LPTSTR) szTargetStationANSI);

    if (pSocket != NULL)
        {
        if (pServiceInfo->GetSockets().GetSize() > 0)
            {
            pSocket->SetReceiveCallback(
                pServiceInfo->GetReceiveCallback());
            }
        else
            {
            pSocket->SetReceiveCallback((RECEIVECALLBACK)
                (LPVOID) TlsReceiveCallback);
            }
        }
    return ((HANDLE) pSocket);
}

extern "C" __declspec(dllexport)
void WINAPI WNetHangup(HANDLE hConnection)
{
    COverlappedSocket *pSocket =
        (COverlappedSocket *) hConnection;

    ASSERT(pSocket != NULL);
    delete pSocket;
}

extern "C" __declspec(dllexport)
void WINAPI WNetShutdown(HANDLE hUser)
{
    CServiceInfo *pServiceInfo =
        (CServiceInfo *) hUser;
    delete pServiceInfo;
}

extern "C" __declspec(dllexport)
```

```
BOOL WINAPI WNetSendDatagram(HANDLE,
                             LPVOID lpTargetStation,
                             LPVOID lpEndpoint,
                             LPVOID lpData,
                             DWORD  dwDataLength)
{
   int nSent = SOCKET_ERROR;

   if (lpEndpoint == NULL)
      {
      lpEndpoint = _T("wnetsrvr");
      }

   LPSERVENT lpServ = getservbyname(
      (LPCTSTR) lpEndpoint,
      "udp");

   if (lpServ != NULL)
      {
      // Have to convert port number to host order
      // SendTo() converts it back to network order
      short sPort = ntohs(lpServ->s_port);

      CAsyncSocket *pSocket = new CAsyncSocket;

      if (pSocket->Socket(SOCK_DGRAM, 0))
         {
         // Now all we have to do is SendTo()
         nSent = pSocket->SendTo(
            lpData, dwDataLength,
            sPort, (LPCTSTR) lpTargetStation);
         }
      delete pSocket;
      }
   return ((nSent != SOCKET_ERROR) && (nSent == (int) dwDataLength));
}

extern "C" __declspec(dllexport)
BOOL WINAPI WNetReceiveDatagram(HANDLE hUser,
                                LPVOID /*lpBuffer*/,
                                DWORD  /*wBufferSize*/
                                )
{
   BOOL bRetcode;

   CServiceInfo *pServiceInfo =
      (CServiceInfo *) hUser;
```

```
    // Already receiving asynchronously?
    // Make sure CServiceInfo object is set up for datagram
    // service
    bRetcode = pServiceInfo->IsReceivingDatagrams();
    return bRetcode;
}
```

Conclusion

Windows Sockets offers a very good programming interface for peer-to-peer communications. It is protocol-independent. In the Win32 environment, it provides connectivity over TCP/IP, IPX/SPX, NetBEUI, and many other protocols. In conjunction with the Service Registration API, it gives you protocol transparency, allowing a single binary image to handle communications over all underlying protocols.

The Sockets API is high-level and generally easy to program. On NT, it is also highly optimized. It offers the fastest data-transfer rate of any peer-to-peer mechanism, particularly using overlapped I/O.

Windows Sockets 2 adds a number of improvements to Windows Sockets 1.1. These include:

- Explicit support for overlapped I/O
- More flexible support for multiple protocols
- A simplified and enhanced Service Registration API
- The ability to request specific qualities of service from the supporting protocols
- The ability to organize sockets into groups
- API hooks for multipoint connections

Suggested Readings

Online References

"Windows Sockets in MFC: Overview," in *Programming MFC: Encyclopedia.*

Network Services Overview in the Win32 SDK online help.

Windows Sockets 2 in the Internet section of the Win32 SDK version 4.0 online help.

Documents available for downloading from the Windows Sockets 2 World Wide Web site (http://www.stardust.com):
"Windows Sockets 2 Application Programming Interface" (WSAPI21.DOC)
"Windows Sockets 2 Protocol-Specific Annex" (WSANX202.DOC)
"Windows Sockets 2 Service Provider Interface" (WSSPI21.DOC)

"Winsock 2 Debug and Trace Facilities" (DBGSPEC.DOC)
Microsoft Knowledge Base for Win32 SDK articles:
"Host Name May Map to Multiple IP Addresses"
"How Database Winsock APIs Are Implemented in Windows NT 3.5"
"How to Use WinSock to Enumerate Addresses"
"Multiprotocol Support for Windows Sockets"
"PRB: Poor TCP/IP Performance When Doing Small Sends"
"Receiving, Sending Multicasts in Windows NT Using WinSock"
"Sockets Applications on Microsoft Windows Platforms"
"Tips for Writing Windows Sockets Apps That Use AF_NETBIOS"
"Windows Sockets API Specification Version"
Microsoft Knowledge Base for Win32 SDK version 4.0 articles:
"BUG: getsockopt for IPX_MAX_ADAPTER_NUM Fails on Windows 95"
"BUG: Incomplete IPX_ADDRESS_DATA Structure Under Windows 95"
"BUG:Invalid Default Interface for IP Multicasting Causes Crash"
"BUG: Timimg Out on recvfrom() Causes Windows 95 to Quit"
"BUG: Windows 95-Based Winsock App Can't Receive IPX Broadcast"
"BUG: Windows 95 Doesn't Allow open_osfhandle on Socket Handles"
"BUG: Winsock App Over IPX/SPX Over RAS Fails to Connect"
"BUG: Winsock Sends IP Packets with TTL 0"
"BUG: WSARecvEx Fails to Set MSG_PARTIAL Flag on Windows 95"
"How to Use the AutoDial Feature in Network and WinSock Apps"
"Receive/Send Multicasts in Windows NT & Win95 Using WinSock"

Chapter 10

Named Pipes and Mailslots

The Named Pipes and Mailslots APIs are high-level, convenient programming interfaces for peer-to-peer communications. Their syntax is the most native to the Win32 environment, since they are implemented as Windows file system drivers. The main part of the data exchange (sending and receiving) uses standard Win32 file I/O. The rest of the interface involves making server applications available to clients. There are also a couple of functions that optimize request-response types of exchanges.

Named Pipes API—The Server Side

The Named Pipes API has always had a rigid, somewhat idiosyncratic notion of who is allowed to do what. Specifically, only certain operating system platforms can support Named Pipes server applications. In the OS/2 environment where Named Pipes originated, only OS/2 could host Named Pipes servers. In the Win32 environment, only NT can. No other communications API enforces this peculiar separation of labor.

Named pipes provide connection-oriented service. Therefore, there must be a way for server applications to listen for connection requests. Servers do this by:

1. Creating a named pipe with a call to CreateNamedPipe()
2. Waiting for clients to request connections by calling ConnectNamedPipe()

Pipes have several characteristics, which are set in the call to CreateNamedPipe():

- **Direction**: A named pipe can be two-way, client-to-server only, or server-to-client only. I've never had occasion to use anything but a two-way pipe.
- **Read mode**: A named pipe can be read in byte or message mode. In byte mode, the data is read and written as a stream of bytes. Reads and writes do not have to be balanced. In message mode, each write to the pipe defines a discrete message, and data must be read as a complete message. Attempts to read more than a message will return only the data comprising the message. Attempts to read a partial message will appear to fail. That is, ReadFile() will return FALSE, though it will retrieve the amount of data that was requested. To indicate that the read fetched an incomplete message, GetLastError() will return ERROR_MORE_DATA.
- **Write mode**: Pipes are also written in byte or message mode. A pipe can be written in message mode and read in byte mode. The reverse is not true, however; if the person transmitting the data has no notion of message boundaries, the receiving station cannot impose them.
- **Blocking mode**: Pipes can be either blocking or nonblocking. This determines whether or not the ConnectNamedPipe() call will block. Nonblocking pipes are obsolete and are included only for backward compatibility with OS/2 Named Pipes.

Like standard files, pipes can be opened for overlapped (asynchronous) I/O. In this case, a pointer to an OVERLAPPED structure is passed to ConnectNamedPipe(), ReadFile(), ReadFileEx(), WriteFile(), WriteFileEx(), and TransactNamedPipe(). Windows 95 does support overlapped I/O against named pipes, but does not support I/O completion ports.

CreateNamedPipe()

CreateNamedPipe() creates a server endpoint. Here is its prototype:

```
HANDLE CreateNamedPipe(
          LPCTSTR lpName,
          DWORD  dwOpenMode,
          DWORD  dwPipeMode,
          DWORD  dwMaxInstances,
          DWORD  dwOutBufferSize,
          DWORD  dwInBufferSize,
          DWORD  dwDefaultTimeout,
          LPSECURITY_ATTRIBUTES lpSecurity);
```

lpName is the name you want to assign to the pipe. Named pipes use pseudodirectory names in UNC format. The first component is the machine name, preceded by two backslashes. The next component must be \PIPE\. CreateNamedPipe() can only create a pipe on the local machine, so the name must use the special syntax \\.\PIPE\<pipe name>. (A dot in the machine name portion is always understood to mean the local machine.) The pipe name portion can contain further path separators; no actual directory or file is created. A useful convention is to make the component following \PIPE\ some kind of application signature, to minimize your chances of picking a name that someone else is using.

It is somewhat puzzling that you have to pass the pipe name in its entirety, even though the first part of it is always \\.\PIPE. The classes I develop later in this chapter relieve you of this burden.

dwOpenMode is similar to the *dwFlagsAndAttributes* argument to CreateFile(). It can be used to request overlapped I/O on the pipe by setting the FILE_FLAG_OVERLAPPED bit. It can also request that writes to byte-mode pipes be immediately transmitted to the partner station by setting the FILE_FLAG_WRITE_THROUGH bit. By default, Windows does not send data on a byte-mode pipe until one of two thresholds is exceeded:

- The amount of data exceeds a certain byte count.
- No data has been sent for a certain amount of time, and there is data to send.

For instance, assume that the byte-count threshold is 512 and the timeout is 500 milliseconds. After 100 milliseconds, 512 bytes have been written to the pipe; Windows will transmit them. Then another 500 milliseconds go by during which only 128 bytes are written; Windows will transmit only those 128 bytes.

dwOpenMode also specifies the direction of the pipe; this is analogous to the read-write access of a file. PIPE_ACCESS_DUPLEX creates a two-way pipe; it is similar to GENERIC_READ | GENERIC_WRITE file access. These are by far the most common pipes. PIPE_ACCESS_INBOUND creates a client-to-server pipe; it is equivalent to GENERIC_READ access. Finally, PIPE_ACCESS_OUTBOUND creates a server-to-client pipe, and corresponds to GENERIC_WRITE access. PIPE_ACCESS_DUPLEX, as you might suspect, is nothing more than PIPE_ACCESS_INBOUND | PIPE_ACCESS_OUTBOUND; you can use either syntax to create a two-way pipe. By the way, even though GENERIC_READ and GENERIC_WRITE mean the same thing as PIPE_ACCESS_INBOUND and PIPE_ACCESS_OUTBOUND, CreateNamedPipe() does not understand them.

dwPipeMode specifies the blocking mode, the read mode, and the write mode of the pipe. Each of these properties has its own set of mutually exclusive flags. The blocking mode is either PIPE_WAIT (0) or PIPE_NOWAIT (1). As I mentioned earlier, PIPE_NOWAIT (nonblocking mode) is an obsolete usage. The read mode is PIPE_READMODE_BYTE (0) or PIPE_READMODE_MESSAGE (2). The write mode is PIPE_TYPE_BYTE (0) or PIPE_TYPE_MESSAGE (4). If you pass *dwPipeMode* as zero, you get a blocking pipe that will be read and written in byte mode. It is permissible to create a pipe that is written in message mode and read in byte mode (PIPE_TYPE_MESSAGE | PIPE_READMODE_BYTE). This makes sense on the server side especially, for the following reasons:

- Because the pipe is being written in message mode, clients can read it in message mode using TransactNamedPipe(), which yields superior performance to WriteFile() followed by ReadFile(). Servers, on the other hand, will be responding to client requests and are less likely to need TransactNamedPipe(). The semantics of TransactNamedPipe() are as follows: ask a question, wait for an answer. Server applications normally provide answers and don't ask questions.
- By reading the pipe in byte mode, the server avoids having to deal with partially read messages. It can read whatever data is available, then go back and get any data that's left. Reading a pipe in message mode requires a little more fancy footwork to make sure you get a complete message.

dwMaxInstances specifies the maximum number of instances of the pipe that can be created. It can be a number from 1 to 254, or the constant PIPE_UNLIMITED_INSTANCES. Each call to CreateNamedPipe() with the same pipe name creates a new instance of the pipe, and each instance can service only one client application. Thus, to service more clients concurrently, create more instances.

dwDefaultTimeout is of marginal importance. It sets the timeout value for client applications that call WaitNamedPipe() and specify a timeout of NMPWAIT_USE_DEFAULT_WAIT. You can pass *dwDefaultTimeout* as zero, which tells Windows "I couldn't care less; you decide."

CreateNamedPipe() is the first function I have presented where you cannot punt on the SECURITY_ATTRIBUTES by passing *lpSecurity* as NULL. Here is the layout of the structure again:

```
typedef struct _SECURITY_ATTRIBUTES
{
   DWORD   nLength;
   LPVOID  lpSecurityDescriptor;
```

```
   BOOL    bInheritHandle;
} SECURITY_ATTRIBUTES;
```

lpSecurity cannot be ignored for the simple reason that passing it as NULL is a significant action; it creates the pipe with "a default security descriptor," according to the Win32 documentation. The effect is to limit access to the pipe to users who are at least as trusted as the user creating it. Thus, if the pipe is created by a user with administrator status, only administrators can connect to it. Passing a non-NULL SECURITY_ATTRIBUTES but setting the *lpSecurityDescriptor* member to NULL is also insufficient. This has the same effect as passing *lpSecurity* as NULL; the only difference is that you can make the handle inheritable. In order to make the pipe accessible to any user wanting to use the server application, you must pass a non-NULL security descriptor containing a NULL discretionary access control list (DACL). The DACL says who is allowed to access the pipe and in what fashion. A non-NULL security descriptor with a NULL DACL allows anyone to access the pipe.

In Chapter 13, I discuss the Win32 Security API in more detail, and develop classes to mask its complexity. For now, I just present the code required to set up the SECURITY_ATTRIBUTES correctly.

```
SECURITY_ATTRIBUTES SecurityAttributes;
SECURITY_DESCRIPTOR SecurityDescriptor;

InitializeSecurityDescriptor(&SecurityDescriptor,
   SECURITY_DESCRIPTOR_REVISION);
SetSecurityDescriptorDacl(&SecurityDescriptor,
                          TRUE,   // DACL is present
                          NULL,   // Allow unlimited access
                          FALSE); // Explicitly specified DACL
SecurityAttributes.nLength =
   sizeof (SECURITY_ATTRIBUTES);
SecurityAttributes.bInheritHandle = FALSE;
SecurityAttributes.lpSecurityDescriptor =
   &SecurityDescriptor;
```

ConnectNamedPipe()

Once you have created instances of a named pipe, you call ConnectNamed-Pipe() to wait for clients to connect.

```
BOOL ConnectNamedPipe(
        HANDLE       hNamedPipeInstance,
        LPOVERLAPPED lpOverlapped);
```

ConnectNamedPipe() behaves differently, depending on how you originally created the pipe. For a blocking pipe that was not created for overlapped I/O, ConnectNamedPipe() does not return until a client tries to connect. In the interim, the calling thread goes to sleep. In many (and perhaps most) situations, this is exactly what you want. There is one special-case situation that may arise—when a client connection request arrives between the server's calls to CreateNamedPipe() and ConnectNamedPipe(). In this case, ConnectNamedPipe() returns FALSE, but GetLastError() indicates ERROR_PIPE_CONNECTED. The connection has been established, and you can proceed to exchange data.

With a nonblocking pipe, ConnectNamedPipe() immediately returns FALSE, and GetLastError() reports ERROR_PIPE_LISTENING. ConnectNamedPipe() will return TRUE when a client request comes in. It will never block. This reduces you to doing polled I/O, which is almost always undesirable in a multitasking environment. Every time you ask, "Okay, is anybody trying to connect?" you use CPU time. Most of the time, the answer will be "No." It is much more effective to use a strategy that puts the calling thread to sleep at some point. Whether it goes to sleep at once when it calls ConnectNamedPipe(), or sometime later (as it will with overlapped I/O) does not matter. The important thing is that you not pester the CPU asking if anything is happening.

On a pipe created for overlapped I/O, you must pass the *lpOverlapped* argument as a pointer to an OVERLAPPED structure:

```
typedef struct _OVERLAPPED
{
   DWORD    Internal;
   DWORD    InternalHigh;
   DWORD    Offset;
   DWORD    OffsetHigh;
   HANDLE   hEvent;
} OVERLAPPED;
```

The only field that ever has any significance for Named Pipes is the event handle (except that the offset fields must be set to zero). When you use standard overlapped techniques, *hEvent* represents a manual-reset event, which will be automatically set to the nonsignalled state when you call any appropriate function. (Apparently, though, Windows 95 forgets to do this.) With an overlapped pipe, ConnectNamedPipe() returns immediately; the event signals when a client connects to you. You detect this by calling one of the wait functions (WaitForSingleObject(), WaitForMultipleObjects(), or MsgWaitForMultipleObjects()). If the pipe is tied to an I/O completion port, then none of the fields are used.

Several strategies for multithreading a Named Pipes server are presented later in this chapter. (In the Win32 online help, see the sections "Multithreaded Server," "Server Using Overlapped Input and Output," and "Server Using Completion Routines" in the *Pipes Overview.*)

Named Pipes API—The Client Side

A client application requests a connection with a Named Pipes server by calling CreateFile() to open the named pipe. The pipe can be on the same machine as the client, in which case it specifies the pipe name as \\.\PIPE\<pipe name>. If it is on a remote machine, the client uses the full UNC name of the pipe, \\<machine name>\PIPE\<pipe name>. You can also connect to a named pipe on the local machine using its full name. However, using \\.\PIPE\ yields a huge improvement in performance, because you bypass the network redirector. When a client station calls CreateFile(), the target server application wakes up from its call to ConnectNamedPipe() (or whatever wait function it is using).

SetNamedPipeHandleState()

CreateFile() knows nothing about pipe-specific attributes (like read mode), so when the client opens the pipe, it starts out as a blocking, byte-read pipe. To change either of these properties, the client calls SetNamedPipeHandleState(). It is often desirable to change the read mode to message mode (PIPE_READMODE_MESSAGE) because this allows you to use TransactNamedPipe(). This function takes advantage of the fact that an answer from the server is as good as an acknowledgment, and thereby eliminates a few steps from the exchange. From what I have seen, TransactNamedPipe() is 10 to 25 percent faster than issuing a WriteFile() followed by a ReadFile(). Here is the prototype for SetNamedPipeHandleState():

```
BOOL SetNamedPipeHandleState(
        HANDLE  hNamedPipe,
        LPDWORD lpMode,
        LPDWORD lpMaxCollectionCount,
        LPDWORD lpCollectDataTimeout);
```

lpMode points to a DWORD that specifies the blocking mode (PIPE_WAIT or PIPE_NOWAIT) and the read mode (PIPE_READMODE_BYTE or PIPE_READMODE_MESSAGE). The client cannot change the write mode; only the server has control over this. If **lpMode* includes the PIPE_TYPE_MESSAGE bit, SetNamedPipeHandleState() fails.

lpMaxCollectionCount and *lpCollectDataTimeout* are the byte-count and timeout thresholds used for buffering data on the sending end of byte-write pipes. Windows collects data on the local station until either of these thresholds is exceeded. You can disable this by setting the FILE_FLAG_WRITE_THROUGH bit in the call to CreateFile().

lpMode, *lpMaxCollectionCount*, and *lpCollectDataTimeout* are pointers so that you can pass NULL for options you are not configuring. In fact, you can pass all three of them as NULL, though it makes no sense to do so.

Named Pipes API—Data Exchange

Once the pipe is connected, the client and server applications use WriteFile() and ReadFile() to exchange data. At this point, the difference between the pipe and a standard disk file is transparent to both parties.

When the communication involves a request-response interaction, you can also use TransactNamedPipe(). This function writes a message to the pipe, then waits for a response. Like ConnectNamedPipe(), ReadFile(), and WriteFile(), it can be called in overlapped mode. As I mentioned, my tests indicate that TransactNamedPipe() provides better performance than just calling WriteFile() followed by ReadFile(), as advertised.

```
BOOL TransactNamedPipe(
        HANDLE       hNamedPipe,
        LPVOID       lpInBuffer,
        DWORD        dwInBufferSize,
        LPVOID       lpOutBuffer,
        DWORD        dwOutBufferSize,
        LPDWORD      lpBytesRead,
        LPOVERLAPPED lpOverlapped);
```

lpInBuffer, *dwInBufferSize*, *lpOutBuffer*, and *dwOutBufferSize* describe the send and receive buffers. If the pipe is not being accessed in overlapped mode, TransactNamedPipe() will block until a response comes in, and **lpBytesRead* will indicate the number of bytes received from the partner station.

Other Client-Side Functions

A Named Pipes server can service only one client for each instance of a pipe. If a client is willing to wait in line, it can call WaitNamedPipe() to wait until an instance becomes available. This function takes the UNC name of the pipe the client wants to access and a timeout value in milliseconds. WaitNamedPipe() does not actually open a client-side handle to the pipe: it merely signals that an instance is available.

```
BOOL WaitNamedPipe(
        LPCTSTR lpPipeName,
        DWORD   dwTimeout);
```

dwTimeout is either the number of milliseconds or NMPWAIT_WAIT_FOREVER (equivalent to INFINITE), which puts the client to sleep indefinitely. Another more esoteric constant is NMPWAIT_USE_DEFAULT_WAIT (0), which says to use the default time-out requested by the server in its call to CreateNamedPipe(). The server can also tell NT to use its own default by passing this value as zero, in which case NMPWAIT_USE_DEFAULT_WAIT means "use the default default."

A return value of TRUE means that an instance is available. You'd better call CreateFile() in a hurry, though; WaitNamedPipe() does not reserve an instance of the pipe for you. It is entirely possible that someone else will get the pipe between your calls to WaitNamedPipe() and CreateFile(). In order to use WaitNamedPipe(), you have to call it in a loop.

```
HANDLE hPipe;
DWORD  dwError;
while (TRUE)
   {
   if (WaitNamedPipe(...), 50000))
      {
      hPipe = CreateFile(...);
      // Have to check for race condition--
      // no guarantee that CreateFile() will
      // succeed
      if (hPipe != INVALID_HANDLE_VALUE)
         break;
      if ((dwError = GetlastError()) != ERROR_PIPE_BUSY)
         ExitProcess(dwError);
      }
   }
```

CallNamedPipe() can be used by a client station on a message-write pipe (one that the server has created with the PIPE_TYPE_MESSAGE bit set in its call to CreateNamedPipe()). It combines calls to WaitNamedPipe(), CreateFile(), TransactNamedPipe(), and CloseHandle(). It is useful when the client only needs to send a single message and receive a single answer, and does not require a long-lived connection.

```
BOOL CallNamedPipe(
        LPCTSTR  lpPipeName,
        LPVOID   lpInBuffer,
        DWORD    dwInBufferSize,
```

```
    LPVOID    lpOutBuffer,
    DWORD     dwOutBufferSize,
    LPDWORD   lpBytesRead,
    DWORD     dwTimeout);
```

The arguments to CallNamedPipe() combine those for TransactNamedPipe() and WaitNamedPipe(). Because the pipe is not yet open, the pipe name, rather than the pipe handle, is required. The five interior arguments are the same as for TransactNamedPipe(); they describe the input and output buffers and provide a variable that returns the number of bytes read. Finally, *dwTimeout* is the same as the timeout argument to WaitNamedPipe(). There is one additional constant, NMPWAIT_NOWAIT (1), which directs CallNamedPipe() to fail if an instance of the pipe is not immediately available.

Terminating a Named Pipes Connection

A Named Pipes connection normally terminates when the client application calls CloseHandle() with its pipe handle. At this point, the server application detects a failure—most likely ReadFile() returns FALSE and GetLastError() says ERROR_PIPE_BROKEN. In response, the server calls DisconnectNamedPipe():

```
BOOL DisconnectNamedPipe(HANDLE hPipe);
```

DisconnectNamedPipe() puts the pipe instance back into the listening state. It does not destroy the pipe. When the server is done using a pipe instance, it calls CloseHandle() with the handle to that instance. NT destroys the pipe when the last instance is closed.

Strategies for Multithreading a Named Pipes Server

There are many ways to service multiple instances of a named pipe. One important consideration is this: a Named Pipes server can assume the identity of a connected client by calling ImpersonateNamedPipeClient(), passing it the handle of the pipe instance to which the client has connected. When the client disconnects, the server calls RevertToSelf() to return to its own security context. Client impersonation affects the security context of the running thread. So to take advantage of this powerful feature, you need to manage each connected instance of a pipe in a separate thread.

One Thread per Instance with a Blocking, Nonoverlapped Pipe

In this scenario, a pipe is created for blocking, nonoverlapped I/O. This permits a very simple, but nonetheless effective, multithreading strategy. For each instance of the pipe you create, you spin off a thread that listens for connection requests, then waits for data after a connection has been established. Here's an example:

```
const short PIPE_INSTANCES = 5;
HANDLE hPipeInstance[PIPE_INSTANCES],
       hPipeThread[PIPE_INSTANCES];

for (int i = 0; i < PIPE_INSTANCES; ++i)
   {
   hPipeInstance[i] = CreateNamedPipe(...);
   if (hPipeInstance[i] != INVALID_HANDLE_VALUE)
      {
      hPipeThread[i] =
         CreateThread(NULL, 0, NamedPipeThread,
            hPipeInstance[i],...);
      }
   }

DWORD WINAPI NamedPipeThread(HANDLE hPipeInstance)
{
   DWORD dwError;
   BYTE  byBuffer[4096];
   DWORD dwBytes;

   while (ConnectNamedPipe(hPipeInstance, NULL) ||
          GetLastError() == ERROR_PIPE_CONNECTED)
      {
      ImpersonateNamedPipeClient(hPipeInstance);
      while (ReadFile(hPipeInstance, byBuffer,
                sizeof (byBuffer), &dwBytes, NULL))
         {
         // Do something with the incoming data
         }
      DisconnectNamedPipe(hPipeInstance);
      RevertToSelf();
      }
   return GetLastError();
}
```

The simplicity of this thread does not argue against its workability: this is a reasonable implementation of a Named Pipes server worker thread. The main capability it sacrifices by not using overlapped I/O is the scaled multiprocessor support offered by I/O completion ports.

One Thread per Instance with an Overlapped Pipe and an I/O Completion Port

Here's a Named Pipes server thread that uses an overlapped pipe and an I/O completion port. It uses the COverlapped class presented in Chapter 6 to determine which operation has completed, and from that it knows what state it is entering (listening or connected).

```
DWORD WINAPI NamedPipesThread(LPVOID lp)
{
   HANDLE       hPipe = (HANDLE) lp;
   HANDLE       hPort;
   COverlapped  ovConnect, ovRead[2];
   TCHAR        szReadBuffer[2][4096];
   DWORD        dwBytesRead;
   DWORD        dwCompletionKey;
   LPOVERLAPPED lpOverlapped;
   int          i;
   COverlapped *lpCOverlapped;

   hPort = CreateIoCompletionPort(hPipe, NULL, 1, 0);

   for (i = 0; i < 2; ++i)
      {
      ovRead[i].SetPreviousOperation(COverlapped::ReadFile);
      ovRead[i].SetBuffer(szReadBuffer[i]);
      }
   ovConnect.SetPreviousOperation(COverlapped::ConnectNamedPipe);
   ConnectNamedPipe(hPipe, &ovConnect);

   while (TRUE)
      {
      if (GetQueuedCompletionStatus(hPort, &dwBytesRead,
            &dwCompletionKey,
            &lpOverlapped, // Pointer to pointer
            INFINITE))
         {
         // An operation completed successfully--see if it
         // was a connect or a read
         lpCOverlapped = (COverlapped *) lpOverlapped;
         if (lpCOverlapped->GetPreviousOperation ==
             COverlapped::ConnectNamedPipe)
            {
            // It was a connect--enter connected state and
            // spin off a couple of reads
            ImpersonateNamedPipeClient(hPipe);
```

```
            ReadFile(hPipe, szReadBuffer[0], sizeof (szReadBuffer[0]),
                &dwBytesRead, &ov[0]);
            ReadFile(hPipe, szReadBuffer[1], sizeof (szReadBuffer[1]),
                &dwBytesRead, &ov[1]);
            }
        else
            {
            // It was a read operation--pick up data and reissue read
            // Data is in lpCOverlapped->GetBuffer();
            // Do something with it, then reissue read
            ReadFile(hPipe, lpCOverlapped->GetBuffer(),
               sizeof (szReadBuffer[0]),
               &dwBytesRead,
               lpCOverlapped);
            }
        }
    else
        {
        // Operation failed--if it was a read, go back
        // to listening state
        if (lpCOverlapped->GetPreviousOperation() !=
             COverlapped::ConnectNamedPipe)
            {
            DisconnectNamedPipe(hPipe);
            RevertToSelf();
            ConnectNamedPipe(hPipe, &ovConnect);
            }
        else
            {
            // Connect failed, time to go home
            break;
            }
        }
    }
  // End of while (TRUE) loop, close I/O completion port
  CloseHandle(hPort);
  return GetLastError();
}
```

Mailslots

Mailslots provide a datagram extension to the connection-oriented services offered by Named Pipes. The protocol is simple:

- The server side creates a mailslot and can only read from it.
- The client side opens a mailslot and can only write to it.

A mailslot can be created only on the local machine. The same process can obtain both server-side (read-only) and client-side (write-only) handles to the mailslot.

The distinction between client and server does not have the same meaning it does for Named Pipes. What this means specifically is that Windows 95 machines can create incoming mailslots.

The Mailslot API

CreateMailslot() creates a mailslot and returns a server-side handle:

```
HANDLE CreateMailslot(
          LPCTSTR lpName,
          DWORD   dwMaxMessageSize,
          DWORD   dwReadTimeout,
          LPSECURITY_ATTRIBUTES lpSecurity);
```

Mailslots use a naming convention similar to Named Pipes. The name must be in the format \\<machine name>\MAILSLOT\<mailslot name>. For CreateMailslot(), the mailslot name must use the machine name ".", since the mailslot can only be created locally.

dwMaxMessageSize specifies the maximum byte count of a message. Passing it as zero tells Windows that messages can be of any size. *dwReadTimeout* gives the number of milliseconds to wait when ReadFile() is called with the mailslot handle. Zero means don't wait; MAILSLOT_WAIT_FOREVER means block indefinitely. This is the only way you can control the behavior of ReadFile(). There is no such thing as an overlapped mailslot, and ReadFile() does not include a timeout argument. The security attributes are used the same as with CreateNamedPipe()—to permit or restrict access to the mailslot. The behavior is also the same—that is, if you pass *lpSecurity* as NULL, only users at least as trusted as you can send messages to the mailslot.

When a client station wants to write to a mailslot, it opens it by calling CreateFile(). The mailslot uses the full UNC format, \\<machine name>\MAILSLOT\<mailslot name>. To obtain a handle that can be used for broadcasting, pass the machine name as "*". For example, to broadcast to all stations that have created the mailslot \MAILSLOT\WNET\WNETSLOT, call CreateFile() as follows:

```
HANDLE hMailslot;
hMailslot =
   CreateFile(TEXT("\\\\*\\MAILSLOT\\WNET\\WNETSLOT"), ...);
```

You can also do multicasts by using an NT Server domain name instead of the name of a specific machine.

The function GetMailslotInfo() gives you a lot of information about a server-side mailslot. For instance, it tells you:

- If there are messages waiting to be read
- How many messages there are
- How big the next message is
- What your ReadFile() timeout is
- What your maximum message size is

```
BOOL GetMailslotInfo(
   HANDLE   hMailslot,
   LPDWORD  lpdwMaxMessageSize,
   LPDWORD  lpdwNextSize,
   LPDWORD  lpdwMessageCount,
   LPDWORD  lpdwReadTimeout);
```

You can also configure the read timeout at any time by calling SetMailslotInfo():

```
BOOL SetMailslotInfo(
   HANDLE hMailslot,
   DWORD  dwReadTimeout);
```

Although GetMailslotInfo() looks like a useful function, it has one serious limitation: it returns immediately, and so forces you to poll the mailslot. This may be reasonable in situations where you don't need to respond quickly (or perhaps don't need to respond at all) to incoming mail. You can put a thread to sleep for, say, 30 seconds, then call GetMailslotInfo() when it wakes up and process all waiting messages. In the multithreaded Win32 environment, it's usually better to call ReadFile() in a background thread and let it block until a message arrives. Note that even though your call to ReadFile() on a mailslot will block, both CreateMailslot() and SetMailslotInfo() can set a finite timeout period. Mailslots are the only objects for which ReadFile() behaves this way.

C++ and MFC Considerations

The Microsoft Foundation Classes do not provide any support for Named Pipes. However, since Named Pipes are native Win32 file objects, pipes can be largely derived from CFile. The Named Pipes API, like Windows Sockets, has two main areas of functionality:

- Connecting clients and servers
- Passing data back and forth

In the last chapter, I effected this division of labor by deriving COverlapped-Socket from COverlappedFile (a class I developed in Chapter 6) to get its I/O capabilities, and embedding within COverlappedSocket a CAsyncSocket-derived object to take care of the Listen, Call, and Hangup operations. The same architecture suggested itself for Named Pipes as well, but did not fall into place quite so comfortably. The main problem I encountered was this: whereas Windows Sockets masquerade as Win32 files, Named Pipes really are Win32 files. Also, since there is no MFC class for Named Pipes (whereas Sockets have CAsyncSocket and CSocket), I had to create one. Its logical base class, of course, is CFile. But this is also the base class for COverlappedFile. For this reason, deriving an overlapped pipes class from COverlappedFile, and embedding a Named Pipes object, was messy—I ended up with two objects that traced their ancestry back to CFile. The specific implication of this was that I had two copies of the file handle to keep track of (and I usually lost track of one of them).

I also considered multiple inheritance. Named Pipes, I reasoned, are files that offer synchronous and asynchronous I/O. The synchronous I/O can inherit what it needs from CFile, adding the communications-related methods. The asynchronous I/O, on the other hand, can use the services of COverlappedFile, and satisfy its communications needs by also deriving from my synchronous pipes class. Figure 10-1 shows this hierarchy starting at CFile.

The problem here is that there are two paths back to CFile. By making COverlappedFile and CNamedPipe virtual subclasses of CFile, you can tell the compiler to only generate a single copy of it. Otherwise, a COverlapped-Pipe object ends up looking like Figure 10-2.

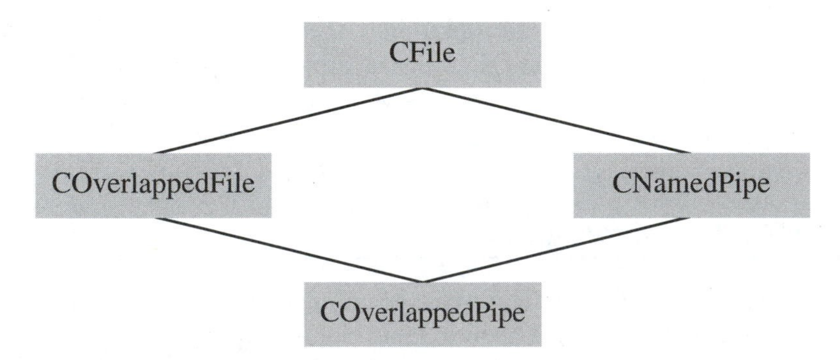

Figure 10-1. Named Pipes Class Hierarchy with Multiple Inheritance

To make classes virtual subclasses, declare them like this:

```
class AFX_EXT_CLASS CNamedPipe      : virtual public CFile
class AFX_EXT_CLASS COverlappedFile : virtual public CFile
```

You should then get a COverlappedPipe object formatted like Figure 10-3. However, this also proved cumbersome to work with.

The CNamedPipe Class

My current design—the one we'll explore in this chapter—derives CNamed-Pipe from COverlappedFile, and COverlappedPipe from CNamedPipe (see Figure 10-4). CNamedPipe implements the communications operations: CreateNamedPipe(), ConnectNamedPipe(), and DisconnectNamedPipe(). It also implements synchronous I/O, primarily by passing NULL OVER-LAPPED pointers to the COverlappedFile Read() and Write() methods. It wraps other Named Pipes-specific calls, like ImpersonateNamedPipe-Client(), RevertToSelf(), TransactNamedPipe(), and CallNamedPipe().

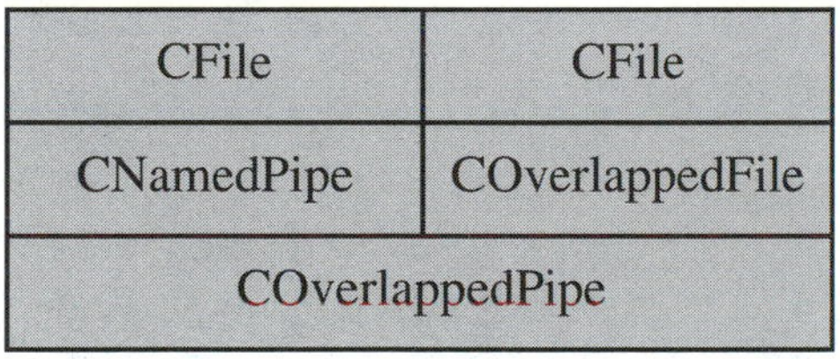

CFile	CFile
CNamedPipe	COverlappedFile
COverlappedPipe	

Figure 10-2. A COverlappedPipe Object with Two CFile Ancestors

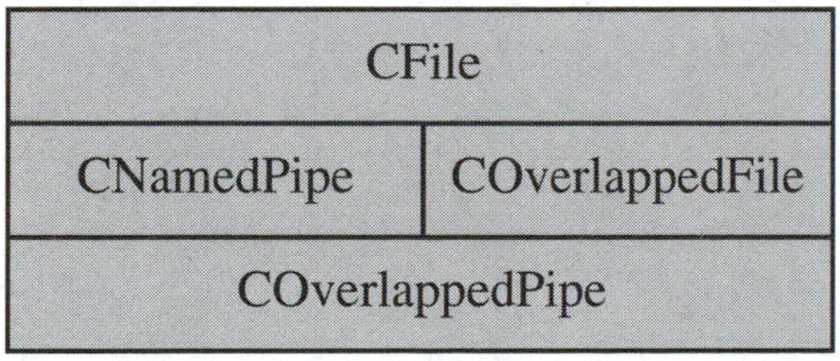

CFile	
CNamedPipe	COverlappedFile
COverlappedPipe	

Figure 10-3. A COverlappedPipe Object with One CFile Ancestor by Virtual Derivation

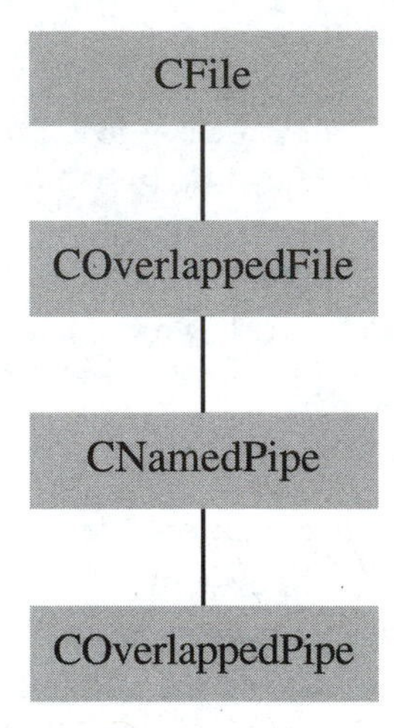

Figure 10-4. Named Pipes Class Hierarchy as Currently Implemented

Here is the class declaration, from the source disk file \WIN32NET\CODE\WIN32OBJ\NAMEPIPE.H:

```
enum PIPE_SIDE
{
   ServerSide,
   ClientSide
};

class AFX_EXT_CLASS CNamedPipe : public COverlappedFile
{
protected:
   int               m_PipeState;
   DWORD             m_dwReadMode;
   CString           m_szPipeName;

public:
   enum PIPE_STATE
      {
      PipeUninitialized        = 0x0001,
      PipeListening            = 0x0002,
      PipeConnected            = 0x0004,
      PipeDisconnected         = 0x0008,
      PipeImpersonatingClient = 0x8000
      };

   CNamedPipe()
      {
      m_PipeState  = PipeUninitialized;
      }
```

```
CNamedPipe(LPCTSTR         lpszPipeName,
           PIPE_SIDE       PipeSide          = ServerSide,
           CStringArray   *paszAllowedUsers = NULL,
           CStringArray   *paszDeniedUsers  = NULL,
           BOOL            bAuditAccess      = FALSE);
virtual ~CNamedPipe() {}

// Server-side
virtual BOOL Create(
            LPCTSTR lpszPipeName,  // No prefix required--will be
                                   // supplied
            DWORD   dwFlags = 0,
            CStringArray *paszAllowedUsers = NULL,
            CStringArray *paszDeniedUsers = NULL,
            BOOL    bAuditAccess = FALSE,
            DWORD   dwMaxInstances = PIPE_UNLIMITED_INSTANCES,
            DWORD   dwDirection = PIPE_ACCESS_DUPLEX,
            DWORD   dwMode = PIPE_WAIT | PIPE_TYPE_MESSAGE |
                             PIPE_READMODE_BYTE,
            BOOL    bInherit    = FALSE,
            DWORD   dwInputBufferSize = 32768,
            DWORD   dwOutputBufferSize = 32768,
            DWORD   dwDefaultTimeout = 0);

virtual BOOL Listen(COverlapped *lpOverlapped = NULL);
virtual BOOL Disconnect(void);
BOOL ImpersonateClient(void);
BOOL RevertToSelf(void);

BOOL GetHandleState(void);
BOOL SetHandleState(
   DWORD dwPipeState = PIPE_WAIT | PIPE_READMODE_MESSAGE);

virtual int GetPipeState(void)
   {
   return m_PipeState;
   }

virtual void SetPipeState(int nPipeState)
   {
   m_PipeState = nPipeState;
   }

CString GetPipeName(void)
   {
   return m_szPipeName;
   }
```

```
   static BOOL Wait(LPCTSTR lpszPipeName,
                    DWORD dwTimeout = NMPWAIT_USE_DEFAULT_WAIT);

   static BOOL Call(LPCTSTR lpszPipeName,
                    LPVOID  lpSendBuffer,
                    DWORD   dwSendSize,
                    LPVOID  lpReceiveBuffer,
                    DWORD   dwReceiveSize,
                    LPDWORD lpdwBytesRead,
                    DWORD   dwTimeout = NMPWAIT_USE_DEFAULT_WAIT);

   virtual BOOL Transact(
            LPVOID       lpSendBuffer,
            DWORD        dwSendSize,
            LPVOID       lpReceiveBuffer,
            DWORD        dwReceiveSize,
            LPDWORD      lpdwBytesRead,
            COverlapped *lpOverlapped = NULL);

   DECLARE_DYNAMIC(CNamedPipe);
};
```

The COverlappedPipe Class

COverlappedPipe is derived from CNamedPipe, but it has little to do. Recall that there is only one thing that differentiates overlapped and nonoverlapped pipes: the FILE_FLAG_OVERLAPPED bit that you pass to CreateNamedPipe() on the server side and CreateFile() on the client side. Once the pipe is open, there is no way to change your mind. All the I/O requirements are provided by COverlappedFile.

COverlappedPipe is declared in \WIN32NET\CODE\WIN32OBJ \OVPIPE.H on the source disk.

```
class AFX_EXT_CLASS COverlappedPipe : public CNamedPipe
{
public:
   COverlappedPipe(
      LPCTSTR         lpszPipeName,
      PIPE_SIDE       PipeSide            = ServerSide,
      CStringArray *paszAllowedUsers = NULL,
      CStringArray *paszDeniedUsers  = NULL,
      BOOL            bAuditAccess        = FALSE);

   virtual ~COverlappedPipe() {}

   DECLARE_DYNAMIC(COverlappedPipe);
};
```

COverlappedPipe overrides only the constructor and the destructor. The constructors of both CNamedPipe and COverlappedPipe are provided so you can create a client or server end of a pipe simply by instantiating an object of either class. The *paszAllowedUsers*, *paszDeniedUsers*, and *bAuditAccess* give the caller very high-level access to the Win32 Security API, and are intended primarily for the server end of the pipe. In both COverlappedPipe and CNamedPipe, the constructor invokes CNamedPipe::Create(). COverlapped-Pipe sets the FILE_FLAG_OVERLAPPED bit; CNamedPipe does not.

Here's how you can create a server-side pipe instance that allows access to the group "Everyone," denies it to the user "JoeEndUser," and generates an audit trail.

```
CNamedPipe *pServerPipe = new CNamedPipe(
   "WNET\WNETPIPE",
   ServerSide,
   "Everyone",
   "JoeEndUser",
   TRUE);
```

The hooks to the Security API are provided by classes implemented in Chapter 13. We'll see the code that uses them when we study the Create() method.

The destructor does nothing, but it allows the CFile destructor, which closes the pipe handle, to be called.

The CNamedPipesServer Class

There is no Named Pipes equivalent to the Windows Sockets Service Registration API. There's no need for one; all remote Named Pipes requests pass through the network redirector layer. The client specifies the target machine name as part of the UNC name of the pipe. The network redirectors are then polled to see which one of them knows how to reach the target server. If one of them says "I do," it in turn does the same type of negotiation with the transport layer drivers to decide which protocol to use. For this reason, Named Pipes are protocol-transparent; you never have to specify an address or protocol family. You don't have to do any name-to-address resolution; there are no equivalents to gethostbyname() and getservbyname(), again because they're unnecessary.

However, we have seen that the Service Registration API greatly simplifies the use of Windows Sockets, once you wrap it in a C++ class. All a server has to do to put itself online is call CServiceInfo::Register() and CServiceInfo::Advertise(). I wanted to provide a class that would simplify the creation of a Named Pipes server in the same way. I call this class CNamedPipesServer. It creates instances of a synchronous named pipe using the CNamedPipe class. For each instance it spins off its static member function ReceiveDataThread() as a background thread, to accept incoming traffic. Here is its class declaration, also from \WIN32NET\CODE\WIN32OBJ \NAMEPIPE.H:

```
struct PIPE_HEADER
{
   CNamedPipe *pPipe;
};

class AFX_EXT_CLASS CNamedPipesServer : public CObject
{
protected:
   DWORD   m_dwInstances;
   PIPE_HEADER **m_pPipeHeader;
   HANDLE *m_pThreadHandles;
   CString m_szPipeName;

public:
   enum {PIPE_INSTANCES = 5};
   CNamedPipesServer(LPTSTR          lpszName,
                     RECEIVECALLBACK lpReceiveCallback,
                     DWORD           dwInstances = PIPE_INSTANCES,
                     CStringArray   *paszAllowedUsers = NULL,
                     CStringArray   *paszDeniedUsers  = NULL,
                     BOOL            bAuditAccess     = FALSE);
   virtual ~CNamedPipesServer();
   static UINT ReceiveDataThread(LPVOID lp);

   DECLARE_DYNAMIC(CNamedPipesServer);
};
```

The PIPE_HEADER structure is used to trick the background threads into going away when the CNamedPipesServer object is deleted. Using the technique I discussed in Chapter 3, the CNamedPipesServer constructor allocates the PIPE_HEADER using VirtualAlloc(). Its destructor calls VirtualFree() to release the memory, then connects to the pipe to wake the thread up. The thread wakes up, suffers an exception, and goes away.

In implementing this class, I discovered anew the elegance and power of the Named Pipes API. It is the best peer-to-peer API that Win32 has to offer. It may not always be the best choice of API, however, for two reasons:

1. Named Pipes applications can only talk to other Named Pipes applications, so they are not as universal as Windows Sockets or RPC applications.
2. Named Pipes do not access the transport layer directly; they go through the network redirectors. For this reason, Windows Sockets over TCP/IP (which do go straight to the transport layer) significantly outperform Named Pipes. This is not true, however, when the client and server reside on the same machine. In this case, Named Pipes is by far the fastest transport mechanism.

Figure 10-5 is a state diagram that compares the Named Pipes and Windows Sockets function calls you have to make to get a server into the connected state.

The Windows Sockets API requires seven function calls, Named Pipes only two. Both vehicles give you a communications channel for exchanging data with a client. The Named Pipes API also gives you a protected endpoint

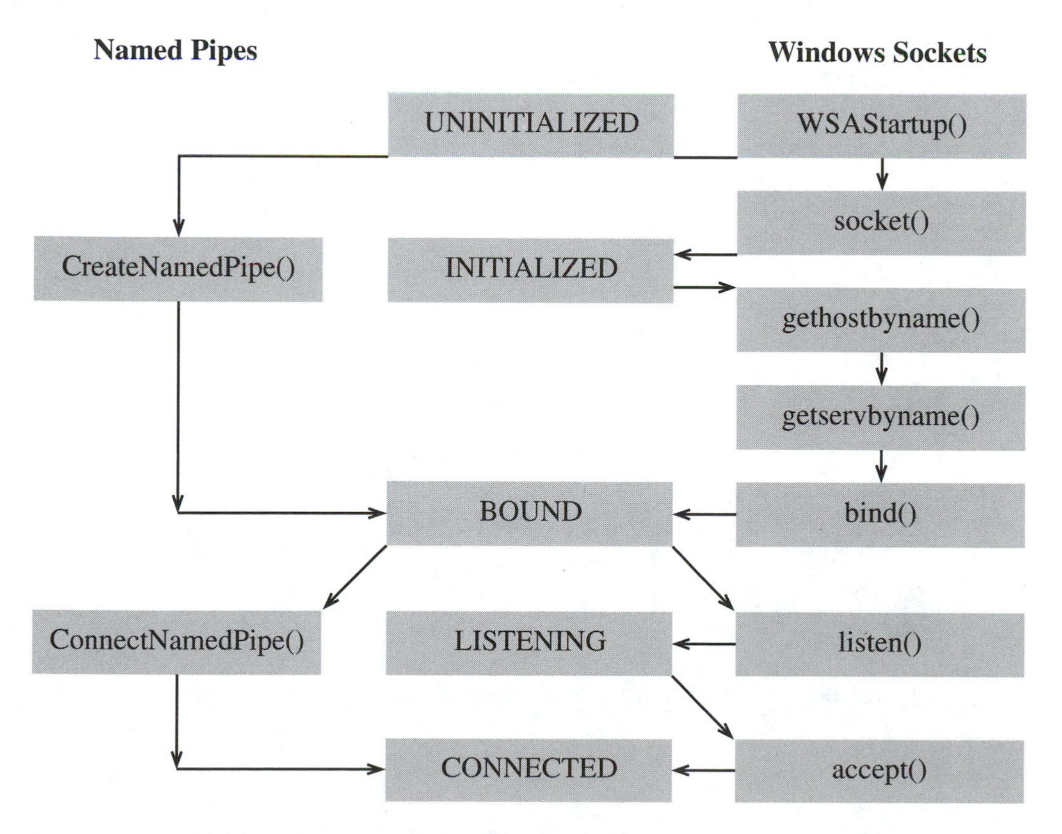

Figure 10-5. State Diagram for Named Pipes and Windows Sockets Servers

for which the system can generate an audit trail. This audit trail can tell you who's using your server, how often, and for how long. It can also tell you who's trying to connect to your server but isn't supposed to. In a future release of NT, it will also be able to generate security alarms, so that the network administrator will be notified immediately when any questionable activity occurs.

So a named pipe is a richer and more powerful object than a Windows Socket. Alas, it's also a slower one, by almost 50 percent (at least over the network). It's also more insular; it can only talk to other Named Pipes objects.

The CMailslot Class

I have wrapped the functionality of mailslots in this class. Mailslots are quite a bit simpler than Named Pipes. For one thing, you can only create one instance of a mailslot. Therefore, I have combined the functionality of CNamedPipe and CNamedPipesServer in CMailslot. For another, as we saw in Chapter 8, there are no Listen, Call, and Hangup operations to be concerned with. All the I/O can be inherited from COverlappedFile, in the same way that CNamedPipe uses it. I have placed CMailslot in my class hierarchy at the same level as CNamedPipe, because they can never be overlapped, but they do need to use the RECEIVECALLBACK function stored in COverlappedFile. Figure 10-6 shows the complete class hierarchy.

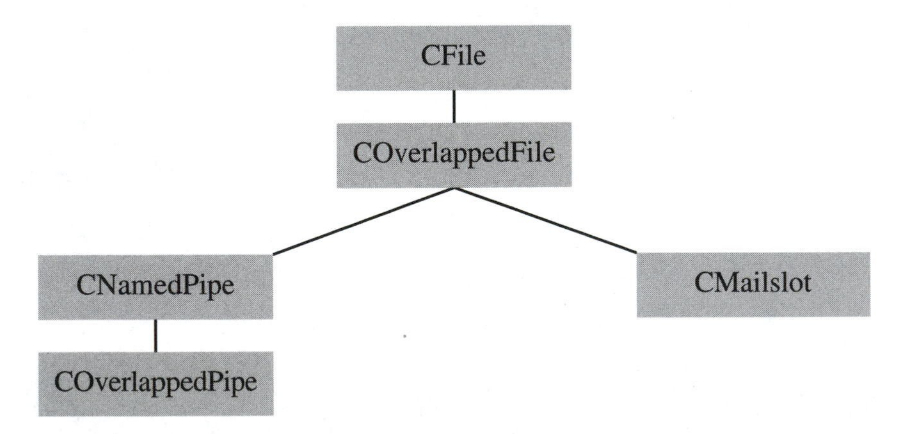

Figure 10-6. Complete Named Pipes and Mailslots Class Hierarchy

Here is the CMailslot class declaration, from \WIN32NET\CODE \WIN32OBJ\MAILSLOT.H:

```
struct MAILSLOT_HEADER
{
   CMailslot *pMailslot;
};

class AFX_EXT_CLASS CMailslot : public COverlappedFile
{
protected:
   CString          m_szMailslotName;
   HANDLE           m_hThread;
   MAILSLOT_HEADER *m_pHeader;
public:
   CMailslot()
      {
      m_hThread = NULL;  // Tells us whether we're server
                         // side or not
      m_pHeader = NULL;
      }
   CMailslot(
      LPCTSTR         lpszMailslotName,
      PIPE_SIDE       PipeSide           = ServerSide,
      RECEIVECALLBACK lpReceiveCallback = NULL, // NULL for
                                                  // client-side
      CStringArray    *paszAllowedUsers  = NULL,
      CStringArray    *paszDeniedUsers   = NULL,
      BOOL            bAuditAccess       = FALSE);
   virtual ~CMailslot();

   // Server-side
   virtual BOOL Create(
            LPCTSTR lpszMailslotName,
            CStringArray *paszAllowedUsers = NULL,
            CStringArray *paszDeniedUsers = NULL,
            BOOL    bAuditAccess = FALSE,
            DWORD   dwMaxMessageSize = 0,
            BOOL    bInherit     = FALSE,
            DWORD   dwReadTimeout =
                      MAILSLOT_WAIT_FOREVER);

   BOOL StartServer(RECEIVECALLBACK lpReceiveCallback);
   static UINT ReceiveDataThread(LPVOID lp);

   BOOL GetInfo(LPDWORD lpdwMaxMessageSize  = NULL,
             LPDWORD lpdwNextMessageSize = NULL,
             LPDWORD lpdwMessageCount    = NULL,
             LPDWORD lpdwReadTimeout     = NULL)
```

```
      {
      return ::GetMailslotInfo(GetFileHandle(),
                              lpdwMaxMessageSize,
                              lpdwNextMessageSize,
                              lpdwMessageCount,
                              lpdwReadTimeout);
      }
   BOOL SetInfo(DWORD dwReadTimeout)
      {
      return ::SetMailslotInfo(GetFileHandle(),
                              dwReadTimeout);
      }
   CString GetMailslotName(void)
      {
      return m_szMailslotName;
      }

   DECLARE_DYNAMIC(CMailslot);
};
```

Class Implementation Specifics

I'd like to focus on what I think are the most revealing and interesting aspects of these classes: CNamedPipe, COverlappedPipe, CNamedPipe-Server, and CMailslot. The complete code listings appear a few pages further on; here we're just going to look at a handlful of the details.

COverlappedPipe::COverlappedPipe()

To begin with, I want to show you the COverlappedPipe constructor. This allows an application that wants Named Pipes support to create either a server- or client-side pipe handle simply by instantiating an object.

```
COverlappedPipe::COverlappedPipe(LPCTSTR      lpszPipeName,
                                 PIPE_SIDE    PipeSide,
                                 CStringArray *paszAllowedUsers,
                                 CStringArray *paszDeniedUsers,
                                 BOOL         bAuditAccess)
{
   m_PipeState = PipeUninitialized;
   switch (PipeSide)
      {
      case ServerSide:
         if (!Create(lpszPipeName, FILE_FLAG_OVERLAPPED,
                     paszAllowedUsers, paszDeniedUsers,
                     bAuditAccess))
```

```
                {
                CFileException::ThrowOsError((LONG)::GetLastError());
                }
            break;
        case ClientSide:
            if (!Open(lpszPipeName,
                    COverlappedFile::modeReadWrite |
                    COverlappedFile::shareExclusive |
                    COverlappedFile::modeNoInherit))
                {
                CFileException::ThrowOsError((LONG)::GetLastError());
                }
            break;
        }
}
```

For a server-side pipe, the pipe name (*lpszPipeName*) is only expected to be the portion of the name following the obligatory \\.\PIPE\, which all pipe names passed to CreateNamedPipe() are required to have. It makes little sense to me that CreateNamedPipe() makes you pass the machine name and the required \PIPE\ component. They are part of the name of every server-side pipe, and can certainly be inferred. CreateNamedPipe() does not infer them; I do. For a client-side pipe, the name must specify the machine where the target pipe resides, and therefore must be spelled out completely.

The second argument, *PipeSide*, uses the PIPE_SIDE enumeration declared as part of the Named Pipes class to say whether the ultimate call should be to CreateNamedPipe() or CreateFile().

The next three arguments—*paszAllowedUsers*, *paszDeniedUsers*, and *bAuditAccess*—allow the calling application to tie specific security characteristics to the pipe. These are available for both server- and client-side pipes, though they really only make sense on the server side. If *paszAllowedUsers* and *paszDeniedUsers* are not passed, or are passed as NULL, the pipe is given a SECURITY_DESCRIPTOR with a NULL discretionary access control list. As we have seen, this allows it to be accessed by any user.

If a server-side pipe is requested, the constructor calls CNamedPipe::Create(), passing the FILE_FLAG_OVERLAPPED flag. For a client-side pipe, it invokes the CFile::Open() method, which has been overridden by COverlappedFile. The override is necessary, as we saw in Chapter 6, because CFile::Open() creates a nonoverlapped file handle, and you have no way of altering its behavior.

CNamedPipe::CNamedPipe()

The CNamedPipe constructor is almost exactly the same as the COverlappedPipe constructor:

```
CNamedPipe::CNamedPipe(LPCTSTR       lpszPipeName,
                       PIPE_SIDE     PipeSide,
                       CStringArray *paszAllowedUsers,
                       CStringArray *paszDeniedUsers,
                       BOOL          bAuditAccess)
{
   m_PipeState = PipeUninitialized;

   switch (PipeSide)
      {
      case ServerSide:
         if (!Create(lpszPipeName, 0, paszAllowedUsers,
                     paszDeniedUsers, bAuditAccess))
            {
            CFileException::ThrowOsError((LONG)::GetLastError());
            }
         break;
      case ClientSide:
         // Bypass COverlappedFile--go directly to CFile
         // COverlappedFile overrides Open() to do overlapped I/O
         if (!CFile::Open(lpszPipeName,
              modeReadWrite | shareExclusive | modeNoInherit))
            {
            CFileException::ThrowOsError((LONG)::GetLastError());
            }
         break;
      }
}
```

It too calls CNamedPipe::Create(), this time without the FILE_FLAG_OVERLAPPED bit. For the client side, just as COverlappedPipe leap-frogged CNamedPipe and went to COverlappedFile, CNamedPipe leap-frogs COverlappedFile and calls CFile::Open(). Here, we want a synchronous, nonoverlapped pipe.

CNamedPipe::Create()

All but two of the other CNamedPipe methods are thin wrappers for the underlying Win32 calls. Although this is true of the Create() method as well, it must do some preparation to set things up for CreateNamedPipe(). What it does is of some interest.

```
BOOL CNamedPipe::Create(
     LPCTSTR       lpszPipeName,  // No prefix required--will be
                                 // supplied
     DWORD         dwFlags,
     CStringArray *paszAllowedUsers,
     CStringArray *paszDeniedUsers,
     BOOL          bAuditAccess,
     DWORD         dwMaxInstances,
     DWORD         dwDirection,
     DWORD         dwMode,
     BOOL          bInherit,
     DWORD         dwInputBufferSize,
     DWORD         dwOutputBufferSize,
     DWORD         dwDefaultTimeout)
{
   CSecurityDescriptor sd(paszAllowedUsers, paszDeniedUsers,
      bAuditAccess);

   CSecurityAttributes sa(bInherit, &sd);
   CString szPipeName;

   m_szPipeName = lpszPipeName;

   m_PipeState = PipeUninitialized;

   szPipeName = _T("\\\\.\\PIPE\\");
   szPipeName += lpszPipeName;

   HANDLE hFile =
      ::CreateNamedPipe(
               szPipeName,
               dwDirection | dwFlags,
               dwMode,
               dwMaxInstances,
               dwOutputBufferSize,
               dwInputBufferSize,
               dwDefaultTimeout,
               &sa);

   BOOL bRetcode = (hFile != INVALID_HANDLE_VALUE);

   m_hFile = (int) hFile;

   return (bRetcode);
}
```

I apologize at once for presenting a function with twelve arguments. Here's my excuse: CreateNamedPipe() requires eight, two of which are packed into its second argument. I have also added arguments to specify allowed and denied users, and to turn auditing on. However, only the pipe name is absolutely necessary. All of the other arguments are likely to take on the same value 95 percent of the time, so we can provide reasonable defaults.

Most of the setting up that Create() does is preparing a SECURITY_DESCRIPTOR. It does so by instantiating a CSecurityDescriptor object, passing along the *paszAllowedUsers*, *paszDeniedUsers*, and *bAuditAccess* arguments. The CSecurityDescriptor class is presented in detail in Chapter 13.

The next step of consequence is to build the full pipe name in a CString object, so callers can just pass the significant portion of the pipe name (the part that distinguishes their pipe from everyone else's).

CNamedPipesServer::CNamedPipesServer()

The CNamedPipesServer class lets an application set up a Named Pipes server just by instantiating a CNamedPipesServer object:

```
CNamedPipesServer::CNamedPipesServer(
                   LPTSTR          lpszName,
                   RECEIVECALLBACK lpReceiveCallback,
                   DWORD           dwInstances /*= PIPE_INSTANCES*/,
                   CStringArray   *paszAllowedUsers /*= NULL*/,
                   CStringArray   *paszDeniedUsers  /*= NULL*/,
                   BOOL            bAuditAccess     /*= FALSE*/)
{
   ASSERT(lpszName != NULL);
   ASSERT(lpReceiveCallback != NULL);

   CWinThread *pThread;

   m_dwInstances    = dwInstances;
   m_pThreadHandles = new HANDLE[dwInstances];
   m_pPipeHeader    = new PIPE_HEADER *[dwInstances];
   m_szPipeName     = _T("\\\\.\\PIPE\\");
   m_szPipeName     += lpszName;

   for (DWORD i = 0; i < dwInstances; ++i)
      {
      // CNamedPipe constructor takes care of everything
      // including failure conditions
      m_pPipeHeader[i] = (PIPE_HEADER *)
         ::VirtualAlloc(NULL, sizeof (PIPE_HEADER),
            MEM_COMMIT, PAGE_READWRITE);
```

```
        if (m_pPipeHeader[i] == NULL)
           AfxThrowMemoryException();

        m_pPipeHeader[i]->pPipe = new CNamedPipe(lpszName,
                                         ServerSide,
                                         paszAllowedUsers,
                                         paszDeniedUsers,
                                         bAuditAccess);
        m_pPipeHeader[i]->pPipe->SetReceiveCallback(lpReceiveCallback);

        pThread =
           AfxBeginThread(ReceiveDataThread,
              (LPVOID) m_pPipeHeader[i]);
        m_pThreadHandles[i] = pThread->m_hThread;
        }
}
```

This constructor creates the number of instances of the pipe requested in *dwInstances*. It VirtualAlloc()'s a PIPE_HEADER structure, then creates a new CNamedPipe object, passing the *lpszName*, *paszAllowedUsers*, *paszDeniedUsers*, and *bAuditAccess* arguments to its constructor. The receive callback function, which we have already talked about in Chapters 6 and 9, is remembered in the COverlappedFile ancestor by calling its SetReceiveCallback() method. This lets the server notify the host application when data arrives over the pipe. Finally, ReceiveDataThread() is started up as a new thread and is passed the PIPE_HEADER pointer that we have just allocated.

The Named Pipes Server Thread

The next method of interest is the background thread itself (CNamedPipesServer::ReceiveDataThread()). It implements the synchronous loop I outlined above, though it uses C++ classes rather than direct Win32 calls. To reiterate, the logic for this loop is:

```
while (ConnectNamedPipe())
   {
   while (ReadFile())
      {
      // Notify host application
      }
   DisconnectNamedPipe();
   }
```

The thread offers some other embellishments, like client impersonation. It also uses the trick I discussed in Chapter 4 to get rid of itself—instead of using a direct pointer to the CNamedPipe object it is managing, it accesses it as a field in a PIPE_HEADER structure. This structure is VirtualAlloc()'d by the CNamedPipesServer constructor, and yanked in ~CNamedPipesServer. Here is the code:

```
UINT CNamedPipesServer::ReceiveDataThread(LPVOID lp)
{
   PIPE_HEADER *pPipeHeader = (PIPE_HEADER *) lp;
   CNamedPipe *pPipe = pPipeHeader->pPipe;
   char *pszBuffer = new char[READSIZE];
   DWORD dwBytesRead;

   try
      {
      // Use pPipeHeader to get to CNamedPipe pointer
      // so we crash when the CNamedPipeServer destructor
      // VirtualFree's it
      while (pPipeHeader->pPipe->Listen(NULL))
         {
         pPipeHeader->pPipe->ImpersonateClient();
         while (pPipeHeader->pPipe->Read(
                 pszBuffer, READSIZE, &dwBytesRead, NULL))
            {
            pPipeHeader->pPipe->CallReceiveCallback(
               (LPBYTE) pszBuffer,
               dwBytesRead,
               (HANDLE) pPipeHeader->pPipe);
            }
         // End of connection
         pPipeHeader->pPipe->RevertToSelf();
         pPipeHeader->pPipe->Disconnect();
         }
      }
   catch (...)
      {
      }

   delete pszBuffer;
   delete pPipe;
   return ::GetLastError();
}
```

The CNamedPipesServer Destructor

CNamedPipesServer::~CNamedPipesServer() shuts the server down. To fool ReceiveDataThread() into going away, it VirtualFree()s the memory that the constructor passed to it originally, then connects to the pipe. This wakes up any threads that are blocked on the CNamedPipe::Listen() call. As soon as they wake up, they try to access the PIPE_HEADER pointer, take an exception, and terminate. Finally, we give the threads a couple seconds to go away, and free all the other memory we allocated.

```
CNamedPipesServer::~CNamedPipesServer()
{
   DWORD i;

   // Trick background threads into going away
   for (i = 0; i < m_dwInstances; ++i)
      {
      ::VirtualFree(m_pPipeHeader[i], 0, MEM_RELEASE);
      }

   HANDLE hPipe;
   do
      {
      hPipe = ::CreateFile((LPCTSTR) m_szPipeName,
         GENERIC_READ,
         FILE_SHARE_READ,
         NULL,
         OPEN_EXISTING,
         0,
         NULL);

      if (hPipe != INVALID_HANDLE_VALUE)
         ::CloseHandle(hPipe);
      }
   while (hPipe != INVALID_HANDLE_VALUE);

   delete [] m_pPipeHeader;

   ::WaitForMultipleObjects(m_dwInstances,
                            m_pThreadHandles,
                            TRUE,
                            2000);

   delete [] m_pThreadHandles;
}
```

The CMailSlot Constructor

The nondefault constructor for the CMailslot class behaves very much like its CNamedPipe and COverlappedPipe counterparts. For server-side mailslots, it also acts like CNamedPipesServer, in that it calls its own StartServer() method to spin off a listening thread. Since you can only create a single instance of a server-side mailslot, I have combined CNamedPipe and CNamedPipesServer functionality into CMailslot.

```
CMailslot::CMailslot(LPCTSTR          lpszMailslotName,
                     PIPE_SIDE        PipeSide,
                     RECEIVECALLBACK lpReceiveCallback,
                     CStringArray    *paszAllowedUsers,
                     CStringArray    *paszDeniedUsers,
                     BOOL             bAuditAccess)
{
   m_hThread = NULL;
   m_pHeader = NULL;

   switch (PipeSide)
      {
      case ServerSide:
         ASSERT(lpReceiveCallback != NULL);
         if (!Create(lpszMailslotName, paszAllowedUsers,
                     paszDeniedUsers, bAuditAccess))
            {
            CFileException::ThrowOsError((LONG)::GetLastError());
            }
         StartServer(lpReceiveCallback);
         break;
      case ClientSide:
         // Bypass COverlappedFile--go directly to CFile
         // COverlappedFile overrides Open() to do overlapped I/O
         if (!CFile::Open(lpszMailslotName,
              modeWrite | shareDenyNone | modeNoInherit))
            {
            CFileException::ThrowOsError((LONG)::GetLastError());
            }
         break;
      }
}
```

CMailslot::StartServer()

StartServer() VirtualAlloc()s a MAILSLOT_HEADER and passes it to ReceiveDataThread(). It also remembers the RECEIVECALLBACK function in its COverlappedFile base class.

```
BOOL CMailslot::StartServer(RECEIVECALLBACK lpReceiveCallback)
{
   CWinThread *pThread;
```

```
    SetReceiveCallback(lpReceiveCallback);
    m_pHeader = (MAILSLOT_HEADER *) ::VirtualAlloc(NULL,
       sizeof (MAILSLOT_HEADER),
       MEM_COMMIT,
       PAGE_READWRITE);
    if (m_pHeader == NULL)
       AfxThrowMemoryException();
    m_pHeader->pMailslot = this;
    pThread =
       AfxBeginThread(ReceiveDataThread, (LPVOID) m_pHeader);

    if (pThread != NULL)
       {
       m_hThread = pThread->m_hThread;
       }
    else
       {
       m_hThread = NULL;
       }
    return (m_hThread != NULL);
}
```

The Mailslot Background Thread

The server thread implements this very simple loop:

```
while (ReadFile())
   {
   Post data upstairs
   }
```

It posts the incoming data by calling the RECEIVECALLBACK function we have remembered in COverlappedFile:

```
UINT CMailslot::ReceiveDataThread(LPVOID lp)
{
   MAILSLOT_HEADER *pMailslotHeader
                           = (MAILSLOT_HEADER *) lp;
   CMailslot *pMailslot = pMailslotHeader->pMailslot;
   char *pszBuffer      =  new char[READSIZE];
   DWORD dwBytesRead;

   try
      {
      // Use pMailslotHeader to get to CMailslot pointer
      // so we crash when the CMailslot destructor
      // VirtualFree's it
```

```
            while (pMailslotHeader->pMailslot->Read(
                    pszBuffer, READSIZE, &dwBytesRead, NULL))
               {
               pMailslotHeader->pMailslot->CallReceiveCallback(
                     (LPBYTE) pszBuffer,
                     dwBytesRead,
                     (HANDLE) pMailslotHeader->pMailslot);
               }
            }
         catch (...)
            {
            }

         delete pszBuffer;
         return ::GetLastError();
      }
```

CMailslot::Create()

The Create() method is quite similar to CNamedPipe::Create(). It sets up a SECURITY_DESCRIPTOR, and expands the mailslot name by prepending \\.\MAILSLOT\ to it. It then calls CreateMailslot() instead of CreateNamed-Pipe().

In preparing the SECURITY_DESCRIPTOR, it is important to see if we're running under Windows 95. The security calls will fail if we are, so we want to use a NULL SECURITY_DESCRIPTOR. (WNetIsWindowsNT() is a helper function in the WNETLVL1.DLL presented in the last chapter.)

```
BOOL CMailslot::Create(
             LPCTSTR       lpszMailslotName,
             CStringArray *paszAllowedUsers /* = NULL*/,
             CStringArray *paszDeniedUsers  /* = NULL*/,
             BOOL          bAuditAccess     /* = FALSE*/,
             DWORD         dwMaxMessageSize /* = 0*/,
             BOOL          bInherit         /* = FALSE*/,
             DWORD         dwReadTimeout    /* =
                                 MAILSLOT_WAIT_FOREVER*/)
{
   CSecurityDescriptor sd(
            paszAllowedUsers,
            paszDeniedUsers,
            bAuditAccess);
   SECURITY_DESCRIPTOR *pSD;

   if (WNetIsWindowsNT())
      pSD = sd.GetSecurityDescriptor();
```

```
    else
       // Security not supported on Windows 95
       pSD = NULL;

    CSecurityAttributes sa(bInherit, pSD);
    CString szMailslotName;

    m_szMailslotName = lpszMailslotName;

    szMailslotName = _T("\\\\.\\MAILSLOT\\");
    szMailslotName += lpszMailslotName;

    HANDLE hFile =
       ::CreateMailslot(
                szMailslotName,
                dwMaxMessageSize,
                dwReadTimeout,
                &sa);

    BOOL bRetcode = (hFile != INVALID_HANDLE_VALUE);

    m_hFile = (int) hFile;
    return (bRetcode);
}
```

The CMailslot Destructor

CMailslot::~CMailslot() has the same responsibility as CNamedPipesServer::~CNamedPipesServer()—to trick the listening thread into going away. It does this by freeing the MAILSLOT_HEADER that StartServer() allocated, opening a client-side handle to the mailslot, then sending it a packet. The server thread wakes up when the data arrives.

```
CMailslot::~CMailslot()
{
   // If we're a server-side mailslot,
   // free our memory, then send ourselves
   // a message.

   // This will trigger an exception in
   // the reading thread
   if (m_pHeader != NULL)
      {
      CString szMailslotName = _T("\\\\.\\MAILSLOT\\");
      szMailslotName += m_szMailslotName;

      ::VirtualFree(m_pHeader, 0, MEM_RELEASE);
```

```
      try
         {
         CMailslot Mailslot(szMailslotName, ClientSide);

         Mailslot.Write(_T("Get out of here"),
            lstrlen(_T("Get out of here")),
            NULL);
         }
      catch (...)
         {
         }
      // Give the guy two seconds to go away
      ::WaitForSingleObject(m_hThread, 2000);
      }
}
```

Code Listings

Here are the full code listings for these classes, from the source disk. \WIN32NET \CODE\WIN32OBJ\NAMEPIPE.H declares CNamedPipe and CNamed-PipesServer; \WIN32NET\CODE\WIN32OBJ\NAMEPIPE.CPP implements them. COverlappedPipe is declared and implemented in \WIN32NET \CODE\ WIN32OBJ\OVPIPE.H and \WIN32NET\CODE\WIN32OBJ\OVPIPE.CPP, and the CMailslot source files are \WIN32NET\CODE\WIN32OBJ\ MAILSLOT.H and \WIN32NET\CODE \WIN32OBJ\MAILSLOT.CPP.

```
/********
*
* NAMEPIPE.H
*
* Copyright (c) 1996 Ralph P. Davis
*
* All Rights Reserved
*
*****/

#ifndef _NAMEPIPE_INCLUDED
#define _NAMEPIPE_INCLUDED

#include "overlap.h"
#include "ovfile.h"

enum PIPE_SIDE
{
   ServerSide,
   ClientSide
};
```

```
enum
{
   READSIZE = 32768
};

class AFX_EXT_CLASS CNamedPipe : public COverlappedFile
{
protected:
   int               m_PipeState;
   DWORD             m_dwReadMode;
   CString           m_szPipeName;

public:
   enum PIPE_STATE
      {
      PipeUninitialized       = 0x0001,
      PipeListening           = 0x0002,
      PipeConnected           = 0x0004,
      PipeDisconnected        = 0x0008,
      PipeImpersonatingClient = 0x8000
      };

   CNamedPipe()
      {
      m_PipeState   = PipeUninitialized;
      }
   CNamedPipe(LPCTSTR        lpszPipeName,
              PIPE_SIDE      PipeSide          = ServerSide,
              CStringArray  *paszAllowedUsers = NULL,
              CStringArray  *paszDeniedUsers  = NULL,
              BOOL           bAuditAccess     = FALSE);
   virtual ~CNamedPipe() {}

   // Server-side
   virtual BOOL Create(
               LPCTSTR lpszPipeName,  // No prefix required--will be
                                      // supplied
               DWORD   dwFlags = 0,
               CStringArray *paszAllowedUsers = NULL,
               CStringArray *paszDeniedUsers = NULL,
               BOOL    bAuditAccess = FALSE,
               DWORD   dwMaxInstances = PIPE_UNLIMITED_INSTANCES,
               DWORD   dwDirection = PIPE_ACCESS_DUPLEX,
               DWORD   dwMode = PIPE_WAIT | PIPE_TYPE_MESSAGE |
                                PIPE_READMODE_BYTE,
               BOOL    bInherit    = FALSE,
               DWORD   dwInputBufferSize = 32768,
               DWORD   dwOutputBufferSize = 32768,
               DWORD   dwDefaultTimeout = 0);
```

```
    virtual BOOL Listen(COverlapped *lpOverlapped = NULL);
    virtual BOOL Disconnect(void);
    BOOL ImpersonateClient(void);
    BOOL RevertToSelf(void);

    BOOL GetState(void);
    BOOL SetState(
       DWORD dwPipeState = PIPE_WAIT | PIPE_READMODE_MESSAGE);

    virtual int GetPipeState(void)
       {
       return m_PipeState;
       }

    virtual void SetPipeState(int nPipeState)
       {
       m_PipeState = nPipeState;
       }

    CString GetPipeName(void)
       {
       return m_szPipeName;
       }

    static BOOL Wait(LPCTSTR lpszPipeName,
                     DWORD dwTimeout = NMPWAIT_USE_DEFAULT_WAIT);

    static BOOL Call(LPCTSTR lpszPipeName,
                     LPVOID  lpSendBuffer,
                     DWORD   dwSendSize,
                     LPVOID  lpReceiveBuffer,
                     DWORD   dwReceiveSize,
                     LPDWORD lpdwBytesRead,
                     DWORD   dwTimeout = NMPWAIT_USE_DEFAULT_WAIT);

    virtual BOOL Transact(
            LPVOID       lpSendBuffer,
            DWORD        dwSendSize,
            LPVOID       lpReceiveBuffer,
            DWORD        dwReceiveSize,
            LPDWORD      lpdwBytesRead,
            COverlapped *lpOverlapped = NULL);

    DECLARE_DYNAMIC(CNamedPipe);
};

struct PIPE_HEADER
```

```
{
   CNamedPipe *pPipe;
};

class AFX_EXT_CLASS CNamedPipesServer : public CObject
{
protected:
   DWORD   m_dwInstances;
   PIPE_HEADER **m_pPipeHeader;
   HANDLE *m_pThreadHandles;
   CString m_szPipeName;

public:
   enum {PIPE_INSTANCES = 5};
   CNamedPipesServer(LPTSTR          lpszName,
                     RECEIVECALLBACK lpReceiveCallback,
                     DWORD           dwInstances = PIPE_INSTANCES,
                     CStringArray   *paszAllowedUsers = NULL,
                     CStringArray   *paszDeniedUsers  = NULL,
                     BOOL            bAuditAccess     = FALSE);
   virtual ~CNamedPipesServer();
   static UINT ReceiveDataThread(LPVOID lp);

   DECLARE_DYNAMIC(CNamedPipesServer);
};
#endif


/********
*
* NAMEPIPE.CPP
*
* Copyright (c) 1996 Ralph P. Davis
*
* All Rights Reserved
*
********/

/*===== Includes =====*/

#include "stdafx.h"
#include "namepipe.h"
#include "security.h"


/*===== Function Definitions =====*/

IMPLEMENT_DYNAMIC(CNamedPipe, COverlappedFile)
IMPLEMENT_DYNAMIC(CNamedPipesServer, CObject)
```

```
CNamedPipe::CNamedPipe(LPCTSTR        lpszPipeName,
                       PIPE_SIDE      PipeSide,
                       CStringArray *paszAllowedUsers,
                       CStringArray *paszDeniedUsers,
                       BOOL           bAuditAccess)
{
   m_PipeState = PipeUninitialized;

   switch (PipeSide)
      {
      case ServerSide:
         if (!Create(lpszPipeName, 0, paszAllowedUsers,
                     paszDeniedUsers, bAuditAccess))
            {
            CFileException::ThrowOsError((LONG)::GetLastError());
            }
         break;
      case ClientSide:
         // Bypass COverlappedFile--go directly to CFile
         // COverlappedFile overrides Open() to do overlapped I/O
         if (!CFile::Open(lpszPipeName,
              modeReadWrite | shareExclusive | modeNoInherit))
            {
            CFileException::ThrowOsError((LONG)::GetLastError());
            }
         break;
      }
}

BOOL CNamedPipe::Create(
     LPCTSTR       lpszPipeName,  // No prefix required--will be
                                  // supplied
     DWORD         dwFlags,
     CStringArray *paszAllowedUsers,
     CStringArray *paszDeniedUsers,
     BOOL          bAuditAccess,
     DWORD         dwMaxInstances,
     DWORD         dwDirection,
     DWORD         dwMode,
     BOOL          bInherit,
     DWORD         dwInputBufferSize,
     DWORD         dwOutputBufferSize,
     DWORD         dwDefaultTimeout)
{
   CSecurityDescriptor sd(paszAllowedUsers, paszDeniedUsers,
      bAuditAccess);

   CSecurityAttributes sa(bInherit, &sd);
   CString szPipeName;
```

```
   m_szPipeName = lpszPipeName;

   m_PipeState = PipeUninitialized;

   szPipeName = _T("\\\\.\\PIPE\\");
   szPipeName += lpszPipeName;

   HANDLE hFile =
   ::CreateNamedPipe(
               szPipeName,
               dwDirection | dwFlags,
               dwMode,
               dwMaxInstances,
               dwOutputBufferSize,
               dwInputBufferSize,
               dwDefaultTimeout,
               &sa);

   BOOL bRetcode = (hFile != INVALID_HANDLE_VALUE);

   m_hFile = (int) hFile;

   return (bRetcode);
}

BOOL CNamedPipe::Listen(COverlapped *lpOverlapped)
{
   BOOL bRetcode;

   m_PipeState = PipeListening;

   if (lpOverlapped != NULL)
      {
      ::ResetEvent(lpOverlapped->GetEventHandle());
      }

   bRetcode = ::ConnectNamedPipe(GetFileHandle(), lpOverlapped);
   if (bRetcode)
      {
      m_PipeState = PipeConnected;
      }
   return bRetcode;
}

BOOL CNamedPipe::Disconnect(void)
{
   Flush();
   BOOL bRetcode = ::DisconnectNamedPipe(GetFileHandle());
```

```
    if (m_PipeState & PipeImpersonatingClient)
        RevertToSelf();

    m_PipeState = PipeDisconnected;
    return bRetcode;
}

BOOL CNamedPipe::ImpersonateClient(void)
{
    BOOL bRetcode = ::ImpersonateNamedPipeClient(GetFileHandle());
    if (bRetcode)
        {
        m_PipeState |= PipeImpersonatingClient;
        }
    return bRetcode;
}

BOOL CNamedPipe::RevertToSelf(void)
{
    BOOL bRetcode = FALSE;
    if (m_PipeState & PipeImpersonatingClient)
        {
        bRetcode = ::RevertToSelf();
        if (bRetcode)
            {
          m_PipeState &= (~PipeImpersonatingClient);
            }
        }
    return bRetcode;
}

BOOL CNamedPipe::GetState()
{
    return ::GetNamedPipeHandleState(
                GetFileHandle(),
                &m_dwReadMode,
                NULL, NULL, NULL, NULL, 0);
}

BOOL CNamedPipe::SetState(DWORD dwPipeState)
{
    m_dwReadMode = dwPipeState;
    return ::SetNamedPipeHandleState(GetFileHandle(),
        &dwPipeState, NULL, NULL);
}

BOOL CNamedPipe::Wait(LPCTSTR lpszPipeName, DWORD dwTimeout)
```

```
{
   return ::WaitNamedPipe(lpszPipeName, dwTimeout);
}

BOOL CNamedPipe::Call(
           LPCTSTR lpszPipeName,
           LPVOID  lpSendBuffer,
           DWORD   dwSendSize,
           LPVOID  lpReceiveBuffer,
           DWORD   dwReceiveSize,
           LPDWORD lpdwBytesRead,
           DWORD   dwTimeout)
{
   return ::CallNamedPipe(
             lpszPipeName,
             lpSendBuffer,
             dwSendSize,
             lpReceiveBuffer,
             dwReceiveSize,
             lpdwBytesRead,
             dwTimeout);
}

BOOL CNamedPipe::Transact(
           LPVOID  lpSendBuffer,
           DWORD   dwSendSize,
           LPVOID  lpReceiveBuffer,
           DWORD   dwReceiveSize,
           LPDWORD lpdwBytesRead,
           COverlapped *lpOverlapped)
{
   DWORD dwReadMode = m_dwReadMode;

   if (~(dwReadMode & PIPE_READMODE_MESSAGE))
      SetState();

   if (lpOverlapped != NULL)
      {
      ::ResetEvent(lpOverlapped->GetEventHandle());
      }

   BOOL bRetcode =
      ::TransactNamedPipe(
              GetFileHandle(),
              lpSendBuffer,
              dwSendSize,
              lpReceiveBuffer,
              dwReceiveSize,
```

```
                lpdwBytesRead,
                lpOverlapped);

   if (dwReadMode != m_dwReadMode)
      SetState(dwReadMode);
   return bRetcode;
}

CNamedPipesServer::CNamedPipesServer(
                    LPTSTR          lpszName,
                    RECEIVECALLBACK lpReceiveCallback,
                    DWORD           dwInstances /*= PIPE_INSTANCES*/,
                    CStringArray   *paszAllowedUsers /*= NULL*/,
                    CStringArray   *paszDeniedUsers  /*= NULL*/,
                    BOOL            bAuditAccess     /*= FALSE*/)
{
   ASSERT(lpszName != NULL);
   ASSERT(lpReceiveCallback != NULL);

   CWinThread *pThread;

   m_dwInstances    = dwInstances;
   m_pThreadHandles = new HANDLE[dwInstances];
   m_pPipeHeader    = new PIPE_HEADER *[dwInstances];
   m_szPipeName     = _T("\\\\.\\PIPE\\");
   m_szPipeName     += lpszName;

   for (DWORD i = 0; i < dwInstances; ++i)
      {
      // CNamedPipe constructor takes care of everything
      // including failure conditions
      m_pPipeHeader[i] = (PIPE_HEADER *)
         ::VirtualAlloc(NULL, sizeof (PIPE_HEADER),
            MEM_COMMIT, PAGE_READWRITE);
      if (m_pPipeHeader[i] == NULL)
         AfxThrowMemoryException();

      m_pPipeHeader[i]->pPipe = new CNamedPipe(lpszName,
                                  ServerSide,
                                  paszAllowedUsers,
                                  paszDeniedUsers,
                                  bAuditAccess);
      m_pPipeHeader[i]->pPipe->SetReceiveCallback(lpReceiveCallback);

      pThread =
         AfxBeginThread(ReceiveDataThread,
            (LPVOID) m_pPipeHeader[i]);
```

```
        m_pThreadHandles[i] = pThread->m_hThread;
        }
}

CNamedPipesServer::~CNamedPipesServer()
{
    DWORD i;

    // Trick background threads into going away
    for (i = 0; i < m_dwInstances; ++i)
        {
        ::VirtualFree(m_pPipeHeader[i], 0, MEM_RELEASE);
        }

    HANDLE hPipe;
    do
        {
        hPipe = ::CreateFile((LPCTSTR) m_szPipeName,
            GENERIC_READ,
            FILE_SHARE_READ,
            NULL,
            OPEN_EXISTING,
            0,
            NULL);

        if (hPipe != INVALID_HANDLE_VALUE)
            ::CloseHandle(hPipe);
        }
    while (hPipe != INVALID_HANDLE_VALUE);

    delete [] m_pPipeHeader;

    ::WaitForMultipleObjects(m_dwInstances,
                             m_pThreadHandles,
                             TRUE,
                             2000);

    delete [] m_pThreadHandles;
}

UINT CNamedPipesServer::ReceiveDataThread(LPVOID lp)
{
    PIPE_HEADER *pPipeHeader = (PIPE_HEADER *) lp;
    CNamedPipe *pPipe = pPipeHeader->pPipe;
    char *pszBuffer = new char[READSIZE];
    DWORD dwBytesRead;
```

```
   try
      {
      // Use pPipeHeader to get to CNamedPipe pointer
      // so we crash when the CNamedPipeServer destructor
      // VirtualFree's it
      while (pPipeHeader->pPipe->Listen(NULL))
         {
         pPipeHeader->pPipe->ImpersonateClient();
         while (pPipeHeader->pPipe->Read(
                pszBuffer, READSIZE, &dwBytesRead, NULL))
            {
            pPipeHeader->pPipe->CallReceiveCallback(
               (LPBYTE) pszBuffer,
               dwBytesRead,
               (HANDLE) pPipeHeader->pPipe);
            }
         // End of connection
         pPipeHeader->pPipe->RevertToSelf();
         pPipeHeader->pPipe->Disconnect();
         }
      }
   catch (...)
      {
      }

   delete pszBuffer;
   delete pPipe;
   return ::GetLastError();
}

/********
*
* OVPIPE.H
*
* Copyright (c) 1996 Ralph P. Davis
*
* All Rights Reserved
*
********/

#ifndef _OVPIPE_INCLUDED
#define _OVPIPE_INCLUDED

#include "namepipe.h"
#include "overlap.h"

class AFX_EXT_CLASS COverlappedPipe : public CNamedPipe
```

```
{
public:
   COverlappedPipe(
      LPCTSTR       lpszPipeName,
      PIPE_SIDE     PipeSide            = ServerSide,
      CStringArray *paszAllowedUsers = NULL,
      CStringArray *paszDeniedUsers  = NULL,
      BOOL          bAuditAccess     = FALSE);

   virtual ~COverlappedPipe() {}

   DECLARE_DYNAMIC(COverlappedPipe);
};

#endif

/********
*
* OVPIPE.CPP
*
* Copyright (c) 1996 Ralph P. Davis
*
* All Rights Reserved
*
********/

/*===== Includes =====*/

#include "stdafx.h"
#include "ovpipe.h"


/*===== Function Definitions =====*/

IMPLEMENT_DYNAMIC(COverlappedPipe, CNamedPipe)

COverlappedPipe::COverlappedPipe(LPCTSTR       lpszPipeName,
                                 PIPE_SIDE     PipeSide,
                                 CStringArray *paszAllowedUsers,
                                 CStringArray *paszDeniedUsers,
                                 BOOL          bAuditAccess)
{
   m_PipeState = PipeUninitialized;
   switch (PipeSide)
      {
      case ServerSide:
         if (!Create(lpszPipeName, FILE_FLAG_OVERLAPPED,
                     paszAllowedUsers, paszDeniedUsers,
                     bAuditAccess))
```

```
            {
            CFileException::ThrowOsError((LONG)::GetLastError());
            }
         break;
      case ClientSide:
         if (!Open(lpszPipeName,
            COverlappedFile::modeReadWrite |
            COverlappedFile::shareExclusive |
            COverlappedFile::modeNoInherit))
            {
            CFileException::ThrowOsError((LONG)::GetLastError());
            }
         break;
      }
}

/********
*
* MAILSLOT.H
*
* Copyright (c) 1996 Ralph P. Davis
*
* All Rights Reserved
*
*****/

#ifndef _MAILSLOT_INCLUDED
#define _MAILSLOT_INCLUDED

#include "overlap.h"
#include "ovfile.h"
#include "namepipe.h"

class CMailslot;

struct MAILSLOT_HEADER
{
   CMailslot *pMailslot;
};

class AFX_EXT_CLASS CMailslot : public COverlappedFile
{
protected:
   CString          m_szMailslotName;
   HANDLE           m_hThread;
   MAILSLOT_HEADER *m_pHeader;
public:
   CMailslot()
```

```
    {
    m_hThread = NULL;  // Tells us whether we're server
                       // side or not
    m_pHeader = NULL;
    }
CMailslot(
    LPCTSTR          lpszMailslotName,
    PIPE_SIDE        PipeSide            = ServerSide,
    RECEIVECALLBACK lpReceiveCallback = NULL, // NULL for
                                                // client-side
    CStringArray   *paszAllowedUsers   = NULL,
    CStringArray   *paszDeniedUsers    = NULL,
    BOOL             bAuditAccess        = FALSE);
virtual ~CMailslot();

// Server-side
virtual BOOL Create(
            LPCTSTR lpszMailslotName,
            CStringArray *paszAllowedUsers = NULL,
            CStringArray *paszDeniedUsers = NULL,
            BOOL     bAuditAccess = FALSE,
            DWORD    dwMaxMessageSize = 0,
            BOOL     bInherit     = FALSE,
            DWORD    dwReadTimeout =
                       MAILSLOT_WAIT_FOREVER);

BOOL StartServer(RECEIVECALLBACK lpReceiveCallback);
static UINT ReceiveDataThread(LPVOID lp);

BOOL GetInfo(LPDWORD lpdwMaxMessageSize  = NULL,
             LPDWORD lpdwNextMessageSize = NULL,
             LPDWORD lpdwMessageCount    = NULL,
             LPDWORD lpdwReadTimeout     = NULL)
    {
    return ::GetMailslotInfo(GetFileHandle(),
                              lpdwMaxMessageSize,
                              lpdwNextMessageSize,
                              lpdwMessageCount,
                              lpdwReadTimeout);
    }
BOOL SetInfo(DWORD dwReadTimeout)
    {
    return ::SetMailslotInfo(GetFileHandle(),
                              dwReadTimeout);
    }
CString GetMailslotName(void)
    {
    return m_szMailslotName;
    }
```

```
   DECLARE_DYNAMIC(CMailslot);
};

#endif


/********
*
* MAILSLOT.CPP
*
* Copyright (c) 1996 Ralph P. Davis
*
* All Rights Reserved
*
********/

/*===== Includes =====*/

#include "stdafx.h"
#include "mailslot.h"
#include "security.h"


/*===== Function Definitions =====*/

IMPLEMENT_DYNAMIC(CMailslot, COverlappedFile)

CMailslot::CMailslot(LPCTSTR         lpszMailslotName,
                     PIPE_SIDE       PipeSide,
                     RECEIVECALLBACK lpReceiveCallback,
                     CStringArray   *paszAllowedUsers,
                     CStringArray   *paszDeniedUsers,
                     BOOL            bAuditAccess)
{
   m_hThread = NULL;
   m_pHeader = NULL;

   switch (PipeSide)
      {
      case ServerSide:
         ASSERT(lpReceiveCallback != NULL);
         if (!Create(lpszMailslotName, paszAllowedUsers,
                     paszDeniedUsers, bAuditAccess))
            {
            CFileException::ThrowOsError((LONG)::GetLastError());
            }
         StartServer(lpReceiveCallback);
         break;
```

```
        case ClientSide:
            // Bypass COverlappedFile--go directly to CFile
            // COverlappedFile overrides Open() to do overlapped I/O
            if (!CFile::Open(lpszMailslotName,
                  modeWrite | shareDenyNone | modeNoInherit))
                {
                CFileException::ThrowOsError((LONG)::GetLastError());
                }
            break;
        }
}

CMailslot::~CMailslot()
{
    // If we're a server-side mailslot,
    // free our memory, then send ourselves
    // a message.

    // This will trigger an exception in
    // the reading thread
    if (m_pHeader != NULL)
        {
        CString szMailslotName = _T("\\\\.\\MAILSLOT\\");
        szMailslotName += m_szMailslotName;

        ::VirtualFree(m_pHeader, 0, MEM_RELEASE);

        try
            {
            CMailslot Mailslot(szMailslotName, ClientSide);

            Mailslot.Write(_T("Get out of here"),
                lstrlen(_T("Get out of here")),
                NULL);
            }
        catch (...)
            {
            }
        // Give the guy two seconds to go away
        ::WaitForSingleObject(m_hThread, 2000);
        }
}

BOOL CMailslot::Create(
                LPCTSTR         lpszMailslotName,
                CStringArray *paszAllowedUsers /* = NULL*/,
                CStringArray *paszDeniedUsers  /* = NULL*/,
                BOOL            bAuditAccess     /* = FALSE*/,
```

```
                DWORD           dwMaxMessageSize /* = 0*/,
                BOOL            bInherit         /* = FALSE*/,
                DWORD           dwReadTimeout    /* =
                                      MAILSLOT_WAIT_FOREVER*/)
{
   CSecurityDescriptor sd(
               paszAllowedUsers,
               paszDeniedUsers,
               bAuditAccess);
   SECURITY_DESCRIPTOR *pSD;

   if (WNetIsWindowsNT())
      pSD = sd.GetSecurityDescriptor();
   else
      // Security not supported on Windows 95
      pSD = NULL;

   CSecurityAttributes sa(bInherit, pSD);
   CString szMailslotName;

   m_szMailslotName = lpszMailslotName;

   szMailslotName = _T("\\\\.\\MAILSLOT\\");
   szMailslotName += lpszMailslotName;

   HANDLE hFile =
      ::CreateMailslot(
               szMailslotName,
               dwMaxMessageSize,
               dwReadTimeout,
               &sa);

   BOOL bRetcode = (hFile != INVALID_HANDLE_VALUE);

   m_hFile = (int) hFile;
   return (bRetcode);
}

BOOL CMailslot::StartServer(RECEIVECALLBACK lpReceiveCallback)
{
   CWinThread *pThread;

   SetReceiveCallback(lpReceiveCallback);
   m_pHeader = (MAILSLOT_HEADER *) ::VirtualAlloc(NULL,
      sizeof (MAILSLOT_HEADER),
      MEM_COMMIT,
      PAGE_READWRITE);
   if (m_pHeader == NULL)
      AfxThrowMemoryException();
```

```
    m_pHeader->pMailslot = this;
    pThread =
       AfxBeginThread(ReceiveDataThread, (LPVOID) m_pHeader);

    if (pThread != NULL)
       {
       m_hThread = pThread->m_hThread;
       }
    else
       {
       m_hThread = NULL;
       }
    return (m_hThread != NULL);
}

UINT CMailslot::ReceiveDataThread(LPVOID lp)
{
    MAILSLOT_HEADER *pMailslotHeader
                         = (MAILSLOT_HEADER *) lp;
    CMailslot *pMailslot = pMailslotHeader->pMailslot;
    char *pszBuffer      =  new char[READSIZE];
    DWORD dwBytesRead;

    try
       {
       // Use pMailslotHeader to get to CMailslot pointer
       // so we crash when the CMailslot destructor
       // VirtualFree's it
       while (pMailslotHeader->pMailslot->Read(
                 pszBuffer, READSIZE, &dwBytesRead, NULL))
          {
          pMailslotHeader->pMailslot->CallReceiveCallback(
                 (LPBYTE) pszBuffer,
                 dwBytesRead,
                 (HANDLE) pMailslotHeader->pMailslot);
          }
       }
    catch (...)
       {
       }
    delete pszBuffer;
    return ::GetLastError();
}
```

Conclusion

Named Pipes and Mailslots are high-level APIs for peer-to-peer communication. Because they are file system drivers, they are tightly integrated into the Win32 environment, and are highly compatible with other Win32 APIs. Data exchange uses the standard file I/O calls WriteFile() and ReadFile(), though Win32 also provides two functions, TransactNamedPipe() and CallNamedPipe(), that optimize request-response transactions.

Ironically, it is precisely their implementation as file system drivers that limits their performance. The Named Pipes API is implemented at the network redirector level. The Windows Sockets API, by contrast, goes straight to the transport driver layer. Named Pipes are also limited in their ability to support internetworking, because they can only talk to other Named Pipes applications.

Nevertheless, the Named Pipes API has some very strong features, of which the most important is security support. A server application can limit client access by passing a security descriptor to CreateNamedPipe(). It can also take on the security context of a connecting client application by calling ImpersonateNamedPipeClient(). The Windows Sockets API does not provide this capability; the only other Win32 API that does is RPC.

Suggested Readings

Online References

Pipes Overview in the Win32 SDK online help.
Mailslots Overview in the Win21 SDK online help.
"Kernel Objects," in the *Handles and Objects Overview* in Win32 SDK online help.
Microsoft Knowledge Base for Win32 SDK articles:
"Client Service for Novell NetWare Doesn't Support Named Pipes"
"Determining the Network Protocol Used by Named Pipes"
"Impersonation Provided by ImpersonateNamedPipeClient()"
"Interprocess Communication on Windows NT, Windows 95, and Win32s"
"Named Pipe Buffer Size"
"PRB: Access Denied When Opening a Named Pipe from a Service"
"Precautions When Passing Security Attributes"
"Restrictions on Named-Pipe Names"
"Security Attributes on Named Pipes"

Chapter 11

Remote Procedure Calls and Win32 Services

Remote procedure calls (RPC) are a paradigm for client-server applications that model the exchange as an API offered by the server. RPC is intended to be hardware- and operating-system–independent so it can provide connectivity among heterogeneous hosts on a network. It is a strategic element in Microsoft's distributed application architecture; much of NT itself is built around RPC.

There are two main RPC specifications in existence today. Microsoft's is based on the RPC defined by the Open Software Foundation (OSF) as part of their Distributed Computing Environment (DCE). OSF/DCE RPC is documented in the OSF publications *OSF DCE Application Development Guide* and *OSF DCE Application Development Reference* (see "Suggested Readings" at the end of this chapter). The *Guide* is an extensive discussion of the OSF operating system architecture, and makes very interesting reading, particularly as background for Microsoft RPC. The *Reference* is just the programming manual for OSF, and is dull as such manuals usually are. The other widely supported RPC is Sun RPC, developed by Sun Microsystems. Unfortunately, the two are not interoperable. An application using Microsoft RPC can communicate with any OSF RPC application, but not with one using Sun RPC.

One important purpose of RPC is to shield applications from the complexities of networks. Communications, error handling, and data-type conversion are handled automatically. We have seen that there are seven basic peer-to-peer operations:

- **Listen** sets up a server so that clients can connect to it.
- **Call** attempts to establish a connection from a client to a server.
- **Send** transmits data over a connection.
- **Receive** waits for data to arrive over a connection.
- **Hangup** terminates a connection between a client and a server.
- **Send Datagram** sends a packet of data using connectionless service.
- **Receive Datagram** looks for datagrams to arrive.

As we saw in previous chapters, Windows Sockets and Named Pipes provide a handful of functions to implement these operations. On first encountering the RPC function suite, you may be somewhat bewildered (I was): though RPC is supposed to simplify things, it provides a suite of over 100 functions. However, most of them are secondary, having to do with configuring the RPC online databases. The essential work of linking clients and servers is done by only a few functions, and the programming interface is very high-level.

RPC gives you the equivalent of the Call, Listen, and Hangup operations that were discussed in Chapter 8. And though you can use datagram-based RPC, the sequence of calls are the same as for connection-oriented RPC. The notions of sending and receiving lose some of their meaning; once a client and server have established a connection (called a **binding** in RPC parlance), the data exchange takes place through the medium of remote procedure calls. The client application issues function calls just as if they were implemented as part of its own code. What the client actually calls, however, is a stub routine that is generated by the RPC compiler. The stub packages the function arguments, ships them to the host, waits for its answer, and returns the results to the client application. On the server side, the function call is received by the RPC server stub, which dispatches the remote procedure call to the server-side function responsible for processing it.

RPC as a Vehicle for Exporting an API

We have already studied one important way of offering an API in Windows—dynamic-link libraries (DLLs). As we saw, they can expose either a C-language function-call interface, or a C++ class-based API. Because RPC is modeled as function calls that are passed from the client to the server,

RPC is another platform for exporting an API. RPC has several advantages over DLLs in this regard:

- RPC is more general-purpose. With DLLs, servers and clients can only be Win32 applications running on a Win32 host. With RPC, they can run on any host supporting the correct RPC implementation.
- RPC applications can offer their APIs both locally and remotely. DLLs are always local.
- RPC servers can be implemented as Win32 services. This allows the operating system to start them up automatically at boot time, giving them a high level of availability. A DLL is not loaded until an application needs it, and there is always a risk that the DLL will not be found. It is precisely because of this symbiotic relationship between RPC servers and Win32 services that I chose to discuss them both in this chapter.

The disadvantages of RPC are:

- It can only offer its API through function calls, not C++ classes.
- Because the client-server exchange crosses process boundaries, and may go over a network, it will not be as fast as a function call handled locally in a DLL.

Microsoft RPC Compliance with OSF/DCE

Microsoft RPC is an implementation of the OSF/DCE specification for remote procedure calls. It differs from OSF RPC in several ways:

- OSF RPC uses UNIX naming conventions for the functions in the RPC runtime libraries (all lowercase letters, words separated by underscores). Microsoft has renamed these functions according to Windows naming conventions (word-break capitalization, no underscores). The OSF function rpc_string_binding_compose(), for instance, becomes RpcStringBindingCompose() in Microsoft RPC.
- In Microsoft RPC, functions report status information through their return values. In OSF, they do this through an output variable.
- Data types are given new names, using all capital letters and *typedefs* for structure types. For example, the OSF type *handle_t* becomes an RPC_BINDING_HANDLE in Microsoft RPC, though the OSF type is also supported.
- Some Microsoft RPC functions have additional Win32-specific arguments, like security descriptors.
- Additional functions and macros in Microsoft RPC provide features like Structured Exception Handling.

Structure of RPC

RPC consists of several components, which I'll cover in detail later in this section.

- *The Interface Definition Language (IDL) compiler.* Microsoft's version is called MIDL, for Microsoft Interface Definition Language. The IDL compiler takes a mandatory Interface Definition Language (.IDL) file and an optional Attribute Configuration (.ACF) file as input and generates C source code for the client and server stubs. These stubs are then submitted to the C compiler and linked with the client- and server-side applications. (By the way, the Microsoft RPC documentation erroneously says that ACF stands for Application Configuration File. However, the OSF documents, which must be considered the authoritative ones, use the term Attribute Configuration File. I will use the OSF term throughout this chapter.)
- *The RPC runtime library.* This is used primarily by server applications to advertise their services, and by clients to locate and connect to servers.
- *The actual remote procedure calls.* To the client application, these appear to be local function calls. The RPC runtime layer takes care of passing the data to the server, calling the correct server function, and passing any return data back to the client.

The Interface Definition Language (.IDL) File

The code in this chapter centers around the WNet RPC Server, a component of my software system that runs as an RPC-based Win32 service. The .IDL file for the WNet RPC server, \WIN32NET\CODE\WNRPC.IDL on the source disk, defines five functions. The client side of these functions is built into the sample applications presented in Chapter 16. Here is a brief description of them:

- *_RpcGetRemoteUser()* returns the name of the user logged in on a machine. The server module retrieves this when it starts up by calling GetUserName().
- The Windows Network Manager, one of the applications discussed in Chapter 16, calls *_RpcSetLocalUser()* when it loads. This is because the WNet RPC Server is started automatically by the operating system, and under NT will report that the logged-in user is SYSTEM unless you tell it otherwise. This function provides an example of using the Local Procedure Call (LPC) facility. LPC is one of the few differences

between RPC on Windows NT and Windows 95; it is only supported in Windows NT. We'll see a little later in this chapter the syntactic implications of this.

- *_RpcWinExec()* runs a program on a remote machine.
- *_RpcGetOSStartupTime()* returns the local time when the WNet RPC Server started up. Because the operating system loads the application, this time is a close approximation for the machine startup time.
- Because RPC provides additional layers of overhead, you would expect there to be a performance penalty for using it. *_RpcBenchmark()* implements an echo client and server, so we can get an idea just how great that penalty is. Data I'll present in Chapter 16 will show that the performance penalty is surprisingly small—in fact, for remote access, RPC over TCP/IP outperforms Named Pipes called directly. Locally, RPC using local RPC is faster than any other protocol, but only half as fast as Named Pipes.

The IDL listing for the WNet RPC Server follows.

```
/********
*
* WNRPC.IDL
*
* Copyright (c) 1993-1996 Ralph P. Davis, All Rights Reserved
*
* Defines interface for WNet RPC Server
*
********/

[ uuid (9534E4E0-1BD6-101A-80FA-00001B3EF36B),
  version(1.0),
  pointer_default(ref)]
interface wnrpc
{
import "wtypes.idl";

void _RpcGetRemoteUser([out, string] wchar_t szString[255],
              [in, out] unsigned long *plLen);
void _RpcSetLocalUser([in, string] wchar_t szUser[255]);
unsigned long _RpcWinExec([in, string] wchar_t szProgram[255],
                  [in] unsigned long nCmdShow);

void _RpcGetOSStartupTime([in, out] SYSTEMTIME *pSystemTime);
void _RpcBenchmark([in] handle_t hServer,
                  [in] unsigned long dwLength,
                  [in,  size_is(dwLength), length_is(dwLength)]
                  unsigned char *pcInBuffer,
```

```
            [out, size_is(dwLength), length_is(dwLength)]
            unsigned char *pcOutBuffer);
}
```

There are several parts to the .IDL file. The first part is the header, contained in square braces. It is followed by the *interface* keyword and the name of your RPC interface. The body of the file is last, in curly braces. In the header, the *uuid* clause provides a unique identifier for the interface. UUID is an OSF acronym for Universal Unique Identifier. UUIDs are 16-byte binary numbers. You generate them with the utility *uuidgen*. It creates a skeletal .IDL file for you if you run it like this:

```
uuidgen -i -o<.IDL filename>
```

This is the file it produces:

```
[
uuid(dc196cc0-7352-11cf-8515-02608c3e9938),
version(1.0)
]
interface INTERFACENAME
{

}
```

You can also create new UUIDs in software by calling the UuidCreate() function.

The interface UUID enables clients to find exactly the RPC server they want. The MIDL compiler incorporates the interface UUID into the C code that it emits, and the RPC runtime layer uses it to match RPC calls to servers that support them. This way, the name of the function you are calling remotely does not have to be unique, which would be an impossibly restrictive requirement. Because they use the UUID to dispatch the remote procedure call, the RPC runtime modules do not get confused if two servers implement an RPC with the same name.

You can use UUIDs to define an even more precise matching between client and server. In addition to the interface UUID, you can also create object UUIDs. You then pass arrays of these UUIDs to the relevant RPC functions. The RPC runtime modules will use the combination of interface UUID and object UUIDs to find the precise server to service a remote procedure call. However, this is a more esoteric usage that is not necessary for many (if not most) RPC applications. I do not consider it further in this chapter, and I pass all relevant arguments as NULL.

UUIDs are exactly the same as the GUIDs used by OLE 2 and the Windows Sockets Service Registration API.

The version number (given here as 1.0) provides for more precise version-specific client-server matching. This allows for the possibility that more than one copy of the same server application might be offering the same interface (as identified by its UUID), but in different versions.

The interface name (in this case, *wnrpc*) is used to generate two global variables: *<interface name>_v<major>_<minor>_c_ifspec* and *<interface name>_v<major>_<minor>_s_ifspec*. The variables generated by my .IDL file are *wnrpc_v1_0_c_ifspec* and *wnrpc_v1_0_s_ifspec*. These are the client- and server-side interface handles. Both of them encapsulate the UUID assigned to the interface. MIDL also generates global variables corresponding to the handles specified in the .ACF file. I have only one, *wnrpc_IfHandle*. This will be used subsequently to represent the client's binding to a particular RPC server.

MIDL also creates the C files *<interface name>_c.c* and *<interface name>_s.c*, and the header file *<interface name>.h*. In my case, it creates the files *wnrpc_c.c, wnrpc_s.c,* and *wnrpc.h. wnrpc_c.c* is compiled and linked with my client applications. *wnrpc_s.c* becomes part of my server.

The body of the .IDL file, contained between the curly braces, contains the prototypes of the remote procedure calls that the interface embodies. The prototypes look like standard C prototypes, but include additional information that tells the compiler whether a given argument is for input (*[in]*), output (*[out]*), or both (*[in, out]*). In the prototype for _RpcBenchmark(), you also see specifiers that tell MIDL how much memory an array requires and how much data to actually transmit. The first argument, *dwLength*, is the number of array elements that we want to be transmitted on a given call. *size_is(dwLength)* says that *dwLength* is the number of bytes required for the array, and *length_is(dwLength)* says to consult *dwLength* to determine how many array elements to transmit. The *string* specifier states that the argument is a null-terminated string.

The Attribute Configuration (.ACF) File

The .ACF file specifies the type of binding handles you will use. Binding handles are the program variables used to represent client-server connections. They have the data type *handle_t* in OSF, or RPC_BINDING_HANDLE by Microsoft conventions.

The Attribute Configuration File has the same structure as the .IDL file (header, interface name, and body). The header declares the type of binding handles you want to use by default. You can override this default in the body of the .ACF file.

Here is the .ACF file for the WNet RPC server, \WIN32NET\CODE \WNRPC.ACF on the source disk:

```
/********
*
* WNRPC.ACF
*
* Attribute Configuration file for WNet RPC Server
*
********/

[implicit_handle(handle_t wnrpc_IfHandle)]
interface wnrpc
{
[explicit_handle] _RpcBenchmark();
}
```

The three types of binding handles are:

- Explicit handles (indicated by the *explicit_handle* keyword that you see above). In this case, each remote procedure call includes a binding handle as its first argument, by OSF convention. Explicit handles allow a client application to target multiple RPC servers. You use explicit handles by declaring variables of the appropriate type, initializing them by connecting to the server, then passing them to your remote procedure calls. _RpcBenchmark() is a good example.

```
void _RpcBenchmark(handle_t hServer,
                unsigned long dwLength,
                [in,  size_is(dwLength), length_is(dwLength)]
                unsigned char *pcInBuffer,
                [out, size_is(dwLength), length_is(dwLength)]
                unsigned char *pcOutBuffer);
```

This allows a benchmark client to query the RPC Name Service database for all the machines running the WNet RPC Server and to do the benchmark test in a round-robin fashion. In the body of the .ACF file, I have stated that this function will not use the default type of handle—implicit handles bound to the global variable *wnrpc_IfHandle*—but will be using an explicit handle instead.

- Implicit handles (*implicit_handle*). The header of my .ACF file states that I will be using implicit handles for all functions not specifically mentioned in the body of the file. The binding handle is a global variable—the one specified in parentheses—that is not included in the function parameter lists. The header file that MIDL generates has an *extern* reference to it, and the actual variable is declared in the client-side stub (*wnrpc_c.c*, in this case).
- Auto handles (*auto_handle*). This imposes the least burden on client applications; they know nothing whatsoever about RPC. The client stub that MIDL creates uses the RPC Name Service database to locate and bind to a server. Auto handles are suitable when you do not care which server handles a remote procedure call. Here is the syntax I would use if I wanted to request auto handles instead of implicit handles.

```
[auto_handle] interface wnrpc
{
}
```

If you do not provide an .ACF file, MIDL will use auto handles for any remote procedure calls that do not pass a binding handle explicitly.

Implicit handles strike a good balance between client RPC awareness and flexibility in the choice of servers.

The RPC Runtime Library (Server Side)

An RPC server must perform three operations to receive incoming RPCs:

1. It must specify the communications protocols over which it wants to be accessible. It can also declare the endpoints it wants to use (TCP ports, named pipes, and so on).
2. It must register its interface UUID with the RPC runtime modules so they can dispatch incoming RPCs.
3. It must put itself into the listening state.

The simplest scenario is when the server knows its own endpoints. It can then initialize itself using three functions:

- RpcServerUseProtseqEp() says that the server wants to support a specific communications protocol, using a known endpoint. The server calls this function for every protocol/endpoint combination it wants to use.
- RpcServerRegisterIf() registers the server's interface UUID.

- RpcServerListen() completes the process by putting the server into the listening state, ready to service RPC requests.

I have wrapped RPC server functionality in my CRpcServer class, and will present excerpts from it to show you how to use the API.

Declaring Communications Protocols. RpcServerUseProtseqEp() tells the RPC runtime layer that the server understands a given communications protocol and will be listening for incoming calls on a well-known endpoint (a pipe name, a TCP port, or whatever term the protocol uses). Here is its prototype:

```
typedef long RPC_STATUS;
#define RPC_ENTRY __stdcall

RPC_STATUS RPC_ENTRY RpcServerUseProtseqEp(
                            PTBYTE       lpProtseq,
                            unsigned int nMaxCalls,
                            PTBYTE       lpEndpoint,
                            LPVOID       lpSecurityDescriptor);
```

lpProtseq is the protocol sequence that you want to register. It is passed as a string. Table 11-1 shows some of the protocols that Microsoft RPC supports.

Table 11-1. Microsoft RPC Protocol Sequences

Protocol Sequence String	Protocol
ncacn_np	Named Pipes (Microsoft extension to OSF)
ncacn_ip_tcp	Connection-oriented service using TCP
ncacn_dnet_nsp	Connection-oriented service using DECnet
ncacn_spx	Connection-oriented service using Novell's SPX (Microsoft extension)
ncalrpc	Local RPC (Microsoft extension)
ncacn_nb_nb	NetBIOS over NetBEUI (Microsoft extension)
ncacn_nb_tcp	NetBIOS over TCP/IP (Microsoft extension)
ncadg_ip_udp	Datagrams over UDP
ncadg_ipx	Datagrams over IPX (Microsoft extension)

For each protocol sequence, endpoints have a specific format. For *ncacn_np*, the endpoint is a pipe name, in the format \PIPE\<rest of pipe name>. For *ncacn_ip_tcp*, the endpoint is a string representation of a TCP port, like "25000". For *ncacn_nb_nb* and *ncacn_nb_tcp*, the endpoint is a string representation of a number between 32 and 255, for instance, "127". (Endpoints below 32 are reserved for system use.) For *ncacn_spx*, the endpoint is an SPX socket between 1 and 65535, also passed as a string. For *ncalrpc*, the endpoint is some kind of string that uniquely identifies the RPC server, like "WNET_RPC_SERVER".

The different protocol sequences also have different ways of representing host names. This is not an issue with server-side calls, but does become important on the client side. Most of the protocols just use the machine name, like NUMBER1. *ncacn_spx* uses the IPX address formatted as a string. For instance, the address of my NT Server machine is "0000000100C0D1800E65".

Additional information on the formatting of host names and endpoints is available in the Win32 online help. You can find each protocol sequence ("ncacn_np", "ncacn_ip_tcp", for example) in the Search dialog box. The reference page has the complete details.

The *nMaxCalls* argument tells the RPC runtime modules what you estimate is the maximum number of concurrent requests you will receive. This is not a ceiling; RPC can accept more requests if the number exceeds this amount. You can request the default number by passing this as RPC_C_PROTSEQ_MAX_REQS_DEFAULT, which is defined as 10. (Many of the RPC constants, like RPC_C_PROTSEQ_MAX_REQS_DEFAULT, will challenge your typing abilities.)

The SECURITY_DESCRIPTOR argument (*lpSecurityDescriptor*) demands some attention. You saw in Chapter 10 that you must supply a security descriptor when you create a named pipe. The same applies to RpcServerUseProtseqEp() when you register *ncacn_np*. In addition, Windows NT provides a security-support module that adds security support for other protocols (shown on the Control Panel Services screen as "NT LM Security Support Provider"). Security is a powerful and highly desirable capability, and RPC offers rich support, up to encrypting all packets passed between a client and a server. (As you might expect, though, security is expensive, as we'll see in Chapter 16.)

Here is a call to RpcServerUseProtseqEp() that registers the Named Pipes protocol and the endpoint \PIPE\WNET\WNRPC. I show you once more how to set up a SECURITY_DESCRIPTOR to allow unlimited access, by tying a NULL discretionary access control list to it.

```
RPC_STATUS RpcStatus;
SECURITY_DESCRIPTOR SecurityDescriptor;
InitializeSecurityDescriptor(&SecurityDescriptor,
   SECURITY_DESCRIPTOR_REVISION);
SetSecurityDescriptorDacl(&SecurityDescriptor,
```

```
   TRUE, NULL, FALSE);

RpcStatus = RpcServerUseProtseqEp(
               TEXT("ncacn_np"),
               RPC_C_PROTSEQ_MAX_REQS_DEFAULT,
               TEXT("\\PIPE\\WNET\\WNRPC",
               &SecurityDescriptor);
if (RpcStatus != RPC_S_OK)
   // Something's wrong here
```

The server can call RpcServerUseProtseqEp() to register as many protocol sequences as it wants to. For RPC servers running on Windows NT, it is a good idea to register the *ncalrpc* protocol. This allows clients to use the Local Procedure Call (LPC) version of RPC, which is considerably faster than using one of the standard network protocols locally.

Dynamic Endpoints. RpcServerUseProtseqEp() registers well-known endpoints—endpoints whose names or numbers you know when you write your application. You can also ask RPC to improvise dynamic endpoints for you by just registering the protocol sequence, without a specific endpoint. The RpcServerUseProtseq() and RpcServerUseAllProtseqs() functions accomplish this.

```
RPC_STATUS RPC_ENTRY RpcServerUseProtseq(
                         LPTSTR       lpProtseq,
                         unsigned int nMaxCalls,
                         LPVOID       lpSecurityDescriptor);

RPC_STATUS RPC_ENTRY RpcServerUseAllProtseqs(
                         unsigned int nMaxCalls,
                         LPVOID       lpSecurityDescriptor);
```

The arguments are the same as for RpcServerUseProtseqEp(), but RpcServerUseProtseq() omits the endpoint, and RpcServerUseAllProtseqs() drops the protocol sequence and the endpoint. With dynamic endpoints, some additional setup is required, as we'll see shortly.

CRpcServer::UseProtocol(). The CRpcServer class has a UseProtocol() method that uses all three of these functions. If both a protocol sequence and endpoint are passed to it, it calls RpcServerUseProtseqEp(). If only a protocol is passed, it uses RpcServerUseProtseq(). If neither is passed, it calls RpcServerUseAllProtseqs(). It also uses the CSecurityDescriptor class (described in Chapter 13) to tie security restrictions to the endpoints, if requested to do so.

The implementation of this method is on the source disk in \WIN32NET \CODE\WIN32OBJ\RPCCLASS.CPP:

```
BOOL CRpcServer::UseProtocol(
                    CStringArray *paszAllowedUsers
                       /*= NULL*/,
                    CStringArray *paszDeniedUsers
                       /*= NULL*/,
                    BOOL          bAuditAccess
                       /*= FALSE*/,
                    PTBYTE        lpszProtocol
                       /*= NULL*/,
                    PTBYTE        lpszEndpoint
                       /*= NULL*/)
{
   CSecurityDescriptor *lpSecurityDescriptor;

   if ((paszAllowedUsers == NULL) &&
       (paszDeniedUsers  == NULL) &&
       !bAuditAccess)
      lpSecurityDescriptor = NULL;
   else
      lpSecurityDescriptor =
         new CSecurityDescriptor(paszAllowedUsers,
                                 paszDeniedUsers,
                                 bAuditAccess);

   RPC_STATUS RpcStatus;

   if (lpszProtocol == NULL)
      {
      // If protocol sequence is NULL, use all of them
      RpcStatus = ::RpcServerUseAllProtseqs(
                     RPC_C_PROTSEQ_MAX_REQS_DEFAULT,
                     lpSecurityDescriptor);
      }
   else if (lpszEndpoint == NULL)
      {
      // If endpoint is NULL, use specified protocol
      // sequence
      RpcStatus = ::RpcServerUseProtseq(
                      lpszProtocol,
                      RPC_C_PROTSEQ_MAX_REQS_DEFAULT,
                      lpSecurityDescriptor);
      }
   else
      {
```

```
        // Both are passed, request specific endpoint
        // for protocol sequence
        RpcStatus = ::RpcServerUseProtseqEp(
                        lpszProtocol,
                        RPC_C_PROTSEQ_MAX_REQS_DEFAULT,
                        lpszEndpoint,
                        lpSecurityDescriptor);
        }

    ::SetLastError(RpcStatus);
    return (RpcStatus == RPC_S_OK);
}
```

Registering the Server's Interface. The next step for the server is to register its interface by calling RpcServerRegisterIf(). This takes the server interface handle that was produced by the MIDL compiler and makes the RPC runtime layer aware of its corresponding UUID. If you look at the stub files that MIDL generates, you will see that the client and server interface handles both incorporate the UUID. Here's how the CRpcServer::Register() method calls RpcServerRegisterIf():

```
RPC_IF_HANDLE hServer;
RPC_STATUS    RpcStatus;

RpcStatus = RpcServerRegisterIf(
                        hServer,
                        NULL,
                        NULL);
```

The second and third arguments to RpcServerRegisterIf() are NULL if the server implements the functions exactly as they are named in the .IDL file. This is the most common usage. If the server requires a higher level of virtualization, the third argument points to a function table containing pointers to the functions that implement the published interface. They can be named anything you want. You can also provide more than one function table for each interface by setting the second argument to a non-NULL value. However, this is quite esoteric; passing both arguments as NULL usually suffices.

Listening for Remote Procedure Calls. At this point, the server is properly initialized and can start listening for RPC requests. The function that opens the incoming channel is RpcServerListen().

```
RPC_STATUS RPC_ENTRY RpcServerListen(
    unsigned int  nMin,
```

```
    unsigned int  nMax,
    unsigned int  bDontWait);
```

Its arguments state the minimum number of threads to spin off, the recommended maximum number, and a flag saying whether RpcServerListen() should return immediately (TRUE) or block (FALSE). As with RpcServerUseProtseq(), RpcServerUseProtseqEp(), and RpcServerUseAllProtseqs(), the maximum number is just a suggestion. If you need more resources than this, the RPC runtime modules will provide them automatically. To request the default, you can pass RPC_C_LISTEN_MAX_CALLS_DEFAULT, defined as 1234.

If you pass the third argument as FALSE, RpcServerListen() does not return until another thread in the server application cancels the Listen by calling RpcMgmtStopServerListening(). Passing it as TRUE, on the other hand, allows the server to do other processing. Eventually, the server must call RpcMgmtWaitServerListen(), which, like RpcServerListen(), blocks until someone calls RpcMgmtStopServerListening(). RpcMgmtWaitServerListen() takes no arguments. The actual remote procedure calls are handled in the background by RPC worker threads.

The CRpcServer::Listen() method uses RpcServerListen() or RpcMgmtWaitServerListen(), depending on the value of its *bWait* argument:

```
BOOL CRpcServer::Listen(BOOL bWait /* = TRUE*/)
{
   RPC_STATUS RpcStatus;

   if (!m_bServerListening)
      {
      if (bWait)
         {
         // Have to set these now, RpcServerListen()
         // won't return until server shuts down
         m_bServerListening = TRUE;
         m_bServerOnLine = TRUE;
         }
      RpcStatus = ::RpcServerListen(
                     1,
                     RPC_C_LISTEN_MAX_CALLS_DEFAULT,
                     !bWait);
      if (!bWait && (RpcStatus == RPC_S_OK))
         {
         m_bServerListening = TRUE;
         }
      else if (bWait && (RpcStatus != RPC_S_OK))
```

```
            {
            m_bServerListening = m_bServerOnLine = FALSE;
            }
        }
    else
        {
        m_bServerOnLine = TRUE;
        RpcStatus = ::RpcMgmtWaitServerListen();

        if (RpcStatus != RPC_S_OK)
            {
            m_bServerOnLine = FALSE;
            }
        }
    ::SetLastError(RpcStatus);
    return (RpcStatus == RPC_S_OK);
```

Server Shutdown. The server withdraws from the listening state by calling RpcMgmtStopServerListening().

```
RPC_STATUS RPC_ENTRY RpcMgmtStopServerListening(
                        RPC_BINDING_HANDLE hBinding);
```

You pass *hBinding* as NULL to shut down your own server application. You can shut down a remote server by passing the handle that represents your binding to that server.

CRpcServer calls RpcMgmtStopServerListening() in its Stop() method. In fact, that's all this method does; but for the updating of a couple of state variables, Stop() could be implemented as an inline call to RpcMgmtStop-ServerListening().

```
BOOL CRpcServer::Stop(void)
{
    RPC_STATUS RpcStatus =
        ::RpcMgmtStopServerListening(NULL);

    if (RpcStatus == RPC_S_OK)
        {
        m_bServerOnLine = m_bServerListening = FALSE;
        }

    ::SetLastError(RpcStatus);
    return (RpcStatus == RPC_S_OK);
}
```

The other steps in cleanup tell the RPC runtime modules that you're going out of service. The only additional required call is RpcServerUnregisterIf(), which reverses the action of RpcServerRegisterIf(). Here is a typical sequence of calls:

```
RPC_IF_HANDLE hServer;

RpcMgmtStopServerListening(NULL);
RpcServerUnregisterIf(hServer, NULL, TRUE);
```

The third argument to RpcServerUnregisterIf() says whether to wait for all current RPCs to complete (TRUE), or to panic and shut down immediately (FALSE). Ordinarily, you want to give all RPCs a chance to complete. The second argument is used only if you passed the second argument of RpcServerRegisterIf() as a non-NULL value, which is, as I stated previously, an esoteric usage. See the RPC online manuals if you are interested in how this works.

Registering with the RPC Name Service and Endpoint Mapper Databases. The RPC runtime suite includes two very important components that permit client applications to browse the network for compatible servers. One is the Endpoint Mapper; the other is the RPC Name Service. The Endpoint Mapper is an essential component; the Name Service is a nice feature, but it is not essential, and is not supported under Windows 95.

The Name Service lists servers and the machines where they reside. Using it, clients can find servers that support an RPC interface they are interested in. The Endpoint Mapper is responsible for routing incoming RPC requests to the correct server process. It is consulted when a client submits what is referred to as a partially bound handle. This can happen for two reasons:

- The server is using dynamically assigned endpoints, so the client has no way of knowing what they are in advance.
- The server is using well-known endpoints, but the client, for some reason, does not know the endpoints.

When an RPC with a partially bound handle arrives, the Endpoint Mapper tries to locate a server on the local machine that offers the interface embodied in the handle (as identified by its UUID). If it succeeds in finding one, it fills in the data structure represented by the handle with the additional information. At this point, the handle is fully bound, and subsequent requests using it go directly to the server application without passing through the Endpoint Mapper.

The server must tell the Name Service and Endpoint Mapper of its existence. To do so, it first calls RpcServerInqBindings() to find out about the endpoints that RPC has created for it. This function takes a single argument, a pointer to a pointer to an RPC_BINDING_VECTOR. This is a structure containing an array of the binding handles (RPC_BINDING_HANDLE) that RPC has created for you. The server does not need to know anything about the contents of the array; its only further responsibility is to free the memory by calling RpcBindingVectorFree() when it is through with the array.

```
RPC_STATUS RPC_ENTRY RpcServerInqBindings(
                        RPC_BINDING_VECTOR **lplpBindingVector);
```

RpcServerInqBindings() allocates the memory and returns the array of binding handles in **lplpBindingVector*. The server then passes this information to the functions that register with the RPC databases, RpcEpRegister() and RpcNsBindingExport().

```
RPC_STATUS RPC_ENTRY RpcEpRegister(
                          RPC_IF_HANDLE        hInterface,
                          RPC_BINDING_VECTOR *lpBindingVector,
                          UUID_VECTOR         *lpUuidVector,
                          LPTSTR               lpComment);
```

RpcEpRegister() takes the server interface handle and the binding vector returned by RpcServerInqBindings(). The third argument can be an array of object UUIDs, or NULL if you are not using objects. The last is a comment string that only has meaning for your application; it is not interpreted by RPC in any way.

The CRpcServer class encapsulates RpcServerInqBindings() and RpcEpRegister() in its Register() method.

```
BOOL CRpcServer::Register(RPC_IF_HANDLE hServer)
{
   m_hServer = hServer;

   RPC_STATUS RpcStatus;
   RpcStatus = ::RpcServerRegisterIf(
                    hServer,
                    NULL,
                    NULL);
```

```
   // If successful, get bindings and pass them to
   // the endpoint mapper
   if (RpcStatus == RPC_S_OK)
      {
      RpcStatus = ::RpcServerInqBindings(
                      &m_pBindingVector);

      if (RpcStatus == RPC_S_OK)
         {
         RpcStatus = ::RpcEpRegister(
                          hServer,
                          m_pBindingVector,
                          NULL,
                          NULL);
         }
      if (RpcStatus != RPC_S_OK)
         {
         Unregister();
         }
      }
   ::SetLastError(RpcStatus);
   return (RpcStatus == RPC_S_OK);
}
```

RpcNsBindingExport() is a little more complicated because it must include a name as the identifier for your server in the database. Here is the prototype:

```
RPC_STATUS RPC_ENTRY RpcNsBindingExport(
                          unsigned long       dwSyntax,
                          LPTSTR              lpszEntryName,
                          RPC_IF_HANDLE       hInterface,
                          RPC_BINDING_VECTOR *lpBindingVector,
                          UUID_VECTOR        *lpUUIDVector);
```

dwSyntax defines the format of the name. The constant RPC_C_NS_SYNTAX_DEFAULT says to use the default syntax for Microsoft RPC. This is stored in the Registry under HKEY_LOCAL_MACHINE\Software\Microsoft\Rpc\NameService\DefaultSyntax. The default syntax is RPC_C_NS_SYNTAX_DCE, standard OSF/DCE name syntax. In this format, the name begins with "/.:/" to designate the local domain, followed by the rest of the name.

hInterface is the server interface handle, and *lpBindingVector* is the RPC_BINDING_VECTOR that was populated by RpcServerInqBindings().

The CRpcServer class wraps RpcNsBindingExport() in its NsExport() method. This method is not automatically invoked by any other methods in the class. Because Name Service registration is optional, CRpcServer lets an application decide whether it wants to use it or not.

DCE names can contain multiple components, separated by forward slashes. NsExport() expects the calling application to pass only the last component of the name. It generates a complete name by prepending the required "/.:/", followed by the local machine name. This way, client applications can look for server applications at a specific location if they need to do so.

```
BOOL CRpcServer::NsExport(PTBYTE lpszEntryName)
{
   // DCE prefix indicating the current domain
   m_szServerNsName = _T("/.:/");

   // Add computer name for more precise name-service
   // lookup
   TCHAR szComputerName[MAX_COMPUTERNAME_LENGTH + 1];
   DWORD dwNameLength = sizeof (szComputerName);

   ::GetComputerName(szComputerName, &dwNameLength);
   m_szServerNsName += szComputerName;

   // Add leaf entry name passed in
   m_szServerNsName += _T("/");
   m_szServerNsName += lpszEntryName;

   RPC_STATUS RpcStatus;

   RpcStatus = ::RpcNsBindingExport(
                   RPC_C_NS_SYNTAX_DEFAULT,
                   (PTBYTE) (LPCTSTR) m_szServerNsName,
                   m_hServer,
                   m_pBindingVector,
                   NULL);

   ::SetLastError(RpcStatus);
   m_bNsRegistered = (RpcStatus == RPC_S_OK);
   return (RpcStatus == RPC_S_OK);
}
```

RpcServerInqBindings(), RpcEpRegister(), and RpcNsBindingExport() have their corresponding cleanup functions. RpcBindingVectorFree() releases the memory allocated by RpcServerInqBindings(). It takes a pointer to the original pointer, not just the pointer. In addition to freeing the memory, it sets the variable to NULL. RpcEpUnregister() tells the RPC Endpoint

Mapper that you are no longer in service. RpcNsBindingUnexport() removes your server name from the Name Service database. Their syntax is similar to their partner functions. CRpcServer wraps them in its Unregister() and NsUnexport() methods.

```
BOOL CRpcServer::Unregister()
{
   RPC_STATUS RpcStatus =
      ::RpcServerUnregisterIf(m_hServer, NULL, TRUE);

   if (RpcStatus == RPC_S_OK && m_pBindingVector != NULL)
      {
      RpcStatus = ::RpcEpUnregister(
                        m_hServer,
                        m_pBindingVector,
                        NULL);
      ::RpcBindingVectorFree(&m_pBindingVector);
      m_pBindingVector = NULL;
      }

   ::SetLastError(RpcStatus);
   return (RpcStatus == RPC_S_OK);
}

BOOL CRpcServer::NsUnexport(void)
{
   BOOL bRetcode;

   if (!m_bNsRegistered)
      {
      bRetcode = FALSE;
      }
   else
      {
      RPC_STATUS RpcStatus;

      RpcStatus = ::RpcNsBindingUnexport(
                       RPC_C_NS_SYNTAX_DEFAULT,
                       (PTBYTE) (LPCTSTR) m_szServerNsName,
                       m_hServer,
                       NULL);

      ::SetLastError(RpcStatus);
      bRetcode = (RpcStatus == RPC_S_OK);
      m_bNsRegistered = !bRetcode;
      }
   return bRetcode;
}
```

Enabling Security Support on the Server Side. To enable security support, the server needs to call RpcServerRegisterAuthInfo(). To request support from the NT security support provider, pass RpcServerRegisterAuthInfo() a name for your server and the authentication-service constant RPC_C_AUTHN_WINNT.

CRpcServer wraps this function in its EnableSecurity() method.

```
BOOL CRpcServer::EnableSecurity(PTBYTE lpszName)
{
   m_szServerSecurityName = lpszName;

   RPC_STATUS RpcStatus =
      ::RpcServerRegisterAuthInfo(
          lpszName,
          RPC_C_AUTHN_WINNT,
          NULL,
          NULL);

   ::SetLastError(RpcStatus);
   return (RpcStatus == RPC_S_OK);
}
```

Additional Security Considerations. An extra layer of security protection is provided by RPC client impersonation. You saw in Chapter 10 that the Named Pipes API provides the ImpersonateNamedPipeClient() function. Similarly, Microsoft RPC offers RpcImpersonateClient():

```
RPC_STATUS RPC_ENTRY RpcImpersonateClient(
                         RPC_BINDING_HANDLE hServerIf);
```

Just as with ImpersonateNamedPipeClient(), RpcImpersonateClient() allows the server-side RPC to take on the security characteristics of the client that it is servicing. *hServerIf* is the server-side interface handle. You can pass it as zero to indicate the client that the current thread is servicing, which is normally what you want. RpcImpersonateClient() does not require that the underlying protocol be Named Pipes, even though Named Pipes is the only networked API to provide an explicit call for client impersonation.

You can see the effect of client impersonation by calling GetUserName() before and after your calls to RpcImpersonateClient(). If your RPC server was started by the operating system, the first call will return “SYSTEM”. If the user JoeEndUser then runs a client application, GetUserName() will return “JoeEndUser” after you call RpcImpersonateClient().

RpcRevertToSelf() returns the server to its own security context.

Code Listing—Server Side

The WNet RPC Server does its server-side initialization and cleanup in the function WNetStartRPCServer(), and uses the services of the CRpcServer class. Actually, the constructor and destructor do most of the work, so I present them first.

```
CRpcServer::CRpcServer(PTBYTE        lpszServerName,
                       RPC_IF_HANDLE hServer,
                       CStringArray *paszAllowedUsers
                          /*= NULL*/,
                       CStringArray *paszDeniedUsers
                          /*= NULL*/,
                       BOOL          bAuditAccess
                          /*= FALSE*/,
                       PTBYTE        lpszProtocol
                          /*= NULL*/,
                       PTBYTE        lpszEndpoint
                          /*= NULL*/)
{
   m_bServerListening = m_bServerOnLine = FALSE;
   m_pBindingVector   = NULL;
   m_bNsRegistered    = FALSE;

   if (!UseProtocol(paszAllowedUsers,
                    paszDeniedUsers,
                    bAuditAccess,
                    lpszProtocol,
                    lpszEndpoint))
      AfxThrowResourceException();

   if (!Register(hServer))
      AfxThrowResourceException();

   if (!EnableSecurity(lpszServerName))
      AfxThrowResourceException();

   // Use same name for Name Service
   // (NsExport() will prefix /.:/<machine name>/ to it)

   NsExport(lpszServerName);
}

CRpcServer::~CRpcServer()
{
   if (m_bServerOnLine)
      {
      Stop();
```

```
        Unregister();
        NsUnexport();
        }

    if (m_pBindingVector != NULL)
        {
        ::RpcBindingVectorFree(&m_pBindingVector);
        }
}
```

WNetStartRPCServer() is found in the source disk file \WIN32NET\CODE\RPCSERV2\WNRPC.CPP. It is declared as DWORD WINAPI because, as we will see, it defines a new thread entry point.

```
CRpcServer *pWNetRpcServer;

DWORD WINAPI WNetStartRPCServer(LPVOID)
{
    DWORD dwError;

    try
        {
        pWNetRpcServer = new CRpcServer(
                                (PTBYTE) TEXT("WNet RPC Server"),
                                wnrpc_v1_0_s_ifspec);
        if (!pWNetRpcServer->Listen())
            {
            dwError = ::GetLastError(),
            WNetStopRPCServer(dwError,
                TEXT("CRpcServer::Listen()"));
            }
        }
    catch (CResourceException *e)
        {
        dwError = ::GetLastError();
        WNetStopRPCServer(::GetLastError(),
            TEXT("CRpcServer::CRpcServer()"));
        e->Delete();
        }
    catch (CMemoryException *e)
        {
        dwError = ::GetLastError();
        WNetStopRPCServer(::GetLastError(),
            TEXT("new CRpcServer()"));
        e->Delete();
        }
```

```
   delete pWNetRpcServer;
   return dwError;
}
```

MIDL_user_allocate() and MIDL_user_free(). RPC applications need to provide callback functions for memory allocation; they must be named MIDL_user_allocate() and MIDL_user_free(). (Actually, you can also call them midl_user_allocate() and midl_user_free(), as the RPC headers provide macros for those spellings.) The stub routines that MIDL creates call these functions when they need to allocate memory. My implementation uses single-step operations with VirtualAlloc() and VirtualFree().

```
void __RPC_FAR * __RPC_API MIDL_user_allocate(size_t len)
{
    return(VirtualAlloc(NULL, len, MEM_COMMIT,
                        PAGE_READWRITE));
}

void __RPC_API MIDL_user_free(void __RPC_FAR * ptr)
{
    VirtualFree(ptr, 0, MEM_RELEASE);
}
```

You will know if you need to provide these functions; your RPC application will not be able to link if the stubs that MIDL generates call them.

A Typical Remote Procedure Call on the Server. The function on the server side that handles a remote procedure call does not differ in any way from a normal local function. Here is the function _RpcGetRemoteUser(), which I use to report the user logged in on the host machine (remembered in the global variable *szUserName*). To achieve the highest level of platform independence, I return the string in Unicode. The client end, WNetGetRemoteUser(), appears in the next section of this chapter.

```
void _RpcGetRemoteUser(WCHAR szString[255], unsigned long
*plLen)
{
   MultiByteToWideChar(CP_ACP,
                       0,
                       szUserName,
                       -1,
                       szString,
                       *plLen);
   *plLen = lstrlen(szUserName);
}
```

Using RPC Function Calls (Client Side)

Two functions suffice to establish the client-server link: RpcStringBindingCompose() and RpcBindingFromStringBinding(). RpcStringBindingCompose() takes separate arguments representing the target machine, the protocol sequence, and the endpoint to use (if the client knows it), and combines them into a specially formatted string. RpcBindingFromStringBinding() parses this string and connects to the host and endpoint that it indicates.

If the client does not know the specific server endpoint, RpcBindingFromStringBinding() creates a partial binding. As we saw above, the first time the client issues an RPC, the Endpoint Mapper on the server machine searches its tables and completes the binding. From that point on, RPCs can be dispatched directly to the server application without going through the endpoint mapper. This activity is not visible to the client application.

The CRpcClient Class. The client-side counterpart to the CRpcServer class is CRpcClient. It invokes RpcStringBindingCompose() and RpcBindingFromStringBinding() in its Connect() method. Here is an excerpt from that method, showing these calls. Notice that RpcStringBindingCompose() takes a pointer to a pointer to a string, and allocates memory for it. You must release the memory by calling RpcStringFree().

```
RPC_IF_HANDLE m_hBinding; // CRpcClient Member variable

BOOL CRpcClient::Connect(RPC_BINDING_HANDLE *pBinding,
                         PTBYTE              lpszServer,
                         PTBYTE              lpszProtocol
                            /*= (PTBYTE) _T("ncacn_ip_tcp")*/,
                         PTBYTE              lpszEndpoint
                            /*= NULL*/,
                         DWORD               dwAuthLevel
                            /*= authDefault*/)
{
   // [...]

   RPC_STATUS RpcStatus;
   PTBYTE     pStringBinding;
   PTBYTE     pOptions;

   if ((CString(lpszProtocol) == CString(_T("ncalrpc"))) ||
       (CString(lpszProtocol) == CString(_T("ncacn_np"))))
      {
      // Security options only significant for
      // Named Pipes and local RPC
```

```
        pOptions = (PTBYTE)
            _T("Security=impersonation dynamic true");
        }
    else
        {
        pOptions = NULL;
        }

    RpcStatus = ::RpcStringBindingCompose(
                    NULL,
                    lpszProtocol,
                    lpszServer,
                    lpszEndpoint,
                    pOptions,
                    &pStringBinding);

    if (RpcStatus == RPC_S_OK)
        {
        RpcStatus = ::RpcBindingFromStringBinding(
                        pStringBinding,
                        &m_hBinding);

        // [...]

        ::RpcStringFree(&pStringBinding);
        }

// [...]
return (RpcStatus == RPC_S_OK);
}
```

Enabling Security Support on the Client Side. We saw above that the server application calls RpcServerRegisterAuthInfo() to request support from the NT LM Security Support Provider. The client, for its part, requests this support by calling RpcBindingSetAuthInfo(). This function has three significant arguments. One is the binding handle that was filled in by RpcBindingFromStringBinding() (or other functions that we'll look at later). Another is the authorization service that you want to use; for NT, it is RPC_C_AUTHN_WINNT. The third is the level of security support you want, ranging from no security at all (RPC_C_AUTHN_LEVEL_NONE) to encryption of all exchanges with the server (RPC_C_AUTHN_LEVEL_PKT_PRIVACY).

CRpcClient defines an enumerated type representing all the levels of security support (with constants that are easier to type than the standard DCE ones. Here is the definition from RPCCLASS.H:

```
enum {authDefault       = RPC_C_AUTHN_LEVEL_DEFAULT,
      authNone          = RPC_C_AUTHN_LEVEL_NONE,
      authConnect       = RPC_C_AUTHN_LEVEL_CONNECT,
      authCall          = RPC_C_AUTHN_LEVEL_CALL,
      authPkt           = RPC_C_AUTHN_LEVEL_PKT,
      authPktIntegrity = RPC_C_AUTHN_LEVEL_PKT_INTEGRITY,
      authPktPrivacy    = RPC_C_AUTHN_LEVEL_PKT_PRIVACY};
```

It calls RpcBindingSetAuthInfo() in its Connect() method after the binding has been successfully established.

```
RpcStatus = ::RpcBindingFromStringBinding(
               pStringBinding,
               &m_hBinding);
if (RpcStatus == RPC_S_OK)
   {
   *pBinding = m_hBinding;

   RpcStatus = ::RpcBindingSetAuthInfo(
                  m_hBinding,
                  NULL,
                  dwAuthLevel,
                  RPC_C_AUTHN_WINNT,
                  NULL,
                  0);
   }
```

To put everything in context, here is the complete listing of CRpcClient::Connect(). The additional code at the beginning of the function uses the *ncalrpc* protocol if the server name is passed as NULL, ".", or the current machine name. It also knows that Windows 95 doesn't support *ncalrpc*, and defaults to using *ncacn_ip_tcp* (TCP/IP) if it detects Windows 95.

```
BOOL CRpcClient::Connect(RPC_BINDING_HANDLE *pBinding,
                         PTBYTE              lpszServer,
                         PTBYTE              lpszProtocol
                            /*= (PTBYTE) _T("ncacn_ip_tcp")*/,
                         PTBYTE              lpszEndpoint
                            /*= NULL*/,
                         DWORD               dwAuthLevel
                            /*= authDefault*/)
{
   // Server name of NULL, '.', or of the local machine
   // will use ncalrpc (highly optimized local RPC)
   // Only on NT, though--Windows 95 doesn't
   // support ncalrpc
```

```
if (*lpszServer == _T('.'))
   lpszServer = NULL;

if (!CWin32Object::IsWindows95())
   {
   if (lpszServer == NULL)
      {
      lpszProtocol = (PTBYTE) _T("ncalrpc");
      lpszEndpoint = NULL;
      }
   else
      {
      // See if server name is our machine

      TCHAR szComputerName[MAX_COMPUTERNAME_LENGTH + 1];
      DWORD dwNameLength = sizeof (szComputerName);

      ::GetComputerName(szComputerName, &dwNameLength);
      if (CString(szComputerName) == CString(lpszServer))
         {
         lpszServer   = NULL;
         lpszProtocol = (PTBYTE) _T("ncalrpc");
         lpszEndpoint = NULL;
         }
      }
   }
if (lpszProtocol == NULL)
   {
   // Default to ncacn_ip_tcp
   lpszProtocol = (PTBYTE) _T("ncacn_ip_tcp");
   }

RPC_STATUS RpcStatus;
PTBYTE     pStringBinding;
PTBYTE     pOptions;

if ((CString(lpszProtocol) == CString(_T("ncalrpc"))) ||
    (CString(lpszProtocol) == CString(_T("ncacn_np"))))
   {
   // Security options only significant for
   // Named Pipes and local RPC
   pOptions = (PTBYTE)
      _T("Security=impersonation dynamic true");
   }
else
   {
   pOptions = NULL;
   }
```

```
    RpcStatus = ::RpcStringBindingCompose(
                    NULL,
                    lpszProtocol,
                    lpszServer,
                    lpszEndpoint,
                    pOptions,
                    &pStringBinding);

    if (RpcStatus == RPC_S_OK)
       {
       RpcStatus = ::RpcBindingFromStringBinding(
                       pStringBinding,
                       &m_hBinding);
       if (RpcStatus == RPC_S_OK)
          {
          *pBinding = m_hBinding;

          RpcStatus = ::RpcBindingSetAuthInfo(
                          m_hBinding,
                          NULL,
                          dwAuthLevel,
                          RPC_C_AUTHN_WINNT,
                          NULL,
                          0);
          if (RpcStatus != RPC_S_OK)
             {
             TRACE(_T("\nRpcBindingSetAuthInfo() failed, status = %d"),
                RpcStatus);
             }
          }
       ::RpcStringFree(&pStringBinding);
       }
    ::SetLastError(RpcStatus);
    return (RpcStatus == RPC_S_OK);
}
```

The Client's View of a Remote Procedure Call. Once the client is bound to the server, it can start sending it remote procedure calls. The client side of _RpcGetRemoteUser() is WNetGetRemoteUser(), included in one of the sample applications developed in Chapter 16. After instantiating a CRpc-Client (which connects to the server), it issues the remote procedure call _RpcGetRemoteUser().

There is one consideration that we cannot avoid here. The RPC client stubs generated by MIDL use Win32 exceptions to report errors that they detect. This is intelligent behavior; the stubs cannot make any assumptions about values that the remote procedure call will return. By raising exceptions, the stubs keep their error-reporting stream separate.

However, because of this, you must issue remote procedure calls within a *__try / __except* or *try / catch* block. In fact, Microsoft RPC provides macros for exception handling. RpcTryExcept introduces the *__try* block. The exception handler is declared using RpcExcept, followed by an exception-filter expression in parentheses. RpcEndExcept closes a *__try / __except* block. There are also macros for Structured Termination Handling—RpcTryFinally, RpcFinally, and RpcEndFinally.

But this becomes a problem when you start wrapping RPC functionality in C++ classes. WNetGetRemoteUser(), for instance, uses a CRpcClient object to talk to the server. Why is it a problem? Because the Microsoft compiler won't let you use C++ objects and Structured Exception Handling in the same function. Here are some possible solutions:

- Connect to the server in one function, then call another function to do the actual remote procedure call.
- Use *try / catch (...)* instead of *__try / __except*. This will trap any exceptions that the stub raises. However, you will not be able to retrieve the exception code for precise error reporting.
- Set up a translator function that maps a Win32 exception to a C++ one. Then you can catch the C++ exception and get any information you need from the object you throw.

I have chosen the last tactic, using the CWin32Exception class I introduced in Chapter 2. So that a user of my CRpcClient class doesn't have to do this, the CRpcClient constructor calls CWin32Exception::SetTranslator() to install the translation routine, and remembers the old one (the return value from CWin32Exception::SetTranslator()). Then the destructor reinstalls the old translation function. CWin32Exception has a method that reports the specific exception code, GetExceptionCode().

```
DWORD WNetGetRemoteUser(LPTSTR  lpszStation,
                        LPTSTR  lpszUserName,
                        LPDWORD lpdwNameLength)
{
   DWORD dwRetcode = NO_ERROR;
   RPC_STATUS RpcStatus = RPC_S_OK;

   try
      {
      CRpcClient RpcClient(wnrpc_v1_0_c_ifspec,
                           (PTBYTE) lpszStation,
                           &wnrpc_IfHandle);
```

```
      RpcClient.SetTimeout(RPC_C_BINDING_MIN_TIMEOUT);
      try
         {
         WCHAR szwUserName[256];

         _RpcGetRemoteUser(szwUserName, lpdwNameLength);
         UnicodeToANSI((LPTSTR) szwUserName, lpszUserName,
            (*lpdwNameLength) + 1);  // +1 for NULL terminator
         RpcStatus = RPC_S_OK;
         }
      catch (CWin32Exception *e)
         {
         RpcStatus = e->GetExceptionCode();
         dwRetcode = ((DWORD) -1);
         e->Delete();
         }
      }
   catch (CResourceException *e)
      {
      // Guess there's nobody home over there
      RpcStatus = ::GetLastError();
      dwRetcode = ((DWORD) -1);
      e->Delete();
      }
   return dwRetcode;
}
```

I want to call your attention to a couple of additional points here. First, notice that WNetGetRemoteUser() connects to the server just by instantiating a CRpcClient object. Here is the constructor that does everything required to get the client and server hooked up:

```
CRpcClient::CRpcClient(RPC_IF_HANDLE       hClient,
                       PTBYTE              lpszServer,
                       RPC_BINDING_HANDLE *pBinding,
                       PTBYTE              lpszProtocol
                          /*= NULL */,
                       PTBYTE              lpszEndpoint
                          /*= NULL*/,
                       DWORD               dwAuthLevel
                          /*= authDefault*/)
{
   m_hBinding             = NULL;
   m_hNameServiceLookup = NULL;
   m_hNameServiceImport = NULL;
   m_pBindingVector      = NULL;
```

```
    m_hClient               = hClient;
    m_pTranslator           = CWin32Exception::SetTranslator();

    if (!Connect(pBinding, lpszServer,
                 lpszProtocol, lpszEndpoint,
                 dwAuthLevel))
       AfxThrowResourceException();
}
```

Because the constructor throws a CResourceException if the Connect() call fails (most likely because the target server isn't running), WNetGetRemoteUser() must be prepared for this.

Second, notice the call to CRpcClient::SetTimeout(). This method invokes the RPC runtime call RpcMgmtSetComTimeout(). I do this because RPC timeouts can be very long if you don't set them explicitly. I have seen RPC clients time out for three minutes—an interminable period for a user waiting for results to appear on the screen. The RpcMgmtSetComTimeout() lets you set the timeout to a value between 0 (RPC_C_BINDING_MIN_TIMEOUT) and 9 (RPC_C_BINDING_MAX_TIMEOUT). These are not absolute timeout periods—they simply represent a relative position in the range of possible timeout values. You can also set it to 10 (RPC_C_BINDING_INFINITE_TIMEOUT) if you can stand to wait forever for an RPC server to respond.

Here is the listing of CRpcClient::SetTimeout():

```
BOOL CRpcClient::SetTimeout(UINT nTimeout /* =
                              RPC_C_BINDING_DEFAULT_TIMEOUT*/)
{
   RPC_STATUS RpcStatus;
   BOOL       bRetcode = FALSE;

   if (m_hBinding != NULL)
      {
      RpcStatus =
         ::RpcMgmtSetComTimeout(m_hBinding, nTimeout);
      bRetcode = (RpcStatus == RPC_S_OK);

      ::SetLastError(RpcStatus);
      }
   return bRetcode;
}
```

Last, my RPC interface passes Unicode strings over the network. The client application I have written prefers ANSI strings, so it has to convert the result by calling my helper function UnicodeToANSI().

The RPC Version of the Hangup Operation. The client hangs up on the server by calling RpcBindingFree(), passing the binding handle returned by RpcBindingFromStringBinding(). CRpcClient offers this through its Hangup() method:

```
BOOL CRpcClient::Hangup()
{
   RPC_STATUS RpcStatus;
   BOOL       bRetcode = FALSE;

   if (m_hBinding != NULL)
      {
      RpcStatus = ::RpcBindingFree(&m_hBinding);

      bRetcode = (RpcStatus == RPC_S_OK);
      ::SetLastError(RpcStatus);
      }
   return bRetcode;
}
```

RpcBindingFree() expects a pointer to the binding handle because it flags it as invalid after freeing it.

WNetGetRemoteUser() does not explicitly call CRpcClient::Hangup(); it doesn't need to. The CRpcClient destructor takes care of this, as you can see.

```
CRpcClient::~CRpcClient()
{
   CWin32Exception::SetTranslator(m_pTranslator);
   Hangup();

   if (m_pBindingVector != NULL)
      ::RpcBindingVectorFree(&m_pBindingVector);

   if (m_hNameServiceLookup != NULL)
      ::RpcNsBindingLookupDone(&m_hNameServiceLookup);

   if (m_hNameServiceImport != NULL)
      ::RpcNsBindingImportDone(&m_hNameServiceImport);
}
```

Because WNetGetRemoteUser() creates its CRpcClient object on the stack, it is automatically destroyed when the function returns.

Using the Name Service Database to Browse for Compatible Servers. The purpose of the Name Service database in the OSF/DCE RPC specification is to allow servers and clients to discover each other. The server reports its presence by calling RpcNsBindingExport().

There are two ways for the client to enumerate RPC servers. One is to import binding handles one at a time by calling RpcNsBindingImportBegin(), RpcNsBindingImportNext(), and RpcNsBindingImportDone(). RpcNsBinding-ImportBegin() opens an enumeration handle that then serves as an input argument to the other two functions. RpcNsBindingImportNext() returns a binding to one of the servers whose interface UUID matches the one passed by the client in its call to RpcNsBindingImportBegin(). Finally, RpcNsBindingImportDone() closes the handle. The other way returns an array of binding handles, using the functions RpcNsBindingLookupBegin(), RpcNsBindingLookupNext(), and RpcNsBindingLookupDone(). The client can then select one binding at a time from the array by calling RpcNsBindingSelect().

CRpcClient models both of these techniques. The NsImport() method uses all the RpcNsBindingImport() functions. The first time it is called, it invokes RpcNsBindingImportBegin(). You can pass RpcNsBindingImportBegin() the name of the server application if you know it (the name it passed to RpcNsBindingExport()). If you don't, you can pass the name as NULL (as I do here). In this case, the client's RPC_IF_HANDLE identifies the servers you want to enumerate, because it contains the UUID of interest.

RpcNsBindingImportBegin() creates a handle typed as an RPC_NS_HANDLE; CRpcClient stores this in its member variable *m_hNameServiceImport*. On subsequent calls, NsImport() calls RpcNsBindingImportNext(). This function takes the RPC_NS_HANDLE created by RpcNsBindingImportBegin() and returns a succession of RPC_BINDING_HANDLEs, one at a time. These are fully bound handles that can be used without modification to send RPCs to the server. When RpcNsBindingImportNext() returns RPC_S_NO_MORE_BINDINGS, indicating that there are no more server entries to report, NsImport() calls RpcNsBindingImportDone() to terminate the query.

```
BOOL CRpcClient::NsImport(RPC_BINDING_HANDLE *pBinding)
{
   RPC_STATUS RpcStatus;
   BOOL       bRetcode = FALSE;

   if (m_hNameServiceImport == NULL)
      {
      RpcStatus = ::RpcNsBindingImportBegin(
                      RPC_C_NS_SYNTAX_DEFAULT,
                      NULL,
```

```
                          m_hClient,
                          NULL,
                          &m_hNameServiceImport);
        }

    if (m_hNameServiceImport != NULL)
        {
        RpcStatus = ::RpcNsBindingImportNext(
                          m_hNameServiceImport,
                          pBinding);

        if (RpcStatus == RPC_S_NO_MORE_BINDINGS) // No more
            {
            ::RpcNsBindingImportDone(&m_hNameServiceImport);
            }
        ::SetLastError(RpcStatus);
        bRetcode = (RpcStatus == RPC_S_OK);
        }
    return bRetcode;
}
```

The technique using RpcNsBindingLookupBegin() is very similar. The difference is that it returns binding information as an RPC_BINDING_VECTOR, which is just an array of RPC_BINDING_HANDLEs. CRpcClient stores this binding vector in its member variable *m_pBindingVector*. The client then iterates over this array by calling RpcNsBindingSelect(). This function removes one binding handle from the array and returns it to the caller.

CRpcClient offers two methods to support this functionality. NsLookup() is a lot like NsImport(). The first time it is called, it calls RpcNsBindingLookupBegin(). This function takes the same arguments as RpcNsBindingImportBegin(), but requires one additional argument (the fifth one) specifying the number of bindings you want to retrieve. Zero requests the default, which the Win32 documentation says is the constant RPC_C_BINDING_MAX_COUNT_DEFAULT—but I haven't found this constant anywhere in the Win32 header files. RpcNsBindingLookupBegin() also creates an RPC_NS_HANDLE, which you then provide to RpcNsBindingLookupNext() and RpcNsBindingLookupDone(). From this point on, NsLookup() calls RpcNsBindingLookupNext(). When it returns a NULL binding vector, NsLookup() calls RpcNsBindingLookupDone() to close the lookup.

```
BOOL CRpcClient::NsLookup(void)
{
   RPC_STATUS RpcStatus;
   BOOL       bRetcode = FALSE;

   if (m_hNameServiceLookup == NULL)
      {
      RpcStatus = ::RpcNsBindingLookupBegin(
                        RPC_C_NS_SYNTAX_DEFAULT,
                        NULL,
                        m_hClient,
                        NULL,
                        0,
                        &m_hNameServiceLookup);
      }

   if (m_hNameServiceLookup != NULL)
      {
      if (m_pBindingVector != NULL)
         {
         ::RpcBindingVectorFree(&m_pBindingVector);
         }

      RpcStatus = ::RpcNsBindingLookupNext(
                        m_hNameServiceLookup,
                        &m_pBindingVector);

      if (m_pBindingVector == NULL) // No more
         {
         ::RpcNsBindingLookupDone(&m_hNameServiceLookup);
         }
      ::SetLastError(RpcStatus);
      bRetcode = (RpcStatus == RPC_S_OK);
      }
   return bRetcode;
}
```

The NsSelect() method calls RpcNsBindingSelect(), passing it the RPC_BINDING_VECTOR returned by RpcNsBindingLookupNext(), and returning an RPC_BINDING_HANDLE representing one of the reported bindings. Because RpcNsBindingLookupNext() actually removes the binding from the array, eventually the array will be depleted. When this happens, RpcNsSelect() returns RPC_S_NO_MORE_BINDINGS, and sets the output binding handle to NULL.

```
BOOL CRpcClient::NsSelect(RPC_BINDING_HANDLE *pBinding)
{
   BOOL       bRetcode = FALSE;
   RPC_STATUS RpcStatus;

   if (m_pBindingVector == NULL)
      {
      NsLookup();
      }

   if (m_pBindingVector != NULL)
      {
      RpcStatus = ::RpcNsBindingSelect(
                     m_pBindingVector,
                     pBinding);
      bRetcode = (RpcStatus == RPC_S_OK);

      if (RpcStatus == RPC_S_NO_MORE_BINDINGS)
         {
         // Last binding has been selected
         ::RpcBindingVectorFree(&m_pBindingVector);
         }
      }
   ::SetLastError(RpcStatus);
   return bRetcode;
}
```

Code Listings

So you can see the CRpcServer and CRpcClient classes in their overall context, I include the full listings of \WIN32NET\CODE\WIN32OBJ\RPCCLASS.H and \WIN32NET\CODE\WIN32OBJ\RPCCLASS.CPP here.

```
/********
*
* RPCCLASS.H
*
* Copyright (c) 1996 Ralph P. Davis
*
* All Rights Reserved
*
*****/

#ifndef RPCCLASS_INCLUDED
#define RPCCLASS_INCLUDED

#include <eh.h>
```

```
class AFX_EXT_CLASS CRpcServer : public CObject
{
protected:
   RPC_IF_HANDLE        m_hServer;
   BOOL                 m_bServerListening;
   BOOL                 m_bServerOnLine;
   RPC_BINDING_VECTOR *m_pBindingVector;
   CString              m_szServerSecurityName;
   CString              m_szServerNsName;
   BOOL                 m_bNsRegistered;
public:
   CRpcServer();
   CRpcServer(PTBYTE        lpszServerName,
              RPC_IF_HANDLE hServer,
              CStringArray *paszAllowedUsers = NULL,
              CStringArray *paszDeniedUsers  = NULL,
              BOOL          bAuditAccess     = FALSE,
              PTBYTE        lpszProtocol     = NULL,
              PTBYTE        lpszEndpoint     = NULL);
   virtual ~CRpcServer();

   BOOL UseProtocol(CStringArray *paszAllowedUsers = NULL,
                    CStringArray *paszDeniedUsers  = NULL,
                    BOOL          bAuditAccess     = FALSE,
                    PTBYTE        lpszProtocol     = NULL,
                    PTBYTE        lpszEndpoint     = NULL);
   BOOL Register(RPC_IF_HANDLE hServer);
   BOOL EnableSecurity(PTBYTE lpszName);
   BOOL Listen(BOOL bWait = TRUE);

   BOOL NsExport(PTBYTE lpszEntryName);
   BOOL NsUnexport(void);
   BOOL Stop(void);
   BOOL Unregister();

   static BOOL ImpersonateClient(void)
      {
      return ::RpcImpersonateClient(0);
      }
   static BOOL RevertToSelf(void)
      {
      return ::RpcRevertToSelf();
      }

   DECLARE_DYNAMIC(CRpcServer)
};

class AFX_EXT_CLASS CRpcClient : public CObject
```

```
{
protected:
   RPC_IF_HANDLE       m_hClient;
   RPC_BINDING_HANDLE  m_hBinding;
   RPC_NS_HANDLE       m_hNameServiceLookup;
   RPC_NS_HANDLE       m_hNameServiceImport;
   RPC_BINDING_VECTOR *m_pBindingVector;
   _se_translator_function
                       m_pTranslator;
public:
   enum {authDefault       = RPC_C_AUTHN_LEVEL_DEFAULT,
         authNone          = RPC_C_AUTHN_LEVEL_NONE,
         authConnect       = RPC_C_AUTHN_LEVEL_CONNECT,
         authCall          = RPC_C_AUTHN_LEVEL_CALL,
         authPkt           = RPC_C_AUTHN_LEVEL_PKT,
         authPktIntegrity = RPC_C_AUTHN_LEVEL_PKT_INTEGRITY,
         authPktPrivacy    = RPC_C_AUTHN_LEVEL_PKT_PRIVACY};

   CRpcClient();
   CRpcClient(RPC_IF_HANDLE       hClient,
              PTBYTE              lpszServer,
              RPC_BINDING_HANDLE *pBinding,
              PTBYTE              lpszProtocol =
                                    (PTBYTE) _T("ncacn_ip_tcp"),
              PTBYTE              lpszEndpoint = NULL,
              DWORD               dwAuthLevel = authDefault);
   virtual ~CRpcClient();

   BOOL Connect(RPC_BINDING_HANDLE *pBinding,
                PTBYTE              lpszServer,
                PTBYTE              lpszProtocol = NULL,
                PTBYTE              lpszEndpoint = NULL,
                DWORD               dwAuthLevel = authDefault);
   BOOL SetTimeout(UINT nTimeout =
      RPC_C_BINDING_DEFAULT_TIMEOUT);
   BOOL Hangup(void);

   BOOL NsLookup(void);
   BOOL NsSelect(RPC_BINDING_HANDLE *pBinding);
   BOOL NsImport(RPC_BINDING_HANDLE *pBinding);

   DECLARE_DYNAMIC(CRpcClient)
};

#endif
```

```
/********
*
* RPCCLASS.CPP
*
* Copyright (c) 1996 Ralph P. Davis
*
* All Rights Reserved
*
*****/

#include "stdafx.h"
#include "rpcclass.h"
#include "security.h"
#include "win32obj.h"
#include "win32exc.h"

IMPLEMENT_DYNAMIC(CRpcServer, CObject)
IMPLEMENT_DYNAMIC(CRpcClient, CObject)

CRpcServer::CRpcServer()
{
   m_bServerListening = m_bServerOnLine = FALSE;
   m_pBindingVector   = NULL;
   m_bNsRegistered    = FALSE;
}

CRpcServer::CRpcServer(PTBYTE        lpszServerName,
                       RPC_IF_HANDLE hServer,
                       CStringArray *paszAllowedUsers
                          /*= NULL*/,
                       CStringArray *paszDeniedUsers
                          /*= NULL*/,
                       BOOL          bAuditAccess
                          /*= FALSE*/,
                       PTBYTE        lpszProtocol
                          /*= NULL*/,
                       PTBYTE        lpszEndpoint
                          /*= NULL*/)
{
   m_bServerListening = m_bServerOnLine = FALSE;
   m_pBindingVector   = NULL;
   m_bNsRegistered    = FALSE;

   if (!UseProtocol(paszAllowedUsers,
                    paszDeniedUsers,
                    bAuditAccess,
                    lpszProtocol,
                    lpszEndpoint))
      AfxThrowResourceException();
```

```
   if (!Register(hServer))
      AfxThrowResourceException();

   if (!EnableSecurity(lpszServerName))
      AfxThrowResourceException();

   // Use same name for Name Service
   // (NsExport() will prefix /.:/<machine name>/ to it)

   NsExport(lpszServerName);
}

CRpcServer::~CRpcServer()
{
   if (m_bServerOnLine)
      {
      Stop();
      Unregister();
      NsUnexport();
      }

   if (m_pBindingVector != NULL)
      {
      ::RpcBindingVectorFree(&m_pBindingVector);
      m_pBindingVector = NULL;
      }
}

BOOL CRpcServer::UseProtocol(
                    CStringArray *paszAllowedUsers
                       /*= NULL*/,
                    CStringArray *paszDeniedUsers
                       /*= NULL*/,
                    BOOL          bAuditAccess
                       /*= FALSE*/,
                    PTBYTE        lpszProtocol
                       /*= NULL*/,
                    PTBYTE        lpszEndpoint
                       /*= NULL*/)
{
   CSecurityDescriptor *lpSecurityDescriptor;

   if ((paszAllowedUsers == NULL) &&
       (paszDeniedUsers  == NULL) &&
       !bAuditAccess)
      lpSecurityDescriptor = NULL;
```

```
    else
        lpSecurityDescriptor =
            new CSecurityDescriptor(paszAllowedUsers,
                                    paszDeniedUsers,
                                    bAuditAccess);

    RPC_STATUS RpcStatus;

    if (lpszProtocol == NULL)
        {
        // If protocol sequence is NULL, use all of them
        RpcStatus = ::RpcServerUseAllProtseqs(
                        RPC_C_PROTSEQ_MAX_REQS_DEFAULT,
                        lpSecurityDescriptor);
        }
    else if (lpszEndpoint == NULL)
        {
        // If endpoint is NULL, use specified protocol
        // sequence
        RpcStatus = ::RpcServerUseProtseq(
                         lpszProtocol,
                         RPC_C_PROTSEQ_MAX_REQS_DEFAULT,
                         lpSecurityDescriptor);
        }
    else
        {
        // Both are passed, request specific endpoint
        // for protocol sequence
        RpcStatus = ::RpcServerUseProtseqEp(
                        lpszProtocol,
                        RPC_C_PROTSEQ_MAX_REQS_DEFAULT,
                        lpszEndpoint,
                        lpSecurityDescriptor);
        }

    ::SetLastError(RpcStatus);
    return (RpcStatus == RPC_S_OK);
}

BOOL CRpcServer::Register(RPC_IF_HANDLE hServer)
{
    m_hServer = hServer;

    RPC_STATUS RpcStatus;
    RpcStatus = ::RpcServerRegisterIf(
                    hServer,
                    NULL,
                    NULL);
```

```
    // If successful, get bindings and pass them to
    // the endpoint mapper
    if (RpcStatus == RPC_S_OK)
       {
       RpcStatus = ::RpcServerInqBindings(
                        &m_pBindingVector);

       if (RpcStatus == RPC_S_OK)
          {
          RpcStatus = ::RpcEpRegister(
                         hServer,
                         m_pBindingVector,
                         NULL,
                         NULL);
          }
       if (RpcStatus != RPC_S_OK)
          {
          Unregister();
          }
       }
    ::SetLastError(RpcStatus);
    return (RpcStatus == RPC_S_OK);
}

BOOL CRpcServer::EnableSecurity(PTBYTE lpszName)
{
    m_szServerSecurityName = lpszName;

    RPC_STATUS RpcStatus =
       ::RpcServerRegisterAuthInfo(
           lpszName,
           RPC_C_AUTHN_WINNT,
           NULL,
           NULL);

    ::SetLastError(RpcStatus);
    return (RpcStatus == RPC_S_OK);
}

BOOL CRpcServer::Listen(BOOL bWait /* = TRUE*/)
{
    RPC_STATUS RpcStatus;

    if (!m_bServerListening)
       {
       if (bWait)
```

```
        {
        // Have to set these now, RpcServerListen()
        // won't return until server shuts down
        m_bServerListening = TRUE;
        m_bServerOnLine = TRUE;
        }
      RpcStatus = ::RpcServerListen(
                    1,
                    RPC_C_LISTEN_MAX_CALLS_DEFAULT,
                    !bWait);
      if (!bWait && (RpcStatus == RPC_S_OK))
        {
        m_bServerListening = TRUE;
        }
      else if (bWait && (RpcStatus != RPC_S_OK))
        {
        m_bServerListening = m_bServerOnLine = FALSE;
        }
      }
   else
      {
      m_bServerOnLine = TRUE;
      RpcStatus = ::RpcMgmtWaitServerListen();

      if (RpcStatus != RPC_S_OK)
        {
        m_bServerOnLine = FALSE;
        }
      }
   ::SetLastError(RpcStatus);
   return (RpcStatus == RPC_S_OK);
}

BOOL CRpcServer::NsExport(PTBYTE lpszEntryName)
{
   // DCE prefix indicating the current domain
   m_szServerNsName = _T("/.:/");

   // Add computer name for more precise name-service
   // lookup
   TCHAR szComputerName[MAX_COMPUTERNAME_LENGTH + 1];
   DWORD dwNameLength = sizeof (szComputerName);

   ::GetComputerName(szComputerName, &dwNameLength);
   m_szServerNsName += szComputerName;

   // Add leaf entry name passed in
   m_szServerNsName += _T("/");
   m_szServerNsName += lpszEntryName;
```

```
   RPC_STATUS RpcStatus;

   RpcStatus = ::RpcNsBindingExport(
                    RPC_C_NS_SYNTAX_DEFAULT,
                    (PTBYTE) (LPCTSTR) m_szServerNsName,
                    m_hServer,
                    m_pBindingVector,
                    NULL);

   ::SetLastError(RpcStatus);
   m_bNsRegistered = (RpcStatus == RPC_S_OK);
   return (RpcStatus == RPC_S_OK);
}

BOOL CRpcServer::NsUnexport(void)
{
   BOOL bRetcode;

   if (!m_bNsRegistered)
      {
      bRetcode = FALSE;
      }
   else
      {
      RPC_STATUS RpcStatus;

      RpcStatus = ::RpcNsBindingUnexport(
                       RPC_C_NS_SYNTAX_DEFAULT,
                       (PTBYTE) (LPCTSTR) m_szServerNsName,
                       m_hServer,
                       NULL);

      ::SetLastError(RpcStatus);
      bRetcode = (RpcStatus == RPC_S_OK);
      m_bNsRegistered = !bRetcode;
      }
   return bRetcode;
}

BOOL CRpcServer::Stop(void)
{
   RPC_STATUS RpcStatus =
      ::RpcMgmtStopServerListening(NULL);

   if (RpcStatus == RPC_S_OK)
      {
      m_bServerOnLine = m_bServerListening = FALSE;
      }
```

```
   ::SetLastError(RpcStatus);
   return (RpcStatus == RPC_S_OK);
}

BOOL CRpcServer::Unregister()
{
   RPC_STATUS RpcStatus =
      ::RpcServerUnregisterIf(m_hServer, NULL, TRUE);

   if (RpcStatus == RPC_S_OK && m_pBindingVector != NULL)
      {
      RpcStatus = ::RpcEpUnregister(
                        m_hServer,
                        m_pBindingVector,
                        NULL);
      ::RpcBindingVectorFree(&m_pBindingVector);
      m_pBindingVector = NULL;
      }

   ::SetLastError(RpcStatus);
   return (RpcStatus == RPC_S_OK);
}

CRpcClient::CRpcClient()
{
   m_hBinding             = NULL;
   m_hNameServiceLookup = NULL;
   m_hNameServiceImport = NULL;
   m_pBindingVector     = NULL;
   m_pTranslator        = CWin32Exception::SetTranslator();
}

CRpcClient::CRpcClient(RPC_IF_HANDLE       hClient,
                       PTBYTE              lpszServer,
                       RPC_BINDING_HANDLE *pBinding,
                       PTBYTE              lpszProtocol
                          /*= NULL */,
                       PTBYTE              lpszEndpoint
                          /*= NULL*/,
                       DWORD               dwAuthLevel
                          /*= authDefault*/)
{
   m_hBinding             = NULL;
   m_hNameServiceLookup = NULL;
   m_hNameServiceImport = NULL;
   m_pBindingVector     = NULL;
   m_hClient            = hClient;
   m_pTranslator        = CWin32Exception::SetTranslator();
```

```
   if (!Connect(pBinding, lpszServer,
                lpszProtocol, lpszEndpoint,
                dwAuthLevel))
      AfxThrowResourceException();
}

CRpcClient::~CRpcClient()
{
   CWin32Exception::SetTranslator(m_pTranslator);
   Hangup();

   if (m_pBindingVector != NULL)
      ::RpcBindingVectorFree(&m_pBindingVector);

   if (m_hNameServiceLookup != NULL)
      ::RpcNsBindingLookupDone(&m_hNameServiceLookup);

   if (m_hNameServiceImport != NULL)
      ::RpcNsBindingImportDone(&m_hNameServiceImport);
}

BOOL CRpcClient::Connect(RPC_BINDING_HANDLE *pBinding,
                         PTBYTE             lpszServer,
                         PTBYTE             lpszProtocol
                            /*= (PTBYTE) _T("ncacn_ip_tcp")*/,
                         PTBYTE             lpszEndpoint
                            /*= NULL*/,
                         DWORD              dwAuthLevel
                            /*= authDefault*/)
{
   // Server name of NULL, '.', or of the local machine
   // will use ncalrpc (highly optimized local RPC)
   // Only on NT, though--Windows 95 doesn't
   // support ncalrpc

   if (*lpszServer == _T('.'))
      lpszServer = NULL;

   if (!CWin32Object::IsWindows95())
      {
      if (lpszServer == NULL)
         {
         lpszProtocol = (PTBYTE) _T("ncalrpc");
         lpszEndpoint = NULL;
         }
      else
         {
         // See if server name is our machine
```

```
        TCHAR szComputerName[MAX_COMPUTERNAME_LENGTH + 1];
        DWORD dwNameLength = sizeof (szComputerName);

        ::GetComputerName(szComputerName, &dwNameLength);
        if (CString(szComputerName) == CString(lpszServer))
           {
           lpszServer   = NULL;
           lpszProtocol = (PTBYTE) _T("ncalrpc");
           lpszEndpoint = NULL;
           }
        }
    }
if (lpszProtocol == NULL)
    {
    // Default to ncacn_ip_tcp
    lpszProtocol = (PTBYTE) _T("ncacn_ip_tcp");
    }

RPC_STATUS RpcStatus;
PTBYTE     pStringBinding;
PTBYTE     pOptions;

if ((CString(lpszProtocol) == CString(_T("ncalrpc"))) ||
     (CString(lpszProtocol) == CString(_T("ncacn_np"))))
    {
    // Security options only significant for
    // Named Pipes and local RPC
    pOptions = (PTBYTE)
       _T("Security=impersonation dynamic true");
    }
else
    {
    pOptions = NULL;
    }

RpcStatus = ::RpcStringBindingCompose(
               NULL,
               lpszProtocol,
               lpszServer,
               lpszEndpoint,
               pOptions,
               &pStringBinding);

if (RpcStatus == RPC_S_OK)
    {
    RpcStatus = ::RpcBindingFromStringBinding(
                   pStringBinding,
                   &m_hBinding);
```

```
      if (RpcStatus == RPC_S_OK)
         {
         *pBinding = m_hBinding;

         RpcStatus = ::RpcBindingSetAuthInfo(
                         m_hBinding,
                         NULL,
                         dwAuthLevel,
                         RPC_C_AUTHN_WINNT,
                         NULL,
                         0);
         if (RpcStatus != RPC_S_OK)
            {
            TRACE(_T("\nRpcBindingSetAuthInfo() failed, status = %d"),
              RpcStatus);
            }
         }
      ::RpcStringFree(&pStringBinding);
      }

   ::SetLastError(RpcStatus);

   return (RpcStatus == RPC_S_OK);
}

BOOL CRpcClient::SetTimeout(UINT nTimeout /* =
                                RPC_C_BINDING_DEFAULT_TIMEOUT*/)
{
   RPC_STATUS RpcStatus;
   BOOL       bRetcode = FALSE;

   if (m_hBinding != NULL)
      {
      RpcStatus =
         ::RpcMgmtSetComTimeout(m_hBinding, nTimeout);
      bRetcode = (RpcStatus == RPC_S_OK);

      ::SetLastError(RpcStatus);
      }
   return bRetcode;
}

BOOL CRpcClient::Hangup()
{
   RPC_STATUS RpcStatus;
   BOOL       bRetcode = FALSE;

   if (m_hBinding != NULL)
```

```
        {
        RpcStatus = ::RpcBindingFree(&m_hBinding);

        bRetcode = (RpcStatus == RPC_S_OK);
        ::SetLastError(RpcStatus);
        }
    return bRetcode;
}

BOOL CRpcClient::NsLookup(void)
{
    RPC_STATUS RpcStatus;
    BOOL       bRetcode = FALSE;

    if (m_hNameServiceLookup == NULL)
        {
        RpcStatus = ::RpcNsBindingLookupBegin(
                        RPC_C_NS_SYNTAX_DEFAULT,
                        NULL,
                        m_hClient,
                        NULL,
                        0,
                        &m_hNameServiceLookup);
        }

    if (m_hNameServiceLookup != NULL)
        {
        if (m_pBindingVector != NULL)
            {
            ::RpcBindingVectorFree(&m_pBindingVector);
            }

        RpcStatus = ::RpcNsBindingLookupNext(
                        m_hNameServiceLookup,
                        &m_pBindingVector);

        if (m_pBindingVector == NULL) // No more
            {
            ::RpcNsBindingLookupDone(&m_hNameServiceLookup);
            }
        ::SetLastError(RpcStatus);
        bRetcode = (RpcStatus == RPC_S_OK);
        }
    return bRetcode;
}

BOOL CRpcClient::NsSelect(RPC_BINDING_HANDLE *pBinding)
```

```
{
   BOOL       bRetcode = FALSE;
   RPC_STATUS RpcStatus;

   if (m_pBindingVector == NULL)
      {
      NsLookup();
      }

   if (m_pBindingVector != NULL)
      {
      RpcStatus = ::RpcNsBindingSelect(
                        m_pBindingVector,
                        pBinding);
      bRetcode = (RpcStatus == RPC_S_OK);

      if (RpcStatus == RPC_S_NO_MORE_BINDINGS)
         {
         // Last binding has been selected
         ::RpcBindingVectorFree(&m_pBindingVector);
         }
      }

   ::SetLastError(RpcStatus);
   return bRetcode;
}

BOOL CRpcClient::NsImport(RPC_BINDING_HANDLE *pBinding)
{
   RPC_STATUS RpcStatus;
   BOOL       bRetcode = FALSE;

   if (m_hNameServiceImport == NULL)
      {
      RpcStatus = ::RpcNsBindingImportBegin(
                        RPC_C_NS_SYNTAX_DEFAULT,
                        NULL,
                        m_hClient,
                        NULL,
                        &m_hNameServiceImport);
      }

   if (m_hNameServiceImport != NULL)
      {
      RpcStatus = ::RpcNsBindingImportNext(
                        m_hNameServiceImport,
                        pBinding);
```

```
        if (RpcStatus == RPC_S_NO_MORE_BINDINGS) // No more
            {
            ::RpcNsBindingImportDone(&m_hNameServiceImport);
            }
        ::SetLastError(RpcStatus);
        bRetcode = (RpcStatus == RPC_S_OK);
        }
    return bRetcode;
}
```

OLE 2 Custom Interfaces

You can also use the Microsoft RPC tools to develop OLE custom interfaces. The Microsoft Interface Definition Language adds a few extensions to the standard OSF/DCE IDL, and generates a different set of files. The key piece that gets generated is a dynamic-link library, referred to in OLE 2 terminology as a **proxy stub DLL**. This contains code that knows how to marshal the arguments for your OLE methods. To emphasize: MIDL generates all the code in this DLL from the .IDL file.

There are some sample applications on both the Visual C++ 4.x and the Win32 SDK CD-ROMs. The one I have used in particular is in the directory SAMPLES\RPC\OBJECT\OHELLO, which presents an OLE custom interface for "Hello world."

As this book goes to press, I am working on several OLE hostings of my WNet API. Hopefully, by the time it reaches the bookstores, I will have finished them, and can at least include them on the source code disk.

Here is the .IDL file that defines my OLE custom interface, \WIN32NET\WNETOLE\CUSTOMIF\WNOLE.IDL on the source disk:

```
/********
*
* WNOLE.IDL
*
* Copyright (c) 1996 Ralph P. Davis
* All Rights Reserved
*
* Interface Definition Language specification
* for WNet OLE 2 custom interface
********/

[
   object,
   uuid(89f01f20-7f32-11cf-83da-08001708e951),
   version(1.0)
]
```

```
/* For an OLE custom interface, you have to specify
   that your interface is a subclass of the
   IUnknown interface.
*/
interface IWNOle : IUnknown
{
   import "unknwn.idl";  /* Defines OLE base types for MIDL */
   import "wtypes.idl";  /* Defines Win32 types for MIDL */

   HRESULT WNetInit([in]           BYTE   *lpReceiveCallback,
                    [in, string]  LPTSTR lpEndpoint,
                    [out]         DWORD *lphUser,
                    [in]          BOOL   bClientOnly,
                    [in]          BOOL   bUseDatagrams);
   HRESULT WNetIsWindowsNT(void);
   HRESULT WNetIsWindows95(void);
   HRESULT WNetListen([in] DWORD hUser);
   HRESULT WNetReceive([in]  DWORD   hConnection,
                       [in]  BYTE    *lpData,
                       [in]  DWORD   dwDataLength,
                       [out] LPDWORD lpdwBytesRead,
                       [in]  DWORD   dwTimeout);
   HRESULT WNetSend([in] DWORD hConnection,
                    [in] BYTE  *lpData,
                    [in] DWORD  dwDataLength,
                    [in] DWORD  dwTimeout);
   HRESULT WNetCall([in]          DWORD  hUser,
                    [in, string] LPTSTR lpTargetStation,
                    [in, string] LPTSTR lpEndpoint,
                    [out] DWORD* phConnection);
   HRESULT WNetHangup([in, out] DWORD* phConnection);
   HRESULT WNetShutdown([in, out] DWORD* phUser);
}
```

The *object* keyword in the header tells MIDL that you are generating an OLE 2 custom interface, rather than an RPC interface. In consequence, it will generate several files:

- A header file declaring your interface, named <*interface name*>.h (mine is WNOLE.H). This header is included in all the source files that use or implement your OLE custom interface.
- A C-language file that associates the UUID of the interface with a C global variable. The file name is <*interface name*>_i.c. This file lets you support requests for your interface in QueryInterface() calls, and is typically linked into both the client and server ends of the interface. Here are the pertinent lines from my generated file, WNOLE_I.C:

```
typedef struct _IID
{
    unsigned long x;
    unsigned short s1;
    unsigned short s2;
    unsigned char  c[8];
} IID;

const IID IID_IWNOle =
{0x89f01f20,0x7f32,0x11cf,
    {0x83,0xda,0x08,0x00,0x17,0x08,0xe9,0x51}
};
```

In the implementation of my interface, I have to provide a QueryInterface() that recognizes this interface ID:

```
HRESULT STDMETHODCALLTYPE
CWNetOLE::QueryInterface(REFIID riid, LPVOID *ppv )
{
   HRESULT hr;

   if (IsEqualGUID(riid, IID_IUnknown) ||
        IsEqualGUID(riid, IID_IWNOle))
       {
       *ppv = (IWNOle *) this;
       AddRef();
       hr = S_OK;
       }
   else
       {
       *ppv = 0;
       hr = E_NOINTERFACE;
       }

   return hr;
}
```

- A C-language file that provides the stub routines required for your interface to be properly marshalled across process boundaries. This file is named <*interface name*>_p.c.
- A C-language file that does the OLE 2 initializations required to plug your DLL into the OLE support modules, called DLLDATA.C.

You must provide an implementation of a class that converts your OLE interface (which is just an abstract base class) into a usable object. I call my class CWNetOLE; it is declared in the header file \WIN32NET\WIN32OLE \CUSTOMIF\WNOLECLS.H:

```
/********
*
* WNOLECLS.H
*
* Copyright (c) 1996 Ralph P. Davis
* All Rights Reserved
*
* Class declaration for CWNetOLE custom interface
*
********/

class CWNetOLE : public IWNOle
{
protected:
   DWORD m_dwRef;

public:
   CWNetOLE();
   virtual ~CWNetOLE();

   // IUnknown methods
   HRESULT STDMETHODCALLTYPE QueryInterface(REFIID riid,
                                            LPVOID *ppv);
   ULONG STDMETHODCALLTYPE AddRef();
   ULONG STDMETHODCALLTYPE Release();

   // IWNOle methods
   // They pass through to the WNet API
   HRESULT STDMETHODCALLTYPE WNetInit(
            BYTE *lpReceiveCallback,
            LPTSTR lpEndpoint,
            DWORD *lphUser,
            BOOL bClientOnly,
            BOOL bUseDatagrams);
   HRESULT STDMETHODCALLTYPE WNetIsWindowsNT(void);
   HRESULT STDMETHODCALLTYPE WNetIsWindows95(void);
   HRESULT STDMETHODCALLTYPE WNetListen(DWORD hUser);
   HRESULT STDMETHODCALLTYPE WNetReceive(
            DWORD hConnection,
            BYTE *lpData,
            DWORD dwDataLength,
            LPDWORD lpdwBytesRead,
            DWORD dwTimeout);
   HRESULT STDMETHODCALLTYPE WNetSend(
            DWORD hConnection,
            BYTE *lpData,
            DWORD dwDataLength,
            DWORD dwTimeout);
```

```
   HRESULT STDMETHODCALLTYPE WNetCall(
            DWORD hUser,
            LPTSTR lpTargetStation,
            LPTSTR lpEndpoint,
            DWORD *phConnection);
   HRESULT STDMETHODCALLTYPE WNetHangup(DWORD *phConnection);
   HRESULT STDMETHODCALLTYPE WNetShutdown(DWORD *phUser);

};
```

This class contains two sets of methods: the IUnknown methods (Query Interface(), AddRef(), and Release()) and the methods that call the WNet API. All of the latter methods are simple pass-throughs to the underlying function. CWNetOLE::WNetInit() is typical:

```
HRESULT STDMETHODCALLTYPE CWNetOLE::WNetInit(
     BYTE *lpReceiveCallback,
     LPTSTR lpEndpoint,
     DWORD *lphUser,
     BOOL bClientOnly,
     BOOL bUseDatagrams)
{
   BOOL bRetcode =
      ::WNetInit((RECEIVECALLBACK) lpReceiveCallback,
                 lpEndpoint,
                 (LPHANDLE) lphUser,
                 bClientOnly,
                 bUseDatagrams);
   return (bRetcode ? S_OK : E_FAIL);
}
```

The rest of the code that I have to provide is just the OLE glue: a class factory that knows how to create and destroy CWNetOLE objects, and a .REG file to add my interface to the Registry.

Win32 Services

I have called this section "Win32 Services" even though, strictly speaking, there is no such thing as a Windows 95 service. The functions and techniques I'm about to discuss apply only to NT. However, you can write applications so they run as a service under NT, and as a standard executable that emulates an NT service under Windows 95. You can also tell Windows 95 to start an application at boot time by making an entry in the Registry. A good way to get this flexibility is to hide the differences in C++ classes. I've created two classes that do this, called CWin32Service and CWin32ComponentService, and will present excerpts from them to illustrate the concepts I discuss. Please assume that everything I discuss here applies only to NT; where pertinent, I will show you the Windows 95 emulation.

Windows NT services are the equivalent of UNIX daemons. They are faceless background processes that can be loaded, paused, resumed, and unloaded at run time. You can also configure services so that the operating system loads them at boot time.

Services are console applications that must follow a small set of rules in order to fit into NT's Service Control Manager scheme. These rules enforce an exact structure on NT services, but the structure is simple. Indeed, services can be built from a template. What gives each service its individual personality are the worker threads you create.

The association between RPC and NT services is a natural one, though it is not compulsory. You can write RPC servers as standard executables, and you can write NT services that do not use RPC. An RPC-based NT service is a powerful vehicle, though, for several reasons:

- The location transparency of RPC allows a service to support client applications anywhere on a network using identical function-call syntax.
- Because services can be started automatically at boot time, you have reasonably high assurance that they will be available when needed.
- The NT Service Control Manager gives the user the flexibility to unload, pause, resume, and reload a service at run time. If this is undesirable, you can also write a service so that the user cannot unload it.

Much of NT's networking software is implemented as RPC services.

The main() Function in an NT Service

Like all console applications, an NT service is entered through its main() function. main() is very simple: all NT requires it to do is call StartServiceCtrlDispatcher(). This function takes an array of SERVICE_ TABLE_ ENTRY structures that define the entry points (referred to as the ServiceMain() function) for each of the logical services included in the executable. The last element in the array must be NULL.

```
typedef struct _SERVICE_TABLE_ENTRY
{
   LPTSTR lpszName;
   LPSERVICE_MAIN_FUNCTION lpServiceMain;
} SERVICE_TABLE_ENTRY;
```

```
BOOL StartServiceCtrlDispatcher(
   LPSERVICE_TABLE_ENTRY lpServiceTableEntries);
```

To emulate StartServiceCtrlDispatcher() in Windows 95, it helps to know what it does. For each service declared in the SERVICE_TABLE_ENTRY array, it creates a new thread and invokes its ServiceMain() function in this thread's context, passing it the *argc* and *argv* that were passed to main(). If successful, StartServiceCtrlDispatcher() does not return until the ServiceMain() function completes.

My CWin32Service class has a Start() method that calls StartServiceCtrlDispatcher() under NT, and emulates its functionality under Windows 95. From main(), I pass it the SERVICE_TABLE_ENTRY array, plus *argc* and *argv*. Here is its listing, from \WIN32NET\CODE\WIN32OBJ \WIN32SRV.CPP on the source disk, along with the thread it spins off under Windows 95 (Win95StartupThread()):

```
struct WIN95STARTUPINFO
{
   LPSERVICE_MAIN_FUNCTION  lpServiceMain;
   int                       argc;
   char                    **argv;
};

BOOL CWin32Service::Start(DWORD dwServices,
                          SERVICE_TABLE_ENTRY Services[],
                          int   argc,
                          char *argv[])
{
   BOOL bRetcode = FALSE;
   if (!m_bWindows95)
      {
      bRetcode = ::StartServiceCtrlDispatcher(Services);
      }
   else
      {
      // Spin off threads to call ServiceMain()
      // functions for each logical service
      WIN95STARTUPINFO *pStartupInfo =
         new WIN95STARTUPINFO[dwServices];
      HANDLE *phThreads = new HANDLE[dwServices];
      DWORD   dwThreadID;

      for (DWORD i = 0; i < dwServices; ++i)
         {
         pStartupInfo[i].lpServiceMain =
            Services[i].lpServiceProc;
```

```
            pStartupInfo[i].argc           = argc;
            pStartupInfo[i].argv           = argv;

            phThreads[i] =
               ::CreateThread(NULL, 0, Win95StartupThread,
               &pStartupInfo[i], 0, &dwThreadID);
            }
         // Sleep till all threads go away
         ::WaitForMultipleObjects(dwServices,
                                  phThreads,
                                  TRUE,
                                  INFINITE);
         delete [] pStartupInfo;
         delete [] phThreads;
         bRetcode = TRUE;
         }
   return bRetcode;
}

DWORD WINAPI CWin32Service::Win95StartupThread(LPVOID lp)
{
   WIN95STARTUPINFO *pStartupInfo =
      (WIN95STARTUPINFO *) lp;

   // Call service main function
   pStartupInfo->lpServiceMain(
                  pStartupInfo->argc,
                  pStartupInfo->argv);
   return 0;
}
```

Here is the main() function from the WNet RPC Server:

```
int main(int argc, char *argv[])
{
   SERVICE_TABLE_ENTRY WNetRPCService[] =
      {
       {TEXT("WNet RPC Server"), WNetRPCServiceMain},
       {NULL, NULL}
      };
   DWORD dwUserNameLength = sizeof (szUserName);

   GetUserName(szUserName, &dwUserNameLength);

   GetLocalTime(&StartupTime);

   // CWin32Service::Start() doesn't return until
   // the service terminates.
```

```
    CWin32Service ThisService;

    if (!ThisService.Start(1, WNetRPCService, argc, argv))
        {
        WNetStopRPCServer(GetLastError(),
            TEXT("CWin32Service::Start()"));
        }
    return (int) dwLastError;
}
```

The ServiceMain() Function

Each logical service in the executable has its own entry point, referred to as the ServiceMain() function.

```
VOID ServiceMain(
    DWORD   dwArgc,
    LPTSTR *lpszArgv);
```

You can name the function anything you want—you tell the Service Control Manager which function to call when you invoke StartServiceCtrlDispatcher(). ServiceMain() has several tasks to accomplish:

1. It registers an additional function (the service control-handling function), by calling RegisterServiceCtrlHandler(). This is the function that is called to pause, resume, or stop the service, or to ask it what its current state is.

   ```
   SERVICE_STATUS_HANDLE RegisterServiceCtrlHandler(
                             LPCTSTR lpszService,
                             LPHANDLER_FUNCTION lpHandler);
   ```

   The SERVICE_STATUS_HANDLE is an opaque type that you will use mostly to report your service's status.
2. It calls SetServiceStatus() to inform the Service Control Manager that it is starting up.

   ```
   BOOL SetServiceStatus(
           SERVICE_STATUS_HANDLE hServiceStatus,
           LPSERVICE_STATUS      lpServiceStatus);
   ```

   hServiceStatus was returned by RegisterServiceCtrlHandler(). *lpServiceStatus* points to a SERVICE_STATUS structure. Its fields are explained in the code listings.

3. It allocates any resources—memory, synchronization objects—that the service needs.
4. It starts the worker threads.
5. It calls SetServiceStatus() once again to notify the Service Control Manager that it is running and to let it know what control commands it will accept.
6. It goes to sleep waiting for the worker threads to complete.
7. It cleans up resources—frees memory, closes handles, and so on.
8. It tells the Service Control Manager that it has stopped.

Once again, there are a couple of things that Windows 95 doesn't support, but that we can emulate without too much difficulty:

- RegisterServiceCtrlHandler() has no meaning in Windows 95; there is no Services applet in its version of Control Panel. You cannot send control commands to a service application running under Windows 95. To emulate this, I install a Control-Break handler. This lets the user kill a service by selecting its console and hitting Ctrl-C or Ctrl-Break.
- There is no Service Control Manager to report your status to, so there is no point in calling SetServiceStatus().

Recall that the ServiceMain() function is called for every logical service contained in the process. Each one of them can have its own control handler. For this reason, I have implemented the registration function in a second class, CWin32ComponentService. My ServiceMain() function (WNetRPC-ServiceMain()) instantiates an object of this class to implement the steps listed above.

CWin32ComponentService::RegisterHandler() encapsulates the call to RegisterServiceCtrlHandler(). Under Windows 95, it calls SetConsoleCtrl-Handler() instead. This function declares an application-defined callback that will be invoked when the user presses Ctrl-C or Ctrl-Break.

```
BOOL CWin32ComponentService::RegisterHandler(
      LPCTSTR              lpszServiceName,
      LPHANDLER_FUNCTION   lpHandler)
{
   BOOL bRetcode;

   if (!CWin32Service::m_bWindows95)
      {
      m_hServiceStatus = ::RegisterServiceCtrlHandler(
                              lpszServiceName,
                              lpHandler);
      bRetcode = (m_hServiceStatus != NULL);
      }
```

```
    else
       {
       g_lpHandler      = lpHandler;
       m_hServiceStatus = NULL;
       ::SetConsoleCtrlHandler(Win95CtrlHandler, TRUE);
       bRetcode = TRUE;
       }
    return bRetcode;
}
```

Notice that the Windows 95 code stores the address of the real control-handling function in the static member variable *g_lpHandler.* The Ctrl-Break handler is invoked asynchronously, and runs in its own thread context. Therefore, the only way to get the address of the original handler function is in a global variable. We can't use Thread Local Storage; the control handler doesn't run in the same thread as ServiceMain(). We can't use a member variable; the control-handling function is called by the operating system, which knows nothing about C++ and the *this* pointer. The only place we can find the handler's address is in some kind of globally visible location.

CWin32ComponentService provides three methods that prepare the SERVICE_STATUS structure for passing to SetServiceStatus(). ReportStatusChange() is used when you go from one state to another, and does the most explicit initialization. SetPendingStatus() sets some fields using intelligent defaults, and frees the caller from having to pass this information. UpdateStatus() just updates the checkpoint field if the checkpoint is greater than zero. The checkpoint, and another field called the wait hint, are used when the service is in a transitional state (like starting up or stopping). The wait hint says how long you expect it will take to complete the transition. The checkpoint is used to reassure the Service Control Manager, which never wants to see the same non-zero checkpoint twice. If it does, it assumes that your service is stuck and throws you out.

Here are the listings for these three methods:

```
BOOL CWin32ComponentService::ReportStatusChange(
                  DWORD dwCurrentState,
                  DWORD dwControlsAccepted
                    /* =
                    SERVICE_ACCEPT_STOP |
                    SERVICE_ACCEPT_PAUSE_CONTINUE
                    SERVICE_ACCEPT_SHUTDOWN */,
                  DWORD dwWaitHint /*= 5000 */,
                  DWORD dwWin32ExitCode
                     /*= NO_ERROR */,
```

```
                DWORD dwProcessSpecificExitCode
                   /*= 0 */)
{
   // The dwCurrentState field reports our current status
   // Possible values are:
   //    SERVICE_START_PENDING--initializing
   //    SERVICE_RUNNING--in service
   //    SERVICE_PAUSE_PENDING--service entering the paused state
   //    SERVICE_PAUSED--service has successfully
   //                entered the paused state
   //    SERVICE_CONTINUE_PENDING--service is returning from
   //                           paused state to running
   //    SERVICE_STOP_PENDING--shutting down
   //    SERVICE_STOPPED--out of service

   m_ServiceStatus.dwCurrentState    = dwCurrentState;

   // The dwControlsAccepted field indicates
   // what control commands (pause, resume, stop) we're willing to
   // accept
   m_ServiceStatus.dwControlsAccepted = dwControlsAccepted;

   // The dwWin32ExitCode and dwServiceSpecificExitCode fields are
   // used to report errors that occur during startup and shutdown
   // If the error is defined by Win32 [like a GetLastError() code
   // or an RPC error], you use dwWin32ExitCode
   // If the error is application-defined, you set dwWin32ExitCode
   // to ERROR_SERVICE_SPECIFIC_ERROR, and put your error code
   // in dwServiceSpecificExitCode

   m_ServiceStatus.dwWin32ExitCode    = dwWin32ExitCode;
   m_ServiceStatus.dwServiceSpecificExitCode =
      dwProcessSpecificExitCode;

   switch (dwCurrentState)
      {
      case SERVICE_START_PENDING:
      case SERVICE_STOP_PENDING:
      case SERVICE_PAUSE_PENDING:
      case SERVICE_CONTINUE_PENDING:
         // The dwCheckPoint and dwWaitHint fields are used
         // to periodically reassure the Service Control Manager
         // while you are in one of the pending states
         // dwWaitHint is the number of milliseconds you
         // expect the operation to take. After that much time,
         // the Service Control Manager will ask you how you're
         // doing. If it does not receive an updated
```

```
            // dwCheckPoint by then,
            // it assumes you've failed and gives up.
            m_ServiceStatus.dwCheckPoint = 1;
            m_ServiceStatus.dwWaitHint   = dwWaitHint;
            break;
         default:
            m_ServiceStatus.dwCheckPoint = 0;
            m_ServiceStatus.dwWaitHint   = 0;
            break;
         }

   BOOL bRetcode = SetStatus();
   return bRetcode;
}

BOOL CWin32ComponentService::SetPendingStatus(
                         DWORD dwCurrentState,
                         DWORD dwWaitHint   /*= 5000 */,
                         DWORD dwCheckPoint /*= 1*/)
{
   m_ServiceStatus.dwCurrentState             = dwCurrentState;


   // We set dwControlsAccepted to zero to disable
   // control requests while in a transitional state

   m_ServiceStatus.dwControlsAccepted         = 0;

   m_ServiceStatus.dwWin32ExitCode            = 0;
   m_ServiceStatus.dwServiceSpecificExitCode = 0;

   m_ServiceStatus.dwWaitHint   = dwWaitHint;
   m_ServiceStatus.dwCheckPoint = dwCheckPoint;

   BOOL bRetcode = SetStatus();
   return bRetcode;
}

BOOL CWin32ComponentService::UpdateStatus(void)
{
   if (m_ServiceStatus.dwCheckPoint > 0)
      {
      ++m_ServiceStatus.dwCheckPoint;
      }

   BOOL bRetcode = SetStatus();
   return bRetcode;
}
```

The SetServiceStatus() function reports our status under Windows NT. Because there is no Service Control Manager under Windows 95, CWin32ComponentService provides a SetStatus() method. Under NT, it calls SetServiceStatus(); under Windows 95, it does nothing.

```
BOOL CWin32ComponentService::SetStatus(void)
{
   BOOL bRetcode;

   if (!CWin32Service::m_bWindows95)
      {
      bRetcode = ::SetServiceStatus(m_hServiceStatus,
                                    &m_ServiceStatus);
      }
   else
      {
      // In Windows 95, we'll just keep track of our status,
      // but there's nobody to report it to.
      bRetcode = TRUE;
      }
   return bRetcode;
}
```

Now that we've looked at the building blocks, let's see the listing for WNetRPCServiceMain():

```
CWin32ComponentService ThisComponent;

VOID WINAPI WNetRPCServiceMain(DWORD dwArgc, LPTSTR *lpArgv)
{
   UNREFERENCED_PARAMETER(dwArgc);
   UNREFERENCED_PARAMETER(lpArgv);
   LPTSTR lpFailedFunction;
   BOOL   bAbnormalTermination = FALSE;

   try
      {
      // Step 1. Register the control handler
      if (!ThisComponent.RegisterHandler(
             TEXT("WNet RPC Server"),
             WNetRPCServiceCtrlHandler))
         {
         lpFailedFunction =
            TEXT("CWin32ComponentService::RegisterHandler()");
         // Throw a dummy exception as a signal to ourselves
         // that we failed
         throw "";
         }
```

```
// Step 2. Tell the Service Control Manager
// that we're starting up by reporting
// status as SERVICE_START_PENDING
if (!ThisComponent.ReportStatusChange(
      SERVICE_START_PENDING,
      0))
   {
   lpFailedFunction = TEXT("SetServiceStatus()");
   throw "";
   }

// Step 3. No other resources needed

// Step 4. Spin off RPC worker threads (only one here)
// Our worker thread is the WNetStartRPCServer function
// that does our RPC initialization
for (short int i = 0; i < nNumThreads; ++i)
   {
   hThreads[i] = ::CreateThread(NULL, 0,
      WNetStartRPCServer, NULL,
      0, &dwThreadID[i]);
   if (hThreads[i] == NULL)
      {
      lpFailedFunction =
         TEXT("CreateThread()");
      throw "";
      }
   }

// Step 5. Tell NT that we're up and running
// We'll accept stop and
// system shutdown control commands.
// Pause and continue don't make sense, because
// the only thing we can do is
// shut down our RPC server startup thread [WNetStartRPCServer()].
// It's already asleep anyhow, blocked on the call
// to RpcServerListen()
// We have no control over the RPC background threads.
if (!ThisComponent.ReportStatusChange(
      SERVICE_RUNNING,
      SERVICE_ACCEPT_STOP | SERVICE_ACCEPT_SHUTDOWN,
      0))
   {
   lpFailedFunction = TEXT("SetServiceStatus()");
   throw "";
   }
```

```
        // Step 6. Block until the server is shutdown by a STOP control
        // (or system shutdown)

        // Wait until all worker threads complete
        ::WaitForMultipleObjects(nNumThreads, hThreads,
            TRUE, INFINITE);
        }
    catch (...)
        {
        bAbnormalTermination = TRUE;
        }

    // We're done--do cleanup
    // Service was already stopped in response to
    // the control command (unless we had a problem
    // during initialization)

    // Step 7. Clean up resources

    // bAbnormalTermination indicates that something in our
    // initialization failed. Write a message to the event log
    if (bAbnormalTermination)
        WNetStopRPCServer(::GetLastError(),
            lpFailedFunction);

    // Close the thread handles
    for (short int i = 0; i < nNumThreads; ++i)
        {
        if (hThreads[i] != NULL)
            {
            ::CloseHandle(hThreads[i]);
            hThreads[i] = NULL;
            }
        }

    // Step 8. Tell Service Control Manager that we're
    // done.
    ThisComponent.ReportStatusChange(
        SERVICE_STOPPED,
        0,
        0,
        dwLastError);

    return;
}
```

The Service Control-Handling Function

The service control-handling function receives control commands from the Service Control Manager (or from any application that makes the appropriate API calls). The commands SERVICE_CONTROL_PAUSE and SERVICE_CONTROL_CONTINUE tell the service to suspend and resume its operations. They can often be implemented by calling SuspendThread() and ResumeThread() with the handles of the worker threads. SERVICE_CONTROL_INTERROGATE asks the service to report its current status. The control command SERVICE_CONTROL_SHUTDOWN indicates that the operating system is shutting down. SERVICE_CONTROL_STOP instructs the service to bring itself out of service. This normally involves at least these steps:

1. Calling SetServiceStatus() to notify the Service Control Manager that you are shutting down.
2. Doing application-specific cleanup.
3. Calling SetServiceStatus() once more to tell the Service Control Manager that you are out of service.

No matter what control command it receives, the control handler is required to report its current status when it exits.

The service control handler for the WNet RPC Server is WNetRPCServiceCtrlHandler(). It responds to SERVICE_CONTROL_STOP and SERVICE_CONTROL_SHUTDOWN commands. SERVICE_CONTROL_PAUSE and SERVICE_CONTROL_RESUME are probably irrelevant here because the only worker thread is already asleep, blocked on its call to RpcServerListen(). Incoming RPCs are being serviced by threads that the RPC runtime layer has created. You have no idea what their handles are, and no control over them.

WNetRPCServiceCtrlHandler() reports our status by invoking the ReportStatusChange() and UpdateStatus() methods on a CWin32ComponentService object, stored in the global variable *ThisComponent*. As I discussed above, I have to use a global variable. This function runs in its own thread context, and has no other way of retrieving the CWin32ComponentService object with which it is associated.

```
VOID WINAPI WNetRPCServiceCtrlHandler(DWORD dwCommand)
{
   switch (dwCommand)
      {
      case SERVICE_CONTROL_STOP:
      case SERVICE_CONTROL_SHUTDOWN:
```

```
            // Tell Service Control Manager that we're coming down
            ThisComponent.ReportStatusChange(
               SERVICE_STOP_PENDING,
               0,
               3000);
            WNetStopRPCServer(0, NULL);
            break;
         }
   ThisComponent.UpdateStatus();
   return;
}
```

Under Windows 95, the operating system does not call the control-handler function. Instead, the Ctrl-Break handler I installed earlier gets activated. It in turn delegates to the control handler, pretending that the user has issued a STOP command (represented by the constant SERVICE_CONTROL_STOP). I implement this function as a static member of CWin32ComponentService.

```
BOOL WINAPI CWin32ComponentService::Win95CtrlHandler(
   DWORD dwControlType)
{
   g_lpHandler(SERVICE_CONTROL_STOP);
   return TRUE;
}
```

The return value of TRUE tells Windows 95 that you have accepted the command.

Code Listings

The complete listings of \WIN32NET\CODE\WIN32OBJ\WIN32SRV.H and \WIN32NET\CODE\WIN32OBJ\WIN32SRV.CPP follow.

```
/********
*
* WIN32SRV.H
*
* Copyright (c) 1996 Ralph P. Davis
*
* All Rights Reserved
*
*****/

#ifndef WIN32SRV_INCLUDED
#define WIN32SRV_INCLUDED
```

```
#include "tls.h"

struct WIN95STARTUPINFO
{
   LPSERVICE_MAIN_FUNCTION  lpServiceMain;
   int                      argc;
   char                   **argv;
};

class AFX_EXT_CLASS CWin32Service : public CObject
{
public:
   static BOOL     m_bWindows95;

   Start(DWORD dwServices,
         SERVICE_TABLE_ENTRY Services[],
         int argc, char *argv[]);
   static DWORD WINAPI Win95StartupThread(LPVOID lp);

   DECLARE_DYNAMIC(CWin32Service)
};

class AFX_EXT_CLASS CWin32ComponentService : public CObject
{
protected:
   SERVICE_STATUS_HANDLE m_hServiceStatus;
   SERVICE_STATUS        m_ServiceStatus;
public:
   static LPHANDLER_FUNCTION g_lpHandler;
   CWin32ComponentService(DWORD dwServiceType =
                          SERVICE_WIN32_OWN_PROCESS);

   BOOL RegisterHandler(LPCTSTR            lpszServiceName,
                        LPHANDLER_FUNCTION lpHandler);

   static BOOL WINAPI Win95CtrlHandler(DWORD dwControlType);
   BOOL ReportStatusChange(
                  DWORD dwCurrentState,
                  DWORD dwControlsAccepted =
                    SERVICE_ACCEPT_STOP |
                    SERVICE_ACCEPT_PAUSE_CONTINUE |
                    SERVICE_ACCEPT_SHUTDOWN,
                  DWORD dwWaitHint      = 5000,
                  DWORD dwWin32ExitCode = NO_ERROR,
                  DWORD dwProcessSpecificExitCode = 0);
   BOOL SetPendingStatus(DWORD dwCurrentState,
                         DWORD dwWaitHint = 5000,
                         DWORD dwCheckPoint = 1);
```

```
   BOOL UpdateStatus(void);
   BOOL SetStatus(void);

   DECLARE_DYNAMIC(CWin32ComponentService)
};
#endif


/********
*
* WIN32SRV.CPP
*
* Copyright (c) 1996 Ralph P. Davis
*
* All Rights Reserved
*
*****/

#include "stdafx.h"
#include "win32obj.h"
#include "win32srv.h"

IMPLEMENT_DYNAMIC(CWin32Service, CObject)
IMPLEMENT_DYNAMIC(CWin32ComponentService, CObject)

LPHANDLER_FUNCTION CWin32ComponentService::g_lpHandler;

BOOL CWin32Service::m_bWindows95 =
   CWin32Object::IsWindows95();

BOOL CWin32Service::Start(DWORD dwServices,
                          SERVICE_TABLE_ENTRY Services[],
                          int   argc,
                          char *argv[])
{
   BOOL bRetcode = FALSE;
   if (!m_bWindows95)
      {
      bRetcode = ::StartServiceCtrlDispatcher(Services);
      }
   else
      {
      // Spin off threads to call ServiceMain()
      // functions for each logical service
      WIN95STARTUPINFO *pStartupInfo =
         new WIN95STARTUPINFO[dwServices];
      HANDLE *phThreads = new HANDLE[dwServices];
      DWORD   dwThreadID;
```

```
      for (DWORD i = 0; i < dwServices; ++i)
         {
         pStartupInfo[i].lpServiceMain =
            Services[i].lpServiceProc;
         pStartupInfo[i].argc          = argc;
         pStartupInfo[i].argv          = argv;

         phThreads[i] =
            ::CreateThread(NULL, 0, Win95StartupThread,
            &pStartupInfo[i], 0, &dwThreadID);
         }
      // Sleep till all threads go away
      ::WaitForMultipleObjects(dwServices,
                               phThreads,
                               TRUE,
                               INFINITE);
      delete [] pStartupInfo;
      delete [] phThreads;
      bRetcode = TRUE;
      }
   return bRetcode;
}

DWORD WINAPI CWin32Service::Win95StartupThread(LPVOID lp)
{
   WIN95STARTUPINFO *pStartupInfo =
      (WIN95STARTUPINFO *) lp;

   // Call service main function
   pStartupInfo->lpServiceMain(
                    pStartupInfo->argc,
                    pStartupInfo->argv);
   return 0;
}

CWin32ComponentService::CWin32ComponentService(
    DWORD dwServiceType /*= SERVICE_WIN32_OWN_PROCESS */)
{
   g_lpHandler      = NULL;
   m_hServiceStatus = NULL;
   ::ZeroMemory(&m_ServiceStatus, sizeof (SERVICE_STATUS));

   // A dwService type of SERVICE_WIN32_OWN_PROCESS
   // means that only one service is defined
   // as part of this process
   //
   // Other possibilities are:
   //   SERVICE_WIN32_SHARE_PROCESS
```

```
   //       Multiple logical services are sharing this process
   //    SERVICE_WIN32_KERNEL_DRIVER
   //       The service is a device driver
   //    SERVICE_WIN32_FILE_SYSTEM_DRIVER
   //       The service is a file-system driver
   //    SERVICE_INTERACTIVE_PROCESS
   //       The service wants to interact with the user
   //       (combined with one of the other flags)
   m_ServiceStatus.dwServiceType = dwServiceType;
}

BOOL CWin32ComponentService::RegisterHandler(
      LPCTSTR             lpszServiceName,
      LPHANDLER_FUNCTION  lpHandler)
{
   BOOL bRetcode;

   if (!CWin32Service::m_bWindows95)
      {
      m_hServiceStatus = ::RegisterServiceCtrlHandler(
                              lpszServiceName,
                              lpHandler);
      bRetcode = (m_hServiceStatus != NULL);
      }
   else
      {
      g_lpHandler      = lpHandler;
      m_hServiceStatus = NULL;
      ::SetConsoleCtrlHandler(Win95CtrlHandler, TRUE);
      bRetcode = TRUE;
      }
   return bRetcode;
}

BOOL WINAPI CWin32ComponentService::Win95CtrlHandler(
   DWORD dwControlType)
{
   g_lpHandler(SERVICE_CONTROL_STOP);
   return TRUE;
}

BOOL CWin32ComponentService::ReportStatusChange(
                  DWORD dwCurrentState,
                  DWORD dwControlsAccepted
                    /* =
                    SERVICE_ACCEPT_STOP |
                    SERVICE_ACCEPT_PAUSE_CONTINUE
                    SERVICE_ACCEPT_SHUTDOWN */,
```

```
                DWORD dwWaitHint /*= 5000 */,
                DWORD dwWin32ExitCode
                   /*= NO_ERROR */,
                DWORD dwProcessSpecificExitCode
                   /*= 0 */)
{
   // The dwCurrentState field reports our current status
   // Possible values are:
   //    SERVICE_START_PENDING--initializing
   //    SERVICE_RUNNING--in service
   //    SERVICE_PAUSE_PENDING--service entering the paused state
   //    SERVICE_PAUSED--service has successfully
   //                entered the paused state
   //    SERVICE_CONTINUE_PENDING--service is returning from
   //                         paused state to running
   //    SERVICE_STOP_PENDING--shutting down
   //    SERVICE_STOPPED--out of service

   m_ServiceStatus.dwCurrentState    = dwCurrentState;

   // The dwControlsAccepted field indicates
   // what control commands (pause, resume, stop) we're willing to
   // accept
   m_ServiceStatus.dwControlsAccepted = dwControlsAccepted;

   // The dwWin32ExitCode and dwServiceSpecificExitCode fields are
   // used to report errors that occur during startup and shutdown
   // If the error is defined by Win32 [like a GetLastError() code
   // or an RPC error], you use dwWin32ExitCode
   // If the error is application-defined, you set dwWin32ExitCode
   // to ERROR_SERVICE_SPECIFIC_ERROR, and put your error code
   // in dwServiceSpecificExitCode

   m_ServiceStatus.dwWin32ExitCode   = dwWin32ExitCode;
   m_ServiceStatus.dwServiceSpecificExitCode =
      dwProcessSpecificExitCode;

   switch (dwCurrentState)
      {
      case SERVICE_START_PENDING:
      case SERVICE_STOP_PENDING:
      case SERVICE_PAUSE_PENDING:
      case SERVICE_CONTINUE_PENDING:
         // The dwCheckPoint and dwWaitHint fields are used
         // to periodically reassure the Service Control Manager
         // while you are in one of the pending states
         // dwWaitHint is the number of milliseconds you
         // expect the operation to take. After that much time,
         // the Service Control Manager will ask you how you're
```

```
            // doing. If it does not receive an updated
            // dwCheckPoint by then,
            // it assumes you've failed and gives up.
            m_ServiceStatus.dwCheckPoint = 1;
            m_ServiceStatus.dwWaitHint   = dwWaitHint;
            break;
        default:
            m_ServiceStatus.dwCheckPoint = 0;
            m_ServiceStatus.dwWaitHint   = 0;
            break;
        }

    BOOL bRetcode = SetStatus();
    return bRetcode;
}

BOOL CWin32ComponentService::SetPendingStatus(
                            DWORD dwCurrentState,
                            DWORD dwWaitHint   /*= 5000 */,
                            DWORD dwCheckPoint /*= 1*/)
{
    m_ServiceStatus.dwCurrentState              = dwCurrentState;

    // We set dwControlsAccepted to zero to disable
    // control requests while in a transitional state

    m_ServiceStatus.dwControlsAccepted          = 0;

    m_ServiceStatus.dwWin32ExitCode             = 0;
    m_ServiceStatus.dwServiceSpecificExitCode = 0;

    m_ServiceStatus.dwWaitHint   = dwWaitHint;
    m_ServiceStatus.dwCheckPoint = dwCheckPoint;

    BOOL bRetcode = SetStatus();
    return bRetcode;
}

BOOL CWin32ComponentService::UpdateStatus(void)
{
    if (m_ServiceStatus.dwCheckPoint > 0)
        {
        ++m_ServiceStatus.dwCheckPoint;
        }

    BOOL bRetcode = SetStatus();
    return bRetcode;
}
```

```
BOOL CWin32ComponentService::SetStatus(void)
{
   BOOL bRetcode;

   if (!CWin32Service::m_bWindows95)
      {
      bRetcode = ::SetServiceStatus(m_hServiceStatus,
                                    &m_ServiceStatus);
      }
   else
      {
      // In Windows 95, we'll just keep track of our status,
      // but there's nobody to report it to.
      bRetcode = TRUE;
      }
   return bRetcode;
}
```

Additional Service-Related Functions

Windows NT also provides a set of functions for service management. They can be used to control services across a network, as well as locally. The REGINST program that I present in Chapter 14 uses almost all of them to install the WNet RPC Server. The actual installation is accomplished by a call to CreateService(), but it will fail if the server already exists. I detect its existence by calling OpenService() to get a handle to it (typed as an SC_HANDLE). If OpenService() returns a non-NULL value, I have to delete the service by calling DeleteService(). However, in order to do this, I have to make sure it isn't currently running; if it is, I have to shut it down. To find out if it's running, I use the ControlService() function to send it a SERVICE_CONTROL_STOP command. If it succeeds, I know the service is currently running, but I have to wait for it to go completely offline. I do this by calling QueryServiceStatus() in a loop until the service reports its status as SERVICE_STOPPED. Finally, after creating the service, I complete the cycle by starting it up, using the function StartService(). Here are the appropriate lines of code.

```
SC_HANDLE hService, hServiceControlManager;
TCHAR     szServiceExecutable[MAX_PATH + 1];

// Install the WNet RPC Server in the Service Control
// Manager's database

hServiceControlManager = OpenSCManager(
```

```
                                NULL, // Local machine
                                TEXT("ServicesActive"),
                                SC_MANAGER_ALL_ACCESS);
if (hServiceControlManager != NULL)
   {
   // First, try to open service
   // If it already exists, we'll stop it,
   // then delete it.
   hService = OpenService(hServiceControlManager,
                          TEXT("WNet RPC Server"),
                          SERVICE_ALL_ACCESS);
   if (hService != NULL)
      {
      SERVICE_STATUS ServiceStatus;
      DWORD          dwCheckPoint = 0xFFFFFFFF;
      DWORD          dwStartTime = GetCurrentTime();

      // Stop it by sending it a STOP command
      if (ControlService(hService, SERVICE_CONTROL_STOP,
                         &ServiceStatus))
         {
         while ((ServiceStatus.dwCurrentState != SERVICE_STOPPED) &&
                 ((GetCurrentTime() - dwStartTime) < 10000))
            {
            if (dwCheckPoint == ServiceStatus.dwCheckPoint)
               // Give up--check point hasn't been incremented
               break;
            dwCheckPoint = ServiceStatus.dwCheckPoint;
            Sleep(ServiceStatus.dwWaitHint);
            QueryServiceStatus(hService, &ServiceStatus);
            }
         if (ServiceStatus.dwCurrentState == SERVICE_STOPPED)
            DeleteService(hService);
         }
      else
         DeleteService(hService);
      CloseServiceHandle(hService);
      }

   hService = CreateService(
                 hServiceControlManager,
                 TEXT("WNet RPC Server"),
                 TEXT("WNet RPC Server"),
                 SERVICE_ALL_ACCESS,
                 SERVICE_WIN32_OWN_PROCESS,
                 SERVICE_AUTO_START,
                 SERVICE_ERROR_NORMAL,
                 szServiceExecutable,
```

```
                    NULL,
                    NULL,
                    NULL,
                    NULL,
                    NULL);
    if (hService != NULL)
        {
        // Start it running
        StartService(hService, 0, NULL);
        CloseServiceHandle(hService);
        printf("\nWNet RPC Server successfully installed\n");
        printf(szServiceExecutable);
        printf("\n");
        }
    else
        {
        printf("\nUnable to install WNet RPC Server, "
                 "GetLastError() = %d\n",
            GetLastError());
        }
    CloseServiceHandle(hServiceControlManager);
    }
else
    {
    printf("\nUnable to access Service Control Manager, "
             "GetLastError() = %d\n",
        GetLastError());
    }
```

Installing a Service under Windows 95

The service-installation functions do not work under Windows 95. It doesn't hurt anything to call them; they just fail. To configure an application for automatic loading at boot time, you add it to the Windows 95 Registry under the key HKEY_LOCAL_MACHINE\SOFTWARE\Microsoft\Windows \CurrentVersion\RunServices. For your service, add a string value whose name is whatever name you want to assign, and whose data is the command string needed to run the application. Figures 11-1 and 11-2 show the Registry Editor screens that display when I add the WNet RPC Server.

The REGINST application includes the function calls that automate this procedure. Because they are discussed in Chapter 14, I don't show the code here.

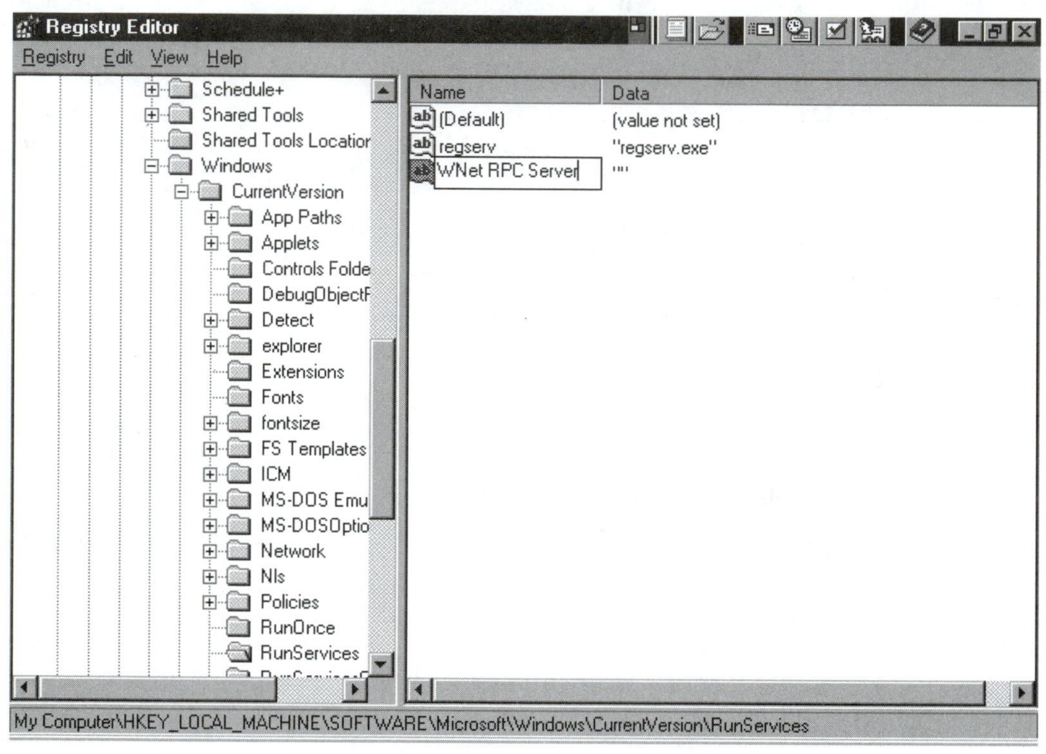

Figure 11-1. Installing a Service in the Windows 95 Registry—Adding the Value

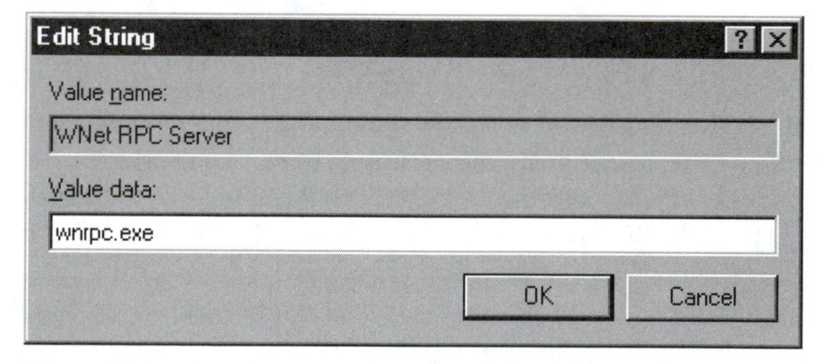

Figure 11-2. Installing a Service in the Windows 95 Registry—Entering the Service Name

Event Logging

Services have no front end. Thus, they cannot display messages, either by calling printf(), as console applications normally can, or with MessageBox(). (Actually, they do have limited access to MessageBox(). See the *Microsoft Knowledge Base for Win32 SDK* article "Access to Display from Win32 Services.") If a service wants to report some condition, its best option is to record an event in the event log. The administrator can then view the information with the Event Viewer. This functionality is only available under Windows NT. I have not taken any heroic measures to emulate it under Windows 95. The function calls I'm about to discuss just fail there; they don't cause any serious problems.

There are three functions you need to call to log an event. RegisterEventSource() obtains a handle to the log file, ReportEvent() deposits a record in the log, and DeregisterEventSource() closes the handle and terminates the log file interaction. If you have message files that are private to your application, you can add an entry to the Registry, telling NT where to find them. The Registry key that stores this information is HKEY_LOCAL_MACHINE\SYSTEM\CurrentControlSet\Services\EventLog\Application. Under this key, you add one naming your service. (See Chapter 14 for details.)

You can use the event log even if you do not register your application. However, doing so allows you to use multilanguage message files, as discussed in Chapter 6. This is the strategy that the WNet RPC Server uses. It has only a single message in the message file (\WIN32NET\CODE\WNETMSGS.MC). Here is the header portion of the file and the definition of the message. As you saw in Chapter 6, this file is processed by the Win32 Message Compiler and eventually produces the DLL WNETMSGS.DLL.

```
;/********
;*
;* WNETMSGS.MC
;*
;*********/

SeverityNames=(Success=0x0:STATUS_SEVERITY_SUCCESS
               Informational=0x1:STATUS_SEVERITY_INFORMATIONAL
               Warning=0x2:STATUS_SEVERITY_WARNING
               Error=0x3:STATUS_SEVERITY_ERROR
              )

LanguageNames=(English=0x0009:MSG00001
              French=0x000c:MSG00002
              Spanish=0x000a:MSG00003
              )
```

```
MessageID=
Severity=Error
SymbolicName=MSG_RPC_SERVER_FAILED
Language=English
%1!s! failed. %2!s!
.
Language=French
%1!s! a manqué. %2!s!
.
Language=Spanish
%1!s! fracasó. %2!s!
.
```

The message has two insertion sequences, designated by *%1!s!* and *%2!s!*. These codes say "Substitute the first and second insertion sequences that I pass you, and expect null-terminated strings." The WNet RPC Server calls its own routine WNetReportEvent() when it encounters a problem. The problem may be merely a warning, or it can be an error that is sufficiently serious to warrant closing the service. The first insertion string is passed to WNetReportEvent() and indicates the function that failed. The second one is built by calling FormatMessage() with the error code represented by the *dwErrorCode* argument. Here is the code for WNetReportEvent():

```
VOID WNetReportEvent(DWORD dwErrorCode, LPTSTR lpszErrorMsg,
                    BOOL bError)
{
   // Services don't have a user interface, so the
   // only way for them to report error conditions
   // is to use the event-logging facility
   // that NT provides.

   // To do this, you call RegisterEventSource() to
   // get a handle, then call ReportEvent() to
   // log the error

   // Finally, you call DeregisterEventSource() to
   // release the handle
   HANDLE hSource;
   TCHAR szLastErrorMsg[1024];
   LPTSTR lpszMessageStrings[2];

   // Look up message string for system error.
   FormatMessage(FORMAT_MESSAGE_FROM_SYSTEM,
                 NULL,
                 dwErrorCode,
```

```
                LANG_USER_DEFAULT,
                szLastErrorMsg,
                sizeof (szLastErrorMsg),
                NULL);

    // RegisterEventSource() takes two arguments--the machine name
    // (NULL means the local machine)
    // and the name of the application logging the event
    hSource = RegisterEventSource(NULL, TEXT("WNet RPC Server"));

    if (hSource != NULL)
        {
        // The lpszMessageStrings array that we pass
        // to ReportEvent() has the insertion sequences
        // for our message.
        lpszMessageStrings[0] = lpszErrorMsg;
        lpszMessageStrings[1] = szLastErrorMsg;

        ReportEvent(hSource,
              bError ? EVENTLOG_ERROR_TYPE :   // Level of severity
                       EVENTLOG_WARNING_TYPE,
              0,                               // Category--we're not
                                               //   using it
              MSG_RPC_SERVER_FAILED,           // Message identifier
              NULL,                            // User security ID (SID)--
                                               //   not using it
              2,                               // Number of insertion
                                               //   strings in
                                               //   lpszMessageStrings
                                               //   array
              0,                               // Number of bytes of
                                               //   binary data to include
              (LPCTSTR *) lpszMessageStrings,  // Messages to log
              NULL);                           // Binary data to log--
                                               //   we're not using any

        DeregisterEventSource(hSource);
        }
}
```

Because I have added information about the WNet RPC Server to the Registry—specifically, which DLL contains its messages—I can pass my own error code to ReportEvent(), and it maps them to the correct message. Figure 11-3 shows how Event Viewer reports an error that I purposely triggered, by registering the OSF RPC protocol sequence "ncadg_ip_udp", representing the User Datagram Protocol (UDP), before NT officially supported it.

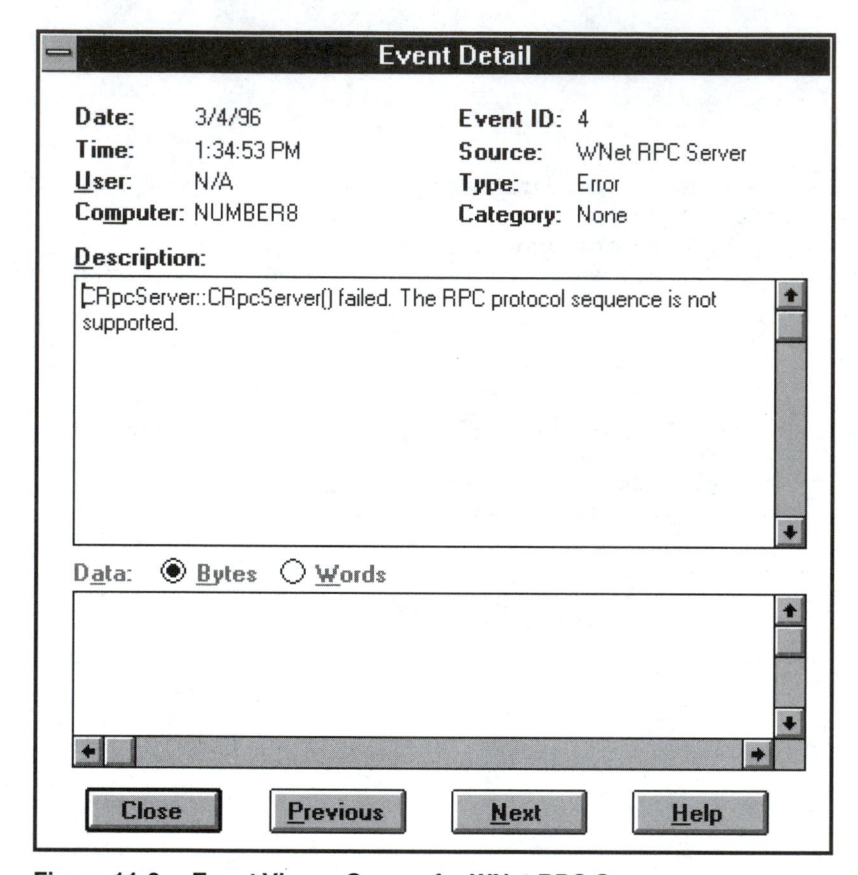

Figure 11-3. Event Viewer Screen for WNet RPC Server

Additional Code Listing

Now that we have covered all the techniques for implementing an RPC server application as a Windows NT service, I present the complete listing of WNRPC.CPP. Notice the remote procedure calls themselves, one of which (_RpcWinExec()) uses client impersonation.

```
/********
*
* WNRPC.CPP
*
* This program demonstrates an RPC server application
* implemented as a Windows NT service.
*
********/
```

```
/*===== Includes =====*/

#include "stdafx.h"
#include "rpcclass.h"
#include "win32obj.h"
#include "win32srv.h"
#include "mailslot.h"
#include "tls.h"

#include "wnrpc.h"

#include "wnetmsgs.h"    // Messages generated by message compiler
#include <stdio.h>


/*===== Global Variables =====*/

TCHAR           szUserName[100];
DWORD           dwLastError = NO_ERROR;
TCHAR           szNsEntryName[256];
SYSTEMTIME      StartupTime;
const short     nNumThreads = 1;
HANDLE          hThreads[nNumThreads];
DWORD           dwThreadID[nNumThreads]  = {0};
CRpcServer     *pWNetRpcServer;


/*===== FORWARD Functions =====*/

extern "C"
VOID  WINAPI WNetRPCServiceMain(DWORD dwArgc, LPTSTR *lpArgv);

extern "C"
VOID  WINAPI WNetRPCServiceCtrlHandler(DWORD dwCommand);

extern "C"
DWORD WINAPI WNetStartRPCServer(LPVOID lpv);

extern "C"
VOID  WNetStopRPCServer(DWORD dwErrorCode, LPTSTR lpszErrorMsg);

extern "C"
VOID  WNetReportEvent(DWORD dwErrorCode, LPTSTR lpszErrorMsg, BOOL
bError);
```

```
/*===== Function Definitions =====*/

extern "C"
int main(int argc, char *argv[])
{
   SERVICE_TABLE_ENTRY WNetRPCService[] =
      {
       {TEXT("WNet RPC Server"), WNetRPCServiceMain},
       {NULL, NULL}
      };
   DWORD dwUserNameLength = sizeof (szUserName);

   GetUserName(szUserName, &dwUserNameLength);

   GetLocalTime(&StartupTime);

   // CWin32Service::Start() doesn't return until
   // the service terminates.

   CWin32Service ThisService;

   if (!ThisService.Start(1, WNetRPCService, argc, argv))
      {
      WNetStopRPCServer(GetLastError(),
         TEXT("CWin32Service::Start()"));
      }
   return (int) dwLastError;
}

CWin32ComponentService ThisComponent;

extern "C"
VOID WINAPI WNetRPCServiceMain(DWORD dwArgc, LPTSTR *lpArgv)
{
   UNREFERENCED_PARAMETER(dwArgc);
   UNREFERENCED_PARAMETER(lpArgv);
   LPTSTR lpFailedFunction;
   BOOL   bAbnormalTermination = FALSE;

   try
      {
      // Step 1. Register the control handler
      if (!ThisComponent.RegisterHandler(
               TEXT("WNet RPC Server"),
               WNetRPCServiceCtrlHandler))
         {
         lpFailedFunction =
            TEXT("CWin32ComponentService::RegisterHandler()");
```

```
    // Throw a dummy exception as a signal to ourselves
    // that we failed
    throw "";
    }

// Step 2. Tell the Service Control Manager
// that we're starting up by reporting
// status as SERVICE_START_PENDING
if (!ThisComponent.ReportStatusChange(
        SERVICE_START_PENDING,
        0))
    {
    lpFailedFunction = TEXT("SetServiceStatus()");
    throw "";
    }

// Step 3. No other resources needed

// Step 4. Spin off RPC worker threads (only one here)
// Our worker thread is the WNetStartRPCServer function
// that does our RPC initialization
for (short int i = 0; i < nNumThreads; ++i)
    {
    hThreads[i] = ::CreateThread(NULL, 0,
        WNetStartRPCServer, NULL,
        0, &dwThreadID[i]);
    if (hThreads[i] == NULL)
        {
        lpFailedFunction =
            TEXT("CreateThread()");
        throw "";
        }
    }

// Step 5. Tell NT that we're up and running
// We'll accept stop and
// system shutdown control commands.
// Pause and continue don't make sense, because
// the only thing we can do is
// shut down our RPC server startup thread [WNetStartRPCServer()].
// It's already asleep anyhow, blocked on the call
// to RpcServerListen()
// We have no control over the RPC background threads.
if (!ThisComponent.ReportStatusChange(
        SERVICE_RUNNING,
        SERVICE_ACCEPT_STOP | SERVICE_ACCEPT_SHUTDOWN))
```

```
            {
            lpFailedFunction = TEXT("SetServiceStatus()");
            throw "";
            }

        // Step 6. Block until the server is shutdown by a STOP control
        // (or system shutdown)

        // Wait until all worker threads complete
        ::WaitForMultipleObjects(nNumThreads, hThreads,
             TRUE, INFINITE);
        }
    catch (...)
        {
        bAbnormalTermination = TRUE;
        }

    // We're done--do cleanup
    // Service was already stopped in response to
    // the control command (unless we had a problem
    // during initialization)

    // Step 7. Cleanup resources

    // bAbnormalTermination indicates that something in our
    // initialization failed. Write a message to the event log
    if (bAbnormalTermination)
        WNetStopRPCServer(dwLastError,
            lpFailedFunction);

    // Close the thread handles
    for (short int i = 0; i < nNumThreads; ++i)
        {
        if (hThreads[i] != NULL)
            {
            ::CloseHandle(hThreads[i]);
            hThreads[i] = NULL;
            }
        }

    // Step 8. Tell Service Control Manager that we're
    // done.
    ThisComponent.ReportStatusChange(
        SERVICE_STOPPED,
        0,
        0,
        dwLastError);
```

```
    delete pWNetRpcServer;
    return;
}

extern "C"
VOID WINAPI WNetRPCServiceCtrlHandler(DWORD dwCommand)
{
    switch (dwCommand)
        {
        case SERVICE_CONTROL_STOP:
        case SERVICE_CONTROL_SHUTDOWN:
            // Tell Service Control Manager that we're coming down
            ThisComponent.ReportStatusChange(
                SERVICE_STOP_PENDING,
                0,
                3000);

            WNetStopRPCServer(0, NULL);
            break;
        }
    ThisComponent.UpdateStatus();
    return;
}

extern "C"
DWORD WINAPI WNetStartRPCServer(LPVOID)
{
    DWORD dwError;

    try
        {
        pWNetRpcServer = new CRpcServer(
                                (PTBYTE) TEXT("WNet RPC Server"),
                                wnrpc_v1_0_s_ifspec);
        if (!pWNetRpcServer->Listen())
            {
            dwError = ::GetLastError();
            WNetStopRPCServer(dwError,
                TEXT("CRpcServer::Listen()"));
            }
        }
    catch (CResourceException *e)
        {
        dwError = ::GetLastError();
        WNetStopRPCServer(::GetLastError(),
            TEXT("CRpcServer::CRpcServer()"));
        e->Delete();
        }
```

```
   catch (CMemoryException *e)
      {
      dwError = ::GetLastError();
      WNetStopRPCServer(::GetLastError(),
         TEXT("new CRpcServer()"));
      e->Delete();
      }

   return dwError;
}

extern "C"
VOID WNetStopRPCServer(DWORD dwErrorCode, LPTSTR lpszErrorMsg)
{
   dwLastError = dwErrorCode;
   if (dwErrorCode != NO_ERROR)
      {
      WNetReportEvent(dwErrorCode, lpszErrorMsg, TRUE);
      }

   pWNetRpcServer->Stop();
}

extern "C"
VOID WNetReportEvent(DWORD dwErrorCode, LPTSTR lpszErrorMsg,
                     BOOL bError)
{
   // Services don't have a user interface, so the
   // only way for them to report error conditions
   // is to use the event-logging facility
   // that NT provides.

   // To do this, you call RegisterEventSource() to
   // get a handle, then call ReportEvent() to
   // log the error

   // Finally, you call DeregisterEventSource() to
   // release the handle

   // Under Windows 95, we'll emulate the functionality
   // by calling FormatMessage() twice, then
   // displaying the message to the user
   TCHAR szLastErrorMsg[1024];
   LPTSTR lpszMessageStrings[2];

   // Look up message string for system error.
   ::FormatMessage(FORMAT_MESSAGE_FROM_SYSTEM,
```

```
   NULL,
   dwErrorCode,
   LANG_USER_DEFAULT,
   szLastErrorMsg,
   sizeof (szLastErrorMsg),
   NULL);

lpszMessageStrings[0] = lpszErrorMsg;   // Passed to function
lpszMessageStrings[1] = szLastErrorMsg; // Formatted by
                                        //   FormatMessage()

if (CWin32Object::IsWindowsNT())
   {
   HANDLE hSource;

   // RegisterEventSource() takes two arguments--the machine name
   // (NULL means the local machine)
   // and the name of the application logging the event
   hSource = ::RegisterEventSource(NULL, TEXT("WNet RPC Server"));

   if (hSource != NULL)
      {
      // The lpszMessageStrings array that we pass
      // to ReportEvent() has the insertion sequences
      // for our message.
      ::ReportEvent(hSource,
         bError ? EVENTLOG_ERROR_TYPE :   // Level of severity
                  EVENTLOG_WARNING_TYPE,
         0,                               // Category--we're not
                                          //   using it
         MSG_RPC_SERVER_FAILED,           // Message identifier
                                          // Defined in WNETMSGS.MC
                                          // and the header file
                                          // WNETMSGS.H that the
                                          // Message Compiler
                                          // generates
         NULL,                            // User security ID (SID)--
                                          //   not using it
         2,                               // Number of insertion
                                          //   strings in
                                          //   lpszMessageStrings
                                          //   array
         0,                               // Number of bytes of
                                          //   binary data to include
         (LPCTSTR *) lpszMessageStrings,  // Messages to log
         NULL);                           // Binary data to log--
                                          //   we're not using any
```

```
        DeregisterEventSource(hSource);
        }
      }
   else
      {
      // Windows 95--load our message DLL and extract
      // the messages from it by calling FormatMessage()
      HINSTANCE hMessageDLL = ::LoadLibrary(TEXT("WNETMSGS.DLL"));
      TCHAR  szMessage[1024];

      if (hMessageDLL != NULL)
         {
         ::FormatMessage(
            FORMAT_MESSAGE_FROM_HMODULE |
            FORMAT_MESSAGE_ARGUMENT_ARRAY,
            (LPCVOID) hMessageDLL,
            MSG_RPC_SERVER_FAILED,
            GetUserDefaultLangID() & 0x00FF,
            szMessage,
            sizeof (szMessage),
            lpszMessageStrings);
         printf("\n%s\n", szMessage);
         printf("\nPress any key to exit...\n");
         getchar();
         }
      ::FreeLibrary(hMessageDLL);
      }
}

extern "C"
void _RpcGetRemoteUser(WCHAR szString[255], unsigned long *plLen)
{
   MultiByteToWideChar(CP_ACP,
                       0,
                       szUserName,
                       -1,
                       szString,
                       *plLen);
   *plLen = lstrlen(szUserName);
}

extern "C"
void _RpcSetLocalUser(WCHAR szUser[255])
{
   CHAR szUserA[256];

   WideCharToMultiByte(CP_ACP, 0, szUser, -1,
      szUserA, sizeof (szUserA), NULL, NULL);
```

```
   lstrcpy(szUserName, szUserA);
}

extern "C"
unsigned long _RpcWinExec(WCHAR szProgram[255],
                          unsigned long uCmdShow)
{
   unsigned long uRetcode;
   CHAR szProgramA[255];
   STARTUPINFO  StartupInfo;
   PROCESS_INFORMATION ProcessInfo;

   WideCharToMultiByte(CP_ACP, 0, szProgram, -1,
      szProgramA, sizeof (szProgramA), NULL, NULL);

   // Assume the identity of the client before execution
   CRpcServer::ImpersonateClient();

   ::ZeroMemory(&StartupInfo, sizeof (StartupInfo));
   StartupInfo.cb = sizeof (STARTUPINFO);

   // Because we're running as a service that gets
   // started by the operating system, we have to
   // force the application to run in the logged-on
   // user's desktop.
   // We do this by setting the lpDesktop field
   // of the STARTUPINFO structure to
   // "WinSta0\\Default", which is the name
   // that NT assigns to the user's desktop.
   //    WinSta0 is window station zero
   //    Default is the default desktop
   //       in that window station
   //
   // This is unnecessary, but harmless, in Windows 95
   StartupInfo.lpDesktop = TEXT("WinSta0\\Default");

   uRetcode = CreateProcess(NULL, szProgramA,
             NULL,
             NULL,
             TRUE,
             CREATE_NEW_CONSOLE,
             NULL,
             NULL,
             &StartupInfo,
             &ProcessInfo);

   // Revert back to server's identity
   CRpcServer::RevertToSelf();
```

```
   return uRetcode;
}

extern "C"
void _RpcBenchmark(handle_t hServer,
             unsigned long dwLength,
             unsigned char *pcInBuffer,
             unsigned char *pcOutBuffer)
{
   // Send it back to the client
   CopyMemory(pcOutBuffer, pcInBuffer, dwLength);
}

extern "C"
void _RpcGetOSStartupTime(SYSTEMTIME *pSystemTime)
{
   *pSystemTime = StartupTime;
}

extern "C"
void __RPC_FAR * __RPC_API MIDL_user_allocate(size_t len)
{
    return(VirtualAlloc(NULL, len, MEM_COMMIT,
                        PAGE_READWRITE));
}

extern "C"
void __RPC_API MIDL_user_free(void __RPC_FAR * ptr)
{
    VirtualFree(ptr, 0, MEM_RELEASE);
}

static BOOL WINAPI MailslotReceiveCallback(
      LPBYTE lpData,
      DWORD dwDataLength,
      HANDLE hConnection)
{
   TCHAR   szComputerName[MAX_COMPUTERNAME_LENGTH + 1];
   DWORD   dwNameLength = sizeof (szComputerName);
   CString szAnswer;
   CString szAnswerStation;

   ::GetComputerName(szComputerName, &dwNameLength);
   szAnswerStation = _T("\\\\");
   szAnswerStation += (LPTSTR) lpData;
   szAnswerStation += _T("\\MAILSLOT\\WNET\\WNETMGR");
```

```
    try
        {
        szAnswer.Format(_T("%s"),
            szComputerName);
        CMailslot Mailslot(
            (LPTSTR) (LPCTSTR) szAnswerStation, ClientSide);
        Mailslot.Write((LPCTSTR) szAnswer,
            szAnswer.GetLength() + 1, NULL);
        }
    catch (...)
        {
        }

    return TRUE;
}

static CMailslot MailslotServer(
            _T("WNET\\WNETMAP"),
            ServerSide,
            MailslotReceiveCallback);
```

Conclusion

Remote Procedure Calls are a powerful paradigm for distributed applications. They hide many of the details of client-server communications. RPCs can access servers either locally or remotely. When talking to a server process on a local machine, the Microsoft protocol *ncalrpc* allows you to take advantage of NT's optimized Local Procedure Call (LPC) facility. For remote communications, Microsoft RPC supports a wide range of protocols that permit connectivity to NT, Windows 95, UNIX, and NetWare hosts.

Win32 services are background processes that you can configure to load when the operating system boots. They are often written as RPC server applications. The combination of RPC and Win32 services is a powerful one. It allows you to place server applications anywhere on a network and have a high level of confidence in their availability. Though users can load and unload services at run time if they want to, you can also write services so they cannot be unloaded, thereby protecting their availability.

As you would expect, RPC is slower than just coding directly to the underlying API. However, in return, RPC gives you true protocol transparency. And surprisingly, the penalty is not as great as you might expect, as we will see in Chapter 16.

RPC is clearly a cornerstone in Microsoft's distributed applications strategy. It is supported with small differences under both Windows NT and Windows 95. It is also the foundation on which Microsoft has implemented 32-bit OLE. Thus, it will probably continue to enjoy a strategic presence, particularly when OLE offers distributed objects.

Suggested Readings

Online References

Services Overview in the Win32 online help.
Event Logging Overview in the Win32 online help.
Desktops and Windows Stations Overview in the Win32 online help.
An Overview of Authenticated RPC in the Win32 online help.
An Overview of the Name Service Entry in the Win32 online help.
Microsoft Knowledge Base for Win32 SDK articles:

- "Accessing the Application Desktop from a Service"
- "Accessing the Event Logs"
- "Adding Categories for Events"
- "Dealing w/ Lengthy Processing in Service Control Handler"
- "Debugging a Service with WinDbg"
- "Detecting Logoff from a Service"
- "Distributed Computing Environment (DCE) Compliance"
- "Determing Whether App Is Running As Service or .EXE"
- "DOCERR: Important Information on RPC 2.0 Missing from the Docs"
- "How to Gracefully Fail at Service Start"
- "How to Start an Application at Boot Time under Windows 95"
- "How to Use the StartService API within a Service"
- "Registering Multiple RPC Server Interfaces"
- "Services and Redirected Drives"
- "Service Control Manager Records Event ID 7023 in the System Log"
- "Sharing Win32 Services"
- "RPC Can Use Multiple Protocols"
- "Using RPC Callback Functions"

Print References

Open Software Foundation. *OSF/DCE Application Development Guide.* Englewood Cliffs, NJ: Prentice-Hall, Inc., 1993.

Open Software Foundation. *OSF/DCE Application Development Reference.* Englewood Cliffs, NJ: Prentice-Hall, Inc., 1993.

Chapter 12

The LAN Manager API for Windows NT

The LAN Manager API is a rich set of functions for network administration. Among its capabilities are calls that let you add, delete, and enumerate users and groups, associate users with groups, share resources, and determine what machines are attached to your network. Since NT Server carries forward (or at least superficially appears to carry forward) much of the network design of LAN Manager, it is natural that the LAN Manager API should follow it.

Why Use the LAN Manager API?

Microsoft prefaces the online help for this API with a dire-sounding disclaimer. Here are the first few paragraphs:

> The Windows Networking APIs specified in this online help are designed to provide some of the API functionality that was available in LAN Manager 2.x. They are not the base Windows NT networking APIs. Windows NT takes some of the functionality that was previously supplied by the networking software and moves this into the base APIs (such as error and audit logging, printing). Windows NT also provides a network independent set of network functions (the WNet functions) that allow network functions to work across different network vendors' products. If a base function or WNet function

exists that could be used by your application, you should convert from the Windows networking function to the public Windows NT equivalent. There are at least three reasons to make the change now:

1. The WNet functions are network independent, while the Windows networking functions work only on LAN Manager networks.
2. Some of the Windows networking functions specified in this document may not be supported in future releases of Windows NT if they have been superseded by base functions or WNet functions. (Of course Microsoft does not plan to remove specific Windows networking functions unless equivalent or better functionality is available from other functions.)
3. The Windows networking functions may not be supported on some other future Microsoft platforms, since they are not part of the Microsoft Win32 application programming interface (API).

Now that you know why you should *not* use the LAN Manager API, here's why you should:

- The LAN Manager API is rich and powerful.
- For many of the services that it provides, there is no other way to accomplish the same thing. For example, there is no other way to add users and groups to the security database, no way to enumerate them, and no way to delete them. These are important network management services.
- The Win32 WNet API continues to be of little significance. The only real service it provides is letting you connect to drives and print queues on remote machines.
- In spite of Microsoft's soft-pedaling the LAN Manager API, it has been improved and expanded for Windows NT. The interface to existing functions is better, and there are whole new API categories.

Because of the sheer size of the LAN Manager API, I am not going to try to cover it in its entirety. Ralph Ryan wrote a complete (and very good) book on the OS/2 LAN Manager API, *Microsoft LAN Manager: A Programmer's Guide*. The official manual is Microsoft's *LAN Manager Programmer's Reference*. (See "Suggested Readings" at the end of this chapter.) Unfortunately, both of these books are almost impossible to find.

I will concentrate on developing C++ classes that expose some of the most important functionality of the LAN Manager API. The Microsoft Foundation Classes provide no support at all for this API. The API is already oriented around specific types of objects, so encapsulating it in C++ classes is not a great leap. These are the objects I will focus on here, and the classes I will implement them in:

- Network servers (CNetServer)
- Users (CNetUser)
- User groups (CNetUserGroup)

I also include a new version of the WNETSVCS sample application from my *Windows NT Network Programming*. The project is on the source disk in the directory \WIN32NET\CODE\LANMAN\WNETSVCS. It provides dialog boxes that mimic the functionality of the NT User Manager. This will give you a chance to become familiar with the LAN Manager API for Windows NT by seeing how some of the most important functions work. Figure 12-1 shows its opening screen.

To give you an idea of the scope of the LAN Manager API, Table 12-1 lists the function categories, along with the functions comprising them and a brief description of their purpose. If a group has been superseded by a Win32 API, I do not list the individual functions.

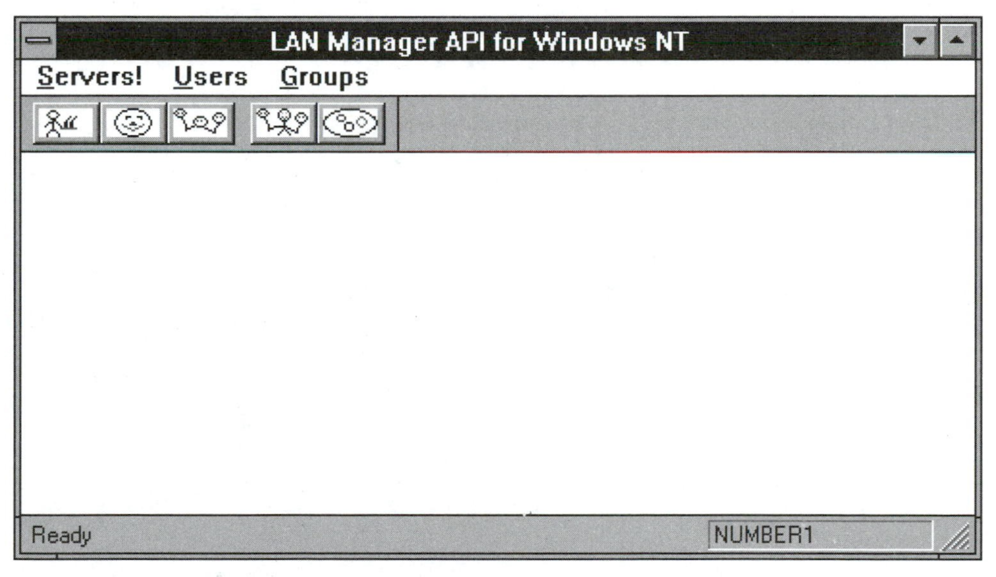

Figure 12-1. WNETSVCS Opening Screen

Table 12-1. LAN Manager API Categories for Windows NT

Category	Component Functions	Purpose	Additional Comments
Access API	<Superseded>	Assigning users permission to files and directories	Replaced by Win32 Security API
Alert API	NetAlertRaise NetAlertRaiseEx	Sending alert messages to network service applications	
Auditing API	<Superseded>	Adding audit trail entries to the system log, reading audit trail	Audit trails are automatically generated by Windows NT when an object has an SACL tied to it, and auditing is enabled. Event Logging API is used to read the logs
Buffer Manipulation API	NetApiBufferAllocate NetApiBufferFree NetApiBufferReallocate NetApiBufferSize	Allocating and releasing memory used for output parameters	New in Windows NT
Configuration API	<Superseded>	Setting machine configuration	Replaced by Registry API
Connection API	<Superseded>	Enumerating connections to remote resources	Replaced by WNetEnumResource()
Domain API	NetGetDCName	Finding out what machine is acting as the domain controller	
Error Logging API	<Superseded>	Reading entries in the system log file	Replaced by Win32 Event Logging API
File API	NetFileEnum NetFileGetInfo NetFileClose	Finding out who currently has files in use, forcing file closing	
Global Group API	NetGroupAdd NetGroupAddUser NetGroupEnum NetGroupGetInfo NetGroupSetInfo NetGroupDel NetGroupDelUser NetGroupGetUsers NetGroupSetUsers	Managing global groups in a domain	Implements the same calls as the LAN Manager Group API, but distinction between local and global groups is new in Windows NT. Global groups only have relevance under Windows NT Server

Table 12-1. LAN Manager API Categories for Windows NT *(continued)*

Category	Component Functions	Purpose	Additional Comments
Local Group API	NetLocalGroupAdd NetLocalGroupAddMember NetLocalGroupEnum NetLocalGroupGetInfo NetLocalGroupSetInfo NetLocalGroupDel NetLocalGroupDelMember NetLocalGroupGetMembers NetLocalGroupSetMembers	Managing local groups	New in Windows NT. Functions that manipulate group members use SIDs, not user names
Message API	NetMessageNameAdd NetMessageNameEnum NetMessageNameGetInfo NetMessageNameDel NetMessageBufferSend	Sending messages to users on the network	
Remote Utility API	NetRemoteTOD	Getting current time from a machine on the network	
Replicator API	NetReplGetInfo NetReplSetInfo	Controlling the NT Directory Replicator service	New in Windows NT
Replicator Export	NetReplExportDirAdd	Setting up directories for export to other machines	New in Windows NT
Directory API	NetReplExportDirDel NetReplExportDirEnum NetReplExportDirGetInfo NetReplExportDirSetInfo NetReplExportDirLock NetReplExportDirUnlock		

continued

Table 12-1. LAN Manager API Categories for Windows NT *(continued)*

Category	Component Functions	Purpose	Additional Comments
Replicator Import Directory API	NetReplImportDirAdd NetReplImportDirDel NetReplImportDirEnum NetReplImportDirGetInfo NetReplImportDirSetInfo NetReplImportDirLock NetReplImportDirUnlock	Setting up directories to be imported from other machines	New in Windows NT
Schedule Service API	NetScheduleJobAdd NetScheduleJobDel NetScheduleJobEnum NetScheduleJobGetInfo	Scheduling jobs for local or remote execution at given times	New in Windows NT
Server API	NetServerEnum NetServerGetInfo NetServerSetInfo NetServerDiskEnum	Enumerating and configuring servers, getting operating statistics	
Service API	<Superseded>	Controlling, starting, and configuring LAN Manager services	Replaced by Win32 Services API
Session API	NetSessionEnum NetSessionGetInfo NetSessionDel	Manipulating sessions, which consist of one or more connections between a resource user and its provider	
Share API	NetShareAdd NetShareEnum NetShareGetInfo NetShareSetInfo NetShareDel NetShareCheck	Managing shared resources	

Table 12-1. LAN Manager API Categories for Windows NT *(continued)*

Category	Component Functions	Purpose	Additional Comments
Statistics API	NetStatisticsGet	Retrieving operating statistics for Server and Redirector	Information retrieved is a subset of that available from Performance Monitoring
Transport API	NetServerTransportAdd NetServerTransportDel NetServerTransportEnum NetWkstaTransportAdd NetWkstaTransportDel NetWkstaTransportEnum	Managing bindings and Redirector and underlying transport layer	New in Windows NT
Use API	<Superseded>	Connecting to remote shared resources	Replaced by Win32 WNet API
User API	NetUserAdd NetUserEnum NetUserGetInfo NetUserSetInfo NetUserDel NetUserGetGroups NetUserGetLocalGroups NetUserSetGroups	Managing user accounts	Distinction between global groups and local groups is new in Windows NT
User Modal API	NetUserModalsGet NetUserModalsSet	Controlling user logon settings and restrictions	
Workstation and Workstation User API	NetWkstaGetInfo NetWkstaSetInfo NetWkstaUserGetInfo NetWkstaUserSetInfo NetWkstaUserEnum	Getting and setting workstation and user configuration information, finding out what users are logged in on a workstation	Workstation User API is new in Windows NT

General Considerations

Before delving into the specifics of the APIs I plan to use, I want to mention a couple of things that apply to the entire LAN Manager API as it is implemented under NT.

Unicode Only

First, only the Unicode character set is supported. For this reason, in my code you will see that I often use the WCHAR and LPWSTR types, which explicitly select Unicode, rather than TCHAR and LPTSTR.

This might lead you to expect that Windows 95 does not support this API. Except for a few functions, this is indeed the case. Unfortunately, though, the way in which Windows 95 "unsupports" it forces you to do some ugly and painful things if you want to be able to accommodate both operating systems. We'll see specifically what I mean when we get to the code.

Buffer Allocation

The NT implementation corrects one of the most awkward features of the OS/2 LAN Manager API. In OS/2, when you ask LAN Manager for information, you have to provide a large enough buffer. Otherwise, the function will return ERROR_MORE_DATA. It will also tell you how much memory you need. You can pass a zero-length buffer to find out how much memory to allocate, then allocate it and call the function again. The NT LAN Manager API set allocates the output buffer for you. All you have to do is pass it a pointer to a pointer, then call NetApiBufferFree() to release the memory when you're through. This is much more convenient and simplifies coding quite a bit.

Global Groups and Local Groups

The distinction between global groups and local groups is new to Windows NT. It has been introduced to support the NT Server notion of trusted domains. Briefly, the difference is that global groups are used to export users from the current NT Server domain; local groups, on the other hand, import users into the domain. Local groups can also be used to give domain users rights on individual NT workstations. Local groups may contain global groups (and other local groups) as members. Global groups may only contain users.

When you install an NT workstation, NT automatically creates the local groups Administrators, Backup Operators, Guests, Power Users, Replicator, and Users. On an NT Server, there is no Power Users group, and three additional local groups: Account Operators, Print Operators, and Server

Operators. The invisible group Everyone is also created; it contains all users defined in the domain, whether they are administrators, normal users, or guests. The Everyone group is invisible in the sense that you don't see it when you are enumerating groups, and the User Manager doesn't show it. However, as you will see in Chapter 13, you can grant and refuse rights to Everyone, and NT normally gives Everyone a default set of rights to files and directories you create. NT workstations have only one global group, called None.

An NT Server will also have the global groups Domain Users, Domain Guests, and Domain Admins, and they will automatically be members of the local groups Users, Guests, and Administrators on all stations in the domain. All NT Servers in a domain share the same security accounts database. One machine is designated the domain controller; the others become backup controllers so that if the domain controller goes down, the others can fill in for it. The domain controller distributes replicas of the security database to all the backup controllers at periodic intervals.

Figure 12-2 shows the groups on my NT Server machine. This is a screen shot taken in WNETSVCS. It includes both local and global groups. Figure 12-3 shows the same screen for an NT workstation.

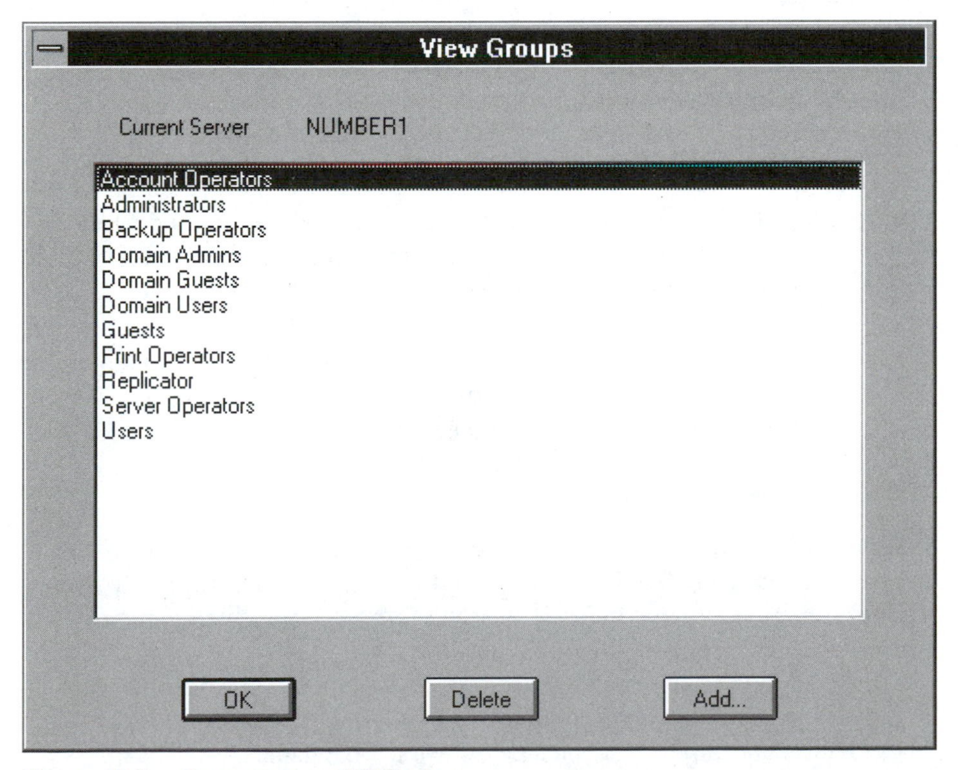

Figure 12-2. Groups on an NT Server

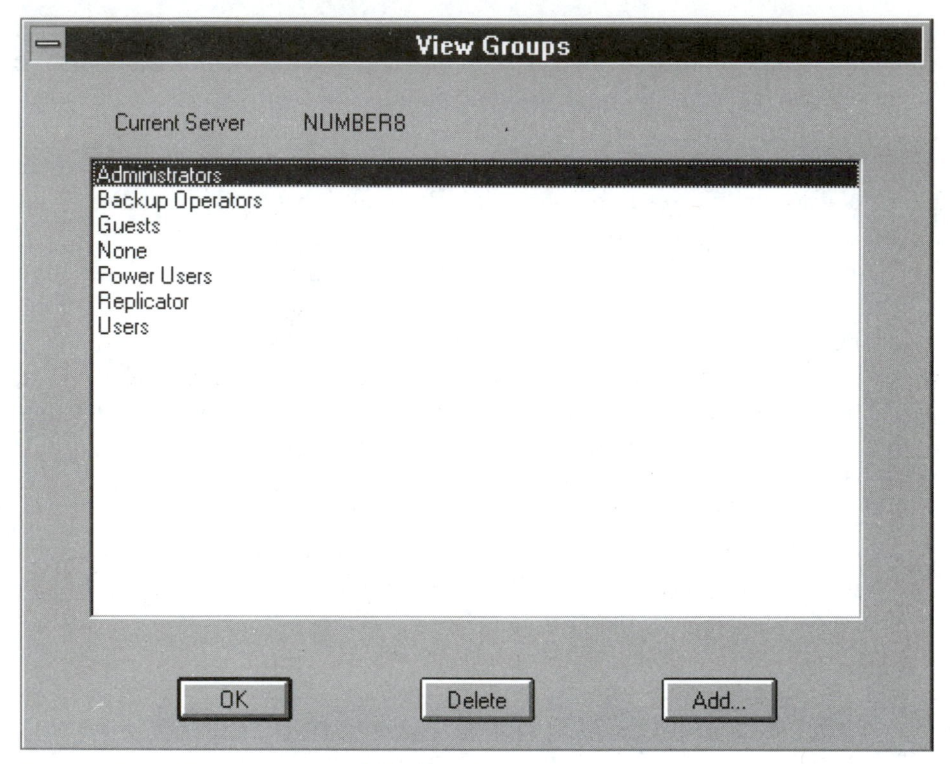

Figure 12-3. Groups on an NT Workstation

OS/2 LAN Manager had no concept of global and local groups. For this reason, the old calls now map to operations on global groups, and a new API set, the Local Group category, has been introduced. All the old LAN Manager group functions take user names as arguments (when you add a member, for instance). The NT local group functions take security identifiers (SIDs). The classes and functions I implement will take user names and translate them to SIDs by calling LookupAccountName(). User-level applications shouldn't have to deal with SIDs.

Machine Name Arguments

Almost all the LAN Manager functions take the target computer name as their first argument. A NULL pointer indicates the local machine. If the target is remote, the name must be in UNC format: \\<machine name>. I will give the calling application a little leeway; it won't need to worry about the "\\", I'll supply it automatically. Because of the superior performance of local Named Pipes and the *ncalrpc* protocol, I include a check to see if the target computer is the current one, then pass the machine name as NULL if it is.

Levels of Detail

Most of the LAN Manager calls include an argument specifying the level of detail that you are providing, or that you want to be returned. Zero represents the lowest level, often including no more than the object name. Each level corresponds to a structure type named for the object in question and the level of detail. For instance, these are the *typedefs* for the USER_INFO_0 and USER_INFO_1 structures from the LAN Manager header file LMACCESS.H:

```
typedef struct _USER_INFO_0
{
    LPWSTR   usri0_name;
} USER_INFO_0, *PUSER_INFO_0, *LPUSER_INFO_0;

typedef struct _USER_INFO_1
{
    LPWSTR   usri1_name;
    LPWSTR   usri1_password;
    DWORD    usri1_password_age;
    DWORD    usri1_priv;
    LPWSTR   usri1_home_dir;
    LPWSTR   usri1_comment;
    DWORD    usri1_flags;
    LPWSTR   usri1_script_path;
} USER_INFO_1, *PUSER_INFO_1, *LPUSER_INFO_1;
```

Include Files and Link Libraries

In any source modules you write that call LAN Manager functions, you need include only LM.H. Like WINDOWS.H, it is a master header file that includes all the other headers needed to use the LAN Manager API.

All of the LAN Manager API is contained in NETAPI32.DLL, so you only need to link with NETAPI32.LIB. Visual C++ does not automatically generate a reference to NETAPI32.LIB, so you have to go into your project's Link settings and add it.

The link to NETAPI32.LIB is problematic with Windows 95. Its version of NETAPI32.DLL, in fact, does not contain one single LAN Manager function. It doesn't even contain stubbed versions of them that return ERROR_CALL_NOT_IMPLEMENTED, as its unsupported Win32 functions do. The DLL that contains the small handful of functions that Windows 95 does support is SVRAPI.DLL, and it has its own import library. If you link at build time to NETAPI32.LIB, your program won't even load under Windows 95. Conversely, if you link to SVRAPI.LIB, it won't work under NT.

If you want a single binary file to support both operating systems, you must load the appropriate DLL at run time by calling LoadLibrary(), then load pointers to the functions you want to call with GetProcAddress(). In my opinion, this is too much monkey business—the support that Windows 95 offers here is so limited that it's not worth jumping through hoops to get it. Therefore, the code in this chapter will only work under Windows NT.

Finding Out about Servers

NetServerEnum() reports the servers that are present on the network. It also illustrates the standard format for the Windows NT LAN Manager enumeration functions.

```
NET_API_STATUS NET_API_FUNCTION
NetServerEnum (
   LPTSTR      lpszServerName,
   DWORD       dwLevel,
   LPBYTE     *lplpBuffer,
   DWORD       dwPreferredMaxLength,
   LPDWORD     lpdwEntriesRead,
   LPDWORD     lpdwTotalEntries,
   DWORD       dwServerType,
   LPTSTR      lpszDomain,
   LPDWORD     lpdwResumeHandle
    );
```

As always, *lpszServerName* indicates the server where the function is to execute, though with NetServerEnum(), this is not that important. The request will be directed to the machine acting as the master browser for the domain. *dwLevel* is the level of information you want returned, and must be 100 or 101. The corresponding structures are a SERVER_INFO_100 and SERVER_INFO_101.

```
typedef struct _SERVER_INFO_100
{
    DWORD           sv100_platform_id;
    LPTSTR          sv100_name;
} SERVER_INFO_100, *PSERVER_INFO_100, *LPSERVER_INFO_100;

typedef struct _SERVER_INFO_101
{
    DWORD           sv101_platform_id;
    LPTSTR          sv101_name;
    DWORD           sv101_version_major;
    DWORD           sv101_version_minor;
    DWORD           sv101_type;
    LPTSTR          sv101_comment;
} SERVER_INFO_101, *PSERVER_INFO_101, *LPSERVER_INFO_101;
```

sv101_platform_id can be either SV_PLATFORM_ID_OS2 or SV_PLATFORM_ID_NT, to indicate whether the reported server is running OS/2 LAN Manager or Windows NT Server. The fields we mainly want to find out about are *sv101_name*, the server's name, and *sv101_type*, a set of bit flags describing the operating system configuration. Table 12-2 shows some of the flags:

Table 12-2. LAN Manager Server Type Flags

Flag	Defined as	Meaning
SV_TYPE_WORKSTATION	(0x00000001)	The host is running the Redirector software.
SV_TYPE_SERVER	(0x00000002)	The host is running the Server software.
SV_TYPE_SQLSERVER	(0x00000004)	The host is running SQL Server.
SV_TYPE_DOMAIN_CTRL	(0x00000008)	The host is an NT Server machine acting as the primary domain controller (the machine that handles logon requests).
SV_TYPE_DOMAIN_BAKCTRL	(0x00000010)	The machine is an NT Server machine serving as a backup domain controller (waiting in the wings to take over should the primary domain controller go down).
SV_TYPE_AFP	(0x00000040)	A machine that understands the Apple FileTalk Protocol.
SV_TYPE_NOVELL	(0x00000080)	A NetWare server.
SV_TYPE_SERVER_UNIX	(0x00000800)	A UNIX machine.
SV_TYPE_NT	(0x00001000)	An NT machine.
SV_TYPE_WFW	(0x00002000)	A Windows for Workgroups workstation.
SV_TYPE_SERVER_NT	(0x00008000)	An NT Server.
SV_TYPE_MASTER_BROWSER	(0x00040000)	The machine is acting as the master browser for the domain. It is the machine responsible for collecting and reporting about active stations.
SV_TYPE_SERVER_OSF	(0x00100000)	A computer running the OSF operating system.
SV_TYPE_SERVER_VMS	(0x00200000)	A VMS host.
SV_TYPE_WINDOWS	(0x00400000)	Windows 95 (96, 97, 98, ...).

You can pass SV_TYPE_ALL (0xFFFFFFFF) to NetServerEnum() to request enumeration of all types of servers.

My machines report the following types:

- NT Server: SV_TYPE_MASTER_BROWSER | SV_TYPE_NT | SV_TYPE_DOMAIN_CTRL | SV_TYPE_SERVER | SV_TYPE_WORKSTATION.
- NT workstation: SV_TYPE_POTENTIAL_BROWSER | SV_TYPE_BACKUP_BROWSER | SV_TYPE_NT | SV_TYPE_SERVER | SV_TYPE_WORKSTATION.
- Windows 95 station: SV_TYPE_WINDOWS | SV_TYPE_POTENTIAL_BROWSER | SV_TYPE_WFW | SV_TYPE_SERVER | SV_TYPE_WORKSTATION.

Getting back to the arguments to NetServerEnum(), the *lplpBuffer, dwPreferredMaxLength, lpdwEntriesRead, lpdwTotalEntries*, and *lpdwResumeHandle* are common to most of the NT LAN Manager enumerators. *lplpBuffer* is a pointer to an LPBYTE, for which NT allocates the requisite amount of memory. On return from NetServerEnum(), it will point to an array of SERVER_INFO_100 or SERVER_INFO_101 structures. *dwPreferred MaxLength* is your preference for the maximum amount of data to be returned, but NT may ignore it. *lpdwEntriesRead* points to a variable that captures the number of elements in the output array. *lpdwTotalEntries* is not significant for NT. (OS/2 LAN Manager used the equivalent argument to tell you how many entries to allocate memory for.) If *lpdwResumeHandle* is not NULL, it points to a DWORD that you initialize to zero. This permits you to call NetServerEnum() several times in a loop if necessary. After the first call, it is automatically reset.

The *lpszDomain* argument indicates the domain whose servers you want to enumerate, with NULL saying that you want to enumerate all available domains.

The CNetServer Class

My CNetServer class will be responsible for all operations that affect servers. This includes adding and deleting users, adding and deleting groups, enumerating users, and enumerating groups. Server enumeration does not target any specific object, so I implement it as a static method on CNetServer. Here is the class declaration, from the source disk \WIN32NET\CODE\LANMAN\LMCLASS\NETSRVR.H. Notice that I keep track of server names using both the Unicode and the ANSI character set. The LAN Manager API requires Unicode, but most of my applications use ANSI. Storing both versions of my object names lets me keep them both happy.

```
/********
*
* NETSRVR.H
*
* Copyright (c) 1996 Ralph P. Davis
*
* All Rights Reserved
*
*****/

#ifndef NETSRVR_INCLUDED
#define NETSRVR_INCLUDED

typedef BOOL (CALLBACK *SERVERENUMPROC)
      (LPTSTR lpszServerName, DWORD dwServerType);

typedef BOOL (CALLBACK *USERENUMPROC)(LPTSTR lpszUserName);

typedef BOOL (CALLBACK *GROUPENUMPROC)(LPTSTR lpszGroupName,
                                       BOOL   bLocal);

class AFX_EXT_CLASS CNetServer : public CObject
{
private:
   CNetServer() {}
protected:
   WCHAR m_szServerNameW[MAX_COMPUTERNAME_LENGTH + 10];
   CHAR  m_szServerNameA[MAX_COMPUTERNAME_LENGTH + 10];
   BOOL  m_bMyName;
   BOOL  m_bTranslated;
public:
   CNetServer(LPCTSTR lpszServerName);

   BOOL IsMyName(void)
      {
      return m_bMyName;
      }

   BOOL IsTranslated(void)
      {
      // Tells us if client application wants
      // ANSI (TRUE) or Unicode (FALSE)
      return m_bTranslated;
      }

   LPSTR GetServerNameA(void)
      {
      return m_szServerNameA;
      }
```

```
    LPWSTR GetServerNameW(void)
        {
        return m_szServerNameW;
        }

    LPTSTR GetServerName(void)
        {
        if (m_bTranslated)
            return (LPTSTR) GetServerNameA();
        else
            return (LPTSTR) GetServerNameW();
        }

    static BOOL EnumServers(SERVERENUMPROC lpServerEnumProc,
                            LPCTSTR        lpszSignature,
                            LPCTSTR        lpszDomain = NULL,
                            DWORD          dwServerType
                                  = SV_TYPE_ALL);

    // User-related methods
    BOOL AddUser(LPCTSTR lpszUserName,
                 LPCTSTR lpszPassword);
    BOOL DeleteUser(LPCTSTR lpszUserName);
    BOOL EnumUsers(USERENUMPROC lpUserEnumProc);

    // Group-related methods
    BOOL AddGroup(LPCTSTR lpszGroupName,
                  BOOL   bLocal = FALSE);
    BOOL DeleteGroup(LPCTSTR lpszUserName,
                     BOOL   bLocal = FALSE);
    BOOL EnumGroups(GROUPENUMPROC lpGroupEnumProc);
    DECLARE_DYNAMIC(CNetServer)
};
#endif
```

The method that reports servers, EnumServers(), calls NetServerEnum() to enumerate the types of servers requested by the caller. It works like a standard Windows enumeration function: for each server it finds, it invokes a callback function, typed as a SERVERENUMPROC in NETSRVR.H:

```
typedef BOOL (CALLBACK *SERVERENUMPROC)
                (LPWSTR lpszServerName, DWORD wServerType);
```

The callback is passed the server name and the type mask returned by NetServerEnum().

Here is the listing for CNetServer::EnumServers(), from \WIN32NET \CODE\LANMAN\LMCLASS\NETSRVR.CPP. There are a couple of additional points you should notice:

- I make no assumptions about the character set that the caller is using. I do know that NetServerEnum() requires Unicode. Before calling NetServerEnum(), I translate the domain name to Unicode. Because the domain name can be passed as NULL, I add an additional argument, a signature string. This can be any string at all, as long as it is passed through the TEXT() or _T() macros. When I report the server name, I use the results of my first translation to determine whether I need to convert the server name back to ANSI. This way, I enumerate it using the same character set that the calling application is using.
- The call to NetApiBufferFree() at the end of the *for* loop releases the memory allocated by NetServerEnum().

```
BOOL CNetServer::EnumServers(
                        SERVERENUMPROC lpServerEnumProc,
                        LPCTSTR         lpszSignature,
                        LPCTSTR         lpszDomain
                                          /* = NULL*/,
                        DWORD          dwServerType
                                          /* = SV_TYPE_ALL */)
{
   WCHAR szDomainNameW[256];
   BOOL  bTranslated = FALSE;

   if (lpszDomain != NULL)
      {
      // Make sure domain name is in Unicode
      // as required by NetServerEnum()
      bTranslated =
         ANSIToUnicode(lpszDomain,
                       szDomainNameW,
                       sizeof (szDomainNameW));
      lpszDomain = (LPCTSTR) szDomainNameW;
      }
   else
      {
      bTranslated =
         ANSIToUnicode(lpszSignature,
                       szDomainNameW,
                       sizeof (szDomainNameW));
      }
```

```
    LPSERVER_INFO_101 lpServerInfo;
    LPWSTR           *lpBuffer;
    DWORD             dwEntries, dwTotal;
    DWORD             i;
    BOOL              bRetcode;
    LPTSTR            lpServerName;
    CHAR              szServerName[MAX_COMPUTERNAME_LENGTH + 10];

    if (NetServerEnum(NULL,    // Local machine
                      101,     // Level 101 (includes server type)
                      (LPBYTE *) &lpBuffer,
                      65536,
                      &dwEntries,
                      &dwTotal,
                      dwServerType,
                      (LPTSTR) lpszDomain,
                      NULL)
              == NERR_Success)
       {
       lpServerInfo = (SERVER_INFO_101 *) lpBuffer;
       for (i = 0; i < dwEntries; ++i)
          {
          // Convert server name back to ANSI
          // if input domain name had to be
          // converted
          if (bTranslated)
             {
             UnicodeToANSI(lpServerInfo[i].sv101_name,
                           szServerName,
                           sizeof (szServerName));
             lpServerName = (LPTSTR) szServerName;
             }
          else
             {
             lpServerName = (LPTSTR) lpServerInfo[i].sv101_name;
             }
          if (!lpServerEnumProc(lpServerName,
                                lpServerInfo[i].sv101_type))
             {
             bRetcode = FALSE;
             break;
             }
          }
       NetApiBufferFree(lpBuffer);
       bRetcode = TRUE;
       }
    return bRetcode;
}
```

WNETSVCS calls CNetServer::EnumServers() with a NULL domain and the type SV_TYPE_ALL, to request enumeration of all known servers. It does this in the CViewServerDlg::OnInitDialog() method. CViewServerDlg is the class that supports the dialog box shown in Figure 12-4.

```
BOOL CViewServerDlg::OnInitDialog()
{
   CDialog::OnInitDialog();

   m_pThis = this;
   UpdateData(TRUE);

   CNetServer::EnumServers(EnumServerCallback,
                           _T("My Signature"));

   return TRUE;
}
```

The callback function (CViewServerDlg::EnumServerCallback()) is a static member function of the same class. It puts the server names into the list box represented by the member variable *m_Servers*, and stores each server's type as its list box item data. It reports the name and type of the currently selected server at the top of the dialog box that you see in Figure 12-4, by invoking the CViewServerDlg::OnSelchangeServers() method.

```
BOOL CALLBACK CViewServerDlg::EnumServerCallback(
      LPTSTR lpszServerName, DWORD dwServerType)
{
   CWnetsvcsApp *pApp = (CWnetsvcsApp *) AfxGetApp();
   int nIndex =
      m_pThis->m_Servers.AddString(lpszServerName);

   if (nIndex >= 0)
      {
      m_pThis->m_Servers.SetItemData(nIndex, dwServerType);

      if (pApp->GetCurrentServer() == CString(lpszServerName))
         {
         // Highlight currently selected server
         m_pThis->m_Servers.SetCurSel(nIndex);
         m_pThis->OnSelchangeServers();
         }
      }
   return TRUE;
}
```

CViewServerDlg::OnSelchangeServers() examines the bits in the selected server's type to determine what operating system it is running. *m_szSelectedServer* is the member variable representing the currently selected item in the list box. *m_szCurrentServer* represents the static text field at the top of the dialog box.

```
void CViewServerDlg::OnSelchangeServers()
{
   UpdateData(TRUE);
   m_szCurrentServer = m_szSelectedServer;

   int nIndex = m_Servers.GetCurSel();
   DWORD dwServerType = m_Servers.GetItemData(nIndex);

   if ((dwServerType & SV_TYPE_DOMAIN_CTRL) ||
       (dwServerType & SV_TYPE_DOMAIN_BAKCTRL))
      {
      m_szCurrentServer += _T(" (NT Server)");
      }
```

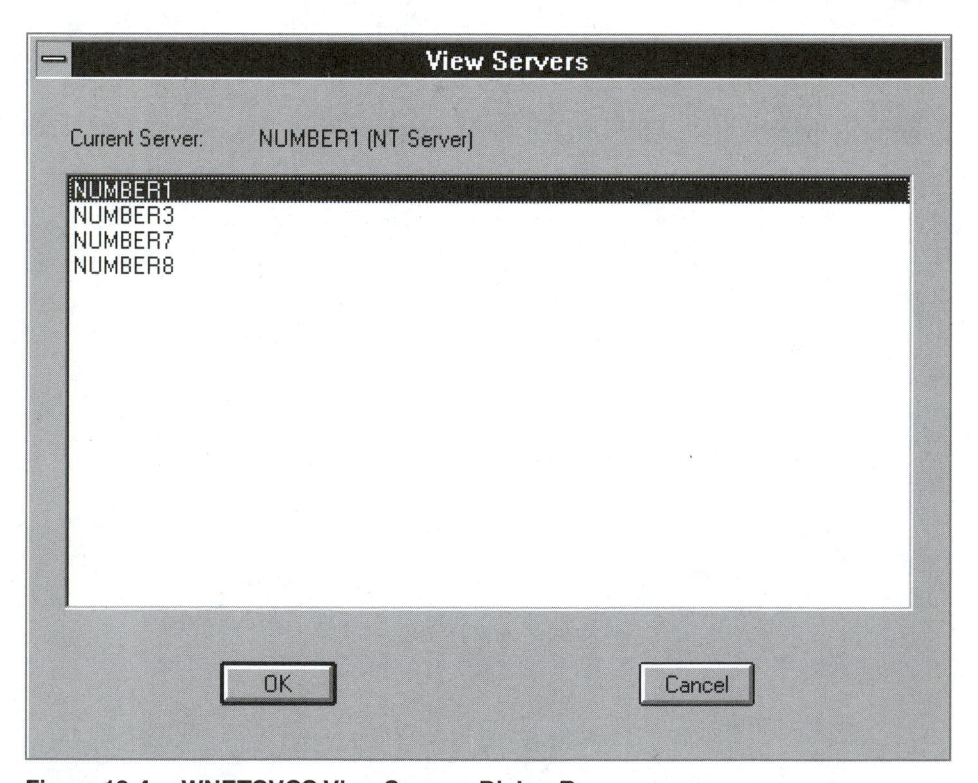

Figure 12-4. WNETSVCS View Servers Dialog Box

```
    else if (dwServerType & SV_TYPE_NT)
       {
       m_szCurrentServer += _T(" (NT Workstation)");
       }
    else if (dwServerType & SV_TYPE_WINDOWS)
       {
       m_szCurrentServer += _T(" (Windows 95 Workstation)");
       }
    else if (dwServerType & SV_TYPE_NOVELL)
       {
       m_szCurrentServer += _T(" (NetWare Server)");
       }
    UpdateData(FALSE);
}
```

Managing Users

A system administrator normally needs to perform three user-related tasks:

- Adding new users
- Deleting existing users
- Listing current users

The LAN Manager API provides a function for each of these: NetUserAdd(), NetUserDel(), and NetUserEnum().

Adding a User

Here is the prototype for NetUserAdd() from LMACCESS.H.

```
NET_API_STATUS NET_API_FUNCTION
NetUserAdd (
    LPWSTR      lpszServerName,
    DWORD       dwLevel,
    LPBYTE      lpBuffer,
    LPDWORD     lpdwParameterInError
    );
```

lpszServerName designates the target machine, with NULL meaning the local computer. If it is not NULL, it must be preceded by \\. *dwLevel* indicates the level of detail you are providing. It must be one, two, or three, corresponding to a USER_INFO_1, USER_INFO_2, or USER_INFO_3 structure. Levels 2 and 3 provide a great deal of detail describing the user's login profile, but a *dwLevel* of 1 is sufficient to create a new user. You can use the User Modals API group to tailor the user's profile more precisely. *lpBuffer* points to the structure appropriate to the level of detail you are providing. *lpdwParameterInError* can be useful in tracking mistakes you make. If NetUserAdd() returns ERROR_INVALID_PARAMETER (87), the variable pointed to by *lpdwParameterInError* will tell you which field of the input structure was incorrect. For the USER_INFO_1, the possible values are:

- USER_NAME_PARMNUM (1)
- USER_PASSWORD_PARMNUM (3)
- USER_PASSWORD_AGE_PARMNUM (4)
- USER_PRIV_PARMNUM (5)
- USER_HOME_DIR_PARMNUM (6)
- USER_COMMENT_PARMNUM (7)
- USER_FLAGS_PARMNUM (8)
- USER_SCRIPT_PATH_PARMNUM (9)

CNetServer::CNetServer()

Because adding, deleting, and enumerating users are operations that target a server, I use the CNetServer class to encapsulate these operations. The corresponding methods are AddUser(), DeleteUser(), and EnumUsers(). The CNetServer constructor builds an object that contains some of the arguments that will be needed by the other methods. Because its default constructor is specified as *private*, everyone using the CNetServer class must pass its constructor the server name. The constructor does four things:

1. It stores the server name as a Unicode string, first adding \\ to the front of the name. This is the format in which the LAN Manager functions require it.
2. It remembers whether the caller is using Unicode or ANSI, by detecting if it had to translate the input string to get its Unicode representation (in the *m_bTranslated* member).
3. It stores the string as an ANSI string. This is how I will need to pass it to functions that are sensitive to the character set I use when I build the DLL (which is the ANSI character set).
4. It checks to see if the machine name is our own, and stores this in the *m_bMyName* member variable.

Here is its listing, from \WIN32NET\CODE\LANMAN\LMCLASS \NETSRVR.CPP:

```
CNetServer::CNetServer(LPCTSTR lpszServerName)
{
   m_szServerNameW[0] = L'\\';
   m_szServerNameW[1] = L'\\';
```

```
    // Unicode version needs leading \\ to pass
    // to LAN Manager functions
    m_bTranslated = ANSIToUnicode(
                        lpszServerName,
                        &m_szServerNameW[2],
                        sizeof (m_szServerNameW) / sizeof (WCHAR));
    UnicodeToANSI((LPTSTR) lpszServerName,
                  m_szServerNameA,
                  sizeof (m_szServerNameA));

    m_bMyName = IsMyComputerName(m_szServerNameA);
}
```

CNetServer::AddUser()

Here is the AddUser() method, which creates a new user on a target server.

```
BOOL CNetServer::AddUser(LPCTSTR lpszUserName,
                         LPCTSTR lpszPassword)
{
   USER_INFO_1    UserInfo;
   NET_API_STATUS dwRetcode;
   DWORD          dwErrorParm;
   WCHAR          szUserNameW[256];
   WCHAR          szPasswordW[256];
   LPTSTR         lpszServerName;

   if (m_bMyName)
      lpszServerName = NULL;
   else
      lpszServerName = (LPTSTR) m_szServerNameW;

   // Force user name to Unicode
   ANSIToUnicode(lpszUserName,
                 szUserNameW,
                 sizeof (szUserNameW) / sizeof (WCHAR));
   lpszUserName = (LPTSTR) szUserNameW;

   // Force password to Unicode
   if (lpszPassword != NULL && (lstrlen(lpszPassword) > 0))
      {
      ANSIToUnicode(lpszPassword,
                    szPasswordW,
                    sizeof (szPasswordW) / sizeof (WCHAR));
      lpszPassword = (LPTSTR) szPasswordW;
      }
   else
      lpszPassword = NULL;
```

```
    ::ZeroMemory(&UserInfo, sizeof (USER_INFO_1));
    UserInfo.usri1_name     = (LPWSTR) lpszUserName;
    UserInfo.usri1_password = (LPWSTR) lpszPassword;
    UserInfo.usri1_priv     = USER_PRIV_USER;
    UserInfo.usri1_flags    = UF_SCRIPT | UF_PASSWD_NOTREQD;

    dwRetcode = NetUserAdd((LPWSTR) lpszServerName,
                           1, // Level
                           (LPBYTE) &UserInfo,
                           &dwErrorParm);
    return (dwRetcode == NERR_Success ||
            dwRetcode == NERR_UserExists);
}
```

I fill in the fields of the USER_INFO_1 structure with all the required information. Incidentally, you cannot make the new user an Administrator by setting the *usri1_priv* field to USER_PRIV_ADMIN. In order to confer administrative status, you have to add the user to either the Administrators local group or the Domain Admins global group on an NT server, which is itself a member of Administrators.

Deleting a User

NetUserDel() is a very simple function:

```
NET_API_STATUS NET_API_FUNCTION
NetUserDel (
   LPWSTR    lpszServerName,
   LPWSTR    lpszUserName
    );
```

It removes user *lpszUserName* from the security accounts database on *lpszServerName*.

CNetServer::DeleteUser()

CNetServer::DeleteUser() reflects the simplicity of NetUserDel(). Most of the code is devoted to normalizing the server name—passing it as NULL if I'm targeting the local machine—and converting the user name to Unicode.

```
BOOL CNetServer::DeleteUser(LPCTSTR lpszUserName)
{
   WCHAR          szUserNameW[256];
   LPTSTR         lpszServerName;
   NET_API_STATUS dwRetcode;
```

```
    if (m_bMyName)
       lpszServerName = NULL;
    else
       lpszServerName = (LPTSTR) m_szServerNameW;

    // Force user name to Unicode
    ANSIToUnicode(lpszUserName,
                  szUserNameW,
                  sizeof (szUserNameW) / sizeof (WCHAR));
    lpszUserName = (LPCTSTR) szUserNameW;

    dwRetcode = NetUserDel((LPWSTR) lpszServerName,
                           (LPWSTR) lpszUserName);
    return (dwRetcode == NERR_Success ||
            dwRetcode == NERR_UserNotFound);
}
```

Enumerating Users

NetUserEnum() allocates memory for an array of USER_INFO_X structures, where X represents the level of detail you want.

```
NET_API_STATUS NET_API_FUNCTION
NetUserEnum (
   LPWSTR      lpszServerName,
   DWORD       dwLevel,
   DWORD       dwFilter,
   LPBYTE     *lplpBuffer,
   DWORD       dwPreferredMaxLength,
   LPDWORD     lpdwEntriesRead,
   LPDWORD     lpdwTotalEntries,
   LPDWORD     lpdwResumeHandle
    );
```

There are several levels of detail you can request with *dwLevel*. Level zero returns an array of USER_INFO_0 structures, which contain a single element, a pointer to the user name.

```
typedef struct _USER_INFO_0
{
    LPWSTR   usri0_name;
} USER_INFO_0, *PUSER_INFO_0, *LPUSER_INFO_0;
```

dwFilter can be used to limit the enumeration to certain types of users. Passing it as zero requests all users. However, when you do this on an NT

Server, you get strange-looking user names that are generated from the names of the NT computers in the domain. These are known as **trust accounts**. A workstation trust account is created for each workstation in the domain. These accounts are enumerated if you set *dwFilter* to FILTER_WORKSTATION_TRUST_ACCOUNT. By the same token, a server trust account is created for any NT Server machine. This corresponds to the filter FILTER_SERVER_TRUST_ACCOUNT. Specifying FILTER_NORMAL_ACCOUNT gives you the same users shown by the NT User Manager, so it is the preferred value to use to avoid startling your users.

lplpBuffer, dwPreferredMaxLength, lpdwEntriesRead, lpdwTotalEntries, and *lpdwResumeHandle* are the standard arguments for the enumeration functions under NT. They behave here just as they do for NetServerEnum(), described earlier in this chapter.

CNetServer::EnumUsers()

The CNetServer::EnumUsers() method calls NetUserEnum() to list users on a given machine. It asks for level zero, as it only needs to report the user names. It passes a filter of FILTER_NORMAL_ACCOUNT, which lists standard users. The callback function that it invokes is a USERENUMPROC, a type that I define as follows in NETSRVR.H:

```
typedef BOOL (CALLBACK *USERENUMPROC)(LPTSTR lpszUserName);
```

Here is the listing of CNetServer::EnumUsers():

```
BOOL CNetServer::EnumUsers(USERENUMPROC lpUserEnumProc)
{
   CHAR            szUserName[256];
   LPUSER_INFO_0   lpBuffer;
   DWORD           dwEntries, dwTotal;
   DWORD           i;
   BOOL            bRetcode = FALSE;
   NET_API_STATUS dwRetcode;
   LPTSTR          lpszUserName;
   LPTSTR          lpszServerName;

   if (m_bMyName)
      lpszServerName = NULL;
   else
      lpszServerName = (LPTSTR) m_szServerNameW;
```

```
    dwRetcode = NetUserEnum((LPWSTR) lpszServerName,
                            0,      // Level zero
                            FILTER_NORMAL_ACCOUNT,
                            (LPBYTE *) &lpBuffer,
                            65536,
                            &dwEntries,
                            &dwTotal,
                            NULL);

    if (dwRetcode == NERR_Success)
       {
       // lpBuffer contains an array of pointers to
       // USER_INFO_0 structures
       bRetcode = TRUE;
       for (i = 0; i < dwEntries; ++i)
          {
          // Convert user name back to caller's
          // character set
          if (m_bTranslated)
             {
             UnicodeToANSI((LPTSTR) lpBuffer[i].usri0_name,
                           (LPTSTR) szUserName,
                           sizeof (szUserName));
             lpszUserName = (LPTSTR) szUserName;
             }
          else
             {
             lpszUserName = (LPTSTR) lpBuffer[i].usri0_name;
             }

          if (!lpUserEnumProc(lpszUserName))
             break;
          }
       NetApiBufferFree(lpBuffer);
       }
    return bRetcode;
}
```

Figure 12-5 shows the WNETSVCS View Users dialog box, listing the users on my Server machine. WNETSVCS populates the list box by calling CNetUser::EnumUsers.

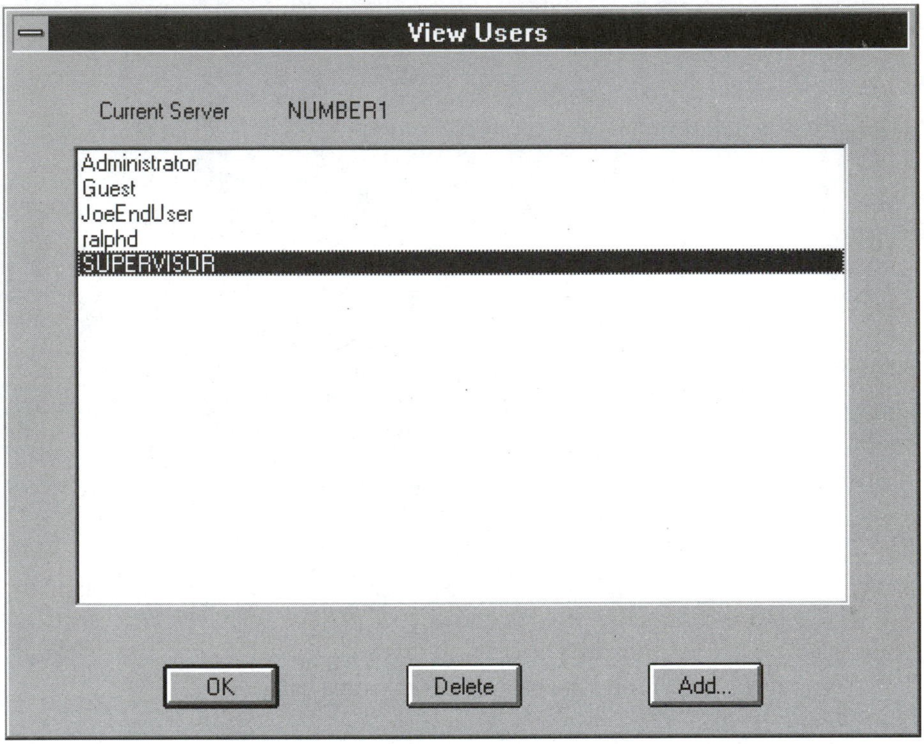

Figure 12-5. WNETSVCS View Users Dialog Box

Managing Groups

An administrator needs to do the same things with groups as with users: create them, delete them, and list them. Because NT has two types of groups, there are two sets of matching functions: NetGroupAdd() and NetLocalGroupAdd(), NetGroupDel() and NetLocalGroupDel(), and NetGroupEnum() and NetLocal-GroupEnum(). To repeat, the difference between the two types of groups is that global groups are used to export users to other domains, and local groups are used to import users and groups either into the current domain or onto an NT workstation participating in a domain. Global groups have meaning only in an NT Server domain. Permission can be granted only to local groups.

Adding a Group

NetGroupAdd() creates a new global group on the specified server. NetLocalGroupAdd() has the same syntax as NetGroupAdd(), but creates a local group instead. By the way, it is not an error to create a global group on an NT workstation. It is just an empty act because you cannot export the group anywhere else.

```
NET_API_STATUS NET_API_FUNCTION
NetGroupAdd (
    LPWSTR   lpServerName,
    DWORD    dwLevel,
    LPBYTE   lpBuffer,
    LPDWORD  lpdwParameterInError
    );

NET_API_STATUS NET_API_FUNCTION
NetLocalGroupAdd (
    LPWSTR   lpServerName,
    DWORD    dwLevel,
    LPBYTE   lpBuffer,
    LPDWORD  lpdwParameterInError
    );
```

dwLevel may be from zero to 2 for NetGroupAdd(), corresponding to a GROUP_INFO_0, GROUP_INFO_1, or GROUP_INFO_2 structure. The level may be only zero or 1 for NetLocalGroupAdd(). Here, the data types are LOCALGROUP_INFO_0 and LOCALGROUP_INFO_1. Both level-zero structures contain just the group name. Level 1 adds a descriptive comment. GROUP_INFO_2 contains two additional fields, one for a group ID and one for its attributes. Unfortunately, there is no explanation of what these fields mean.

CNetServer::AddGroup()

CNetServer::AddGroup() calls either NetGroupAdd() or NetLocalGroup-Add(), depending on the setting of its *bLocal* argument.

```
BOOL CNetServer::AddGroup(LPCTSTR lpszGroupName,
                          BOOL    bLocal /* = FALSE */)
{
   NET_API_STATUS dwRetcode;
   WCHAR          szGroupNameW[256];
   DWORD          dwErrorParm;
   LPTSTR         lpszServerName;

   if (m_bMyName)
      lpszServerName = NULL;
   else
      lpszServerName = (LPTSTR) m_szServerNameW;
```

```
    // Force group name to Unicode
    ANSIToUnicode(lpszGroupName,
                  szGroupNameW,
                  sizeof (szGroupNameW) / sizeof (WCHAR));
    lpszGroupName = (LPCTSTR) szGroupNameW;

    if (bLocal)
       {
       LOCALGROUP_INFO_0 LocalGroupInfo;

       LocalGroupInfo.lgrpi0_name = (LPWSTR) lpszGroupName;
       dwRetcode = NetLocalGroupAdd(
                      (LPWSTR) lpszServerName,
                      0,          // Level
                      (LPBYTE) &LocalGroupInfo,
                      &dwErrorParm);
       }
    else
       {
       GROUP_INFO_0 GroupInfo;

       GroupInfo.grpi0_name = (LPWSTR) lpszGroupName;
       dwRetcode = NetGroupAdd(
                      (LPWSTR) lpszServerName,
                      0,
                      (LPBYTE) &GroupInfo,
                      &dwErrorParm);
       }
    return (dwRetcode == NERR_Success ||
            dwRetcode == NERR_GroupExists);
}
```

Deleting Groups

NetGroupDel() and NetLocalGroupDel() are a syntactically identical pair of functions that delete global and local groups, respectively.

```
NET_API_STATUS NET_API_FUNCTION
NetGroupDel (
    LPWSTR   lpszServerName,
    LPWSTR   lpszGroupName
    );

NET_API_STATUS NET_API_FUNCTION
NetLocalGroupDel (
    LPWSTR   lpszServerName,
    LPWSTR   lpszGroupName
    );
```

CNetServer::DeleteGroup()

CNetServer::DeleteGroup() calls either NetGroupDel() or NetLocalGroup-Del(), again basing its decision on the *bLocal* input parameter.

```
BOOL CNetServer::DeleteGroup(LPCTSTR lpszGroupName,
                             BOOL   bLocal /* = FALSE */)
{
   WCHAR          szGroupNameW[256];
   LPTSTR         lpszServerName;
   NET_API_STATUS dwRetcode;

   if (m_bMyName)
      lpszServerName = NULL;
   else
      lpszServerName = (LPTSTR) m_szServerNameW;

   // Force group name to Unicode
   ANSIToUnicode(lpszGroupName,
                 szGroupNameW,
                 sizeof (szGroupNameW) / sizeof (WCHAR));
   lpszGroupName = (LPCTSTR) szGroupNameW;

   if (bLocal)
      {
      dwRetcode = NetLocalGroupDel((LPWSTR) lpszServerName,
                                   (LPWSTR) lpszGroupName);
      }
   else
      {
      dwRetcode = NetGroupDel((LPWSTR) lpszServerName,
                              (LPWSTR) lpszGroupName);
      }

   return (dwRetcode == NERR_Success ||
           dwRetcode == NERR_GroupNotFound);
}
```

Enumerating Groups

NetGroupEnum() and NetLocalGroupEnum() are also twin functions that behave exactly like the other enumerators we have already seen, NetServer-Enum() and NetUserEnum().

```
NET_API_STATUS NET_API_FUNCTION
NetGroupEnum (
```

```
    LPWSTR       lpServerName,
    DWORD        dwLevel,
    LPBYTE      *lplpBuffer,
    DWORD        dwPreferredMaxLength,
    LPDWORD      lpdwEntriesRead,
    LPDWORD      lpdwTotalEntries,
    LPDWORD      lpdwResumeHandle
    );

NET_API_STATUS NET_API_FUNCTION
NetLocalGroupEnum (
    LPWSTR       lpServerName,
    DWORD        dwLevel,
    LPBYTE      *lplpBuffer,
    DWORD        dwPreferredMaxLength,
    LPDWORD      lpdwEntriesRead,
    LPDWORD      lpdwTotalEntries,
    LPDWORD      lpdwResumeHandle
    );
```

Only levels zero and 1 may be requested here. NetGroupEnum() will return an array of GROUP_INFO_0 or GROUP_INFO_1 structures, and NetLocalGroup-Enum() returns LOCALGROUP_INFO_0 and LOCALGROUP_INFO_1.

CNetServer::EnumGroups()

To make sure it enumerates all groups on the target server, CNet-Server::EnumGroups() calls one of these functions, then the other. Its callback function is a GROUPENUMPROC.

```
typedef BOOL (CALLBACK *GROUPENUMPROC)(LPTSTR lpszGroupName,
                                       BOOL    bLocal);
```

The *bLocal* item passed to the callback tells it what kind of group is being listed. WNETSVCS puts the group name into a list box and stores the group type (local or global) as list box item data. When WNETSVCS needs to manipulate the group in some way—to delete it, for instance, or to add and remove members—it retrieves the *bLocal* flag from the list box item data where it stored it.

```
BOOL CNetServer::EnumGroups(GROUPENUMPROC lpGroupEnumProc)
{
   CHAR             szGroupName[256];
   LPLOCALGROUP_INFO_0
                    lpGroupInfo;
```

```
DWORD           dwEntries, dwTotal;
DWORD           i;
BOOL            bRetcode = FALSE;
LPTSTR          lpszGroupName;
LPTSTR          lpszServerName;

if (m_bMyName)
   lpszServerName = NULL;
else
   lpszServerName = (LPTSTR) m_szServerNameW;

if (NetLocalGroupEnum((LPWSTR) lpszServerName,
                      0,      // Level zero
                      (LPBYTE *) &lpGroupInfo,
                      65536,
                      &dwEntries,
                      &dwTotal,
                      NULL) == NERR_Success)
   {
   bRetcode = TRUE;

   // lpGroupInfo contains an array of pointers
   // to the Group names
   for (i = 0; i < dwEntries; ++i)
      {
      // Convert group name back to caller's
      // character set
      if (m_bTranslated)
         {
         UnicodeToANSI((LPTSTR) lpGroupInfo[i].lgrpi0_name,
                       (LPTSTR) szGroupName,
                       sizeof (szGroupName));
         lpszGroupName = (LPTSTR) szGroupName;
         }
      else
         {
         lpszGroupName = (LPTSTR) lpGroupInfo[i].lgrpi0_name;
         }

      if (!lpGroupEnumProc(lpszGroupName,
                           TRUE))
         break;
      }
   NetApiBufferFree(lpGroupInfo);
   }
```

```
    if (NetGroupEnum((LPWSTR) lpszServerName,
                     0,        // Level zero
                     (LPBYTE *) &lpGroupInfo,
                     65536,
                     &dwEntries,
                     &dwTotal,
                     NULL) == NERR_Success)
       {
       bRetcode = TRUE;

       for (i = 0; i < dwEntries; ++i)
          {
          if (m_bTranslated)
             {
             UnicodeToANSI((LPTSTR) lpGroupInfo[i].lgrpi0_name,
                           (LPTSTR) szGroupName,
                           sizeof (szGroupName));
             lpszGroupName = (LPTSTR) szGroupName;
             }
          else
             {
             lpszGroupName = (LPTSTR) lpGroupInfo[i].lgrpi0_name;
             }

          if (!lpGroupEnumProc(lpszGroupName,
                               FALSE))
             break;
          }
       NetApiBufferFree(lpGroupInfo);
       }
    return bRetcode;
}
```

Associating Users and Groups

Groups have a major role to play in network administration. They make it much easier to assign permissions to users because you can group many related users into a few groups. Thus, you need to grant permissions only to a handful of groups, rather than to an enormous number of users. Also, if a user's organizational affiliation changes, you don't have to go all over your server trying to find files to which the user has rights—you just change the group membership. Therefore, the functions that let you associate users and groups are very important. Here are these functions:

- NetGroupAddUser() and NetLocalGroupAddMember() add a new member to a group. The difference in the names is significant: NetGroupAddUser() expects a user name, whereas NetLocalGroupAddMember() requires the new member's SID.
- NetGroupDelUser() and NetLocalGroupDelMember() remove a group member.
- NetGroupGetUsers() and NetLocalGroupGetMembers() return arrays describing the current group members.

Adding a User to a Group

NetGroupAddUser() and NetLocalGroupAddMember() are simple functions, as their prototypes show.

```
NET_API_STATUS NET_API_FUNCTION
NetGroupAddUser (
    LPWSTR   lpszServerName,
    LPWSTR   lpszGroupName,
    LPWSTR   lpszUserName
    );

NET_API_STATUS NET_API_FUNCTION
NetLocalGroupAddMember (
    LPWSTR   lpszServerName,
    LPWSTR   lpszGroupName,
    PSID     pMemberSID
    );
```

The CNetUserGroup Class

The CNetUserGroup class supports the operations that affect groups—adding, deleting, and enumerating members. It is defined in \WIN32NET\CODE\LANMAN\LMCLASS\NETGROUP.H on the source disk:

```
/********
*
* NETGROUP.H
*
* Copyright (c) 1996 Ralph P. Davis
*
* All Rights Reserved
*
*****/

#ifndef NETGROUP_INCLUDED
#define NETGROUP_INCLUDED
```

```
#include "netsrvr.h"

class AFX_EXT_CLASS CNetUserGroup : public CObject
{
private:
   CNetUserGroup() {}
protected:
   WCHAR        m_szGroupNameW[256];
   CHAR         m_szGroupNameA[256];
   BOOL         m_bLocal;
   CNetServer *m_pServer;
public:
   CNetUserGroup(LPCTSTR     lpszGroupName,
                 CNetServer *pServer,
                 BOOL        bLocal = TRUE);

   CNetServer *GetServer(void)
      {
      return m_pServer;
      }
   BOOL IsLocal(void)
      {
      return m_bLocal;
      }
   LPWSTR GetGroupNameW(void)
      {
      return m_szGroupNameW;
      }
   LPSTR GetGroupNameA(void)
      {
      return m_szGroupNameA;
      }
   LPTSTR GetGroupName(void)
      {
      if (m_pServer->IsTranslated())
         return (LPTSTR) GetGroupNameA();
      else
         return (LPTSTR) GetGroupNameW();
      }

   BOOL AddMember(LPCTSTR lpszUserName);
   BOOL DeleteMember(LPCTSTR lpszUserName);
   BOOL EnumMembers(USERENUMPROC lpMemberEnumProc);
   BOOL IsMemberOf(CNetUserGroup *pGroup);
   DECLARE_DYNAMIC(CNetUserGroup)
};
#endif
```

CNetUserGroup::AddMember()

The only complication here is that NetLocalGroupAddMember() expects the new member's SID, and I want to support human-readable group names in CNetUserGroup::AddMember(). This obliges me to call LookupAccountName() (discussed in Chapter 13) to convert the user's name to its underlying SID.

To add members to groups, I instantiate a CNetUserGroup object, then invoke its AddMember() method for each new member. The CNetUserGroup constructor expects the group name, a CNetServer object representing its host server, and a boolean flag indicating whether it is local or not. The constructor takes its string arguments and stores them in both Unicode and ANSI. We need them in Unicode to call the LAN Manager functions, and in ANSI to call LookupAccountName() (since I'm building the DLL using the ANSI character set). The ANSI version is stored without the leading \\, since only the LAN Manager functions require it.

```
CNetUserGroup::CNetUserGroup(LPCTSTR     lpszGroupName,
                             CNetServer *pServer,
                             BOOL        bLocal
                                          /*= TRUE*/)
{
   ANSIToUnicode(lpszGroupName,
                 m_szGroupNameW,
                 sizeof (m_szGroupNameW) / sizeof (WCHAR));

   UnicodeToANSI(lpszGroupName,
                 m_szGroupNameA,
                 sizeof (m_szGroupNameA));

   m_pServer = pServer;
   m_bLocal  = bLocal;
}
```

Here is the listing for CNetUserGroup::AddMember(), from \WIN32NET \CODE\LANMAN\LMCLASS\NETGROUP.CPP:

```
BOOL CNetUserGroup::AddMember(LPCTSTR lpszUserName)
{
   NET_API_STATUS dwRetcode;
   LPTSTR lpszServerName;
   WCHAR  szUserNameW[256];
   CHAR   szUserNameA[256];

   // We need the user name in Unicode for
   // NetGroupAddUser()
   // and in ANSI for LookupAccountName()
```

```
ANSIToUnicode(lpszUserName,
              szUserNameW,
              sizeof (szUserNameW) / sizeof (WCHAR));

UnicodeToANSI(lpszUserName,
              szUserNameA,
              sizeof (szUserNameA));

if (m_pServer->IsMyName())
   {
   lpszServerName = NULL;
   }
else
   {
   lpszServerName = m_pServer->GetServerNameW();
   }

if (m_bLocal)
   {
   // LookupAccountName() to translate the
   // name to a SID
   BYTE  bySIDBuffer[1024];
   DWORD dwSIDSize = sizeof (bySIDBuffer);
   CHAR szDomain[256];
   DWORD dwDomainSize = sizeof (szDomain);
   SID_NAME_USE SidNameUse;

   if (lpszServerName != NULL)
      lpszServerName = (LPTSTR) m_pServer->GetServerNameA();

   if (!LookupAccountName(lpszServerName,
                          szUserNameA,
                          (PSID) bySIDBuffer,
                          &dwSIDSize,
                          szDomain,
                          &dwDomainSize,
                          &SidNameUse))
      {
      dwRetcode = FALSE;
      }
   else
      {
      if (lpszServerName != NULL)
         lpszServerName = m_pServer->GetServerNameW();
```

```
            dwRetcode = NetLocalGroupAddMember(
                           (LPWSTR) lpszServerName,
                           (LPWSTR) m_szGroupNameW,
                           bySIDBuffer);
            }
         }
      else
         {
         if (lpszServerName != NULL)
            lpszServerName = m_pServer->GetServerNameW();

         dwRetcode = NetGroupAddUser(
                           (LPWSTR) lpszServerName,
                           (LPWSTR) m_szGroupNameW,
                           (LPWSTR) szUserNameW);
         }
      return (dwRetcode == NERR_Success ||
              dwRetcode == NERR_UserInGroup);
}
```

Deleting a Group Member

The delete functions, NetGroupDelUser() and NetLocalGroupDelMember(), are syntactically the same as NetGroupAddUser() and NetLocalGroupAdd-Member(), with the latter function also requiring a SID, not a name.

```
NET_API_STATUS NET_API_FUNCTION
NetGroupDelUser (
    LPWSTR   lpszServerName,
    LPWSTR   lpszGroupName,
    LPWSTR   lpszUserName
    );

NET_API_STATUS NET_API_FUNCTION
NetLocalGroupDelMember (
    LPWSTR   lpszServerName,
    LPWSTR   lpszGroupName,
    PSID     pMemberSID
    );
```

CNetUserGroup::DeleteMember()

This function is the mirror image of CNetUserGroup::AddMember(); just use the opposite verb.

```
BOOL CNetUserGroup::DeleteMember(LPCTSTR lpszUserName)
{
   NET_API_STATUS dwRetcode;
   LPTSTR lpszServerName;
   WCHAR  szUserNameW[256];
   CHAR   szUserNameA[256];

   // We need the user name in Unicode for
   // NetGroupAddUser()
   // and in ANSI for LookupAccountName()

   ANSIToUnicode(lpszUserName,
                 szUserNameW,
                 sizeof (szUserNameW) / sizeof (WCHAR));

   UnicodeToANSI(lpszUserName,
                 szUserNameA,
                 sizeof (szUserNameA));

   if (m_pServer->IsMyName())
      {
      lpszServerName = NULL;
      }
   else
      {
      lpszServerName = m_pServer->GetServerNameW();
      }

   if (m_bLocal)
      {
      BYTE  bySIDBuffer[1024];
      DWORD dwSIDSize = sizeof (bySIDBuffer);
      CHAR szDomain[256];
      DWORD dwDomainSize = sizeof (szDomain);
      SID_NAME_USE SidNameUse;

      if (lpszServerName != NULL)
         lpszServerName =
            (LPTSTR) m_pServer->GetServerNameA();

      if (!LookupAccountName(lpszServerName,
                             szUserNameA,
                             (PSID) bySIDBuffer,
                             &dwSIDSize,
                             szDomain,
                             &dwDomainSize,
                             &SidNameUse))
```

```
            {
            dwRetcode = FALSE;
            }
         else
            {
            if (lpszServerName != NULL)
               lpszServerName = m_pServer->GetServerNameW();

            dwRetcode = NetLocalGroupDelMember(
                           (LPWSTR) lpszServerName,
                           (LPWSTR) m_szGroupNameW,
                           bySIDBuffer);
            }
         }
      else
         {
         if (lpszServerName != NULL)
            lpszServerName = m_pServer->GetServerNameW();

         dwRetcode = NetGroupDelUser(
                           (LPWSTR) lpszServerName,
                           (LPWSTR) m_szGroupNameW,
                           (LPWSTR) szUserNameW);
         }
      return (dwRetcode == NERR_Success ||
            dwRetcode == NERR_UserNotInGroup);
}
```

Listing Group Members

Here again, I convert LAN Manager enumerators, where one call returns an array of objects, to Windows ones, where for each object I invoke a callback function. The relevant LAN Manager functions are NetGroupGetUsers() and NetLocalGroupGetMembers(). Here are the prototypes for these two functions.

```
NET_API_STATUS NET_API_FUNCTION
NetGroupGetUsers (
    LPWSTR     lpszServerName,
    LPWSTR     lpszGroupName,
    DWORD      dwLevel,
    LPBYTE    *lplpBuffer,
    DWORD      dwPreferredMaxLength,
    LPDWORD    lpdwEntriesRead,
    LPDWORD    lpdwTotalEntries,
    LPDWORD    lpdwResumeHandle
    );
```

```
NET_API_STATUS NET_API_FUNCTION
NetLocalGroupGetMembers
    LPWSTR     lpszServerName,
    LPWSTR     lpszGroupName,
    DWORD      dwLevel,
    LPBYTE    *lplpBuffer,
    DWORD      dwPreferredMaxLength,
    LPDWORD    lpdwEntriesRead,
    LPDWORD    lpdwTotalEntries,
    LPDWORD    lpdwResumeHandle
    );
```

The array returned at **lplpBuffer* consists of GROUP_USERS_INFO_0 or GROUP_USERS_INFO_1 structures for NetGroupGetUsers(), and LOCAL-GROUP_MEMBERS_INFO_0 or LOCALGROUP_MEMBERS_INFO_1 for NetLocalGroupGetMembers(). If we ask the latter function for level 1, we don't have to worry about converting a SID to a name; the name is supplied in the structure. The level-zero structure has only the SID.

```
typedef struct _LOCALGROUP_MEMBERS_INFO_1
{
     PSID          lgrmi1_sid;
     SID_NAME_USE lgrmi1_sidusage;
     LPWSTR        lgrmi1_name;
} LOCALGROUP_MEMBERS_INFO_1;
```

For global groups, the GROUP_USERS_INFO_X structures report the user name. GROUP_USERS_INFO_1 includes attributes, but they are not explained anywhere; I have no idea what they pertain to.

```
typedef struct _GROUP_USERS_INFO_0 {
     LPWSTR  grui0_name;
} GROUP_USERS_INFO_0;

typedef struct _GROUP_USERS_INFO_1 {
     LPWSTR  grui1_name;
     DWORD   grui1_attributes;
} GROUP_USERS_INFO_1;
```

CNetUserGroup::EnumMembers()

CNetUserGroup::EnumMembers() just calls NetGroupGetUsers() or Net-LocalGroupGetMembers(), depending on its *bLocal* argument, and reports everyone it encounters. The callback function is a USERENUMPROC, which enumerates the user names. Notice that I call NetUserGetInfo() to make sure I enumerate normal users, and not trust accounts.

```
BOOL CNetUserGroup::EnumMembers(
                         USERENUMPROC lpMemberEnumProc)
{
   LPLOCALGROUP_MEMBERS_INFO_1 lpLocalGroupInfo = NULL;
   DWORD         dwEntriesRead = 0, dwTotalAvail = 0;
   DWORD         i;
   BOOL          bRetcode = FALSE;
   CHAR          szMemberNameA[256];
   LPTSTR        lpszServerName;
   LPTSTR        lpszMemberName;
   USER_INFO_1 *lpUserInfo;

   if (m_pServer->IsMyName())
      lpszServerName = NULL;
   else
      lpszServerName = m_pServer->GetServerNameW();

   if (m_bLocal)
      {
      bRetcode = TRUE;

      if (NetLocalGroupGetMembers(
          (LPWSTR) lpszServerName,
          m_szGroupNameW,
          1,
          (LPBYTE *) &lpLocalGroupInfo,
          65536,
          &dwEntriesRead,
          &dwTotalAvail,
          NULL) == NERR_Success)
         {
         for (i = 0; i < dwEntriesRead; ++i)
            {
            // Make sure we're enumerating a normal user
            // (not some kind of a trust account)
            NetUserGetInfo((LPWSTR) lpszServerName,
                           lpLocalGroupInfo[i].lgrmi1_name,
                           1,
                           (LPBYTE *) &lpUserInfo);

            if (lpUserInfo->usri1_flags &
                UF_NORMAL_ACCOUNT)
```

```
                {
                if (m_pServer->IsTranslated())
                    {
                    UnicodeToANSI(
                        (LPTSTR) lpLocalGroupInfo[i].lgrmi1_name,
                        szMemberNameA,
                        sizeof (szMemberNameA));
                    lpszMemberName = (LPTSTR) szMemberNameA;
                    }
                else
                    lpszMemberName =
                        (LPTSTR) lpLocalGroupInfo[i].lgrmi1_name;

                if (!lpMemberEnumProc(lpszMemberName))
                    break;
                }
            NetApiBufferFree(lpUserInfo);
            }
        NetApiBufferFree(lpLocalGroupInfo);
        }
    }
else
    {
    LPGROUP_USERS_INFO_0 lpGroupInfo = NULL;

    if (NetGroupGetUsers((LPWSTR) lpszServerName,
                         m_szGroupNameW,
                         0,
                         (LPBYTE *) &lpGroupInfo,
                         65536,
                         &dwEntriesRead,
                         &dwTotalAvail,
                         NULL) == NERR_Success)
        {
        bRetcode = TRUE;

        for (i = 0; i < dwEntriesRead; ++i)
            {
            NetUserGetInfo((LPWSTR) lpszServerName,
                           lpGroupInfo[i].grui0_name,
                           1,
                           (LPBYTE *) &lpUserInfo);

            if (lpUserInfo->usri1_flags &
                 UF_NORMAL_ACCOUNT)
                {
```

```
                if (m_pServer->IsTranslated())
                   {
                   UnicodeToANSI(
                      (LPTSTR) lpGroupInfo[i].grui0_name,
                      szMemberNameA,
                      sizeof (szMemberNameA));
                   lpszMemberName = (LPTSTR) szMemberNameA;
                   }
                else
                   lpszMemberName =
                      (LPTSTR) lpGroupInfo[i].grui0_name;
                if (!lpMemberEnumProc(lpszMemberName))
                   break;
                }
             NetApiBufferFree(lpUserInfo);
             }
          NetApiBufferFree(lpGroupInfo);
          }
       }
   return bRetcode;
}
```

Determining If a User Belongs to a Group

Before discussing how to enumerate all the groups to which a user belongs, I want to show you how I determine if a given user is already in a group or not. This is an operation affecting a user object, so I implement it in the CNetUser class, declared in \WIN32NET\CODE\LANMAN\LMCLASS \NETUSER.H on the source disk. It also applies to CNetUserGroup, since both local and global groups can belong to local groups.

```
/********
*
* NETUSER.H
*
* Copyright (c) 1996 Ralph P. Davis
*
* All Rights Reserved
*
*****/

#ifndef NETUSER_INCLUDED
#define NETUSER_INCLUDED
```

```
#include "netsrvr.h"
#include "netgroup.h"

class AFX_EXT_CLASS CNetUser : public CObject
{
private:
   CNetUser() {}
protected:
   CHAR  m_szUserNameA[256];
   WCHAR m_szUserNameW[256];
public:
   CNetUser(LPCTSTR lpszUserName);
   BOOL IsMemberOf(CNetUserGroup *pGroup);
   BOOL EnumGroups(GROUPENUMPROC lpGroupEnumProc,
                   CNetServer   *pServer);
   DECLARE_DYNAMIC(CNetUser)
};
#endif
```

There is no direct way, no single API call, to accomplish this. My solution is to call NetGroupGetUsers() or NetLocalGroupGetMembers() and compare the enumerated users with the user I'm looking for. I do that in the CNetUser::IsMemberOf() method. It expects to be passed a CNetUserGroup object designating the group of interest.

```
BOOL CNetUser::IsMemberOf(CNetUserGroup *pGroup)
{
   LPTSTR lpszServerName;
   LPLOCALGROUP_MEMBERS_INFO_1 lpLocalGroupInfo = NULL;
   DWORD  dwEntriesRead = 0, dwTotalAvail = 0;
   DWORD  i;
   BOOL   bRetcode = FALSE;
   CHAR   szMemberNameA[256];

   if (pGroup->GetServer()->IsMyName())
      lpszServerName = NULL;
   else
      lpszServerName =
         pGroup->GetServer()->GetServerNameW();

   if (pGroup->IsLocal())
      {
      if (NetLocalGroupGetMembers(
          (LPWSTR) lpszServerName,
          pGroup->GetGroupNameW(),
          1,
```

```
                (LPBYTE *) &lpLocalGroupInfo,
                65536,
                &dwEntriesRead,
                &dwTotalAvail,
                NULL) == NERR_Success)
            {
            // See if our boy is here
            for (i = 0; (i < dwEntriesRead) && !bRetcode; ++i)
               {
               UnicodeToANSI(
                  (LPTSTR) lpLocalGroupInfo[i].lgrmi1_name,
                  szMemberNameA,
                  sizeof (szMemberNameA));
               if (lstrcmp(szMemberNameA, m_szUserNameA) == 0)
                  bRetcode = TRUE;
               }
            }
         }
      else
         {
         LPGROUP_USERS_INFO_0 lpGroupInfo = NULL;

         if (NetGroupGetUsers((LPWSTR) lpszServerName,
                              pGroup->GetGroupNameW(),
                              0,
                              (LPBYTE *) &lpGroupInfo,
                              65536,
                              &dwEntriesRead,
                              &dwTotalAvail,
                              NULL) == NERR_Success)
            {
            for (i = 0; (i < dwEntriesRead) && !bRetcode; ++i)
               {
               UnicodeToANSI(
                  (LPTSTR) lpGroupInfo[i].grui0_name,
                  szMemberNameA,
                  sizeof (szMemberNameA));
               if (lstrcmp(szMemberNameA, m_szUserNameA) == 0)
                  bRetcode = TRUE;
               }
            }
         }
   return bRetcode;
}
```

Determining If a Group Is a Member of Another Group

On an NT Server network, groups can belong to other groups. Specifically, local groups can contain other groups, both local and global. Therefore, the test for group membership is also relevant for group objects. The CNetUserGroup has an IsMemberOf() method also, similar to CNetUser::IsMemberOf(). It is somewhat simpler, since it only needs to check for membership in local groups.

```
BOOL CNetUserGroup::IsMemberOf(CNetUserGroup *pGroup)
{
   LPTSTR lpszServerName;
   LPLOCALGROUP_MEMBERS_INFO_1 lpLocalGroupInfo = NULL;
   DWORD  dwEntriesRead = 0, dwTotalAvail = 0;
   DWORD  i;
   BOOL   bRetcode = FALSE;
   CHAR   szMemberNameA[256];

   lpszServerName = pGroup->GetServer()->GetServerNameW();

   if (pGroup->IsLocal())
      {
      if (NetLocalGroupGetMembers(
           (LPWSTR) lpszServerName,
           pGroup->GetGroupNameW(),
           1,
           (LPBYTE *) &lpLocalGroupInfo,
           65536,
           &dwEntriesRead,
           &dwTotalAvail,
           NULL) == NERR_Success)
         {
         // See if this group is here
         for (i = 0; (i < dwEntriesRead) && !bRetcode; ++i)
            {
            UnicodeToANSI(
               (LPTSTR) lpLocalGroupInfo[i].lgrmi1_name,
               szMemberNameA,
               sizeof (szMemberNameA));
            if (lstrcmp(szMemberNameA, m_szGroupNameA) == 0)
               bRetcode = TRUE;
            }
         }
      }
   else
      {
      // Nonlocal groups can't contain other groups
```

```
        bRetcode = FALSE;
        }
    return bRetcode;
}
```

Listing Member Groups

The LAN Manager functions of interest here are NetUserGetGroups() and NetUserGetLocalGroups(). These functions are not quite the same.

```
NET_API_STATUS NET_API_FUNCTION
NetUserGetGroups (
    LPWSTR     lpszServerName,
    LPWSTR     lpszUserName,
    DWORD      dwLevel,
    LPBYTE    *lplpBuffer,
    DWORD      dwPreferredMaxLength,
    LPDWORD    lpdwEntriesRead,
    LPDWORD    lpdwTotalEntries
    );

NET_API_STATUS NET_API_FUNCTION
NetUserGetLocalGroups (
    LPWSTR     lpszServerName,
    LPWSTR     lpszUserName,
    DWORD      dwLevel,
    DWORD      dwFlags,
    LPBYTE    *lplpBuffer,
    DWORD      dwPreferredMaxLength,
    LPDWORD    lpdwEntriesRead,
    LPDWORD    lpdwTotalEntries
    );
```

The first function populates an array of GROUP_USERS_INFO_0 or GROUP_USERS_INFO_1 structures. The second generates a LOCAL-GROUP_MEMBERS_INFO_0 or LOCALGROUP_MEMBERS_ INFO_1 array. The *dwFlags* argument that you pass to NetUserGetLocalGroup() says whether to report groups that the user actually belongs to (by passing *dwFlags* as zero), or to also include groups to which the user belongs by virtue of being in a group that belongs to it (in which case, you pass *dwFlags* as LG_INCLUDE_INDIRECT).

CNetUser::EnumGroups()

CNetUser::EnumGroups() calls NetUserGetLocalGroups() and NetUserGetGroups() to report the local and global groups to which a user belongs directly.

```
BOOL CNetUser::EnumGroups(GROUPENUMPROC lpGroupEnumProc,
                          CNetServer   *pNetServer)
{
   LPLOCALGROUP_USERS_INFO_0 lpLocalGroupInfo = NULL;
   DWORD        dwEntriesRead = 0,
                dwTotalAvail = 0;
   DWORD        i;
   BOOL         bRetcode = FALSE;
   LPTSTR       lpszServerName;
   CHAR         szGroupName[256];
   LPTSTR       lpszGroupName;

   if (pNetServer->IsMyName())
      lpszServerName = NULL;
   else
      lpszServerName = pNetServer->GetServerNameW();

   if (NetUserGetLocalGroups((LPWSTR) lpszServerName,
                             m_szUserNameW,
                             0,
                             0,
                             (LPBYTE *) &lpLocalGroupInfo,
                             65536,
                             &dwEntriesRead,
                             &dwTotalAvail) == NERR_Success)
      {
      bRetcode = TRUE;
      for (i = 0; i < dwEntriesRead; ++i)
         {
         if (pNetServer->IsTranslated())
            {
            UnicodeToANSI(
               (LPTSTR) lpLocalGroupInfo[i].lgrui0_name,
               szGroupName,
               sizeof (szGroupName));
            lpszGroupName = szGroupName;
            }
         else
            {
            lpszGroupName =
               (LPTSTR) lpLocalGroupInfo[i].lgrui0_name;
            }
```

```
            if (!lpGroupEnumProc(lpszGroupName,
                                 TRUE))
               break;
            }
         NetApiBufferFree(lpLocalGroupInfo);
         }

   LPGROUP_INFO_0 lpGroupInfo = NULL;

   if (NetUserGetGroups((LPWSTR) lpszServerName,
                        m_szUserNameW,
                        0,
                        (LPBYTE *) &lpGroupInfo, 65536,
                        &dwEntriesRead,
                        &dwTotalAvail) == NERR_Success)
      {
      bRetcode = TRUE;
      for (i = 0; i < dwEntriesRead; ++i)
         {
         if (pNetServer->IsTranslated())
            {
            UnicodeToANSI(
               (LPTSTR) lpGroupInfo[i].grpi0_name,
               szGroupName,
               sizeof (szGroupName));
            lpszGroupName = szGroupName;
            }
         else
            {
            lpszGroupName =
               (LPTSTR) lpGroupInfo[i].grpi0_name;
            }
         if (!lpGroupEnumProc(lpszGroupName,
                              FALSE))
            break;
         }
      NetApiBufferFree(lpGroupInfo);
      }
   return bRetcode;
}
```

With these methods in place, WNETSVCS can display users and the groups to which they belong. Figure 12-6 shows the User Groups dialog box. On this screen, the user can change the groups that a user belongs to by selecting them in the right-hand list boxes, then clicking the appropriate push button.

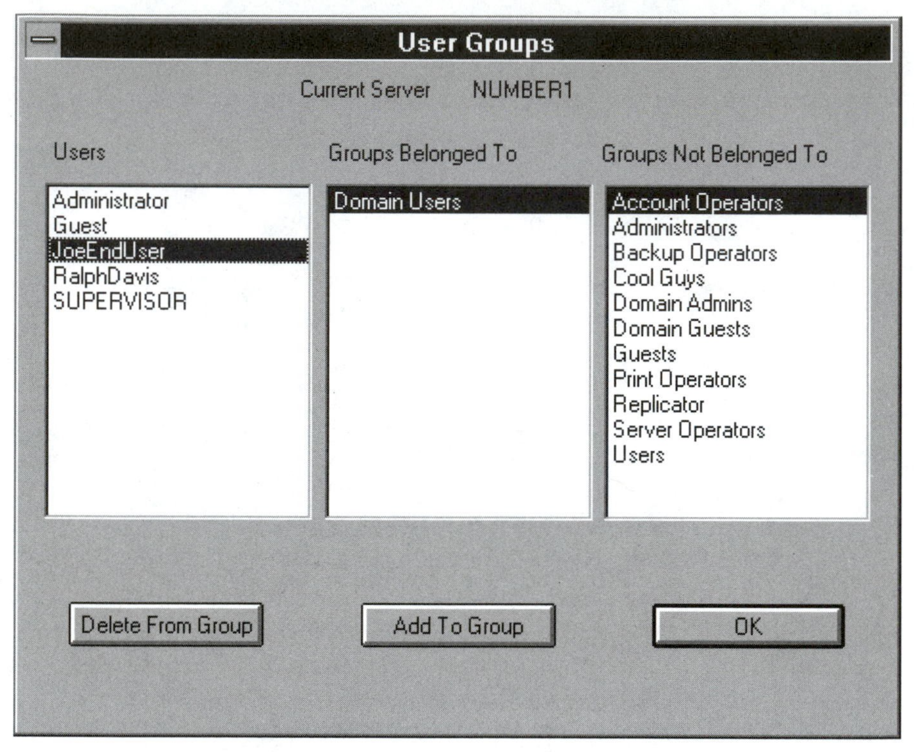

Figure 12-6. The WNETSVCS User Groups Dialog Box

The class that supports this dialog box is CUserGroupDlg. It populates the user list box in its OnInitDialog() method by invoking CNetServer::EnumUsers(). The two group list boxes are filled by OnSelchangeUsers(). This class is defined in \WIN32NET\CODE\LANMAN\WNETSVCS\USERGRP.H and implemented in USERGRP.CPP. Here are the OnInitDialog() method and the EnumUsersCallback() function that it passes to CNetServer::EnumUsers().

```
CUserGroupsDlg *CUserGroupsDlg::m_pThis;

BOOL CUserGroupsDlg::OnInitDialog()
{
   CDialog::OnInitDialog();

   m_pThis = this;
   UpdateData(TRUE);

   CNetServer TargetServer(m_szCurrentServer);
```

```
    TargetServer.EnumUsers(EnumUsersCallback);
    OnSelchangeUsers();

    return TRUE;
}

BOOL CALLBACK CUserGroupsDlg::EnumUsersCallback(
        LPTSTR lpszUserName)
{
    int nIndex =
        m_pThis->m_Users.AddString(lpszUserName);

    if (nIndex >= 0)
        {
        if (nIndex == 0)
            m_pThis->m_Users.SetCurSel(nIndex);
        }
    return TRUE;
}
```

There are a couple of things to notice. First, OnInitDialog() stores the *this* pointer in a static member variable, *m_pThis*. EnumUsersCallback() is a static member function, as all callbacks must be. For this reason, it does not get passed a *this* pointer; we have to pass it some other way. Using a static member variable is a reasonable solution here; this is a modal dialog box, so we don't have to worry about it getting reentered.

The *m_Users* member variable is a CListbox object generated by Class Wizard to represent the user's list box. EnumUsersCallback() calls its AddString() method to put each reported user into the list box, and SetCurSel() to highlight the first item.

Populating the group list boxes is easy. I just enumerate all the groups on the target server, then call CNetUser::IsMemberOf() for each group. If it says yes, I put the group in the Groups Belonged To list; otherwise, it goes in Groups Not Belonged To. OnSelchangeUsers(), called whenever the user changes the selection in the Users list box, does the group enumeration. Its callback function, EnumGroupsCallback(), decides where to put each enumerated group.

```
void CUserGroupsDlg::OnSelchangeUsers()
{
    UpdateData(TRUE);  // Get selected user

    m_GroupsIn.ResetContent();
    m_GroupsNotIn.ResetContent();
```

```
   CNetServer TargetServer(m_szCurrentServer);

   TargetServer.EnumGroups(EnumGroupsCallback);
   m_AddUser.EnableWindow(m_GroupsNotIn.GetCount() > 0);
   m_DeleteUser.EnableWindow(m_GroupsIn.GetCount() > 0);
}

BOOL CALLBACK CUserGroupsDlg::EnumGroupsCallback(
   LPTSTR lpszGroupName, BOOL bLocal)
{
   // See if selected user is a member of the group

   CNetServer TargetServer(m_pThis->m_szCurrentServer);
   CNetUser SelectedUser(m_pThis->m_szSelectedUser);

   CNetUserGroup ThisGroup(
      lpszGroupName,
      &TargetServer,
      bLocal);

   int nIndex;

   if (SelectedUser.IsMemberOf(&ThisGroup))
      {
      // Put it in the Group In list box
      nIndex = m_pThis->m_GroupsIn.AddString(lpszGroupName);
      if (nIndex >= 0)
         {
         m_pThis->m_GroupsIn.SetItemData(nIndex, bLocal);
         if (nIndex == 0)
            {
            m_pThis->m_GroupsIn.SetCurSel(nIndex);
            }
         }
      }
   else
      {
      // Put it in the Group Not In list box
      nIndex = m_pThis->m_GroupsNotIn.AddString(lpszGroupName);
      if (nIndex >= 0)
         {
         m_pThis->m_GroupsNotIn.SetItemData(nIndex, bLocal);
         if (nIndex == 0)
            {
            m_pThis->m_GroupsNotIn.SetCurSel(nIndex);
            }
         }
```

```
        }

    return TRUE;
}
```

Figure 12-7 shows the Group Members dialog box.

The logic by which the Group Members dialog box populates itself is very similar to the User Groups dialog box, but it has to make a few more decisions about what it puts in the list boxes. The class supporting this dialog box is CGroupMembersDlg, and its source files on disk are \WIN32NET\CODE \LANMAN\WNETSVCS\MMBRSDLG.H and MMBRSDLG.CPP. I omit the OnInitDialog() and EnumGroupsCallback() functions, as they differ little from the CUserGroupsDlg class. Here is the OnSelchangeGroups() method.

```
void CGroupMembersDlg::OnSelchangeGroups()
{
    UpdateData(TRUE);  // Get selected group
```

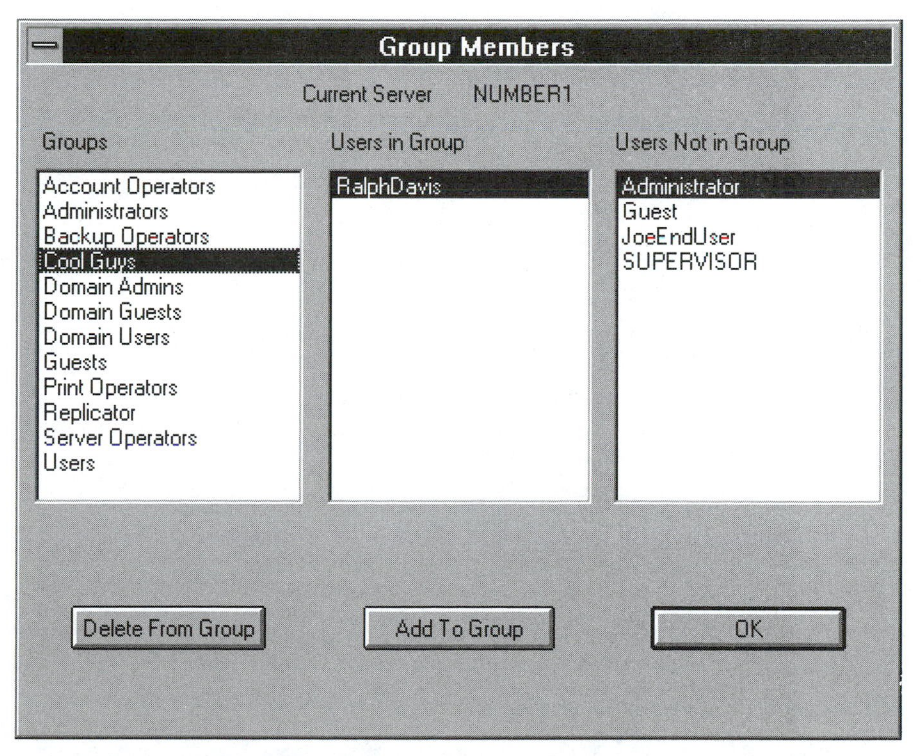

Figure 12-7. The WNETSVCS Group Members Dialog Box

```
   m_Members.ResetContent();
   m_NonMembers.ResetContent();

   CNetServer TargetServer(m_szCurrentServer);

   TargetServer.EnumUsers(EnumUsersCallback);
   TargetServer.EnumGroups(EnumContainedGroupsCallback);
   m_AddUser.EnableWindow(m_NonMembers.GetCount() > 0);
   m_DeleteUser.EnableWindow(m_Members.GetCount() > 0);
}
```

Notice that it must enumerate not only users, but also groups—after all, groups can contain other groups. First, let's look at EnumUsersCallback(), which decides where to post the enumerated users.

```
CGroupMembersDlg *CGroupMembersDlg::m_pThis;


BOOL CALLBACK CGroupMembersDlg::EnumUsersCallback(
   LPTSTR lpszUserName)
{
   // See if user is a member of the selected group

   CNetServer TargetServer(m_pThis->m_szCurrentServer);
   CNetUserGroup SelectedGroup(m_pThis->m_szSelectedGroup,
      &TargetServer,
      m_pThis->m_Groups.GetItemData(
         m_pThis->m_Groups.GetCurSel()));

   CNetUser ThisUser(lpszUserName);
   int nIndex;

   if (ThisUser.IsMemberOf(&SelectedGroup))
      {
      // Put him in the Members list box
      nIndex = m_pThis->m_Members.AddString(lpszUserName);
      if (nIndex == 0)
         {
         m_pThis->m_Members.SetCurSel(nIndex);
         }
      }
   else
      {
      // Put him in the non-members list box
      nIndex = m_pThis->m_NonMembers.AddString(lpszUserName);
      if (nIndex == 0)
```

```
            {
            m_pThis->m_NonMembers.SetCurSel(nIndex);
            }
         }

      return TRUE;
   }
```

This is just the flip side of what the User Groups dialog box did. The only extra wrinkle is the fact that list boxes containing groups store a boolean flag in list box item data, which is TRUE if the group is local, FALSE if it's global.

However, the group enumeration function (EnumContainedGroupsCallback()) has a few more things to worry about. It needs to know if the group that is being enumerated is a member of the group that's currently selected in the Groups list box. For this to happen, the selected group has to be local. It also does not want to tell the user that the currently selected group is not a member of itself; that goes without saying. So a third check makes sure that the two groups are different.

```
BOOL CALLBACK CGroupMembersDlg::EnumContainedGroupsCallback(
   LPTSTR lpszGroupName, BOOL bLocal)
{
   // See if group is a member of the selected group
   CNetServer TargetServer(m_pThis->m_szCurrentServer);
   CNetUserGroup SelectedGroup(m_pThis->m_szSelectedGroup,
      &TargetServer,
      m_pThis->m_Groups.GetItemData(
         m_pThis->m_Groups.GetCurSel()));

   CNetUserGroup ThisGroup(lpszGroupName,
                           &TargetServer,
                           bLocal);

   // Only local groups can contain other groups
   // Also, screen for the case where the
   // group being enumerated is the
   // group that's been selected.
   if (SelectedGroup.IsLocal() &&
       (lstrcmp(lpszGroupName, SelectedGroup.GetGroupName()))
         != 0)
      {
      int nIndex;

      if (ThisGroup.IsMemberOf(&SelectedGroup))
         {
         // Put it in the Members list box
```

```
            nIndex = m_pThis->m_Members.AddString(lpszGroupName);
            if (nIndex == 0)
               {
               m_pThis->m_szSelectedMember = lpszGroupName;
               m_pThis->m_Members.SetCurSel(nIndex);
               }
            }
         else
            {
            // Put it in the non-members list box
            nIndex = m_pThis->m_NonMembers.AddString(lpszGroupName);
            if (nIndex == 0)
               {
               m_pThis->m_szSelectedNonMember = lpszGroupName;
               m_pThis->m_NonMembers.SetCurSel(nIndex);
               }
            }
         }
      return TRUE;
}
```

Conclusion

In enhancing and expanding the original OS/2 LAN Manager API, Microsoft has improved it quite a bit. The LAN Manager API for Windows NT is a rich, large, powerful, and versatile set of functions that gives a solid base of support for network management and configuration applications. There are many areas of functionality that are not available through any other API set. These include:

- Adding, deleting, and enumerating users
- Adding, deleting, and enumerating groups
- Adding users to groups, removing them from groups, and finding out what users belong to what groups
- Raising network alert messages
- Finding out who is using a given file
- Sending console messages to users on the network
- Replicating directories from one machine on the network to other machines
- Scheduling remote applications for execution
- Finding out what machines are attached to the network
- Sharing local resources
- Adding, deleting, and enumerating transport drivers

- Controlling when users may log in, and from what workstations
- Finding out who's logged in where

Suggested Readings

Online References

LAN Manager Functions Overview in the Win32 online help.
Microsoft Knowledge Base for Win32 SDK articles:
"Creating/Managing User Accounts Programmatically"
"How to Look Up a User's Full Name"
"Windows 95 Support for LAN Manager APIs"

Print References

Ryan, Ralph. *Microsoft LAN Manager—A Programmer's Guide*. Redmond, WA: Microsoft Press, 1990.
Microsoft Corporation. *Microsoft LAN Manager Programmer's Reference*. Redmond, WA: Microsoft Press, 1990.

Chapter 13

The Win32 Security API

The Win32 Security API is austere, intimidating, and one of the most difficult API sets you will have to contend with in your work with Windows NT. However, let me at once present two mitigating factors: you probably won't have to use it that much, and it's child's play next to OLE 2.

The Win32 Security API does not work in Windows 95. The functions discussed in this chapter fail in that environment, and set the last error code to ERROR_CALL_NOT_IMPLEMENTED (120).

The Windows NT Security Model

Security is a pervasive element in the Windows NT environment. Many of the key building blocks of NT applications are NT objects of one sort or another. Files, pipes, threads, processes, synchronization objects, shared memory, and windows are some of the most important. In previous chapters, you saw that the functions that create these objects (with the exception of windows) include one argument that points to a SECURITY_ATTRIBUTES structure. This structure is the highest-level entry point into the NT security system and governs two aspects of an object: its inheritability and its accessibility. Here's how it's typed:

```
typedef struct _SECURITY_ATTRIBUTES
{
   DWORD  nLength;
   LPVOID lpSecurityDescriptor;
   BOOL    bInheritHandle;
} SECURITY_ATTRIBUTES;
```

nLength will always be set to *sizeof (SECURITY_ATTRIBUTES);* presumably this field is for version control. *lpSecurityDescriptor* points to a SECURITY_DESCRIPTOR. Setting it to NULL is the same as passing the SECURITY_ATTRIBUTES as NULL. It causes the affected object to acquire security characteristics by default mechanisms that I examine in this chapter. *bInheritHandle*, if set to TRUE, allows child processes to inherit the handle of the object you are creating.

Table 13-1 lists some of the functions that take a SECURITY_ATTRIBUTES pointer and refers you to the relevant chapters in this book.

Table 13-1. Functions That Take SECURITY_ATTRIBUTES

Function Name	Where Discussed in This Book
CreateFile	Chapter 6, "Win32 File I/O" Chapter 10, "Named Pipes and Mailslots"
CreateMailslot	Chapter 10, "Named Pipes and Mailslots"
CreateProcess	Not discussed
CreateProcessAsUser	Not discussed
CreateConsoleScreenBuffer	Not discussed
CreateDesktop	Not discussed
CreateDirectory(Ex)	Chapter 6, "Win32 File I/O"
CreateEvent	Chapter 5, "Synchronization Objects"
CreateFileMapping	Chapter 7, "Dynamic-Link Libraries"
CreateMutex	Chapter 5, "Synchronization Objects"
CreateNamedPipe	Chapter 10, "Named Pipes and Mailslots"
CreatePipe	Not discussed
CreateRemoteThread	Not discussed
CreateSemaphore	Chapter 5, "Synchronization Objects"
CreateThread	Chapter 4, "Multithreading"
CreateWindowStation	Not discussed
RegCreateKeyEx	Chapter 14, "The Registry and Performance Monitoring"
RegSaveKey	Chapter 14, "The Registry and Performance Monitoring"

Other functions involve an implicit attachment of security properties. Perhaps one of the most surprising is CreateWindow(). There are no SECURITY_ATTRIBUTES as such involved, but windows in NT belong to a hierarchy of screen-based objects. The top of the hierarchy is the process window station, created when you start a process. The threads spawned by that process are assigned to desktops, and these in turn create windows. Window handles—the familiar HWNDs—do not play a direct role in any Win32 Security APIs, but you can control the security characteristics of window stations and desktops. Then, when you call CreateWindow(), the resultant HWND inherits the security settings from the window station and its thread desktop.

Figure 13-1 shows a process window station with desktops for two threads. The first thread has created two windows, and the second owns one.

In many of the code examples in previous chapters, I ignored the SECURITY_ATTRIBUTES by passing it as a NULL pointer. However, as I hinted on several occasions, this is not an empty action. You will see in this chapter that it has a very specific meaning that may not always be what you intend. Another use of the SECURITY_ATTRIBUTES is to create a handle that can be inherited by child processes. In this case, you often set the *bInheritHandle* field to TRUE, and *lpSecurityDescriptor* to NULL. This too is a significant action.

There are no functions that manipulate SECURITY_ATTRIBUTES. The format of the structure is exposed, and you can set and read the fields directly.

Security Descriptors

The most important field in the SECURITY_ATTRIBUTES is *lpSecurityDescriptor*, which points to a SECURITY_DESCRIPTOR. Unlike the SECURITY_ATTRIBUTES, the internal layout of this structure is not

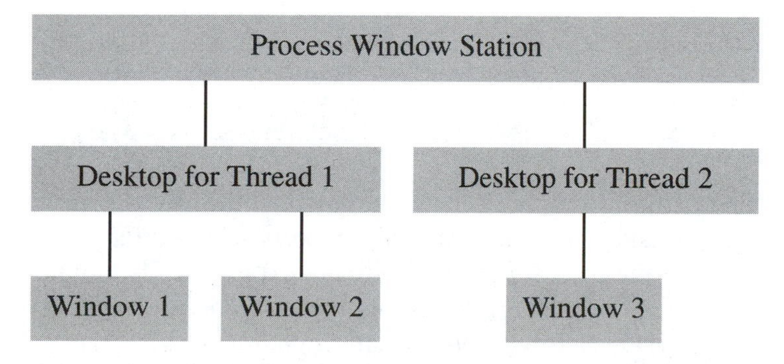

Figure 13-1. Hierarchy of Screen-Based Object Classes

documented. You can think of a SECURITY_DESCRIPTOR as a single record in the security database. For each protected object, there exists at most one SECURITY_DESCRIPTOR. It carries the information needed to regulate attempts to use the object. Each item in the SECURITY_DESCRIPTOR has paired Get() and Set() functions.

Information Stored in a Security Descriptor. These are the data items and the functions you use to manipulate a security descriptor:

- The object's owner (GetSecurityDescriptorOwner() and SetSecurityDescriptorOwner()). This is represented by the Security Identifier (SID) of the owner. I will discuss SIDs in more detail shortly.
- The primary group to which the owner belongs (GetSecurityDescriptorGroup() and SetSecurityDescriptorGroup)). This is the group to which NT automatically assigns you when your account is first created. It is also identified by its SID.
- The **discretionary access control list (DACL)**, which determines who may do what with the object (GetSecurityDescriptorDacl() and SetSecurityDescriptorDacl()).
- The **system access control list (SACL)**, which specifies how you want to audit the use of the object (GetSecurityDescriptorSacl() and SetSecurityDescriptorSacl()).

Because the security database represents users and groups in the same way as SIDs, the owner- and group-related functions have identical syntax. Similarly, because the last two groups of functions work with access control lists, they are syntactically the same. Of all these functions, the most important are GetSecurityDescriptorDacl() and SetSecurityDescriptorDacl(); they allow you to control who can use an object. They are discussed extensively through the rest of the chapter, so I will only show the syntax for the owner-related functions here.

```
BOOL GetSecurityDescriptorOwner(
        PSECURITY_DESCRIPTOR lpSecurityDescriptor,
        PSID                *ppSID,
        LPBOOL               lpbOwnerDefaulted);
```

A pointer to the security identifier (SID) of the object's owner is returned in **ppSID*, and **lpbOwnerDefaulted* reports whether the owner was determined by some default mechanism or set explicitly. The pointer returned in **ppSID* is not allocated; it is an address within the security descriptor. If GetSecurityDescriptorOwner() or any function in the Security API returns FALSE, consult GetLastError() to find out what the exact problem is.

```
BOOL SetSecurityDescriptorOwner(
        PSECURITY_DESCRIPTOR lpSecurityDescriptor,
        PSID                 pSID,
        BOOL                 bOwnerDefaulted);
```

The owner of the object is changed to the object with the SID to which *pSID* points. SIDs are binary data; you will see shortly how you match human-readable names to their underlying SIDs, and vice versa.

Initializing a Security Descriptor. When creating a new object, you assemble its security descriptor from scratch. In this case, the first function you call is InitializeSecurityDescriptor(). This takes a pointer to the security descriptor and a constant specifying the security descriptor revision:

```
BOOL InitializeSecurityDescriptor(
        PSECURITY_DESCRIPTOR lpSecurityDescriptor,
        DWORD                dwRevision);
```

It is suggested that you pass *dwRevision* as SECURITY_DESCRIPTOR_REVISION, currently defined as 1. Presumably, if Microsoft comes out with a new SECURITY_DESCRIPTOR layout, the constant will be redefined, but existing code that uses existing objects will not break because both are version-stamped.

Self-Relative versus Absolute Security Descriptors. Security descriptors may be in either **self-relative** or **absolute** format. In self-relative format, the individual fields are represented as offsets from the beginning of the SECURITY_DESCRIPTOR. In absolute format, they are actual pointers. The self-relative format is useful for putting security descriptors into places where pointers have no meaning, like on disk or in a network packet. Certain types of securable objects are permanent, that is, they continue to exist even when NT is shut down. These include file objects, Registry keys, and NT services, and may also include private objects. It therefore stands to reason that when you retrieve a security descriptor, you get it in self-relative format. However, if you alter the contents of a security descriptor, you do so by passing pointers to your own program variables. The security descriptor incorporates the information you are putting into it by adding your pointers. Therefore, with functions like SetSecurityDescriptorDacl() or SetSecurityDescriptorSacl(), the security descriptor must be in absolute format. InitializeSecurityDescriptor() creates an absolute descriptor.

For example, if you want to read the security descriptor of a file in order to grant rights to someone, you have to convert the security descriptor from self-relative to absolute format. Win32 provides functions for making these conversions, MakeAbsoluteSD() and MakeSelfRelativeSD(). MakeSelfRelativeSD() is simple, but MakeAbsoluteSD() is cumbersome. Because you have to provide locations for all of the pieces of the security descriptor, it requires 11 arguments.

Let's take a closer look at discretionary access control lists and the functions that manage them.

Access-Control Lists (ACLs) and Access Control Entries (ACEs)

Access-control lists (ACLs) are the most important data structure in the Security API because they determine who can and cannot use an object, and the precise manner in which it can be used. They are made up in turn of **access-control entries (ACEs)**, one for each user (or group) being granted or denied access. The ACL structure type defines an access control list.

```
typedef struct _ACL
{
    BYTE AclRevision;  // Set this to the constant ACL_REVISION
    BYTE Sbz1;
    WORD AclSize;
    WORD AceCount;
    WORD Sbz2;
} ACL;
```

This is just a header. *AclSize* is the byte size of the entire list, including all the access-control entries. *AceCount* is the number of ACEs following the ACL. The ACEs in turn consist of an ACE_HEADER followed by the access-control information.

```
typedef struct _ACE_HEADER
{
    BYTE AceType;
    BYTE AceFlags;
    WORD AceSize;
} ACE_HEADER;
```

The *AceType* indicates what this ACE is doing—allowing access, denying it, or requesting an audit trail. The appropriate constants are ACCESS_ALLOWED_ACE_TYPE, ACCESS_DENIED_ACE_TYPE, and SYSTEM_AUDIT_ACE_TYPE. A fourth type, SYSTEM_ALARM_ ACE_TYPE, is not yet supported. *AceSize* is the size of the ACE, including the ACE_HEADER. This is necessary because security identifiers are of variable length.

The rest of the ACE contains two pieces of information: the rights being conferred, withheld, or audited, and the security identifier of the user or group in question. Here is the type definition of an ACCESS_ALLOWED_ACE, which is typical:

```
typedef struct _ACCESS_ALLOWED_ACE
{
    ACE_HEADER Header;
    ACCESS_MASK Mask;
    DWORD SidStart;
} ACCESS_ALLOWED_ACE;
```

The ACCESS_MASK is a DWORD whose bits represent the appropriate permissions. Because of the large number of object types, there can be a wide difference in meaning. For this reason, Win32 provides generic masks that you can pass; it then takes care of translating them to the specific rights that are relevant for a given object. These masks are GENERIC_READ, GENERIC_WRITE, GENERIC_EXECUTE, and GENERIC_ALL, and they occupy the high four bits of the ACCESS_MASK. You will see how these get translated when we examine some actual DACLs.

Security Identifiers (SIDs)

The atomic unit of representation in the Windows NT security database is the **security identifier**, or **SID**. This is a binary number, whose format can be rather complex. It is intended to be an opaque data type, which applications are not supposed to access directly.

SID Representation in Memory. The following *typedef* for a SID appears in WINNT.H.

```
#define ANYSIZE_ARRAY 1
typedef struct _SID_IDENTIFIER_AUTHORITY
{
   BYTE Value[6];
} SID_IDENTIFIER_AUTHORITY, *PSID_IDENTIFIER_AUTHORITY;

typedef struct _SID
{
   BYTE Revision;
   BYTE SubAuthorityCount;
   SID_IDENTIFIER_AUTHORITY IdentifierAuthority;
   DWORD SubAuthority[ANYSIZE_ARRAY];
} SID;
```

The subject of how SIDs are represented is complex and esoteric, and unlikely to affect your life as a programmer. If you are interested, there are good discussions elsewhere. The *Security Overview* in the Win32 online help is helpful. Look for the section called "Security Identifiers."

Converting SIDs to Names and Names to SIDs. Users, of course, have little patience with binary network addresses, binary security identifiers—binary anythings, really—nor should they. They want to see user and group names that make sense to them. However, NT, as operating systems are wont to do, likes dealing with compact, symbolic representations like SIDs. We developers are caught in the middle, and have to please both users and the operating system. Fortunately, Win32 provides two very useful functions that map names to SIDs and SIDs to names: LookupAccountName() and LookupAccountSid(). LookupAccountName() takes a name in user-readable format, like the group "Everyone" or user "ralphd" and returns the corresponding SID. Every legitimate name will have a SID that the system knows about. LookupAccountSid() takes a SID and returns its name. This is useful for dumping ACLs to the user, for instance. The access-control entries consist of rights masks and SIDs, so you need to convert the SIDs to human-readable format to display them. It may surprise you to learn that not all SIDs have a matching name. When you log on to NT, it assigns you a **logon SID**, which is used for the duration of your NT session, and has no name to go with it. It is this SID that receives rights to the process window station and the thread desktop and, through them, to all windows created by processes that the user runs.

I will make considerable use of LookupAccountName() and LookupAccountSid() in the code examples here. Here are their prototypes:

```
BOOL LookupAccountName(
        LPCTSTR lpszMachineName,
        LPCTSTR lpszAccountName,
        PSID    pSID,
        LPDWORD lpdwSIDSize,
        LPTSTR  lpszReferencedDomain,
        LPDWORD lpdwReferencedDomain,
        PSID_NAME_USE pSidNameUse);

BOOL LookupAccountSid(
        LPCTSTR lpszMachineName,
        PSID    pSID,
        LPTSTR  lpszAccountName,
        LPDWORD lpdwAccountSize,
        LPTSTR  lpszReferencedDomain,
        LPDWORD lpdwReferencedDomain,
        PSID_NAME_USE pSidNameUse);
```

The *lpszMachineName* argument may tip you off to the fact that these functions can be executed on remote computers. If you pass it as NULL, the function queries the local database. *lpszAccountName* and *pSID* are the input or output data, depending on the function, and *lpdwSIDSize* is used to report the length of the SID. The other arguments are of less interest, but you have to supply them—the functions won't accept NULL pointers. *pSidNameUse* points to a variable of the enumerated type SID_NAME_USE, which gives you an idea of the types of objects NT supports.

```
typedef enum tagSID_NAME_USE
{
    SidTypeUser = 1,
    SidTypeGroup,
    SidTypeDomain,
    SidTypeAlias,
    SidTypeWellKnownGroup,
    SidTypeDeletedAccount,
    SidTypeInvalid,
    SidTypeUnknown
} SID_NAME_USE;
```

Using the Win32 Security Functions

In this section, we will look closely at how you use the Win32 Security API for various tasks. We will also see how some of the functions mentioned in Table 13-1 behave. I have divided the code samples into groups according to the kinds of objects they work with. NT recognizes these categories of securable objects, and provides different functions for manipulating their security descriptors:

- **File objects** include standard disk files, named pipes, and mailslots (GetFileSecurity() and SetFileSecurity()).
- **Kernel objects** consist primarily of synchronization objects, file-mapping objects, and process and thread handles (GetKernelObject-Security() and SetKernelObjectSecurity()).
- **Private objects** are objects known only to your application. You can use them to protect server applications where no built-in security exists. The functions are CreatePrivateObjectSecurity(), GetPrivate-ObjectSecurity(), SetPrivateObjectSecurity(), and DestroyPrivateOb-jectSecurity().
- **User objects** are process window stations, thread desktops, and the windows and menus that are their descendants. The relevant functions are GetUserObjectSecurity() and SetUserObjectSecurity().

- **Registry keys** are records in the NT configuration database. The functions that manipulate their security descriptors are RegGetKeySecurity() and RegSetKeySecurity(), which are discussed in Chapter 14.
- **Shares** are directories and print queues that you are making available for remote users. The relevant functions are NetShareGetInfo() and NetShareSetInfo(). They are part of the LAN Manager API, which was presented in Chapter 12 (though these functions were not discussed).
- **NetDDE shares** are aliases for DDEML service and topic pairs. They are used by the NetDDE communications protocol. The functions that read and write their security descriptors are NDdeGetShareSecurity() and NDdeSetShareSecurity(). NetDDE is presented briefly in Chapter 15.
- **Service objects** are the services known to the Service Control Manager, which we looked at in Chapter 11. With their DACLs, you can control who is allowed to start, stop, pause, and configure a service. The functions, which are documented in the Services group, are QueryServiceObjectSecurity() and SetServiceObjectSecurity(). Because they are more narrowly specialized than the others, I do not discuss them further.

File Objects—Named Pipes

File objects are a very important topic for this book. First of all, one of the things you most need to do in a network environment is control who can access files stored on a server. Second, because Named Pipes and Mailslots are file systems, they are treated as file objects for security purposes. When writing a server application, you need to be able to control access to your service endpoints. With Named Pipes and Mailslots, this protection is built in. You may never need to control the security properties of a disk file in a program, since interactive tools allow you to do this. However, there is no analogous tool for Pipes and Mailslots; because they are invisible program objects, you must use the Security API to regulate their use.

If you don't add security descriptors to file objects, NT adds them for you. You will see exactly how it does that in the sample applications in this chapter.

Creating a Named Pipe with NULL Security Attributes. The first sample, \WIN32NET\CODE\SECURITY\PIPE1\PIPE1.CPP, creates a named pipe, \\.\PIPE\WNET\PIPE1, passing a NULL SECURITY_ATTRIBUTES pointer to CreateNamedPipe(). It then dumps the pipe's DACL to see who has been assigned rights to it. Here is what it finds if you're logged on as *Administrator*:

```
Access rights 001F01FF granted to Administrators on \\.\PIPE\WNET\PIPE1
Access rights 001F01FF granted to SYSTEM on \\.\PIPE\WNET\PIPE1
```

As you can see, you did not get a pipe with unrestricted access. Rather, both the group Administrators and the user SYSTEM (denoting the operating system itself) have access rights 0x001F01FF. Let's see what this rights mask means and how it got there.

If you browse through WINNT.H, you will find this definition for FILE_ALL_ACCESS:

```
#define FILE_ALL_ACCESS (STANDARD_RIGHTS_REQUIRED | SYNCHRONIZE | 0x1FF)
```

The 0x1FF in this definition accounts for the low 16 bits of the access rights listed above. It corresponds to the constants FILE_ GENERIC_READ | FILE_GENERIC_WRITE | FILE_GENERIC_ EXECUTE, which confer all possible rights to the file itself.

Later in the file, STANDARD_RIGHTS_REQUIRED is defined as 0x000F0000L, and SYNCHRONIZE is 0x00100000L. SYNCHRONIZE access, which was discussed in Chapter 5, gives you permission to use the object's handle for synchronization purposes. STANDARD_RIGHTS_REQUIRED is a combination of other bits that grant DELETE, READ_CONTROL, WRITE_DAC, and WRITE_OWNER access. DELETE lets you delete an object. READ_CONTROL permits you to read its security descriptor. WRITE_DAC lets you change the discretionary access control list in the security descriptor. WRITE_OWNER allows you to change the object's owner.

That accounts for all the bits in the access mask. We now know that all members of the group Administrators, and the special user SYSTEM, have all possible rights to the named pipe. Let's look at the code that tells us that, then see how they got the rights.

The first part of main() creates the pipe and calls the routine RunTests().

```
void main(int argc, char *argv[])
{
   HANDLE hFile;
   SECURITY_INFORMATION SecurityInformation;

   // Create pipe using NULL SECURITY_ATTRIBUTES
   hFile = CreateNamedPipe("\\\\.\\PIPE\\WNET\\PIPE1",
                           PIPE_ACCESS_DUPLEX,
                           PIPE_TYPE_MESSAGE |
                           PIPE_READMODE_BYTE |
                           PIPE_WAIT,
```

```
                              1, 0, 0, 0,
                              NULL);
    if (hFile == INVALID_HANDLE_VALUE)
       {
       printf("\nUnable to create pipe, GetLastError() = %d\n",
          GetLastError());
       ExitProcess(1);
       }

    SecurityInformation = DACL_SECURITY_INFORMATION;
    RunTests("\\\\.\\PIPE\\WNET\\PIPE1",
       &SecurityInformation);

    CloseHandle(hFile);
```

Getting a File Object's Security Descriptor. The variable *SecurityInformation* that is passed to RunTests() is set to indicate that you want to read the discretionary access control list (DACL) of the object. RunTests() calls GetFileSecurity() to read the pipe's security descriptor.

```
BOOL GetFileSecurity(LPTSTR lpFileName,
                     SECURITY_INFORMATION SecurityInformation,
                     PSECURITY_DESCRIPTOR lpSecurityDescriptor,
                     DWORD                dwSecDescSize,
                     LPDWORD              lpdwSecDescActualSize);
```

To read a file's security descriptor, you pass the filename *(lpFileName)*, rather than a handle to an open file. *SecurityInformation* includes bits that tell GetFileSecurity() how much information we need. By setting it to DACL_SECURITY_INFORMATION, you say that you want only the discretionary access control list. *dwSecDescSize* is the size of the buffer at *lpSecurityDescriptor*. If this is merely *sizeof* (SECURITY_DESCRIPTOR), the function is likely to fail. SECURITY_DESCRIPTORs are variable-length structures because they contain access control lists and SIDs, both of which are structures containing open-ended arrays. If *dwSecDescSize* is too small to hold all the output information, GetFileSecurity() returns FALSE, and GetLastError() reports ERROR_INSUFFICIENT_BUFFER. In this case, **lpdwSecDescActualSize* tells you exactly how much memory you need. This is the cleanest way to retrieve a security descriptor, but for the sake of brevity, I just create a large output buffer (8192 bytes) on the stack. Here is RunTests().

```
VOID RunTests(LPTSTR lpName, SECURITY_INFORMATION *pSecurityInfo)
{
   BYTE   bySDBuffer[8192];
   PSECURITY_DESCRIPTOR lpSecurityDescriptor =
      (PSECURITY_DESCRIPTOR) bySDBuffer;
   DWORD  dwSDSize;

   dwSDSize = sizeof (bySDBuffer);

   if (!GetFileSecurity(lpName, *pSecurityInfo,
      lpSecurityDescriptor, dwSDSize, &dwSDSize))
      {
      printf("\nGetFileSecurity() failed, GetLastError() = %d",
         GetLastError());
      return;
      }
   DumpDACL(lpName, lpSecurityDescriptor);
}
```

Reading the Discretionary Access Control List. Once RunTests() has fetched the security descriptor, it passes it to DumpDACL(), which prints all the entries in the discretionary access control list. DumpDACL(), like Run-Tests(), calls one Win32 function, GetSecurityDescriptorDacl(), and one local function, DumpACEs(). GetSecurityDescriptorDacl() returns a pointer to the DACL.

```
BOOL GetSecurityDescriptorDacl(
        PSECURITY_DESCRIPTOR lpSecurityDescriptor,
        LPBOOL                lpbDaclPresent,
        PACL                 *ppDACL,
        LPBOOL                lpbDaclDefaulted);
```

ppDACL points to a PACL (ACL*) that GetSecurityDescriptorDacl() fills in with the address of the DACL. This pointer is not dynamically allocated; it points to the actual location of the DACL in the security descriptor.When the function completes, **lpbDaclPresent* will be set to TRUE if a DACL is present. If it's FALSE, **ppDACL* does not contain a valid address.

Here is the listing of DumpDACL(). Along with other auxiliary functions, it is contained in \WIN32NET\CODE\SECURITY\SECUHLPR.CPP.

```
VOID DumpDACL(LPTSTR lpFileName, PSECURITY_DESCRIPTOR pSD)

{
   PACL pACL = NULL;
   BOOL bDACLPresent;
   BOOL bDACLDefaulted;
```

```
    if (!GetSecurityDescriptorDacl(pSD, &bDACLPresent,
       &pACL, &bDACLDefaulted))
       {
       printf("\nGetSecurityDescriptorDacl() failed, "
              "GetlastError() = %d",
          GetLastError());
       return;
       }

    if (pACL != NULL)
       DumpACEs(pACL, lpFileName);
    else
       printf("\n%s has a NULL DACL", lpFileName);
    printf("\n");
}
```

Walking the Discretionary Access Control List. DumpACEs() examines each access control entry in the DACL and displays its type, the user or group name, and the rights mask. Because you do not know the format of the access control list in advance, you have to declare it as a raw BYTE array, then parse it based on the information you find in the headers. The list header is contained in the ACL structure that begins the list; each ACE has its own ACE_HEADER.

DumpACEs() uses two Win32 functions: GetAclInformation() and GetAce(). Among other things, GetAclInformation() reports the number of ACEs in the list.

```
BOOL GetAclInformation(PACL   pACL,
                       LPVOID lpOutputBuffer,
                       DWORD  dwOutputSize,
                       ACL_INFORMATION_CLASS ACLInfo);
```

ACL_INFORMATION_CLASS is an enumeration type whose two possible values are AclRevisionInformation and AclSizeInformation. If you ask it for the size information, which is what you're interested in here, it fills *lpOutputBuffer* with an ACL_SIZE_INFORMATION structure.

```
typedef struct _ACL_SIZE_INFORMATION
{
    DWORD   AceCount;
    DWORD   AclBytesInUse;
    DWORD   AclBytesFree;
} ACL_SIZE_INFORMATION;
```

AceCount is the number of ACEs comprising the list. For each of these, DumpACEs() calls GetAce() to get a pointer to its contents.

```
BOOL GetAce(PACL    pACL,
            DWORD   dwIndex,
            LPVOID *lpACE);
```

dwIndex says which element in the list you want, starting with zero. *lpACE* points to a VOID pointer; on output, it will contain the address of the requested ACE. Just as with GetSecurityDescriptorDacl(), this pointer is not allocated; it is the address of the ACE within the DACL.

With a pointer to the ACE in hand, DumpACEs() looks at the ACE_HEADER to determine what kind of ACE it's looking at, then skips past the header to examine the access mask and the SID. It calls a local routine, DumpSID(), to convert the SID in the ACE to a user-readable account name.

Here's the full code for DumpACEs(), also from \WIN32NET\CODE \SECURITY\SECUHLPR.CPP.

```
VOID DumpACEs(PACL pACL, LPTSTR lpFileName)
{
   BYTE byBuffer[1024];
   ACL_SIZE_INFORMATION *pACLSize =
      (ACL_SIZE_INFORMATION *) byBuffer;
   LPVOID pACE;
   ACE_HEADER *pACEHeader;
   LPBYTE lpTemp;
   TCHAR  szSIDName[256];
   TCHAR  szNameType[256];
   DWORD  dwAccessMask;
   PSID   pSID;
   LPTSTR lpVerb;

   if (pACL == NULL)
      {
      printf("\nDumpACEs() passed a NULL ACL pointer");
      return;
      }

   if (!GetAclInformation(pACL, byBuffer, sizeof (byBuffer),
      AclSizeInformation))
      {
      printf("\nGetAclInformation() failed, GetLastError() = %d",
         GetLastError());
      return;
      }
```

```
    for (DWORD i = 0; i < pACLSize->AceCount; ++i)
        {
        if (!GetAce(pACL, i, &pACE))
            {
            printf("\nGetAce() failed, GetLastError() = %d",
                GetLastError());
            continue;
            }
        pACEHeader = (ACE_HEADER *) pACE;
        lpTemp = (LPBYTE) pACE;

        lpTemp += sizeof (ACE_HEADER);
        dwAccessMask = *(ACCESS_MASK *) lpTemp;
        lpTemp += sizeof (ACCESS_MASK);
        pSID = (PSID) lpTemp;

        switch (pACEHeader->AceType)
            {
            case ACCESS_ALLOWED_ACE_TYPE:
                lpVerb = "granted to";
                break;
            case ACCESS_DENIED_ACE_TYPE:
                lpVerb = "denied to";
                break;
            case SYSTEM_AUDIT_ACE_TYPE:
                lpVerb = "being audited for";
                break;
            case SYSTEM_ALARM_ACE_TYPE:
                lpVerb = "being audited for";
                break;
            }
        if (DumpSID(pSID, szSIDName, szNameType))
            {
            printf("\nAccess rights %08X %s %s on %s",
                dwAccessMask, lpVerb,
                szSIDName, lpFileName);
            }
        }
}
```

Mapping a SID to an Account Name. DumpSID() calls LookupAccountSid() to translate the SID passed to it into a readable name.

```
static LPTSTR SidNames[] =
{
    NULL,
    TEXT("User"),
    TEXT("Group"),
```

```
    TEXT("Domain"),
    TEXT("Alias"),
    TEXT("Well-known group"),
    TEXT("Deleted account"),
    TEXT("Invalid"),
    TEXT("Unknown")
};

BOOL DumpSID(PSID pSID, LPTSTR lpSIDName, LPTSTR lpNameType)
{
    TCHAR szAccount[256];
    DWORD dwAccountSize = sizeof (szAccount);
    TCHAR szDomain[256];
    DWORD dwDomainSize = sizeof (szDomain);
    SID_NAME_USE SidNameUse;

    if (!LookupAccountSid(NULL, pSID, szAccount,&dwAccountSize,
            szDomain, &dwDomainSize, &SidNameUse))
        {
        printf("\nLookupAccountSid() failed, GetLastError() = %d",
            GetLastError());
        return FALSE;
        }
    sprintf(lpSIDName, "%s", szAccount);
    if (lpNameType != NULL)
        sprintf(lpNameType, "%s", SidNames[SidNameUse]);
    return TRUE;
}
```

Default Assignment of Security Descriptors. So far we have seen that a named pipe created by the Administrator with NULL SECURITY_ATTRIBUTES ends up with all access granted to Administrators and SYSTEM. We also looked at the code that determines that. How did Administrators and SYSTEM get assigned rights to this pipe?

When you log on to Windows NT, it generates a logon SID for you, then creates an access token that gets attached to every process you run. This token contains all the security-related information NT needs to judge your requests to use protected objects. These include your user SID, your primary group, and any other groups you belong to. Another piece of information the token carries is called the default discretionary access control list. The documentation for CreateNamedPipe() is a little vague on what happens if you pass a NULL SECURITY_ATTRIBUTES: "If this parameter is NULL, the pipe is created with a default security descriptor." However, it is reasonable to surmise that there is a connection between the default DACL in the token and the DACL that eventually gets assigned. The second test that PIPE1 performs, in the last half of main(), checks this hypothesis. To do so, it reads the process token by calling GetTokenInformation() and asking for the default DACL.

```
BOOL GetTokenInformation(
        HANDLE                  hToken,
        TOKEN_INFORMATION_CLASS TokenInfo,
        LPVOID                  lpOutputBuffer,
        DWORD                   dwOutputSize,
        PDWORD                  lpdwActualOutputSize);
```

The token handle is retrieved by calling OpenProcessToken() as follows.

```
HANDLE hToken;
OpenProcessToken(GetCurrentProcess(),
                 TOKEN_ALL_ACCESS,
                 &hToken);
```

TOKEN_INFORMATION_CLASS is an enumerated type. The value that asks for the default DACL is TokenDefaultDacl. The information is returned in a TOKEN_DEFAULT_DACL structure, typed as follows.

```
typedef struct _TOKEN_DEFAULT_DACL
{
    PACL DefaultDacl;
} TOKEN_DEFAULT_DACL;
```

After obtaining this information, PIPE1 calls DumpACEs() again to display the contents of the token's default DACL.

```
/*=======================================================*/
   // Part II.
   // Let's get the default DACL for our process' token
   // This is where the DACL came from that got
   // tied to the named pipe we created

   HANDLE hToken = NULL;
   OpenProcessToken(GetCurrentProcess(),
                    TOKEN_ALL_ACCESS,
                    &hToken);

   if (hToken != NULL)
      {
      BYTE   byACLBuffer[4096];
      DWORD  dwACLSize = sizeof (byACLBuffer);
```

```
        TOKEN_DEFAULT_DACL *pTokenDefaultDACL =
           (TOKEN_DEFAULT_DACL *) byACLBuffer;

        // Get the DACL for the token and dump it.
        if (!GetTokenInformation(hToken, TokenDefaultDacl,
           byACLBuffer, dwACLSize, &dwACLSize))
           {
           printf("\nGetTokenInformation() failed, "
                  "GetLastError() = %d",
                 GetLastError());
           }
        else
           {
           DumpACEs(pTokenDefaultDACL->DefaultDacl,
              "Process token default DACL");
           }
        }
     fflush(stdout);
     ExitProcess(0);
}
```

This is what DumpACEs() tells us:

```
Access rights 10000000 granted to Administrators on Process token
default DACL
Access rights 10000000 granted to SYSTEM on Process token default DACL
```

This looks very much like the information that results from dumping the pipe's DACL. Indeed, the only difference is the rights mask. Here, you see 0x10000000; before, we saw 0x001F01FF. The fact that only one bit is set in the rights mask might lead you to suspect that a single *#define* describes it. This is exactly right. Here is the relevant line from WINNT.H:

```
#define GENERIC_ALL  (0x10000000L)
```

Here's what has happened: the default DACL in the token represents the rights using their generic description because the DACL may be applied to more than one type of object. When the process owning the token creates a named pipe without specifying a security descriptor, NT allocates one and copies the token's default DACL into it. At this time, it maps the generic rights in the token to the specific rights for the object. Here, GENERIC_ALL (0x10000000L) becomes FILE_ALL_ACCESS (0x001F01FFL).

Here's the significance of this discovery: if you create a named pipe with a NULL security descriptor, only users belonging to your primary group (and services started by the operating system) will be able to connect to it.

Creating a Pipe Object with Unrestricted Access. The solution to this was presented in Chapters 10 and 11: assign the pipe a security descriptor with a NULL DACL. Here's how you do this:

```
SECURITY_ATTRIBUTES SecurityAttributes;
SECURITY_DESCRIPTOR SecurityDescriptor;

InitializeSecurityDescriptor(&SecurityDescriptor,
   SECURITY_DESCRIPTOR_REVISION);
SetSecurityDescriptorDacl(&SecurityDescriptor,
                          TRUE,
                          NULL,    // No DACL
                          FALSE);
SecurityAttributes.lpSecurityDescriptor = &SecurityDescriptor;
```

This makes the pipe available to anyone. The server can still protect itself by calling ImpersonateNamedPipeClient() when a connection is established. This assures that the server will run in the security context of the client for the duration of their interaction. When the client disconnects, the server can return to its own security environment by calling RevertToSelf().

The next sample application shows how to create a more precisely crafted DACL for the pipe, denying access to some users while allowing it to others.

Controlling Access to a Named Pipe. Next, we are going to specifically grant rights to the named pipe when creating it. Let's say you want to allow broad access to all users except those belonging to the Guests group. You simply add an ACE that denies GENERIC_ALL access to Guests, and follow it with one that gives Everyone GENERIC_ALL access. Even though members of Guests also belong to Everyone, they will be denied access to the pipe because we explicitly forbid them to use it.

Once again, we will use InitializeSecurityDescriptor() to create an empty security descriptor as shown in the preceding code block. But before calling SetSecurityDescriptorDacl(), we will invoke InitializeAcl(), AddAccessDeniedAce(), and AddAccessAllowedAce(). These functions create the necessary access control list. InitializeAcl() requires a pointer to the buffer that it will format as an ACL; it needs to know the size of the buffer; and it needs the ACL revision number. The last item is represented by the Win32 constant ACL_REVISION. Here is the call to InitializeAcl() from \WIN32NET \CODE\SECURITY\PIPE2\PIPE2.CPP:

```
InitializeAcl((PACL) byACLBuffer, sizeof (byACLBuffer),
   ACL_REVISION);
```

AddAccessDeniedAce() and AddAccessAllowedAce() have the same argument lists, which include a pointer to the ACL, the ACL revision, the rights you are granting or denying, and the SID of the affected account. Here is how I call AddAccessDeniedAce():

```
// Add access denied ACE first, by convention
// Get SID for "Guests"
if (NameToSID("Guests", (PSID) bySIDBuffer, &dwSIDSize))
   {
   AddAccessDeniedAce((PACL) byACLBuffer, ACL_REVISION,
      GENERIC_ALL, bySIDBuffer);
   }
```

Here is the main() function from PIPE2.CPP. RunTests() is the same as in PIPE1.CPP, and is shown earlier in this chapter. It calls GetFileSecurity() to collect the DACL of the pipe, then calls DumpDACL().

```
void main(int argc, char *argv[])
{
   HANDLE hFile;
   SECURITY_INFORMATION SecurityInformation;
   BYTE   byACLBuffer[4096];
   DWORD  dwACLSize = sizeof (byACLBuffer);
   SECURITY_DESCRIPTOR SecurityDescriptor;
   SECURITY_ATTRIBUTES SecurityAttributes;
   BYTE   bySIDBuffer[1024];
   DWORD  dwSIDSize = sizeof (bySIDBuffer);

   SecurityInformation = DACL_SECURITY_INFORMATION;

   InitializeSecurityDescriptor(&SecurityDescriptor,
      SECURITY_DESCRIPTOR_REVISION);

   // Set up ACL with two ACEs
   InitializeAcl((PACL) byACLBuffer, sizeof (byACLBuffer),
      ACL_REVISION);

   // Add access denied ACE first, by convention
   // Get SID for "Guests"
   if (NameToSID("Guests", (PSID) bySIDBuffer, &dwSIDSize))
      {
      AddAccessDeniedAce((PACL) byACLBuffer, ACL_REVISION,
         GENERIC_ALL, bySIDBuffer);
      }
```

```
    dwSIDSize = sizeof (bySIDBuffer);
    // Now add access allowed ACE for "Everyone"
    if (NameToSID("Everyone", (PSID) bySIDBuffer, &dwSIDSize))
       {
       AddAccessAllowedAce((PACL) byACLBuffer, ACL_REVISION,
          GENERIC_ALL, bySIDBuffer);
       }

    // Insert the DACL into the SECURITY_DESCRIPTOR
    if (!SetSecurityDescriptorDacl(&SecurityDescriptor,
       TRUE, (PACL) byACLBuffer, FALSE))
       printf("\nSetSecurityDescriptorDacl() failed, "
              "GetLastError() = %d",
             GetLastError());

    // Create pipe using non-NULL SECURITY_ATTRIBUTES
    SecurityAttributes.nLength = sizeof (SECURITY_ATTRIBUTES);
    SecurityAttributes.lpSecurityDescriptor =
       &SecurityDescriptor;
    SecurityAttributes.bInheritHandle = FALSE;

    hFile = CreateNamedPipe("\\\\.\\PIPE\\WNET\\PIPE2",
                            PIPE_ACCESS_DUPLEX,
                            PIPE_TYPE_MESSAGE |
                            PIPE_READMODE_BYTE |
                            PIPE_WAIT,
                            1, 0, 0, 0,
                            &SecurityAttributes);

    if (hFile == INVALID_HANDLE_VALUE)
       {
       printf("\nUnable to create pipe, GetLastError() = %d\n",
          GetLastError());
       ExitProcess(1);
       }
    RunTests("\\\\.\\PIPE\\WNET\\PIPE2",
       &SecurityInformation);

    CloseHandle(hFile);

    ExitProcess(0);
}
```

Here is the output from PIPE2.EXE:

```
Access rights 001F01FF denied to Guests on \\.\PIPE\WNET\PIPE2
Access rights 001F01FF granted to Everyone on \\.\PIPE\WNET\PIPE2
```

The rights explicitly assigned have superseded the default DACL from the process token. Notice that the GENERIC_ALL (0x10000000L) rights mask that was passed to AddAccessDeniedAce() and AddAccessAllowedAce() has again been translated to FILE_ALL_ACCESS (0x001F01FF).

Mapping an Account Name to a SID. Building the ACEs requires finding out the SIDs for Guests and Everyone. NameToSID() is another helper routine in \WIN32NET\CODE\SECURITY\SECUHLPR.CPP. It uses LookupAccountName() to perform the conversion.

```
BOOL NameToSID(LPTSTR lpName, PSID pSID, LPDWORD lpdwSIDSize)
{
   TCHAR szDomain[256];
   DWORD dwDomainSize = sizeof (szDomain);
   SID_NAME_USE SidNameUse;

   if (!LookupAccountName(NULL, lpName, pSID, lpdwSIDSize,
         szDomain, &dwDomainSize, &SidNameUse))
      {
      printf("\nLookupAccountName() failed, GetLastError() = %d",
         GetLastError());
      return FALSE;
      }
   return TRUE;
}
```

File Objects—Standard Disk Files

Disk files behave very much like named pipes. The next sample application, \WIN32NET\CODE\SECURITY\FILES\FILES.CPP, explores what happens when you create a disk file without SECURITY_ATTRIBUTES. FILES differs very little from PIPE1. Instead of calling CreateNamedPipe(), it calls CreateFile() to create the file passed as *argv[1]*. Here is main() from \WIN32NET\CODE\SECURITY\FILES\FILES.CPP:

```
void main(int argc, char *argv[])
{
   HANDLE hFile;
   SECURITY_INFORMATION SecurityInformation =
      DACL_SECURITY_INFORMATION;

   // Open temporary file with NULL SECURITY_ATTRIBUTES
   hFile = CreateFile(argv[1],
              GENERIC_ALL,
              0,
```

```
                NULL,
                CREATE_NEW,
                FILE_ATTRIBUTE_NORMAL,
                NULL);
    if (hFile == INVALID_HANDLE_VALUE)
        {
        printf("\nUnable to create file,  GetLastError() = %d\n",
            GetLastError());
        ExitProcess(1);
        }
    CloseHandle(hFile);

    RunTests(argv[1],
        &SecurityInformation);

    fflush(stdout);
    ExitProcess(0);
}
```

RunTests() is the same as for PIPE1.CPP and PIPE2.CPP; see the listing earlier in this chapter. Here is the program's output.

```
Access rights 001F01FF granted to Administrators on filetest.fil
Access rights 001301BF granted to Everyone on filetest.fil
Access rights 001F01FF granted to Administrators on filetest.fil
Access rights 001F01FF granted to SYSTEM on filetest.fil
```

We have more entries than we did when we created a named pipe. Administrators and SYSTEM are both still there, with FILE_ALL_ACCESS rights. We also have an entry for Everyone, and an extra ACE for Administrators. The additional ACEs are inherited from the file's parent directory. Figure 13-2 shows the File Manager permissions screen for E:\NTNET\CODE \SECURITY\FILES, the directory in which I ran this test.

The only one of the trusted users that did not propagate to the temporary file is CREATOR OWNER. However, you can see in Figure 13-2 that the directory's owner is none other than the group Administrators.

This is concrete evidence of how the NT File System handles inheritance of rights, and it's an important part of operating system policy; system administrators don't want to assign rights to every single file that every user on their systems create. Therefore, in the absence of any other restrictions—which, in our context, means when you pass NULL SECURITY_ ATTRIBUTES to CreateFile()—the DACL of the parent directory propagates to newly created files and directories. Actually, a walk of the directory's DACL reveals that, in addition to the ACEs that grant rights to the

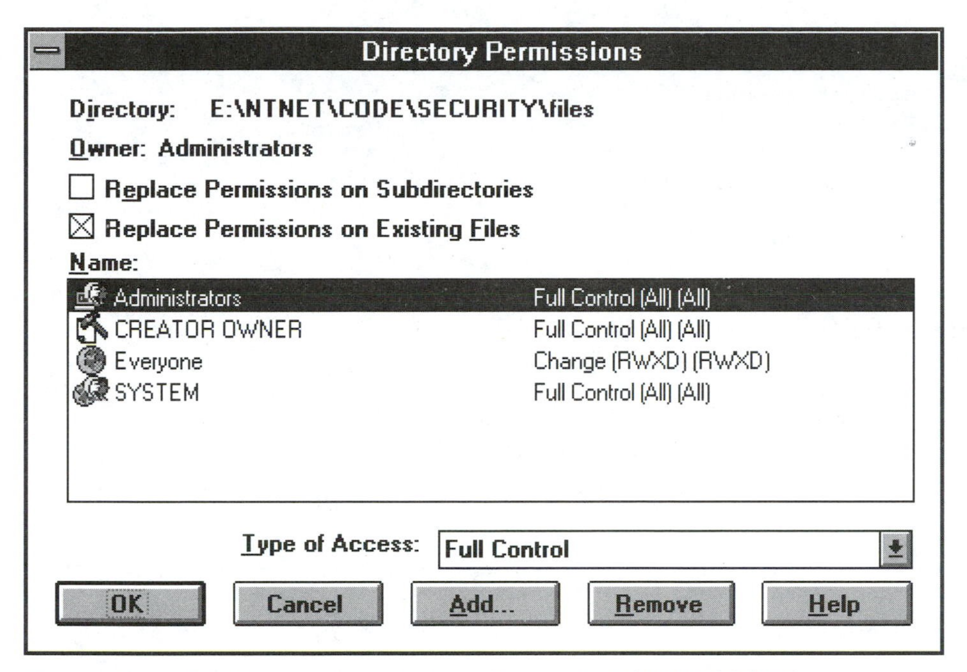

Figure 13-2. File Manager Permissions Screen for E:\NTNET\CODE\SECURITY\FILES

directory itself, there are others flagged as INHERIT_ONLY_ACEs (in the AceFlags field of the ACE_HEADER). These describe the rights that contained objects inherit.

Kernel Objects

The next sample application, KRNLOBJS, demonstrates that things are a little different with kernel objects. It creates four kernel objects—a mutex, an event, a shared-memory object, and a thread—with NULL SECURITY_ATTRIBUTES, then dumps their DACLs. Here is main() from \WIN32NET\CODE\SECURITY\KRNLOBJS\KRNLOBJS.CPP.

```
void main(int argc, char *argv[])
{
   HANDLE hMutex;
   SECURITY_INFORMATION SecurityInformation;

   hMutex = CreateMutex(NULL, FALSE,
      "/MUTEX/WNET/NICE_LITTLE_MUTEX");
   if (hMutex == NULL)
```

```
      {
      printf("\nUnable to create mutex, GetLastError() = %d\n",
         GetLastError());
      ExitProcess(1);
      }
   RunTests(hMutex, &SecurityInformation, “Mutex”);

   CloseHandle(hMutex);

/*============================================*/
   // Test with an event
   HANDLE hEvent;

   hEvent = CreateEvent(NULL, TRUE, FALSE,
      "/EVENT/WNET/NICE_LITTLE_EVENT");

   if (hEvent == NULL)
      {
      printf("\nUnable to create event, GetLastError() = %d\n",
         GetLastError());
      ExitProcess(1);
      }
   RunTests(hEvent, &SecurityInformation, "Event");

   CloseHandle(hEvent);

/*============================================*/
   // Test with shared memory
   HANDLE hSharedMemory;

   hSharedMemory =
      CreateFileMapping((HANDLE) 0xFFFFFFFF,
                        NULL,
                        PAGE_READWRITE,
                        0,
                        4096,
                        "/SHARED_MEM/WNET/NICE_SHARED_MEMORY");
   RunTests(hSharedMemory, &SecurityInformation,
      "Shared Memory");

   CloseHandle(hSharedMemory);

/*============================================*/
   // Test with a thread
   HANDLE hThread;
   DWORD  dwThreadID;

   hThread = CreateThread(NULL, 0, TestThread, NULL, 0, &dwThreadID);
   if (hThread == NULL)
```

```
      {
      printf("\nUnable to create thread, GetLastError() = %d\n",
         GetLastError());
      ExitProcess(1);
      }
   RunTests(hThread, &SecurityInformation, "Thread");

   CloseHandle(hThread);

   ExitProcess(0);
}
```

RunTests() differs from previous versions in that it calls GetKernelObjectSecurity() instead of GetFileSecurity(). GetKernelObjectSecurity() takes an object HANDLE as its first argument, instead of the filename that GetFileSecurity() wants.

```
BOOL GetKernelObjectSecurity(
        HANDLE                 hObject,
        SECURITY_INFORMATION SecurityInformation,
        PSECURITY_DESCRIPTOR lpSecurityDescriptor,
        DWORD                  dwOutBufferSize,
        LPDWORD                lpdwOutBufferActualSize);
```

This is RunTests() as KRNLOBJS.CPP implements it:

```
VOID RunTests(HANDLE hObject, SECURITY_INFORMATION *pSecurityInfo,
              LPTSTR lpObjectType)
{
   BYTE   bySDBuffer[8192];
   PSECURITY_DESCRIPTOR lpSecurityDescriptor =
      (PSECURITY_DESCRIPTOR) bySDBuffer;
   DWORD  dwSDSize;

   dwSDSize = sizeof (bySDBuffer);

   if (!GetKernelObjectSecurity(hObject, *pSecurityInfo,
      lpSecurityDescriptor, dwSDSize, &dwSDSize))
      {
      printf("\nGetKernelObjectSecurity() failed, "
             "GetLastError() = %d",
         GetLastError());
      return;
      }

   DumpDACL(lpObjectType, lpSecurityDescriptor);
}
```

The output generated by KRNLOBJS is sparse.

```
Mutex has a NULL DACL

Event has a NULL DACL

Shared Memory has a NULL DACL

Thread has a NULL DACL
```

So kernel objects behave differently from file objects. When you create one with NULL SECURITY_ATTRIBUTES, you actually get an object with no security restrictions.

Private Objects

Private objects are a more sophisticated use of the Win32 Security API. They allow you to implement protection in situations where NT itself does not provide it, by building objects from scratch.

With private objects, there are two additional functions: CreatePrivate-ObjectSecurity() and DestroyPrivateObjectSecurity(). The first generates a new SECURITY_DESCRIPTOR that can take its initial characteristics from several sources:

- The default DACL of the process's token, if no other sources exist
- A template SECURITY_DESCRIPTOR that you provide to Create-PrivateObjectSecurity()
- The object's parent, if the concept has meaning for the object

PRIVATE1 demonstrates the first, PRIVATE2 the second, and PRIVATE3 the third.

Defining How Generic Rights Map to Object-Specific Rights. When you create a private object, you must define how generic rights translate into specific rights. You do this by setting the fields of a GENERIC_MAPPING structure.

```
typedef struct _GENERIC_MAPPING
{
    ACCESS_MASK GenericRead;    // What does GENERIC_READ mean?
    ACCESS_MASK GenericWrite;   // How about GENERIC_WRITE?
    ACCESS_MASK GenericExecute; // GENERIC_EXECUTE?
    ACCESS_MASK GenericAll;     // GENERIC_ALL?
} GENERIC_MAPPING;
```

You populate each field with the specific rights that correspond to the generic constant. In PRIVATE1 and PRIVATE2, I use the rights appropriate for file objects. After all, NT has no preconceptions about the object, so it lets me create the object any way I want to. Here are the lines from \WIN32NET\CODE\SECURITY\PRIVATE1.CPP, including the call to CreatePrivateObjectSecurity():

```
GenericMapping.GenericRead    = FILE_GENERIC_READ;
GenericMapping.GenericWrite   = FILE_GENERIC_WRITE;
GenericMapping.GenericExecute = FILE_GENERIC_EXECUTE;
GenericMapping.GenericAll     = FILE_ALL_ACCESS;

if (!CreatePrivateObjectSecurity(NULL, NULL,
      &pSecurityDescriptor, FALSE, hToken, &GenericMapping))
   {
   printf("\nCreatePrivateObjectSecurity() failed, "
         "GetLastError() = %d",
        GetLastError());
   ExitProcess(GetLastError());
   }
```

Creating a Private Object with Default Security. The first two arguments to CreatePrivateObjectSecurity() are the parent and template security descriptors. The third points to a pointer to a SECURITY_DESCRIPTOR for which CreatePrivateObjectSecurity() allocates memory. Passing the first two parameters as NULL is the same as creating a file with no SECURITY_ATTRIBUTES. You must also pass a HANDLE to your process's token. The default DACL will be taken from this token. Here is the complete listing of the first part of main(), up to the point where it calls RunTests():

```
void main(int argc, char *argv[])
{
   SECURITY_INFORMATION SecurityInformation;
   PSECURITY_DESCRIPTOR pSecurityDescriptor;
   GENERIC_MAPPING GenericMapping;
   HANDLE hToken;

   SecurityInformation = DACL_SECURITY_INFORMATION;

   hToken = GetProcessToken();
   if (hToken == NULL)
      {
      ExitProcess(GetLastError());
      }
```

```
      GenericMapping.GenericRead    = FILE_GENERIC_READ;
      GenericMapping.GenericWrite   = FILE_GENERIC_WRITE;
      GenericMapping.GenericExecute = FILE_GENERIC_EXECUTE;
      GenericMapping.GenericAll     = FILE_ALL_ACCESS;

      if (!CreatePrivateObjectSecurity(NULL, NULL,
         &pSecurityDescriptor, FALSE, hToken, &GenericMapping))
         {
         printf("\nCreatePrivateObjectSecurity() failed, "
                "GetLastError() = %d",
               GetLastError());
         ExitProcess(GetLastError());
         }
      RunTests(pSecurityDescriptor,
         &SecurityInformation);
```

RunTests() retrieves the object's security descriptor by calling GetPrivateObjectSecurity(). Just as you pass GetFileSecurity() the filename and GetKernelObjectSecurity() the object HANDLE, you give GetPrivateObjectSecurity() the SECURITY_DESCRIPTOR generated by CreatePrivateObjectSecurity().

```
VOID RunTests(PSECURITY_DESCRIPTOR pSecurityDescriptor,
              SECURITY_INFORMATION *pSecurityInfo)
{
   BYTE   bySDBuffer[8192];
   PSECURITY_DESCRIPTOR lpSecurityDescriptor =
      (PSECURITY_DESCRIPTOR) bySDBuffer;
   DWORD  dwSDSize;

   dwSDSize = sizeof (bySDBuffer);

   if (!GetPrivateObjectSecurity(pSecurityDescriptor, *pSecurityInfo,
      lpSecurityDescriptor, dwSDSize, &dwSDSize))
      {
      printf("\nGetPrivateObjectSecurity() failed, "
             "GetLastError() = %d, dwSDSize = %d",
         GetLastError(), dwSDSize);
      return;
      }

   DumpDACL("Private Object", lpSecurityDescriptor);
}
```

The output from PRIVATE1 follows.

```
Access rights 001F01FF granted to Administrators on Private Object
Access rights 001F01FF granted to SYSTEM on Private Object
```

This is exactly what we saw with a named pipe created with no security attributes. The private object inherits the default DACL of the process's token. The rights that have been granted are also the same (0x001F01FF, corresponding to FILE_ALL_ACCESS). This is because the custom mapping uses the same scheme as file objects.

Creating a Standalone Private Object with Explicit Security. In PRIVATE2, I create a private object from a security descriptor template and assign the template a DACL that denies GENERIC_ALL access to Guests and grants it to Everyone. main() has a little more work to do because it must initialize the security descriptor and populate its DACL. By the way, instead of calling NameToSID() to get the SIDs for Guests and Everyone, I build their SIDs from scratch by calling AllocateAndInitializeSid(). The *Security Identifiers* topic in the Win32 online help tells you how to do this, and explains how SIDs are constructed.

```
void main(int argc, char *argv[])
{
   SECURITY_INFORMATION SecurityInformation;
   SECURITY_DESCRIPTOR  SecurityDescriptor;
   PSECURITY_DESCRIPTOR pSecurityDescriptor;
   GENERIC_MAPPING GenericMapping;
   HANDLE hToken;
   BYTE   byACLBuffer[1024];

   hToken = GetProcessToken();

   if (hToken == NULL)
      ExitProcess(GetLastError());

   SecurityInformation = DACL_SECURITY_INFORMATION;

   // With a standalone private object, we first create a
   // template SECURITY_DESCRIPTOR that has
   // the characteristics we want.
   // In this case, we'll use it to build
   // a DACL that denies access to "Guests"
   // and permits it to "Everyone"
   InitializeSecurityDescriptor(&SecurityDescriptor,
      SECURITY_DESCRIPTOR_REVISION);

   // Set up ACL with two ACEs
```

```
InitializeAcl((PACL) byACLBuffer, sizeof (byACLBuffer),
   ACL_REVISION);

// Add access denied ACE first, by convention
// This time, we'll build the SIDs from scratch

// Create the SID for "Guests". This is NT authority, the built-in
// domain, and the Guests alias
SID_IDENTIFIER_AUTHORITY SIAWindowsNT =
   SECURITY_NT_AUTHORITY;

PSID pGuestSID;

if (!AllocateAndInitializeSid(&SIAWindowsNT,
                              2,    // 2 subauthorities
                              SECURITY_BUILTIN_DOMAIN_RID,
                              DOMAIN_ALIAS_RID_GUESTS,
                              0, 0, 0, 0, 0, 0,
                              &pGuestSID))
   {
   printf("\nAllocateAndInitializeSid() failed, "
          "GetLastError() = %d",
      GetLastError());
   ExitProcess(GetLastError());
   }

AddAccessDeniedAce((PACL) byACLBuffer, ACL_REVISION,
   GENERIC_ALL, pGuestSID);

FreeSid(pGuestSID);

// Create the SID for "Everyone". This uses world
// authority, rather than NT authority
SID_IDENTIFIER_AUTHORITY SIAWorld =
   SECURITY_WORLD_SID_AUTHORITY;
PSID pEveryoneSID;

if (!AllocateAndInitializeSid(&SIAWorld,
                              1,    // 1 subauthority
                              SECURITY_WORLD_RID,
                              0, 0, 0, 0, 0, 0, 0,
                              &pEveryoneSID))
   {
   printf("\nAllocateAndInitializeSid() failed, "
          "GetLastError() = %d",
      GetLastError());
   ExitProcess(GetLastError());
   }
```

```
// Now add access allowed ACE for "Everyone"
AddAccessAllowedAce((PACL) byACLBuffer, ACL_REVISION,
   GENERIC_ALL, pEveryoneSID);

FreeSid(pEveryoneSID);

// Insert the DACL into the SECURITY_DESCRIPTOR
if (!SetSecurityDescriptorDacl(&SecurityDescriptor,
   TRUE, (PACL) byACLBuffer, FALSE))
   printf("\nSetSecurityDescriptorDacl() failed, "
          "GetLastError() = %d",
         GetLastError());

// Set generic-to-specific access mapping as if
// this object were a file
GenericMapping.GenericRead    = FILE_GENERIC_READ;
GenericMapping.GenericWrite   = FILE_GENERIC_WRITE;
GenericMapping.GenericExecute = FILE_GENERIC_EXECUTE;
GenericMapping.GenericAll     = FILE_ALL_ACCESS;

// Now when we call CreatePrivateObjectSecurity(),
// we pass the second argument as a pointer to
// our template security descriptor, instead of
// as a NULL pointer.
if (!CreatePrivateObjectSecurity(NULL,
   &SecurityDescriptor,
   &pSecurityDescriptor, FALSE, hToken, &GenericMapping))
   {
   printf("\nCreatePrivateObjectSecurity() failed, "
          "GetLastError() = %d",
         GetLastError());
   ExitProcess(GetLastError());
   }

RunTests(pSecurityDescriptor,
   &SecurityInformation);
```

The program's output reflects the new DACL that we have created.

```
Access rights 001F01FF denied to Guests on Private Object
Access rights 001F01FF granted to Everyone on Private Object
```

Creating a Contained Private Object with Inherited Security. To create a private object that is a descendant of another object, you pass the security descriptor of the parent as the first argument of CreatePrivateObjectSecurity(). PRIVATE3 makes its object a child of the \WIN32NET\CODE directory, getting its security descriptor by invoking GetFileSecurity() as follows:

```
// We'll create this object as a child of the
// directory \WIN32NET\CODE.
BYTE byParentSecurityDescriptor[1024];
DWORD dwParentSDSize =
   sizeof (byParentSecurityDescriptor);

GetFileSecurity("\\WIN32NET\\CODE",
                DACL_SECURITY_INFORMATION,
                byParentSecurityDescriptor,
                dwParentSDSize,
                &dwParentSDSize);
```

The call to CreatePrivateObjectSecurity() changes accordingly.

```
// Now when we call CreatePrivateObjectSecurity(),
// we pass the first argument as a pointer to
// the parent object's security descriptor, instead of
// as a NULL pointer. The second argument becomes
// NULL.
PSECURITY_DESCRIPTOR pSecurityDescriptor;

if (!CreatePrivateObjectSecurity(
   (PSECURITY_DESCRIPTOR) byParentSecurityDescriptor,
   NULL,
   &pSecurityDescriptor, FALSE, hToken, &GenericMapping))
```

So does the program's output.

```
Access rights 001F01FF granted to Administrators on Private Object
Access rights 001301BF granted to Everyone on Private Object
Access rights 001F01FF granted to Administrators on Private Object
Access rights 001F01FF granted to SYSTEM on Private Object
```

Checking a Request to Access a Private Object. To demonstrate how to validate an attempt to access a private object, I added code at the end of main() in PRIVATE1, PRIVATE2, and PRIVATE3. This code calls the AccessCheck() function, which compares the DACL in a security descriptor with a token and a requested access mask. Here is the excerpt from PRIVATE1.CPP:

```
if (!AccessCheck(pSecurityDescriptor, // Has DACL of interest
    hNewToken,                        // Contains user and group info
    dwAccessRequested,                // Must have been translated
                                      // so it contains no generic
                                      // rights
    &GenericMapping,                  // Tells NT how to map any
                                      // generic rights it encounters
```

```
     (PPRIVILEGE_SET) byPrivilegeSet,   // Throwaway arguments,
     &dwPrivilegeSetSize,               // but they're required
     &dwAccessGranted,                  // Returns granted rights
     &bStatus))                         // Returns yes or no
    {
    // Function failed
    }
else
    {
    // Function succeeded, bStatus says yes or no
    if (bStatus)
        {
        // You're OK, dwAccessGranted says what rights
        // you have
        }
    else
        {
        // Get lost--but ask GetLastError() why you were rejected
        }
    }
```

Impersonating Yourself. Things get a little esoteric with AccessCheck(). Notice the argument that I call *hNewToken*. The name is intended to tip you off to the fact that this is not the process's token; it is an impersonation token that the current thread is using. AccessCheck() requires an impersonation token. To get an impersonation token in this situation, you have to impersonate yourself. Here's how you do that:

1. Call ImpersonateSelf() to begin the impersonation.
2. Call OpenThreadToken() to get a HANDLE to the impersonation token. You must use OpenThreadToken() because OpenProcessToken() returns the original token of the process.
3. Do whatever you need to with the token. In this particular case, that involves a call to AccessCheck().
4. Call RevertToSelf() to end the impersonation.

All of this is done within the main thread of the application; I have not spun off any secondary threads. The call to ImpersonateSelf() generates a new token and attaches it to the current thread. However, the original process token is still in existence. The only difference between the new token and the old is that the old one is a primary token and the new one is an impersonation token.

Here's the code that precedes the call to AccessCheck():

```
if (!ImpersonateSelf(SecurityImpersonation))
   printf("\nImpersonateSelf() failed, "
          "GetLastError() = %d",
         GetLastError());

hNewToken = GetThreadToken();

dwAccessRequested = GENERIC_ALL;
MapGenericMask(&dwAccessRequested,
   &GenericMapping);
if (!AccessCheck(pSecurityDescriptor, ...))
```

Finally, here is the output of PRIVATE1 when run by the domain Administrator:

```
Access rights 001F01FF granted to Administrators on Private Object
Access rights 001F01FF granted to SYSTEM on Private Object

Access permitted, access mask is 001F01FF
```

I requested GENERIC_ALL access, and I was awarded FILE_ ALL_ACCESS rights—which is exactly how I specified that GENERIC_ ALL rights should be mapped.

Impersonating Another User. You can use a similar technique to test the access granted to a remote user. Instead of calling ImpersonateSelf() in Step 1 above, you call LogonUser(), passing it the user's login name and password, then call ImpersonateLoggedOnUser(). From this point on, Steps 2, 3, and 4 are the same. For LogonUser() to succeed, the user running the application must have been given the "Act as part of the operating system" privilege. The *Win32 SDK Knowledge Base* article "How to Assign Privileges to Accounts for API Calls" tells you how to do this.

The PRIVATE4 application demonstrates the use of LogonUser() and ImpersonateLoggedOnUser(); here's the new code:

```
LPTSTR lpPassword;
if (argc < 4)
   lpPassword = NULL;
else
   lpPassword = (LPTSTR) argv[3];

if (!LogonUser(argv[1], argv[2], lpPassword,
    LOGON32_LOGON_INTERACTIVE,
    LOGON32_PROVIDER_DEFAULT,
    &hToken))
```

```
      {
      printf("\nLogonUser() failed, "
             "GetLastError() = %d",
            GetLastError());
      ExitProcess(GetLastError());
      }

   if (!ImpersonateLoggedOnUser(hToken))
      {
      printf("\nImpersonateLoggedOnUser() failed, "
             "GetLastError() = %d",
            GetLastError());
      ExitProcess(GetLastError());
      }
   hNewToken = GetThreadToken();

   dwAccessRequested = GENERIC_ALL;
   MapGenericMask(&dwAccessRequested,
      &GenericMapping);
   if (!AccessCheck(pSecurityDescriptor, ...))
```

If I run PRIVATE4 and tell it to log me in as the Administrator, I get the exact same output as I get from PRIVATE3. However, if I tell it to log me in as the Guest user, I get these results:

```
Access rights 001F01FF denied to Guests on Private Object
Access rights 001F01FF granted to Everyone on Private Object

Access denied, GetLastError() = 5
```

User Objects

User objects are the windows that the user actually sees on the screen. Windows themselves cannot be protected directly. There are no security hooks in the functions that create or manipulate windows; if you pass a window handle to GetUserObjectSecurity() or SetUserObjectSecurity(), the function fails. The securable objects are the parent and grandparent classes of visible windows—the thread desktop and the process window station.

The thread desktop is represented by an object of type HDESK.You can find out its handle by passing the current thread ID to GetThreadDesktop().

```
HDESK hDesktop =
   GetThreadDesktop(GetCurrentThreadId());
```

GetProcessWindowStation() tells you the handle of your process's window station, typed as an HWINSTA.

```
HWINSTA hWindowStation = GetProcessWindowStation();
```

These are the handles that you pass to GetUserObjectSecurity() and SetUserObjectSecurity() as their first argument. The other arguments are the same as for GetFileSecurity(), GetKernelObjectSecurity(), and GetPrivateObjectSecurity(), except that the second argument, the SECURITY_INFORMATION that says what part of the security descriptor you are interested in, is passed as a pointer instead of by value.

USEROBJS, the application that demonstrates user object security, is the only one of this suite of applications that runs in a window. This is not required—you get the same results with a console application. However, because we are dealing with user objects, I wanted to create the most germane environment.

RunTests() does two cycles of tests, one with the process window station and one with the thread desktop. For both objects, it calls GetUserObjectSecurity() to get the security descriptor, then a private version of DumpDACL() that writes its findings to the window. Here is RunTests():

```
VOID RunTests(HDC hDC,
             SECURITY_INFORMATION *pSecurityInfo)
{
   BYTE   bySDBuffer[8192];
   PSECURITY_DESCRIPTOR lpSecurityDescriptor =
      (PSECURITY_DESCRIPTOR) bySDBuffer;
   DWORD  dwSDSize;
   HDESK  hDesktop;
   HWINSTA hWindowStation;

   nYPosition = 0;
   hCurrentDC = hDC;

   hWindowStation = GetProcessWindowStation();
   dwSDSize = sizeof (bySDBuffer);

   if (!GetUserObjectSecurity((HANDLE) hWindowStation, pSecurityInfo,
      lpSecurityDescriptor, dwSDSize, &dwSDSize))
      {
      printfConsole("GetUserObjectSecurity() failed, "
                    "GetLastError() = %d",
         GetLastError());
      return;
      }

   DumpDACL("Window Station", lpSecurityDescriptor);

   hDesktop = GetThreadDesktop(GetCurrentThreadId());
   dwSDSize = sizeof (bySDBuffer);
```

```
    if (!GetUserObjectSecurity((HANDLE) hDesktop, pSecurityInfo,
       lpSecurityDescriptor, dwSDSize, &dwSDSize))
       {
       printfConsole("GetUserObjectSecurity() failed, "
                     "GetLastError() = %d",
          GetLastError());
       return;
       }

    DumpDACL("Thread Desktop", lpSecurityDescriptor);
}
```

Let's look at what this produces. USEROBJS displays the information somewhat differently from the other samples because you can't convert one of the SIDs in the DACL to a name. For this user, USEROBJS does a hexadecimal dump of the SID instead of the user name, as you can see in Figure 13-3.

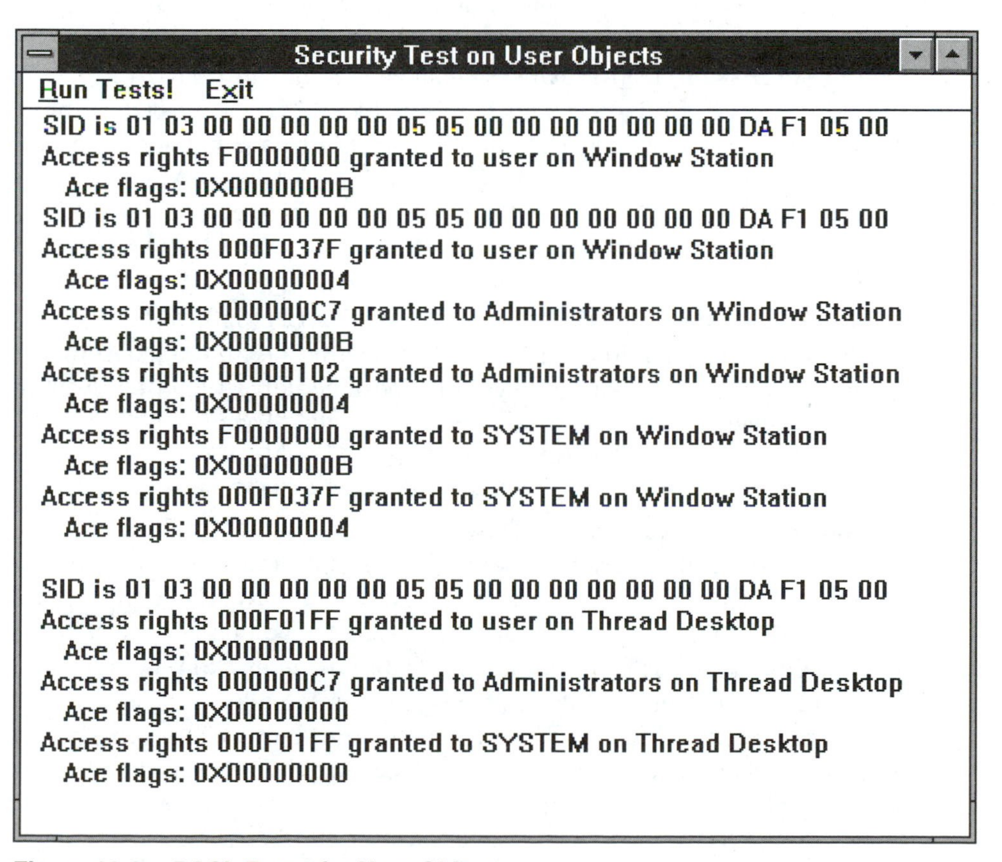

Figure 13-3. DACL Dump for User Objects

Although you can create window stations and desktops by calling CreateWindowStation() and CreateDesktop(), normally you don't need to. They are created for you when you start up a process or thread, and the security descriptor is created at that time. The first SID found in the DACL is the logon SID, generated when you log on. This SID does not correspond to any account name in the security database; when you call LookupAccountSid(), the function fails and GetLastError() returns ERROR_NONE_MAPPED.

All the users referred to by the window station's ACL have two sets of rights. The rights whose ACE flags are 0x0000000B are those that are inherited by descendant objects (like windows and menus). The ACE flags of 0x00000004 are the rights that the user has to the window station itself.

The first set of rights granted the logged-in user—0xF0000000—is GENERIC_READ (0x80000000) | GENERIC_WRITE (0x40000000) | GENERIC_EXECUTE (0x20000000) | GENERIC_ALL (0x10000000). This means that all the generic sets of rights are inheritable. The rights that the user has to the window station are the specific mapping of GENERIC_ALL for window station objects. The high 16 bits are STANDARD_RIGHTS_REQUIRED, that is, WRITE_DAC | READ_ CONTROL | WRITE_OWNER | DELETE (0x000F0000), described in more detail earlier in this chapter. The low 16 bits differ from what you have seen before. They are defined in WINUSER.H as WINSTA_ ENUMDESKTOPS | WINSTA_READATTRIBUTES | WINSTA_ACCESSCLIPBOARD | WINSTA_CREATEDESKTOP | WINSTA_WRITE-ATTRIBUTES | WINSTA_ACCESSGLOBALATOMS | WINSTA_EXIT-WINDOWS | WINSTA_ENUMERATE | WINSTA_READSCREEN (0x0000037F).

The other users mentioned in the window station's ACL are the Administrators group and the operating system. The inheritable rights for Administrators pertain to desktops, not window stations. They are DESKTOP_ WRITEOBJECTS | DESKTOP_ENUMERATE | DESKTOP_ CREATEMENU | DESKTOP_CREATEWINDOW | DESKTOP_READOBJECTS (0x000000C7). You can see that these are the exact same rights that Administrators have to the thread desktop. The Administrators group only has WINSTA_ENUMERATE and WINSTA_ READATTRIBUTES (0x00000102) rights to the window station itself. The operating system, as you would expect, has free rein: its inheritable rights mask allows all rights to propagate, and it enjoys all possible rights to the window station.

For the thread desktop, you can see that there is only one set of rights for each user—their rights to the desktop object itself. Furthermore, all three sets of rights have been inherited from the window station. The rights granted to SYSTEM and to the logged-in user are the specific mapping of GENERIC_ALL. Besides STANDARD_RIGHTS_REQUIRED, they include DESKTOP_READOBJECTS | DESKTOP_CREATEWINDOW | DESKTOP_CREATEMENU | DESKTOP_HOOKCONTROL | DESKTOP_JOURNALRECORD | DESKTOP_JOURNALPLAYBACK | DESKTOP_ENUMERATE | DESKTOP_WRITEOBJECTS | DESKTOP_ SWITCHDESKTOP (0x000001FF). The rights mask for Administrators (0x000000C7) is exactly the same as the inheritable rights assigned at the window-station level.

System Access Control Lists

Although system access control lists (SACLs) are not as important as DACLs, no serious discussion of the Win32 Security API can ignore them altogether. By tying an SACL to an object, you generate audit trail messages so that you can determine how objects of yours are being used.

SACLs look very much like DACLs, and the associated functions have the same syntax. To assign an SACL to an object:

1. Enable the SE_SECURITY_NAME privilege for your token by calling AdjustTokenPrivileges(). Administrative users have this privilege, but it is disabled unless you explicitly enable it. Whereas rights confer access to objects, privileges permit you to perform operations.
2. Initialize a security descriptor by calling InitializeSecurityDescriptor().
3. Initialize an ACL by calling InitializeAcl().
4. Instead of adding access allowed and access denied ACEs, you add system audit ACEs. The function that does this is AddSystemAuditAce().
5. To place the SACL into the security descriptor, call SetSecurityDescriptorSacl().
6. For an existing object, call the Set<Object Type>Security() function. If you are creating a new object, put a pointer to the new security descriptor into a SECURITY_ATTRIBUTES structure and call the Create<Object>() function.
7. To restore the previous state of the environment, call AdjustTokenPrivileges() once again to return your privileges to their former setting.

In the remainder of this section, I present a sample application, SACLS, that adds an SACL to a file or dumps its SACL. This is the only sample with command-line arguments. You run it as follows:

```
SACLS <filename> [<dump SACL>]
```

SACLS does not care what the second argument is. If there is more than one argument, it reports the current SACL but does not change it.

Enabling Token Privileges

\WIN32NET\CODE\SECURITY\SECUHLPR.CPP contains a routine called TurnPrivilegeOn(), which enables a requested privilege. It calls LookupPrivilegeValue() to convert the string name of the privilege into its binary value, called its Locally Unique ID (LUID). Then, after obtaining a HANDLE to the process's token, it calls AdjustTokenPrivileges(). For some reason, you are cautioned not to test the return value of AdjustTokenPrivileges() but to immediately ask GetLastError() how things went. That is the reason for the fancy footwork at the end of the listing.

```
BOOL TurnPrivilegeOn(LPTSTR lpPrivilegeName,
                     PTOKEN_PRIVILEGES pCurrentPrivileges)
{
   HANDLE hToken;

   hToken = GetProcessToken();

   if (hToken == NULL)
      return FALSE;

   LUID PrivilegeValue;

   // Get value of privilege name
   if (!LookupPrivilegeValue(
          NULL,
          lpPrivilegeName,
          &PrivilegeValue))
      {
      printf("\nLookupPrivilegeValue() failed, "
             "GetLastError() = %d",
            GetLastError());
      return FALSE;
      }

   // Set TOKEN_PRIVILEGES structure
   // to enable the requested privilege
   TOKEN_PRIVILEGES NewPrivilegeSet;
   NewPrivilegeSet.PrivilegeCount = 1;
   NewPrivilegeSet.Privileges[0].Luid = PrivilegeValue;
   NewPrivilegeSet.Privileges[0].Attributes =
      SE_PRIVILEGE_ENABLED;

   DWORD dwOutLength;

   AdjustTokenPrivileges(hToken, FALSE,
      &NewPrivilegeSet, sizeof (TOKEN_PRIVILEGES),
```

```
      pCurrentPrivileges, &dwOutLength);
   return (GetLastError() == NO_ERROR);
}
```

Steps 2 and 3, in which you initialize a security descriptor and an ACL, are no different from how these tasks were done earlier in this chapter.

Adding a System Audit ACE

AddAuditAccessAce() adds a new access control entry to the SACL.

```
BOOL AddAuditAccessAce(
    PACL pAcl,
    DWORD dwAceRevision,
    DWORD dwAccessMask,
    PSID pSid,
    BOOL bAuditSuccess,
    BOOL bAuditFailure);
```

Its first four arguments are the same as for AddAccessAllowedAce() and AddAccessDeniedAce(). They identify the buffer where you are assembling the ACL, the ACL revision, the kinds of access you want to audit, and the SID of the user or group whose access you want to audit. AddAuditAccess-Ace() takes two additional arguments, boolean flags that state whether to audit successful accesses, failed accesses, or both. The access mask must include the flag ACCESS_SYSTEM_SECURITY. SACLs don't work if you don't set this bit.

Here are the pertinent lines of code from SACLS.CPP:

```
// Add a system audit ACE for "Everyone"
// Audit all successful and unsuccessful access attempts.

if (NameToSID("Everyone", (PSID) bySIDBuffer, &dwSIDSize))
   {
   if (!AddAuditAccessAce((PACL) byACLBuffer, ACL_REVISION,
         ACCESS_SYSTEM_SECURITY | GENERIC_READ |
         GENERIC_WRITE | GENERIC_EXECUTE |
         STANDARD_RIGHTS_REQUIRED,
         bySIDBuffer, TRUE, TRUE))
      {
      printf("\nAddAuditAccessAce() failed, "
            "GetLastError() = %d",
            GetLastError());
      }
   }
```

The combination ACCESS_SYSTEM_SECURITY | GENERIC_READ | GENERIC_WRITE | GENERIC_EXECUTE | STANDARD_RIGHTS_REQUIRED produces the same access mask that File Manager gives you if you check all the check boxes in Figure 13-4.

Here is the output from SACLS when I ask it to dump the SACL that File Manager produces:

```
SACL is present

SACL explicitly assigned

System audit ace
Access rights 011F01BF being audited for Everyone on PRIVATE2.out
```

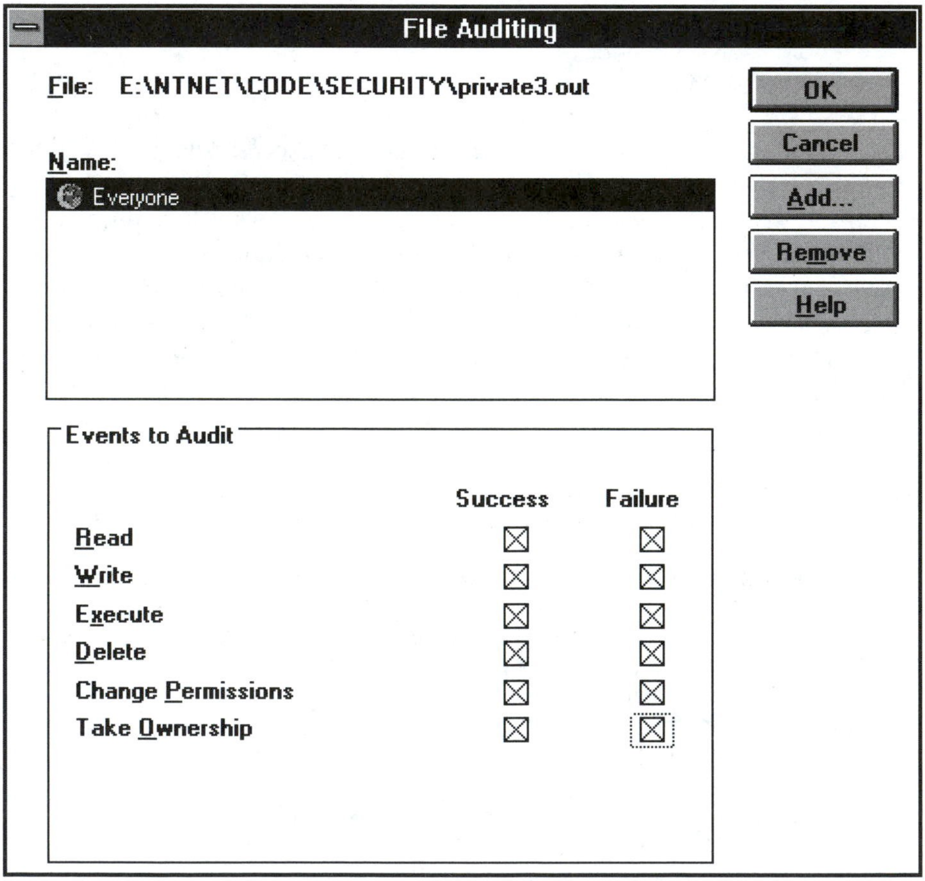

Figure 13-4. File Manager File Auditing Screen

I get the exact same output when I tell SACLS to create a new SACL. In the access mask, GENERIC_READ, GENERIC_WRITE, and GENERIC_EXECUTE have been mapped to FILE_GENERIC_READ (0x00120089), FILE_GENERIC_WRITE (0x00120116), and FILE_GENERIC_ EXECUTE (0x00120028). The mask 0x011F01BF corresponds to ACCESS_SYSTEM_SECURITY | SYNCHRONIZE | STANDARD_RIGHTS_REQUIRED | FILE_WRITE_ATTRIBUTES | FILE_READ_ ATTRIBUTES | FILE_EXECUTE | FILE_WRITE_EA | FILE_READ_EA | FILE_APPEND_DATA | FILE_WRITE_DATA | FILE_READ_DATA.

Here is the main() function from \WIN32NET\CODE\SECURITY \SACLS.CPP:

```
void main(int argc, char *argv[])
{
   SECURITY_INFORMATION SecurityInformation =
      SACL_SECURITY_INFORMATION;
   BYTE   byACLBuffer[4096];
   DWORD  dwACLSize = sizeof (byACLBuffer);
   SECURITY_DESCRIPTOR SecurityDescriptor;
   BYTE   bySIDBuffer[1024];
   DWORD  dwSIDSize = sizeof (bySIDBuffer);

   if (argc == 1)
      {
      printf("\nUsage:  secutst8 <filename>");
      ExitProcess(1);
      }

   // We have to enable the SE_SECURITY_NAME
   // privilege in order to play with SACLs
   TOKEN_PRIVILEGES CurrentPrivileges;

   TurnPrivilegeOn(SE_SECURITY_NAME, &CurrentPrivileges);

   SecurityInformation = SACL_SECURITY_INFORMATION;

   // The presence of a second command-line argument says to read the
   // SACL, not alter it
   if (argc <= 2)
      {
      InitializeSecurityDescriptor(&SecurityDescriptor,
         SECURITY_DESCRIPTOR_REVISION);

      // Set up ACL with one ACE
      InitializeAcl((PACL) byACLBuffer, sizeof (byACLBuffer),
         ACL_REVISION);
```

```
        dwSIDSize = sizeof (bySIDBuffer);

        // Add a system audit ACE for "Everyone"
        // Audit all successful and unsuccessful access attempts.

        if (NameToSID("Everyone", (PSID) bySIDBuffer, &dwSIDSize))
           {
           if (!AddAuditAccessAce((PACL) byACLBuffer, ACL_REVISION,
                 ACCESS_SYSTEM_SECURITY | GENERIC_READ |
                 GENERIC_WRITE | GENERIC_EXECUTE |
                 STANDARD_RIGHTS_REQUIRED,
                 bySIDBuffer, TRUE, TRUE))
              {
              printf("\nAddAuditAccessAce() failed, "
                    "GetLastError() = %d",
                    GetLastError());
              }
           }

        // Insert the SACL into the SECURITY_DESCRIPTOR
        if (!SetSecurityDescriptorSacl(&SecurityDescriptor,
           TRUE, (PACL) byACLBuffer, FALSE))
           printf("\nSetSecurityDescriptorSacl() failed, "
                 "GetLastError() = %d",
                 GetLastError());

        // Tie the SACL to the file
        if (!SetFileSecurity(argv[1], SecurityInformation,
              &SecurityDescriptor))
           {
           printf("\nSetFileSecurity() failed, "
                 "GetLastError() = %d",
                 GetLastError());
           }
        }
     RunTests(argv[1], &SecurityInformation);

     RestorePrivileges(&CurrentPrivileges);

     fflush(stdout);
     ExitProcess(0);
}
```

C++ and MFC Considerations

There are no MFC classes encapsulating the Win32 Security API. However, wrapping some of the functionality in C++ objects can save us some trouble. Because this is a book about Win32 network programming, I have created classes to do the things I am most likely to need to do—that is, tie security descriptors to server-application endpoints in order to:

- Grant universal access
- Grant and deny access to specific users or groups
- Request the generation of an audit trail

There are three types of objects that I need for these purposes:

- SECURITY_ATTRIBUTES structures, which are required by many of the pertinent functions.
- SECURITY_DESCRIPTOR structures, which embody the actual security information.
- Access control lists (ACLs), specifying who may do what and what events are to be audited. ACLs are further divided into discretionary ACLs (DACLs), which grant access, and system ACLs (SACLs), which request auditing.

These are the objects I will model in the remainder of this chapter.

The CSecurityAttributes Class

This class does very little. In fact, the only method it offers is a constructor that sets the fields of the SECURITY_ATTRIBUTES structure from which it is derived. Here are the declarations of SECURITY_ATTRIBUTES, from WINBASE.H, and of the CSecurityAttributes class, from \WIN32NET \CODE\WIN32OBJ\SECURITY.H:

```
typedef struct _SECURITY_ATTRIBUTES
{
   DWORD  nLength;
   LPVOID lpSecurityDescriptor;
   BOOL    bInheritHandle;
} SECURITY_ATTRIBUTES;

class AFX_EXT_CLASS CSecurityAttributes : public SECURITY_ATTRIBUTES
{
public:
   CSecurityAttributes(BOOL bInherit           = FALSE,
                       SECURITY_DESCRIPTOR *lp = NULL)
      {
      nLength              = sizeof (SECURITY_ATTRIBUTES);
      bInheritHandle       = bInherit;
      lpSecurityDescriptor = lp;
      }
};
```

The constructor copies its arguments to the fields of the SECURITY_ATTRIBUTES structure.

The CSecurityDescriptor Class

The workhorse of the group is the CSecurityDescriptor class, since it contains the key data object, a pointer to a SECURITY_DESCRIPTOR (*m_pSD*). It also contains data members that point to its ACLs, *m_pDACL* for its discretionary access control list and *m_pSACL* for its system ACL. Because the Win32 headers define the SECURITY_DESCRIPTOR as an LPVOID, I have not derived this class from it. Rather, the class contains an embedded pointer to a SECURITY_DESCRIPTOR in its *m_pSD* member variable.

```
class AFX_EXT_CLASS CSecurityDescriptor
{
protected:
   CDacl *m_pDACL;
   CSacl *m_pSACL;
   SECURITY_DESCRIPTOR *m_pSD;
public:
   // The sole purpose of this constructor is so
   // we can construct an empty CSecurityDescriptor
   // We have to provide an argument so the
   // compiler can distinguish it from
   // the second version
   CSecurityDescriptor(BOOL bNotUsed)
      {
      m_pDACL = NULL;
      m_pSACL = NULL;
      m_pSD   = NULL;
      }

   CSecurityDescriptor(
      CStringArray *paszAllowedUsers = NULL,
      CStringArray *paszDeniedUsers  = NULL,
      BOOL          bAuditAccess     = FALSE);
   virtual ~CSecurityDescriptor();

   SECURITY_DESCRIPTOR *GetSecurityDescriptor(void)
      {
      return m_pSD;
      }

   void SetSecurityDescriptor(
      PSECURITY_DESCRIPTOR pSecurityDescriptor)
```

```
      {
      m_pSD = (SECURITY_DESCRIPTOR *) pSecurityDescriptor;
      }
   CDacl *GetDacl(void)
      {
      return m_pDACL;
      }
   CSacl *GetSacl(void)
      {
      return m_pSACL;
      }
   BOOL SetDacl(CDacl *pDacl           = NULL,
                BOOL   bDaclPresent    = TRUE,
                BOOL   bDaclDefaulted  = FALSE);
   BOOL SetSacl(CSacl *pSacl           = NULL,
                BOOL   bSaclPresent    = TRUE,
                BOOL   bSaclDefaulted  = FALSE);

   static BOOL NameToSID(
        LPTSTR lpName,
        PSID pSID,
        LPDWORD lpdwSIDSize);
   static HANDLE GetProcessToken(void);
   static HANDLE GetThreadToken(void);
   static CSecurityDescriptor* CreatePrivateObject(
      CStringArray *paszAllowedUsers = NULL,
      CStringArray *paszDeniedUsers  = NULL,
      BOOL          bAuditAccess     = FALSE);
   BOOL DestroyPrivateObject(void);
};
```

The most interesting member functions are the constructor, SetDacl() and SetSacl(), and the static member function CreatePrivateObject(). These wrap much of the functionality that we have already seen in this chapter.

The CSecurity Descriptor Constructor. The CSecurityDescriptor constructor offers a very high-level interface by allowing you to pass allowed and denied users as pointers to CStringArray objects. You can also request an audit trail by passing *bAuditAccess* as TRUE. Auditing will be requested for the group "Everyone."

```
CSecurityDescriptor::CSecurityDescriptor(
   CStringArray *paszAllowedUsers,
   CStringArray *paszDeniedUsers,
   BOOL          bAuditAccess)
```

```
{
   m_pDACL = NULL;
   m_pSACL = NULL;

   LPBYTE lp = new BYTE[16384];
   m_pSD = (SECURITY_DESCRIPTOR *) lp;

   if (!::InitializeSecurityDescriptor(
         m_pSD,
         SECURITY_DESCRIPTOR_REVISION))
      {
      // Windows 95?
      if (::GetLastError() != ERROR_CALL_NOT_IMPLEMENTED)
         AfxThrowResourceException();
      return;
      }

   // Add denied ACEs to ACL first
   if (paszDeniedUsers != NULL)
      {
      if (m_pDACL == NULL)
         m_pDACL = new CDacl;

      for (int i = 0; i < paszDeniedUsers->GetSize(); ++i)
         {
         m_pDACL->DenyUserAccess(
            (LPTSTR) (LPCTSTR) paszDeniedUsers->GetAt(i));
         }
      }

   if (paszAllowedUsers != NULL)
      {
      if (m_pDACL == NULL)
         m_pDACL = new CDacl;

      for (int i = 0; i < paszAllowedUsers->GetSize(); ++i)
         {
         m_pDACL->AllowUserAccess(
            (LPTSTR) (LPCTSTR) paszAllowedUsers->GetAt(i));
         }
      }
   if ((paszAllowedUsers != NULL) ||
       (paszDeniedUsers  != NULL))
      {
      SetDacl(m_pDACL);
      }

   LPTSTR lpAuditUsers = _T("Everyone");
```

```
    m_pSACL = NULL;

    if (bAuditAccess)
        {
        m_pSACL = new CSacl(1, &lpAuditUsers);
        SetSacl(m_pSACL);
        }
}
```

We first allocate memory for the SECURITY_DESCRIPTOR. Notice that I allocate an array of 16,384 bytes, instead of saying:

```
m_pSD = new SECURITY_DESCRIPTOR;
```

The SECURITY_DESCRIPTOR is a variable-length object, and in some cases function calls will fail if you don't provide a large enough buffer—in particular, the functions that retrieve an object's current security characteristics (GetFileSecurity(), GetKernelObjectSecurity(), and so on).

Next I call InitializeSecurityDescriptor(), as required. Under Windows 95, it will fail, and GetLastError() will return ERROR_CALL_NOT_ IMPLEMENTED. I simply ignore this error; that makes using security objects straightforward under Windows 95. They don't work, but they're harmless.

Next, I scan the arrays of denied and allowed users. By convention, access-denied ACEs come first in an ACL. I pass each element of the arrays to the appropriate method of the CDacl class, DenyUserAccess() or AllowUserAccess() (which I'll show in a minute). After this, I call CSecurityDescriptor::SetDacl() to add the DACL to the SECURITY_DESCRIPTOR.

Finally, if auditing is requested, I instantiate a new CSacl object, and call CSecurityDescriptor::SetSacl().

SetDacl() / SetSacl(). These CSecurityDescriptor methods call the corresponding Win32 functions SetSecurityDescriptorDacl() and SetSecurityDescriptorSacl(). Because the two are so similar, I only show SetDacl() here.

```
BOOL CSecurityDescriptor::SetDacl(
                CDacl *pDacl           /*= NULL*/,
                BOOL   bDaclPresent    /*= TRUE*/,
                BOOL   bDaclDefaulted /*= FALSE*/)
{
    PACL pACL = NULL;

    if (pDacl != NULL)
```

```
        {
        pACL = pDacl->GetACL();
        }

    BOOL bRetcode
        = ::SetSecurityDescriptorDacl(
                m_pSD,
                bDaclPresent,
                pACL,
                bDaclDefaulted);
    return bRetcode;
}
```

CreatePrivateObject(). I provide this member function for my own future use (or yours). Private objects are how you add security protection to communications endpoints where the native API doesn't support it. I don't do any more with them now, because there are issues that I haven't thought through completely—like how to avoid passing an unencrypted password across the network. However, I can implement this function easily enough just by stealing code from the PRIVATE sample applications I've shown earlier in this chapter.

There are three ways to create a private object. One uses a container object, and inherits its ACLs. Another takes on the default DACL of the running process. The third—the one I implement here—creates a private object from a template SECURITY_DESCRIPTOR. CreatePrivateObject() takes allowed users, denied users, and audit-enabling as its arguments, builds a template CSecurityDescriptor from them, then creates a private object based on the template.

```
CSecurityDescriptor *CSecurityDescriptor::CreatePrivateObject(
      CStringArray *paszAllowedUsers /* = NULL*/,
      CStringArray *paszDeniedUsers  /* = NULL*/,
      BOOL           bAuditAccess     /* = FALSE*/)
{
   // Create a template SECURITY_DESCRIPTOR
   // from the input arguments
   CSecurityDescriptor TemplateSD(
      paszAllowedUsers,
      paszDeniedUsers,
      bAuditAccess);

   CSecurityDescriptor *pNewSD = NULL;
   PSECURITY_DESCRIPTOR pSecurityDescriptor;
   GENERIC_MAPPING      GenericMapping;
   HANDLE               hToken;
```

```
  hToken = CSecurityDescriptor::GetProcessToken();

  if (hToken != NULL)
     {

     // Set generic-to-specific access mapping as if
     // this object were a file
     GenericMapping.GenericRead    = FILE_GENERIC_READ;
     GenericMapping.GenericWrite   = FILE_GENERIC_WRITE;
     GenericMapping.GenericExecute = FILE_GENERIC_EXECUTE;
     GenericMapping.GenericAll     = FILE_ALL_ACCESS;

     // When we call CreatePrivateObjectSecurity(),
     // we pass the second argument as a pointer to
     // our template security descriptor
     if (CreatePrivateObjectSecurity(NULL,
        TemplateSD.GetSecurityDescriptor(),
        &pSecurityDescriptor, FALSE, hToken, &GenericMapping))
        {
        pNewSD = new CSecurityDescriptor(TRUE);
        pNewSD->SetSecurityDescriptor(pSecurityDescriptor);
        if (paszAllowedUsers != NULL ||
            paszDeniedUsers  != NULL)
           {
           // CreatePrivateObjectSecurity() has already
           // created ACEs
           // All we need is a CDacl object
           pNewSD->SetDacl(new CDacl(0, NULL));
           }

        if (bAuditAccess)
           {
           // CreatePrivateObjectSecurity() has already
           // create the system ACEs
           // All we need is a CSacl object
           pNewSD->SetSacl(new CSacl(0, NULL));
           }
        }
     }
  return pNewSD;
}
```

The CAcl, CDacl, and CSacl Classes

These classes represent access control lists. CAcl is a generic ACL, and serves as the base class for both of the others. Here are their declarations:

```
class AFX_EXT_CLASS CAcl
{
protected:
   PACL m_pACL;
public:
   CAcl();
   virtual ~CAcl();

   PACL GetACL(void)
      {
      return m_pACL;
      }
};

class AFX_EXT_CLASS CDacl : public CAcl
{
public:
   CDacl() {}
   CDacl(DWORD dwUsers,
         LPTSTR lpUsers[],
         DWORD dwAccess = GENERIC_ALL | STANDARD_RIGHTS_REQUIRED);

   BOOL AllowUserAccess(
          LPTSTR lpUser,
          DWORD  dwAccess = GENERIC_ALL | STANDARD_RIGHTS_REQUIRED);
   BOOL AllowUserAccess(
            DWORD  dwUserCount,
            LPTSTR lpUsers[],
            DWORD  dwAccess = GENERIC_ALL |
                              STANDARD_RIGHTS_REQUIRED);

   BOOL DenyUserAccess(
          LPTSTR lpUser,
          DWORD  dwAccess = GENERIC_ALL | STANDARD_RIGHTS_REQUIRED);
   BOOL DenyUserAccess(
            DWORD  dwUserCount,
            LPTSTR lpUsers[],
            DWORD  dwAccess = GENERIC_ALL |
                              STANDARD_RIGHTS_REQUIRED);

};

class AFX_EXT_CLASS CSacl : public CAcl
{
protected:
   TOKEN_PRIVILEGES m_CurrentPrivileges;
   BOOL             TurnPrivilegeOn(LPTSTR lpPrivilegeName);
   BOOL             RestorePrivileges(void);
```

```
public:
   CSacl(DWORD dwUsers,
         LPTSTR lpUsers[],
         DWORD dwAccess = GENERIC_ALL | STANDARD_RIGHTS_REQUIRED
                              | ACCESS_SYSTEM_SECURITY);

   virtual ~CSacl();

   BOOL AuditUserAccess(
           LPTSTR lpUser,
           DWORD  dwAccess = GENERIC_ALL | STANDARD_RIGHTS_REQUIRED
                              | ACCESS_SYSTEM_SECURITY);
   BOOL AuditUserAccess(
             DWORD  dwUserCount,
             LPTSTR lpUsers[],
             DWORD  dwAccess = GENERIC_ALL |
                               STANDARD_RIGHTS_REQUIRED |
                               ACCESS_SYSTEM_SECURITY);

};
```

The constructors for CDacl and CSacl allow you to pass an arrow of LPTSTRs, indicating the users to grant access to (for CDacl objects), and users to audit (for CSacl objects). Both classes also offer member functions that:

- Allow or deny user access, singly or en masse
- Audit users, also one-at-a-time or as a group

The methods of interest are the one-user-at-a-time version of CDacl::AllowUserAccess(), CDacl::DenyUserAccess(), and CSacl::AuditUserAccess(). Each calls its corresponding Win32 function—AddAccessAllowedAce(), AddAccessDeniedAce(), and AddSystemAuditAce(). First, though, they convert the user name to its Security Identifier (SID) by calling CSecurityDescriptor::NameToSID(). This is a static member function taken from the same helper function we saw earlier in this chapter. CDacl::AllowUserAccess() is typical.

```
BOOL CDacl::AllowUserAccess(
   LPTSTR lpUser,
   DWORD  dwAccess)
{
   SECURITY_INFORMATION SecurityInformation =
      DACL_SECURITY_INFORMATION;
   BYTE   bySIDBuffer[1024];
   DWORD  dwSIDSize = sizeof (bySIDBuffer);
   BOOL   bRetcode  = FALSE;
```

```
   dwSIDSize = sizeof (bySIDBuffer);

   dwAccess;

   if (CSecurityDescriptor::NameToSID(
         lpUser, (PSID) bySIDBuffer, &dwSIDSize))
      {
      bRetcode = ::AddAccessAllowedAce(m_pACL, ACL_REVISION,
                    dwAccess,
                    bySIDBuffer);
      }
   return bRetcode;
}
```

Code Listings

The complete code listings for my security-related classes follow. The header file is \WIN32NET\CODE\WIN32OBJ\SECURITY.H, and the implementation file is \WIN32NET\CODE\WIN32OBJ\SECURITY.CPP.

```
/********
*
* SECURITY.H
*
* Copyright (c) 1996 Ralph P. Davis
*
* All Rights Reserved
*
*****/

#ifndef _SECURITY_INCLUDED
#define _SECURITY_INCLUDED

extern CWinApp *g_pMyApp;

class CSecurityAttributes;
class CSecurityDescriptor;
class CAcl;
class CDacl;
class CSacl;

class AFX_EXT_CLASS CSecurityAttributes : public SECURITY_ATTRIBUTES
{
public:
   CSecurityAttributes(BOOL bInherit            = FALSE,
                       SECURITY_DESCRIPTOR *lp = NULL)
```

```
        {
        nLength               = sizeof (SECURITY_ATTRIBUTES);
        bInheritHandle        = bInherit;
        lpSecurityDescriptor = lp;
        }

};

class AFX_EXT_CLASS CSecurityDescriptor
{
protected:
   CDacl *m_pDACL;
   CSacl *m_pSACL;
   SECURITY_DESCRIPTOR *m_pSD;
public:
   // The sole purpose of this constructor is so
   // we can construct an empty CSecurityDescriptor
   // We have to provide an argument so the
   // compiler can distinguish it from
   // the second version
   CSecurityDescriptor(BOOL bNotUsed)
      {
      m_pDACL = NULL;
      m_pSACL = NULL;
      m_pSD   = NULL;
      }

   CSecurityDescriptor(
      CStringArray *paszAllowedUsers = NULL,
      CStringArray *paszDeniedUsers  = NULL,
      BOOL          bAuditAccess     = FALSE);
   virtual ~CSecurityDescriptor();

   SECURITY_DESCRIPTOR *GetSecurityDescriptor(void)
      {
      return m_pSD;
      }

   void SetSecurityDescriptor(
      PSECURITY_DESCRIPTOR pSecurityDescriptor)
      {
      m_pSD = (SECURITY_DESCRIPTOR *) pSecurityDescriptor;
      }
   CDacl *GetDacl(void)
      {
      return m_pDACL;
      }
   CSacl *GetSacl(void)
```

```
      {
      return m_pSACL;
      }
   BOOL SetDacl(CDacl *pDacl          = NULL,
                BOOL   bDaclPresent   = TRUE,
                BOOL   bDaclDefaulted = FALSE);
   BOOL SetSacl(CSacl *pSacl          = NULL,
                BOOL   bSaclPresent   = TRUE,
                BOOL   bSaclDefaulted = FALSE);

   static BOOL NameToSID(
        LPTSTR lpName,
        PSID pSID,
        LPDWORD lpdwSIDSize);
   static HANDLE GetProcessToken(void);
   static HANDLE GetThreadToken(void);
   static CSecurityDescriptor* CreatePrivateObject(
      CStringArray *paszAllowedUsers = NULL,
      CStringArray *paszDeniedUsers  = NULL,
      BOOL          bAuditAccess     = FALSE);
   BOOL DestroyPrivateObject(void);
};

class AFX_EXT_CLASS CAcl
{
protected:
   PACL m_pACL;
public:
   CAcl();
   virtual ~CAcl();

   PACL GetACL(void)
      {
      return m_pACL;
      }
};

class AFX_EXT_CLASS CDacl : public CAcl
{
public:
   CDacl() {}
   CDacl(DWORD dwUsers,
         LPTSTR lpUsers[],
         DWORD dwAccess = GENERIC_ALL | STANDARD_RIGHTS_REQUIRED);

   BOOL AllowUserAccess(
           LPTSTR lpUser,
           DWORD  dwAccess = GENERIC_ALL | STANDARD_RIGHTS_REQUIRED);
```

```
   BOOL AllowUserAccess(
             DWORD  dwUserCount,
             LPTSTR lpUsers[],
             DWORD  dwAccess = GENERIC_ALL |
                               STANDARD_RIGHTS_REQUIRED);

   BOOL DenyUserAccess(
           LPTSTR lpUser,
           DWORD  dwAccess = GENERIC_ALL | STANDARD_RIGHTS_REQUIRED);
   BOOL DenyUserAccess(
             DWORD  dwUserCount,
             LPTSTR lpUsers[],
             DWORD  dwAccess = GENERIC_ALL |
                               STANDARD_RIGHTS_REQUIRED);

};

class AFX_EXT_CLASS CSacl : public CAcl
{
protected:
   TOKEN_PRIVILEGES m_CurrentPrivileges;
   BOOL             TurnPrivilegeOn(LPTSTR lpPrivilegeName);
   BOOL             RestorePrivileges(void);
public:
   CSacl(DWORD dwUsers,
         LPTSTR lpUsers[],
         DWORD dwAccess = GENERIC_ALL | STANDARD_RIGHTS_REQUIRED
                        | ACCESS_SYSTEM_SECURITY);

   virtual ~CSacl();

   BOOL AuditUserAccess(
           LPTSTR lpUser,
           DWORD  dwAccess = GENERIC_ALL | STANDARD_RIGHTS_REQUIRED
                           | ACCESS_SYSTEM_SECURITY);
   BOOL AuditUserAccess(
             DWORD  dwUserCount,
             LPTSTR lpUsers[],
             DWORD  dwAccess = GENERIC_ALL |
                               STANDARD_RIGHTS_REQUIRED |
                               ACCESS_SYSTEM_SECURITY);

};

#endif
```

```
/********
*
* SECURITY.CPP
*
* Copyright (c) 1996 Ralph P. Davis
*
* All Rights Reserved
*
*****/

/*===== Includes =====*/

#include "stdafx.h"
#include "security.h"

CSecurityDescriptor::CSecurityDescriptor(
   CStringArray *paszAllowedUsers,
   CStringArray *paszDeniedUsers,
   BOOL          bAuditAccess)
{
   m_pDACL = NULL;
   m_pSACL = NULL;

   LPBYTE lp = new BYTE[16384];
   m_pSD = (SECURITY_DESCRIPTOR *) lp;

   if (!::InitializeSecurityDescriptor(
         m_pSD,
         SECURITY_DESCRIPTOR_REVISION))
      {
      // Windows 95?
      if (::GetLastError() != ERROR_CALL_NOT_IMPLEMENTED)
         AfxThrowResourceException();
      return;
      }

   // Add denied ACEs to ACL first
   if (paszDeniedUsers != NULL)
      {
      if (m_pDACL == NULL)
         m_pDACL = new CDacl;

      for (int i = 0; i < paszDeniedUsers->GetSize(); ++i)
         {
         m_pDACL->DenyUserAccess(
            (LPTSTR) (LPCTSTR) paszDeniedUsers->GetAt(i));
         }
      }
```

```
    if (paszAllowedUsers != NULL)
        {
        if (m_pDACL == NULL)
            m_pDACL = new CDacl;

        for (int i = 0; i < paszAllowedUsers->GetSize(); ++i)
            {
            m_pDACL->AllowUserAccess(
                (LPTSTR) (LPCTSTR) paszAllowedUsers->GetAt(i));
            }
        }
    if ((paszAllowedUsers != NULL) ||
         (paszDeniedUsers  != NULL))
        {
        SetDacl(m_pDACL);
        }

    LPTSTR lpAuditUsers = _T("Everyone");

    m_pSACL = NULL;

    if (bAuditAccess)
        {
        m_pSACL = new CSacl(1, &lpAuditUsers);
        SetSacl(m_pSACL);
        }
}

CSecurityDescriptor::~CSecurityDescriptor()
{
    delete m_pDACL;
    delete m_pSACL;
    delete m_pSD;
}

BOOL CSecurityDescriptor::NameToSID(
      LPTSTR lpName,
      PSID pSID,
      LPDWORD lpdwSIDSize)
{
    TCHAR szDomain[256];
    DWORD dwDomainSize = sizeof (szDomain);
    SID_NAME_USE SidNameUse;

    BOOL bRetcode = LookupAccountName(NULL, lpName, pSID,
          lpdwSIDSize, szDomain, &dwDomainSize, &SidNameUse);

    return bRetcode;
}
```

```
HANDLE CSecurityDescriptor::GetProcessToken(void)
{
   HANDLE hToken;
   BOOL   bRetval;
   DWORD  dwError;

   bRetval = ::OpenProcessToken(::GetCurrentProcess(),
                 TOKEN_ALL_ACCESS,
                 &hToken);

   dwError = ::GetLastError();

   if (!bRetval)
      {
      return NULL;
      }
   return hToken;
}

HANDLE CSecurityDescriptor::GetThreadToken(void)
{
   HANDLE hToken;
   BOOL   bRetval;
   DWORD  dwError;

   bRetval = ::OpenThreadToken(::GetCurrentThread(),
                 TOKEN_ALL_ACCESS,
                 TRUE, &hToken);

   dwError = ::GetLastError();

   if (!bRetval)
      {
      return NULL;
      }
   return hToken;
}

BOOL CSecurityDescriptor::SetDacl(
                 CDacl *pDacl           /*= NULL*/,
                 BOOL   bDaclPresent    /*= TRUE*/,
                 BOOL   bDaclDefaulted  /*= FALSE*/)
{
   PACL pACL = NULL;

   if (pDacl != NULL)
```

```
      {
      pACL = pDacl->GetACL();
      }

   BOOL bRetcode
      = ::SetSecurityDescriptorDacl(
           m_pSD,
           bDaclPresent,
           pACL,
           bDaclDefaulted);
   return bRetcode;
}

BOOL CSecurityDescriptor::SetSacl(
                CSacl *pSacl,
                BOOL   bSaclPresent   /*= TRUE*/,
                BOOL   bSaclDefaulted /*= FALSE*/)
{
   PACL pACL = NULL;

   if (pSacl != NULL)
      {
      pACL = pSacl->GetACL();
      }

   BOOL bRetcode
      = ::SetSecurityDescriptorSacl(
           m_pSD,
           bSaclPresent,
           pACL,
           bSaclDefaulted);
   return bRetcode;
}

CSecurityDescriptor *CSecurityDescriptor::CreatePrivateObject(
      CStringArray *paszAllowedUsers /* = NULL*/,
      CStringArray *paszDeniedUsers  /* = NULL*/,
      BOOL          bAuditAccess     /* = FALSE*/)
{
   // Create a template SECURITY_DESCRIPTOR
   // from the input arguments
   CSecurityDescriptor TemplateSD(
      paszAllowedUsers,
      paszDeniedUsers,
      bAuditAccess);

   CSecurityDescriptor *pNewSD = NULL;
   PSECURITY_DESCRIPTOR pSecurityDescriptor;
```

```
   GENERIC_MAPPING      GenericMapping;
   HANDLE               hToken;

   hToken = CSecurityDescriptor::GetProcessToken();

   if (hToken != NULL)
      {

      // Set generic-to-specific access mapping as if
      // this object were a file
      GenericMapping.GenericRead    = FILE_GENERIC_READ;
      GenericMapping.GenericWrite   = FILE_GENERIC_WRITE;
      GenericMapping.GenericExecute = FILE_GENERIC_EXECUTE;
      GenericMapping.GenericAll     = FILE_ALL_ACCESS;

      // When we call CreatePrivateObjectSecurity(),
      // we pass the second argument as a pointer to
      // our template security descriptor
      if (CreatePrivateObjectSecurity(NULL,
         TemplateSD.GetSecurityDescriptor(),
         &pSecurityDescriptor, FALSE, hToken, &GenericMapping))
         {
         pNewSD = new CSecurityDescriptor(TRUE);
         pNewSD->SetSecurityDescriptor(pSecurityDescriptor);
         if (paszAllowedUsers != NULL ||
             paszDeniedUsers  != NULL)
            {
            // CreatePrivateObjectSecurity() has already
            // created ACEs
            // All we need is a CDacl object
            pNewSD->SetDacl(new CDacl(0, NULL));
            }

         if (bAuditAccess)
            {
            // CreatePrivateObjectSecurity() has already
            // created the system ACEs
            // All we need is a CSacl object
            pNewSD->SetSacl(new CSacl(0, NULL));
            }
         }
      }
   return pNewSD;
}

BOOL CSecurityDescriptor::DestroyPrivateObject()
{
   PSECURITY_DESCRIPTOR pSecurityDescriptor =
      (PSECURITY_DESCRIPTOR) GetSecurityDescriptor();
```

```
   BOOL bRetcode =
      ::DestroyPrivateObjectSecurity(&pSecurityDescriptor);

   m_pSD = NULL;
   delete this;
   return bRetcode;
}

CAcl::CAcl()
{
   LPBYTE lpb = new BYTE[16384];

   m_pACL = (PACL) lpb;

   if (!::InitializeAcl((PACL) m_pACL, 16384,
            ACL_REVISION))
      {
      if (::GetLastError() != ERROR_CALL_NOT_IMPLEMENTED)
         AfxThrowResourceException();
      return;
      }
}

CAcl::~CAcl()
{
   delete m_pACL;
}

CDacl::CDacl(DWORD  dwUserCount,
             LPTSTR lpUsers[],
             DWORD  dwAccess /*= STANDARD_RIGHTS_REQUIRED |
                                 GENERIC_ALL*/)
{
   for (DWORD i = 0; i < dwUserCount; ++i)
      {
      if (!AllowUserAccess(lpUsers[i], dwAccess))
         {
         if (::GetLastError() != ERROR_CALL_NOT_IMPLEMENTED)
            AfxThrowResourceException();
         return;
         }
      }
}

BOOL CDacl::AllowUserAccess(
   LPTSTR lpUser,
   DWORD  dwAccess)
```

```
{
   SECURITY_INFORMATION SecurityInformation =
      DACL_SECURITY_INFORMATION;
   BYTE    bySIDBuffer[1024];
   DWORD   dwSIDSize = sizeof (bySIDBuffer);
   BOOL    bRetcode  = FALSE;

   dwSIDSize = sizeof (bySIDBuffer);

   dwAccess;

   if (CSecurityDescriptor::NameToSID(
         lpUser, (PSID) bySIDBuffer, &dwSIDSize))
      {
      bRetcode = ::AddAccessAllowedAce(m_pACL, ACL_REVISION,
                     dwAccess,
                     bySIDBuffer);
      }
   return bRetcode;
}

BOOL CDacl::AllowUserAccess(DWORD  dwUserCount,
             LPTSTR lpUsers[],
             DWORD  dwAccess /*= STANDARD_RIGHTS_REQUIRED |
                                 GENERIC_ALL*/)
{
   BOOL bRetcode = FALSE;
   for (DWORD i = 0; i < dwUserCount; ++i)
      {
      bRetcode |= AllowUserAccess(lpUsers[i], dwAccess);
      }
   return bRetcode;
}

BOOL CDacl::DenyUserAccess(
   LPTSTR lpUser,
   DWORD  dwAccess)
{
   SECURITY_INFORMATION SecurityInformation =
      DACL_SECURITY_INFORMATION;
   BYTE    bySIDBuffer[1024];
   DWORD   dwSIDSize = sizeof (bySIDBuffer);
   BOOL    bRetcode  = FALSE;

   dwSIDSize = sizeof (bySIDBuffer);

   dwAccess;
```

```
    if (CSecurityDescriptor::NameToSID(
            lpUser, (PSID) bySIDBuffer, &dwSIDSize))
        {
        bRetcode = ::AddAccessDeniedAce(m_pACL, ACL_REVISION,
                        dwAccess,
                        bySIDBuffer);
        }
    return bRetcode;
}

BOOL CDacl::DenyUserAccess(DWORD  dwUserCount,
             LPTSTR lpUsers[],
             DWORD  dwAccess /*= STANDARD_RIGHTS_REQUIRED |
                                 GENERIC_ALL*/)
{
    BOOL bRetcode = FALSE;
    for (DWORD i = 0; i < dwUserCount; ++i)
        {
        bRetcode |= DenyUserAccess(lpUsers[i], dwAccess);
        }
    return bRetcode;
}

CSacl::CSacl(DWORD  dwUserCount,
             LPTSTR lpUsers[],
             DWORD  dwAccess /*= STANDARD_RIGHTS_REQUIRED |
                                 GENERIC_ALL |
                                 ACCESS_SYSTEM_SECURITY */)
{
    for (DWORD i = 0; i < dwUserCount; ++i)
        {
        if (!AuditUserAccess(lpUsers[i], dwAccess))
            {
            if (::GetLastError() != ERROR_CALL_NOT_IMPLEMENTED)
                AfxThrowResourceException();
            return;
            }
        }
}

CSacl::~CSacl()
{
    RestorePrivileges();
}

BOOL CSacl::AuditUserAccess(
    LPTSTR lpUser,
    DWORD  dwAccess)
```

```
{
   SECURITY_INFORMATION SecurityInformation =
      SACL_SECURITY_INFORMATION;
   BYTE    bySIDBuffer[1024];
   DWORD   dwSIDSize = sizeof (bySIDBuffer);
   BOOL    bRetcode  = FALSE;

   // We have to enable the SE_SECURITY_NAME
   // privilege in order to play with SACLs
   TurnPrivilegeOn(SE_SECURITY_NAME);

   SecurityInformation = SACL_SECURITY_INFORMATION;

   dwSIDSize = sizeof (bySIDBuffer);

   dwAccess |= ACCESS_SYSTEM_SECURITY;

   if (CSecurityDescriptor::NameToSID(
         lpUser, (PSID) bySIDBuffer, &dwSIDSize))
      {
      bRetcode = ::AddAuditAccessAce(m_pACL, ACL_REVISION,
                   dwAccess,
                   bySIDBuffer, TRUE, TRUE);
      }
   return bRetcode;
}

BOOL CSacl::AuditUserAccess(
             DWORD  dwUserCount,
             LPTSTR lpUsers[],
             DWORD  dwAccess /*= STANDARD_RIGHTS_REQUIRED |
                                GENERIC_ALL |
                                ACCESS_SYSTEM_SECURITY */)
{
   BOOL bRetcode = FALSE;
   for (DWORD i = 0; i < dwUserCount; ++i)
      {
      bRetcode |= AuditUserAccess(lpUsers[i], dwAccess);
      }
   return bRetcode;
}

BOOL CSacl::TurnPrivilegeOn(LPTSTR lpPrivilegeName)
{
   HANDLE hToken;

   hToken = CSecurityDescriptor::GetProcessToken();
```

```
    if (hToken == NULL)
       return FALSE;

    LUID PrivilegeValue;

    // Get value of privilege name
    if (!::LookupPrivilegeValue(
            NULL,
            lpPrivilegeName,
            &PrivilegeValue))
       {
       return FALSE;
       }

    // Set TOKEN_PRIVILEGES structure
    // to enable the requested privilege
    TOKEN_PRIVILEGES NewPrivilegeSet;

    NewPrivilegeSet.PrivilegeCount = 1;
    NewPrivilegeSet.Privileges[0].Luid = PrivilegeValue;
    NewPrivilegeSet.Privileges[0].Attributes =
       SE_PRIVILEGE_ENABLED;

    DWORD dwOutLength;

    ::AdjustTokenPrivileges(hToken, FALSE,
       &NewPrivilegeSet, sizeof (TOKEN_PRIVILEGES),
       &m_CurrentPrivileges, &dwOutLength);
    return (GetLastError() == NO_ERROR);
}

BOOL CSacl::RestorePrivileges(void)
{
    HANDLE hToken;

    hToken = CSecurityDescriptor::GetProcessToken();

    if (hToken == NULL)
       return FALSE;

    ::AdjustTokenPrivileges(hToken, FALSE,
       &m_CurrentPrivileges, sizeof (TOKEN_PRIVILEGES),
       NULL, NULL);
    return (GetLastError() == NO_ERROR);
}
```

Conclusion

The Win32 Security API is very powerful, but very complex. It is somewhat thinly documented, so you are often on your own to figure out how things really work. Nevertheless, correct addition of security features to server applications can greatly enhance their value. They can protect server endpoints from unauthorized access and audit the usage of sensitive objects.

Part of my purpose in this chapter has been to see what happens when you pass NULL pointers for SECURITY_ATTRIBUTES or SECURITY_DESCRIPTOR arguments. Here is what I discovered:

- File objects and Registry keys inherit the security characteristics of the directory or containing key where they reside. More precisely, a new DACL is built for them containing all the inheritable ACEs in the DACL of the owner.
- Although a named pipe is a file object (because Named Pipes are an NT file system), a named pipe takes on the default DACL of the access token belonging to the process that calls CreateNamedPipe(). Presumably, this is because the concept of an owning directory has no meaning for a named pipe.
- Kernel objects created with NULL security attributes are unprotected. Some important objects in this category are mutexes, events, semaphores, threads, processes, and file mappings.

Private objects—those whose meaning is known only to your application—can inherit a parent's security, can take on the security of the process's token, or can be created with a brand new set of security characteristics.

User objects—windows and menus—inherit security from the process windowstation and the thread desktop. There is rarely a reason to set explicit security restrictions here.

Suggested Readings

Online References

Security Overview in the Win32 API online help.
Microsoft Knowledge Base for Win32 SDK articles:
"Administrator Access to Files"
"Checking for Administrators Group"
"Computing the Size of a New ACL"
"Creating a World SID"
"Creating Access Control Lists for Directories"

"Definition of a Protected Server"
"Determining the Maximum Allowed Access for an Object"
"Determining Whether the User Is an Administrator"
"Extracting the SID from an ACE"
"FILE_READ_EA and FILE_WRITE_EA Specific Types"
"Gaining Access to ACLs"
"How CREATOR_OWNER and CREATOR_GROUP Affect Security"
"How to Add an Access-Allowed ACE to a File"
"How to Assign Privileges to Accounts for API Calls"
"How to Create Inheritable Win32 Handles in Windows 95"
"How to Manage User Privileges Programmatically in Windows NT"
"How to Obtain a Handle to Any Process with SeDebugPrivilege"
"Impersonation Provided by ImpersonateNamedPipeClient()"
"Listing Account Privileges"
"Looking Up the Current User and Domain"
"New Owner in Take-Ownership Operation"
"Owners Have Special Access to Their Objects"
"Passing Security Information to SetFileSecurity()"
"PRB: Access Denied When Opening a Named Pipe from a Service"
"Precautions When Passing Security Attributes"
"Security and Screen Savers"
"Security Attributes on Named Pipes"
"Security Context of Child Processes"
"Setting File Permissions"
"Sharing Objects with a Service"
"System GENERIC_MAPPING Structures"
"Taking Ownership of Registry Keys"
"Validating User Accounts (Impersonation)"
"Validating User Account Password under Windows NT"

Chapter 14

The Registry and Performance Monitoring

The Registry was introduced in Windows 3.1 as a means for OLE clients and servers to discover each other. Its focus was quite narrow, and you could spend your entire professional life writing Windows programs without finding out about it. With the advent of Windows NT, the importance of the Registry increased a great deal. It became a general-purpose configuration database to keep track of everything Windows NT needed to know about your hardware, software, and user environment. In the process, it became a critical cornerstone of the operating system. Although Windows 95 puts less stringent demands on the Registry than Windows NT, Windows 95 uses the NT model.

With the move from Windows 3.1 to Win32, several functions in the Registry API have been superseded by extended versions. These functions, and their new names, are:

- RegCreateKey() / RegCreateKeyEx()
- RegEnumKey() / RegEnumKeyEx()
- RegOpenKey() / RegOpenKeyEx()
- RegQueryValue() / RegQueryValueEx()
- RegSetValue() / RegSetValueEx()

In this chapter, I will cover and use only the new versions.

The Registry as a Hierarchical Database

Two types of entities are stored in the Registry: keys and values. **Keys** identify the individual database records, and **values** are the attributes (or fields) of those records. Keys exist in a hierarchical framework, very much like a directory tree. There are two trees, each with its own responsibilities:

- One tree keeps track of user profiles, which are the WIN.INI settings for all of the users known on the current machine. It is rooted at the key HKEY_USERS. The special key HKEY_CURRENT_USER points to the branch of HKEY_USERS that stores the profile of the currently logged-in user.
- The other tree keeps track of the hardware and software configuration of your machine, and contains the security database. It is rooted in the key HKEY_LOCAL_MACHINE. The special key HKEY_CLASSES_ROOT is an alias for HKEY_LOCAL_MACHINE\SOFTWARE\Classes, which maps filename extensions to the applications that process them and stores OLE object information.

The Registry Editor (REGEDT32.EXE in NT; REGEDIT.EXE in Windows 95) is handy for familiarizing yourself with the structure of the Registry. Use it with caution—if you delete the wrong keys, you can wreck Windows so thoroughly that your only remedy is to reinstall it. REGEDT32 has an item on its Options menu that lets you explore the Registry in read-only mode. Turning this on is a good idea if you are browsing the contents of the Registry and want to keep yourself from accidentally deleting information.

Figures 14-1 and 14-2 show the NT Registry Editor screens for the level of detail immediately beneath HKEY_LOCAL_MACHINE and HKEY_USERS. In Figure 14-1, SAM and SECURITY contain the security database; they are off limits, even to Administrators. In Figure 14-2, there are two entries—one a default user profile, and the other specific to Administrator, and identified by his or her SID.

The trees branch out very quickly, so you don't have to go very far down before the Registry Editor display won't fit on a single screen. Our primary interest will be HKEY_LOCAL_MACHINE\SOFTWARE. The key that contains much of NT's configuration is HKEY_LOCAL_MACHINE\SOFTWARE\Microsoft\Windows NT\CurrentVersion. For Windows 95, the corresponding key is HKEY_LOCAL_MACHINE\SOFTWARE\Microsoft\Windows\CurrentVersion.

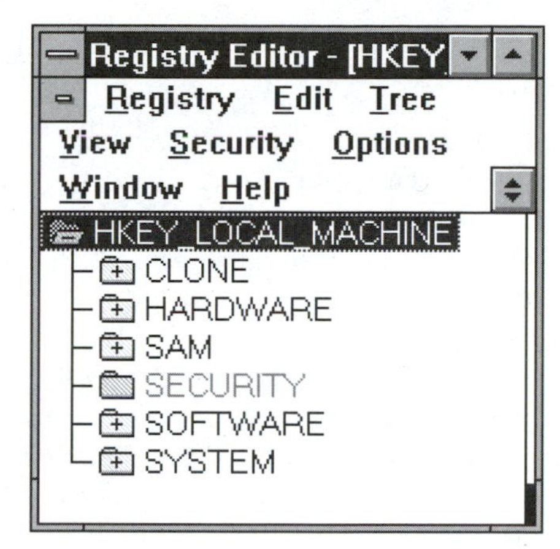

Figure 14-1. The HKEY_LOCAL_MACHINE Registry Node

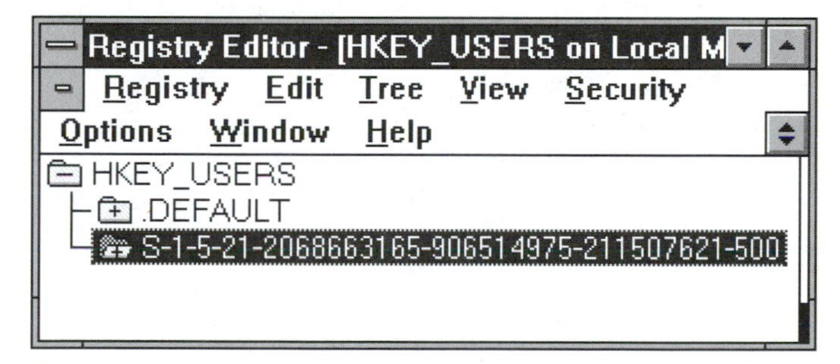

Figure 14-2. The HKEY_USERS Registry Node

The Win32 Registry API

Table 14-1 lists the Win32 Registry functions. Because the Registry is a database, many of these functions perform the standard database management operations—add, update, query, and delete.

Table 14-1. Win32 Registry Functions

Function Name	Description
RegCloseKey	Closes a Registry key when you are finished using it
RegConnectRegistry	Connects to the Registry on a remote machine
RegCreateKeyEx	Adds a new record to the Registry
RegDeleteKey	Deletes an existing record
RegDeleteValue	Deletes an attribute (value) of a record (key)
RegEnumKeyEx	Enumerates the keys that are immediate children of a given key

Table 14-1. Win32 Registry Functions *(continued)*

Function Name	Description
RegEnumValue	Enumerates the values belonging to a given key
RegFlushKey	Forces write of an open key to disk
RegGetKeySecurity	Retrieves the security descriptor of a Registry key
RegLoadKey	Restores a branch of the Registry tree from a backup file created by RegSaveKey
RegNotifyChangeKeyValue	Requests notification of changes in the Registry
RegOpenKeyEx	Opens an existing key in the Registry
RegQueryInfoKey	Gets all information about a key, including what subkeys it has, what values it possesses, its security descriptor, and when it was last modified
RegQueryMultipleValues	Reads an array of attributes of an open key
RegQueryValueEx	Reads a named attribute of an open key
RegReplaceKey	Changes the file that backs up a branch of the Registry
RegRestoreKey	Overwrites the contents of an existing key with information saved in a Registry backup file (created by RegSaveKey)
RegSaveKey	Saves a branch of the Registry to a file
RegSetKeySecurity	Provides a new security descriptor for a Registry key
RegSetValueEx	Adds or modifies an attribute of an existing key
RegUnLoadKey	Unloads a Registry branch that was installed by calling Reg-LoadKey

Adding a Record

To add a record to the Registry, you create a new key relative to an existing open key, or to one of the predefined keys (HKEY_LOCAL_MACHINE, HKEY_USERS, HKEY_CURRENT_USER, or HKEY_CLASSES_ROOT), which are always open. The function that does this is RegCreateKeyEx().

```
LONG RegCreateKeyEx(
        HKEY                    hTopLevelKey,
        LPCTSTR                 lpszNewKeyName,
        DWORD                   dwReserved,       // Has to be zero
        LPTSTR                  lpszKeyClass,
        DWORD                   dwOptions,
        REGSAM                  SAMDesiredAccess,
        LPSECURITY_ATTRIBUTES lpSecurityAttributes,
        PHKEY                   phNewKey,
        LPDWORD                 lpdwDisposition);
```

hTopLevelKey is the already existing key under which the new key will be created. *lpszNewKeyName* specifies the path to the new key and may contain several components. For instance, if you are creating the key HKEY_LOCAL_MACHINE\SOFTWARE\My Company\MyS oftware\CurrentVersion, you do not have to create *My Company*, then *My Software*, then *CurrentVersion*. A single call installs the entire Registry branch.

lpszKeyClass specifies the class of data that the key embodies and is a string representation of one of the Registry types. The most common types are:

- "REG_SZ": A null-terminated string
- "REG_MULTI_SZ": An array of null-terminated strings, terminated by an empty string
- "REG_EXPAND_SZ": A null-terminated string containing environment variables, like "%SystemRoot%\system32"
- "REG_DWORD": A 32-bit data item
- "REG_BINARY": Raw binary data, whose format is interpreted by the application that uses the data. For instance, security identifiers are stored in this format

NT allows you to distinguish between volatile and non-volatile keys. *dwOptions* states whether the information stored in the key is volatile (REG_OPTION_VOLATILE) or non-volatile (REG_OPTION_NON_VOLATILE). Volatile keys are destroyed when you shut down the system and are not restored at startup. On the other hand, NT calls RegSaveKey() to save non-volatile keys to a file when you shut down, then rebuilds the Registry from the file at startup. All the keys describing your hardware configuration are volatile, and are regenerated when you restart your system. Windows 95 only supports non-volatile keys; if you pass *dwOptions* as REG_OPTION_VOLATILE, it just ignores it.

SAMDesiredAccess states what kind of access you want to the key handle. Registry keys are protected objects, so your access request must be consistent with the security attributes of the key. RegCreateKeyEx() can be used to open existing keys, as well as for creating new ones. Possible values are KEY_ALL_ACCESS, KEY_CREATE_LINK, KEY_CREATE_SUB_KEY, KEY_ENUMERATE_SUB_KEYS, KEY_EXECUTE, KEY_NOTIFY, KEY_QUERY_VALUE, KEY_READ, KEY_SET_VALUE, and KEY_WRITE. As always, you get better performance by requesting only the level of access you actually need. The Win32 online documentation tells you what rights you need to perform what operations; out of laziness, I frequently just say KEY_ALL_ACCESS.

lpSecurityAttributes allows you to control the inheritability and accessibility of the key handle. To limit access, you build a security descriptor using the techniques discussed in Chapter 13 and point the *lpSecurityDescriptor* field of the SECURITY_ATTRIBUTES to it. The C++ classes presented in Chapter 13 facilitate this process. If you pass the security attributes as NULL, the new key inherits the security restrictions of the key under which it is added.

Finally, the variable pointed to by *phNewKey* will return the new key handle, and **lpdwDisposition* will tell you whether a new key was created (REG_CREATED_NEW_KEY) or an existing one was opened (REG_OPENED_EXISTING_KEY).

In a departure from normal Win32 usage (where a return value of TRUE or FALSE indicates success or failure, and GetLastError() reports specific error conditions) RegCreateKeyEx()—and all the Registry functions—return the actual error code if they fail, or ERROR_SUCCESS (0) if they succeed.

Opening an Existing Record

RegCreateKeyEx() can be used to open existing keys and to create new ones. You can also call RegOpenKeyEx() to open a key.

```
LONG RegOpenKeyEx(
       HKEY      hAncestorKey,
       LPCTSTR   lpszKeyPath,
       DWORD     dwReserved,  // Must be zero
       REGSAM    SAMDesiredAccess,
       PHKEY     phOpenedKey);
```

The arguments are the same as for RegCreateKeyEx(), with the omission of those that do not apply.

Updating a Record

In Registry terms, updating a record means setting the values associated with a key. Figure 14-3 shows the Registry entry describing File Manager extensions. The full key is HKEY_LOCAL_MACHINE\SOFTWARE\Microsoft \Windows NT\CurrentVersion\File Manager\AddOns. The right-hand side of the screen indicates that this key has one value, "Mail File Manager Extension," whose type is REG_SZ. The data stored in that value is "SendFI32.dll." For me, it helps clarify the issue to refer to values as attributes, using the more common terminology from database theory.

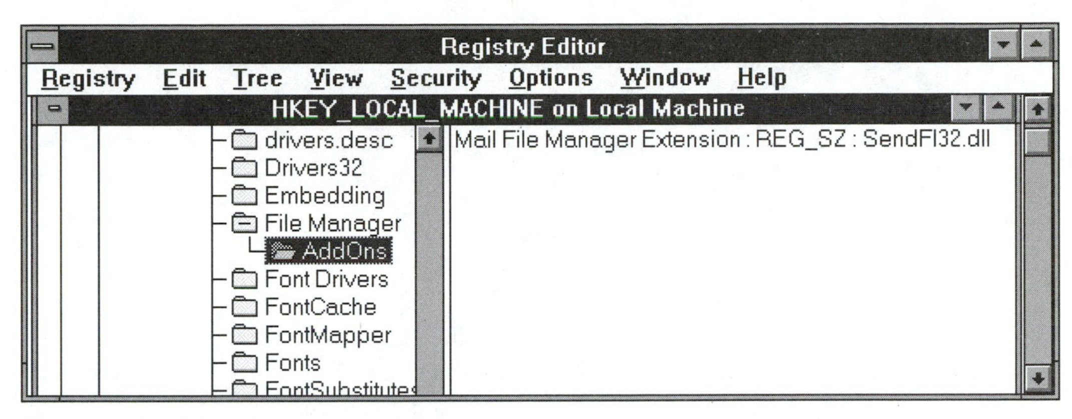

Figure 14-3. A Registry Key and Its Value

RegSetValueEx() changes the data stored in a key's value and creates the value if it does not already exist.

```
LONG RegSetValueEx(
        HKEY          hOpenKey,
        LPCTSTR       lpszValueName,
        DWORD         dwReserved,      // Must be zero
        DWORD         dwType,
        CONST BYTE *lpbyData,
        DWORD         dwDataSize);
```

hOpenKey will have been generated by RegCreateKeyEx() or RegOpen-KeyEx(). *lpszValueName* is the name of the value you want to add, or whose data you want to change. *dwType* is the Registry type of the data. Again, this is most commonly REG_SZ, REG_MULTI_SZ, REG_EXPAND_SZ, REG_DWORD, or REG_BINARY. *lpbyData* points to the data, and *dwDataSize* tells Windows how much data is there. If *lpbyData* points to a Unicode string, as it often will, *dwDataSize* must be ((lstrlen((LPCTSTR) lpbyData) + 1) * sizeof (TCHAR)).

Querying a Record

The functions you will use most often to retrieve Registry key data are Reg-EnumKeyEx(), which reports all the keys that are children of a given key; RegQueryValueEx(), which retrieves the data associated with an attribute; and RegQueryMultipleValues(), which returns an array of attributes. If you know nothing about the structure of a branch, you can call RegQueryIn-foKey() to find out how many subkeys and values a key has, and RegEnum-Value() to enumerate a key's values.

```
LONG RegEnumKeyEx(
         HKEY      hParentKey,
         DWORD     dwIndex,
         LPTSTR    lpszKeyName,
         LPDWORD   lpdwKeyNameSize,
         LPDWORD   lpdwReserved,    // Must be NULL
         LPTSTR    lpszClassName,
         LPDWORD   lpdwClassNameSize,
         PFILETIME pLastWriteTime);
```

dwIndex is used to iterate over all the subkeys belonging to *hParentKey*. The first time you call RegEnumKeyEx(), pass it as zero, then increment it for each subsequent call. (It is not bumped automatically.) *lpszKeyName* returns the name of the key. *lpdwKeyNameSize* points to a DWORD that has the length of the buffer at *lpszKeyName* on input and the actual length of the key name on output. You have to reset it each time you call RegEnumKeyEx(). *lpszKeyName* will report only the subkey component, not the full Registry path name. *lpszClassName* and *lpdwClassNameSize* tell you the class that the subkey belongs to, and *pLastWriteTime* tells you when it was last modified. The last three may be passed as NULL. As long as RegEnumKeyEx() returns ERROR_SUCCESS, you can keep asking it for more information. When there are no more subkeys to enumerate, it returns ERROR_NO_MORE_ITEMS.

RegQueryValueEx() fetches the data associated with a key value (or attribute).

```
LONG RegQueryValueEx(
        HKEY          hTargetKey,
        LPTSTR        lpszValueName,
        LPDWORD       lpdwReserved,    // Must be NULL
        LPDWORD       lpdwDataType,
        LPBYTE        lpbyData,
        LPDWORD       lpdwDataSize);
```

hTargetKey is the key whose value *lpszValueName* you want to read. The variable pointed to by *lpdwDataType* returns the type of the data as a numeric code (most often REG_SZ, REG_MULTI_SZ, REG_EXPAND_SZ, REG_DWORD, or REG_BINARY). *lpbyData* renders the data, and **lpdwDataSize* reports the number of bytes in the data, if the data type does not imply it.

You will see later in this chapter that RegQueryValueEx() *is* the Performance Monitoring API.

RegQueryMultipleValues() returns data for an array of attributes.

```
LONG RegQueryMultipleValues(
        HKEY    hTargetKey,
        PVALENT lpValueEntries,
        DWORD   dwNumberOfValues,
        LPTSTR  lpDataBuffer,
        LPDWORD lpdwBufferSize);
```

lpValueEntries points to an array of VALENT structures.

```
typedef struct value_ent {
    LPTSTR ve_valuename;
    DWORD  ve_valuelen;
    DWORD  ve_valueptr;
    DWORD  ve_type;
} VALENT;
```

Before you call RegQueryMultipleValues(), you must set the *ve_valuename* field of each entry in the array to the name of the attribute that you want to read. *lpDataBuffer* points to the memory location where you want the information returned; **lpdwBufferSize* says how much space you are providing. When the call completes, the output information will be deposited in *lpDataBuffer*. For each element in the VALENT array, the *ve_valueptr* field of the VALENT will contain the offset into *lpDataBuffer* where the data for this attribute can be found. *ve_valuelen* tells you how much data is there, and *ve_type* tells you the Registry type of the data. **lpdwBufferSize* informs you of how much data was passed back. If your input buffer is too small, RegQueryMultipleValues() returns ERROR_MORE_DATA, and sets **lpdwBufferSize* to tell you how much memory you need.

Closing and Deleting a Key

When you are done with your Registry operations, you close the key you have been using by passing RegCloseKey() its handle.

```
LONG RegCloseKey(HKEY hKey);
```

You can also delete keys from the Registry by calling RegDeleteKey().

```
LONG RegDeleteKey(
        HKEY    hTopLevelKey,
        LPCTSTR lpszKeyPath);
```

To remove a value that you have associated with a key, call RegDeleteValue().

```
LONG RegDeleteValue(
        HKEY  hTargetKey,
        LPTSTR lpszValueName);
```

Connecting to the Registry on a Remote Machine

You can open Registry keys across a network by calling RegConnectRegistry().

```
LONG RegConnectRegistry(
        LPTSTR    lpszComputerName,
        HKEY      hRootKey,     // Must be HKEY_LOCAL_MACHINE
                                // or HKEY_USERS
        PHKEY     phAssignedKey);
```

From this point on, you perform your Registry manipulations using the handle returned through *phAssignedKey*. This is a powerful capability; it allows you to write distributed configuration management systems.

Security and the Registry

Because the Registry is of such crucial importance, it must be protected. For this reason, Windows NT attaches security descriptors to Registry keys when you create them. If you call RegCreateKeyEx() with either a NULL SECURITY_ATTRIBUTES or a SECURITY_ATTRIBUTES containing a NULL *lpSecurityDescriptor*, the new key inherits the security characteristics of its containing key. RegGetKeySecurity() and RegSetKeySecurity() retrieve and change a Registry key's security descriptor.

```
LONG RegGetKeySecurity(
        HKEY                     hKeyOfInterest,
        SECURITY_INFORMATION SecurityInfo,
        PSECURITY_DESCRIPTOR lpSecurityDescriptor,
        LPDWORD                  lpDescriptorSize);

LONG RegSetKeySecurity(
        HKEY                     hKeyOfInterest,
        SECURITY_INFORMATION SecurityInfo,
        PSECURITY_DESCRIPTOR lpSecurityDescriptor);
```

The arguments to RegGetKeySecurity() are the same as for the other functions explored in Chapter 13 (GetFileSecurity(), GetKernelObjectSecurity(), GetPrivateObjectSecurity(), and GetUserObjectSecurity()), except that the first is the handle of the key you are interested in. Notice again that the return values follow Registry API usage, rather than normal Win32 convention, because they return the Win32 error code, not TRUE or FALSE.

Using the Registry

The purposes to which the Registry can be applied are innumerable. In this section, I will discuss some of the things I have found the Registry useful for, and show you the corresponding code. Besides Performance Monitoring, which is covered in the final section of the chapter, I have used the Registry for:

- Initialization-file mapping
- Locating dynamic-link libraries at run time
- Registering applications to use the NT Event Logger

Initialization-File Mapping

When all users run their own copies of Windows 95, it is acceptable for their personal preferences to be stored in .INI files, either on their local hard disks or in personal network directories. However, with a protected, multiuser operating system like Windows NT, this invites problems. Therefore, the NT Registry provides a key that you can use to map .INI file references to the Registry, HKEY_LOCAL_MACHINE\SOFTWARE\Microsoft\Windows NT\CurrentVersion\IniFileMapping. This key in turn contains subkeys named for the .INI files they replace. Figure 14-4 shows the IniFileMapping node on my machine.

This is how .INI files are formatted, using the WIN.INI shown in Figure 14-4 as an example.

```
[Network]
ExpandLogonDomain=yes
```

Network is called the **section**, and *ExpandLogonDomain* the **key**. Under the Registry keys representing the .INI files, there are keys for each section in the file. For instance, the WIN.INI file in Figure 14-4 has two sections, the *Network* section just shown and another one called *Windows*.

For each section key, the .INI-file keys themselves are stored as values. The values, though, do not contain the actual information. Instead, they point to another location in the Registry where the information resides. The string for the *ExpandLogonDomain* value of the WIN.INI *Network* key, for example, is

```
SYS:Microsoft\Windows NT\CurrentVersion\Network\
World Full Access Shared Parameters
```

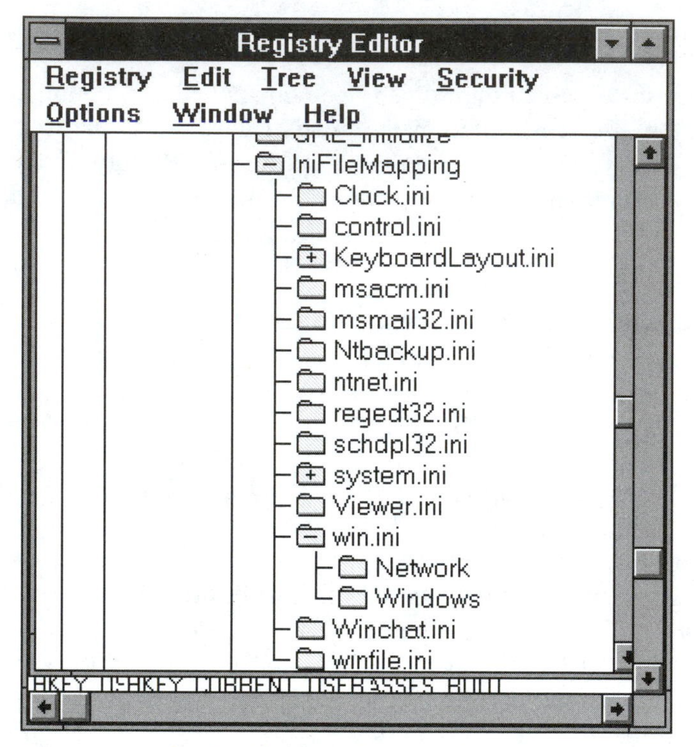

Figure 14-4. IniFileMapping Registry Node

The SYS: that you see here is an alias for HKEY_LOCAL_MACHINE \SOFTWARE\. What we're being told is: go to Registry key HKEY_ LOCAL_MACHINE\SOFTWARE\Microsoft\Windows NT\CurrentVersion \Network and look up its key "World Full Access Shared Parameters." Figure 14-5 shows the SYS:Microsoft\Windows NT\CurrentVersion\Network node.

The value of *ExpandLogonDomain* for the "World Full Access Shared Parameters" key is "yes," as you can see in Figure 14-6.

Once you have mapped an .INI file, all function calls that refer to that file are actually directed to the Registry, unbeknownst to you. Thus, you can continue to store and retrieve the information using calls like WritePrivateProfileString() and GetPrivateProfileString(), and NT will automatically go to the Registry on your behalf.

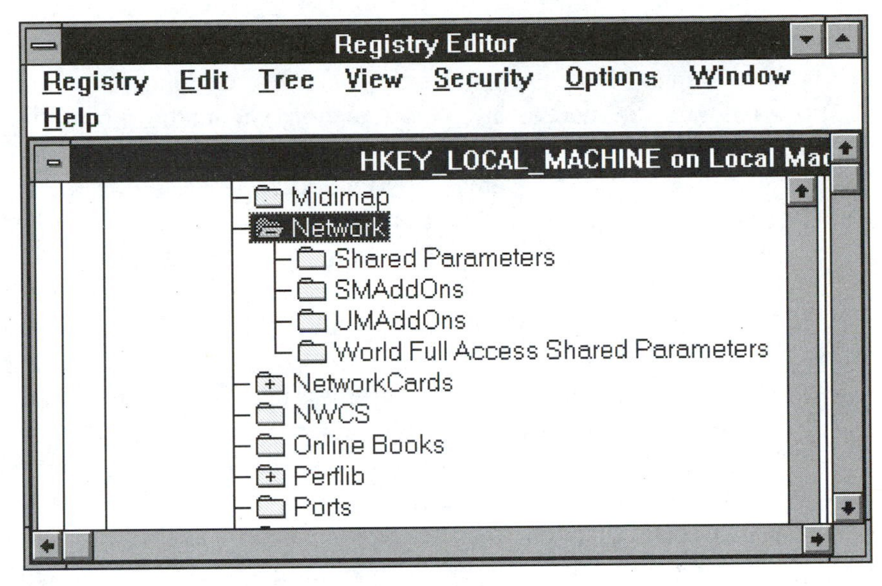

Figure 14-5. The Network Registry Node

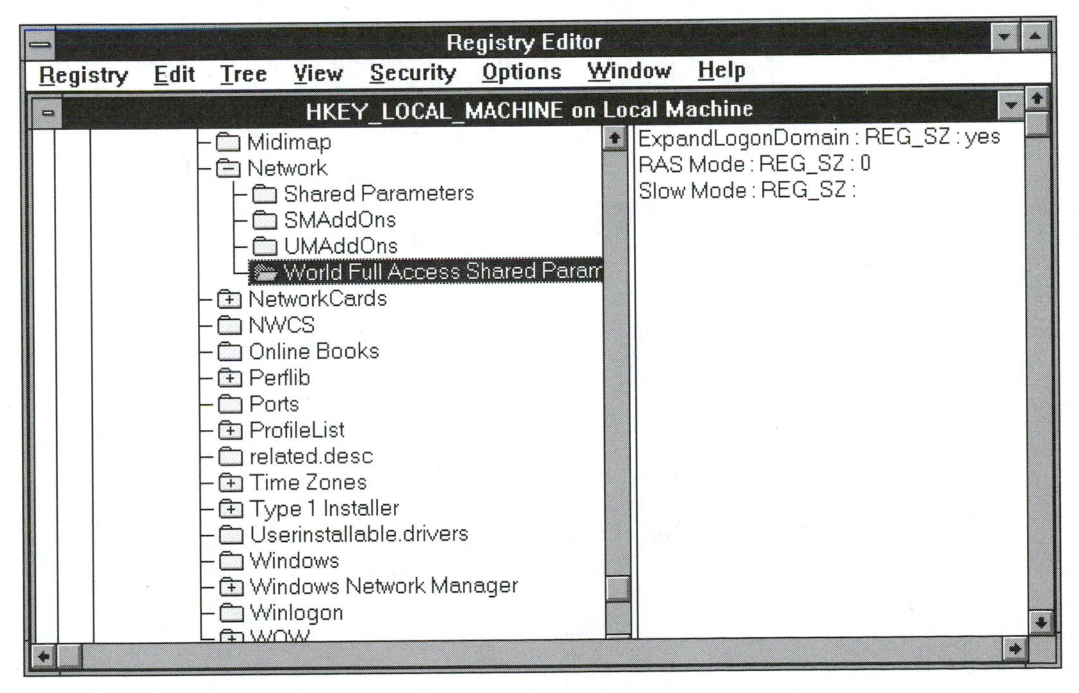

Figure 14-6. The ExpandLogonDomain Registry Value

Registering an Application for Event Logging

In Chapter 11, we examined the use of Event Logging in NT Services. When a service (or, indeed, any NT application) encounters a condition it wants to report in a permanent log, it can do so by calling RegisterEventSource(), ReportEvent(), and DeregisterEventSource(). By telling the Event Logger about your application, you can have it place formatted error messages into the log file for you, reading them from a message DLL that you provide. You do this by adding a Registry entry under the key HKEY_LOCAL_MACHINE\SYSTEM\CurrentControlSet\Services\EventLog\Application. The key that you add names your service or application and tells the Event Logger which DLL contains your messages. Then you call RegisterEventSource(), passing it the name you added to the Registry. ReportEvent() will now accept your error codes and translate them into the corresponding messages, adding insertion sequences as appropriate. Here is the WNetReportEvent() function from Chapter 11, shown again for ease of reference. Notice that Windows 95 does not have Event Logging; we have to emulate it.

```
VOID WNetReportEvent(DWORD dwErrorCode, LPTSTR lpszErrorMsg,
                     BOOL bError)
{
   // Services don't have a user interface, so the
   // only way for them to report error conditions
   // is to use the event-logging facility
   // that NT provides.

   // To do this, you call RegisterEventSource() to
   // get a handle, then call ReportEvent() to
   // log the error

   // Finally, you call DeregisterEventSource() to
   // release the handle

   // Under Windows 95, we'll emulate the functionality
   // by calling FormatMessage() twice, then
   // displaying the message to the user
   TCHAR szLastErrorMsg[1024];
   LPTSTR lpszMessageStrings[2];

   // Look up message string for system error.
   ::FormatMessage(FORMAT_MESSAGE_FROM_SYSTEM,
      NULL,
      dwErrorCode,
      LANG_USER_DEFAULT,
      szLastErrorMsg,
      sizeof (szLastErrorMsg),
```

```
        NULL);

    lpszMessageStrings[0] = lpszErrorMsg;   // Passed to function
    lpszMessageStrings[1] = szLastErrorMsg; // Formatted by
                                            //   FormatMessage()

    if (CWin32Object::IsWindowsNT())
        {
        HANDLE hSource;

        // RegisterEventSource() takes two arguments--the machine name
        // (NULL means the local machine)
        // and the name of the application logging the event
        hSource = ::RegisterEventSource(NULL, TEXT("WNet RPC Server"));

        if (hSource != NULL)
            {
            // The lpszMessageStrings array that we pass
            // to ReportEvent() has the insertion sequences
            // for our message.
            ::ReportEvent(hSource,
                bError ? EVENTLOG_ERROR_TYPE :   // Level of severity
                         EVENTLOG_WARNING_TYPE,
                0,                               // Category--we're not
                                                 //   using it
                MSG_RPC_SERVER_FAILED,           // Message identifier
                                                 // Defined in WNETMSGS.MC
                                                 // and the header file
                                                 // WNETMSGS.H that the
                                                 // Message Compiler
                                                 // generates
                NULL,                            // User security ID (SID)--
                                                 //   not using it
                2,                               // Number of insertion
                                                 //   strings in
                                                 //   lpszMessageStrings
                                                 //   array
                0,                               // Number of bytes of
                                                 //   binary data to include
                (LPCTSTR *) lpszMessageStrings,  // Messages to log
                NULL);                           // Binary data to log--
                                                 //   we're not using any

            DeregisterEventSource(hSource);
            }
        }
    else
```

```
        {
        // Windows 95--load our message DLL and extract
        // the messages from it by calling FormatMessage()
        HINSTANCE hMessageDLL = ::LoadLibrary(TEXT("WNETMSGS.DLL"));
        TCHAR  szMessage[1024];

        if (hMessageDLL != NULL)
           {
           ::FormatMessage(
              FORMAT_MESSAGE_FROM_HMODULE |
              FORMAT_MESSAGE_ARGUMENT_ARRAY,
              (LPCVOID) hMessageDLL,
              MSG_RPC_SERVER_FAILED,
              GetUserDefaultLangID() & 0x00FF,
              szMessage,
              sizeof (szMessage),
              lpszMessageStrings);
           printf("\n%s\n", szMessage);
           printf("\nPress any key to exit...\n");
           getchar();
           }
        ::FreeLibrary(hMessageDLL);
        }
}
```

Figure 14-7 shows the Event Logger Application node. You can see that there is an entry for WNet RPC Server, which is also the second argument that WNetReportEvent() passes to RegisterEventSource().

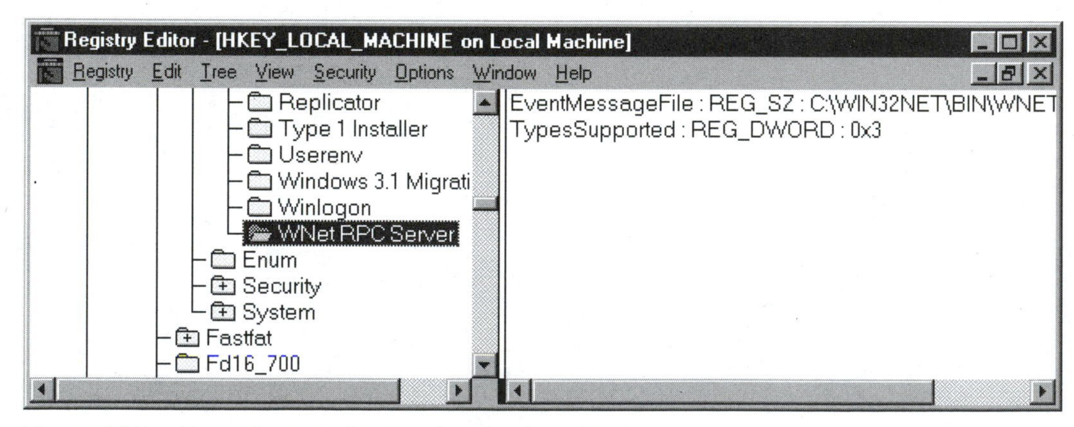

Figure 14-7. Event Logger Application Registry Node

The registered applications have well-known attributes (that is, Registry keys that mean something to the Event Logger) that enable the Event Logger to map their error codes. The WNet RPC Server uses two of them: *EventMessageFile* and *TypesSupported*. *EventMessageFile* describes the path to our message DLL, and *TypesSupported* indicates the kinds of messages we will be inserting. The WNet RPC Server has only two kinds: warning and error messages.

In Chapter 11, I introduced you briefly to the REGINST application (found in \WIN32NET\CODE\REGISTRY). In that chapter, I used REGINST to install my service. In this chapter, I use it to register my service for Event Logging.

I add these entries to the Registry in the InstallNT() function in REGINST.CPP. Because the *EventMessageFile* entry (%HOMEDRIVE%\WIN32NET\BIN\WNETMSGS.DLL) contains an environment variable, I expand it first by calling ExpandEnvironmentStrings(). I could also make its Registry type REG_EXPAND_SZ instead of REG_SZ.

```
// Next, add an Event Log entry for the WNet RPC Server
// so we can use event logging the right way
DWORD dwDisposition;
TCHAR     szMessageFile[MAX_PATH + 100];  // Leave lots of room
DWORD dwEventTypes = EVENTLOG_ERROR_TYPE | EVENTLOG_WARNING_TYPE;

RegDeleteKey(HKEY_LOCAL_MACHINE,
      TEXT("SYSTEM\\CurrentControlSet\\Services\\EventLog")
      TEXT("\\Application\\WNet RPC Server"));
if (RegCreateKeyEx(HKEY_LOCAL_MACHINE,
      TEXT("SYSTEM\\CurrentControlSet\\Services\\EventLog")
      TEXT("\\Application\\WNet RPC Server"),
      0,
      TEXT("REG_SZ"),
      REG_OPTION_NON_VOLATILE,
      KEY_ALL_ACCESS,
      NULL,
      &hRegistryKey,
      &dwDisposition) == ERROR_SUCCESS)
   {
   ExpandEnvironmentStrings(
      TEXT("%HOMEDRIVE%\\WIN32NET\\BIN\\WNETMSGS.DLL"),
      szMessageFile,
      sizeof (szMessageFile));
   RegSetValueEx(hRegistryKey,
      TEXT("EventMessageFile"),
      0,
      REG_SZ,
```

```
      (LPBYTE) szMessageFile,
      ((lstrlen(szMessageFile) + 1) * sizeof (TCHAR)));
   RegSetValueEx(hRegistryKey,
      TEXT("TypesSupported"),
      0,
      REG_DWORD,
      (LPBYTE) &dwEventTypes,
      sizeof (DWORD));
   RegCloseKey(hRegistryKey);
   }
}
```

All accesses to WNETMSGS.DLL are indirect. WNetReportEvent() shows how you retrieve a string for Event Logging—you never actually mention the DLL, except to install it in the Registry. RegisterEventSource() looks up your application name in the Registry and knows from the *EventMessageFile* value which DLL to load. Your call to ReportEvent() then extracts the appropriate string, based on the constant that the Message Compiler emitted for you.

Windows 95

Windows 95 does not support event logging. However, it is not difficult to emulate the functionality using the techniques I presented in Chapter 6. As we saw there, you can call LoadLibrary() to load the message library, then pass FormatMessage() its handle and the message identifier for any string it contains. This is exactly what WNetReportEvent() does; here are the relevant lines of code:

```
// Under Windows 95, we'll emulate the functionality
// by calling FormatMessage() twice, then
// displaying the message to the user
TCHAR szLastErrorMsg[1024];
LPTSTR lpszMessageStrings[2];

// Look up message string for system error.
::FormatMessage(FORMAT_MESSAGE_FROM_SYSTEM,
   NULL,
   dwErrorCode,
   LANG_USER_DEFAULT,
   szLastErrorMsg,
   sizeof (szLastErrorMsg),
   NULL);

lpszMessageStrings[0] = lpszErrorMsg;
lpszMessageStrings[1] = szLastErrorMsg;
```

```
if (CWin32Object::IsWindowsNT())
   {
   // [...]
   }
else
   {
   // Windows 95--load our message DLL and extract
   // the messages from it by calling FormatMessage()
   HINSTANCE hMessageDLL = ::LoadLibrary(TEXT("WNETMSGS.DLL"));
   TCHAR  szMessage[1024];

   if (hMessageDLL != NULL)
      {
      ::FormatMessage(
         FORMAT_MESSAGE_FROM_HMODULE |
         FORMAT_MESSAGE_ARGUMENT_ARRAY,
         (LPCVOID) hMessageDLL,
         MSG_RPC_SERVER_FAILED,
         GetUserDefaultLangID() & 0x00FF,
         szMessage,
         sizeof (szMessage),
         lpszMessageStrings);
      printf("\n%s\n", szMessage);
      printf("\nPress any key to exit...\n");
      getchar();
      }
   ::FreeLibrary(hMessageDLL);
   }
```

Performance Monitoring

Performance Monitoring is a capability built into Windows NT that allows you to keep track of system usage. This makes it possible to identify problems and bottlenecks, and correct them before they turn into crises. It is of particular interest to network programming and administration because you can obtain a great deal of information about your network. In Chapter 16, I will show you how I have used NT's Performance Monitoring services to validate benchmark data (and, indeed, to catch some bugs).

Table 14-2 shows the Windows NT objects related to network management that you can monitor. The descriptions are taken directly from the Registry. I collected most of this data by running the sample application shown in the Performance Monitoring Overview in the Win32 online help under the topic "Displaying Object, Counter, and Instance Names." The rest of it I got from Volume 4 of the *Windows NT Resource Kit*, "Optimizing Windows NT." That book is a critical piece of documentation if you are interested in using Performance Monitoring. (See "Suggested Readings" at the end of this chapter.)

Table 14-2. Performance Monitoring Objects Related to Network Management

Object Name	Description
AppleTalk	AppleTalk Protocol counters.
Browser	Browser Statistics
Client Service for NetWare	Client Service For NetWare object type.
FTP Server	The FTP Server object type includes counters specific to the FTP Server service.
Gateway Service for NetWare	Gateway Service for NetWare object type.
ICMP	The ICMP Object Type includes those counters that describe the rates that ICMP Messages are received and sent by a certain entity using the ICMP protocol. It also describes various error counts for the ICMP protocol.
IP	The IP Object Type includes those counters that describe the rates that IP datagrams are received and sent by a certain computer using the IP protocol. It also describes various error counts for the IP protocol.
MacFile Server Object	Services for Macintosh AFP File Server counters.
NBT Connection	The NBT Connection Object Type includes those counters that describe the rates that bytes are received and sent over a single NBT connection connecting the local computer with some remote computer. The connection is identified by the name of the remote computer.
NetBEUI	The NetBEUI protocol handles data transmission for that network activity which follows the NetBIOS End User Interface standard.
NetBEUI Resource	The NetBEUI Resource object tracks the use of resources (that is, buffers) by the NetBEUI protocol
Network Interface	The Network Interface Object Type includes those counters that describe the rates that bytes and packets are received and sent over a Network TCP/IP connection. It also describes various error counts for the same connection.
Network Segment	Provides Network Statistics for the local network segment via the Network Monitor Service.
NWLink IPX	The NWLink IPX transport handles datagram transmission to and from computers using the IPX protocol.
NWLink NetBIOS	The NWLink NetBIOS protocol layer handles the interface to applications communicating over the IPX transport.
NWLink SPX	The NWLink SPX transport handles data transmission and session connections for computers using the SPX protocol.

Table 14-2. Performance Monitoring Objects Related to Network Management *(continued)*

Object Name	Description
RAS Port	The RAS Object Type handles individual ports of the RAS device on your system.
RAS Total	The RAS Object Type handles all combined ports of the RAS device on your system.
Redirector	The Redirector is the object that manages network connections to other computers that originate from your own computer.
Server	Server is the process that interfaces the services from the local computer to the network services.
Server Work Queues	[No description exists.]
TCP	The TCP Object Type includes those counters that describe the rates that TCP Segments are received and sent by a certain entity using the TCP protocol. In addition, it describes the number of TCP connections that are in each of the possible TCP connection states.
UDP	The UDP Object Type includes those counters that describe the rates that UDP datagrams are received and sent by a certain entity using the UDP protocol. It also describes various error counts for the UDP protocol.
WINS Server	The WINS Server object type includes counters specific to the WINS Server service.

The Performance Monitoring API

There is no Win32 Performance Monitoring API as such. A single call to RegQueryValueEx(), with the special key HKEY_PERFORMANCE_DATA, collects the data you request. The tricks here are knowing what to ask for and what to do with the information you get. I will first show you how to request data, then how to analyze it.

Objects and Counters

The Registry does not actually store any performance data. The call to RegQueryValueEx() for HKEY_PERFORMANCE_DATA causes NT to gather the data from the management agents. The Registry stores information on what types of objects can be monitored, as well as the data items, called **counters**, that track a specific aspect of the object's behavior. These are stored as REG_MULTI_SZ strings—arrays of null-terminated Unicode strings—in whatever languages are supported on the host machine. They reside under the key HKEY_LOCAL_MACHINE\SOFTWARE\Microsoft

\Windows NT\CurrentVersion\Perflib. Each supported language is represented by an additional subkey, named for the code identifying the language. For English, this is 009. You don't need to hard-code language values into a program; you can get this value by asking for LOBYTE(GetUserDefaultLangID()). The language-specific key has two REG_MULTI_SZ values: *Counter* and *Help*, as shown in Figure 14-8.

Counter stores the names of all the objects and counter types and their numeric identifiers. The layout is

```
<ID>\0<name>\0<ID>\0<name>\0 ... <ID>\0<name>\0\0
```

Figure 14-9 shows the dialog box that appears when you double-click on the *Counter* value. I have scrolled down into the list box to show you the

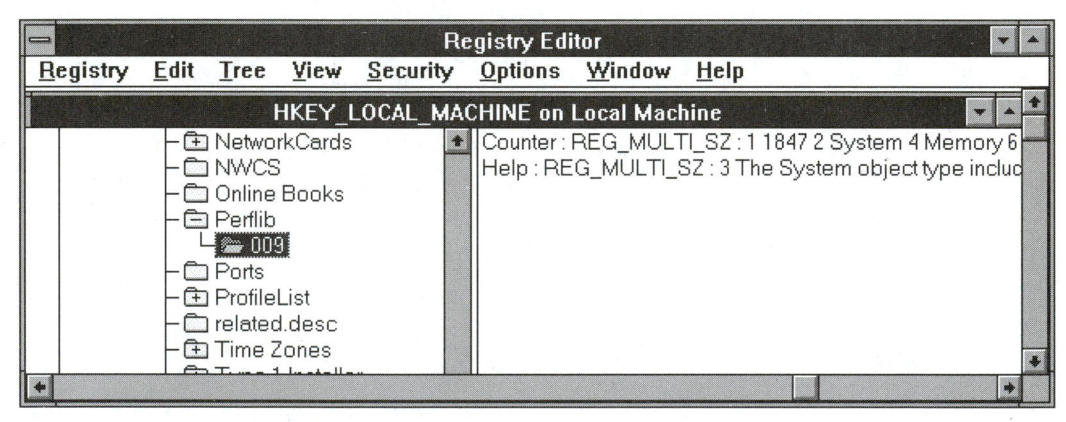

Figure 14-8. The Perflib Registry Key for the English Language

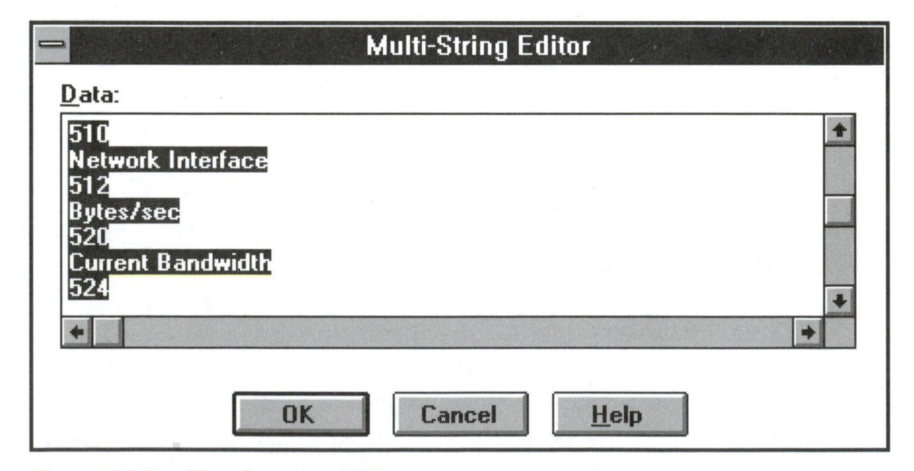

Figure 14-9. The Counters Value

Network Interface object. (This is the object that reports performance statistics for TCP/IP.)

In Figure 14-9, 510 is the identifier for *Network Interface*, 512 for *Bytes/sec*, and 520 for *Current Bandwidth*. *Network Interface* is an object, while *Bytes/sec* and *Current Bandwidth* are counters.

Explain Text

The second named value in Figure 14-8 is *Help*. This stores text that provides a brief description of what each of the objects and counters represents, referred to as "Explain text." Like the object and counter names, it is stored as a contiguous array of null-terminated Unicode strings. Here, too, you have identifier/text pairs. The descriptions shown in Table 14-2 are, in fact, the Explain text stored in the Registry.

Retrieving Performance Data

When calling RegQueryValueEx() to get performance data, several choices are available for the value name that you request:

- TEXT("Global") asks for all data, except that which the system considers costly to retrieve.
- A string in the format TEXT("nnn xx yy"), where *nnn*, *xx*, and *yy* are identifiers for objects that you want, retrieves performance data for those objects and any related objects. For example, threads cannot exist without processes, so if you ask for information on threads, you will also find out about the processes that own them.
- TEXT("Foreign ssss") requests performance data for a remote machine, designated by *ssss*.
- TEXT("Foreign ssss nnn xx yy") asks for object-specific statistics on machine *ssss*.
- TEXT("Costly") says you want the data for objects that are considered expensive.

The data is returned in a rather complex arrangement. The structures are well documented in several places. The *Performance Monitoring Overview* in the Win32 online help is quite good, and includes sample programs that you can copy to disk, compile, and run. Another excellent source is *Optimizing Windows NT*, the fourth volume of the *Windows NT Resource Kit* (see "Suggested Readings" at the end of this chapter). Chapter 12 of that book discusses "Writing a Custom Windows NT Performance Monitor." The book's author, Russ Blake, wrote the Performance Monitor, an excellent management tool provided with Windows NT, and he knows what he's talking about. The source code to Performance Monitor itself comes with the Win32 SDK, in \MSTOOLS\SAMPLES\SDKTOOLS\PERFMON. Finally, the SDK header file WINPERF.H is extensively commented and offers some of the best explanations of the data structures you will find.

Not only is there a large amount of data available, there is considerable variation in the types of data reported. Because one of the goals of Performance Monitoring is to be system-independent, the data describes itself. That is, it tells you how big the data items are, where to find them, what their data types are, and how to interpret and present the information. This is the most daunting aspect of writing code that uses Performance Monitoring. I found the functions in the online help to be very useful in figuring out what exactly is going on (not to mention numerous debugging sessions).

Data Structures Returned by the System

The first structure in the data returned by RegQueryValueEx() is a PERF_DATA_BLOCK.

```
typedef struct _PERF_DATA_BLOCK
{
    WCHAR         Signature[4];  // Unicode "PERF"
    DWORD         LittleEndian;
    DWORD         Version;
    DWORD         Revision;
    DWORD         TotalByteLength;
    DWORD         HeaderLength;
    DWORD         NumObjectTypes;
    DWORD         DefaultObject;
    SYSTEMTIME    SystemTime;
    LARGE_INTEGER PerfTime;
    LARGE_INTEGER PerfFreq;
    LARGE_INTEGER PerfTime100nSec;
    DWORD         SystemNameLength;
    DWORD         SystemNameOffset;
} PERF_DATA_BLOCK;
```

Five fields are of particular interest:

- *TotalByteLength* is the size of the entire block returned by RegQueryValueEx().
- *HeaderLength* is the offset to the next portion of the block, which contains an array of object descriptions.

- *NumObjectTypes* is the number of elements in the array that follows the PERF_DATA_BLOCK.
- *SystemTime* is a SYSTEMTIME structure that reports the time the sample is taken.
- *PerfTime* is the value of the high-resolution counter at the time of the sample. Not all machines have such a counter, though, which is why the SYSTEMTIME is also provided. When you retrieve a counter value, its type tells you which value to use in computing elapsed time.

The Object Description Array. Following the PERF_DATA_BLOCK is an array that describes all the pertinent objects, their counters and the current values of the counters. The first structure you find is a PERF_OBJECT_TYPE. Here is how you navigate to it from the PERF_DATA_BLOCK.

```
BYTE byData[100000];            // Buffer that RegQueryValueEx() fills
PPERF_DATA_BLOCK  pPerfData;
PPERF_OBJECT_TYPE pObjectType;
PBYTE             pTemp;        // For computing byte offsets

pPerfData   = (PPERF_DATA_BLOCK) byData;
pTemp       = byData;
pObjectType = (PPERF_OBJECT_TYPE) (pTemp + pPerfData->HeaderLength);
```

The block of data headed by the PERF_OBJECT_TYPE structure contains information on the object, followed by descriptions of its counters, then followed by the counter data. If the object supports multiple instances (like threads and processes), the counter data is presented on a per-instance basis, along with structures describing the object instance. Let's look at the PERF_OBJECT_TYPE structure first, then consider the simplest case, an object that does not support instances.

```
typedef struct _PERF_OBJECT_TYPE
{
    DWORD  TotalByteLength;
    DWORD  DefinitionLength;
    DWORD  HeaderLength;
    DWORD  ObjectNameTitleIndex;
    LPWSTR ObjectNameTitle;
    DWORD  ObjectHelpTitleIndex;
    LPWSTR ObjectHelpTitle;
    DWORD  DetailLevel;
    DWORD  NumCounters;
    DWORD  DefaultCounter;
    DWORD  NumInstances;
    DWORD  CodePage;
```

```
    LARGE_INTEGER PerfTime;
    LARGE_INTEGER PerfFreq;
} PERF_OBJECT_TYPE;
```

The following fields are of greatest interest:

- *TotalByteLength* is the size of this complete object description. The next object description in the array is at this offset.
- *DefinitionLength* is the size of the PERF_OBJECT_TYPE structure and all the counter definitions that follow it. It is therefore the offset to the actual counter data for an object that cannot have multiple instances, or to the array of object instance descriptors.
- *HeaderLength* is the size of the PERF_OBJECT_TYPE structure, so it is the offset to the counter definitions that follow.
- *ObjectNameTitleIndex* is the numeric identifier for this object. This is the number associated with the object name in Figure 14-9. This field is important because when you are looking for information on a single object, you have to scan the object descriptions for the correct *Object-NameTitleIndex*.
- *NumCounters* tells you the number of counters describing this object.
- *NumInstances* is the number of instances of the object, with –1 indicating that the object cannot have multiple instances.

Here is a *for* loop that steps through the array of object descriptions. I use a simple BYTE pointer (*pTemp*), because it eliminates the necessity for a lot of type casting, which is both hard to read and easy to do wrong.

```
BYTE byData[100000];            // Buffer that RegQueryValueEx() fills
PPERF_DATA_BLOCK  pPerfData;
PPERF_OBJECT_TYPE pObjectType;
PBYTE             pTemp;        // For computing byte offsets

pPerfData   = (PPERF_DATA_BLOCK) byData;
pTemp       = byData;
pObjectType = (PPERF_OBJECT_TYPE) (pTemp + pPerfData->HeaderLength);
pTemp       = (PBYTE) pObjectType;

for (DWORD i = 0;
     i < pPerfData->NumObjectTypes;
     ++i,
     // Find next object description
     pObjectType = (PPERF_OBJECT_TYPE)
                   (pTemp += pObjectType->TotalByteLength))
   {
   // Process each element
   }
```

The Counter Definitions. Immediately following the PERF_OBJECT_TYPE is an array of structures describing all the counters for that object. The structure is typed as a PERF_COUNTER_DEFINITION. This array can be thought of as the Performance Monitoring database schema for the object. The data itself is not presented here, but this structure tells you where to find it, what it looks like, and how big it is.

```
typedef struct _PERF_COUNTER_DEFINITION
{
    DWORD  ByteLength;
    DWORD  CounterNameTitleIndex;
    LPWSTR CounterNameTitle;
    DWORD  CounterHelpTitleIndex;
    LPWSTR CounterHelpTitle;
    DWORD  DefaultScale;
    DWORD  DetailLevel;
    DWORD  CounterType;
    DWORD  CounterSize;
    DWORD  CounterOffset;
} PERF_COUNTER_DEFINITION;
```

The most important fields here are as follows:

- *ByteLength* is the size of the counter definition structure and the offset to the next PERF_COUNTER_DEFINITION in the array.
- *CounterNameTitleIndex* plays the same role as *ObjectNameTitleIndex* in the PERF_OBJECT_TYPE structure. It is the identifier associated with the counter name as shown in Figure 14-9.
- *CounterType* tells you how to interpret, evaluate, and format the data. There are many predefined types. Table 12-4 in Chapter 12 of *Optimizing Windows NT* lists them, and it goes on for four pages.
- *CounterSize* specifies the number of bytes occupied by the counter data.
- *CounterOffset* indicates the byte offset of the counter data in the counter block structure. If an object does not support instances, this follows the counter definition arrays. Otherwise, each object instance has its own counter block.

Looking up the Counter Data. For an object without instances, there is only one more structure to contend with, the PERF_COUNTER_BLOCK. It has only one field.

```
typedef struct _PERF_COUNTER_BLOCK
{
    DWORD ByteLength;
} PERF_COUNTER_BLOCK;
```

This structure is followed by the actual counter data. *ByteLength* indicates the total size of the block containing the data. The information for each individual counter can be fetched using the *CounterOffset* information provided in the PERF_COUNTER_DEFINITION. This offset is from the beginning of the PERF_COUNTER_BLOCK. *The CounterSize* field indicates the number of bytes to copy out of the block.

Here is a typical scenario (and the one I will be using). Suppose you want to get the data for one counter belonging to one object type. For instance, you need to retrieve the Bytes Total/sec counter (number 388) for the Redirector object (number 262). To do so you:

1. Call RegQueryValueEx() to fill the PERF_DATA_BLOCK. RegQueryValueEx() will return ERROR_MORE_DATA if the buffer you provide is not large enough for all the data you could possibly retrieve. Even though one of its arguments points to the size of the buffer, it will not set it to reflect the amount of memory it actually needs. You have to either keep trying for more, or allocate a very large buffer, then reallocate it to shrink it. When RegQueryValueEx() finally succeeds, it tells you how much data it actually provided.
2. Use the *HeaderLength* field of the PERF_DATA_BLOCK to find the first PERF_OBJECT_TYPE.
3. Scan through the array of object types for the one whose *ObjectNameTitleIndex* matches the one you want, each time increasing a running BYTE pointer by the *TotalByteLength* field of the PERF_OBJECT_TYPE structure.
4. When you find the object you're looking for, remember its address, then go to the array of PERF_COUNTER_DEFINITION structures. This is calculated from the *HeaderLength* field in the PERF_OBJECT_TYPE.
5. Scan the counter definitions for the correct *CounterNameTitleIndex*. Each time through the loop, add the *ByteLength* that you find in the PERF_COUNTER_DEFINITION structure. When you find the one you want, take the PERF_OBJECT_TYPE pointer you remembered in Step 4, and add the *DefinitionLength* field of the structure to its base address. This gives you the address of the PERF_COUNTER_BLOCK containing the data you need.

6. Use the *CounterOffset* and *CounterSize* fields of the PERF_COUNTER_DEFINITION to determine where in the counter block your data resides, and how many bytes of data you need.

Here is a code fragment that continues the previous one. It implements the six steps just outlined.

```
BYTE                byData[100000];  // Buffer that RegQueryValueEx()
                                     // fills
DWORD               dwDataSize = sizeof (byData);
PPERF_DATA_BLOCK    pPerfData;
PPERF_OBJECT_TYPE pObjectType;
PBYTE               pTemp;           // For computing byte offsets

DWORD               dwType;

// Step 1. Get performance data from RegQueryValueEx()
RegQueryValueEx(HKEY_PERFORMANCE_DATA,
                TEXT("262"),      // Redirector
                NULL,
                &dwType,
                byData,
                &dwDataSize);

pPerfData   = (PPERF_DATA_BLOCK) byData;
pTemp       = byData;

// Step 2. Find PERF_OBJECT_TYPE array
pObjectType = (PPERF_OBJECT_TYPE) (pTemp + pPerfData->HeaderLength);
pTemp       = (PBYTE) pObjectType;

// Step 3. Scan the array looking for the object we're
//         interested in. The Redirector is object
//         number 262.
for (DWORD i = 0;
     i < pPerfData->NumObjectTypes;
     ++i,
     pObjectType = (PPERF_OBJECT_TYPE)
                   (pTemp += pObjectType->TotalByteLength))
   {
   // Is pObjectType->ObjectNameTitleIndex the one we want?
   // Then look for the counter we need
   if (pObjectType->ObjectNameTitleIndex == 262)
      {
      // Step 4. pObjectType holds the address of the object
      //         Index to PERF_COUNTER_DEFINITIONs
      PPERF_COUNTER_DEFINITION pCounterDefinition;
```

```
    pTemp += pObjectType->HeaderLength;
    pCounter = (PPERF_COUNTER_DEFINITION) pTemp;

    // Step 5. Scan PERF_COUNTER_DEFINITIONs for the
    //         counter we want. For Bytes Total/sec,
    //         we want 388
    for (DWORD j = 0;
         j < pObjectType->NumCounters;
         ++j,
         pCounter = (PPERF_COUNTER_DEFINITION)
                      (pTemp +=  pCounter->ByteLength))
       {
       // Is it the one we're looking for?
       if (pCounter->CounterNameTitleIndex == 388)
          {
          PBYTE pCounterData;

          // Step 6. pCounter->CounterOffset tells us
          //         where the data is,
          //         pCounter->CounterSize tells us
          //         how much of it there is
          pTemp = (PBYTE) pObjectType;
          pCounterData = pTemp +
                         pObjectType->DefinitionLength +
                         pCounter->CounterOffset;

          PBYTE pOutputData =
                (PBYTE) HeapAlloc(GetProcessHeap(),
                           HEAP_ZERO_MEMORY |
                           HEAP_GENERATE_EXCEPTIONS,
                           pCounter->CounterSize);
          CopyMemory(pOutputData, pCounterData,
                     pCounter->CounterSize);
          return pOutputData;
          }
       }
    }
  return NULL;  // Object or counter not found
  }
```

Reading Counter Data for an Object Type with Instances. When an object type may have multiple instances, the situation is more complicated. Now, the counter definition array is followed by an array of instance descriptions. Each of these consists of a PERF_INSTANCE_DEFINITION structure and a PERF_COUNTER_BLOCK, containing the counter data for each instance.

```
typedef struct _PERF_INSTANCE_DEFINITION
{
    DWORD ByteLength;
    DWORD ParentObjectTitleIndex;
    DWORD ParentObjectInstance;
    DWORD UniqueID;
    DWORD NameOffset;
    DWORD NameLength;
} PERF_INSTANCE_DEFINITION;
```

The only field of concern is *ByteLength*. This is the offset to the PERF_COUNTER_BLOCK for this instance. To find the next instance in the array, add the *ByteLength* of the PERF_INSTANCE_DEFINITION and the *ByteLength* of the PERF_COUNTER_BLOCK to the address of the current instance definition.

GetPerformanceCounterData()

Next, I want to show you the function GetPerformanceCounterData() that encapsulates all the logic discussed in the previous section. It is in the file \WIN32NET\CODE\MFCSOCK\PERFHLPR.CPP on the source disk. It takes strings representing the object and counter information that the caller needs, a pointer to a pointer that it allocates for the output data, and references to two C++ objects that return the *SystemTime* and the *PerfTime* from the PERF_DATA_BLOCK. The caller then has the option of using either of these. If the machine supports a high-resolution counter, it will use the more precise *SampleTime*.

```
/*******
*
* GetPerformanceCounter() reads a requested counter value
* It allocates an array for the output information
*
* Its return value is the number of instances
* for which the counter is returned.
*
********/

LONG GetPerformanceCounterData(LPWSTR lpwObject,
                               LPWSTR lpwCounter,
                               LPBYTE *lplpOutputData,
                               CSystemTime& SystemTime,
                               CLargeInt&   SampleTime)
{
```

```
WCHAR  szwObjectIndex[100];
WCHAR  szwCounterIndex[100];
LPBYTE lpOutputData;
LONG   lNumInstances = 0;

// Get performance monitoring data
DWORD  dwType;
LPBYTE pbyData;
DWORD  dwDataBytes = 163840;

pbyData = (LPBYTE) HeapAlloc(GetProcessHeap(),
                             HEAP_ZERO_MEMORY |
                             HEAP_GENERATE_EXCEPTIONS,
                             dwDataBytes);

while (TRUE)
   {
   DWORD dwError;

   // RegQueryValueEx() will not tell you how
   // much memory you need to allocate if the
   // buffer you initially provide is too small.
   // Therefore, you have to call it in a loop,
   // providing a successively larger buffer until
   // it doesn't return ERROR_MORE_DATA any more.
   if ((dwError = RegQueryValueExW(HKEY_PERFORMANCE_DATA,
         lpwObject,
         NULL,
         &dwType,
         pbyData,
         &dwDataBytes)) == ERROR_MORE_DATA)
      {
      pbyData = (LPBYTE) HeapReAlloc(GetProcessHeap(),
                             HEAP_ZERO_MEMORY,
                             pbyData,
                             dwDataBytes += 4096);
      }
   else if (dwError == ERROR_SUCCESS)
      break;
   else
      return -1;
   }

// Shrink data buffer down
// It looks like RegQueryValueEx() makes you
// pass it a buffer big enough to hold
// all possible output data
pbyData = (LPBYTE) HeapReAlloc(GetProcessHeap(),
```

```
                        HEAP_ZERO_MEMORY,
                        pbyData,
                        dwDataBytes);

*lplpOutputData = (LPBYTE)
   HeapAlloc(GetProcessHeap(),
             HEAP_ZERO_MEMORY |
             HEAP_GENERATE_EXCEPTIONS,
             dwDataBytes);

lpOutputData = *lplpOutputData;

// Look for requested object
PPERF_DATA_BLOCK pPerfData =
   (PPERF_DATA_BLOCK) pbyData;
DWORD                     dwThisObject;   // count of objects
PPERF_OBJECT_TYPE         pThisObject;    // pointer to
                                          // object structure
PPERF_COUNTER_DEFINITION pThisCounter;
PBYTE                     pTempObject = pbyData;

// Remember the sample time as SYSTEMTIME
// and high-resolution counter time
SystemTime = pPerfData->SystemTime;
SampleTime = pPerfData->PerfTime;

// Beginning of object array is indicated
// by the HeaderLength field of the PERF_DATA_BLOCK
pThisObject = (PPERF_OBJECT_TYPE) (pTempObject +
   pPerfData->HeaderLength);

pTempObject = (PBYTE) pThisObject;

BOOL   bFound = FALSE;

// Scan through the object array looking for the
// one the caller wants.
// To navigate to each successive element, add
// the TotalByteLength field of the PERF_OBJECT_TYPE
// structure to the address of the current
// PERF_OBJECT_TYPE
for (dwThisObject = 0;
     !bFound && (dwThisObject < pPerfData->NumObjectTypes);
     dwThisObject++,
        pThisObject = (PPERF_OBJECT_TYPE)
                      (pTempObject +=
                       pThisObject->TotalByteLength))
```

```
{
swprintf(szwObjectIndex, L"%-d",
   pThisObject->ObjectNameTitleIndex);

// Is this the object we want?
if (CompareStringW(GetUserDefaultLCID(), 0,
     szwObjectIndex, -1, lpwObject, -1) != 2) // Equal strings?
     continue;

// We've found our object, let's find
// the requested counter
DWORD dwThisCounter;
PBYTE pTempCounter;

// The PERF_COUNTER_DEFINITION array starts
// at the address indicated by the HeaderLength
// field of the PERF_OBJECT_TYPE structure
pTempCounter = pTempObject +
               pThisObject->HeaderLength;
pThisCounter =
   (PPERF_COUNTER_DEFINITION) pTempCounter;

// Loop through the counter definitions
// To navigate to the next counter, add the
// ByteLength field of the PERF_COUNTER_DEFINITION
// structure to the address of the current
// PERF_COUNTER_DEFINITION
for (dwThisCounter = 0;
      dwThisCounter < pThisObject->NumCounters;
      dwThisCounter++,
         pThisCounter = (PPERF_COUNTER_DEFINITION)
                        (pTempCounter +=
                         pThisCounter->ByteLength))
   {
   swprintf(szwCounterIndex, L"%-d",
      pThisCounter->CounterNameTitleIndex);

   // Is this the counter we're looking for?
   if (CompareStringW(GetUserDefaultLCID(), 0,
       szwCounterIndex, -1, lpwCounter, -1) == 2) // Equal
                                                   // strings?
      {
      lNumInstances += pThisObject->NumInstances;
      bFound = TRUE;
      break;
      }
   }
```

```
if (bFound && pThisObject->NumInstances >= 0)
   {
   PPERF_INSTANCE_DEFINITION pThisInstance;
   PPERF_COUNTER_BLOCK       pCounterBlock;
   DWORD  dwThisInstance;
   PBYTE  pTempInstance;
   PBYTE  pTempCounterData;

   // This is a multiple-instance object
   // We have to scan the PERF_INSTANCE_DEFINITION
   // array
   // The beginning of the array is found by
   // adding the DefinitionLength field of the
   // PERF_OBJECT_TYPE to the address of the
   // current PERF_OBJECT_TYPE
   pTempInstance = pTempObject +
      pThisObject->DefinitionLength;
   pThisInstance = (PPERF_INSTANCE_DEFINITION)
      pTempInstance;

   for (dwThisInstance = 0;
      dwThisInstance < (DWORD) pThisObject->NumInstances;
      dwThisInstance++)
      {
      // The PERF_COUNTER_BLOCK for this instance
      // is found by adding the ByteLength field of
      // the PERF_INSTANCE_DEFINITION structure to
      // the address of the current
      // PERF_INSTANCE_DEFINITION
      pTempCounterData = pTempInstance +
                         pThisInstance->ByteLength;
      // pTempCounterData now pointing to PERF_COUNTER_BLOCK

      pCounterBlock = (PPERF_COUNTER_BLOCK)
         pTempCounterData;

      // Data is at pThisCounter->CounterOffset
      pTempCounterData += pThisCounter->CounterOffset;

      // pThisCounter->CounterSize tells us how many
      // bytes are contained in the data
      CopyMemory(lpOutputData, pTempCounterData,
         pThisCounter->CounterSize);
      lpOutputData += pThisCounter->CounterSize;

      // Move to next element in the instance array.
      // We add the ByteLength field of the
      // PERF_INSTANCE_DEFINITION structure and
```

```
            // the ByteLength field of the
            // PERF_COUNTER_BLOCK to the address of
            // the current PERF_INSTANCE_DEFINITION
            pTempInstance += (pCounterBlock->ByteLength +
                              pThisInstance->ByteLength);
            pThisInstance = (PPERF_INSTANCE_DEFINITION)
                             pTempInstance;
            }
         }
      else if (pThisObject->NumInstances ==
               (PERF_NO_INSTANCES))
         {
         // Object has no instances
         // Counter definition is followed by the counter data
         PBYTE pTempCounterData;
         pTempCounterData = pTempObject +
                            pThisObject->DefinitionLength;
         pTempCounterData += pThisCounter->CounterOffset;
         CopyMemory(lpOutputData, pTempCounterData,
            pThisCounter->CounterSize);
         lpOutputData += pThisCounter->CounterSize;
         lNumInstances = 1;
         }
      }
   return lNumInstances;
}
```

I will use GetPerformanceCounterData() extensively in the Win32 benchmark sample application I present in Chapter 16. Each benchmark client calls GetPerformanceCounterData() to retrieve Performance Monitoring statistics, then computes the data transfer rate that these statistics indicate. The trick is finding out which objects and counters to use for which protocols. As it turns out, Network Interface (object number 510) collects data for TCP/IP, and Redirector (number 262) does the same for Named Pipes.

The Bytes Total/sec Counter

The counter of interest for both the Network Interface object and the Redirection object is Bytes Total/sec, with identifier number 388. For the Redirector object, Bytes Total/sec has the type PERF_COUNTER_BULK_COUNT. This is a composite type, defined as PERF_SIZE_LARGE | PERF_TYPE_COUNTER | PERF_COUNTER_RATE | PERF_TIMER_TICK | PERF_DELTA_COUNTER | PERF_DISPLAY_PER_SEC. The PERF_SIZE_LARGE flag indicates that the counter data is reported as a LARGE_INTEGER, a Win32 type that contains two DWORD parts. The other flags mean that this counter is to be computed by taking successive snapshots and capturing the counter value and the high-resolution performance counter. The value reported is the change in the counter value divided by the change in the timer.

For the Network Interface object, Bytes Total/sec is a PERF_COUNTER_COUNTER. The only difference between PERF_COUNTER_COUNTER and PERF_COUNTER_BULK_COUNT is that the former returns a DWORD instead of a LARGE_INTEGER.

Some Useful C++ Objects

The code that calculates the byte transfer rate uses two C++ classes that I have defined, CLargeInt and CSystemTime. In both cases, the main reason I use a C++ object is so that I can overload the binary minus operator. You cannot perform standard arithmetic on LARGE_INTEGER and SYSTEMTIME structures. I need to subtract LARGE_INTEGER values, because for Named Pipes, the counter is reported that way; if I am using the high-resolution performance counter, its value is also returned as a LARGE_INTEGER. I don't use the CSystemTime class unless there is no high-resolution performance counter on the host machine. In that case, I subtract the end time from the start time by converting the time portion of their SYSTEMTIME structures to milliseconds.

Here are the declarations of these two classes, taken from \WIN32NET\CODE\MFCSOCK\PERFHLPR.H on the source disk. Notice that CLargeInt is not a subclass of LARGE_INTEGER, as CSystemTime is a subclass of SYSTEMTIME. This is because the LARGE_INTEGER type is a union containing a structure, not a simple structure.

```
class CLargeInt
{
   private:
      DWORD LowPart;
      DWORD HighPart;
   public:
      CLargeInt()
         {
         LowPart = 0;
         HighPart = 0;
         }
      CLargeInt(LARGE_INTEGER LargeInt)
         {
         LowPart = LargeInt.LowPart;
         HighPart = LargeInt.HighPart;
         }
```

```
      operator DWORD()
         {
         return LowPart;
         }
      CLargeInt operator-(const CLargeInt& nl);
};

class CSystemTime : public SYSTEMTIME
{
   public:
      CSystemTime();
      CSystemTime(SYSTEMTIME st);
      double operator-(const CSystemTime& cs);
};
```

Here are the class implementations, from \WIN32NET\CODE\MFC-SOCK\PERFHLPR.CPP.

```
CLargeInt CLargeInt::operator-(const CLargeInt& nl)
{
   CLargeInt nlResult;

   if (LowPart < nl.LowPart)
      --HighPart;

   nlResult.LowPart = LowPart - nl.LowPart;
   nlResult.HighPart = HighPart - nl.HighPart;
   return nlResult;
}

CSystemTime::CSystemTime()
{
   wMilliseconds = wSecond = wMinute = wHour = 0;
   wDay = wDayOfWeek = wMonth = wYear = 0;
}

CSystemTime::CSystemTime(SYSTEMTIME st)
{
   wYear         = st.wYear;
   wMonth        = st.wMonth;
   wDayOfWeek    = st.wDayOfWeek;
   wDay          = st.wDay;
   wHour         = st.wHour;
   wMinute       = st.wMinute;
   wSecond       = st.wSecond;
   wMilliseconds = st.wMilliseconds;
}
```

```
double CSystemTime::operator-(const CSystemTime& cs)
{
   // This routine won't work if
   // start time and end time
   // aren't on the same day
   double dStartMilliseconds, dEndMilliseconds;

   dStartMilliseconds =
      ((double)  cs.wMilliseconds) +
      (((double) cs.wSecond) * 1000.0) +
      (((double) cs.wMinute) * 1000.0 * 60.0) +
      (((double) cs.wHour) * 1000.0 * 60.0 * 24.0);
   dEndMilliseconds =
      ((double)  wMilliseconds) +
      (((double) wSecond) * 1000.0) +
      (((double) wMinute) * 1000.0 * 60.0) +
      (((double) wHour) * 1000.0 * 60.0 * 24.0);

   return dEndMilliseconds - dStartMilliseconds;
}
```

Calculating the Byte-Transfer Rate

To calculate the byte-transfer rate using Performance Monitoring statistics, I call GetPerformanceCounterData() just before I start my test, then immediately after I finish it. I then subtract the first counter value from the last one, and the start time from the end time. The QueryPerformanceFrequency() function populates a LARGE_INTEGER with the scale factor for the timer. It reports the number of times a second the high-resolution counter increments.

Here is a code excerpt from \WIN32NET\CODE\MFCSOCK\MFC-SODLG.CPP, which is discussed in Chapter 16. It gets the Bytes Total/sec for Network Interface.

```
double       dMilliSeconds;
DWORD       *lpCounterStart;
DWORD       *lpCounterStop;
DWORD        dwCounterDelta;
CSystemTime SystemTime[2];
CLargeInt   SampleTime[2];
DWORD        dwInstances;

// [Initialize client and connect to server]
```

```
GetPerformanceCounterData(
      NETWORK_INTERFACE,            // Defined as L"510" in PERFHLPR.H
      BYTES_TOTAL_PER_SEC,          // Defined as L"388" in PERFHLPR.H
      (LPBYTE *) &lpCounterStart,
      SystemTime[0],
      SampleTime[0]);

// [Send data to server and wait for it to come back]

dwInstances = GetPerformanceCounterData(
      NETWORK_INTERFACE,
      BYTES_TOTAL_PER_SEC,
      (LPBYTE *) &lpCounterStop,
      SystemTime[1],
      SampleTime[1]);

RegCloseKey(HKEY_PERFORMANCE_DATA);

// [Calculate transfer rate using my own statistics]

LARGE_INTEGER PerformanceFrequency;

if (QueryPerformanceFrequency(&PerformanceFrequency))
   dMilliSeconds =
      ((double) (((DWORD) SampleTime[1]) -
                 ((DWORD) SampleTime[0]))) /
      ((double) (PerformanceFrequency.LowPart))
      * 1000.0;
else
   dMilliSeconds = SystemTime[1] - SystemTime[0];

for (DWORD j = 0; j < dwInstances; ++j)
   {
   dwCounterDelta = lpCounterStop[j] -
                    lpCounterStart[j];
   if (dwCounterDelta != 0)
      break;
   }
}
```

Conclusion

The Windows Registry stores a great deal of information on behalf of the operating system and applications that choose to use it. Important uses of the Registry are:

- Mapping initialization-file reads and writes to the Registry so that .INI files, which are problematic in a secure environment, can be eliminated. (Only available on Windows NT.)
- Informing the Event Logger of the existence of your application so that you can use multilingual message files and application-defined events to write entries to the event log. (Also only under Windows NT.)
- Storing information that your program uses directly, thereby allowing it to be reconfigured without any recompilation of code. (Available in both Win32 environments.)
- Retrieving Performance Monitoring information. (Only available under NT.)

Performance Monitoring is a powerful, self-correcting capability included in Windows NT. It allows system administrators to precisely diagnose problems and bottlenecks; it also gives developers a hook for obtaining system information for their own purposes. Of special interest for network programming are the many objects and counters that pertain to network management.

Suggested Readings

Online References

Registry Overview in the Win32 SDK online help.
Performance Monitoring Overview in the Win32 SDK online help.
Event Logging Overview in the Win32 SDK online help.
Microsoft Knowledge Base for Win32 SDK articles:
"Accessing the Event Logs"
"Adding Categories for Events"
"Calculating String Length in Registry"
"FormatMessage() Converts GetLastError() Codes"
"How to Back Up the Windows NT Registry"
"How to Delete Keys from the Windows NT Registry"
"Mapping .INI File Entries to the Registry"
"RegSaveKey() Requires SeBackupPrivilege"
"Retrieving Counter Data from the Registry"
"Setting the Console Configuration"

Print References

Blake, Russ. *Optimizing Windows NT.* Windows NT Resource Kit, Volume 4. Redmond, WA: Microsoft Press, 1995.

Windows NT Resource Guide, Chapters 10–14. *Windows NT Resource Kit.* Volume 1. Redmond, WA: Microsoft Press, 1995.

Chapter 15

Additional Network APIs

In this chapter, I discuss some API sets that are too important to ignore, but that, for one reason or another, are not included in other chapters. The reasons are varied: perhaps the API is of minor importance, but merits my telling you why I think so (for example, the built-in WNet API). The API may be powerful and useful, but waning in importance (for example, NetDDE). Or perhaps, the API is relevant, useful, and maybe even here to stay, but not one I have much experience with (for example, the Messaging API (MAPI)).

Each of these APIs has some code devoted to it in either the Windows Network Manager (presented in Chapter 16) or the WNETRSC application, included as \WIN32NET\CODE\WNETRSC\WNETRSC.CPP on the code disk. I will cover these topics only briefly here, show you the relevant code excerpts, and let the APIs speak for themselves as much as possible.

The Built-In WNet Functions

The Windows WNet functions have been around for a long time. They were originally introduced in Windows 3.0 as functions in the network driver, which you could access either by loading the driver or by generating an import library from it. In Windows 3.1, three functions moved into USER.EXE, and joined the documented API—WNetAddConnection(), WNetCancelConnection(), and WNetGetConnection(). In 32-bit Windows, the WNet API is the province of the Multiple Provider Router (MPR), and the functions reside in MPR.DLL. This operating system component takes requests that use redirected drive letters and calls to the WNet functions, and determines which network provider should handle them. This is why Microsoft refers to this API as network-independent; it gives all your installed network providers a chance to respond to function calls. However, it is quite limited and narrowly focused; its network independence does not buy you much.

Connecting to Remote Resources

Here are the Win32 prototypes for WNetAddConnection(), WNetCancel-Connection(), and WNetGetConnection():

```
DWORD WNetAddConnection(LPTSTR lpszRemoteName,
                        LPTSTR lpPassword,
                        LPTSTR lpszLocalName);
DWORD WNetCancelConnection(LPTSTR lpszName,
                           BOOL   bForce);
DWORD WNetGetConnection(LPTSTR  lpszLocalName,
                        LPTSTR  lpRemoteName,
                        LPDWORD lpdwBufferSize);
```

WNetAddConnection() maps a local device (such as F:, G:, or LPT1) to a network resource. WNetCancelConnection() restores a mapped device to its local setting. WNetGetConnection() retrieves the network mapping of a local device.

Windows NT and Windows 95 add the functions WNetAddConnection2() and WNetAddConnection3(). They provide the same service as WNet-AddConnection(), but have some syntactic differences:

- The local and remote resource names are passed in a NETRESOURCE structure, instead of as separate arguments.
- An optional argument is added to specify a different user name than the one under which you are logged in.
- You can specify that the new connection is to be remembered for the user, and restored every time he or she logs on.
- WNetAddConnnection3() adds an argument to pass a window handle to the network provider. This gives it an owning window for any dialog boxes it wants to post.

Here are the prototypes for WNetAddConnection2 and WNetAdd-Connection3:

```
DWORD WNetAddConnection2(LPNETRESOURCE lpResourceInformation,
                         LPTSTR        lpszPassword,
                         LPTSTR        lpszNewUserName,
                         DWORD         dwFlags);

DWORD WNetAddConnection3(HWND          hOwnerWindow,
                         LPNETRESOURCE lpResourceInformation,
                         LPTSTR        lpszPassword,
                         LPTSTR        lpszNewUserName,
                         DWORD         dwFlags);
```

The NETRESOURCE structure is typed as follows:

```
typedef struct _NETRESOURCE
{
    DWORD  dwScope;
    DWORD  dwType;
    DWORD  dwDisplayType;
    DWORD  dwUsage;
    LPTSTR lpLocalName;
    LPTSTR lpRemoteName;
    LPTSTR lpComment;
    LPTSTR lpProvider;
} NETRESOURCE;
```

The *lpLocalName* and *lpRemoteName* fields of the NETRESOURCE structure specify the local device (say F:) and the remote resource (such as \\NUMBER1\CDROM). *dwType* can specify RESOURCETYPE_DISK, RESOURCETYPE_PRINT, or RESOURCETYPE_ANY. You can pass *lpProvider* as a non-NULL pointer if you know the name of the network where the resource resides, but usually it is advisable to pass *lpProvider* as NULL. When you do so, the Multiple Provider Router (MPR) takes care of locating the correct network provider.

You will pass *lpszNewUserName* to WNetAddConnection2() and WNetAddConnection3() as non-NULL only when you use a name that differs from the logged-in user.

The *dwFlags* argument can take on one non-zero value, CONNECT_UPDATE_PROFILE, which will cause the new connection to be remembered.

Breaking a Connection to a Remote Resource

Win32 also adds WNetCancelConnection2() for disconnecting from a remote resource. It has one more argument than WNetCancelConnection(), specifying whether the connection should be dropped from the user's list of persistent connections (those that NT automatically restores when the user logs in).

```
DWORD WNetCancelConnection2(
         LPTSTR  lpszLocalOrRemoteName,
         DWORD   dwFlags,
         BOOL    bForce);
```

lpszLocalOrRemoteName can be passed as either the redirected local device or as the remote resource to which it is connected. In the latter case, all the user's connections to the resource are terminated. If *dwFlags* is passed as CONNECT_UPDATE_PROFILE, the connection loses its persistent status. Passing *dwFlags* as zero causes no such side effect. Under most circumstances, you want to pass *bForce* as FALSE. It tells NT whether it should break the connection even if the user has files currently open on that connection. If *bForce* is FALSE and files are open, then WNetCancelConnection2() fails. If it is TRUE, the connection is broken, and the files are left to fend for themselves.

Finding Out Your User Name

WNetGetUser() is a complementary function to WNetAddConnection2() and WNetAddConnection3().

```
DWORD WNetGetUser(
         LPTSTR    lpszLocalDevice,
         LPTSTR    lpszUserName,
         LPDWORD   lpdwNameSize);
```

If *lpszLocalDevice* is not NULL, WNetGetUser() tells you the user name you used to connect to the resource that *lpszLocalDevice* names. Otherwise, it informs you of your login name, and is the same as calling GetUserName().

Connection Dialog Boxes

The WNet API gives you canned dialog boxes you can present to your end users to let them connect and disconnect drives and printers. They are shown in Figures 15-1 and 15-2.

These dialogs can be quite useful; not only do they give your users a standardized interface for connecting to network disks, they also do all the work of browsing the network and making the connection. The only thing you have to do is call WNetConnectionDialog() or WNetDisconnectDialog().

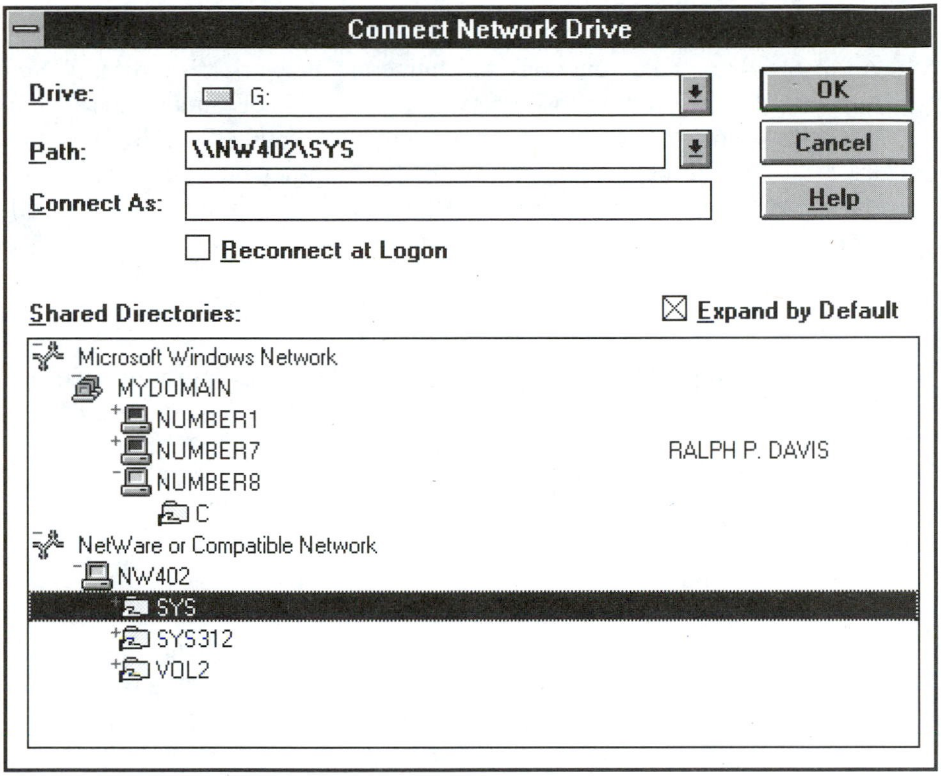

Figure 15-1. The WNetConnectionDialog() Screen

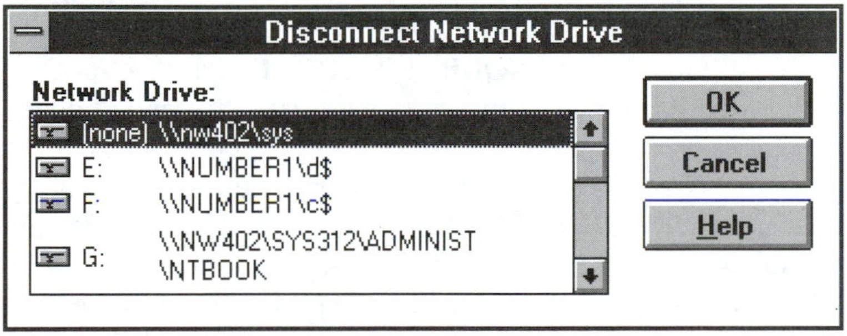

Figure 15-2. The WNetDisconnectDialog() Screen

Both functions take the handle of the owner window and a constant defining the resource as a disk (RESOURCETYPE_DISK) or a printer (RESOURCETYPE_PRINT). WNetConnectionDialog() only supports connections to remote directories. WNetDisconnectDialog() will also disconnect you from a printer.

Network Resource Enumeration

Win32 provides three functions to enumerate network resources: WNetOpenEnum(), WNetEnumResource(), and WNetCloseEnum(). These functions allow you to determine what network resources, such as shared directories and print queues, are available. You can take the information returned and pass it unaltered to WNetAddConnection() or WNetAddConnection2() to connect to the resource.

WNetOpenEnum().

WNetOpenEnum() begins a resource enumeration. It has five arguments:

```
DWORD WNetOpenEnum(
        DWORD          dwScope,
        DWORD          dwType,
        DWORD          dwUsage,
        LPNETRESOURCE  lpNetResource,
        LPHANDLE       lphEnum);
```

The scope of the enumeration, specified by *dwScope*, can be all resources on the network (represented by the constant RESOURCE_GLOBALNET), currently connected resources (RESOURCE_CONNECTED), or persistent connections (RESOURCE_REMEMBERED). (Persistent connections are automatically restored when you log on.)

dwType indicates whether you want to enumerate disk resources (RESOURCETYPE_DISK), print resources (RESOURCETYPE_PRINT), or all resources (RESOURCETYPE_ANY).

If *dwScope* is not RESOURCE_GLOBALNET, then *dwUsage* is ignored. Otherwise, passing *dwUsage* as zero indicates that you want to enumerate all resources. The value RESOURCEUSAGE_CONNECTABLE says that you want all connectable resources (shared resources on your own or other machines). RESOURCEUSAGE_CONTAINER requests enumeration of container resources, like domains, workgroups, and servers.

If *dwScope* is RESOURCE_CONNECTED, *lpNetResource* must be NULL. Otherwise, it may point to a NETRESOURCE structure, shown again here for ease of reference:

```
typedef struct _NETRESOURCE
{
    DWORD  dwScope;
    DWORD  dwType;
    DWORD  dwDisplayType;
    DWORD  dwUsage;
```

```
    LPTSTR lpLocalName;
    LPTSTR lpRemoteName;
    LPTSTR lpComment;
    LPTSTR lpProvider;
} NETRESOURCE;
```

dwScope and *dwType* are the same as the arguments to WNetOpen-Enum(). *dwDisplayType* gives you further information about the nature of the resource. Its most important values are:

- RESOURCEDISPLAYTYPE_DOMAIN: The resource is a domain.
- RESOURCEDISPLAYTYPE_SERVER: The resource is a server machine.
- RESOURCEDISPLAYTYPE_SHARE: The resource is a share being offered for public access over the network.

If *dwScope* is RESOURCE_GLOBALNET, *dwUsage* tells you whether the resource is a container (RESOURCEUSAGE_CONTAINER), like a domain or a server, in which case you can enumerate its contained resources, or is a connectable resource (RESOURCEUSAGE_CONNECTABLE), like a shared directory or print queue. If it is connectable, you can pass a pointer to the NETRESOURCE to WNetAddConnection2() or WNetAdd-Connection3() without modification.

If *dwScope* is RESOURCE_CONNECTED or RESOURCE_ REMEM-BERED, then *lpLocalName* reports the name of the redirected local device (F:, LPT1, or whatever). Finally, *lpProvider* is a string identifying the network provider responsible for this resource. Because the WNet API is network-independent, you may see resources on non-Windows machines, like Net-Ware servers.

The last argument, *lphEnum,* returns an enumeration handle that you then use as input to WNetEnumResource() and WNetCloseEnum().

The first time you call WNetOpenEnum(), set *lpNetResource* to NULL. Then, when you call WNetEnumResource(), it returns an array of NET-RESOURCE structures. For any container resources that WNetEnum-Resource() reports, you can call WNetOpenEnum() with a non-NULL *lpNetResource* to do a recursive search for resources.

WNetEnumResource(). WNetEnumResource() uses the handle returned by WNetOpenEnum(). Note from the prototype that WNetEnumResource() behaves like a LAN Manager enumerator, rather than a Windows enumerator like EnumWindows() or EnumFontFamilies(). That is, it populates an output buffer with an array of object descriptions; it does not call an enumeration function.

```
DWORD WNetEnumResource(
        HANDLE     hEnum,
        LPDWORD    lpdwEntries,
        LPVOID     lpBuffer,
        LPDWORD    lpdwBufferSize);
```

hEnum is the enumeration handle returned by WNetOpenEnum(). On input, **lpdwEntries* specifies the number of entries you want to get back; a value of 0xFFFFFFFF means you want all possible values. On output, it will report the number of entries actually returned. *lpBuffer* will be filled with an array of NETRESOURCE structures. *lpdwBufferSize* points to a DWORD describing the size of *lpBuffer*. If the buffer is too small to hold even a single entry, WNetEnumResource() will return ERROR_MORE_DATA, and **lpdwBufferSize* will tell you how much memory you need.

WNetEnumResource() returns NO_ERROR as long as it has more information to report. When it has enumerated all requested resources, it returns ERROR_NO_MORE_ITEMS.

You can do nested enumerations on the NETRESOURCE structures returned by WNetEnumResource(). If the *dwScope* argument to WNetOpenEnum() is RESOURCE_GLOBALNET, the *dwScope* field of the NETRESOURCE structure is the same, and the *dwUsage* field has the RESOURCEUSAGE_CONTAINER flag set, you can call WNetOpenEnum() again, this time pointing *lpNetResource* to the array element you are looking at. You'll see an example of this shortly.

WNetCloseEnum(). WNetCloseEnum() closes an enumeration. Its only argument is the handle returned by WNetOpenEnum().

```
DWORD WNetCloseEnum(HANDLE hEnum);
```

An Example: EnumNetworkResources(). The WNETRSC sample application contains a function that enumerates network resources and performs recursive enumeration on container resources, EnumNetworkResources(). Here is the listing of that function, taken from \WIN32NET\CODE \WNETRSC\WNETRSC.CPP on the code disk.

```
void EnumNetworkResources(LPNETRESOURCE lpNet, int nLevel,
           DWORD dwScope,
           DWORD dwResourceType, DWORD dwUsageType)
{
   static char *szResourceTypes[] = {"",
                 "Domain or Workgroup",
                 "Server",
```

```
                "Share",
                "File",
                "Group",
                "Network",
                "Root",
                "Administrative Share",
                "Directory",
                "Tree"};
DWORD  dwRetcode;
HANDLE hEnum;
char   szBuffer[1000];
DWORD  dwEntries = 0xFFFFFFFF;
DWORD  dwBytes = 163840;
DWORD  i;
LPNETRESOURCE lpBuffer;

lpBuffer = (LPNETRESOURCE) VirtualAlloc(NULL, 163840,
          MEM_COMMIT,
          PAGE_READWRITE);

if (lpBuffer == NULL)
   {
   printf("\nMemory allocation error\n");
   ExitProcess(1);
   }

dwRetcode = WNetOpenEnum(dwScope,
          dwResourceType,
          dwUsageType,
          lpNet,  // NULL the first time
          &hEnum);

if (dwRetcode == NO_ERROR)
   {
   while (WNetEnumResource(hEnum, &dwEntries, lpBuffer, &dwBytes)
     == NO_ERROR)
      {
      for (i = 0; i < dwEntries; ++i)
         {
         ZeroMemory(szBuffer, sizeof (szBuffer));
         if (nLevel > 0)
             FillMemory(szBuffer, nLevel * 5, ' ');
    sprintf(&szBuffer[strlen(szBuffer)],
       "Local name:  %s  remote name:  %s\t(%s)",
       (lpBuffer[i].lpLocalName != NULL ?
        lpBuffer[i].lpLocalName : ""),
       (lpBuffer[i].lpRemoteName != NULL ?
        lpBuffer[i].lpRemoteName : ""),
```

```
            szResourceTypes[lpBuffer[i].dwDisplayType]);
        printf("\n%s", szBuffer);

        // Do recursive enumeration of container resource
        if (lpBuffer[i].dwUsage & RESOURCEUSAGE_CONTAINER)
            {
            EnumNetworkResources(&lpBuffer[i], ++nLevel,
         dwScope, dwResourceType, dwUsageType);
            --nLevel;
            }
        }
    dwBytes = 163840;
    dwEntries = 0xFFFFFFFF;
    }
      WNetCloseEnum(hEnum);
      }
   VirtualFree(lpBuffer, 0, MEM_RELEASE);
}
```

The main() function calls EnumNetworkResources() twice: once to enumerate all network resources, and once to scan your connections to remote resources. Here are the calls.

```
printf("\n===== Enumerating All Network Resources =====\n");
EnumNetworkResources(NULL, 0, RESOURCE_GLOBALNET,
RESOURCETYPE_ANY, 0);

printf("\n\n===== Enumerating Current Connections =====\n");
EnumNetworkResources(NULL, 0, RESOURCE_CONNECTED,
RESOURCETYPE_DISK, RESOURCEUSAGE_CONNECTABLE);
```

Here is its output for the Microsoft portion of my network. The output for NetWare enumerates every single directory on every NetWare server I have.

```
===== Enumerating All Network Resources =====

Local name:    remote name:  Microsoft Windows Network
     Local name:    remote name:  RPDOMAIN        (Domain or Workgroup)
          Local name:    remote name:  \\NUMBER1  (Server)
               Local name:    remote name:  \\NUMBER1\NETLOGON (Share)
          Local name:    remote name:  \\NUMBER10 (Server)
          Local name:    remote name:  \\NUMBER2  (Server)
               Local name:    remote name:  \\NUMBER2\C (Share)

===== Enumerating Current Connections =====

Local name:  H:  remote name:  \\number10\c$
```

Extended Error Reporting

When one of the WNet functions fails, your first step is to call GetLastError(). If it returns ERROR_EXTENDED_ERROR, you can find out the extended network error by calling WNetGetLastError(). This will return a network-specific error code and a printable string that you can display to the user. The kinds of errors that may occur vary greatly from one network provider to another, so WNetGetLastError() is a good way to shield yourself from these details.

```
DWORD WNetGetLastError(
      LPDWORD     lpdwErrorCode,       // Captures network-specific
                                       // error code
      LPTSTR      lpszErrorString,     // Returns printable error
                                       // message
      DWORD       dwErrorStringSize,   // Size of message buffer
      LPTSTR      lpszProviderName,    // Returns name of network
                                       // provider
      DWORD       dwProviderNameSize); // Size of provider buffer
```

That, then, is the built-in WNet API. It is a decent API as far as it goes, but it is not a rich one. There are many more things a developer needs to do on a network than connect to remote drives.

NetDDE

NetDDE is an extension to the DDE Management Library (DDEML) interface. Client and server applications use DDEML calls to communicate with each other, and there is very little difference in how they use DDEML.

When NetDDE was first introduced into the Windows 3.x environment, it seemed like quite an innovation. But in the Win32 environment, where Windows Sockets, Named Pipes, and RPC offer powerful vehicles for network communications, NetDDE begins to fade into the background. It is not a bad API; it's just not a general-purpose or versatile one. I used to use it for only one thing—installing remote group boxes in Program Manager. Even with that usage, I had to plug in my own NetDDE agents; Program Manager doesn't know about NetDDE. I have since dropped remote group box installation, and no longer use NetDDE. My guess is that you won't need to use it, either.

NetDDE is also problematic for 32-bit applications running under Windows 95. Its NetDDE support DLL, NDDEAPI.DLL, only comes in a 16-bit version. To use NetDDE from a 32-bit application, you have to write a 32-bit to 16-bit thunking layer. That's a lot of trouble for a tool of minor significance.

Connecting to a NetDDE Server

One slight variation between DDEML and NetDDE is that the client must provide the name of the target station when it starts a conversation. Also, the target application is always NDDE$, the name used by the NetDDE server. Standard DDEML uses topics and items to further identify the individual pieces of data involved in an exchange. For example, in a conversation with Excel, the name of a spreadsheet might constitute a topic, and cells A1, A2, A3, and A4 might be individual items. A DDE server application that wishes to offer its services over a network creates a share name that represents the service (or application), topic, and item names that it would use for local DDE. The client application then uses this share name as the topic in its call to DdeConnect(). If the application you are trying to access is not running on the server machine, NetDDE can start it for you. For example, to create group boxes in Program Manager, you connect to it using the application and topic name "PROGMAN". Suppose Program Manager creates the NetDDE share "PROGMAN$". (It does not, by the way). A client application on \\NUMBER10 would connect to Program Manager on \\NUMBER1 as follows.

```
#include <ddeml.h>

extern HINSTANCE hInst;      // Assume a global exists
DWORD  dwDDE;
HSZ    hszProgman, hszTopic;
HCONV  hProgmanConv;

if (DdeInitialize(&dwDDE, MyDDECallback, APPCLASS_CLIENTONLY,
                  CBF_SKIP_REGISTRATIONS | CBF_SKIP_UNREGISTRATIONS)
    == DMLERR_NO_ERROR)
   {
   // Use the application name \\NUMBER1\NDDE$
   hszProgman = DdeCreateStringHandle(dwDDE, "\\\\NUMBER1\\NDDE$",
                   CP_WINANSI);

   // Use topic name PROGMAN
   hszTopic = DdeCreateStringHandle(dwDDE, "PROGMAN$", CP_WINANSI);

   // Try to connect
   hProgmanConv = DdeConnect(dwDDE, hszProgman, hszTopic, NULL);

   if (hProgmanConv != NULL)
      // Proceed with DdeClientTransaction() calls for
      // XTYP_EXECUTE transactions
   }
```

Once the client is connected to the server, the DDE conversation proceeds just as if it were a local interaction; there are no further differences.

Incidentally, it has been my experience that NetDDE does not like it if you pass Unicode strings to DdeCreateStringHandle(). Specifically, the DdeConnect() fails, apparently because the target machine name gets garbled.

Making a DDE Server NetDDE-Aware

As I stated above, a DDE server that wants to make itself available to clients across a network must create NetDDE shares that symbolize its service and topic pairs. In other words, a server application must be NetDDE-aware in order for NetDDE clients to connect to it. This, as it turns out, is the greatest weakness in NetDDE; only a few DDE servers know anything about NetDDE. Unless more major applications add NetDDE awareness, it seems likely that NetDDE will be eclipsed by the other APIs discussed in this book. The very existence of those other APIs makes it unlikely that many serious server applications will choose to support NetDDE.

The NetDDE DLL, NDDEAPI.DLL, provides functions for adding, deleting, and enumerating DDE shares: NDdeShareAdd(), NDdeShareDel(), and NDdeShareEnum(). NDdeShareGetInfo() returns more detailed information about a share reported by NDdeShareEnum(). The prototypes, data types, and constants are defined in NDDEAPI.H.

\WIN32NET\CODE\WNETRSC\WNETRSC.CPP includes a section that enumerates the currently existing DDE shares, then adds the share WNPM$. In an earlier version of my software, the Windows Network Manager used WNPM$ to field remote XTYP_EXECUTE requests for the Program Manager. Since Program Manager is not NetDDE-aware, it used NetDDE to establish a connection to the Windows Network Manager on the target machine, which was NetDDE-aware. The Windows Network Manager then connected to the Program Manager on the local machine and sent along the command strings that it received from the partner application.

Here is the code that creates the WNPM$ share. I first delete the share if it already exists by calling NDdeShareDel(), then call NDdeShareAdd() to recreate it. Among other things, NDdeShareAdd() needs a pointer to an NDDESHAREINFO structure.

```
typedef struct _NDDESHAREINFO
{
    LONG                        lRevision;
    LPTSTR                      lpszShareName;
    LONG                        lShareType;
    LPTSTR                      lpszAppTopicList;
```

```
    LONG                        fSharedFlag;
    LONG                        fService;
    LONG                        fStartAppFlag;
    LONG                        nCmdShow;
    LONG                        qModifyId[2];
    LONG                        cNumItems;
    LPTSTR                      lpszItemList;
} NDDESHAREINFO;
```

After this, I call NDdeSetTrustedShare(). This is required because I set the *fService* flag in the NDDESHAREINFO to FALSE. Frankly, I don't know why this works like this, but I know that it does. After this, just out of curiosity, I call NDdeGetShareSecurity() to see what kind of security descriptor NT generated in response to NDdeShareAdd(), to which I passed a NULL security descriptor. Notice the use of NDdeGetErrorString() to convert a function return value into a printable string.

```
NDdeShareDel(NULL, "WNPM$", 0);

ZeroMemory(lpShareInfo, sizeof (NDDESHAREINFO));
lpShareInfo->lRevision = 1;
lpShareInfo->lpszShareName = "WNPM$";
lpShareInfo->lpszAppTopicList =
   "\0\0WNET|WNETPM\0";                      // Note the two leading
                                             // \0s. This is not
                                             // clearly documented,
                                             // but it
                                             // is required.
                                             // The first one is for
                                             // the DDE app and topic,
                                             // the second is for
                                             // the OLE app and topic.
                                             // We're using a static
                                             // app and topic,
                                             // which comes in the
                                             // third position.

                                             // The Service and topic
                                             // are separated by
                                             // a vertical bar (|)
lpShareInfo->lShareType = SHARE_TYPE_STATIC; // I don't know what this
                                             // means, but this is
                                             // how the other DDE
                                             // shares are typed
lpShareInfo->fSharedFlag = TRUE;             // Allow remote users
                                             // to connect
lpShareInfo->fService = FALSE;               // Must make this a
```

```
                                                  // trusted share before
                                                  // it can be used
lpShareInfo->fStartAppFlag = TRUE;                // Allow automatic
                                                  // startup of application
lpShareInfo->nCmdShow = SW_SHOWNORMAL;            // Show screen in
                                                  // normalized state
lpShareInfo->cNumItems = 0;                       // Share all items
lpShareInfo->lpszItemList = "";                   //   under this topic

uDDEError = NDdeShareAdd(
     NULL,                                        // Execute locally
     2,                                           // Info level, must be 2
     NULL,                                        // No security descriptor
                                                  // Inherits security
                                                  //   from somebody
     (LPBYTE) lpShareInfo,                        // Pointer to NDDESHAREINFO
     sizeof (NDDESHAREINFO));

if (uDDEError != NDDE_NO_ERROR)
   {
   NDdeGetErrorString(uDDEError, szDDEError,
      sizeof (szDDEError));
   printf("\nCannot add DDE share WNPM$: %s", szDDEError);
   }

// We have to call NDdeSetTrustedShare() since we
// set the fService flag in the NDDESHAREINFO to FALSE
uDDEError = NDdeSetTrustedShare(
               NULL,                              // Execute locally
               "WNPM$",                           // Share name
               NDDE_TRUST_SHARE_START |           // Let NetDDE
                                                  // start the app
               NDDE_TRUST_SHARE_INIT);            // and initialize it
if (uDDEError != NDDE_NO_ERROR)
   {
   NDdeGetErrorString(uDDEError, szDDEError, sizeof (szDDEError));
   printf("\nCannot make WNPM$ a trusted share: %s", szDDEError);
   }

if ((uDDEError =
   NDdeGetShareSecurity(
      NULL,                                       // Machine name
      "WNPM$",                                    // Share name
      DACL_SECURITY_INFORMATION,
      (PSECURITY_DESCRIPTOR) bySDBuffer,
      dwSDSize, &dwSDSize))
    == NDDE_NO_ERROR)
   DumpDACL("WNPM$", (PSECURITY_DESCRIPTOR) bySDBuffer);
```

```
else
   {
   NDdeGetErrorString(uDDEError, szDDEError, sizeof (szDDEError));
   printf("\nCan't read share's security descriptor: %s",
      szDDEError);
   }
```

Here's the output from DumpDACL().

```
DACL explicitly assigned
Access allowed ace
Access rights 0000023D granted to Everyone on WNPM$
Access allowed ace
Access rights 000F03FF granted to Administrators on WNPM$
```

This looks like an inherited DACL, though I don't know where it's inherited from. The default DACL in my access token gives GENERIC_ALL rights to SYSTEM and Administrators. SYSTEM does not appear in this DACL, and Everyone does. The rights masks are represented by constants in NDDESEC.H. For Everyone, the flags are NDDE_SHARE_GENERIC_READ | NDDE_SHARE_INITIATE_LINK. For Administrators, they are NDDE_SHARE_GENERIC_ALL.

Obtaining NetDDE Share Information

To obtain information about NetDDE shares, call NDdeShareEnum() to retrieve their names, then call NDdeShareGetInfo() for each one.

```
UINT NDdeShareEnum(LPTSTR    lpServer,
                   UINT      uLevel,
                   LPBYTE    lpNameBuffer,
                   DWORD     dwNameBufferSize,
                   LPDWORD   lpdwEntriesRead,
                   LPDWORD   lpdwTotalAvailable);
```

Set *lpszServer* to NULL to enumerate NetDDE shares on the local machine. *uLevel* must be zero. NDdeShareEnum() works like a LAN Manager enumerator; it returns an array of null-terminated share names in *lpNameBuffer*, with two nulls at the end. On input, *dwNameBufferSize* says how large the buffer at *lpNameBuffer* is. On output, **lpdwEntriesRead* reports the number of shares enumerated; **lpdwTotalAvailable* returns the number of bytes of information available. If the original buffer was too small, NDdeShareEnum() returns NDDE_BUF_TOO_SMALL, and you can allocate the memory required.

You can get the original NDDESHAREINFO structure for each share in the array by calling NDdeShareGetInfo().

```
UINT NDdeShareGetInfo(LPTSTR  lpszServer,
                      LPTSTR  lpszShareName,
                      UINT    uLevel,
                      LPBYTE  lpShareInfo,
                      DWORD   dwShareInfoSize,
                      LPDWORD lpdwTotalAvailable,
                      LPDWORD lpdwItems);
```

As usual, *lpszServer* must be NULL to get share information on your own machine. *uLevel* must be two, just as it was in the initial call to NDdeShare-Add(). *lpdwItems* must be NULL at this time. *lpszShareName* is the name of the share for which you are requesting information. *lpShareInfo* points to an NDDESHAREINFO structure, and *dwShareInfoSize* is the size of the buffer at *lpShareInfo*. Any items that are included in the share will also be returned in the buffer pointed to by *lpShareInfo*; if the buffer is only *sizeof* (NDDE-SHAREINFO) bytes large, NDdeShareGetInfo() may well return NDDE_BUF_TOO_SMALL. **lpdwTotalAvailable* returns the total number of bytes needed to capture all of the output information.

WNETRSC enumerates existing NetDDE shares and analyzes their application/topic pairs. Here's the code, followed by the program's output.

```
printf("\n===== DDE Shares on %s =====\n", lpStation);
ZeroMemory(szDDEShares, sizeof (szDDEShares));
NDdeShareEnum(
    NULL,                               // Enumerate locally
    0,                                  // Level must be zero
    (LPBYTE) szDDEShares,               // Output buffer
    sizeof (szDDEShares),
    &dwEntries,
    &dwBytes);

// Output is an array of contiguous null-terminated strings,
// terminated by two null bytes
for (i = 0; szDDEShares[i] != '\0'; i += (lstrlen(&szDDEShares[i]) + 1))
   {
   printf("\nShare name: %s", &szDDEShares[i]);
   dwBytes = sizeof (szShareInfoBuffer);
   wShares = 0;
   if (NDdeShareGetInfo(
         NULL,                          // Local machine
         &szDDEShares[i],               // Pointer to current
                                        // share name
         2,                             // Level must be two
```

```
         (LPBYTE) szShareInfoBuffer,      // Output NDDESHAREINFO
         sizeof (szShareInfoBuffer),
         &dwBytes,
         &wShares)
      == 0)
      {
      // App and topic are delimited by a |
      // For example, WNET|WNETPM
      // For SHARE_TYPE_STATIC, first two bytes
      // are '\0'
      while (*lpShareInfo->lpszAppTopicList == '\0')
         ++lpShareInfo->lpszAppTopicList;
      lpszAppName = strtok(lpShareInfo->lpszAppTopicList, "|");
      lpszTopicName = strtok(NULL, "");
      printf("\n\tApp name: %s, Topic name: %s", lpszAppName,
         lpszTopicName);
      }
   }

===== DDE Shares on \\NUMBER1 =====

Share name: Chat$
   App name: WinChat, Topic name: Chat
Share name: CLPBK$
   App name: ClipSrv, Topic name: System
Share name: Hearts$
   App name: MSHearts, Topic name: Hearts
Share name: WNPM$
   App name: WNET, Topic name: WNETPM
```

Only WinChat, the Clipbook Server, and MSHearts are NetDDE-aware. This means you cannot use NetDDE to talk to any other major Windows applications. You can, of course, use NetDDE to build your own distributed systems, and it does have some appealing features. It is built on top of DDEML, which is by and large a very usable, cleanly structured API. It offers securable endpoints. It will execute a remote server application if it is not running when a NetDDE request comes in. This is a very nice feature that no other API offers, but you can get the same effect by writing an NT service. However, it seems likely that if some major applications don't become NetDDE-aware soon, NetDDE will wither on the vine.

Other NetDDE Functions

Table 15-1 lists the other NetDDE functions.

Table 15-1. Other NetDDE Functions

Function	Purpose
NDdeGetErrorString	Retrieves text for a NetDDE error
NDdeGetShareSecurity	Gets the security descriptor for a NetDDE share
NDdeGetTrustedShare	Gets trust information on a share
NDdeIsValidAppTopicList	Verifies the syntax of a string containing applications and topics delimited by |
NDdeIsValidShareName	Checks that a share name is in correct format (does not mean that the share exists)
NDdeSetShareSecurity	Sets the security descriptor belonging to a share
NDdeSetTrustedShare	Gives a share trusted status, and defines the startup operations that a client will be allowed to do
NDdeShareSetInfo	Changes the information pertaining to a share
NDdeTrustedShareEnum	Enumerates shares that are trusted in the security context of the calling process

The Messaging API (MAPI)

There are currently two levels of the Messaging API available: simple MAPI and extended MAPI. Simple MAPI has been around for several years. It offers an interface consisting of 12 functions. For a user needing to send mail, most of the work is handled by MAPISendDocument() and MAPISendMail().

Extended MAPI is a set of OLE 2 interfaces. By basing itself on OLE, extended MAPI allows much more flexibility. Because messaging service providers can offer their services using standard interfaces, it is possible for a much greater range of service providers to make themselves available.

The Microsoft Foundation Classes also offer rudimentary client-side support for MAPI. When you generate a project, you can ask Visual C++ to add MAPI support to your application. It adds a Send... item to your File menu. It is supported by the CDocument::OnFileSendMail() method, which in turn uses simple MAPI.

In this chapter, I will discuss simple MAPI and MFC's support for it. I will not discuss extended MAPI, for a couple of reasons:

- I have no personal experience or expertise with it, and do not want to try your patience with my ignorance.
- I do not want to add the complexity of OLE 2 to the material I cover in this book, which is complex enough.

Simple MAPI

Simple MAPI allows applications to easily add electronic mail capabilities. It provides a set of functions for using the Microsoft mail system. Most of the functions put up a canned dialog box, which in turn handles all the details of constructing, interpreting, and sending e-mail messages. Because the level of service is so high, applications can become mail-enabled with little trouble. With Visual C++, a simple click on a check box gives you complete outgoing mail capabilities.

Table 15-2 lists the MAPI function calls. The MAPI header file (MAPI.H) that defines their prototypes is provided with the Win32 SDK.

Table 15-2. MAPI Functions

Function	Operation
MAPIAddress	Presents a dialog box to get list of recipients from user
MAPIDeleteMail	Deletes a message retrieved by MAPIFindNext()
MAPIDetails	Presents a dialog box giving detailed information on a recipient
MAPIFindNext	Scans mailbox for incoming messages
MAPIFreeBuffer	Frees memory allocated by MAPIAddress(), MAPIResolveName(), and MAPIReadMail()
MAPILogoff	Logs user off the mail system
MAPILogon	Logs user onto the mail system
MAPIReadMail	Reads a message retrieved by MAPIFindNext()
MAPIResolveName	Retrieves information on a user known to the MS-Mail system; may also present a dialog box asking the user to resolve an ambiguous name
MAPISaveMail	Updates a mail message
MAPISendDocuments	Presents a dialog box to send files to remote user
MAPISendMail	Presents a dialog box to send mail to remote user

Under both Win32 operating systems, the functions reside in MAPI32.DLL. The import library MAPI32.LIB is also provided for build-time linking, although it is common MAPI programming practice to load the DLL by calling LoadLibrary().

Word for Windows includes a Send... item on its File menu. Selecting that option as I type this text puts up the dialog box shown in Figure 15-3; this is also the dialog box you see when you select Send... in an MFC application with MAPI support. It is none other than the dialog box belonging to MAPISendDocuments() (or MAPISendMail() with document attachments).

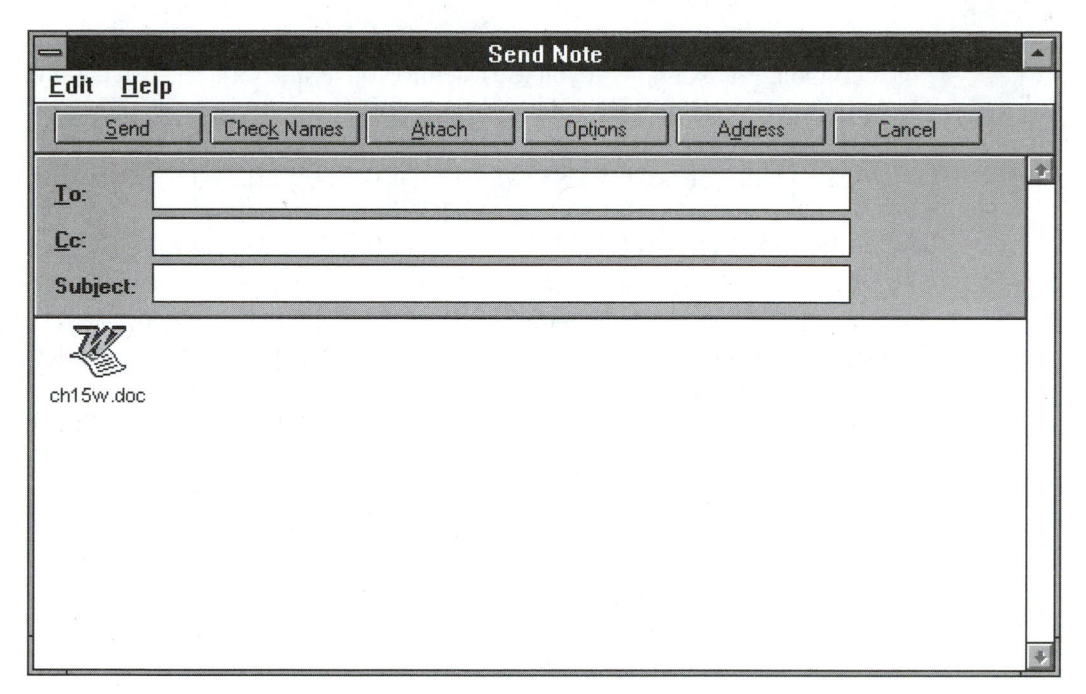

Figure 15-3. Word for Windows Send Note Dialog Box

This is the easiest way to mail-enable an application. The recommended procedure is to do it just as Word for Windows has—add a Send... option to your File menu (or let Visual C++ generate one for you).

MAPISendDocuments()

When users select Send..., you might want to ask if they want to send the active document, selected documents, or all open documents. MAPISendDocuments() handles everything else for you. By the way, the LPSTRs in the prototype tell you that MAPI does not support Unicode.

```
ULONG MAPISendDocuments(
   ULONG ulUIParam,
   LPSTR lpszDelimChar,
   LPSTR lpszFilePaths,
   LPSTR lpszFileNames,
   ULONG ulReserved);       // Pass as zero
```

ulUIParam is the handle of the window that will own the MAPI dialog boxes, cast to a ULONG. To pass multiple filenames, you build concatenated strings in *lpszFilePaths* and *lpszFilenames*. The character in *lpszDelimChar* is the delimiter. For example, if you use a semicolon as a delimiter when passing H:\WIN32NET\CODE\WIN32OBJ\WIN32OBJ.H and H:\WIN32NET \CODE\WIN32OBJ\WIN32OBJ.CPP, then *lpszDelimChar* will be ";", *lpszFilePaths* will be "H:\WIN32NET\CODE\WIN32OBJ\WIN32OBJ.H;H: \WIN32NET\CODE\WIN32OBJ\WIN32OBJ.CPP", and *lpszFileNames* will be "WIN32OBJ.H;WIN32OBJ.CPP". Notice that *lpszFileNames* and *lpszFilePaths* both include the filenames. *lpszFileNames* lists the filenames without their paths. If passed as empty strings or NULL pointers, no files will be transmitted; however, the user can still compose an e-mail message or select files for transmission.

The implication of this is: MAPISendDocuments() is the only MAPI call you ever need to use, unless you want to read incoming e-mail. MAPISendDocuments() does its work by presenting canned dialogs to your users and letting them make the selections they want. It corresponds to a series of calls to the other MAPI functions. For this reason, once you have entered the mail system by calling MAPISendDocuments(), you do not need to make any other MAPI calls. For the remainder of this chapter, we'll look at the succession of dialog boxes that appear, and the functions associated with them.

MAPILogon()

MAPILogon() posts the dialog box that you see in Figure 15-4. It is prototyped as follows:

```
ULONG FAR PASCAL MAPILogon(
   ULONG     ulUIParam,
   LPSTR     lpszName,
   FLAGS     flFlags,
   ULONG     ulReserved,
   LPLHANDLE lplhSession);
```

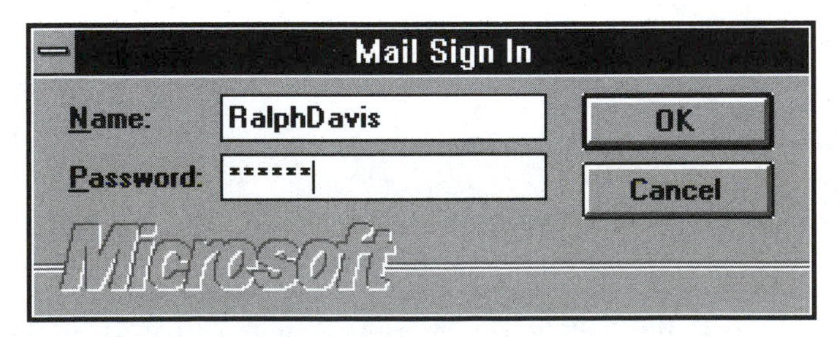

Figure 15-4. MAPI Login Dialog Box

ulUIParam designates the window that will own the dialog box. You can use MAPILogon() to log in without the dialog box by passing an explicit user name in *lpszName*. If *lpszName* is a NULL pointer or an empty string, MAPILogon() will present the logon dialog box (provided that *flFlags* is set appropriately). There are three possible settings for *flFlags*: MAPI_LOGON_UI, MAPI_NEW_SESSION, and MAPI_FORCE_DOWNLOAD. MAPI_LOGON_UI specifies that you want the logon dialog box to be presented. MAPI_NEW_SESSION specifies that you want MAPI to create a new mail session. Otherwise, it will try to use an existing one. MAPI_FORCE_DOWNLOAD requests MAPI to immediately download new mail from the mail server. MAPILogon() returns a session handle through *lplhSession*. This handle will be used in subsequent calls to MAPI functions.

MAPISendMail()

The next screen that appears is the Send dialog box (shown earlier in Figure 15-3). This is produced by a call to MAPISendMail(). Because it came up in response to a File Send command, it has a file attachment. The user can enter text to accompany the file, or select more files for transmission by clicking the Attach button.

Here is the prototype for MAPISendMail():

```
ULONG FAR PASCAL MAPISendMail(
   LHANDLE        lhSession,
   ULONG          ulUIParam,
   lpMapiMessage lpMessage,
   FLAGS          flFlags,
   ULONG          ulReserved);
```

lhSession is the session handle returned by MAPILogon(). *lpMessage* points to a MapiMessage structure. Here is its type definition from MAPI.H.

```
typedef struct
{
    ULONG ulReserved;                // Reserved for future use
                                     // Pass as zero
    LPSTR lpszSubject;               // Message subject
    LPSTR lpszNoteText;              // Message text
    LPSTR lpszMessageType;           // Message class
                                     // Normally passed as NULL
    LPSTR lpszDateReceived;          // in YYYY/MM/DD HH:MM format
    LPSTR lpszConversationID;        // conversation thread ID
                                     // pass as NULL
```

```
    FLAGS flFlags;                    // unread,return receipt
    lpMapiRecipDesc lpOriginator; // Originator descriptor
    ULONG nRecipCount;                // Number of recipients
    lpMapiRecipDesc lpRecips;         // Recipient descriptors
    ULONG nFileCount;                 // # of file attachments
    lpMapiFileDesc lpFiles;           // Attachment descriptors
} MapiMessage, FAR * lpMapiMessage;
```

lpszSubject denotes the subject of the message; it appears in the Subject field of the dialog box in Figure 15-3. *lpszNoteText* points to the body of the message. Paragraphs in the message should be terminated with a CR/LF. If *lpszNoteText* is NULL or an empty string, it is taken to mean no message. The user can still type a message into the edit box in Figure 15-3. *flFlags* for MAPISendMail() can be zero, or can have the MAPI_RECEIPT_REQUESTED bit set to request receipt notification.

The fields from *lpOriginator* to *lpRecips* describe the message sender and recipients. You do not need to initialize the fields in these structures before you call MAPISendMail(); MAPI will fill them in for you. You may do so if you want to, but it is much easier to let the user fill them in using the MAPI dialog boxes.

The *lpFiles* field describes any file attachments. It, too, will be populated for you when you call MAPISendDocuments(). It is filled in automatically when you read a message that has file attachments.

MAPIAddress()

The Address button that you see in Figure 15-3 calls MAPIAddress().

```
ULONG FAR PASCAL MAPIAddress(
    LHANDLE                 lhSession,
    ULONG                   ulUIParam,
    LPSTR                   lpszCaption,
    ULONG                   nEditFields,
    LPSTR                   lpszLabels,
    ULONG                   nRecips,
    lpMapiRecipDesc         lpRecips,
    FLAGS                   flFlags,
    ULONG                   ulReserved,
    LPULONG                 lpnNewRecips,
    lpMapiRecipDesc FAR *lppNewRecips);
```

MAPIAddress() brings up the dialog box shown in Figure 15-5.

lpszCaption is the caption that the dialog box will display. If it is NULL or zero-length, the caption "Address Book" will be assigned by default.

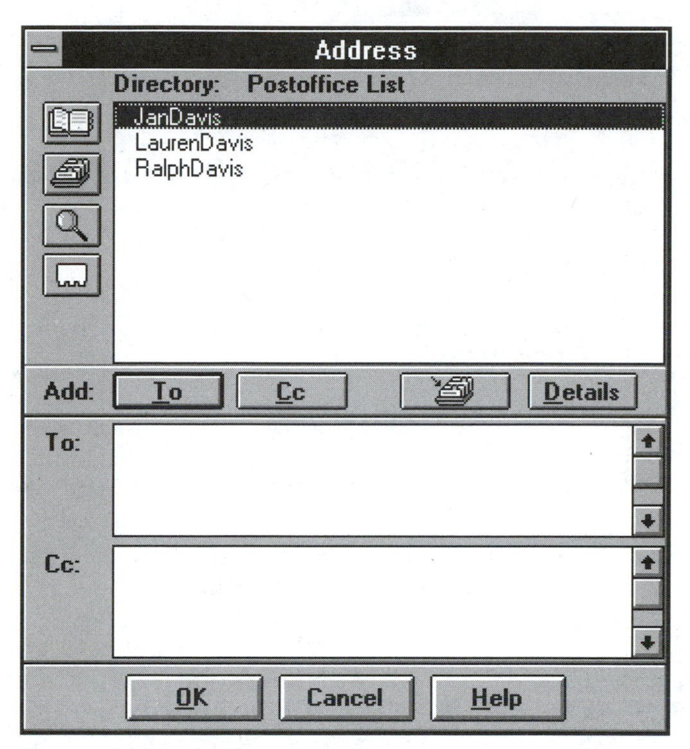

Figure 15-5. MAPI Address Dialog Box

flFlags can be MAPI_LOGON_UI to present the logon dialog box (if the user is not already logged on), and MAPI_NEW_SESSION to force a new logon. MAPI_NEW_SESSION will be ignored if *lhHandle* is not NULL, and represents a valid mail session. The meanings of *nEditFields* and *lpszLabels* is somewhat esoteric. Basically, pass *nEditFields* as zero if you want to prevent the user from modifying the initial recipient list (indicated by *lpRecips*). Otherwise, pass 4. *lpRecips* is an array of MapiRecipDesc structures that will be used to initialize the address list on the dialog box. *nRecips* is the number of entries in *lpRecips*. If *nRecips* is zero, the list is initially empty. *lpnNewRecips* and *lppNewRecips* are used to return the final list of recipients. **lpnNewRecips* reports the number of recipients in the list; the list itself is returned through *lppNewRecips*. This is a pointer to an array of MapiRecipDesc structures, and will be allocated by MAPI on your behalf. It includes addressees designated as primary recipients, and those getting carbon copies. To free the memory allocated, call MAPIFreeBuffer().

```
ULONG FAR PASCAL MAPIFreeBuffer(LPVOID pv);
```

pv is the pointer than MAPIAddress() returned in **lppNewRecips*.

MAPIDetails()

The Details button in Figure 15-5 calls MAPIDetails(), which presents the dialog box shown in Figure 15-6.

```
ULONG FAR PASCAL MAPIDetails(
   LHANDLE          lhSession,
   ULONG            ulUIParam,
   lpMapiRecipDesc lpRecip,
   FLAGS            flFlags,
   ULONG            ulReserved);
```

lpRecip points to a MapiRecipDesc structure that describes the recipient whose details are to be displayed. *flFlags* can be MAPI_LOGON_UI or MAPI_NEW_SESSION, which mean the same thing as they did before. Another possible flag is MAPI_AB_NOMODIFY, which specifies that the dialog box should be read-only (as is the one in Figure 15-6).

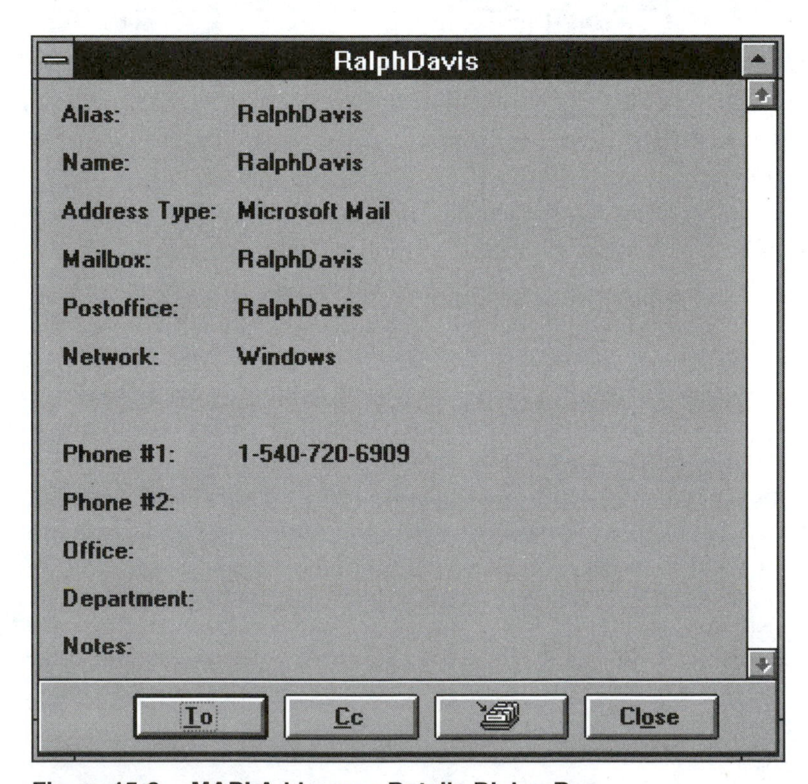

Figure 15-6. MAPI Addressee Details Dialog Box

MAPIResolveName()

MAPIResolveName() serves two purposes: it can be used to convert a recipient name into a complete MapiRecipDesc structure, and it can be used to ask the user which recipient an ambiguous name should resolve to.

```
ULONG FAR PASCAL MAPIResolveName(
   LHANDLE                 lhSession,
   ULONG                   ulUIParam,
   LPSTR                   lpszName,
   FLAGS                   flFlags,
   ULONG                   ulReserved,
   lpMapiRecipDesc FAR *lppRecip);
```

lpszName is the name you want resolved. *flFlags* includes the MAPI_LOGON_UI and MAPI_NEW_SESSION bits we have already seen. You can also set the MAPI_DIALOG flag, which requests presentation of a dialog box if an ambiguous name can only be resolved by user intervention. A pointer to a fully resolved description of the user is returned through *lppRecip*. Use MAPIFreeBuffer() to free it.

MAPIFindNext()

To read mail, scan incoming messages with MAPIFindNext().

```
ULONG FAR PASCAL MAPIFindNext(
   LHANDLE lhSession,
   ULONG   ulUIParam,
   LPSTR   lpszMessageType,
   LPSTR   lpszSeedMessageID,
   FLAGS   flFlags,
   ULONG   ulReserved,
   LPSTR   lpszMessageID);
```

lpszMessageType should be passed as NULL. *lpszSeedMessageID* and *lpszMessageID* should point to buffers that are at least 64 bytes long. To iterate over all messages, pass *lpszSeedMessageID* as an empty string initially. Then, before each subsequent call, copy the message ID returned in *lpszMessageID* to *lpszSeedMessageID*. The value returned in *lpszMessageID* will be used as input to MAPIReadMail(), MAPIDeleteMail(), and MAPISaveMail(). *flFlags* can be MAPI_UNREAD_ONLY, to limit the scan to unread mail, and MAPI_GUARANTEE_FIFO, to read the messages in the order in which they were received.

Having obtained a message ID, you can read, save, or delete the message.

MAPIReadMail()

MAPIReadMail() retrieves a message from the message store.

```
ULONG FAR PASCAL MAPIReadMail(
   LHANDLE            lhSession,
   ULONG              ulUIParam,
   LPSTR              lpszMessageID,
   FLAGS              flFlags,
   ULONG              ulReserved,
   lpMapiMessage FAR *lppMessageOut);
```

lpszMessageID must be a message ID returned by MAPIFindNext() or MAPISaveMail(). *lppMessageOut* points to a pointer to a MapiMessage structure. MAPIReadMail() allocates the memory for this structure; it must be freed by calling MAPIFreeBuffer().

The *flFlags* field controls the information read from the message. MAPI_ENVELOPE_ONLY reads only the header of the message. That is, it will not copy any files that were sent, nor will it return the body of the message. MAPI_SUPPRESS_ATTACH causes MAPI to return a pointer to the message text in the *lpszNoteText* field, but will not copy any attached files. If MAPI_BODY_AS_FILE is set, MAPI will not return the message text, but will write it to a temporary file. MAPI_PEEK returns the message, but does not flag it as read. It will continue to be returned by MAPIFindNext() calls that specify MAPI_UNREAD_ONLY.

MAPISaveMail()

Call MAPISaveMail() if you want to change some of the information in the message or copy it to a new message.

```
ULONG FAR PASCAL MAPISaveMail(
   LHANDLE       lhSession,
   ULONG         ulUIParam,
   lpMapiMessage lpMessage,
   FLGS          flFlags,
   ULONG         ulReserved,
   LPSTR         lpszMessageID);
```

lpszMessageID is the ID originally returned by MAPIFindNext(). If you pass an empty string, MAPI will create a new message and return its new ID through *lpszMessageID*. The buffer must be at least 64 bytes in length. *lpMessage* points to a MapiMessage structure. You can change the information in the MapiMessage structure after reading it with MAPIReadMail(), then save it as a new message, or replace the old one. The only supported values for *flFlags* are MAPI_LOGON_UI and MAPI_NEW_SESSION.

The message ID that MAPISaveMail() returns can be used in subsequent calls to MAPIReadMail() and MAPIDeleteMail().

If files were attached to the message, they are written to temporary files. The *lpFiles* array of the MapiMessage structure gives the names under which the files were saved.

MAPIDeleteMail()

MAPIDeleteMail() deletes a message fetched by MAPIFindNext(), or saved by MAPISaveMail().

```
ULONG FAR PASCAL MAPIDeleteMail(
   LHANDLE lhSession,
   ULONG   ulUIParam,
   LPSTR   lpszMessageID,
   FLAGS   flFlags,
   ULONG   ulReserved);
```

Again, *lpszMessageID* is the ID returned by MAPIFindNext() or MAPISaveMail(). The flags are not used, and should be passed as zero.

MAPILogoff()

MAPILogoff() terminates a mail session.

```
ULONG FAR PASCAL MAPILogoff(
   LHANDLE lhSession,
   ULONG ulUIParam,
   FLAGS flFlags,
   ULONG ulReserved);
```

Only *lhSession* and *ulUIParam* are used. As always, they are the session handle returned by MAPILogon(), and the handle of the window that will own any dialog boxes. *flFlags* and *ulReserved* should be passed as zero.

Enabling MFC E-Mail Capabilities

MFC allows you to send a file you are editing by selecting a Send... item on the File menu. This item can be generated by Visual C++ when you create your application, or you can add it later by hand. It is very easy to do. You only need to add this message-map entry for your document class:

```
ON_COMMAND(ID_FILE_SEND_MAIL, OnFileSendMail)
```

You do not need to implement OnFileSendMail() yourself; the CDocument class contains a complete version (in the MFC source file DOCMAPI.CPP). This function loads MAPI32.DLL, gets a pointer to MapiSendMail(), then passes it information about the document.

Conclusion

The built-in WNet API set is small and provides little useful functionality. NetDDE offers valuable services, but at present has not been widely adopted and is unlikely to be. MAPI is a high-level standard dialog API that allows applications to become mail-enabled with a minimum of effort. The Microsoft Foundation Classes offer transparent MAPI support through CDocument::OnFileSendMail(). You can ask Visual C++ to automatically include this support in projects that it generates.

In addition to simple MAPI, there are two other APIs that provide messaging services. One is extended MAPI, based on a set of OLE 2 interfaces. The other is the Common Messaging Calls API, based on the X.400 specification. E-mail APIs like these are highly relevant for network programming today, and are likely to remain so for the foreseeable future.

Suggested Readings

Online References

Networks Overview in the Win32 online help.
Win32 Messaging (MAPI) Overview and Reference in the Win32 online help.
Microsoft Knowledge Base for Win32 SDK articles:
"BUG: WNetGetUniversalName Fails Under Windows 95"
"Enumerating Network Connections"
"Location of WNet* API Functions"
"Trusted DDE Shares"
"Windows 95 Support for Network DDE"

Chapter 16

Sample Applications

In this chapter, we will look at a couple of sample applications that use many of the techniques we've studied in the last eight chapters. The new version of my Windows Network Manager uses the WNet DLLs to send remote message boxes, and uses RPC for a variety of purposes. It also installs a Program Manager group box for the software on the code disk. MFCSOCK does benchmark tests using Windows Sockets, Named Pipes, my WNet DLLs, and RPC. It also collects Performance Monitoring statistics to corroborate its own data. Both applications are provided on the source code disk.

The Windows Network Manager

It is somewhat pretentious of me to call this sample application the Windows Network Manager; it's not really a network manager, it just demonstrates some network programming techniques. However, the name is catchy, and someday maybe I'll really do something with it.

These are the main things that the Windows Network Manager illustrates:

- It uses the WNet DLLs to send message boxes to remote stations. It also provides the receiving side of this exchange to unwrap a remote MessageBox() call and post a message box locally.

- It uses RPC for several purposes. It calls _RpcSetLocalUser() to tell the WNet RPC Server who the current user is. It calls _RpcGetRemoteUser() to find out the user logged in on the station selected in the Stations list box. It calls _RpcGetOSStartupTime() to find out when the WNet RPC Server was loaded on the target machine. Finally, it calls _RpcWinExec() when the user clicks the Execute a Program... push button.
- It uses NetServerEnum() to populate the Stations list box. If it is running under Windows 95 (where NetServerEnum() isn't supported), it uses a broadcast mailslot to announce its presence and to detect the presence of other stations.

Figure 16-1 shows the Windows Network Manager dialog box.

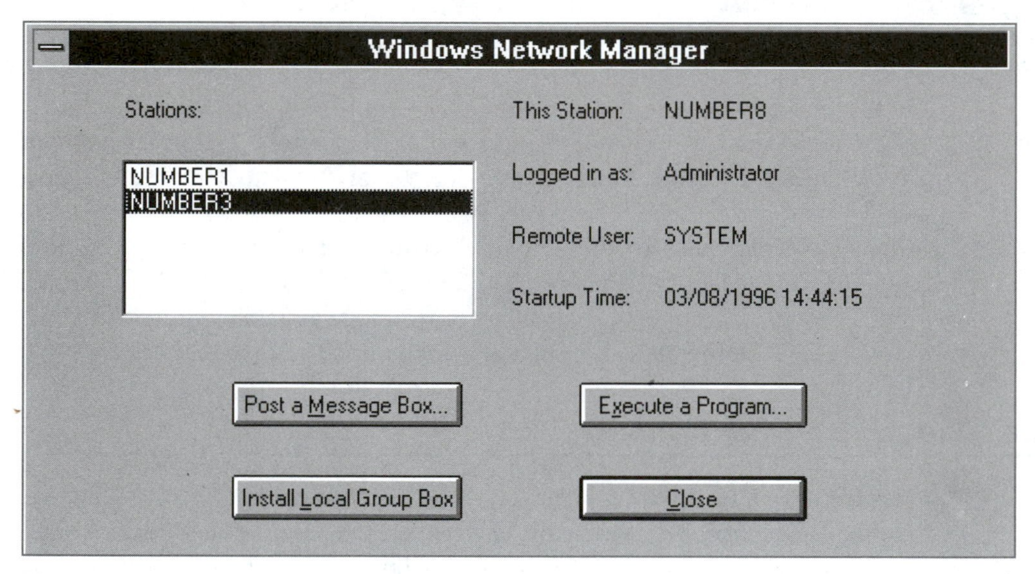

Figure 16-1. The Windows Network Manager Dialog Box

CWNetDlg::OnInitDialog()

Many of the calls in the Windows Network manager are done in CWNetDlg::OnInitDialog(). Here is an excerpt showing the pertinent lines of code. The source files for this class are \WIN32NET\CODE\WNETNEW\WNETDLG.H and WNETDLG.CPP.

```
TCHAR szUserName[256];
DWORD dwSize = sizeof (szUserName);
```

```
::GetUserName(szUserName, &dwSize);
m_szUserName = szUserName;

// Find out who is out there
WNetEnumServers(ServerEnumProc, m_StationsWnd);

// Tell WNet RPC Server who we are
WNetSetLocalUser((LPTSTR) (LPCTSTR) m_szUserName);

// Register with WNet DLLs
WNetInit(ReceiveCallback, NULL, &m_hWNetUser);

TCHAR szRemoteUser[256];
dwSize = sizeof (szRemoteUser);

// m_szTargetStation is the currently selected
// station in the Stations list box
// (Set by WNetEnumServers())
// Ask WNet RPC Server who's logged in over there
// He may say SYSTEM if the user hasn't run
// the Windows Network Manager on that machine
if (WNetGetRemoteUser((LPTSTR) (LPCTSTR) m_szTargetStation,
                      szRemoteUser,
                      &dwSize) == NO_ERROR)
   {
   m_szRemoteUser = szRemoteUser;
   }
else
   {
   m_szRemoteUser = _T("");
   }

// Find out when the WNet RPC Server started
// on the target station
SYSTEMTIME SystemTime;
if (WNetGetStartupTime(
      (LPTSTR) (LPCTSTR) m_szTargetStation,
      &SystemTime) == NO_ERROR)
   {
   m_szSystemTime.Format(_T("%02d/%02d/%04d %02d:%02d:%02d"),
       SystemTime.wMonth, SystemTime.wDay, SystemTime.wYear,
       SystemTime.wHour, SystemTime.wMinute,
SystemTime.wSecond);
   }
else
   {
   m_szSystemTime = _T("");
   }
```

Remote Message Boxes

To post message boxes on remote stations, the Windows Network Manager provides a WNetMessageBox() function. It is implemented on top of the WNet DLLs, and uses a higher-level protocol that I have dubbed Distributed Function Calls (DFC), mostly to distinguish it from Remote Procedure Calls. These are Win32 functions that I have written to run on remote stations—WNetSendMessage(), WNetPostMessage(), WNetFindWindow(), and WNetMessageBox(). They were a centrally important focus of my earlier book, *Windows Network Programming*, but I have moved away from them over the last several years. However, I have kept WNetMessageBox() to demonstrate the DFC protocol.

The packet that I send includes a header that stamps the packet as one of mine using a signature string of "WNET$$$." It is padded to a length of eight (including the null terminator) so the next field is properly aligned on RISC machines. After that, there is a code telling the receiving station what function it is to execute. The function arguments are passed in the body of the message.

WNetMessageBox() is coded in \WIN32NET\CODE\WNETNEW\WNETMBOX.CPP.

```
#define WNET_SIGNATURE_UNICODE      L"WNET$$$"
#define WNET_SIG_LENGTH             (8 * sizeof (WCHAR))

enum WNET_REQUEST
{
   POST_MESSAGE,
   SEND_MESSAGE,
   FIND_WINDOW,
   ENUM_STATIONS,
   ENUM_STATION_RESPONSE,
   MESSAGE_BOX
};

#pragma pack(1)

struct WNET_MSG
{
   TCHAR        szSignature[WNET_SIG_LENGTH];
   WNET_REQUEST WNetRequest;
   MSG          Message;
   BOOL         bIsLParamPtr;
   WORD         wDataLength;
   WORD         wOutDataLength;
};
```

```
#pragma pack()

int WNetMessageBox(HANDLE  hConnection,
                   HWND    hOwnerWnd,
                   LPCTSTR lpszMessage,
                   LPCTSTR lpszCaption,
                   UINT    uType,
                   BOOL    bWaitForResponse)
{
   int     nResult = -1;
   LPTSTR  lpBuffer, lpTemp;
   DWORD   dwLength;
   DWORD   dwTempAddress;

   if (lpszMessage == NULL)
      {
      return -1;
      }

   dwLength = WNET_SIG_LENGTH +
              sizeof (WNET_REQUEST) +
              sizeof (HWND) +
              lstrlen(lpszMessage) + 1 +
              (lpszCaption == NULL ? 1 :
               lstrlen(lpszCaption) + 1) +
              sizeof (UINT) + sizeof (BOOL) +
              sizeof (UINT);  // Padding for RISC chips

   lpBuffer = new CHAR[dwLength * sizeof (WCHAR)];
   lpTemp = lpBuffer;

   // Write our signature (L"WNET$$$") to the packet
   ::CopyMemory(lpTemp, WNET_SIGNATURE_UNICODE,
      WNET_SIG_LENGTH);
   lpTemp += WNET_SIG_LENGTH;

   // Indicate that we want to issue a remote MessageBox()
   *((WNET_REQUEST *) lpTemp) = MESSAGE_BOX;
   lpTemp += (sizeof (WNET_REQUEST) * sizeof (WCHAR));

   // Send handle of owning window on remote station
   *((HWND *) lpTemp) = hOwnerWnd;

   lpTemp += ((sizeof (HWND)) * sizeof (WCHAR));

   // We're going to transmit the message and
   // the window caption in Unicode
```

```
    WCHAR szwMessage[256];
    ANSIToUnicode((LPSTR) lpszMessage,
       szwMessage, sizeof (szwMessage) / sizeof (WCHAR));

    ::CopyMemory(lpTemp, szwMessage,
       ((lstrlen(lpszMessage) + 1) * sizeof (WCHAR)));
    lpTemp += ((lstrlen(lpszMessage) + 1) * sizeof (WCHAR));

    if (lpszCaption == NULL)
       lpszCaption = TEXT("");

    WCHAR szwCaption[256];
    ANSIToUnicode((LPSTR) lpszCaption,
       szwCaption, sizeof (szwCaption) / sizeof (WCHAR));

    ::CopyMemory(lpTemp, szwCaption,
       ((lstrlen(lpszCaption) + 1) * sizeof (WCHAR)));

    lpTemp += ((lstrlen(lpszCaption) + 1) * sizeof (WCHAR));

    // Align lpTemp on DWORD boundary for
    // RISC chips
    dwTempAddress = (DWORD) lpTemp;
    while (dwTempAddress % (sizeof (UINT)) != 0)
       ++dwTempAddress;
    lpTemp = (LPTSTR) dwTempAddress;

    // Tell other side what kind of push buttons
    // we want
    // Include a question mark if caller wants
    // an answer
    if (bWaitForResponse)
       uType += MB_ICONQUESTION;

    *((UINT *) lpTemp) = uType;
    lpTemp += (sizeof (UINT) * sizeof (WCHAR));
    *((BOOL *) lpTemp) = bWaitForResponse;

    // Send the packet
    if (WNetSend(hConnection, lpBuffer, dwLength * sizeof
(WCHAR)))
       {
       if (bWaitForResponse)
          {
          // Wait for an answer (but get bored after 5 seconds)
          DWORD dwBytesReceived;
          if (!WNetReceive(hConnection, &nResult,
```

```
            sizeof (nResult), &dwBytesReceived, 5000))
          nResult = -1;
        }
      else
        {
        nResult = IDOK;
        }
      }
   delete [] lpBuffer;
   return nResult;
}
```

To receive incoming message boxes, the CWNetDlg class provides two methods. One is ReceiveCallback(), the callback function we pass to WNetInit(). This function looks at the packet, makes sure the signature string is correct, then examines the command code. If it is MESSAGE_BOX, it calls the OnMessageBox() method. This function reverses the action of WNetMessageBox()—it removes the arguments from the packet and passes them to MessageBox().

```
BOOL CALLBACK CWNetDlg::ReceiveCallback(LPBYTE lpReceivedData,
                                         DWORD  dwDataLength,
                                         HANDLE hConnection)
{
   LPBYTE    lpPacket;
   WNET_MSG *lpMsgHeader;
   BOOL      bRetcode;

   lpPacket = (LPBYTE) ::VirtualAlloc(NULL,
      dwDataLength, MEM_COMMIT, PAGE_READWRITE);

   // Pull the packet into our own local storage
   CopyMemory(lpPacket, lpReceivedData, dwDataLength);
   lpMsgHeader = (WNET_MSG *) lpPacket;

   CHAR szMsgHeader[25];

   // Convert the signature to ANSI
   // The packet is passed using Unicode,
   // but we're using ANSI so we work under
   // Windows 95
   UnicodeToANSI((LPTSTR) lpMsgHeader, szMsgHeader,
      sizeof (szMsgHeader));

   // If the packet doesn't begin with our signature,
   // we got it by accident
   if (lstrcmp(szMsgHeader, WNET_SIGNATURE) != 0)
```

```
        {
        return FALSE;
        }

    switch (lpMsgHeader->WNetRequest)
        {
        case MESSAGE_BOX:
            OnMessageBox(hConnection,
                (LPTSTR) lpPacket + WNET_SIG_LENGTH +
                         (sizeof (WNET_REQUEST) * sizeof
                                 (WCHAR)));
            bRetcode = TRUE;
            ::VirtualFree(lpPacket, 0, MEM_RELEASE);
            break;
        default:
            // Starts with our signature, but an
            // unknown command code...chuck it
            bRetcode = FALSE;
            break;
        }
    return bRetcode;
}

void CWNetDlg::OnMessageBox(HANDLE hConnection, LPTSTR
lpPacket)
{
    HWND            hOwnerWnd;
    LPCTSTR         lpszMessage;
    LPCTSTR         lpszCaption;
    UINT            uType;
    int             nRetVal;
    BOOL            bWaitForResponse;
    DWORD           dwPacketAddress;
    CHAR            szMessage[512];
    CHAR            szCaption[512];

    hOwnerWnd = *((HWND *) lpPacket);

    if (hOwnerWnd == NULL)
        hOwnerWnd = theApp.m_pDialogWnd->GetSafeHwnd();

    // Activate the window's top-level parent
    // (if it isn't already active)
    if (::GetActiveWindow() != ::GetTopLevelParent(hOwnerWnd))
        ::SetActiveWindow(::GetTopLevelParent(hOwnerWnd));

    lpPacket += (sizeof (HWND) * sizeof (WCHAR));
    lpszMessage = (LPCTSTR) lpPacket;
```

```
    // Network packets use UNICODE
    UnicodeToANSI((LPTSTR) lpszMessage, szMessage,
                  sizeof (szMessage));
    lpszMessage = szMessage;

    lpPacket += ((lstrlen(lpszMessage) + 1) * sizeof (WCHAR));

    lpszCaption = (LPCTSTR) lpPacket;
    UnicodeToANSI((LPTSTR) lpszCaption, szCaption,
       sizeof (szCaption));
    lpszCaption = szCaption;

    lpPacket += ((lstrlen(lpszCaption) + 1) * sizeof (WCHAR));

    // Sender translates a NULL caption into
    // a zero-length string
    if (*lpszCaption == TEXT('\0'))
       lpszCaption = NULL;

    // Make sure lpPacket is aligned on a DWORD boundary
    // for RISC chips
    dwPacketAddress = (DWORD) lpPacket;
    while (dwPacketAddress % (sizeof (UINT)) != 0)
       ++dwPacketAddress;
    lpPacket = (LPTSTR) dwPacketAddress;

    // Find out what push buttons we're supposed to display
    uType = *((UINT *) lpPacket);
    lpPacket += (sizeof (UINT) * sizeof (WCHAR));

    // Sender can tell us that it wants to
    // know which push button the user clicked
    bWaitForResponse = *((BOOL *) lpPacket);

    nRetVal = ::MessageBox(hOwnerWnd, lpszMessage,
              lpszCaption, uType);

    ::SetFocus(hOwnerWnd);

    if (bWaitForResponse)
       {
       // Caller wants an answer, send it back
       WNetSend(hConnection, (LPVOID) &nRetVal, sizeof (int));
       }
}
```

Remote Program Execution

The Execute a Program... push button uses the services of the WNet RPC Server to execute a program on a remote machine. The RPC of interest is _RpcWinExec(); the Windows Network Manager wrapper is WNetWin-Exec(), contained in \WIN32NET\CODE\WNETNEW\WNETWEXC.CPP. It is very similar to other RPC client code I presented in Chapter 11. Most of these wrapper functions differ very little from each other, because the setup sequence is usually the same. In this function, as in the ones shown in Chapter 11, I instantiate a CRpcClient object to establish my link to the server.

```
UINT WNetWinExec(LPTSTR      lpszStation,
                 LPTSTR      lpszCommand,
                 UINT        uCmdShow)

{
   DWORD dwRetcode = NO_ERROR;
   RPC_STATUS RpcStatus = RPC_S_OK;

   try
      {
      CRpcClient RpcClient(wnrpc_v1_0_c_ifspec,
                           (PTBYTE) lpszStation,
                           &wnrpc_IfHandle);
      RpcClient.SetTimeout(RPC_C_BINDING_MIN_TIMEOUT);
      try
         {
         WCHAR szwCommand[4096];

         ANSIToUnicode(lpszCommand, szwCommand,
            sizeof (szwCommand) / sizeof (WCHAR));
         dwRetcode = _RpcWinExec(szwCommand, uCmdShow);
         RpcStatus = RPC_S_OK;
         }
      catch (CWin32Exception *e)
         {
         RpcStatus = e->GetExceptionCode();
         dwRetcode = ((DWORD) -1);
         e->Delete();
         }
      }
   catch (CResourceException *e)
      {
      RpcStatus = ::GetLastError();
      dwRetcode = ((DWORD) -1);
      e->Delete();
      }
   return dwRetcode;
}
```

Enumerating Servers

We saw in Chapter 12 that you can enumerate the stations on a network by calling NetServerEnum(). I also wrapped NetServerEnum() in the CNetServer::EnumServer() method. That would be an appropriate solution here as well, except that it would make it impossible for this application to run under Windows 95. NETAPI32.DLL, which exports the LAN Manager API for Windows NT, contains nothing but the Netbios() function in Windows 95. So I can't link to it at build time; I have to load it dynamically at run time.

The Windows Network Manager includes a function WNetEnumServers() that delegates to the appropriate subroutine for Windows NT or Windows 95.

```
BOOL WNetEnumServers(SERVERENUMPROC lpServerEnumProc,
                     CListBox& ListBox)
{
   if (WNetIsWindowsNT())
      NTEnumServers(lpServerEnumProc, ListBox);
   else
      Win95EnumServers(lpServerEnumProc, ListBox);
   return TRUE;
}
```

Server Enumeration under NT. NTEnumServers() loads a pointer to NetServerEnum() from NETAPI32.DLL, then calls the function and reports its findings. It also needs a pointer to NetApiBufferFree() so it can release the memory allocated by NetServerEnum().

```
// We have to do this because of Windows 95
typedef NET_API_STATUS (NET_API_FUNCTION *NET_SERVER_ENUM)(
       LPTSTR      servername,
       DWORD       level,
       LPBYTE      *bufptr,
       DWORD       prefmaxlen,
       LPDWORD     entriesread,
       LPDWORD     totalentries,
       DWORD       servertype,
       LPTSTR      domain,
       LPDWORD     resume_handle);
typedef NET_API_STATUS (NET_API_FUNCTION *NET_BUFFER_FREE)(
    LPVOID Buffer);

static HINSTANCE hLib = ::LoadLibrary(TEXT("NETAPI32.DLL"));
static NET_SERVER_ENUM lpNetServerEnum =
   (NET_SERVER_ENUM) ::GetProcAddress(hLib, "NetServerEnum");
static NET_BUFFER_FREE lpNetApiBufferFree =
   (NET_BUFFER_FREE) ::GetProcAddress(hLib,
"NetApiBufferFree");
```

```
static void NTEnumServers(
           SERVERENUMPROC lpServerEnumProc,
           CListBox& ListBox)
{
   LPSERVER_INFO_101 lpServerInfo;
   LPWSTR *lpBuffer;
   DWORD dwEntries, dwTotal;
   DWORD i;

   if (lpNetServerEnum(NULL, 101, (LPBYTE *) &lpBuffer, 65536,
                  &dwEntries, &dwTotal,
                  SV_TYPE_ALL, NULL, NULL) ==
          NERR_Success)
      {
      CHAR szServerName[256];

      lpServerInfo = (SERVER_INFO_101 *) lpBuffer;
      for (i = 0; i < dwEntries; ++i)
         {
         ::WideCharToMultiByte(CP_ACP,
                               0,
                               (LPCWSTR)
                                  lpServerInfo[i].sv101_name,
                               -1,
                               szServerName,
                               sizeof (szServerName),
                               NULL,
                               NULL);
         if (!lpServerEnumProc(szServerName,
                   ListBox))
            break;
         }
      }
   lpNetApiBufferFree(lpBuffer);
}
```

Server Enumeration under Windows 95. The first thing I tried under Windows 95 was the built-in WNet API—WNetOpenEnum(), WNetEnumResource(), and WNetCloseEnum(). However, when I used code that works just fine under NT (the WNETRSC sample application I showed you in Chapter 15) Windows 95 got stuck in an infinite loop. I thought about locating NetServerEnum() in a remote procedure call, but the problem there was keeping the local Windows 95 station from trying to respond. Finally, I used a technique I first developed for *Windows Network Programming*—sending out a broadcast diagram to say, "Hi, I'm here," then collecting the responses when they come in. Win95EnumServers() creates an incoming mailslot called \\.\MAILSLOT\WNET\WNETMGR, and opens a broadcast mailslot called *\MAILSLOT\WNET\WNETMAP. The WNet RPC Server provides the server side of the WNETMAP mailslot, so the chances are pretty good that if a station is running, I'll find out about it. Both partners use the CMailslot class I created in Chapter 10. It creates a thread to handle incoming traffic, and invokes the callback function that was passed to its constructor. In this case, the callback function adds the new station to the Stations list box, if it isn't already there.

```
static SERVERENUMPROC g_lpEnumProc;
static CListBox *g_pListBox;

static TCHAR g_szComputerName[MAX_COMPUTERNAME_LENGTH + 1];
static DWORD g_dwNameLength = sizeof (g_szComputerName);

static BOOL WINAPI MailslotReceiveCallback(
      LPBYTE lpData,
      DWORD dwDataLength,
      HANDLE hConnection)
{
   // If this station isn't already in the list box,
   // enumerate it

   if (g_pListBox->FindStringExact(-1, (LPCTSTR) lpData) ==
       LB_ERR)
      {
      g_lpEnumProc((LPTSTR) lpData, *g_pListBox);
      }

   return TRUE;
}

// This is all we have to do to get incoming
// mailslot capabilities (besides implementing
// the receive callback)
static CMailslot MailslotServer(
         _T("WNET\\WNETMGR"),
         ServerSide,
         MailslotReceiveCallback);

static void Win95EnumServers(
           SERVERENUMPROC lpServerEnumProc,
           CListBox& ListBox)
```

```
{
   ::GetComputerName(g_szComputerName, &g_dwNameLength);
   g_lpEnumProc     = lpServerEnumProc;
   g_pListBox       = &ListBox;

   // Find out who's here
   try
      {
      CString szMessage;

      CMailslot Mailslot(_T("\\\\*\\MAILSLOT\\WNET\\WNETMAP"),
            ClientSide);

      szMessage.Format(_T("%s"), (LPCTSTR) g_szComputerName);
      Mailslot.Write((LPCTSTR) szMessage,
                     szMessage.GetLength() + 1,
                     NULL);
      }
   catch (...)
      {
      }
}
```

Win32 Benchmark Tests

The MFCSOCK application tests the performance of several APIs, and the different ways of using them. Its project files are in \WIN32NET\CODE\MFCSOCK. It got its name from the fact that I originally used it to compare the different ways of programming Windows Sockets:

- Standard blocking Berkeley calls
- Overlapped I/O using the Sockets API directly
- The two MFC classes (CAsyncSocket and CSocket)
- CServiceInfo and COverlappedSocket in overlapped mode

Subsequently, I expanded it to do testing for Named Pipes, my WNet DLLs, and RPC, but I kept the original name.

Figure 16-2 shows the dialog box that MFCSOCK presents when it first starts up.

Benchmark Procedure

The benchmark tests use a simple echo mechanism: get the current tick count, send a certain number of packets of a certain size, get the tick count again, and divide the total number of bytes sent and received by the amount

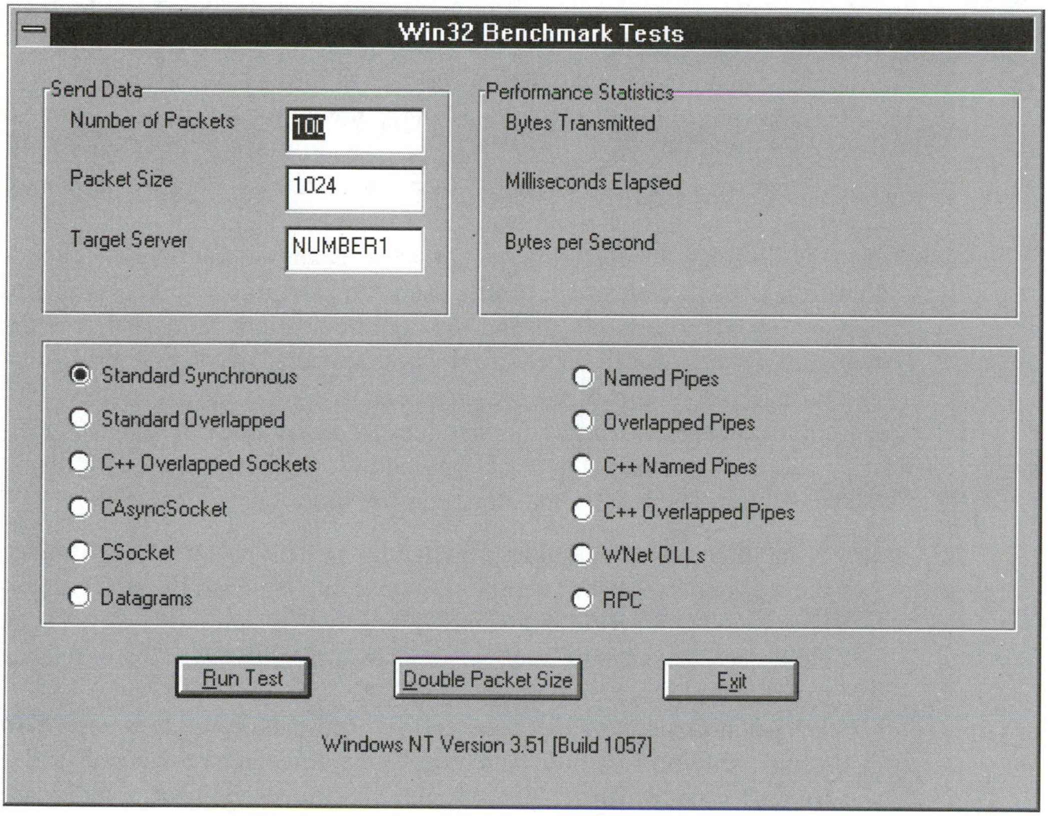

Figure 16-2. The Win32 Benchmark Application Dialog Box

of time it took. Immediately before calling GetCurrentTime() the first time, and immediately after calling it the second time, the tests call GetPerformanceCounterData() (shown in Chapter 14) to capture the Performance Monitoring counters.

I usually run the tests using packet sizes of 1024, 2048, 4096, 8192, 16384, and 32768. One thing I want to test is if the data transfer rate increases with the packet size. My hypothesis is that it should, because the more data we send, the higher the ratio of application data to protocol data, and the better our effective data transfer rate.

The dialog box is supported by the CMfcsockDlg class. Clicking on one of the radio buttons shown in Figure 16-2 sets a variable indicating which vehicle you want to test. Clicking the Run Test push button then calls the appropriate routine, named Do<vehicle>(). For Berkeley Sockets, the routine is DoStandardSynchronous(). For overlapped sockets, it is DoStandardOverlapped(). For C++ overlapped sockets, it is DoCPPOverlapped().

For the most part, I will confine the code listings to the Do<vehicle>() functions. I'll take the MFC glue for granted, except where it isn't obvious; our topic of interest is how to use the various APIs and C++ objects.

Please keep in mind that benchmarking is not a precise science, although Performance Monitoring corroboration helps keep it from erring too wildly. The comparisons between the numbers are what are of interest, and I have seen them in enough environments that I have confidence in them. This is also why I display the operating system version and build number at the bottom of the screen; benchmark results can change from one build number to another. My purpose is not to find the communications vehicle that is the obvious choice to use in all circumstances. Rather, I want to consider the benefits and tradeoffs involved. Nevertheless, in my travels around the country training developers, one of the first questions I get asked is, "What's fastest?" I'll answer that right now: Windows Sockets, especially using overlapped I/O. There are some other relevant questions:

- What other advantages does a particular vehicle have that might make the slower performance worth it (like security support)? This is particularly relevant for RPC and Named Pipes.
- How does the use of C++ objects instead of native C variables affect performance?
- What kind of communications are you most likely to be doing? Will you be sending very little data most of the time, then occasionally need to send a large chunk? (This is the way most end-user applications work, because the user spends most of his or her time in what the computer considers idle mode.) It may be that a data-transfer rate that looks pitiful in a benchmark test (which bombards the network) would be perfectly acceptable—that is, it would not be perceived as slow by the users of your application.
- Do you need to communicate outside of your immediate environment? If you do, your choices narrow considerably, because only Sockets and RPC can give you this kind of universality.

If you run these tests in your environment, and your results vary significantly from mine, please let me know. My phone number is 540-720-6909, and my CompuServe address is 71161,1060 (from the Internet, 71161.1060@compuserve.com).

Windows Sockets

The Sockets tests take advantage of the TCP *echo* service, provided as part of the Simple TCP/IP Services package. MFCSOCK opens the client end of the connection, sends the packets, and computes the timings. *echo* can service datagrams as well as connection-oriented transmissions, so I test that also.

Standard Blocking Berkeley Calls. The first test uses standard blocking Berkeley calls—socket(), connect(), send(), and recv(). This is its logic:

1. Open a TCP/IP stream socket by calling socket() and passing it AF_INET and SOCK_STREAM.
2. Get the addressing information for *echo* on the target machine (captured in the member variable *m_szTargetServer*). The GetHostAddress() method issues the appropriate calls (gethostbyname(), getservbyname()).

```
BOOL CMfcsockDlg::GetHostAddress(LPCSTR lpszHost,
                                 LPCSTR lpszService,
                                 LPCSTR lpszProto)
{
   LPHOSTENT lpHost;
   LPSERVENT lpServ;

   lpHost = ::gethostbyname(lpszHost);
   if (lpHost != NULL)
      {
      m_sin.sin_family = PF_INET;
      ::CopyMemory(&m_sin.sin_addr, lpHost->h_addr_list[0],
                   lpHost->h_length);
      lpServ = ::getservbyname(lpszService, lpszProto);
      if (lpServ != NULL)
         {
         m_sin.sin_port = lpServ->s_port;
         ::ZeroMemory(m_sin.sin_zero, sizeof
         (m_sin.sin_zero));
         return TRUE;
         }
      }
   return FALSE;
}
```

3. Call connect() to establish the connection.
4. Send a dummy packet of 100 bytes, and wait for it to come back. Here and later in the actual timing loop, accumulate the number of bytes received to make sure it totals the number sent. In this case, it's probably not necessary; a 100-byte packet won't get fragmented. But later, when we're sending packets ranging from 1K to 32K, it most definitely is necessary; TCP/IP will fragment the packets. Here's the receiving loop:

```
nBytes = ::send(sCall, (LPCSTR) szBuffer, 100, 0);

for (nTotalReceived = nReceived = 0;
     nBytes != SOCKET_ERROR &&
     nTotalReceived < nBytes;
    )
   {
   nReceived = ::recv(sCall, (LPSTR) szBuffer, nBytes, 0);
   if (nReceived != SOCKET_ERROR)
      nTotalReceived += nReceived;
   }
```

5. Call GetPerformanceCounterData() to get the current value of BYTES_TOTAL_PER_SEC (counter number 388) for NETWORK_INTERFACE (object number 510). This returns a snapshot of the number of bytes that have been sent and received up to this point.
6. Call GetCurrentTime() to get the current tick count (number of milliseconds since Windows started up), then start the timing loop.
7. In the loop, send() the packet, then call recv() until we've gotten back all the data we sent.
8. After the loop, capture the current time again. Then call GetPerformanceCounterData() to get the second Performance Monitor snapshot.
9. Close the socket by calling closesocket(), and close the Performance Monitoring Registry key HKEY_PERFORMANCE_DATA.
10. Compute the results and display them.

Here's the code, from \WIN32NET\CODE\MFCSOCK\MFCSODLG.CPP:

```
void CMfcsockDlg::DoStandardSynchronous()
{
   SOCKET      sCall = INVALID_SOCKET;
   CString     szMessage;
   int         nTotalReceived, nReceived, nBytes;
   BYTE        szBuffer[32768];
   DWORD       dwStartTime, dwEndTime;
   UINT        i;
   DWORD       dwBytesTransmitted;
   DWORD      *lpCounterStart;
   DWORD      *lpCounterStop;
   DWORD       dwCounterDelta;
   CSystemTime SystemTime[2];
   CLargeInt   SampleTime[2];
   DWORD       dwInstances;

   sCall = socket(AF_INET, SOCK_STREAM, 0);
```

```
if (sCall == INVALID_SOCKET)
    {
    szMessage.Format(TEXT("socket() failed, WSAGetLastError() = %d"),
        WSAGetLastError());
    AfxMessageBox(szMessage);
    return;
    }

if (!GetHostAddress(m_szTargetServer, "echo", "tcp"))
    {
    szMessage.Format(TEXT("Address query failed, WSAGetLastError() =
        %d"),
        WSAGetLastError());
    ::closesocket(sCall);
    AfxMessageBox(szMessage);
    return;
    }

if (::connect(sCall, (LPSOCKADDR) &m_sin, sizeof (SOCKADDR_IN)) != 0)
    {
    szMessage.Format(TEXT("connect failed, WSAGetLastError() = %d"),
        WSAGetLastError());
    ::closesocket(sCall);
    AfxMessageBox(szMessage);
    return;
    }
nBytes = ::send(sCall, (LPCSTR) szBuffer, 100, 0);

for (nTotalReceived = nReceived = 0;
      nBytes != SOCKET_ERROR &&
      nTotalReceived < nBytes;
     )
    {
    nReceived = ::recv(sCall, (LPSTR) szBuffer, nBytes, 0);
    if (nReceived != SOCKET_ERROR)
        nTotalReceived += nReceived;
    }

GetPerformanceCounterData(NETWORK_INTERFACE,
    BYTES_TOTAL_PER_SEC,
    (LPBYTE *) &lpCounterStart, SystemTime[0],
    SampleTime[0]);

for (i = 0, dwStartTime = ::GetCurrentTime();
      i < m_nNumPackets; ++i)
    {
    if ((nBytes = ::send(sCall, (LPCSTR) szBuffer, m_nPacketSize, 0))
            != SOCKET_ERROR)
```

```
            {
            for (nReceived = 0, nTotalReceived = 0;
                  nTotalReceived < nBytes; )
               {
               if ((nReceived = ::recv(sCall, (LPSTR) szBuffer, nBytes, 0))
                     == SOCKET_ERROR)
                  break;
               nTotalReceived += nReceived;
               }
            dwBytesTransmitted += (DWORD) nTotalReceived;
            }
         }
   dwEndTime = GetCurrentTime();

   dwInstances =
      GetPerformanceCounterData(NETWORK_INTERFACE,
         BYTES_TOTAL_PER_SEC,
         (LPBYTE *) &lpCounterStop, SystemTime[1],
         SampleTime[1]);

   RegCloseKey(HKEY_PERFORMANCE_DATA);

   ::closesocket(sCall);

   double dMilliSeconds;
   LARGE_INTEGER PerformanceFrequency;

   if (QueryPerformanceFrequency(&PerformanceFrequency))
      dMilliSeconds =
         ((double) (((DWORD) SampleTime[1]) -
                    ((DWORD) SampleTime[0]))) /
         ((double) (PerformanceFrequency.LowPart))
         * 1000.0;
   else
      dMilliSeconds = SystemTime[1] - SystemTime[0];

   for (DWORD j = 0; j < dwInstances; ++j)
      {
      dwCounterDelta = lpCounterStop[j] -
                       lpCounterStart[j];

      if (dwCounterDelta != 0)
         break;

      }
   DisplayResults(dwStartTime, dwEndTime, dMilliSeconds,
      dwCounterDelta,
      (((double) dwCounterDelta) * 1000.0) / dMilliSeconds);
```

```
    ::HeapFree(::GetProcessHeap(), 0, lpCounterStart);
    ::HeapFree(::GetProcessHeap(), 0, lpCounterStop);
}
```

Figure 16-3 shows the dialog box for the packet size yielding the fastest transfer rate. All numbers here are two-way; we transmitted 6,553,600 bytes because we sent 3,267,800 and got that many back.

In the Performance Statistics group box, the numbers in parentheses are those generated by Performance Monitoring. We want to see a consistently close correspondence here, and indeed we do. We expect the number of milliseconds to be greater than what we compute, because we call GetPerformanceCounterData() first and last. The number of bytes transmitted should NEVER be less than what we report; if it is, there's a bug in our code.

TCP/IP is a well-behaved protocol; it performs better and better as packets grow in size. At a packet size of 1K, I get a byte-transfer rate of around

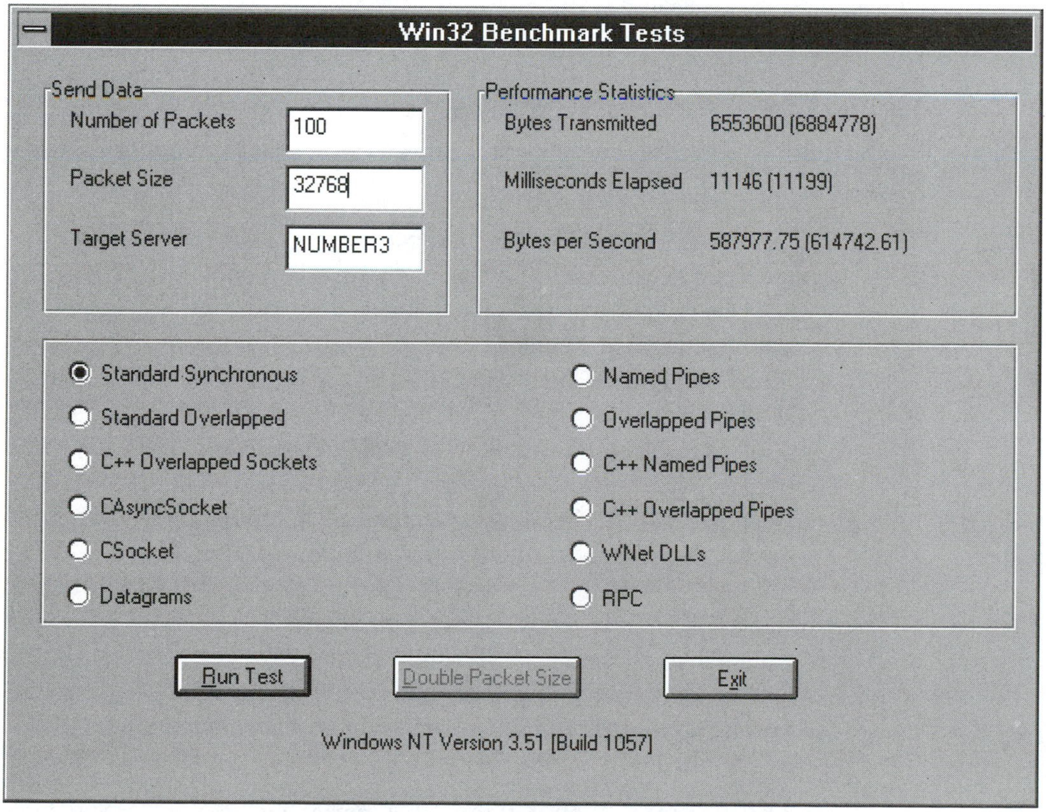

Figure 16-3. Benchmark Results for Standard Synchronous Sockets

260K. By the time we get to 32K packets, our transfer rate is 588K. For each increase in the packet size, the transfer rate increases.

Overlapped Sockets. Microsoft claims that the fastest way to do Sockets is using overlapped I/O. As we'll see, their claims are valid. The routine that does this test is DoStandardOverlapped(). It is based on a version of this test sent to me by David Treadwell of Microsoft. I am greatly indebted to him for showing me how to do this.

DoStandardOverlapped() uses standard overlapped techniques, with manual-reset events. The logic of the timing loop is:

1. Get the Performance Monitoring snapshot and the current time.
2. Call setsockopt() to disable send buffering (by setting the send buffer size to 0). Similarly, make the incoming buffer large (65,000 bytes) so it can cache a fair amount of data.
3. Spin off two overlapped ReadFile() calls. We do ReadFile() first so buffer space is already available when we do the first transmission. That way, we can start receiving data as soon as the server is ready to send it to us.
4. Issue two overlapped WriteFile()s.

From this point on, everything is done in response to WaitForMultipleObjects().

5. If WaitForMultipleObjects() indicates that a ReadFile() has completed, add the number of bytes read to the total number received. If it equals the packet size times the number of packets, we're done. Otherwise, issue another ReadFile().
6. If WaitForMultipleObjects() tells us that a WriteFile() is completing, add the number of bytes written to the total sent. If it equals the packet size times the number of packets—MINUS THE SIZE OF ONE PACKET—we reset the event and go to the top of the loop. Otherwise, we call WriteFile() once more. The reason why the check must be for bytes transmitted so far equal to ((packet size) * (number of packets – 1)) is this: we have two asynchronous write operations in progress. If we just check for bytes transmitted equal to ((packet size) * (number of packets)), we'll send too many packets. The reason for resetting the event is to prevent WaitForMultipleObjects() from ever reporting this operation again. As soon as the other one completes, we'll be finished.

Here is the listing. I omit things that are the same as DoStandardSynchronous().

```
void CMfcsockDlg::DoStandardOverlapped()
{
   SOCKET      sCall = INVALID_SOCKET;
   CString     szMessage;
   int         nTotalReceived, nReceived, nBytes;
   char szBuffer[4][32768];
   DWORD       dwStartTime, dwEndTime;
   UINT        i;
   DWORD       dwBytesTransmitted, dwBytesReceived;
   HANDLE      hEvents[4];
   OVERLAPPED  ov[4];
   DWORD       dwTotalBytes;
   DWORD       dwIoBytes;
   BOOL        bSuccess;
   DWORD      *lpCounterStart;
   DWORD      *lpCounterStop;
   DWORD       dwCounterDelta;
   CSystemTime SystemTime[2];
   CLargeInt   SampleTime[2];
   DWORD       dwInstances;

   sCall = socket(AF_INET, SOCK_STREAM, 0);

   // [Make sure sCall is valid]

   // Create events to use for standard overlapped I/O
   // Put them into OVERLAPPED structures
   for ( i = 0; i < 4; i++ )
      {
      hEvents[i] = ::CreateEvent( NULL, TRUE, FALSE, NULL );
      if ( hEvents[i] == NULL )
         {
         szMessage.Format(
            TEXT("CreateEvent() failed, GetLastError() = %d"),
               ::GetLastError());
         ::closesocket(sCall);
         AfxMessageBox(szMessage);
         return;
         }
      ov[i].Internal = 0;
      ov[i].InternalHigh = 0;
      ov[i].Offset = 0;
      ov[i].OffsetHigh = 0;
      ov[i].hEvent = hEvents[i];
      }

   if (!GetHostAddress(m_szTargetServer, "echo", "tcp"))
```

```
    {
    szMessage.Format(
       TEXT("Address query failed, WSAGetLastError() = %d"),
          WSAGetLastError());
    ::closesocket(sCall);
    AfxMessageBox(szMessage);
    return;
    }

if (::connect(sCall, (LPSOCKADDR) &m_sin, sizeof (SOCKADDR_IN)) != 0)
    {
    szMessage.Format(TEXT("connect failed, WSAGetLastError() = %d"),
       WSAGetLastError());
    ::closesocket(sCall);
    AfxMessageBox(szMessage);
    return;
    }

// [Send dummy packet, wait for it to come back]

// Disable buffering on the send side by setting
// the send buffer size to zero
i = 0;
if (::setsockopt(sCall, SOL_SOCKET, SO_SNDBUF, (LPSTR) &i, sizeof (i))
    == SOCKET_ERROR)
    {
    szMessage.Format(
       TEXT("::setsockopt(SO_SNDBUF) failed, WSAGetLastError() = %d"),
          WSAGetLastError());
    ::closesocket(sCall);
    AfxMessageBox(szMessage);
    return;
    }

// Configure socket to cache 65,000 bytes
// of incoming data
i = 65000;
if (::setsockopt(sCall, SOL_SOCKET, SO_RCVBUF, (LPSTR) &i, sizeof (i))
   == SOCKET_ERROR)
    {
    szMessage.Format(
       TEXT("::setsockopt(SO_RCVBUF) failed, WSAGetLastError() = %d"),
          WSAGetLastError());
    ::closesocket(sCall);
    AfxMessageBox(szMessage);
    return;
    }

dwTotalBytes = (DWORD) (m_nNumPackets * m_nPacketSize);
```

```
// [Call GetPerformanceCounterData() to get
//  starting Performance Monitoring snapshot]

dwStartTime = GetCurrentTime();

// Spin off overlapped operations
// Do reads first so we have buffer space available
// to receive answers from the server
::ReadFile((HANDLE)sCall, szBuffer[RECV_1], m_nPacketSize,
           &dwIoBytes, &ov[RECV_1]);
::ReadFile((HANDLE)sCall, szBuffer[RECV_2], m_nPacketSize,
           &dwIoBytes, &ov[RECV_2]);

::WriteFile((HANDLE)sCall, szBuffer[SEND_1], m_nPacketSize,
            &dwIoBytes, &ov[SEND_1]);
::WriteFile((HANDLE)sCall, szBuffer[SEND_2], m_nPacketSize,
            &dwIoBytes, &ov[SEND_2]);
dwBytesTransmitted = dwBytesReceived = 0;
while ( TRUE )
   {
   // Wait for an I/O call to complete.

   i = ::WaitForMultipleObjects( 4, hEvents, FALSE, INFINITE );

   if (i >= 4)
      {
      szMessage.Format(
         TEXT("::WaitForMultipleObjects() failed, GetLastError() =
          %d"),
           GetLastError());
      ::closesocket(sCall);
      AfxMessageBox(szMessage);
      return;
      }

   bSuccess = GetOverlappedResult((HANDLE)sCall, &ov[i], &dwIoBytes,
              FALSE);
   if (!bSuccess)
      {
      szMessage.Format(
         TEXT("WriteFile/ReadFile[%d] failed, WSAGetLastError() =
          %d"),
           i, GetLastError());
      ::closesocket(sCall);
      AfxMessageBox(szMessage);
      return;
      }
```

```
// Is a read completing?
if ( i == RECV_1 || i == RECV_2 )
   {
   // Yes--add byte count to total received
   dwBytesReceived += dwIoBytes;

   // If byte count exceeds or equals packet size
   // times number of packets, terminate the loop
   if ((dwBytesReceived >= dwTotalBytes) )
      {
      break;
      }

   // Theoretically, we shouldn't have to call
   // ResetEvent() here.  Docs say that event
   // is automatically reset when operation returns.
   // However, it appears that Windows 95 forgets
   // to do this.
   ::ResetEvent(hEvents[i]);

   // Recycle the operation
   bSuccess = ::ReadFile((HANDLE)sCall, szBuffer[i], m_nPacketSize,
                         &dwIoBytes, &ov[i]);

   // If operation completes synchronously, make sure
   // the event is in the signalled state.
   // We'll go back to the top of the loop, and
   // WaitForMultipleObjects() will immediately wake up.
   if (bSuccess)
      ::SetEvent(hEvents[i]);

   if ((bSuccess && dwIoBytes == 0) ||
       (!bSuccess && (::GetLastError() != ERROR_IO_PENDING)))
      {
      // Operation failed, we're outa here
      break;
      }
   }
else if (i == SEND_1 || i == SEND_2)
   {
   // Write completed, add number of bytes to
   // total written
   dwBytesTransmitted += dwIoBytes;

   // Check for termination is a little different here
   // Because we're overlapping two operations, we want
   // to stop sending when the total written equals
```

```
        // the packet size times the number of packets,
        // minus the size of one packet.
        // If we just compare dwBytesTransmitted to dwTotalBytes,
        // we send too many packets
        if ( dwBytesTransmitted >= (dwTotalBytes - m_nPacketSize))
           {
           // Resetting the event is important here.
           // We don't submit a new operation, so
           // once we reset the event, there's no
           // way it can ever signal. Therefore,
           // it won't cause WaitForMultipleObjects()
           // to wake up again, and we won't hear from it any more.
           ::ResetEvent( hEvents[i] );
           continue;
           }
        // Here, we reset the event just to help out Windows 95--
        // because it's so good-looking
        ::ResetEvent(hEvents[i]);
        bSuccess = ::WriteFile((HANDLE)sCall, szBuffer[i],
        m_nPacketSize,
                                       &dwIoBytes, &ov[i]);
        if (bSuccess)
           ::SetEvent(hEvents[i]);
        if ((bSuccess && dwIoBytes == 0) ||
            (!bSuccess && (::GetLastError() != ERROR_IO_PENDING)))
           {
           ::ResetEvent( hEvents[i] );
           continue;
           }
        }
     }
  dwEndTime = GetCurrentTime();

  // [Capture second Performance Monitoring snapshot]
  RegCloseKey(HKEY_PERFORMANCE_DATA);

  ::closesocket(sCall);

  // [Do arithmetic]
  DisplayResults(dwStartTime, dwEndTime, dMilliSeconds,
     dwCounterDelta,
     (((double) dwCounterDelta) * 1000.0) / dMilliSeconds);

  ::HeapFree(::GetProcessHeap(), 0, lpCounterStart);
  ::HeapFree(::GetProcessHeap(), 0, lpCounterStop);
}
```

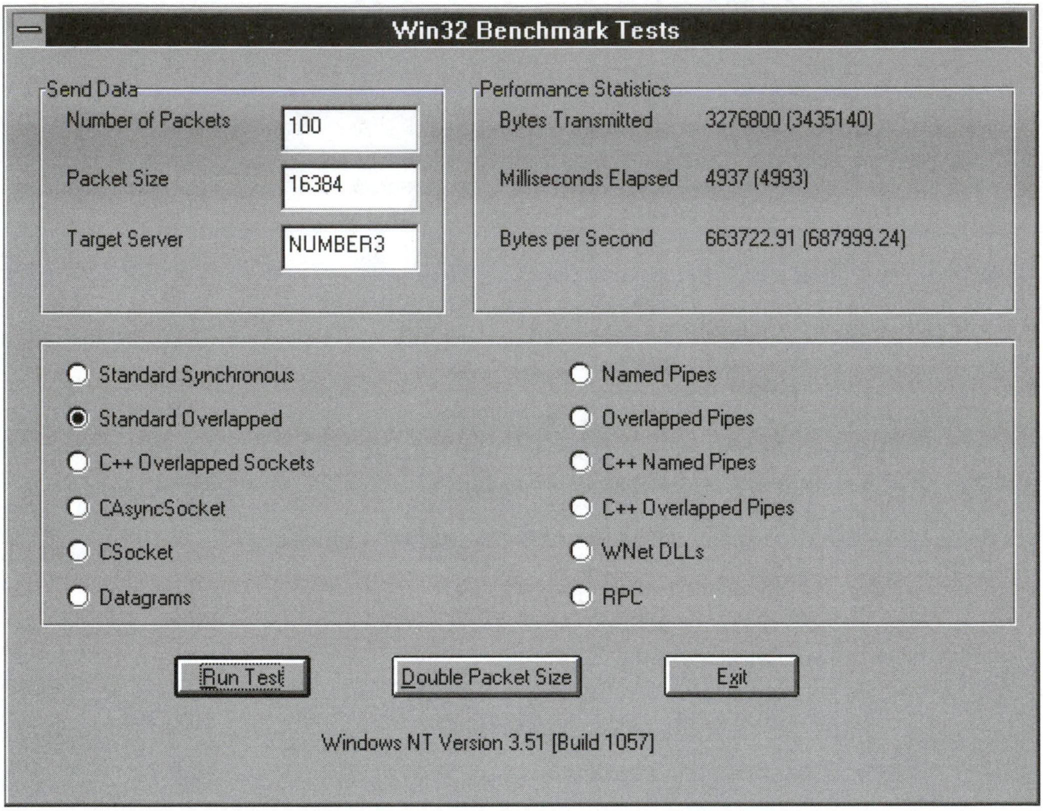

Figure 16-4. Benchmark Results for Standard Overlapped Sockets

Figure 16-4 shows the screen for the fastest time reported, 663K at a packet size of 16K. That is about 80K faster than with blocking Berkeley calls. No other mechanism will equal this transfer rate.

A couple of comments: yes, overlapped I/O is the fastest way to transmit data over Windows Sockets. But the code, as you can see, is a lot more complex. Is the complexity worth the faster transfer rate?

Second, I have not observed any improvement in performance from using overlapped I/O on the server side. I have no idea how the *echo* server is implemented. But I have experimented with my own servers and found that it is the client's use of overlapped I/O that causes the transfer rate to go up. I asked Dave Treadwell at Microsoft about this, and his interpretation makes sense—the client is the limiting factor in the speed of the exchange. Making the client faster and smarter, therefore, gives us the performance boost we're looking for.

Windows Sockets 2. Because Windows Sockets 2 makes overlapped sockets part of the standard, I have translated DoStandardOverlapped() so it uses the appropriate Sockets 2 functions. Many of the translations—those having to do with overlapped I/O—are optional. The native Win32 calls and data types work just fine once you have used WSASocket() to open a socket for overlapped I/O. The Sockets wrappers are provided for portability to the Win16 environment, not something I care very much about. Thus:

- Events change from HANDLEs to WSAEVENTs (optional).
- Buffer pointers are passed as an array of WSABUF structures (required by WSASend() and WSARecv(), though the use of these functions is optional).
- The OVERLAPPED structure becomes a WSAOVERLAPPED structure (optional).
- socket() becomes WSASocket().
- The FILE_FLAG_OVERLAPPED bit is passed to WSASocket() as WSA_FLAG_OVERLAPPED (optional; WSA_FLAG_OVERLAPPED is defined as FILE_FLAG_OVERLAPPED).
- CreateEvent() is replaced by WSACreateEvent() (optional).
- connect() becomes WSAConnect() (optional; but only WSAConnect() can piggyback data onto the connection request).
- WriteFile() turns into WSASend(), and ReadFile() into WSARecv() (optional).
- WaitForMultipleObjects() becomes WSAWaitForMultipleEvents() (optional).
- GetOverlappedResult() should become WSAGetOverlappedResult(), but in the beta version of NT 4.0 that I tested it with (build number 1234), WSAGetOverlappedResult() threw an undocumented exception (0xC0000264). GetOverlappedResult() worked just fine. (Even if WSAGetOverlappedResult() worked, this would be an optional translation.)
- ResetEvent() is replaced by WSAResetEvent(), and SetEvent() by WSASetEvent() (optional).
- CloseHandle() becomes WSACloseEvent() (optional).

Here is the Sockets 2 version of DoStandardOverlapped(). To avoid having to load function pointers (which makes for ugly code), I use a compile switch and a different Visual C++ project to create the binary image for Sockets 2.

```
void CMfcsockDlg::DoStandardOverlapped()
{
   SOCKET          sCall = INVALID_SOCKET;
   CString         szMessage;
   DWORD           dwTotalReceived, dwReceived, dwBytes;
   int             nError;
   char            szBuffer[4][32768];
   WSABUF          WSABuffer[4];
   DWORD           dwStartTime, dwEndTime;
   UINT            i;
   DWORD           dwBytesTransmitted, dwBytesReceived;
   WSAEVENT        hEvents[4];
   WSAOVERLAPPED ov[4];
   DWORD           dwTotalBytes;
   DWORD           dwIoBytes;
   DWORD           dwWSAFlags = 0;
   BOOL            bSuccess;
   DWORD          *lpCounterStart;
   DWORD          *lpCounterStop;
   DWORD           dwCounterDelta;
   CSystemTime     SystemTime[2];
   CLargeInt       SampleTime[2];
   DWORD           dwInstances;

   sCall = ::WSASocket(AF_INET, SOCK_STREAM, 0, NULL, 0,
      WSA_FLAG_OVERLAPPED);

   if (sCall == INVALID_SOCKET)
      {
      szMessage.Format(TEXT("WSAsocket() failed, "
                            "WSAGetLastError() = %d"),
         ::WSAGetLastError());
      AfxMessageBox(szMessage);
      return;
      }

   // Create events to use for standard overlapped I/O
   // Put them into WSAOVERLAPPED structures
   for ( i = 0; i < 4; i++ )
      {
      WSABuffer[i].len = m_nPacketSize;
      WSABuffer[i].buf = szBuffer[i];

      hEvents[i] = ::WSACreateEvent();
      if ( hEvents[i] == NULL )
         {
         szMessage.Format(TEXT("WSACreateEvent() failed, "
                               "WSAGetLastError() = %d"),
```

```
            ::WSAGetLastError());
         ::closesocket(sCall);
         AfxMessageBox(szMessage);
         return;
         }
      ov[i].Internal = 0;
      ov[i].InternalHigh = 0;
      ov[i].Offset = 0;
      ov[i].OffsetHigh = 0;
      ov[i].hEvent = hEvents[i];
      }

   if (!GetHostAddress(m_szTargetServer, "echo", "tcp"))
      {
      szMessage.Format(TEXT("Address query failed, "
                            "WSAGetLastError() = %d"),
         ::WSAGetLastError());
      ::closesocket(sCall);
      AfxMessageBox(szMessage);
      return;
      }

   if (::WSAConnect(sCall,
                    (LPSOCKADDR) &m_sin,
                    sizeof (SOCKADDR_IN),
                    NULL,
                    NULL,
                    NULL,
                    NULL) != 0)
      {
      szMessage.Format(TEXT("WSAConnect() failed, "
                            "WSAGetLastError() = %d"),
         ::WSAGetLastError());
      ::closesocket(sCall);
      AfxMessageBox(szMessage);
      return;
      }

   // Send non-overlapped dummy packet
   WSABuffer[0].len = 100;
   nError = ::WSASend(sCall, &WSABuffer[0], 1, &dwBytes,
        0, NULL, NULL);

   if (nError != 0)
      {
      szMessage.Format(TEXT("WSASend() of dummy packet failed, "
                            "error = %d"), nError);
      ::closesocket(sCall);
```

```
        AfxMessageBox(szMessage);
        return;
        }

    for (dwTotalReceived = dwReceived = 0;
          dwTotalReceived < dwBytes;
         )
        {
        nError = ::WSARecv(sCall, &WSABuffer[0], 1, &dwReceived,
              &dwWSAFlags, NULL, NULL);
        if (nError != 0)
           {
           szMessage.Format(TEXT("WSARecv() of dummy packet failed, "
                                 "WSAGetLastError() = %d"),
              ::WSAGetLastError());
           ::closesocket(sCall);
           AfxMessageBox(szMessage);
           return;
           }
        dwTotalReceived += dwReceived;
        }

    WSABuffer[0].len = m_nPacketSize;

    // Disable buffering on the send side by setting
    // the send buffer size to zero
    i = 0;
    if (::setsockopt(sCall, SOL_SOCKET, SO_SNDBUF,
         (LPSTR) &i, sizeof (i))
        == SOCKET_ERROR)
        {
        szMessage.Format(TEXT("::setsockopt(SO_SNDBUF) failed, "
                              "WSAGetLastError() = %d"),
           ::WSAGetLastError());
        ::closesocket(sCall);
        AfxMessageBox(szMessage);
        return;
        }

    // Configure socket to cache 65,000 bytes
    // of incoming data
    i = max(65000, 2 * m_nPacketSize);

    if (::setsockopt(sCall, SOL_SOCKET, SO_RCVBUF,
         (LPSTR) &i, sizeof (i))
       == SOCKET_ERROR)
```

```
   {
   szMessage.Format(TEXT("::setsockopt(SO_RCVBUF) failed, "
                          "WSAGetLastError() = %d"),
      ::WSAGetLastError());
   ::closesocket(sCall);
   AfxMessageBox(szMessage);
   return;
   }

dwTotalBytes = (DWORD) (m_nNumPackets * m_nPacketSize);

GetPerformanceCounterData(NETWORK_INTERFACE,
   BYTES_TOTAL_PER_SEC,
   (LPBYTE *) &lpCounterStart, SystemTime[0],
   SampleTime[0]);

dwStartTime = GetCurrentTime();

// Spin off overlapped operations
// Do reads first so we have buffer space available
// to receive answers from the server
::WSARecv(sCall, &WSABuffer[RECV_1], 1,
          &dwIoBytes, &dwWSAFlags, &ov[RECV_1], NULL);

::WSARecv(sCall, &WSABuffer[RECV_2], 1,
          &dwIoBytes, &dwWSAFlags, &ov[RECV_2], NULL);

::WSASend(sCall, &WSABuffer[SEND_1], 1,
          &dwIoBytes, 0, &ov[SEND_1], NULL);

::WSASend(sCall, &WSABuffer[SEND_2], 1,
          &dwIoBytes, 0, &ov[SEND_2], NULL);

dwBytesTransmitted = dwBytesReceived = 0;
while ( TRUE )
   {
   // Wait for an I/O call to complete.

   i = ::WSAWaitForMultipleEvents(4, hEvents, FALSE, INFINITE,
           FALSE);

   if (i >= 4)
      {
      szMessage.Format(
         TEXT("::WSAWaitForMultipleEvents() failed, "
              "WSAGetLastError() = %d"),
         ::WSAGetLastError());
      ::closesocket(sCall);
```

```
    AfxMessageBox(szMessage);
    return;
    }

// In beta build 1234 of NT 4.0,
// WSAGetOverlappedResult() provokes exception
// 0xC0000264 (undocumented)
// GetOverlappedResult() works just fine
bSuccess = ::GetOverlappedResult((HANDLE) sCall, &ov[i],
                &dwIoBytes, FALSE);
if (!bSuccess)
    {
    szMessage.Format(TEXT("WSASend/WSARecv[%d] failed, "
                          "WSAGetLastError() = %d"),
        i, ::WSAGetLastError());
    ::closesocket(sCall);
    AfxMessageBox(szMessage);
    return;
    }

// Is a read completing?
if ( i == RECV_1 || i == RECV_2 )
    {
    // Yes--add byte count to total received
    dwBytesReceived += dwIoBytes;

    // If byte count exceeds or equals packet size
    // times number of packets, terminate the loop
    if ((dwBytesReceived >= dwTotalBytes) )
        {
        break;
        }

    // Theoretically, we shouldn't have to call
    // WSAResetEvent() here.  Docs say that event
    // is automatically reset when operation returns.
    // However, it appears that Windows 95 forgets
    // to do this.
    ::WSAResetEvent(hEvents[i]);

    // WSARecv() returns 0 if it completes synchronously
    // SOCKET_ERROR (-1) otherwise
    // Bump return value by 1 to convert to boolean
    bSuccess = ::WSARecv(sCall, &WSABuffer[i], 1,
                 &dwIoBytes, &dwWSAFlags, &ov[i], NULL) + 1;

    // If operation completes synchronously, make sure
    // the event is in the signalled state.
```

```
        // We'll go back to the top of the loop, and
        // WSAWaitForMultipleEvents() will immediately wake up.
        if (bSuccess)
            ::WSASetEvent(hEvents[i]);

        if ((bSuccess && dwIoBytes == 0) ||
             (!bSuccess && (::WSAGetLastError() != WSA_IO_PENDING)))
            {
            // Operation failed, we're outa here
            break;
            }
        }
    else if (i == SEND_1 || i == SEND_2)
        {
        // Write completed, add number of bytes to
        // total written
        dwBytesTransmitted += dwIoBytes;

        // Check for termination is a little different here
        // Because we're overlapping two operations, we want
        // to stop sending when the total written equals
        // the packet size times the number of packets,
        // minus the size of one packet.
        // If we just compare dwBytesTransmitted to dwTotalBytes,
        // we send too many packets
        if ( dwBytesTransmitted >= (dwTotalBytes - m_nPacketSize))
            {
            // Resetting the event is important here.
            // We don't submit a new operation, so
            // once we reset the event, there's no
            // way it can ever signal. Therefore,
            // it won't cause WaitForMultipleObjects()
            // to wake up again, and we won't hear from it any more.
            ::WSAResetEvent(hEvents[i]);
            continue;
            }

        // Here, we reset the event just to help out Windows 95--
        // because it's so good-looking
        ::WSAResetEvent(hEvents[i]);
        bSuccess = ::WSASend(sCall, &WSABuffer[i], 1,
                      &dwIoBytes, 0, &ov[i], NULL) + 1;
        if (bSuccess)
            ::WSASetEvent(hEvents[i]);
        if ((bSuccess && dwIoBytes == 0) ||
             (!bSuccess && (::WSAGetLastError() != WSA_IO_PENDING)))
            {
            ::WSAResetEvent( hEvents[i] );
```

```
            continue;
            }
         }
      }
   dwEndTime = GetCurrentTime();

   dwInstances =
      GetPerformanceCounterData(NETWORK_INTERFACE,
         BYTES_TOTAL_PER_SEC,
         (LPBYTE *) &lpCounterStop, SystemTime[1],
         SampleTime[1]);

   RegCloseKey(HKEY_PERFORMANCE_DATA);

   ::closesocket(sCall);

   // Close event handles
   for (i = 0; i < 4; ++i)
      {
      ::WSACloseEvent(hEvents[i]);
      }

   double dMilliSeconds;
   LARGE_INTEGER PerformanceFrequency;

   // [Do arithmetic]
   DisplayResults(dwStartTime, dwEndTime, dMilliSeconds,
      dwCounterDelta,
      (((double) dwCounterDelta) * 1000.0) / dMilliSeconds);

   ::HeapFree(::GetProcessHeap(), 0, lpCounterStart);
   ::HeapFree(::GetProcessHeap(), 0, lpCounterStop);
}
```

Using CAsyncSocket. The MFC CAsyncSocket class provides a thin wrapper over the Sockets API. To test it, I override its asynchronous behavior to force it to behave like a standard blocking socket. The difference between this test and DoStandardSynchronous() is the use of CAsyncSocket methods instead of direct Windows Sockets function calls.

Here is a stripped-down listing of the function (DoCAsyncSocket()), showing where the CAsyncSocket method calls replace Sockets functions.

```
void CMfcsockDlg::DoCAsyncSocket()
{
   CAsyncSocket sCall;
   CString      szMessage;
   int          nTotalReceived, nReceived, nBytes;
```

```
BYTE         szBuffer[32768];
DWORD        dwStartTime, dwEndTime;
UINT         i;
DWORD        dwBytesTransmitted;
DWORD       *lpCounterStart;
DWORD       *lpCounterStop;
DWORD        dwCounterDelta;
CSystemTime SystemTime[2];
CLargeInt   SampleTime[2];
DWORD        dwInstances;

// Create socket with no notifications
if (!sCall.Create(0, SOCK_STREAM, 0))
   {
   szMessage.Format(TEXT("CAsyncSocket::Create() failed,
      WSAGetLastError() = %d"),
      sCall.GetLastError());
   AfxMessageBox(szMessage);
   return;
   }

DWORD dwBlockingIO = FALSE;
sCall.IOCtl(FIONBIO, &dwBlockingIO); // Set not-non-blocking I/O

// [Call GetHostAddress() to get server's addressing information]
if (!sCall.Connect((const SOCKADDR *) &m_sin, sizeof (SOCKADDR_IN)))
   {
   szMessage.Format(TEXT("CAsyncSocket::Connect() failed,
      WSAGetLastError() = %d"),
      sCall.GetLastError());
   AfxMessageBox(szMessage);
   sCall.Close();
   return;
   }

// [Send and receive dummy packet]
// [Get first Performance Monitoring snapshot]

for (i = 0, dwStartTime = ::GetCurrentTime();
     i < m_nNumPackets; ++i)
   {
   if ((nBytes = sCall.Send((const void *) szBuffer, m_nPacketSize))
        != SOCKET_ERROR)
      {
      for (nReceived = 0, nTotalReceived = 0;
           nTotalReceived < nBytes; )
```

```
                {
                if ((nReceived = sCall.Receive((LPVOID) szBuffer, nBytes))
                    == SOCKET_ERROR)
                    break;
                    nTotalReceived += nReceived;
                }
            dwBytesTransmitted += (DWORD) nTotalReceived;
            }
        }
    dwEndTime = GetCurrentTime();

    // [Get second Performance Monitoring snapshot]
    sCall.Close();

    // [Do arithmetic]
    DisplayResults(dwStartTime, dwEndTime, dMilliSeconds,
        dwCounterDelta,
        (((double) dwCounterDelta) * 1000.0) / dMilliSeconds);

    ::HeapFree(::GetProcessHeap(), 0, lpCounterStart);
    ::HeapFree(::GetProcessHeap(), 0, lpCounterStop);
}
```

Figure 16-5 shows the fastest transfer rate for CAsyncSocket.

It's faster than the results shown in Figure 16-3 for standard blocking Berkeley calls! However, the difference (3K) is not statistically significant. The conclusion is not that CAsyncSocket is faster than standard Berkeley; rather, it is that there is no appreciable difference between the two. This may seem surprising at first blush, but it makes sense. CAsyncSocket is a thin wrapper, especially for client-side operations. Many of its methods are implemented as inline calls to the corresponding Sockets functions. The two methods that affect the transfer rate are CAsyncSocket::Send() and CAsyncSocket::Receive(). In MFC 4.0, these are not inline calls, but they do nothing—*nothing*—but call send() and recv(). Since I coerced the socket into blocking mode by calling CAsyncSocket::IOCtl(), I'm really just doing standard synchronous sockets.

What we can conclude is that you can use CAsyncSocket and the Sockets API interchangeably, for blocking client-side operations. Where CAsyncSocket diverges from the direct use of the Sockets API is on the server side. That is where its asynchronous behavior becomes important.

Using CSocket. As we saw in Chapter 9, CSocket virtualizes a synchronous interface by calling the corresponding CAsyncSocket method, then pumping messages until it gets the message indicating that the call has completed. With

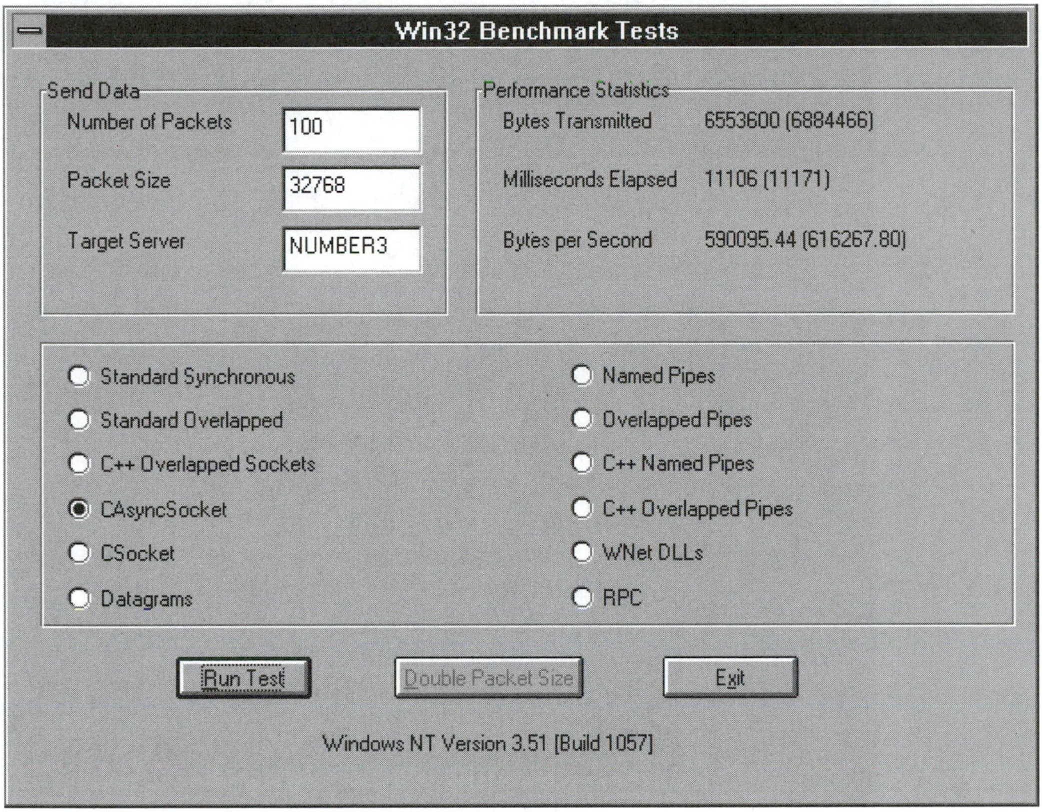

Figure 16-5. Benchmark Results for CAsyncSocket

this level of overhead, you would expect a deterioration in performance, and indeed you get one. The differences in the code are minor, so I will not display the listing of DoCSocket(). Instead of declaring *sCall* as a CAsyncSocket object, you make it a CSocket.

Figure 16-6 shows the fastest transfer rate achieved by CSocket—537K at a packet size of 16K. This is quite comparable to CAsyncSocket. At other packet sizes, CSocket is also pretty respectable, but its behavior is somewhat more erratic, showing peaks and valleys rather than linear improvement. At 32K, its performance degrades completely, falling to around 80K per second.

Overlapped I/O with the COverlappedSocket Class. In Chapter 9, I presented two classes to encapsulate both the Sockets API and the Service Registration API, COverlappedSocket and CServiceInfo. The DoCPPOverlapped() method implements the same logic as DoStandardOverlapped(), but uses my classes instead.

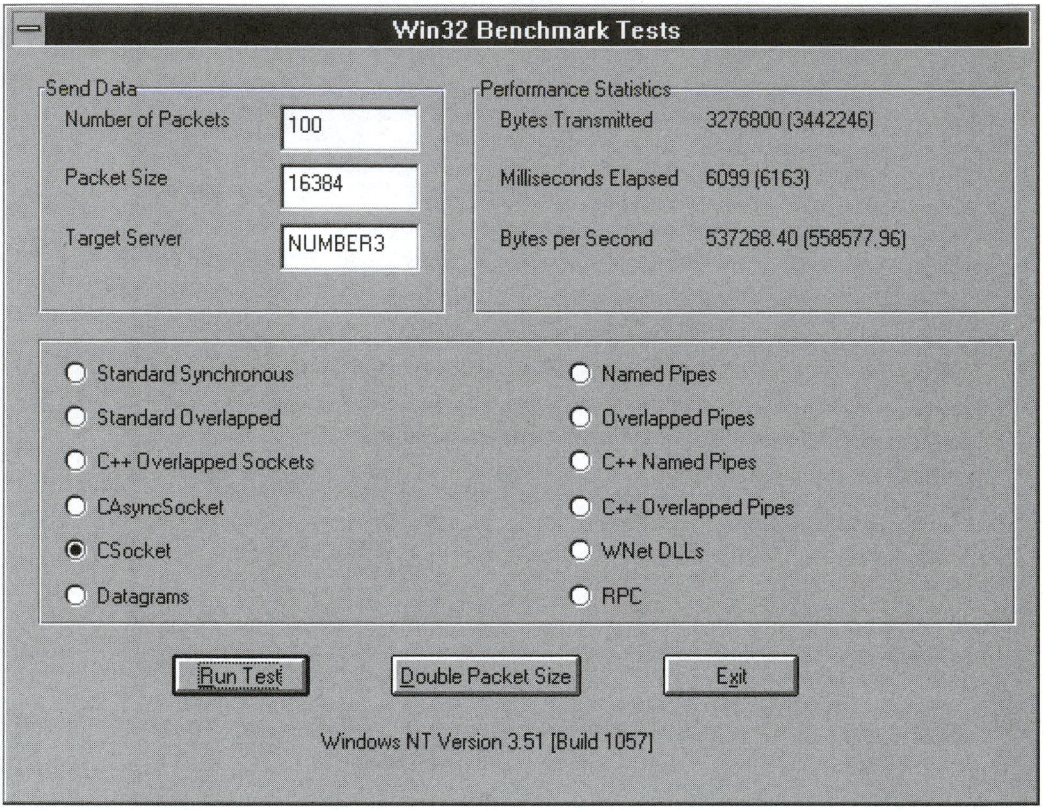

Win32 Benchmark Tests

Send Data
Number of Packets 100
Packet Size 16384
Target Server NUMBER3

Performance Statistics
Bytes Transmitted 3276800 (3442246)
Milliseconds Elapsed 6099 (6163)
Bytes per Second 537268.40 (558577.96)

Standard Synchronous
Standard Overlapped
C++ Overlapped Sockets
CAsyncSocket
CSocket
Datagrams
Named Pipes
Overlapped Pipes
C++ Named Pipes
C++ Overlapped Pipes
WNet DLLs
RPC

Run Test | Double Packet Size | Exit

Windows NT Version 3.51 (Build 1057)

Figure 16-6. Benchmark Results for CSocket

Now, we can connect to the *echo* server using its GUID, defined in SVCGUID.H as SVCID_ECHO_TCP. We don't have to call GetHost-Address(); the CServiceInfo::Connect() method takes care of all address resolution. The rest of the code is further simplified by the use of my COverlapped class, presented in Chapter 6. The sockets calls look very much like DoCAsyncSocket(); COverlappedSocket() uses its methods through its embedded *m_AsyncSocket* member.

Here is the code, including the excerpts that highlight this approach:

```
void CMfcsockDlg::DoCPPOverlapped()
{
   CString     szMessage;
   int         nTotalReceived, nReceived, nBytes;
   char szBuffer[4][32768];
   DWORD       dwStartTime, dwEndTime;
   UINT        i;
```

```
DWORD        dwBytesTransmitted, dwBytesReceived;
COverlapped ov[4];
DWORD        dwTotalBytes;
DWORD        dwIoBytes;
BOOL         bSuccess;
static GUID EchoGuid = SVCID_ECHO_TCP;
CServiceInfo MyService;
DWORD         dwLastError;
DWORD       *lpCounterStart;
DWORD       *lpCounterStop;
DWORD        dwCounterDelta;
CSystemTime SystemTime[2];
CLargeInt    SampleTime[2];
DWORD        dwInstances;

COverlappedSocket *lpSocket =
   MyService.Connect(&EchoGuid, (LPTSTR) (const char *)m_szTargetServer);

if (lpSocket == NULL)
   {
   szMessage.Format(TEXT("socket() failed, WSAGetLastError() = %d"),
                    ::GetLastError());
   AfxMessageBox(szMessage);
   return;
   }

HANDLE hEvent[4];
for ( i = 0; i < 4; i++ )
   {
   hEvent[i] = ::CreateEvent(NULL, TRUE, FALSE, NULL);
   ov[i].SetEventHandle(hEvent[i]);
   }

// [Send and receive dummy packet]
i = 0;

// Disable buffering of sends by setting send buffer size
// to zero
if (!lpSocket->GetSocket().SetSockOpt(
        SO_SNDBUF, (const void *) &i, sizeof (i)))
   {
   szMessage.Format(TEXT("::setsockopt(SO_SNDBUF) failed,
      WSAGetLastError() = %d"),
      lpSocket->GetSocket().GetLastError());
   lpSocket->Close();
   delete lpSocket;
```

```
      AfxMessageBox(szMessage);
      return;
      }

   // Make receive buffer 65000, so drivers can cache
   // a lot of incoming packets for us
   i = 65000;
   if (!lpSocket->GetSocket().SetSockOpt(
           SO_RCVBUF, (const void *) &i, sizeof (i)))
      {
      szMessage.Format(TEXT("::setsockopt(SO_RCVBUF) failed,
         WSAGetLastError() = %d"),
         lpSocket->GetSocket().GetLastError());
      lpSocket->Close();
      delete lpSocket;
      AfxMessageBox(szMessage);
      return;
      }

   int nSuccessfulReads = 0, nSuccessfulWrites = 0;
   dwTotalBytes = (DWORD) (m_nNumPackets * m_nPacketSize);

   // [Get first Performance Monitoring snapshot]

   dwStartTime = GetCurrentTime();

   if (lpSocket->Read(szBuffer[RECV_1], m_nPacketSize,
            &dwIoBytes, &ov[RECV_1] ) ||
         ::GetLastError() == ERROR_IO_PENDING)
      ++nSuccessfulReads;
   else
      dwLastError = ::GetLastError();

   if (lpSocket->Read(szBuffer[RECV_2], m_nPacketSize,
            &dwIoBytes, &ov[RECV_2] ) ||
         ::GetLastError() == ERROR_IO_PENDING)
      ++nSuccessfulReads;
   else
      dwLastError = ::GetLastError();

   if (lpSocket->Write(szBuffer[SEND_1], m_nPacketSize,
            &ov[SEND_1] ) ||
         ::GetLastError() == ERROR_IO_PENDING)
      ++nSuccessfulWrites;
   else
      dwLastError = ::GetLastError();
```

```
if (lpSocket->Write(szBuffer[SEND_2], m_nPacketSize,
         &ov[SEND_2] ) ||
      ::GetLastError() == ERROR_IO_PENDING)
   ++nSuccessfulWrites;
else
   dwLastError = ::GetLastError();
dwBytesTransmitted = dwBytesReceived = 0;

BOOL bContinue = (nSuccessfulReads > 0 && nSuccessfulWrites > 0);
while (bContinue)
   {
   i = ::WaitForMultipleObjects(4, hEvent, FALSE, 5000);
   if (i >= 4)
      {
      szMessage.Format(
         TEXT("::WaitForMultipleObjects() failed, GetLastError() = %d"),
            GetLastError());
      lpSocket->Close();
      AfxMessageBox(szMessage);
      delete lpSocket;
      return;
      }

   bSuccess = ov[i].GetResult(&dwIoBytes, FALSE );
   if ( !bSuccess )
      {
      szMessage.Format(
         TEXT("WriteFile/ReadFile[%d] failed, WSAGetLastError() = %d"),
            i, GetLastError());
      lpSocket->Close();
      AfxMessageBox(szMessage);
      delete lpSocket;
      return;
      }

   if (ov[i].GetPreviousOperation() == COverlapped::ReadFile)
      {
      dwBytesReceived += dwIoBytes;
      if ( dwBytesReceived >= dwTotalBytes )
         {
         break;
         }
      ::ResetEvent(hEvent[i]);
      }
   else   // WriteFile() completed
      {
      dwBytesTransmitted += dwIoBytes;
```

```
        if ( dwBytesTransmitted >= (dwTotalBytes - m_nPacketSize))
           {
           ::ResetEvent(hEvent[i]);
           continue;
           }
        ::ResetEvent(hEvent[i]);
        }
     bSuccess = ov[i].Recycle(m_nPacketSize, &dwIoBytes);
     if (bSuccess)
        ::SetEvent(hEvent[i]);
     else if (::GetLastError() != ERROR_IO_PENDING)
        {
        szMessage.Format(TEXT("::ReadFile() failed, ::GetLastError() = %d"),
                         ::GetLastError());
        lpSocket->Close();
        AfxMessageBox(szMessage);
        delete lpSocket;
        return;
        }
     }
  dwEndTime = GetCurrentTime();

  // [Get second Performance Monitoring snapshot]
  lpSocket->Close();

  delete lpSocket;

  // [Do arithmetic]
  DisplayResults(dwStartTime, dwEndTime, dMilliSeconds,
     dwCounterDelta,
     (((double) dwCounterDelta) * 1000.0) / dMilliSeconds);

  ::HeapFree(::GetProcessHeap(), 0, lpCounterStart);
  ::HeapFree(::GetProcessHeap(), 0, lpCounterStop);
}
```

Figure 16-7 shows the transfer rate at 32K, 657K bytes per second.

The conclusion seems clear: C++ encapsulation doesn't impose a high level of overhead, if indeed it imposes any overhead at all.

Using Datagrams. The datagram version uses synchronous Berkeley calls. Because it is very similar to DoStandardSynchronous(), I don't show the listing. These are the differences:

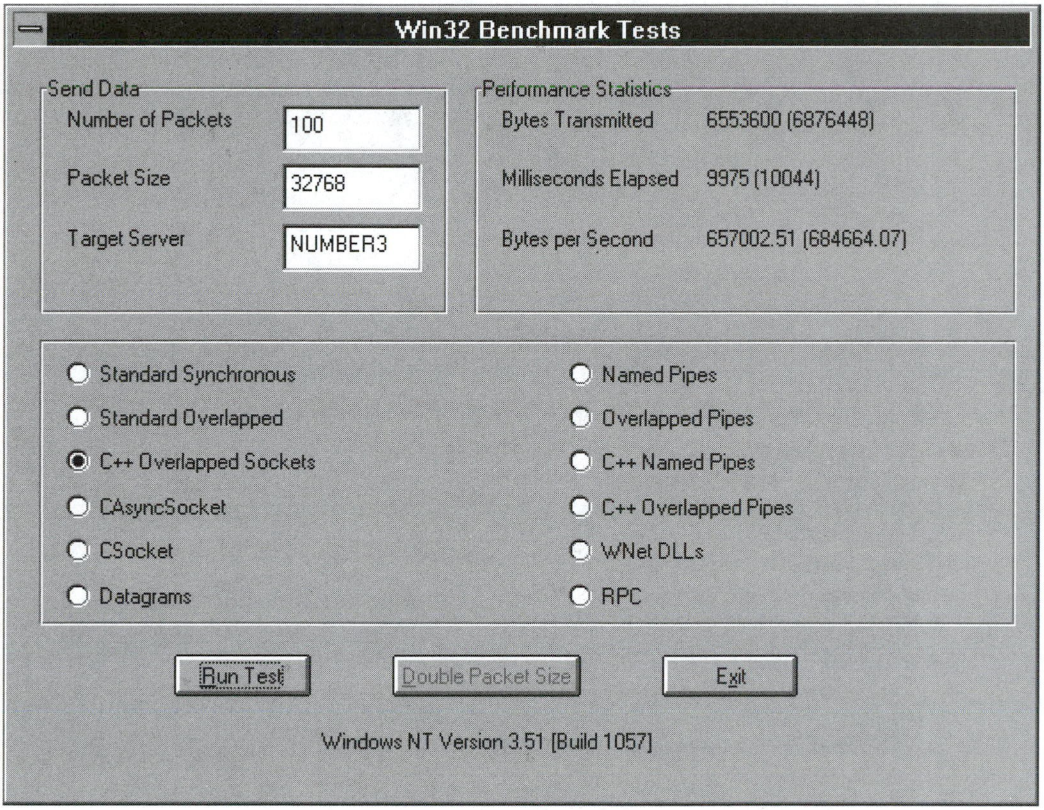

Figure 16-7. Benchmark Results with COverlappedSocket

- When you open a socket, you ask for a SOCK_DGRAM socket type instead of a SOCK_STREAM.
- The call to GetHostAddress() asks for the *echo* service using the protocol string "udp".
- Instead of using send() and recv() we use sendto() and recvfrom().

You might expect that datagram service would leave connection-oriented transmissions in the dust. However, this is not the case. Figure 16-8 shows the fastest transfer rate achieved by datagrams.

The transfer rate shown here is roughly comparable to standard synchronous TCP sockets. But above a packet size of 8192, MFCSOCK goes to sleep and never wakes up—it blocks forever on the recvfrom() call.

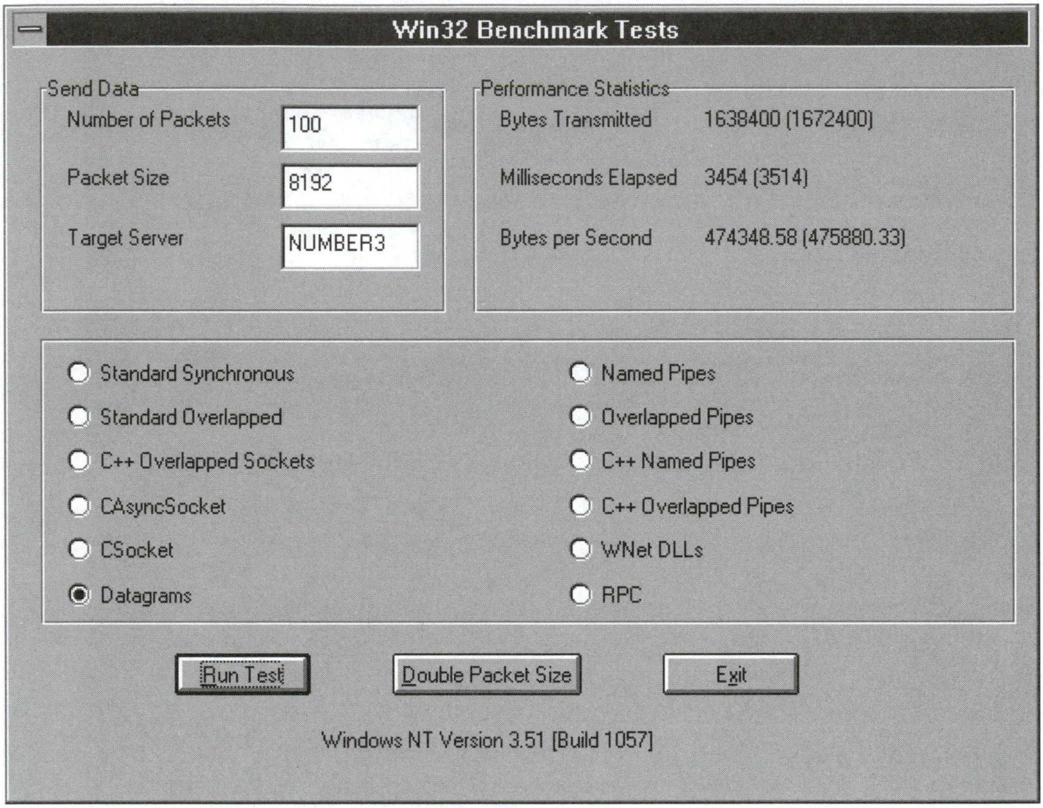

Figure 16-8. Benchmark Results with UDP Datagrams

Named Pipes

To support the Named Pipes benchmarks, MFCSOCK spins off a Named Pipes server thread when it starts up. It does this by instantiating an object of the CNamedPipesServer class I discussed in Chapter 10. To test my classes that encapsulate the Win32 Security API, I allow access to the group Everyone, deny it to JoeEndUser, and disable auditing. The receive callback function for this object sends back the data that it receives. I don't care if I can't create the Named Pipes server. It's not a critical piece of functionality, and may indicate that I'm running under Windows 95 (which cannot support Named Pipes servers).

Here are the lines of code in CMfcsockDlg::OnInitDialog() that start the server:

```
CStringArray aszAllowedUsers;
CStringArray aszDeniedUsers;
```

```
aszAllowedUsers.Add(CString(_T("Everyone")));
aszDeniedUsers.Add(CString(_T("JoeEndUser")));

try
   {
   m_pNamedPipesServer = new CNamedPipesServer(
      _T("WNET\\WNETBNCH"),
      PipesReceiveCallback,
      5,
      &aszAllowedUsers,
      &aszDeniedUsers,
      FALSE);  // Don't audit
   }
catch (...)
   {
   // Couldn't start Pipes server--on Windows 95, maybe
   m_pNamedPipesServer = NULL;
   }
```

I have several variations on the Named Pipes client. The first uses the native Win32 API with a non-overlapped pipe. The second uses an overlapped pipe, still with the Win32 API. Then I do the same tests with the CNamedPipe and COverlappedPipe classes I developed in Chapter 10.

Keep in mind that Named Pipes are at a higher level of the protocol stack than Windows Sockets. Named Pipes are an NT file system. When a client opens a named pipe, the Multiple Provider Router asks the network redirectors if any of them knows how to reach the target machine. When one of them claims that it can, it is given responsibility for the pipe. It then finds a transport protocol that it and the target understand. Although Named Pipes have historically been associated with NetBEUI, they are completely protocol-transparent; the caller never knows what protocol it uses, and has no control over this. In fact, for the tests that follow, I'm using TCP/IP; I haven't even installed NetBEUI. I'll anticipate things a little bit and tell you that, from what I've seen, the transfer rate of Named Pipes is not dependent on the transport protocol. It appears that their performance is bound by the network redirector they use.

For Performance Monitoring corroboration, we have to query the redirector object (number 262), and the same counter we examined for TCP/IP, Bytes Total/sec (number 388). The arithmetic is a little different, because the byte count is returned as a LARGE_INTEGER (wrapped in a CLargeInt object). For Network Interface (the appropriate object for TCP/IP), it comes back as a DWORD.

Non-Overlapped Pipes Using Native Win32 Calls. Here is the CMfc-sockDlg::DoNamedPipes() method, which performs the first test. It uses a message read/write pipe and TransactNamedPipe().

```
void CMfcsockDlg::DoNamedPipes()
{
   HANDLE       hPipe = INVALID_HANDLE_VALUE;
   CString      szMessage;
   BYTE         szBuffer[32768];
   DWORD        dwStartTime, dwEndTime;
   UINT         i;
   DWORD        dwBytesTransmitted;
   CString      szPipe;
   LARGE_INTEGER *lpCounterStart;
   LARGE_INTEGER *lpCounterStop;
   CLargeInt CounterDelta;
   CSystemTime SystemTime[2];
   CLargeInt   SampleTime[2];

   szPipe = _T("\\\\");
   szPipe += m_szTargetServer;
   szPipe += _T("\\PIPE\\WNET\\WNETBNCH");

   hPipe = ::CreateFile(
               szPipe,
               GENERIC_READ | GENERIC_WRITE,
               0,
               NULL,
               OPEN_EXISTING,
               0,
               NULL);

   if (hPipe == INVALID_HANDLE_VALUE)
      {
      szMessage.Format(_T("Couldn't connect to pipe %s, GetLastError()
         = %d"),
         (LPCTSTR) szPipe, ::GetLastError());
      AfxMessageBox(szMessage);
      return;
      }

   // At this point, we should be connected to the server
   DWORD dwMode = PIPE_WAIT | PIPE_READMODE_MESSAGE;

   ::SetNamedPipeHandleState(hPipe, &dwMode, NULL, NULL);

   GetPerformanceCounterData(REDIRECTOR,
      BYTES_TOTAL_PER_SEC,
```

```
    (LPBYTE *) &lpCounterStart, SystemTime[0],
    SampleTime[0]);

for (i = 0, dwStartTime = ::GetCurrentTime();
     i < m_nNumPackets; ++i)
    {
    if (!::TransactNamedPipe(hPipe,
          szBuffer,
          m_nPacketSize,
          szBuffer,
          m_nPacketSize,
          &dwBytesTransmitted,
          NULL))
        {
        szMessage.Format(_T("TransactNamedPipe() failed,
           GetLastError() = %d"),
           GetLastError());
        AfxMessageBox(szMessage);
        ::CloseHandle(hPipe);
        return;
        }
    }
dwEndTime = GetCurrentTime();

GetPerformanceCounterData(REDIRECTOR,
    BYTES_TOTAL_PER_SEC,
    (LPBYTE *) &lpCounterStop, SystemTime[1],
    SampleTime[1]);

RegCloseKey(HKEY_PERFORMANCE_DATA);

CounterDelta = CLargeInt(*lpCounterStop) -
               CLargeInt(*lpCounterStart);

double dMilliSeconds;
LARGE_INTEGER PerformanceFrequency;

if (QueryPerformanceFrequency(&PerformanceFrequency))
    dMilliSeconds =
        ((double) (((DWORD) SampleTime[1]) -
                   ((DWORD) SampleTime[0]))) /
        ((double) (PerformanceFrequency.LowPart))
        * 1000.0;
else
    dMilliSeconds = SystemTime[1] - SystemTime[0];

::CloseHandle(hPipe);
DisplayResults(dwStartTime, dwEndTime,
```

```
        dMilliSeconds,
        (DWORD) CounterDelta,
        (((double) ((DWORD) CounterDelta)) * 1000.0)
        / dMilliSeconds);

    ::HeapFree(::GetProcessHeap(), 0, lpCounterStart);
    ::HeapFree(::GetProcessHeap(), 0, lpCounterStop);
}
```

Figure 16-9 shows the top speed achieved, 395K per second at a 32K packet size. This is not impressive; in fact, Named Pipes will prove to be the slowest transfer mechanism we have. What's more, the transfer rate plateaus around 4K; increasing the packet size after that increases the speed only marginally. It also makes no difference if the server has no security restrictions.

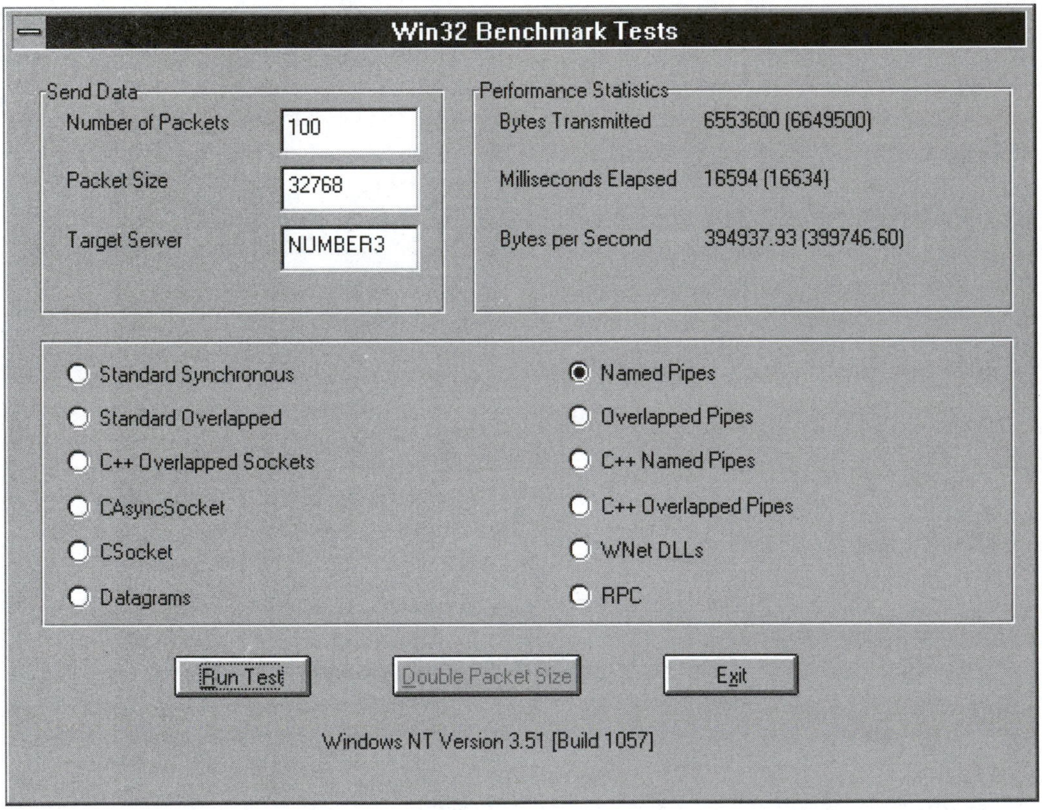

Win32 Benchmark Tests

Send Data

Number of Packets: 100

Packet Size: 32768

Target Server: NUMBER3

Performance Statistics

Bytes Transmitted: 6553600 (6649500)

Milliseconds Elapsed: 16594 (16634)

Bytes per Second: 394937.93 (399746.60)

- Standard Synchronous
- Standard Overlapped
- C++ Overlapped Sockets
- CAsyncSocket
- CSocket
- Datagrams
- Named Pipes (selected)
- Overlapped Pipes
- C++ Named Pipes
- C++ Overlapped Pipes
- WNet DLLs
- RPC

Run Test | Double Packet Size | Exit

Windows NT Version 3.51 [Build 1057]

Figure 16-9. Benchmark Results with Win32 Synchronous Named Pipes

If this were the end of the story, Named Pipes might well be irrelevant. However, take a look at Figure 16-10. This is the fastest speed recorded when the target machine is ".", the local machine.

The number you see is not a mistake—the transfer rate is approximately 8 megabytes per second. No other transport mechanism comes anywhere near this. Blocking Berkeley Sockets with a target machine of "localhost" gets up to 2.5MB at a packet size of 32K. Pipes' nearest rival is RPC using the *ncal-rpc* protocol suite. We'll see how that performs fairly soon.

(By the way, the numbers in parentheses are zero because local Named Pipes bypasses the Network Redirector, and therefore no Performance Monitoring data is generated.)

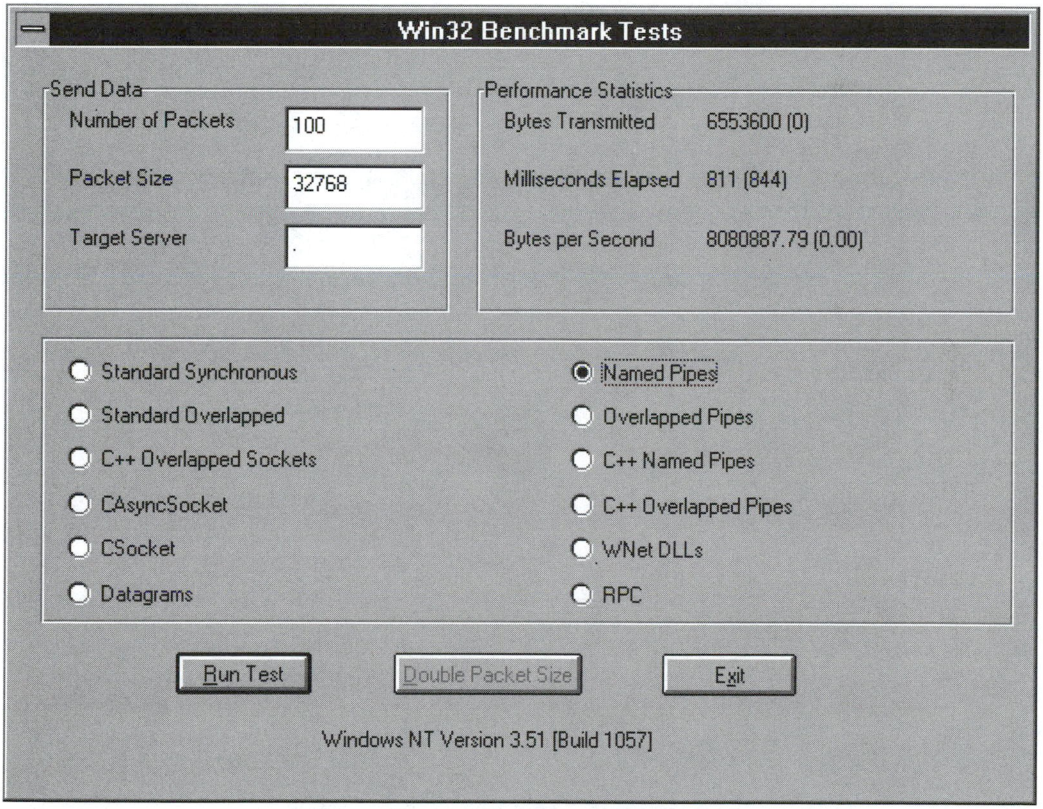

Win32 Benchmark Tests

Send Data
Number of Packets 100
Packet Size 32768
Target Server .

Performance Statistics
Bytes Transmitted 6553600 (0)
Milliseconds Elapsed 811 (844)
Bytes per Second 8080887.79 (0.00)

Standard Synchronous
Standard Overlapped
C++ Overlapped Sockets
CAsyncSocket
CSocket
Datagrams
Named Pipes
Overlapped Pipes
C++ Named Pipes
C++ Overlapped Pipes
WNet DLLs
RPC

Run Test
Double Packet Size
Exit

Windows NT Version 3.51 [Build 1057]

Figure 16-10. Benchmark Results Using Local Named Pipes

Overlapped Pipes Using Win32 Calls. Just as we saw with Windows Sockets, overlapped I/O provides a significant performance boost with Named Pipes. The DoOverlappedPipes() method is very similar to DoStandardOverlapped(). The only differences, in fact, are in the calls that establish the connection to the server. From that point on, as far as the Win32 API is concerned, we're just doing I/O on file handles. The timing loop is EXACTLY the same, except that the name of the variable becomes *hPipe* instead of *sCall*. For this reason, I won't display the code here.

Figure 16-11 shows the transfer rate for 32K packets. Now we're almost up to 500K per second. This is still 150K slower than overlapped sockets, but sockets don't have built-in security.

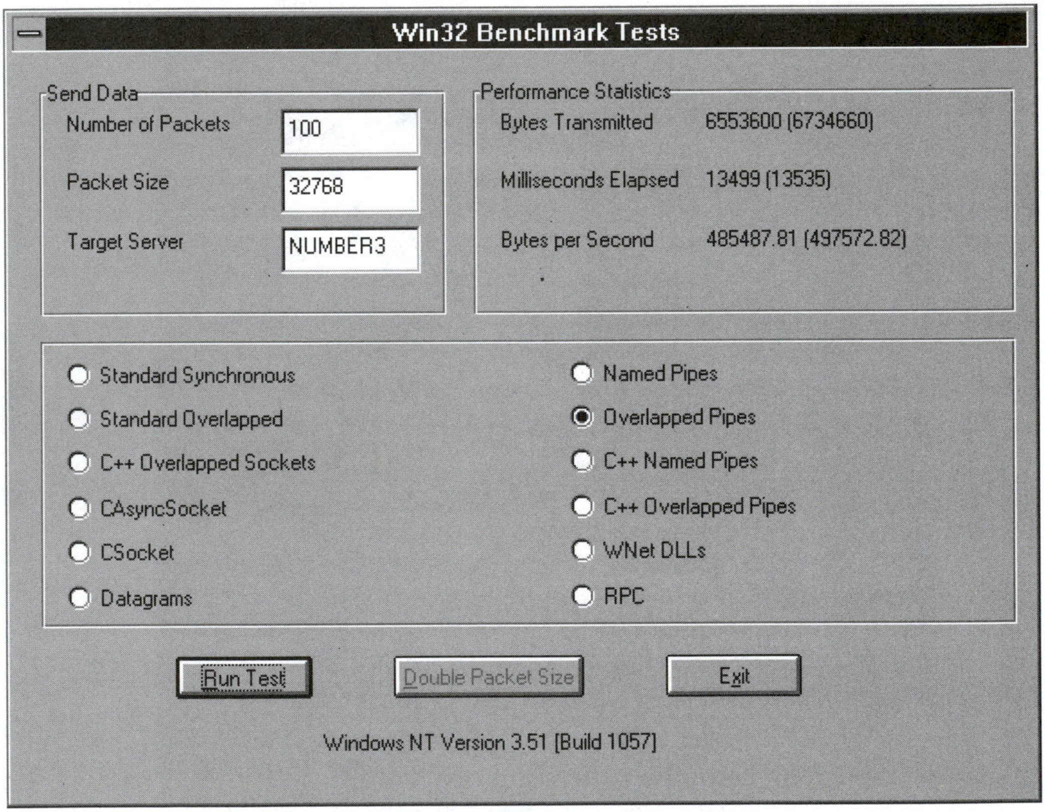

Figure 16-11. Benchmark Results Using Overlapped Win32 Sockets

C++ Named Pipes. This test uses the CNamedPipe class I developed in Chapter 10. The rest of the function is very close to DoNamedPipes(). In the listing that follows, I show only the calls to CNamedPipe methods (and their immediate context).

```
void CMfcsockDlg::DoCPPNamedPipes()
{
   CNamedPipe   *lpNamedPipe;
   CString      szMessage;
   BYTE         szBuffer[32768];
   DWORD        dwStartTime, dwEndTime;
   UINT         i;
   DWORD        dwBytesTransmitted;
   CString      szPipe;
   LARGE_INTEGER *lpCounterStart;
   LARGE_INTEGER *lpCounterStop;
   CLargeInt CounterDelta;
   CSystemTime SystemTime[2];
   CLargeInt   SampleTime[2];

   szPipe = _T("\\\\");
   szPipe += m_szTargetServer;
   szPipe += _T("\\PIPE\\WNET\\WNETBNCH");

   try
      {
      lpNamedPipe = new CNamedPipe(szPipe,
                      ClientSide);
      }
   catch(...)
      {
      szMessage.Format(TEXT("Unable to connect, GetLastError() = %d"),
         ::GetLastError());
      AfxMessageBox(szMessage);
      return;
      }

   // [...]

   for (i = 0, dwStartTime = ::GetCurrentTime();
        i < m_nNumPackets; ++i)
      {
      if (!lpNamedPipe->Transact(
           szBuffer,
           m_nPacketSize,
           szBuffer,
           m_nPacketSize,
           &dwBytesTransmitted))
```

```
            {
            szMessage.Format(_T("TransactNamedPipe() failed,
               GetLastError() = %d"),
               GetLastError());
            AfxMessageBox(szMessage);
            delete lpNamedPipe;
            return;
            }
        }
    dwEndTime = GetCurrentTime();

    // [...]
    delete lpNamedPipe;
}
```

The timings are the same as for synchronous Win32 Named Pipes, as you can see in Figure 16-12.

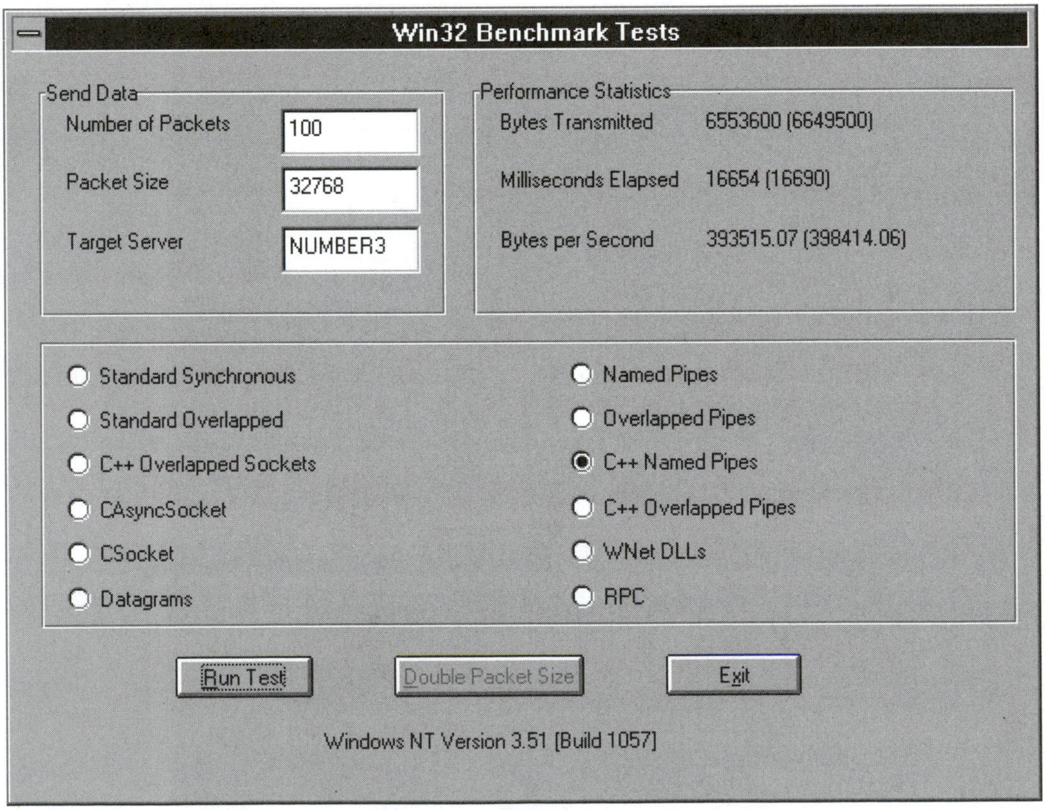

Figure 16-12. Benchmark Results With C++ Overlapped Pipes

C++ Overlapped Pipes. The CMfcsockDlg::DoCPPOverlappedPipes() method uses the COverlappedPipe class from Chapter 10. This code is quite similar to DoCPPOverlapped(), which uses the COverlappedSocket class. Once again, as far as the underlying Win32 calls are concerned, the only difference is in how you get the client and the server connected. After that, it's just file I/O.

The timings are the same as for Win32 overlapped pipes—the top transfer rate is just shy of 500K per second.

Using the WNet DLLs

The WNet DLLs, presented in Chapters 8 and 9, add another layer on top of my C++ classes. We would therefore expect them to perform more slowly.

When MFCSOCK starts up, it issues the WNetInit() call to set itself as a server. The client routine is DoWNetDLLs(), shown here:

```
void CMfcsockDlg::DoWNetDlls()
{
   HANDLE  hConnection;
   CString szMessage;
   DWORD   dwStartTime, dwEndTime;
   BYTE    szBuffer[2][65536];
   DWORD   i;
   DWORD       *lpCounterStart;
   DWORD       *lpCounterStop;
   DWORD        dwCounterDelta;
   CSystemTime SystemTime[2];
   CLargeInt    SampleTime[2];
   DWORD        dwInstances;

   hConnection = WNetCall(m_hWNetUser,
                          (LPVOID) (LPCTSTR) m_szTargetServer,
                          _T("wnetbnch"));
   if (hConnection == NULL)
      {
      szMessage.Format(TEXT("WNetCall() failed, ::GetLastError() = %d"),
         ::GetLastError());
      AfxMessageBox(szMessage);
      return;
      }

   // [Get first Performance Monitoring snapshot]

   for (i = 0, dwStartTime = ::GetCurrentTime();
        i < m_nNumPackets; ++i)
```

```
      {
      if (WNetSend(hConnection, szBuffer[0], m_nPacketSize))
         {
         if (!WNetReceive(hConnection, szBuffer[1], m_nPacketSize,
               NULL))
            {
            szMessage.Format(TEXT("WNetReceive() failed,
               ::GetLastError() = %d"),
               ::GetLastError());
            AfxMessageBox(szMessage);
            WNetHangup(hConnection);
            return;
            }
         }
      else
         {
         szMessage.Format(TEXT("WNetSend() failed, ::GetLastError() =
            %d"),
            ::GetLastError());
         AfxMessageBox(szMessage);
         WNetHangup(hConnection);
         return;
         }
      }
   dwEndTime = GetCurrentTime();

   // [Get second Performance Monitoring snapshot]

   WNetHangup(hConnection);

   // [Do arithmetic]
   DisplayResults(dwStartTime, dwEndTime, dMilliSeconds,
      dwCounterDelta,
      (((double) dwCounterDelta) * 1000.0) / dMilliSeconds);

   ::HeapFree(::GetProcessHeap(), 0, lpCounterStart);
   ::HeapFree(::GetProcessHeap(), 0, lpCounterStop);
}
```

Figure 16-13 shows the top speed: 520K at a packet size of 32K.

RPC

The last test uses the _RpcBenchmark() function that I presented in Chapter 11. It sends data to the WNet RPC Server, which bounces it right back. If the

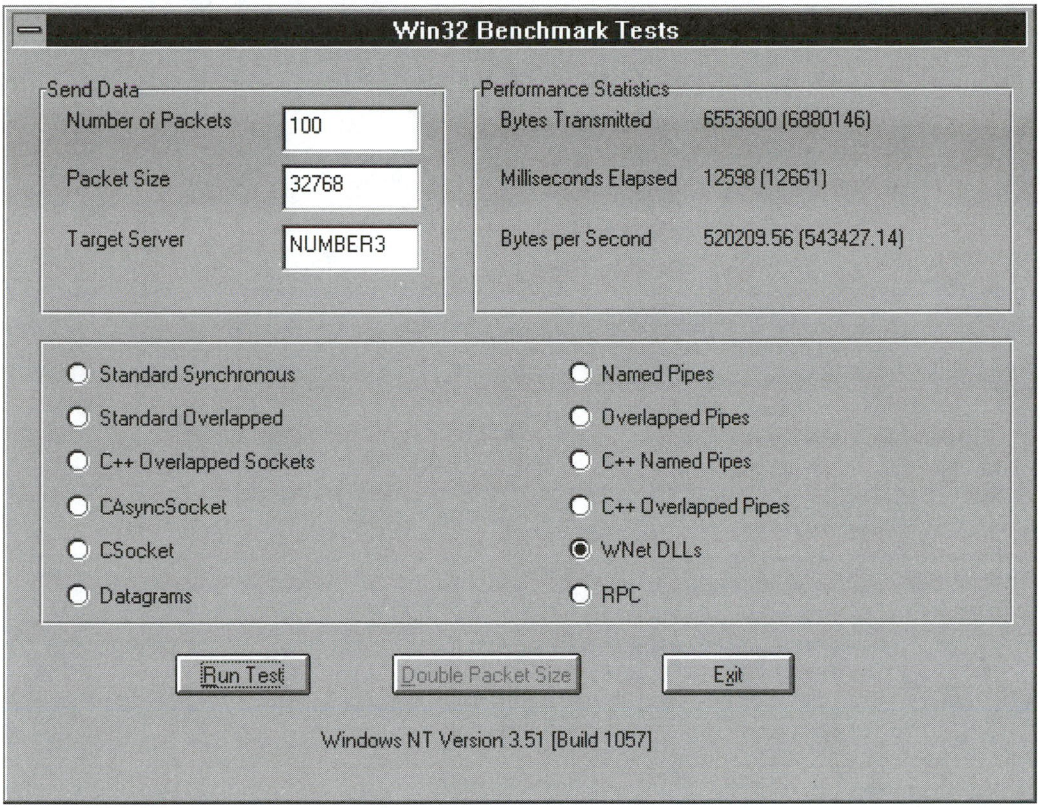

Figure 16-13. Benchmark Results Using the WNet DLLs

server is running locally, it uses the *ncalrpc* protocol (but only on NT, as Windows 95 doesn't support *ncalrpc*). Otherwise, it uses *ncacn_ip_tcp* (TCP/IP).

The DoRPC() method takes advantage of the CRpcClient class I developed in Chapter 11, and the CWin32Exception class from Chapter 2. To get the best performance, it passes the CRpcClient constructor the *CRpcClient::authNone* constant to disable security on the RPC binding. With default security in place, the transfer rate is only about half what it is with security disabled. Because the server uses dynamic endpoints (it registers itself by calling RpcServerUseAllProtseqs()), the initial binding to the server will be partial. Therefore, DoRPC() sends one dummy packet to the server. This will be intercepted by the RPC Endpoint Mapper on the target machine, which will complete the binding. All subsequent calls to _RpcBenchmark() can then be dispatched directly to the server.

The use of a C++ object (CRpcClient) here should not affect performance in any way. Its sole purpose is to connect to the server. Once the connection is in place, _RpcBenchmark() is called directly.

```
void CMfcsockDlg::DoRPC()
{
   BYTE        byInBuffer[60000];
   BYTE        byOutBuffer[60000];
   DWORD       dwStartTime, dwEndTime;
   double      dMilliSeconds;
   DWORD      *lpCounterStart;
   DWORD      *lpCounterStop;
   DWORD       dwCounterDelta;
   CSystemTime SystemTime[2];
   CLargeInt   SampleTime[2];
   DWORD       dwInstances;
   RPC_BINDING_HANDLE hBenchmark;
   RPC_STATUS  RpcStatus = RPC_S_OK;
   PTBYTE      lpServer;
   PTBYTE      lpProtocol;
   UINT        i;

   lpServer = (LPBYTE) (LPCTSTR) m_szTargetServer;

   // For machine name of '.', use ncalrpc
   // Otherwise, use ncacn_ip_tcp
   if (*lpServer == _T('.'))
      {
      lpServer   = NULL;
      lpProtocol = (PTBYTE) _T("ncalrpc");
      }
   else
      lpProtocol = (PTBYTE) _T("ncacn_ip_tcp");

   try
      {
      CRpcClient RpcClient(wnrpc_v1_0_c_ifspec,
                           lpServer,
                           &hBenchmark,
                           lpProtocol,
                           NULL,
                           CRpcClient::authNone);

      RpcClient.SetTimeout(RPC_C_BINDING_MIN_TIMEOUT);

      // Send a few bytes to make sure the
      // binding is resolved
```

```
try
   {
   _RpcBenchmark(hBenchmark,
      100, (LPBYTE) byInBuffer,
      (LPBYTE) byOutBuffer);
   }
catch (CWin32Exception *e)
   {
   e->Delete();
   }
GetPerformanceCounterData(NETWORK_INTERFACE,
   BYTES_TOTAL_PER_SEC,
   (LPBYTE *) &lpCounterStart, SystemTime[0],
   SampleTime[0]);

for (i = 0, dwStartTime = GetCurrentTime();
    i < m_nNumPackets; ++i)
   {
   try
      {
      _RpcBenchmark(hBenchmark,
         m_nPacketSize, (LPBYTE) byInBuffer,
         (LPBYTE) byOutBuffer);
      }
   catch (CWin32Exception *e)
      {
      RpcStatus = e->GetExceptionCode();
      delete e;
      }
   }
dwEndTime = GetCurrentTime();
dwInstances =
   GetPerformanceCounterData(NETWORK_INTERFACE,
      BYTES_TOTAL_PER_SEC,
      (LPBYTE *) &lpCounterStop, SystemTime[1],
      SampleTime[1]);

RegCloseKey(HKEY_PERFORMANCE_DATA);

LARGE_INTEGER PerformanceFrequency;

if (QueryPerformanceFrequency(&PerformanceFrequency))
   dMilliSeconds =
      ((double) (((DWORD) SampleTime[1]) -
                 ((DWORD) SampleTime[0]))) /
      ((double) (PerformanceFrequency.LowPart))
      * 1000.0;
```

```
        else
           dMilliSeconds = SystemTime[1] - SystemTime[0];

        for (DWORD j = 0; j < dwInstances; ++j)
           {
           dwCounterDelta = lpCounterStop[j] -
                            lpCounterStart[j];

           if (dwCounterDelta != 0)
              break;

           }
        }
     catch (CResourceException *e)
        {
        RpcStatus = ::GetLastError();
        e->Delete();
        }

     if (RpcStatus == RPC_S_OK)
        {
        DisplayResults(dwStartTime, dwEndTime, dMilliSeconds,
           dwCounterDelta,
           (((double) dwCounterDelta) * 1000.0) / dMilliSeconds);
        }
     else
        {
        CString szMessage;
        szMessage.Format(_T("RPC Error %d has occurred"),
           RpcStatus);
        AfxMessageBox(szMessage);
        }

     ::HeapFree(::GetProcessHeap(), 0, lpCounterStart);
     ::HeapFree(::GetProcessHeap(), 0, lpCounterStop);
}
```

Figure 16-14 shows the fastest speed achieved: 450K with 32K packets.

Local RPC Using the *ncalrpc* Protocol Suite. Figure 16-15 shows the fastest data-transfer rate achieved using the *ncalrpc* protocol suite—almost 5 megabytes a second.

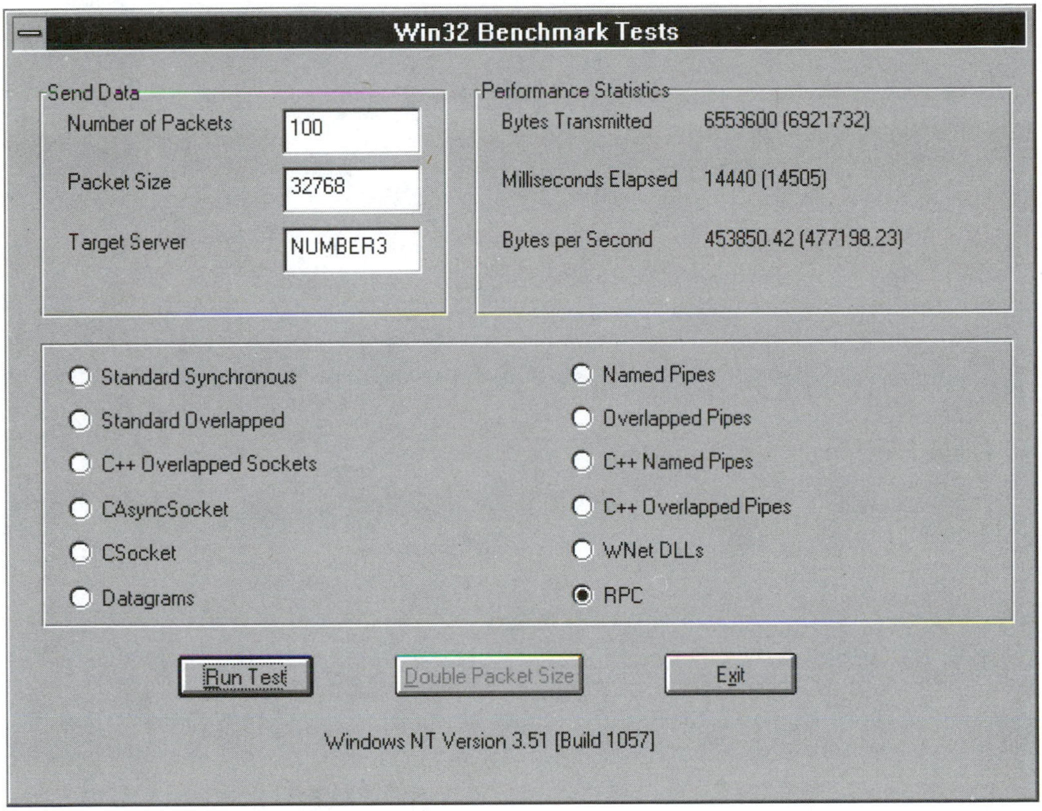

Figure 16-14. Benchmark Results Using RPC

Other Protocol Suites

I have also benchmarked Windows Sockets over Microsoft's version of the IPX/SPX suite, and found that it performs quite well. Using standard blocking Berkeley calls, I have observed data transfer rates in the 465K per second range at a packet size of 32K. With overlapped I/O, I have gotten up to 640K per second. I corroborated these numbers using the Performance Monitoring object NWLink SPX (490).

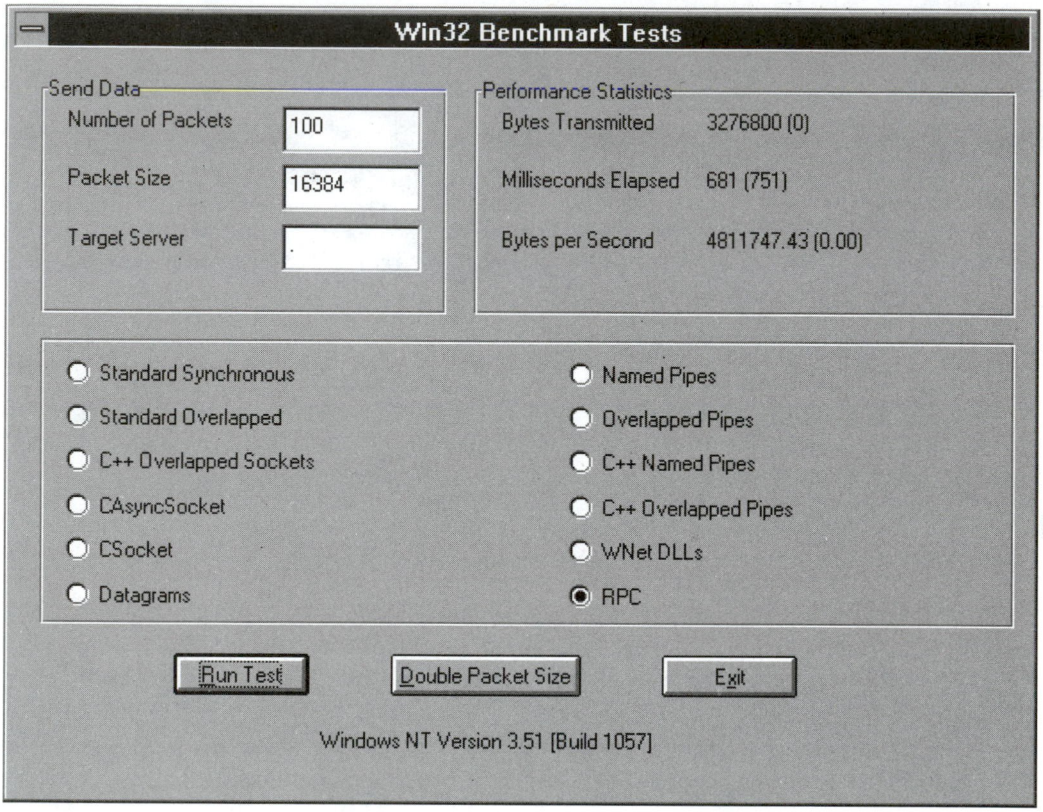

Figure 16-15. Benchmark Results Using Local RPC

Conclusion

With the data presented in this chapter, we can make some definitive statements.

- Overlapped I/O provides a significant improvement. With Windows Sockets over TCP/IP, Windows Sockets over IPX/SPX, and Named Pipes the transfer rate is consistently higher. Furthermore, the difference is enough to be statistically significant, and in every case is corroborated by Performance Monitoring statistics.
- Windows Sockets over TCP/IP yields the best all-around performance for both synchronous and overlapped I/O.
- There is no performance advantage to using the UDP datagram protocol. However, if you need to broadcast packets, then datagrams are your only choice.
- There is no performance penalty for using C++ objects.

- For local interprocess communication, Named Pipes is far and away the best vehicle. RPC using *ncalrpc* performs quite well also.

Finally, I will venture to say that the performance of all these vehicles is reasonable, and that your choice of which one to use should be based on your specific requirements.

- Windows Sockets over TCP/IP probably offers the most universal connectivity, given the wide availability of TCP/IP. It lacks one significant feature, though: security. There are additional software layers that can provide this, such as the Secure Sockets Layer (SSL) technology.
- RPC provides a high level of support and a high-level interface. It also provides good wide-world connectivity, but only to hosts that support OSF RPC. RPC has strong built-in security features.
- Windows Sockets over IPX/SPX is valuable for communicating with applications running on NetWare servers, particularly NLMs. NetWare supports the TLI programming interface over the IPX/SPX protocol. It also supports TCP/IP, and many NetWare installations will have it installed.
- Named Pipes provide a high level of built-in security and a convenient programming interface. Their wide-world connectivity is quite limited, because a Named Pipes client can only communicate with a Named Pipes server. Pipes are excellent for communications on a local area network, or between client and server applications running on the same machine.

Index

Addison-Wesley warrants the enclosed disk to be free of defects in materials and faulty workmanship under normal use for a period of ninety days after purchase. If a defect is discovered in the disk during this warranty period, a replacement disk can be obtained at no charge by sending the defective disk, postage prepaid, with proof of purchase to:

Addison-Wesley Publishing Company
Editorial Department
Developers Press
One Jacob Way
Reading, MA 01867

After the 90-day period, a replacement will be sent upon receipt of the defective disk and a check or money order for $10.00, payable to Addison-Wesley Publishing Company.

Addison-Wesley makes no warranty or representation, either express or implied, with respect to this software, its quality, performance, merchantability, or fitness for a particular purpose. In no event will Addison-Wesley, its distributors, or dealers be liable for direct, indirect, special, incidental, or consequential damages arising out of the use or inability to use the software. The exclusion of implied warranties is not permitted in some states. Therefore, the above exclusion may not apply to you. This warranty provides you with specific legal rights. There may be other rights that you may have that vary from state to state.